Houghton
Mifflin
Harcourt

Volume 1

Made in the United States
Text printed on 100%
recycled paper

Houghton Mifflin Harcourt

2017 Edition

Copyright © by Houghton Mifflin Harcourt Publishing Company

Printed in the U.S.A.

ISBN 978-0-544-71058-0

12 0877 20

4500789750   D E F G

Dear Students and Families,

Welcome to **Go Math!**, Grade 3! In this exciting mathematics program, there are hands-on activities to do and real-world problems to solve. Best of all, you will write your ideas and answers right in your book. In **Go Math!**, writing and drawing on the pages helps you think deeply about what you are learning, and you will really understand math!

By the way, all of the pages in your **Go Math!** book are made using recycled paper. We wanted you to know that you can Go Green with **Go Math!**

Sincerely,

The Authors

Made in the United States
Text printed on 100% recycled paper

GO MATH!

Authors

Juli K. Dixon, Ph.D.
Professor, Mathematics Education
University of Central Florida
Orlando, Florida

Edward B. Burger, Ph.D.
President, Southwestern University
Georgetown, Texas

Steven J. Leinwand
Principal Research Analyst
American Institutes for
    Research (AIR)
Washington, D.C.

Contributor

Rena Petrello
Professor, Mathematics
Moorpark College
Moorpark, CA

Matthew R. Larson, Ph.D.
K-12 Curriculum Specialist for
    Mathematics
Lincoln Public Schools
Lincoln, Nebraska

Martha E. Sandoval-Martinez
Math Instructor
El Camino College
Torrance, California

English Language Learners Consultant

Elizabeth Jiménez
CEO, GEMAS Consulting
Professional Expert on English
    Learner Education
Bilingual Education and
    Dual Language
Pomona, California

VOLUME 1
Whole Number Operations

Big Idea Develop a conceptual understanding of whole number operations and data. Use strategies for addition and subtraction within 1,000 and multiplication and division within 100.

① Addition and Subtraction Within 1,000   3

② Represent and Interpret Data   85

Big Idea

GO DIGITAL

Go online! Your math lessons are interactive. Use *i*Tools, Animated Math Models, the Multimedia *e*Glossary, and more.

Chapter 1 Overview

In this chapter, you will explore and discover answers to the following **Essential Questions**:

- How can you add and subtract whole numbers and decide if an answer is reasonable?
- How do you know when an estimate will be close to an exact answer?
- When do you regroup to add or subtract whole numbers?
- How might you decide which strategy to use to add or subtract?

Chapter 2 Overview

In this chapter, you will explore and discover answers to the following **Essential Questions**:

- How can you represent and interpret data?
- What are some ways to organize data so it is easy to use?
- How can analyzing data in graphs help you solve problems?

Chapter 3 Overview

In this chapter, you will explore and discover answers to the following **Essential Questions**:

• How can you use multiplication to find how many in all?
• What models can help you multiply?
• How can you use skip counting to help you multiply?
• How can multiplication properties help you find products?
• What types of problems can be solved by using multiplication?

Practice and Homework

Lesson Check and Spiral Review in every lesson

Chapter 4 Overview

In this chapter, you will explore and discover answers to the following **Essential Questions**:

• What strategies can you use to multiply?
• How are patterns and multiplication related?
• How can multiplication properties help you find products?
• What types of problems can be solved by using multiplication?

5 Use Multiplication Facts 259

Chapter 5 Overview

In this chapter, you will explore and discover answers to the following **Essential Questions**:

• How can you use multiplication facts, place value, and properties to solve multiplication problems?

• How are patterns and multiplication related?

• How can multiplication properties help you find products?

• What types of problems can be solved by using multiplication?

6 Understand Division 299

Chapter 6 Overview

In this chapter, you will explore and discover answers to the following **Essential Questions**:

• How can you use division to find how many in each group or how many equal groups?

• How are multiplication and division related?

• What models can help you divide?

• How can subtraction help you divide?

Chapter 7 Overview

In this chapter, you will explore and discover answers to the following **Essential Questions:**

- What strategies can you use to divide?
- How can you use a related multiplication fact to divide?
- How can you use factors to divide?
- What types of problems can be solved by using division?

VOLUME 2
Fractions

Big Idea Develop a conceptual understanding of fractions and fraction concepts, including fraction comparisons and equivalence.

8 Understand Fractions 441

9 Compare Fractions 505

Big Idea

GO DIGITAL

Go online! Your math lessons are interactive. Use *i*Tools, Animated Math Models, the Multimedia *e*Glossary, and more.

Chapter 8 Overview

In this chapter, you will explore and discover answers to the following **Essential Questions**:

- How can you use fractions to describe how much or how many?
- Why do you need to have equal parts for fractions?
- How can you solve problems that involve fractions?

Chapter 9 Overview

In this chapter, you will explore and discover answers to the following **Essential Questions**:

- How can you compare fractions?
- What models can help you compare and order fractions?
- How can you use the size of the pieces to help you compare and order fractions?
- How can you find equivalent fractions?

Measurement

Big Idea Develop a conceptual understanding of measurement, including time, linear, and liquid measures. Develop concepts of area and perimeter.

Geometry

Big Idea Describe, analyze, and compare two-dimensional shapes. Develop a conceptual understanding of dividing shapes into equal areas and writing the area as a fraction.

Big Idea

GO DIGITAL

Go online! Your math lessons are interactive. Use *i*Tools, Animated Math Models, the Multimedia eGlossary, and more.

Chapter 12 Overview

In this chapter, you will explore and discover answers to the following **Essential Questions**:

- What are some ways to describe and classify two-dimensional shapes?

- How can you describe the angles and sides in polygons?

- How can you use sides and angles to describe quadrilaterals and triangles?

- How can you use properties of shapes to classify them?

- How can you divide shapes into equal parts and use unit fractions to describe the parts?

Personal Math Trainer
Online Assessment and Intervention

© Houghton Mifflin Harcourt Publishing Company

xi

Big Idea Whole Number Operations

BIG IDEA Develop a conceptual understanding of whole number operations and data. Use strategies for addition and subtraction within 1,000 and multiplication and division within 100.

Some Baby Abuelita dolls sing Spanish rhymes and lullabies.

Inventing Toys

The dolls in the picture are called Abuelitos. Some of them are grandmother and grandfather dolls that were designed to sing lullabies. They and the grandchildren dolls have music boxes inside them. You squeeze their hands to start them singing!

Get Started   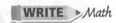 WRITE ▸ *Math*

Suppose you and a partner work in a toy store. You want to order enough dolls to fill two shelves in the store. Each shelf is 72 inches long. How many cartons of dolls will fill the two shelves? Use the Important Facts to help you.

Important Facts

- Each Abuelita doll comes in a box that is 8 inches wide.
- There are 4 boxes in 1 carton.
- Abuelita Rosa sings 6 songs.
- Abuelito Pancho sings 4 songs.
- Javier sings 5 songs.
- Baby Andrea and Baby Tita each sing 5 songs.
- Baby Mimi plays music but does not sing.

8 in.

_____

_____

_____

_____

_____

_____

_____

Completed by _____

Chapter 1 Addition and Subtraction Within 1,000

 Show What You Know

 **Personal Math Trainer** Online Assessment and Intervention

Check your understanding of important skills.

Name _____

▶ **Think Addition to Subtract** Write the missing numbers.

1. $9 - 4 = \blacksquare$

Think: $4 + \blacksquare = 9$

$4 + \underline{} = 9$

So, $9 - 4 = \underline{}$.

2. $13 - 7 = \blacksquare$

Think: $7 + \blacksquare = 13$

$7 + \underline{} = 13$

So, $13 - 7 = \underline{}$.

3. $17 - 9 = \blacksquare$

Think: $9 + \blacksquare = 17$

$9 + \underline{} = 17$

So, $17 - 9 = \underline{}$.

▶ **Addition Facts** Find the sum.

4. $\begin{array}{r} 4 \\ +\ 3 \\ \hline \end{array}$

5. $\begin{array}{r} 2 \\ +\ 7 \\ \hline \end{array}$

6. $\begin{array}{r} 8 \\ +\ 6 \\ \hline \end{array}$

7. $\begin{array}{r} 9 \\ +\ 4 \\ \hline \end{array}$

8. $\begin{array}{r} 7 \\ +\ 9 \\ \hline \end{array}$

▶ **Subtraction Facts** Find the difference.

9. $\begin{array}{r} 8 \\ -\ 5 \\ \hline \end{array}$

10. $\begin{array}{r} 11 \\ -\ 2 \\ \hline \end{array}$

11. $\begin{array}{r} 10 \\ -\ 6 \\ \hline \end{array}$

12. $\begin{array}{r} 18 \\ -\ 9 \\ \hline \end{array}$

13. $\begin{array}{r} 15 \\ -\ 7 \\ \hline \end{array}$

 **Math in the Real World**

Manuel's puppy chewed part of this homework paper. Two of the digits in his math problem are missing. Help Manuel figure out the missing digits. What digits are missing?

© Houghton Mifflin Harcourt Publishing Company

Vocabulary Builder

▶ **Visualize It** ••••••••••••••••••••••••••••••••••••••

Sort the review words with a ✓ into the Venn diagram.

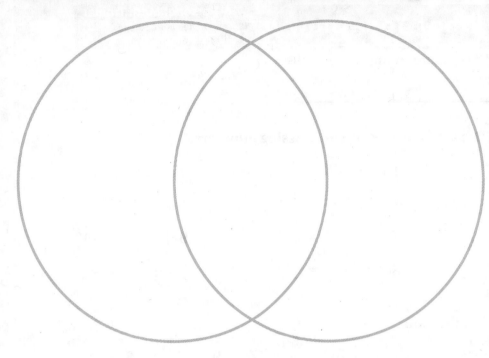

Addition Words   **Subtraction Words**

© Houghton Mifflin Harcourt Publishing Company

Review Words

✓ add
✓ difference
even
✓ hundreds
odd
✓ ones
✓ regroup
✓ subtract
✓ sum
✓ tens

Preview Words

Associative Property of Addition
Commutative Property of Addition
compatible numbers
estimate
Identity Property of Addition
pattern
round

▶ **Understand Vocabulary** ••••••••••••••••••••••••••••

Complete the sentences by using preview words.

1. A number close to an exact number is called an _____.

2. You can _____ a number to the nearest ten or hundred to find a number that tells *about* how much or *about* how many.

3. _____ are numbers that are easy to compute mentally.

4. The _____ states that you can add two or more numbers in any order and get the same sum.

• **Interactive Student Edition**
• **Multimedia eGlossary**

Chapter 1 Vocabulary

Associative Property of Addition

Propiedad asociativa de la suma

5

Commutative Property of Addition

Propiedad conmutativa de la suma

8

compatible numbers

números compatibles

10

difference

diferencia

12

estimate

estimar

24

Identity Property of Addition

Propiedad de identidad de la suma

34

Pattern

patrón

57

round

redondear

72

The property that states that you can add two or more numbers in any order and get the same sum

Example: $6 + 7 = 7 + 6$

The property that states that you can group addends in different ways and still get the same sum

Example: $(2 + 3) + 4 = 2 + (3 + 4)$

The answer to a subtraction problem

Example: $6 - 3 = 3$

difference

Numbers that are easy to compute with mentally

The property that states that when you add zero to a number, the result is that number

Example: $17 + 0 = 17$

To find about how many or how much

To replace a number with another number that tells about how many or how much

Example:

42	→	40
+16	→	+20
58		60

An ordered set of numbers or objects in which the order helps you predict what will come next

Examples: 2, 4, 6, 8, 10, 2, 4, 6, 8, 10

Going to New York City

© Houghton Mifflin Harcourt Publishing Company • Image Credits: (bg) ©Jeremy Woodhouse/PhotoDisc/Getty Images

Word Box

Associative
  Property of
  Addition
Commutative
  Property of
  Addition
compatible
  numbers
difference
estimate
Identity Property
  of Addition
pattern
round

For 2 to 4 players

Materials

- 1 red playing piece
- 1 blue playing piece
- 1 green playing piece
- 1 yellow playing piece
- 1 number cube
- Clue Cards

How to Play

1. Each player puts a playing piece on START.

2. If you land on these spaces:

   Green Space Follow the directions printed in the space.

   Blue Space Round the number to the nearest hundred.
   If you round it correctly, move ahead 1.

   Red Space The player to your right draws a Clue Card and
   reads you the question. If you answer correctly, move
   ahead 1. Return the Clue Card to the bottom of the pile.

3. The first player to reach FINISH wins.

Game

START

Visit the Empire State Building. Move ahead 1.

New York, NY

Visit the Statue of Liberty. Take another turn.

149

285

CLUE CARD

CLUE CARD

424

Get lost in Central Park. Lose 1 turn.

CLUE CARD

FINISH

CLUE CARD

777

Visit the American Museum of Natural History. Move ahead 1.

CLUE CARD

BROADWAY

See a Broadway show. Trade places with another player.

CLUE CARD

Hear a concert at Madison Square Garden. Go back 1.

CLUE CARD

561

CLUE CARD

© Houghton Mifflin Harcourt Publishing Company • Image Credits: (Statue of Liberty) ©upthebanner/Shutterstock; (park) ©Getty Images/Medioimages; (curtains) ©Getty Images/Medioimages; (Broadway sign) ©Getty Images; (museum) ©Creatas/Jupiterimages/Getty Images; ©Phil Crow/Alamy;

Game

Chapter 1 4C

The Write Way

Reflect

Choose one idea. Write about it.

- Draw and explain two ways to add 3-digit numbers. Use a separate piece of paper for your drawing.
- Elena and Han rounded 469 to the nearest hundred. Which solution is correct? Tell how you know.
- *Elena's solution*: 470, because 469 is closer to 470 than 460 on a number line.
- *Han's solution*: 500, 469 is closer to 500 than 400 because the tens digit is 6.
- Explain the Associative Property of Addition so a younger child would understand it.

Name _____

Number Patterns

Essential Question How can you use properties to explain patterns on the addition table?

Learning Objective You will find and describe number patterns on an addition table using properties.

Unlock the Problem

A **pattern** is an ordered set of numbers or objects. The order helps you predict what will come next.

You can use the addition table to explore patterns.

Activity 1

Materials ■ orange and green crayons

- Look across each row and down each column. What pattern do you see?

  _____

  _____

+	0	1	2	3	4	5	6	7	8	9	10
0	0	1	2	3	4	5	6	7	8	9	10
1	1	2	3	4	5	6	7	8	9	10	11
2	2	3	4	5	6	7	8	9	10	11	12
3	3	4	5	6	7	8	9	10	11	12	13
4	4	5	6	7	8	9	10	11	12	13	14
5	5	6	7	8	9	10	11	12	13	14	15
6	6	7	8	9	10	11	12	13	14	15	16
7	7	8	9	10	11	12	13	14	15	16	17
8	8	9	10	11	12	13	14	15	16	17	18
9	9	10	11	12	13	14	15	16	17	18	19
10	10	11	12	13	14	15	16	17	18	19	20

- Shade the row and column orange for the addend 0. Compare the shaded squares to the yellow row and the blue column. What pattern do you see?

  _____

  What happens when you add 0 to a number?

  _____

- Shade the row and column green for the addend 1. What pattern do you see?

  _____

  What happens when you add 1 to a number?

  _____

  _____

The **Identity Property of Addition** states that the sum of any number and zero is that number.

$$7 + 0 = 7$$

Math Talk Math Processes and Practices ⑦

Look for a Pattern What other patterns can you find in the addition table?

Activity 2

Materials ■ orange crayon

- Shade all the sums of 5 orange. What pattern do you see?

_____

_____

- Write two addition sentences for each sum of 5. The first two are started for you.

$5 + 0 =$ _____ and $0 + 5 =$ _____

_____ + _____ = _____ and _____ + _____ = _____

_____ + _____ = _____ and _____ + _____ = _____

- What pattern do you see?

_____

_____

+	0	1	2	3	4	5	6	7	8	9	10
0	0	1	2	3	4	5	6	7	8	9	10
1	1	2	3	4	5	6	7	8	9	10	11
2	2	3	4	5	6	7	8	9	10	11	12
3	3	4	5	6	7	8	9	10	11	12	13
4	4	5	6	7	8	9	10	11	12	13	14
5	5	6	7	8	9	10	11	12	13	14	15
6	6	7	8	9	10	11	12	13	14	15	16
7	7	8	9	10	11	12	13	14	15	16	17
8	8	9	10	11	12	13	14	15	16	17	18
9	9	10	11	12	13	14	15	16	17	18	19
10	10	11	12	13	14	15	16	17	18	19	20

The **Commutative Property of Addition** states that you can add two or more numbers in any order and get the same sum.

$$3 + 4 = 4 + 3$$
$$7 = 7$$

Activity 3

Materials ■ orange and green crayons

- Shade a diagonal from left to right orange. Start with a square for 1. What pattern do you see?

_____

- Shade a diagonal from left to right green. Start with a square for 2. What pattern do you see?

_____

- Write addition sentences for the shaded boxes. Write *even* or *odd* under each addend.

Remember

Even numbers end in 0, 2, 4, 6, or 8. Odd numbers end in 1, 3, 5, 7, or 9.

Math Talk Math Processes and Practices ⑥

Describe how you know when the sum of two numbers will be odd.

_____ + _____ = 6   _____ + _____ = 7   _____ + _____ = 8
↑   ↑   ↑   ↑   ↑   ↑   ↑   ↑   ↑
_____ + _____ = even   _____ + _____ = odd   _____ + _____ = even

6

Share and Show · MATH BOARD

Use the addition table on page 6 for 1–9.

1. Complete the addition sentences to show the Commutative Property of Addition.

   3 + _____ = _____   4 + _____ = _____

Math Talk   Math Processes and Practices ②

Reason Abstractly Explain why you can use the Commutative Property of Addition to write a related addition sentence.

Find the sum. Then use the Commutative Property of Addition to write the related addition sentence.

☑ 2.   8 + 5 = _____   3.   7 + 9 = _____   4.   10 + 4 = _____

   _____ + _____ = _____   _____ + _____ = _____   _____ + _____ = _____

Is the sum even or odd? Write *even* or *odd*.

5. 8 + 1 _____   6. 3 + 9 _____   ☑ 7. 4 + 8 _____

Problem Solving · Applications Real World

8. THINKSMARTER   Look back at the shaded diagonals in Activity 2. Why does the orange diagonal show only odd numbers? Explain.

   _____

   _____

9. GO DEEPER   Find the sum 15 + 0. Then write the name of the property that you used to find the sum.

   _____

10. THINKSMARTER   Select the number sentences that show the Commutative Property of Addition. Mark all that apply.

    Ⓐ 27 + 4 = 31   Ⓒ 27 + 0 = 0 + 27

    Ⓑ 27 + 4 = 4 + 27   Ⓓ 27 + (4 + 0) = (27 + 4) + 0

Sense or Nonsense?

11. **(Math Processes and Practices 3) Make Arguments** Whose statement makes sense? Whose statement is nonsense? Explain your reasoning.

The sum of an odd number and an odd number is odd.

The sum of an even number and an even number is even.

Joey's Work

Kayley's Work

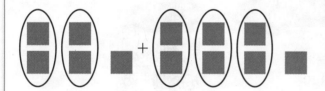

$$odd + odd = odd$$
$$5 + 7$$

I can circle pairs of tiles in each addend and there is 1 left over in each addend. So, the sum will be odd.

_____

_____

_____

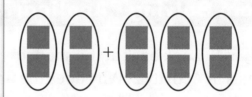

$$even + even = even$$
$$4 + 6$$

I can circle pairs of tiles with no tiles left over. So, the sum is even.

_____

_____

_____

• For the statement that is nonsense, correct the statement.

_____

Number Patterns

Learning Objective You will find and describe number patterns on an addition table using properties.

Find the sum. Then use the Commutative Property of Addition to write the related addition sentence.

1. 9 + 2 = _11_   3.   3 + 10 = ____   5.   8 + 9 = ____

    _2_ + _9_ = _11_   ___ + ___ = ___   ___ + ___ = ___

2. 4 + 7 = ____   4.   6 + 7 = ____   6.   0 + 4 = ____

    ___ + ___ = ___   ___ + ___ = ___   ___ + ___ = ___

Is the sum even or odd? Write *even* or *odd*.

7. 5 + 2 _____   8. 6 + 4 _____   9. 1 + 0 _____

10. 5 + 5 _____   11. 3 + 8 _____   12. 7 + 7 _____

Problem Solving

13. Ada writes 10 + 8 = 18 on the board. Maria wants to use the Commutative Property of Addition to rewrite Ada's addition sentence. What number sentence should Maria write?

    _____

    _____

    _____

14. Jackson says he has an odd number of model cars. He has 6 cars on one shelf and 8 cars on another shelf. Is Jackson correct? **Explain**.

    _____

    _____

    _____

15. **WRITE** ▸*Math* Write the definitions of the Identity Property of Addition and the Commutative Property of Addition. Use the addition table to provide examples of each.

    _____

    _____

Lesson Check

1. Marvella writes the addition problem 5 + 6. Is this sum even or odd?

   _____

2. What related number sentence shows the Commutative Property of Addition?

   $$3 + 9 = 12$$

   _____

Spiral Review

3. Amber has 2 quarters, 1 dime, and 3 pennies. How much money does Amber have?

   _____

   _____

4. Josh estimates the height of his desk. What is a reasonable estimate?

   _____

   _____

Use the bar graph for 5–6.

5. Who read the most books?

   _____

6. Who read 3 more books than Bob?

   _____

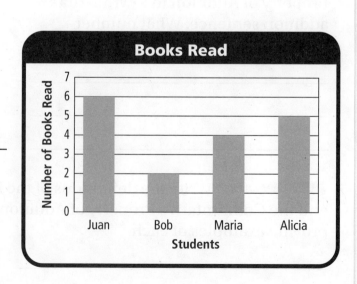

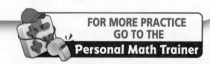

FOR MORE PRACTICE
GO TO THE
Personal Math Trainer

Round to the Nearest Ten or Hundred

Essential Question How can you round numbers?

Learning Objective You will use number lines and place value understanding to round 2- and 3-digit numbers to the nearest ten or hundred.

🔑 Unlock the Problem · Real World

When you **round** a number, you find a number that tells you *about* how much or *about* how many.

Mia's baseball bat is 32 inches long. What is its length rounded to the nearest ten inches?

🔒 One Way Use a number line to round.

Ⓐ Round 32 to the nearest ten.

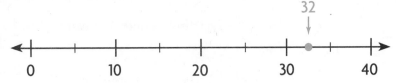

Find which tens the number is between.

32 is between _____ and _____.

32 is closer to _____ than it is to _____.

32 rounded to the nearest ten is _____.

So, the length of Mia's bat rounded to the nearest ten inches is _____ inches.

Math Talk

Math Processes and Practices ①

Analyze Relationships How is rounding to the nearest ten similar to rounding to the nearest hundred?

Ⓑ Round 174 to the nearest hundred.

Find which hundreds the number is between.

174 is between _____ and _____.

174 is closer to _____ than it is to _____.

So, 174 rounded to the nearest hundred is _____.

Try This! Round 718 to the nearest ten and hundred.
Locate and label 718 on the number lines.

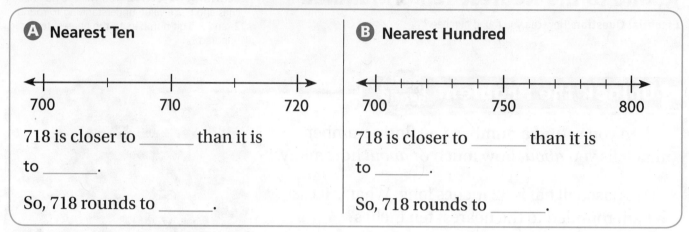

A Nearest Ten

718 is closer to _____ than it is

to _____.

So, 718 rounds to _____.

B Nearest Hundred

718 is closer to _____ than it is

to _____.

So, 718 rounds to _____.

🔑 Another Way Use place value.

A Round 63 to the nearest ten.

Think: The digit in the ones place tells if
the number is closer to 60 or 70.

3 ◯ 5

63

↑

So, the tens digit stays the same. Write 6 as the
tens digit.

Write zero as the ones digit.

So, 63 rounded to the nearest ten

is _____.

- Find the place to which you want to round.
- Look at the digit to the right.
- If the digit is less than 5, the digit in the rounding place stays the same.
- If the digit is 5 or greater, the digit in the rounding place increases by one.
- Write zeros for the digits to the right of the rounding place.

B Round 457 to the nearest hundred.

Think: The digit in the tens place tells if
the number is closer to 400 or 500.

5 ◯ 5

457

↑

So, the hundreds digit increases by one.
Write 5 as the hundreds digit.

Write zeros as the tens and ones digits.

So, 457 rounded to the nearest hundred

is _____.

Math Talk

Math Processes and Practices ⑥

Make Connections
Explain how using
place value is similar to
using a number line.

Name _____

Locate and label 46 on the number line.
Round to the nearest ten.

Use Reasoning What is the greatest number that rounds to 50 when rounded to the nearest ten? What is the least number? Explain.

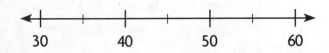

1. 46 is between _____ and _____.

2. 46 is closer to _____ than it is to _____.

3. 46 rounded to the nearest ten is _____.

Round to the nearest ten.

4. 19 _____   5. 66 _____   ✓ 6. 51 _____

Round to the nearest hundred.

✓ 7. 463 _____   8. 202 _____   9. 658 _____

On Your Own

Locate and label 548 on the number line.
Round to the nearest hundred.

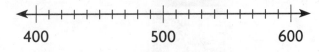

10. 548 is between _____ and _____.

11. 548 is closer to _____ than it is to _____.

12. 548 rounded to the nearest hundred is _____.

13. **GO DEEPER** There are 372 workers at a software company. There are 483 workers at a lumber company. When rounding to the nearest hundred, which company has 400 workers?

_____

Problem Solving • Applications

Use the table for 14–16.

14. On which day did about 900 visitors come to the giraffe exhibit?

_____

15. **GO DEEPER** On which two days did about 400 visitors come to the giraffe exhibit each day?

_____

16. **GO DEEPER** On which two days did about 800 visitors come to the giraffe exhibit each day?

_____

Visitors to the Giraffe Exhibit	
Day	**Number of Visitors**
Sunday	894
Monday	793
Tuesday	438
Wednesday	362
Thursday	839
Friday	725
Saturday	598

17. **Math Processes and Practices ③ Make Arguments** Cole said that 555 rounded to the nearest ten is 600. What is Cole's error? Explain.

_____

_____

_____

WRITE *Math* • Show Your Work

18. **THINK SMARTER** Write five numbers that round to 360 when rounded to the nearest ten.

_____

_____

19. **THINK SMARTER** Select the numbers that round to 100. Select all that apply.

Ⓐ 38   Ⓒ 109

Ⓑ 162   Ⓓ 83

Round to the Nearest Ten or Hundred

Learning Objective You will use number lines and place value understanding to round 2- and 3-digit numbers to the nearest ten or hundred.

**Locate and label 739 on the number line.
Round to the nearest hundred.**

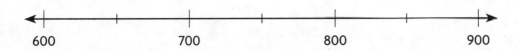

600   700   800   900

1. 739 is between __700__ and __800__.

2. 739 is closer to _____ than it is to _____.

3. 739 rounded to the nearest hundred is _____.

Round to the nearest ten and hundred.

4. 66 _____

5. 829 _____

6. 572 _____

_____

_____

_____

7. 209 _____

8. 663 _____

9. 949 _____

_____

_____

_____

Problem Solving

10. The baby elephant weighs 435 pounds. What is its weight rounded to the nearest hundred pounds?

_____

11. Jayce sold 218 cups of lemonade at his lemonade stand. What is 218 rounded to the nearest ten?

_____

12. **WRITE** ▸*Math* Describe how to round 678 to the nearest hundred.

_____

_____

Lesson Check

1. One day, 758 people visited the Monkey House at the zoo. What is 758 rounded to the nearest hundred?

   _____

2. Sami ordered 132 dresses for her store. What is 132 rounded to the nearest ten?

   _____

Spiral Review

3. What property describes the number sentence?

   $$6 + 0 = 6$$

   _____

   _____

4. Is the sum even or odd?

   $$2 + 6$$

   _____

   _____

5. What name describes this shape?

   _____

6. What word describes the equal shares of the shape?

   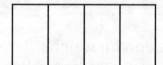

   _____

FOR MORE PRACTICE
GO TO THE
Personal Math Trainer

Estimate Sums

Essential Question How can you use compatible numbers and rounding to estimate sums?

Learning Objective You will use compatible numbers and rounding to estimate sums.

🔑 Unlock the Problem

The table shows how many dogs went to Pine Lake Dog Park during the summer months. About how many dogs went to the park during June and August?

You can estimate to find *about* how many or *about* how much. An **estimate** is a number close to an exact amount.

Pine Lake Dog Park

Month	Number of Dogs
June	432
July	317
August	489

🔒 One Way Use compatible numbers.

Compatible numbers are numbers that are easy to compute mentally and are close to the real numbers.

$$
\begin{array}{rcl}
432 & \rightarrow & 425 \\
+\ 489 & \rightarrow & +\ 475 \\
\end{array}
$$

So, about _____ dogs went to Pine Lake Dog Park during June and August.

Math Processes and Practices ②

Reason Quantitatively Will the sum of the compatible numbers 425 and 475 be greater than or less than the exact sum? Explain.

---

1. What other compatible numbers could you have used?

_____

2. About how many dogs went to the park during July and August? What compatible numbers could you use to estimate?

_____

 **Another Way** Use place value to round.

432 + 489 = ■

First, find the place to which you want to round.
Round both numbers to the same place.
The greatest place value of 432 and 489 is
hundreds. So, round to the nearest hundred.

Remember
When you round a number,
you find a number that tells
about how many or *about*
how much.

STEP 1 Round 432 to the nearest hundred.

- Look at the digit to the right of the
  hundreds place.

- Since 3 < 5, the digit 4 stays the same.

- Write zeros for the tens and ones digits.

$$\begin{array}{c} 4\ 3\ 2 \\ \uparrow \end{array} \qquad \begin{array}{c} 4\ 3\ 2 \\ +\ 4\ 8\ 9 \end{array} \rightarrow \quad + \underline{\qquad}$$

STEP 2 Round 489 to the nearest hundred.

- Look at the digit to the right of the
  hundreds place.

- Since 8 > 5, the digit 4 increases by one.

- Write zeros for the tens and ones digits.

$$\begin{array}{c} 4\ 8\ 9 \\ \uparrow \end{array} \qquad \begin{array}{c} 4\ 3\ 2 \\ +\ 4\ 8\ 9 \end{array} \begin{array}{c} \rightarrow \\ \rightarrow \end{array} \begin{array}{c} 4\ 0\ 0 \\ + \underline{\qquad} \end{array}$$

STEP 3 Find the sum of the rounded numbers.

$$\begin{array}{c} 4\ 3\ 2 \\ +\ 4\ 8\ 9 \end{array} \begin{array}{c} \rightarrow \\ \rightarrow \end{array} \begin{array}{c} 4\ 0\ 0 \\ +\ 5\ 0\ 0 \end{array}$$

So, 432 + 489 is about _____.

 Math Talk Math Processes and Practices ②

Use Reasoning How can a
number rounded to the nearest
ten be greater than the same
number rounded to the nearest
hundred?

Try This! Estimate the sum.

A Use compatible numbers.

$$\begin{array}{c} 47 \\ +23 \end{array} \begin{array}{c} \rightarrow \\ \rightarrow \end{array} \begin{array}{c} \\ +25 \end{array}$$

B Use rounding.

$$\begin{array}{c} 304 \\ +494 \end{array} \begin{array}{c} \rightarrow \\ \rightarrow \end{array} \begin{array}{c} 300 \\ + \end{array}$$

Name _____

1. Use compatible numbers to complete the problem. Then estimate the sum.

$$\begin{array}{r} 428 \\ +286 \end{array} \rightarrow \quad +$$

Math Talk

Math Processes and Practices ①

Evaluate What other compatible numbers could you use for 428 and 286?

Use rounding or compatible numbers to estimate the sum.

2. $\begin{array}{r} 65 \\ +23 \end{array}$ +_____

✓ 3. $\begin{array}{r} 421 \\ +218 \end{array}$ +_____

✓ 4. $\begin{array}{r} 369 \\ +480 \end{array}$ +_____

On Your Own

Use rounding or compatible numbers to estimate the sum.

5. $\begin{array}{r} 19 \\ +54 \end{array}$ +_____

6. $\begin{array}{r} 39 \\ +42 \end{array}$ +_____

7. $\begin{array}{r} 327 \\ +581 \end{array}$ +_____

8. Seth bought a pair of sneakers for $48 and a jacket for $64. Explain how you can estimate to find the total amount that he spent for the sneakers and jacket.

_____

_____

9. Elena drove 255 miles last week and 342 miles this week. About how many miles did Elena drive for the two weeks, rounded to the nearest hundred?

_____

10. **GO DEEPER** There are 187 kindergarten students, 203 first-grade students, and 382 second-grade students. About how many students are in the three grades, rounded to the nearest ten? How does the answer change if you round each number to the nearest hundred?

_____

Problem Solving • Applications

Use the table for 11–13.

Dan's Pet Supplies Sold

Month	Pet Bowls	Bags of Pet Food
June	91	419
July	57	370
August	76	228

11. **Math Processes and Practices ② Use Reasoning** About how many pet bowls were sold in June and July altogether?

_____

12. **GO DEEPER** Would you estimate there were more pet bowls sold in June or in July and August combined? Explain.

_____

_____

13. **THINK SMARTER** Dan estimated the lowest-monthly sales of both pet bowls and bags of pet food to be about 300. What month had the lowest sales? Explain.

_____

_____

_____

14. **THINK SMARTER** Write each number sentence in the box below the better estimate of the sum.

263 + 189 = ■ 305 + 72 = ■ 195 + 238 = ■ 215 + 289 = ■

400	500

Name _____

Estimate Sums

Learning Objective You will use compatible numbers and rounding to estimate sums.

Use rounding or compatible numbers to estimate the sum.

1.
$$\begin{array}{r} 171 \\ + 727 \\ \hline \end{array}$$
$$\begin{array}{r} 175 \\ + 725 \\ \hline 900 \end{array}$$

2.
$$\begin{array}{r} 87 \\ + 34 \\ \hline \end{array}$$
$$\begin{array}{r} \underline{} \\ + \underline{} \\ \hline \end{array}$$

3.
$$\begin{array}{r} 222 \\ + 203 \\ \hline \end{array}$$
$$\begin{array}{r} \underline{} \\ + \underline{} \\ \hline \end{array}$$

4.
$$\begin{array}{r} 52 \\ + 39 \\ \hline \end{array}$$
$$\begin{array}{r} \underline{} \\ + \underline{} \\ \hline \end{array}$$

5.
$$\begin{array}{r} 256 \\ + 321 \\ \hline \end{array}$$
$$\begin{array}{r} \underline{} \\ + \underline{} \\ \hline \end{array}$$

6.
$$\begin{array}{r} 302 \\ + 412 \\ \hline \end{array}$$
$$\begin{array}{r} \underline{} \\ + \underline{} \\ \hline \end{array}$$

7. $325 + 458$

_____ + _____ = _____

8. $620 + 107$

_____ + _____ = _____

Problem Solving · Real World

9. Stephanie read 72 pages on Sunday and 83 pages on Monday. About how many pages did Stephanie read during the two days?

_____

10. Matt biked 345 miles last month. This month he has biked 107 miles. Altogether, about how many miles has Matt biked last month and this month?

_____

11. **WRITE** ▸Math Explain how to estimate $368 + 231$ two different ways.

_____

_____

Lesson Check

1. The McBrides drove 317 miles on one day and 289 miles on the next day. Estimate the number of miles the McBrides drove during the two days.

_____

_____

2. Ryan counted 63 birds in his backyard last week. This week, he counted 71 birds in his backyard. About how many birds did Ryan count?

_____

_____

Spiral Review

3. What name describes this shape?

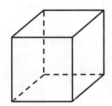

_____

4. Is the sum even or odd?

$$6 + 7$$

_____

5. What is 503 rounded to the nearest hundred?

_____

6. What is 645 rounded to the nearest ten?

_____

FOR MORE PRACTICE
GO TO THE
Personal Math Trainer

Name _____

Mental Math Strategies for Addition

Essential Question What mental math strategies can you use to find sums?

Learning Objective You will use mental math strategies to find sums.

🔑 Unlock the Problem Real World

The table shows how many musicians are in each section of a symphony orchestra. How many musicians play either string or woodwind instruments?

Orchestra Musicians

Section	Number
Brass	12
Percussion	13
String	57
Woodwind	15

🔑 One Way Count by tens and ones to find 57 + 15.

A Count on to the nearest ten. Then count by tens and ones.

Think: $3 + \blacksquare = 15$

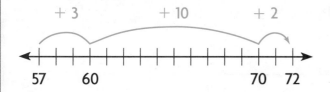

$+3 \qquad +10 \qquad +2$

57   60   70   72

B Count by tens. Then count by ones.

Think: $10 + 5 = 15$

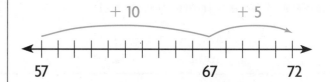

$+10 \qquad\qquad +5$

57   67   72

$57 + 15 = $ _____

So, _____ musicians play either string or woodwind instruments.

Math Idea
Count on from the greater addend, 57.

Try This! Find 43 + 28. Draw jumps and label the number line to show your thinking.

So, $43 + 28 = $ _____.

Math Talk

Math Processes and Practices ④

Use Diagrams Explain another way you can draw the jumps.

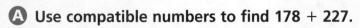 Other Ways

A Use compatible numbers to find 178 + 227.

STEP 1 Break apart the addends to make them compatible.

Think: 178 = 175 + 3   175 and 225 are
227 = 225 + 2   compatible numbers.

STEP 2 Find the sums.

178	→	175	+	3
+ 227	→	225	+	2
			+	

STEP 3 Add the sums.   _____ + _____ = _____

So, 178 + 227 = _____.

Math Talk

Math Processes and Practices ❶

Describe another way to use friendly numbers to find the sum.

B Use friendly numbers and adjust to find 38 + 56.

STEP 1 Make a friendly number.   38 + 2 = _____

Think: Add to 38 to make a number with 0 ones.

STEP 2 Since you added 2 to 38, you have to subtract 2 from 56.   56 − 2 = _____

STEP 3 Find the sum.   _____ + _____ = _____

So, 38 + 56 = _____.

Share and Show

1. Count by tens and ones to find 63 + 27. Draw jumps and label the number line to show your thinking.

Think: Count by tens and ones from 63.

```
←—|————————————————————————→
  63
```

63 + 27 = _____

Name _____

2. Use compatible numbers to find 26 + 53.

Think: 26 = 25 + 1   26 + 53 = _____
      53 = 50 + 3

Math Talk

Math Processes and Practices ⑧

Generalize Explain when it is most helpful to use compatible numbers to solve a problem.

Count by tens and ones to find the sum.
Use the number line to show your thinking.

✓ **3.** 34 + 18 = _____

✓ **4.** 22 + 49 = _____

<--->   <--->

On Your Own

Use mental math to find the sum.
Draw or describe the strategy you use.

5. 116 + 203 = _____

6. 18 + 57 = _____

7. (Math Processes and Practices ⑥) **Explain a Method** On Friday, 376 people attended the school concert. On Saturday, 427 people attended. On Sunday, 254 people attended. Explain how you can use mental math to find which two nights more people attended the concert.

_____

_____

_____

8. **GO DEEPER** There are 14 more girls than boys in the school orchestra. There are 19 boys. How many students are in the school orchestra?

_____

Problem Solving • Applications Real World

Use the table for 9–12

9. **Math Processes and Practices ① Analyze** How many girls attended school on Monday and Tuesday?

_____

10. **What's the Question?** The answer is 201 students.

_____

_____

11. **THINK SMARTER** How many students attended school on Tuesday and Wednesday? Explain how you can find your answer.

_____

_____

_____

_____

_____

Harrison School Attendance		
Day	Boys	Girls
Monday	92	104
Tuesday	101	96
Wednesday	105	93
Thursday	99	102
Friday	97	103

12. **GO DEEPER** On which day did the most students attend school?

_____

_____

13. **THINK SMARTER** On Monday, 46 boys and 38 girls bought lunch at school. How many students bought lunch? Explain one way to solve the problem.

_____

_____

Mental Math Strategies for Addition

Learning Objective You will use mental math strategies to find sums.

Count by tens and ones to find the sum.
Use the number line to show your thinking.

1. 29 + 14 = ___43___

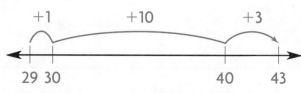

2. 36 + 28 = _____

Use mental math to find the sum.
Draw or describe the strategy you use.

3. 52 + 19 = _____

4. 122 + 306 = _____

Problem Solving Real World

5. Shelley spent 17 minutes washing the dishes. She spent 38 minutes cleaning her room. **Explain** how you can use mental math to find how long Shelley spent on the two tasks.

_____

_____

_____

_____

6. It took Marty 42 minutes to write a book report. Then he spent 18 minutes correcting his report. **Explain** how you can use mental math to find how long Marty spent on his book report.

_____

_____

_____

_____

7. **WRITE** ▸*Math* Which method do you prefer to use to find sums—count by tens and ones, use compatible numbers, or use friendly numbers and adjust? Explain why.

_____

Lesson Check

1. Sylvia spent 36¢ for a pencil and 55¢ for a notepad. Use mental math to find how much she spent.

_____

2. Will spent 24 minutes putting together a model plane. Then he spent 48 minutes painting the model. How long did Will spend working on the model plane?

_____

Spiral Review

3. What name describes this shape?

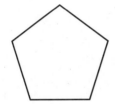

_____

4. What word describes the equal shares of the shape?

_____

5. Tammy wrote the addition problem 5 + 6. Is this sum even or odd?

_____

6. Greg counted 83 cars and 38 trucks in the mall parking lot. Estimate the total number of cars and trucks Greg counted.

_____

FOR MORE PRACTICE
GO TO THE
Personal Math Trainer

Name _____

Use Properties to Add

Essential Question How can you add more than two addends?

Learning Objective You will use the Commutative and Associative Properties of Addition to add more than two numbers.

CONNECT You have learned the Commutative Property of Addition. You can add two or more numbers in any order and get the same sum.

$$16 + 9 = 9 + 16$$

The **Associative Property of Addition** states that you can group addends in different ways and still get the same sum. It is also called the Grouping Property.

$$(16 + 7) + 23 = 16 + (7 + 23)$$

Math Idea

You can change the order or the grouping of the addends to make combinations that are easy to add.

🔑 Unlock the Problem Real World

Mrs. Gomez sold 23 cucumbers, 38 tomatoes, and 42 peppers at the Farmers' Market. How many vegetables did she sell in all?

Find 23 + 38 + 42.

• Will the sum be closer to 90 or 100?

_____

🔑 **Look for an easy way to add.**

STEP 1 Line up the numbers by place value.	**STEP 2** Group the ones to make them easy to add.	**STEP 3** Group the tens to make them easy to add.
	Think: Make a ten.	Think: Make doubles.
$\begin{array}{r} 2\,3 \\ 3\,8 \\ +\,4\,2 \\ \hline \end{array}$	$\begin{array}{r} \overset{1}{2}\,3 \\ 3\,8 \\ +\,4\,2 \\ \hline 3 \end{array}$ ⎬ 10	$5 < \ 5 < \begin{array}{r} \overset{1}{2}\,3 \\ 3\,8 \\ +\,4\,2 \\ \hline 1\,0\,3 \end{array}$

23 + 38 + 42 = _____

So, Mrs. Gomez sold _____ vegetables in all.

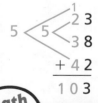

Math Talk   Math Processes and Practices ②

Reason Abstractly Explain how to group the digits to make them easy to add.

🔑 Example Use properties to find 36 + 37 + 51.

STEP 1 Line up the numbers by place value.	**STEP 2** Change the grouping.	**STEP 3** Add.
	Think: Adding 37 + 51 first would be easy because there is no regrouping needed.	
3 6 3 7 + 5 1	3 6 3 7 ⎱ + 5 1 ⎰ 88	▨ 3 6 + 8 8 ▨

So, 36 + 37 + 51 = _____ .

Try This! Use properties to add.

Ⓐ Find 11 + 16 + 19 + 14.	**Ⓑ** Find 17 + (33 + 45).
Think: Use the Commutative Property of Addition to change the order.	Think: Use the Associative Property of Addition to change the grouping.

1 1
1 6 → 1 1 ⎱ 10
1 9   1 9 ⎰
+1 4   1 6 ⎱ 10
         +1 4 ⎰
         ▨
	1 7 ⎱ 50
	3 3 ⎰ 5 0
	+4 5 → +4 5
	              ▨

Math Talk Math Processes and Practices ⑥

Explain how the Commutative and Associative Properties of Addition are alike and how they are different.

Share and Show [MATH BOARD]

1. Find the sum. Write the addition property you used.

STEP 1	STEP 2	STEP 3	STEP 4
4 6 5 5 +2 4	5 5 ▨ + 2 4	5 5 4 6 +2 4 ⎱ ▨	5 5 +7 0 ▨
_____ Property of Addition		_____ Property of Addition	

Use addition properties and strategies to find the sum.

☑ **2.** $13 + 26 + 54 =$ _____

☑ **3.** $57 + 62 + 56 + 43 =$ _____

On Your Own

Use addition properties and strategies to find the sum.

4. $18 + 39 + 32 =$ _____

5. $13 + 49 + 87 =$ _____

6. **GO DEEPER** There was a food drive at the school fair. Two local grocery stores each donated 75 boxes of pasta and 30 cans of soup. How many packages of food did both stores donate altogether?

_____

7. **GO DEEPER** Mrs. Jackson and Mrs. Reed each brought 25 packages of cups, 32 packages of plates, and 25 packages of napkins for the school picnic. How many packages of paper goods did the two mothers bring to the school picnic?

_____

8. Change the order and the grouping of the addends so that you can use mental math to find the sum. Then find the sum.

$43 + 39 + 43 + 11 =$ _____

_____ + _____ + _____ + _____ = _____

Problem Solving • Applications

9. **GO DEEPER** Mr. Arnez bought 32 potatoes, 29 onions, 31 tomatoes, and 28 peppers to make salads for his deli. How many vegetables did he buy?

_____

10. **GO DEEPER** A local community donated books to a school to sell at the school fair. On Wednesday, 74 books were donated. On Thursday, 62 books were donated. On Friday, 36 books were donated. Were more books donated on Wednesday and Thursday or on Thursday and Friday?

_____

11. **Math Processes and Practices ②** **Reason Abstractly** What is the unknown number? Which property did you use?

$$(\blacksquare + 8) + 32 = 49$$

_____

12. **THINK SMARTER** Change the order or grouping to find the sum. Explain how you used properties to find the sum.

$$63 + 86 + 77$$

_____
_____

13. **THINK SMARTER** For numbers 13a–13d, choose Yes or No to tell whether the number sentence shows the Associative Property of Addition.

13a. $(86 + 7) + 93 = 86 + (7 + 93)$ ○ Yes   ○ No

13b. $86 + 7 = 7 + 86$ ○ Yes   ○ No

13c. $86 + 0 = 86$ ○ Yes   ○ No

13d. $86 = 80 + 6$ ○ Yes   ○ No

Name _____

Use Properties to Add

Learning Objective You will use the Commutative and Associative Properties of Addition to add more than two numbers.

Use addition properties and strategies to find the sum.

1. $34 + 62 + 51 + 46 =$ ___193___

$$
\begin{array}{r}
34 \\
46 \\
62 \\
+51 \\
\hline
193
\end{array}
$$

with groupings: 34 and 46 = 10, 10 and 62... (bracket labels 10, 10)

2. $27 + 68 + 43 =$ _____

3. $42 + 36 + 18 =$ _____

4. $74 + 35 + 16 + 45 =$ _____

Problem Solving Real World

5. A pet shelter has 26 dogs, 37 cats, and 14 gerbils. How many of these animals are in the pet shelter in all?

_____

6. The pet shelter bought 85 pounds of dog food, 50 pounds of cat food, and 15 pounds of gerbil food. How many pounds of animal food did the pet shelter buy?

_____

7. **WRITE** *Math* Give an example of an addition problem in which you would and would not group the addends differently to add.

_____

_____

Lesson Check

1. At summer camp there are 52 boys, 47 girls, and 18 adults. How many people are at summer camp?

_____

2. At camp, 32 children are swimming, 25 are fishing, and 28 are canoeing. How many children are swimming, fishing, or canoeing?

_____

Spiral Review

3. Hank estimated the width of the door to his classroom in feet. What is a reasonable estimate?

_____

_____

4. Garth estimated the height of the door to his classroom in meters. What is a reasonable estimate?

_____

_____

5. Jeff's dog weighs 76 pounds. What is the dog's weight rounded to the nearest ten pounds?

_____

_____

6. Ms. Kirk drove 164 miles in the morning and 219 miles in the afternoon. Estimate the total number of miles she drove that day.

_____

_____

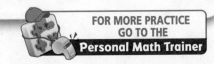

**FOR MORE PRACTICE
GO TO THE
Personal Math Trainer**

Use the Break Apart Strategy to Add

Essential Question How can you use the break apart strategy to add 3-digit numbers?

Learning Objective You will use the break apart strategy to add 3-digit numbers.

🔑 Unlock the Problem

There are more zoos in Germany than in any other country. At one time, there were 355 zoos in the United States and 414 zoos in Germany. How many zoos were there in the United States and Germany altogether?

You can use the break apart strategy to find sums.

Math Talk

Math Processes and Practices ②

Use Reasoning Do you think the sum will be greater than or less than 800? Explain.

🔒 Example 1 Add. 355 + 414

STEP 1 Estimate. 400 + 400 = _____

STEP 2 Break apart the addends.
Start with the hundreds.
Then add each place value.

$$\begin{array}{rcl} 355 & = & 300 + \boxed{} + 5 \\ + 414 & = & \underline{ + 10 + 4} \\ & & 700 + 60 + 9 \end{array}$$

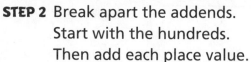

STEP 3 Add the sums.

    700 + 60 + 9 = _____

So, there were _____ zoos in the United States and Germany altogether.

🔒 Example 2 Add. 467 + 208

STEP 1 Estimate. 500 + 200 = _____

STEP 2 Break apart the addends.
Start with the hundreds.
Then add each place value.

$$\begin{array}{rcl} 467 & = & 400 + \boxed{} + \boxed{} \\ + 208 & = & \underline{\boxed{} + 0 + 8} \\ & & 600 + 60 + 15 \end{array}$$

STEP 3 Add the sums.

    600 + 60 + 15 = _____

So, 467 + 208 = _____ .

Try This! Use the break apart strategy to find 343 + 259.

Estimate. 300 + 300 = _____

$$
\begin{array}{rcl}
343 & = & 300 + \boxed{} + \boxed{} \\
+ 259 & = & \underline{\boxed{} + \boxed{} + \boxed{}} \\
 & & \boxed{} + \boxed{} + \boxed{} = \boxed{}
\end{array}
$$

1. **Math Processes and Practices ⑥** **Explain** why there is a zero in the tens place in the sum.

_____

_____

_____

_____

2. How do you know your answer is reasonable?

_____

_____

Share and Show MATH BOARD

1. Complete.
   Estimate: 400 + 400 = _____

$$
\begin{array}{rcl}
425 & = & 400 + \boxed{} + 5 \\
+ 362 & = & \underline{\boxed{} + 60 + \boxed{}} \\
 & & 700 + \boxed{} + 7 = \boxed{}
\end{array}
$$

So, 425 + 362 = _____.

2. Write the numbers the break apart strategy shows.

$$
\begin{array}{rcl}
\boxed{} & = & 100 + 30 + 4 \\
+ \boxed{} & = & \underline{200 + 40 + 9} \\
\boxed{} & = & 300 + 70 + 13
\end{array}
$$

Math Talk Math Processes and Practices ②

Reason Abstractly
Explain how the break apart strategy uses expanded forms of numbers.

36

Estimate. Then use the break apart strategy to find the sum.

✓ **3.** Estimate: _____

$$142 =$$
$$+\,436 =$$

✓ **4.** Estimate: _____

$$459 =$$
$$+\,213 =$$

5. Estimate: _____

$$291 =$$
$$+\,420 =$$

6. Estimate: _____

$$654 =$$
$$+\,243 =$$

On Your Own

Estimate. Then use the break apart strategy to find the sum.

7. Estimate: _____

$$435 =$$
$$+\,312 =$$

8. Estimate: _____

$$163 =$$
$$+\,205 =$$

9. There are three baby giraffes at the zoo. One weighs 148 pounds, one weighs 125 pounds, and the other weighs 137 pounds. What is their combined weight?

_____

10. During one week, a bowling alley had 348 customers on Thursday night and 465 customers on Friday night. The following week, the bowling alley had 212 customers on Thursday and 318 customers on Friday. About how many customers did the bowling alley have during those 4 days?

_____

Practice: Copy and Solve **Estimate. Then solve.**

11. 163 + 205

12. 543 + 215

13. 213 + 328

14. 372 + 431

15. 152 + 304

16. 268 + 351

17. 413 + 257

18. 495 + 312

Problem Solving · Applications

Use the table for 19–20.

Number of Students	
School	**Number**
Harrison	304
Montgomery	290
Bryant	421

19. **GO DEEPER** Which two schools together have fewer than 600 students? Explain.

_____

_____

_____

20. **THINK SMARTER** The number of students in Collins School is more than double the number of students in Montgomery School. What is the least number of students that could attend Collins School?

_____

21. **What's the Error?** Lexi used the break apart strategy to find 145 + 203. Describe her error. What is the correct sum?

$$100 + 40 + 5$$
$$+ 200 + 30 + 0$$
$$\overline{300 + 70 + 5 = 375}$$

_____

22. **Math Processes and Practices 5** **Communicate** Is the sum of 425 and 390 less than or greater than 800? How do you know?

_____

_____

23. **THINK SMARTER** What is the sum of 421 and 332? Show your work.

_____

Use the Break Apart Strategy to Add

Learning Objective You will use the break apart strategy to add 3-digit numbers.

Estimate. Then use the break apart strategy to find the sum.

1. Estimate: ___800___

$$\begin{array}{ll} 325 & = \quad 300 + 20 + 5 \\ + \ 494 & = \quad 400 + 90 + 4 \\ \hline & \quad \ \ 700 + 110 + 9 \end{array}$$

2. Estimate: _____

$$\begin{array}{ll} 518 & = \\ + \ 372 & = \end{array}$$

3. Estimate: _____

$$\begin{array}{ll} 731 & = \\ + \ 207 & = \end{array}$$

4. Estimate: _____

$$\begin{array}{ll} 495 & = \\ + \ 254 & = \end{array}$$

Problem Solving Real World

Use the table for 5–6.

5. Laura is making a building using Set A and Set C. How many blocks can she use in her building?

_____

6. Clark is making a building using Set B and Set C. How many blocks can he use in his building?

_____

Build-It Blocks	
Set	**Number of Blocks**
A	165
B	188
C	245

7. **WRITE** ▸Math Explain how to use the break apart strategy to find $247 + 358$.

_____

_____

Lesson Check

1. Arthur read two books last week. One book has 216 pages. The other book has 327 pages. Altogether, how many pages are in the two books?

   _____

2. One skeleton in a museum has 189 bones. Another skeleton has 232 bones. How many bones are in the two skeletons?

   _____

Spiral Review

3. Culver has 1 quarter, 3 dimes, and 1 penny. How much money does he have?

   _____

4. Felicia has 34 quarters, 25 dimes, and 36 pennies. How many coins does Felicia have?

   _____

5. Jonas wrote 9 + 8 = 17. What number sentence shows the Commutative Property of Addition?

   _____

6. At Kennedy School there are 37 girls and 36 boys in the third grade. How many students are in the third grade at Kennedy School?

   _____

FOR MORE PRACTICE
GO TO THE
Personal Math Trainer

Use Place Value to Add

Essential Question How can you use place value to add 3-digit numbers?

Learning Objective You will use place value to add 3-digit numbers.

 Unlock the Problem *Real World*

Dante is planning a trip to Illinois. His airplane leaves from Dallas, Texas, and stops in Tulsa, Oklahoma. Then it flies from Tulsa to Chicago, Illinois. How many miles does Dante fly?

Chicago

585 miles

Tulsa

236 miles

Dallas

🔑 **Use place value to add two addends.**

Add. 236 + 585

Estimate. 200 + 600 = _____

STEP 1	**STEP 2**	**STEP 3**
Add the ones. Regroup the ones as tens and ones.	Add the tens. Regroup the tens as hundreds and tens.	Add the hundreds.
$\begin{array}{r} \overset{1}{2}\ 3\ 6 \\ +\ 5\ 8\ 5 \\ \hline \end{array}$	$\begin{array}{r} \overset{1}{2}\ \overset{1}{3}\ 6 \\ +\ 5\ 8\ 5 \\ \hline 1 \end{array}$	$\begin{array}{r} \overset{1}{2}\ \overset{1}{3}\ 6 \\ +\ 5\ 8\ 5 \\ \hline 2\ 1 \end{array}$

236 + 585 = _____

So, Dante flies _____ miles.

Since _____ is close to the estimate of _____ , the answer is reasonable.

 ERROR Alert

Remember to add the regrouped ten and hundred.

• You can also use the Commutative Property of Addition to check your work. Change the order of the addends and find the sum.

$\begin{array}{r} 5\ 8\ 5 \\ +\ 2\ 3\ 6 \\ \hline \end{array}$

Try This! Find 563 + 48 in two ways.

Estimate. 550 + 50 = _____

Ⓐ Use the break apart strategy.

$$563 = 500 + \boxed{} + \boxed{}$$
$$+\ 48 = \qquad\qquad 40 + \boxed{}$$

$$\boxed{} + \boxed{} + \boxed{} = \boxed{}$$

Ⓑ Use place value.

$$563$$
$$+\ 48$$
$$\boxed{}$$

🔑 **Use place value to add three addends.**

Ⓐ Add. 140 + 457 + 301

Estimate. 150 + 450 + 300 = _____

STEP 1 Add the ones.

```
  1 4 0
  4 5 7
+ 3 0 1
  ▢
```

STEP 2 Add the tens.

```
  1 4 0
  4 5 7
+ 3 0 1
  ▢ 8
```

STEP 3 Add the hundreds.

```
  1 4 0
  4 5 7
+ 3 0 1
  ▢ 9 8
```

So, 140 + 457 + 301 = _____.

Ⓑ Add. 173 + 102 + 328

Estimate. 200 + 100 + 300 = _____

STEP 1 Add the ones. Regroup the ones as tens and ones.

```
  1
  1 7 3
  1 0 2
+ 3 2 8
  ▢
```

STEP 2 Add the tens. Regroup the tens as hundreds and tens.

```
  1 1
  1 7 3
  1 0 2
+ 3 2 8
  ▢ 3
```

STEP 3 Add the hundreds.

```
  1 1
  1 7 3
  1 0 2
+ 3 2 8
  ▢ 0 3
```

So, 173 + 102 + 328 = _____.

42

Name _____

Share and Show

1. Circle the problem in which you need to regroup.
   Use the strategy that is easier to find the sum.

   a. 496 + 284

   b. 482 + 506

Estimate. Then find the sum.

2. Estimate: _____

$$\begin{array}{r} 251 \\ +345 \\ \hline \end{array}$$

3. Estimate: _____

$$\begin{array}{r} 479 \\ +395 \\ \hline \end{array}$$

4. Estimate: _____

$$\begin{array}{r} 686 \\ +314 \\ \hline \end{array}$$

5. Estimate: _____

$$\begin{array}{r} 231 \\ 410 \\ +158 \\ \hline \end{array}$$

Math Talk — Math Processes and Practices ①

Evaluate How can you compute 403 + 201 mentally?

On Your Own

Practice: Copy and Solve Estimate. Then solve.

6. 253 + 376

7. 654 + 263

8. 321 + 439 + 112

9. 182 + 321

10. 701 + 108

11. 543 + 372 + 280

Math Processes and Practices ② Use Reasoning Algebra Find the unknown digits.

12.
$$\begin{array}{r} 1\ \square\ 4 \\ +\ \square\ 3\ \square \\ \hline 2\ 5\ 7 \end{array}$$

13.
$$\begin{array}{r} \square\ 7\ \square \\ +6\ \square\ 4 \\ \hline 9\ 8\ 6 \end{array}$$

14.
$$\begin{array}{r} 2\ \square\ \square \\ +\ \square\ 2\ 9 \\ \hline 6\ 8\ 2 \end{array}$$

15.
$$\begin{array}{r} 3\ \square\ \square \\ +\ \square\ 1\ 7 \\ \hline 9\ 0\ 3 \end{array}$$

16. There are 431 crayons in a box and 204 crayons on the floor. About how many fewer than 1,000 crayons are there? Estimate. Then solve.

Unlock the Problem

17. **THINK SMARTER** A plane flew 187 miles from New York City, New York, to Boston, Massachusetts. It then flew 273 miles from Boston to Philadelphia, Pennsylvania. The plane flew the same distance on the return trip. How many miles did the plane fly?

a. What do you need to find?

_____

b. What is an estimate of the total distance?

_____

c. Show the steps you used to solve the problem.

d. How do you know your answer is reasonable?

_____

_____

e. The total distance is _____ miles round trip.

---

18. **THINK SMARTER** Help Max find the sum of the problem.

```
   4 5 1
   2 4 6
 + 2 2 2
```

For numbers 18a–18d, choose Yes or No to tell if Max should regroup.

18a. Regroup the ones.   ○ Yes   ○ No

18b. Add the regrouped ten.   ○ Yes   ○ No

18c. Regroup the tens.   ○ Yes   ○ No

18d. Add the regrouped hundred. ○ Yes   ○ No

Name _____

Use Place Value to Add

Learning Objective You will use place value to add 3-digit numbers.

Estimate. Then find the sum.

1. Estimate: _____
$$\begin{array}{r} {}^{1} \\ 324 \\ +\ 285 \\ \hline 609 \end{array}$$

2. Estimate: _____
$$\begin{array}{r} 519 \\ +\ 347 \\ \hline \end{array}$$

3. Estimate: _____
$$\begin{array}{r} 323 \\ +\ 151 \\ \hline \end{array}$$

4. Estimate: _____
$$\begin{array}{r} 169 \\ +\ 354 \\ \hline \end{array}$$

5. Estimate: _____
$$\begin{array}{r} 127 \\ +\ 290 \\ \hline \end{array}$$

6. Estimate: _____
$$\begin{array}{r} 258 \\ +\ 565 \\ \hline \end{array}$$

7. Estimate: _____
$$\begin{array}{r} 311 \\ +\ 298 \\ \hline \end{array}$$

8. Estimate: _____
$$\begin{array}{r} 534 \\ +\ 256 \\ \hline \end{array}$$

Problem Solving · Real World

9. Mark has 215 baseball cards. Emily has 454 baseball cards. How many baseball cards do Mark and Emily have altogether?

10. Jason has 330 pennies. Richie has 268 pennies. Rachel has 381 pennies. Which two students have more than 700 pennies combined?

_____

11. **WRITE** *Math* Explain one way to add 3-digit numbers.

_____

_____

Lesson Check

1. There are 167 students in the third grade. The same number of students is in the fourth grade. How many third graders and fourth graders are there?

   _____

2. Jamal read a book with 128 pages. Then he read a book with 179 pages. How many pages did Jamal read?

   _____

Spiral Review

3. Adam travels 248 miles on Monday. He travels 167 miles on Tuesday. Estimate the total number of miles Adam travels.

   _____

   _____

4. Wes made $14, $62, $40, and $36 mowing lawns. How much did he make mowing lawns?

   _____

   _____

5. There are 24 students in Mrs. Cole's class and 19 students in Mr. Garmen's class. How many students are in the two classes?

   _____

6. There were 475 children at the baseball game on Sunday. What is 475 rounded to the nearest ten?

   _____

FOR MORE PRACTICE
GO TO THE
Personal Math Trainer

Name _____

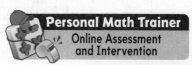
Vocabulary

Choose the best term from the box.

1. A _____ is an ordered set of numbers or objects in which the order helps you predict what comes next. (p. 5)

2. The _____ states that when you add zero to any number, the sum is that number. (p. 5)

Concepts and Skills

Is the sum even or odd? Write *even* or *odd*.

3. 8 + 5 _____ | 4. 9 + 7 _____ | 5. 4 + 6 _____

Use rounding or compatible numbers to estimate the sum.

6. 56
   +32   + ____

7. 271
   +425   + ____

8. 328
   +127   + ____

Use mental math to find the sum.

9. 46 + 14 = _____ | 10. 39 + 243 = _____ | 11. 326 + 402 = _____

Estimate. Then find the sum.

12. Estimate: _____

    356
   +442

13. Estimate: _____

    164
   +230

14. Estimate: _____

    545
   +139

15. Estimate: _____

    437
   +184

16. Nancy planted 77 daisies, 48 roses, and 39 tulips. About how many roses and tulips did she plant?

_____

17. Tomas collected 139 cans for recycling on Monday, and twice that number on Tuesday. How many cans did he collect on Tuesday?

_____

18. There are 294 boys and 332 girls in the Hill School. How many students are in the school?

_____

19. **GO DEEPER** Monday's art group made 25 paper models. Tuesday's group made 32 paper models. Wednesday's group made 15 paper models. How many paper models did the groups make?

_____

48

Estimate Differences

Essential Question How can you use compatible numbers and rounding to estimate differences?

Learning Objective You will use compatible numbers and rounding to estimate differences.

⚷ Unlock the Problem

The largest yellowfin tuna caught by fishers weighed 387 pounds. The largest grouper caught weighed 436 pounds. About how much more did the grouper weigh than the yellowfin tuna?

You can estimate to find *about* how much more.

- Does the question ask for an exact answer? How do you know?

_____

_____

- Circle the numbers you need to use.

⚷ One Way Use compatible numbers.

Think: Compatible numbers are numbers that are easy to compute mentally and are close to the real numbers.

$$
\begin{array}{ccc}
4\,3\,6 & \to & 4\,2\,5 \\
-\,3\,8\,7 & \to & -\,3\,7\,5 \\
\end{array}
$$

So, the grouper weighed about

_____ pounds more than the yellowfin tuna.

Yellowfin tuna

Grouper

- What other compatible numbers could you have used?

_____

Try This! Estimate. Use compatible numbers.

A	$73 \to 75$	**B**	$376 \to$
	$-22 \to -$		$-148 \to -150$

🔒 Another Way Use place value to round.

436 − 387 = ▪

STEP 1 Round 436 to the nearest ten.

> **Think:** Find the place to which you want to round. Look at the digit to the right.

- Look at the digit in the ones place.
- Since 6 > 5, the digit 3 increases by one.
- Write a zero for the ones place.

$$
4\,3\underset{\uparrow}{6} \qquad \begin{array}{r} 4\,3\,6 \\ -\,3\,8\,7 \\ \hline \end{array} \rightarrow \begin{array}{r} \\ - \\ \hline \end{array}
$$

STEP 2 Round 387 to the nearest ten.

- Look at the digit in the ones place.
- Since 7 > 5, the digit 8 increases by one.
- Write a zero for the ones place.

$$
3\,8\underset{\uparrow}{7} \qquad \begin{array}{r} 4\,3\,6 \\ -\,3\,8\,7 \\ \hline \end{array} \rightarrow \begin{array}{r} 4\,4\,0 \\ - \\ \hline \end{array}
$$

STEP 3 Find the difference of the rounded numbers.

$$
\begin{array}{r} 4\,3\,6 \\ -\,3\,8\,7 \\ \hline \end{array} \rightarrow \begin{array}{r} 4\,4\,0 \\ -\,3\,9\,0 \\ \hline \end{array}
$$

So, 436 − 387 is about _____.

Try This! Estimate. Use place value to round.

Ⓐ
$$
\begin{array}{r} 761 \\ -528 \\ \hline \end{array} \rightarrow \begin{array}{r} 800 \\ - \\ \hline \end{array}
$$

> **Think:** Round both numbers to the same place value.

Ⓑ
$$
\begin{array}{r} 642 \\ -287 \\ \hline \end{array} \rightarrow \begin{array}{r} \\ -300 \\ \hline \end{array}
$$

Math Talk Math Processes and Practices ❸

Compare Strategies Describe how estimating differences is both the same as and different from estimating sums.

Name _____

1. Use compatible numbers to complete the problem. Then estimate the difference.

$$546 \rightarrow \quad 550$$
$$-209 \rightarrow -\_\_\_\_$$

 Math Talk Math Processes and Practices ⑥

Explain a Method How does rounding help you to estimate?

Use rounding or compatible numbers to estimate the difference.

2.
$$\begin{array}{r} 57 \\ -21 \end{array} \qquad -$$

✓3.
$$\begin{array}{r} 642 \\ -137 \end{array} \qquad -$$

✓4.
$$\begin{array}{r} 374 \\ -252 \end{array} \qquad -$$

On Your Own

Use rounding or compatible numbers to estimate the difference.

5.
$$\begin{array}{r} 67 \\ -24 \end{array} \qquad -$$

6.
$$\begin{array}{r} 81 \\ -39 \end{array} \qquad -$$

7.
$$\begin{array}{r} 936 \\ -421 \end{array} \qquad -$$

8. There are 298 students in the third grade. If 227 students take the bus to school, about how many students do not take the bus?

9. *GO DEEPER* A museum has 324 oil paintings, 227 watercolors paintings, and 158 statues. About how many more oil and watercolor paintings does the museum have than statues?

10. *GO DEEPER* There are 262 students in the second grade and 298 students in the third grade. If 227 students ride their bikes to school, about how many students do not ride their bikes?

Problem Solving • Applications

Use the table for 11–13.

11. (Math Processes and Practices 3) **Use Counterexamples** Melissa said the estimated difference between the weight of the Pacific halibut and the yellowfin tuna is zero. Do you agree or disagree? Explain.

_____

_____

_____

Largest Saltwater Fish Caught	
Type of Fish	**Weight in Pounds**
Pacific Halibut	459
Conger	133
Yellowfin Tuna	387

12. **What's the Question?** The answer is about 500 pounds.

_____

_____

WRITE ▸Math • **Show Your Work**

13. (THINK SMARTER) About how much more is the total weight of the Pacific halibut and conger than the weight of the yellowfin tuna? Explain.

_____

_____

_____

_____

Personal Math Trainer

14. (THINK SMARTER +) A total of 907 people went to a fishing tournament. Of these people, 626 arrived before noon. Alina estimates that fewer than 300 people arrived in the afternoon. How did she estimate? Explain.

_____

_____

Name _____

Estimate Differences

Learning Objective You will use compatible numbers and rounding to estimate differences.

Use rounding or compatible numbers to estimate the difference.

1.   40   40
   − 13   − 10
            30

2.   762   ___
   − 332   − ___

3.   823   ___
   − 242   − ___

4.   98   ___
   − 49   − ___

5.   287   ___
   − 162   − ___

6.   359   ___
   − 224   − ___

7. 771 − 531

   ___ − ___ = ___

8. 299 − 61

   ___ − ___ = ___

Problem Solving Real World

9. Ben has a collection of 812 stamps. He gives his brother 345 stamps. About how many stamps does Ben have left?

_____

_____

10. Savannah's bakery sold 284 loaves of bread in September. In October the bakery sold 89 loaves. About how many more loaves of bread did Savannah's bakery sell in September than in October?

_____

_____

11. **WRITE** ▸Math Explain how to estimate 586 − 321 two different ways.

_____

_____

Lesson Check

1. Jorge has 708 baseball cards and 394 basketball cards. About how many more baseball cards than basketball cards does Jorge have?

   _____

   _____

2. Danika is making necklaces. She has 512 silver beads and 278 blue beads. About how many more silver than blue beads does Danika have?

   _____

   _____

Spiral Review

3. A store manager ordered 402 baseball caps and 122 ski caps. Estimate the total number of caps the manager ordered.

   _____

   _____

4. Autumn collected 129 seashells at the beach. What is 129 rounded to the nearest ten?

   _____

   _____

5. Find the sum.

   $$\begin{array}{r} 585 \\ + 346 \\ \hline \end{array}$$

6. Julie made $22, $55, $38, and $25 babysitting. How much did she make babysitting?

   _____

FOR MORE PRACTICE
GO TO THE
Personal Math Trainer

Mental Math Strategies for Subtraction

Essential Question What mental math strategies can you use to find differences?

Learning Objective You will use mental math strategies to find differences.

Unlock the Problem

A sunflower can grow to be very tall. Dylan is 39 inches tall. She watered a sunflower that grew to be 62 inches tall. How many inches shorter was Dylan than the sunflower?

One Way Use a number line to find 62 − 39.

A Count up by tens and then ones.

Think: Start at 39. Count up to 62.

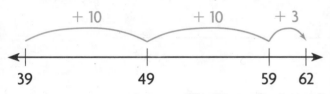

Add the lengths of the jumps to find the difference.

$10 + 10 + 3 =$ _____

$62 - 39 =$ _____

So, Dylan was _____ inches shorter than the sunflower.

B Take away tens and ones.

Think: Start at 62. Count back 39.

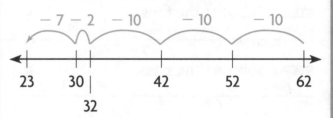

Take away lengths of jumps to end on the difference.

Math Talk

Math Processes and Practices ③

Compare Representations Compare the number lines. Explain where the answer is on each one.

Other Ways

A Use friendly numbers and adjust to find 74 − 28.

STEP 1 Make the number you subtract a friendly number.

Think: Add to 28 to make a number with 0 ones.

$28 + 2 =$ _____

STEP 2 Since you added 2 to 28, you have to add 2 to 74.

$74 + 2 =$ _____

STEP 3 Find the difference.

_____ − _____ = _____

So, $74 - 28 =$ _____ .

Try This! Use friendly numbers to subtract 9 and 99.

- Find 36 – 9.

  Think: 9 is 1 less than 10.

  Subtract 10.   36 – 10 = _____

  Then add 1.   _____ + 1 = _____

  So, 36 – 9 = _____ .

- Find 423 – 99.

  Think: 99 is 1 less than 100.

  Subtract 100.   423 – 100 = _____

  Then add 1.   _____ + 1 = _____

  So, 423 – 99 = _____ .

B Use the break apart strategy to find 458 – 136.

STEP 1 Subtract the hundreds.   400 – 100 = _____

STEP 2 Subtract the tens.   50 – 30 = _____

STEP 3 Subtract the ones.   8 – 6 = _____

STEP 4 Add the differences.   _____ + _____ + _____ = _____

So, 458 – 136 = _____ .

Share and Show  MATH BOARD

1. Find 61 – 24. Draw jumps and label the number line to show your thinking.

   Think: Take away tens and ones.

61

61 – 24 = _____

2. Use friendly numbers to find the difference.

   86 – 42 = _____   Think: 42 – 2 = 40
                              86 – 2 = 84

 Math Talk   Math Processes and Practices ⑥

Describe the break apart strategy for subtracting numbers.

Use mental math to find the difference.
Draw or describe the strategy you use.

✅ **3.** 56 − 38 = _____

✅ **4.** 435 − 121 = _____

Problem Solving • Applications (Real World)

5. (Math Processes and Practices ③) **Make Arguments** Erica used friendly numbers to find 43 − 19. She added 1 to 19 and subtracted 1 from 43. What is Erica's error? Explain.

_____

_____

6. THINK SMARTER The farm shop had 68 small bags of bird treats and 39 large bags of bird treats on a shelf. If Jill buys 5 small bags and 1 large bag, how many more small bags than large bags of bird treats are left on the shelf?

_____

_____

_____

7. THINK SMARTER There were 87 sunflowers at the flower shop in the morning. There were 56 sunflowers left at the end of the day. How many sunflowers were sold? Explain a way to solve the problem.

_____

_____

Compare and Contrast

Emus and ostriches are the world's largest birds. They are alike in many ways and different in others.

When you compare things, you decide how they are alike. When you contrast things, you decide how they are different.

The table shows some facts about emus and ostriches. Use the information on this page to compare and contrast the birds.

Facts About Emus and Ostriches		
	Emus	**Ostriches**
Can they fly?	No	No
Where do they live?	Australia	Africa
How much do they weigh?	About 120 pounds	About 300 pounds
How tall are they?	About 72 inches	About 108 inches
How fast can they run?	About 40 miles per hour	About 40 miles per hour

Ostrich

8. How are emus and ostriches alike?
   How are they different?

   Alike: 1. _____

             2. _____

   Different: 1. _____

             2. _____

             3. _____

9. **GO DEEPER** What if two emus weigh 117 pounds and 123 pounds, and an ostrich weighs 338 pounds. How much more does the ostrich weigh than the two emus?

   _____

Emu

Name _____

Mental Math Strategies for Subtraction

Learning Objective You will use mental math strategies to find differences.

Use mental math to find the difference. Draw or describe the strategy you use.

1. $74 - 39 = $ _____35_____

-5 -4 -10 -10 -10

35 40 44   54   64   74

2. $93 - 28 = $ _____

3. $51 - 12 = $ _____

4. $76 - 23 = $ _____

Problem Solving Real World

5. Ruby has 78 books. Thirty-one of the books are on shelves. The rest are still packed in boxes. How many of Ruby's books are still in boxes?

_____

6. Kyle has 130 pins in his collection. He has 76 of the pins displayed on his wall. The rest are in a drawer. How many of Kyle's pins are in a drawer?

_____

7. **WRITE** ▸Math Give one example of when you would use the friendly numbers strategy to subtract. Explain why.

_____

_____

© Houghton Mifflin Harcourt Publishing Company

Lesson Check

1. One day, a baker made 54 fruit pies. At the end of the day, only 9 of the pies were NOT sold. How many pies were sold that day?

   _____

2. George's father bought a 50-pound bag of wild bird seed. At the end of two weeks, 36 pounds of seed were left in the bag. How many pounds of seed had been used?

   _____

Spiral Review

3. For a party, Shaun blew up 36 red balloons, 28 white balloons, and 24 blue balloons. How many total balloons did he blow up?

   _____

4. Tiffany has read 115 pages of her book. She has 152 pages left to read. How many pages are in the book?

   _____

5. The flower shop had 568 flowers on Monday. By Tuesday, the shop had 159 flowers left. About how many flowers had been sold?

   _____

6. There are 383 books in one section of the school library. Of the books, 165 are fiction books. Estimate the number of books in that section that are NOT fiction.

   _____

FOR MORE PRACTICE
GO TO THE
Personal Math Trainer

Name _____

Use Place Value to Subtract

Essential Question How can you use place value to subtract 3-digit numbers?

Learning Objective You will use place value to subtract 3-digit numbers.

 Unlock the Problem

Ava sold 473 tickets for the school play. Kim sold 294 tickets. How many more tickets did Ava sell than Kim?

🔑 **Use place value to subtract.**

Subtract. 473 − 294

Estimate. 475 − 300 = _____

- Do you need to combine or compare the number of tickets sold?

  _____

- Circle the numbers you will need to use.

STEP 1

Subtract the ones.
3 < 4, so regroup.

7 tens 3 ones =

6 tens _____ ones

```
  6 13
  4 7 3
- 2 9 4
```

STEP 2

Subtract the tens.
6 < 9, so regroup.

4 hundreds 6 tens =

3 hundreds _____ tens

```
    16
  3 6 13
  4 7 3
- 2 9 4
      9
```

STEP 3

Subtract the hundreds.
Add to check your answer.

```
    16
  3 6 13        1 1
  4 7 3         1 7 9
- 2 9 4       + 2 9 4
    7 9         4 7 3
```

So, Ava sold _____ more tickets than Kim.

Since _____ is close to the estimate of _____, the answer is reasonable.

Math Idea
Addition and subtraction undo each other. So you can use addition to check subtraction.

Try This! Use place value to subtract. Use addition to check your work.

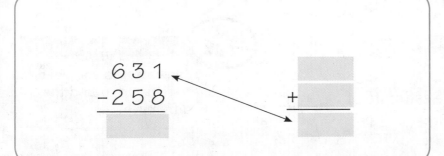

```
  6 3 1            
- 2 5 8         +   
```

① Example Use place value to find 890 − 765.

Estimate. 900 − 750 = _____

STEP 1	**STEP 2**	**STEP 3**
Subtract the ones. Regroup the tens as tens and ones.	Subtract the tens.	Subtract the hundreds. Add to check your answer.

STEP 1:
```
   8 10
  8 9 0̸
 −7 6 5
 ───────
```

STEP 2:
```
   8 10
  8 9 0̸
 −7 6 5
 ───────
      5
```

STEP 3:
```
   8 10
  8 9 0̸          1 2 5
 −7 6 5         +7 6 5
 ───────        ───────
   2 5
```

So, 890 − 765 = _____.

Math Talk

Math Processes and Practices ①

Describe Reasonableness How do you know your answer is reasonable?

Try This! Circle the problem in which you need to regroup. Find the difference.

Ⓐ	Ⓑ	Ⓒ
894 −583	521 −301	918 −427

Share and Show MATH BOARD

1. Estimate. Then use place value to find 627 − 384. Add to check your answer.

Estimate. _____ − _____ = _____

```
 6 2 7           
−3 8 4         +3 8 4
───────        ───────
```

Math Talk

Math Processes and Practices ①

Evaluate Did you need to regroup to find the difference?

Since _____ is close to the estimate of _____, the answer is reasonable.

62

© Houghton Mifflin Harcourt Publishing Company

Name _____

Estimate. Then find the difference.

2. Estimate: _____

$$\begin{array}{r} 386 \\ -123 \\ \hline \end{array}$$

3. Estimate: _____

$$\begin{array}{r} 519 \\ -205 \\ \hline \end{array}$$

4. Estimate: _____

$$\begin{array}{r} 456 \\ -217 \\ \hline \end{array}$$

5. Estimate: _____

$$\begin{array}{r} 642 \\ -159 \\ \hline \end{array}$$

6. Estimate: _____

$$\begin{array}{r} 242 \\ -220 \\ \hline \end{array}$$

7. Estimate: _____

$$\begin{array}{r} 870 \\ -492 \\ \hline \end{array}$$

8. Estimate: _____

$$\begin{array}{r} 654 \\ -263 \\ \hline \end{array}$$

9. Estimate: _____

$$\begin{array}{r} 937 \\ -618 \\ \hline \end{array}$$

Math Talk Math Processes and Practices ❶

Make Sense of Problems Which exercises can you compute mentally? Explain why.

On Your Own

10. Darius has 127 photos. Jillian has 467 photos. How many more photos does Jillian have than Darius?

_____

11. Beth, Dan, and Yoshi collect stamps. Beth has 157 stamps. Dan has 265 stamps. Yoshi has 79 fewer stamps than Beth and Dan do combined. How many stamps does Yoshi have?

_____

Practice: Copy and Solve Estimate. Then solve.

12. $568 - 276$ 13. $761 - 435$ 14. $829 - 765$ 15. $974 - 285$

Math Processes and Practices ❷ **Use Reasoning** **Algebra** Find the unknown number.

16.
$$\begin{array}{r} 86 \\ - \\ \hline 62 \end{array}$$

17.
$$\begin{array}{r} 372 \\ - \\ \hline 240 \end{array}$$

18.
$$\begin{array}{r} 537 \\ - \\ \hline 172 \end{array}$$

19.
$$\begin{array}{r} 629 \\ - \\ \hline 335 \end{array}$$

Problem Solving • Applications

Use the table for 20–21.

20. **THINK SMARTER** Alicia sold 59 fewer tickets than Jenna and Matt sold together. How many tickets did Alicia sell? Explain.

_____

_____

_____

School Play Tickets Sold	
Student	**Number of Tickets**
Jenna	282
Matt	178
Sonja	331

21. **GO DEEPER** How many more tickets would each student need to sell so that each student sells 350 tickets?

_____

_____

22. Nina says to check subtraction, add the difference to the number you subtracted from. Does this statement make sense? Explain.

_____

_____

_____

23. **Math Processes and Practices 5** **Communicate** Do you have to regroup to find $523 - 141$? Explain. Then solve.

_____

_____

Personal Math Trainer

24. **THINK SMARTER +** Students want to sell 400 tickets to the school talent show. They have sold 214 tickets. How many more tickets do they need to sell to reach their goal? Show your work.

_____

Use Place Value to Subtract

Learning Objective You will use place value to subtract 3-digit numbers.

Estimate. Then find the difference.

1. Estimate: __500__

$$\begin{array}{r} \overset{7\ \ 15}{5\cancel{8}5} \\ -\ 119 \\ \hline \end{array}$$

2. Estimate: _____

$$\begin{array}{r} 738 \\ -\ 227 \\ \hline \end{array}$$

3. Estimate: _____

$$\begin{array}{r} 651 \\ -\ 376 \\ \hline \end{array}$$

4. Estimate: _____

$$\begin{array}{r} 815 \\ -\ 281 \\ \hline \end{array}$$

5. Estimate: _____

$$\begin{array}{r} 627 \\ -\ 253 \\ \hline \end{array}$$

6. Estimate: _____

$$\begin{array}{r} 862 \\ -\ 419 \\ \hline \end{array}$$

7. Estimate: _____

$$\begin{array}{r} 726 \\ -\ 148 \\ \hline \end{array}$$

8. Estimate: _____

$$\begin{array}{r} 543 \\ -\ 358 \\ \hline \end{array}$$

Problem Solving

9. Mrs. Cohen has 427 buttons. She uses 195 buttons to make puppets. How many buttons does Mrs. Cohen have left?

10. There were 625 ears of corn and 247 tomatoes sold at a farm stand. How many more ears of corn were sold than tomatoes?

_____

_____

11. **WRITE** ▸ *Math* Explain how to subtract 247 from 538.

_____

_____

_____

Lesson Check

1. On Saturday, 453 people go to a school play. On Sunday, 294 people go to the play. How many more people go to the play on Saturday?

   _____

2. Corey has 510 marbles. He fills one jar with 165 marbles. How many of Corey's marbles are NOT in the jar?

   _____

Spiral Review

3. Pattie brought 64 peppers to sell at the farmers' market. There were 12 peppers left at the end of the day. How many peppers did Pattie sell?

   _____

4. An airplane flies 617 miles in the morning. Then it flies 385 miles in the afternoon. About how many more miles does the airplane fly in the morning?

   _____

5. What is the unknown number?

   $(\blacksquare + 4) + 59 = 70$

6. Dexter has 128 shells. He needs 283 more shells for his art project. How many shells will Dexter use for his art project?

   _____

FOR MORE PRACTICE
GO TO THE
Personal Math Trainer

Combine Place Values to Subtract

Essential Question How can you use the combine place values strategy to subtract 3-digit numbers?

Learning Objective You will use the combine place values strategy to subtract 3-digit numbers.

 Unlock the Problem Real World

Elena collected 431 bottles for recycling. Pete collected 227 fewer bottles than Elena. How many bottles did Pete collect?

• What do you need to find?

_____

• Circle the numbers you need to use.

🔑 **Combine place values to find the difference.**

Ⓐ **Subtract.** 431 − 227

Estimate. 400 − 200 = _____

STEP 1 Look at the ones place. Since 7 > 1, combine place values. Combine the tens and ones places. There are 31 ones and 27 ones. Subtract the ones. Write 0 for the tens.

$$\begin{array}{r} 4\,\boxed{3\;1} \\ -\,2\,\boxed{2\;7} \\ \hline \end{array}$$ **Think:** 31 − 27

STEP 2 Subtract the hundreds.

So, Pete collected _____ bottles.

Since _____ is close to the estimate

of _____ , the answer is reasonable.

$$\begin{array}{r} 4\,3\,1 \\ -\,2\,2\,7 \\ \hline 0\,4 \end{array}$$

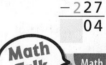 **Math Talk**

Math Processes and Practices ①

Analyze Explain why there is a zero in the tens place.

Ⓑ **Subtract.** 513 − 482

Estimate. 510 − 480 = _____

STEP 1 Subtract the ones.

$$\begin{array}{r} 5\,1\,3 \\ -\,4\,8\,2 \\ \hline \end{array}$$

STEP 2 Look at the tens place. Since 8 > 1, combine place values. Combine the hundreds and tens places. There are 51 tens and 48 tens. Subtract the tens.

$$\begin{array}{r} \boxed{5\;1}\,3 \\ -\,\boxed{4\;8}\,2 \\ \hline 1 \end{array}$$ **Think:** 51 − 48

So, 513 − 482 = _____ .

🔑 Example Combine place values to find 500 − 173.

Estimate. 500 − 175 = _____

STEP 1 Look at the ones and tens places. Since 3 > 0 and 7 > 0 , combine the hundreds and tens.

There are 50 tens. Regroup 50 tens as 49 tens 10 ones.

```
  4 9 10
  5 0 0
-   1 7 3
```

STEP 2 Subtract the ones.

Think: 10 − 3

```
  4 9 10
  5 0 0
-   1 7 3
```

STEP 3 Subtract the tens.

Think: 49 − 17

```
  4 9 10
  5 0 0
-   1 7 3
        7
```

So, 500 − 173 = _____ .

Math Talk

Math Processes and Practices ⑧

Use Repeated Reasoning Explain why you combined the hundreds and tens.

Try This! Find 851 − 448 in two ways.

Estimate. 850 − 450 = _____

Ⓐ Use place value.

```
  8 5 1
- 4 4 8
```

Ⓑ Combine place values.

```
  8 5 1
- 4 4 8
```

Think: Combine tens and ones.

1. When does the combine place values strategy make it easier to find the difference? Explain.

_____

_____

_____

2. Which strategy would you use to find 431 − 249? Explain.

_____

_____

Name _____

Share and Show MATH BOARD

1. Combine place values to find 406 − 274.

$$406$$
$$-274$$

Think: Subtract the ones. Then combine the hundreds and tens places.

Estimate. Then find the difference.

☑ **2.** Estimate: _____

$$595$$
$$-286$$

3. Estimate: _____

$$728$$
$$-515$$

4. Estimate: _____

$$543$$
$$-307$$

☑ **5.** Estimate: _____

$$600$$
$$-453$$

On Your Own

Estimate. Then find the difference.

6. Estimate: _____

$$438$$
$$-257$$

7. Estimate: _____

$$706$$
$$-681$$

8. Estimate: _____

$$839$$
$$-754$$

9. Estimate: _____

$$916$$
$$-558$$

10. GO DEEPER A train travels a distance of 872 miles. Then it travels another 342 miles. The train then travels another 403 miles. How many more miles does the train travel on the first part of the trip than on the second and third trips combined?

_____

11. Denzel wants to subtract 517 − 183. How can he combine the place values to find the difference?

_____

_____

Practice: Copy and Solve Estimate. Then solve.

12. 457 − 364

13. 652 − 341

14. 700 − 648

15. 963 − 256

Problem Solving • Applications

Use the table for 16–18.

Roller Coaster Heights		
Roller Coaster	**State**	**Height in Feet**
Titan	Texas	245
Kingda Ka	New Jersey	456
Intimidator 305	Virginia	305
Top Thrill Dragster	Ohio	420

16. **Math Processes and Practices 5** **Use Appropriate Tools** The table shows the heights of some roller coasters in the United States. How much taller is Kingda Ka than Titan?

_____

17. **Go DEEPER** Jason rode two roller coasters with a difference in height of 115 feet. Which roller coasters did Jason ride?

_____

WRITE *Math* • **Show Your Work**

18. **THINK SMARTER** What if another roller coaster was 500 feet tall? Which roller coaster would be 195 feet shorter?

_____

19. **THINK SMARTER** Owen solves this problem. He says the difference is 127. Explain the mistake Owen made. What is the correct difference?

$$\begin{array}{r} 335 \\ -218 \end{array}$$

_____

_____

_____

Combine Place Values to Subtract

Learning Objective You will use the combine place values strategy to subtract 3-digit numbers.

Estimate. Then find the difference.

1. Estimate: __200__
    $$\begin{array}{r} 476 \\ - \ 269 \\ \hline \end{array}$$

2. Estimate: _____
    $$\begin{array}{r} 615 \\ - \ 342 \\ \hline \end{array}$$

3. Estimate: _____
    $$\begin{array}{r} 508 \\ - \ 113 \\ \hline \end{array}$$

4. Estimate: _____
    $$\begin{array}{r} 716 \\ - \ 229 \\ \hline \end{array}$$

5. Estimate: _____
    $$\begin{array}{r} 826 \\ - \ 617 \\ \hline \end{array}$$

6. Estimate: _____
    $$\begin{array}{r} 900 \\ - \ 158 \\ \hline \end{array}$$

7. Estimate: _____
    $$\begin{array}{r} 607 \\ - \ 568 \\ \hline \end{array}$$

8. Estimate: _____
    $$\begin{array}{r} 973 \\ - \ 869 \\ \hline \end{array}$$

Problem Solving Real World

9. Bev scored 540 points. This was 158 points more than Ike scored. How many points did Ike score?

10. A youth group earned $285 washing cars. The group's expenses were $79. How much profit did the group make washing cars?

_____

_____

11. **WRITE** ▸*Math* Explain how to use the combine place values strategy to find 223 − 119.

_____

_____

Lesson Check

1. A television program lasts for 120 minutes. Of that time, 36 minutes are taken up by commercials. What is the length of the actual program without the commercials?

   _____

2. Syd spent 215 minutes at the library. Of that time, he spent 120 minutes on the computer. How much of his time at the library did Sid NOT spend on the computer?

   _____

Spiral Review

3. Xavier's older brother has 568 songs on his music player. To the nearest hundred, about how many songs are on the music player?

   _____

4. The students traveled to the zoo in 3 buses. One bus had 47 students. The second bus had 38 students. The third bus had 43 students. How many total students were on the three buses?

   _____

5. Callie has 83 postcards in her collection. Of the postcards, 24 are from Canada. The rest of the postcards are from the United States. How many of the postcards are from the United States?

   _____

6. There were 475 seats set up for the school play. At one performance, 189 of the seats were empty. How many seats were filled at that performance?

   _____

© Houghton Mifflin Harcourt Publishing Company

FOR MORE PRACTICE
GO TO THE
Personal Math Trainer

Name _____

Problem Solving •
Model Addition and Subtraction

Essential Question How can you use the strategy *draw a diagram* to solve one- and two-step addition and subtraction problems?

Learning Objective You will use the strategy *draw a diagram* to solve real-world addition and subtraction problems by drawing bar models.

Unlock the Problem

Sami scored 84 points in the first round of a new computer game. He scored 21 more points in the second round than in the first round. What was Sami's total score?

Read the Problem

What do I need to find?	**What information do I need to use?**	**How will I use the information?**
I need to find _____.	Sami scored _____ points in the first round. He scored _____ more points than that in the second round.	I will draw a bar model to show the number of points Sami scored in each round. Then I will use the bar model to decide which operation to use.

Solve the Problem

- Complete the bar model to show the number of points Sami scored in the second round.

  ☐ points

  Round 1 | _____ points

  Round 2 | ■ points

  _____ + _____ = ■

  _____ = ■

- Complete another bar model to show Sami's total score.

  _____ points | _____ points

  ▲ points

  _____ + _____ = ▲

  _____ = ▲

1. How many points did Sami score in the second round? _____

2. What was Sami's total score? _____

Try Another Problem

Anna scored 265 points in a computer game. Greg scored 142 points. How many more points did Anna score than Greg?

You can use a bar model to solve the problem.

Read the Problem

What do I need to find?	What information do I need to use?	How will I use the information?

Solve the Problem

Record the steps you used to solve the problem.

Anna _____ points

Greg _____ points

■ points

3. How many more points did Anna score than Greg?

_____

4. How do you know your answer is reasonable?

_____

_____

_____

5. How did your drawing help you solve the problem?

_____

_____

Math Talk

Math Processes and Practices 6

Make Connections Explain how the length of each bar in the model would change if Greg scored more points than Anna but the totals remained the same.

74

Name _____

Unlock the Problem

✓ Use the problem solving MathBoard.
✓ Choose a strategy you know.

✓ **1.** Sara received 73 votes in the school election. Ben received 25 fewer votes than Sara. How many students voted?

First, find how many students voted for Ben.

Think: 73 − 25 = ■

Write the numbers in the bar model.

So, Ben received _____ votes.

Next, find the total number of votes.

Think: 73 + 48 = ▲

Write the numbers in the bar model.

So, _____ students voted.

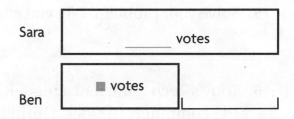

Sara [_____ votes]

Ben [■ votes] [ ]

_____ votes

■ = _____ votes

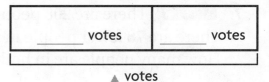

[_____ votes | _____ votes]

▲ votes

▲ = _____ votes

✓ **2.** If Ben received 73 votes and Sara received 25 fewer votes than Ben, how would your bar models change? Would the total votes be the same? Explain.

_____

_____

_____

3. *THINK SMARTER* What if there were 3 students in another election and the total number of votes was the same? What would the bar model for the total number of votes look like? How many votes might each student get?

Math on the Spot

_____

_____

_____

© Houghton Mifflin Harcourt Publishing Company

4. **Pose a Problem** Use the bar model at the right. Write a problem to match it.

89	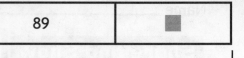

157

_____

_____

5. Solve your problem. Will you add or subtract?

_____

6. Tony's Tech Store had a big sale. The store had 142 computers in stock. During the sale, 91 computers were sold. How many computers were not sold?

_____

7. **GO DEEPER** There are 208 people in one movie theater. There are 78 fewer people in the next movie theater. How many people are in both movie theaters?

_____

8. **GO DEEPER** In one week, 128 cell phones were sold. The following week, 37 more cell phones were sold than the week before. How many cell phones were sold in those two weeks?

_____

9. **Math Processes and Practices 6** On Monday, the number of customers in the store, rounded to the nearest hundred, was 400. What is the greatest number of customers that could have been in the store? **Explain.**

_____

_____

10. **THINK SMARTER** There are 306 people at the fair on Saturday. There are 124 fewer people on Sunday. How many people are at the fair during the two days?

_____

Name _____

Problem Solving • Model Addition and Subtraction

Learning Objective You will use the strategy *draw a diagram* to solve real-world addition and subtraction problems by drawing bar models.

Use the bar model to solve the problem.

1. Elena went bowling. Elena's score in the first game was 127. She scored 16 more points in the second game than in the first game. What was her total score?

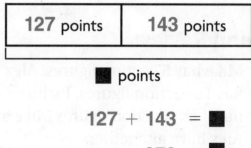

16 points

Game 1 | **127** points

Game 2 | ▲ points

127 + 16 = ▲

143 = ▲

__270 points__

127 points | 143 points

■ points

127 + 143 = ■

270 = ■

2. Mike's Music sold 287 CDs on the first day of a 2-day sale. The store sold 96 more CDs on the second day than on the first day. How many CDs in all were sold during the 2-day sale?

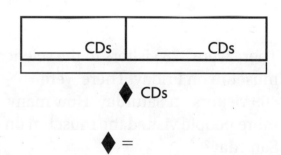

_____ CDs

Day 1 | _____ CDs

Day 2 | ✦ CDs

✦ =

_____ CDs | _____ CDs

◆ CDs

◆ =

_____

3. **WRITE** ▸*Math* Write an addition or subtraction problem and draw a diagram to solve it.

_____

_____

Lesson Check

1. Ms. Hinely picked 46 tomatoes from her garden on Friday. On Saturday, she picked 17 tomatoes. How many tomatoes did she pick?

_____

2. Rosa read 57 pages of a book in the morning. She read 13 fewer pages in the afternoon. How many pages did Rosa read in the afternoon?

_____

Spiral Review

3. Mike has 57 action figures. Alex has 186 action figures. Estimate the number of action figures Mike and Alex have altogether.

_____

_____

4. There are 500 sheets of paper in the pack Hannah bought. She has used 137 sheets already. How many sheets of paper does Hannah have left?

_____

_____

5. There were 378 visitors to the science museum on Friday. There were 409 visitors on Saturday. How many more people visited the museum on Saturday?

_____

6. Ravi scores 247 points in a video game. How many more points does he need to score a total of 650?

_____

FOR MORE PRACTICE
GO TO THE
Personal Math Trainer

✓ Chapter 1 Review/Test

Personal Math Trainer
Online Assessment
and Intervention

1. For numbers 1a–1d, choose Yes or No to tell whether the sum is even.

   1a. $5 + 8$ ○ Yes   ○ No

   1b. $9 + 3$ ○ Yes   ○ No

   1c. $6 + 7$ ○ Yes   ○ No

   1d. $9 + 5$ ○ Yes   ○ No

2. Select the number sentences that show the Commutative Property of Addition. Mark all that apply.

   Ⓐ $14 + 8 = 22$

   Ⓑ $8 + 14 = 14 + 8$

   Ⓒ $8 + (13 + 1) = (8 + 13) + 1$

   Ⓓ $(5 + 9) + 8 = (9 + 5) + 8$

3. Select the numbers that round to 300 when rounded to the nearest hundred. Mark all that apply.

   Ⓐ   238

   Ⓑ   250

   Ⓒ   283

   Ⓓ   342

   Ⓔ   359

4. There are 486 books in the classroom library. Complete the chart to show 486 rounded to the nearest 10.

Hundreds	Tens	Ones

© Houghton Mifflin Harcourt Publishing Company

GO DIGITAL   Assessment Options
Chapter Test

5. Write each number sentence in the box below the better estimate of the sum.

393 + 225 = ▪   481 + 215 = ▪

352 + 328 = ▪   309 + 335 = ▪

600	700

6. GO DEEPER Diana sold 336 muffins at the bake sale. Bob sold 287 muffins. Bob estimates that he sold 50 fewer muffins than Diana. How did he estimate? Explain.

7. The table shows how many books each class read.

Reading Contest	
Class	Number of Books
Mr. Lopez	273
Ms. Martin	402
Mrs. Wang	247

For numbers 7a–7d, select True or False for each statement.

7a. Ms. Martin's class read about 100 more books than Mr. Lopez's class.   ○ True   ○ False

7b. The 3 classes read over 900 books altogether.   ○ True   ○ False

7c. Mrs. Wang's class read about 50 fewer books than Mr. Lopez's class.   ○ True   ○ False

7d. Ms. Martin's and Mrs. Wang's class read about 700 books.   ○ True   ○ False

80

Name _____

8. Janna buys 2 bags of dog food for her dogs. One bag weighs 37 pounds. The other bag weighs 15 pounds. How many pounds do both bags weigh? Explain how you solved the problem.

9. Choose the property that makes the statement true.

The Identity / Commutative / Associative Property of addition states that you

can group addends in different ways and get the same sum.

Use the table for 10–12.

Susie's Sweater Shop	
Month	Number of Sweaters Sold
January	402
February	298
March	171

10. The table shows the number of sweaters sold online in three months. How many sweaters were sold in January and February?

_____ sweaters

11. How many more sweaters were sold in January than March?

_____ sweaters

12. How many more sweaters were sold in February and March than in January?

_____ sweaters

© Houghton Mifflin Harcourt Publishing Company

Chapter 1 81

13. Help Dana find the sum.

$$
\begin{array}{r}
346 \\
421 \\
+\ 152 \\
\hline
\end{array}
$$

For numbers 13a–13d, select Yes or No to tell Dana
when to regroup.

13a.   Regroup the ones.   ○ Yes   ○ No

13b.   Add the regrouped
        ten.   ○ Yes   ○ No

13c.   Regroup the tens.   ○ Yes   ○ No

13d.   Add the regrouped
        hundred.   ○ Yes   ○ No

14. Alexandra has 78 emails in her inbox. She deletes
47 emails. How many emails are left in her inbox? Draw
jumps and label the number line to show your thinking.

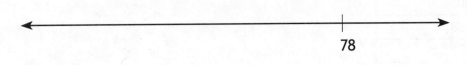

78

_____ emails

15. Daniel has 402 pieces in a building set. He uses
186 pieces to build a house. How many pieces does
he have left? Show your work.

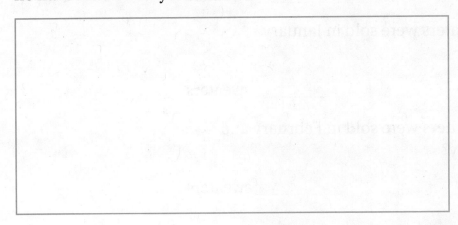

16. Luke solves this problem. He says the difference is 214. Explain the mistake Luke made. What is the correct difference?

$$
\begin{array}{r}
352 \\
- 148 \\
\hline
\end{array}
$$

17. Sunnyday Elementary School is having its annual Read-a-thon. The third graders have read 573 books so far. Their goal is to read more than 900 books. What is the least number of books they need to read to reach their goal? Explain.

18. **THINK SMARTER +** There are 318 fiction books in the class library. The number of nonfiction books is 47 less than the number of fiction books.

Personal Math Trainer

Part A

About how many nonfiction books are there in the class library? Explain.

Part B

How many fiction and nonfiction books are there in the class library altogether? Show your work.

19. GO DEEPER Alia used $67 + 38 = 105$ to check her subtraction. Which math problem could she be checking? Mark all that apply.

Ⓐ $67 - 38 = \blacksquare$

Ⓑ $105 - 67 = \blacksquare$

Ⓒ $105 + 38 = \blacksquare$

Ⓓ $105 - 38 = \blacksquare$

20. Alexa and Erika collect shells. The tables show the kinds of shells they collected.

Alexa's Shells	
Shell	Number of Shells
Scallop	36
Jingle	95
Clam	115

Erika's Shells	
Shell	Number of Shells
Scallop	82
Clam	108
Whelk	28

Part A

Who collected more shells? How many did she collect? About how many more is that? Explain how you solved the problem.

Part B

Alexa and Erika have the greatest number of what kind of shell? How many shells of that kind do they have? Show your work.

Represent and Interpret Data

Show What You Know

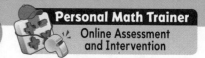

Personal Math Trainer
Online Assessment
and Intervention

Check your understanding of important skills.

Name _____

▶ **Numbers to 20** Circle the number word. Write the number.

1.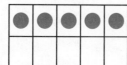

2.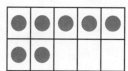

fourteen _____   seventeen _____

fifteen   eighteen

▶ **Skip Count** Skip count to find the missing numbers.

3. Count by twos. 2, 4, ____, ____, 10, ____, ____, 16

4. Count by fives. 5, 10, ____, ____, ____, 30, ____

▶ **Addition and Subtraction Facts** Find the sum or difference.

5. $12 - 4 =$ ____   6. $9 + 8 =$ ____   7. $11 - 7 =$ ____

Paige helps to sell supplies in the school store. Each month she totals all the sales and makes a bar graph. The graph shows sales through December. Help to find the month during which the hundredth sale was made.

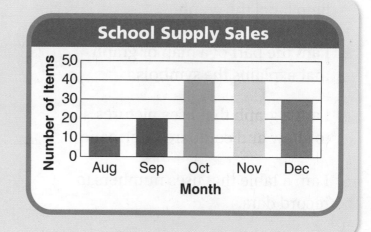

Vocabulary Builder

▶ **Visualize It** •••••••••••••••••••••••••••••••••••

Complete the bubble map by using the words with a ✓.

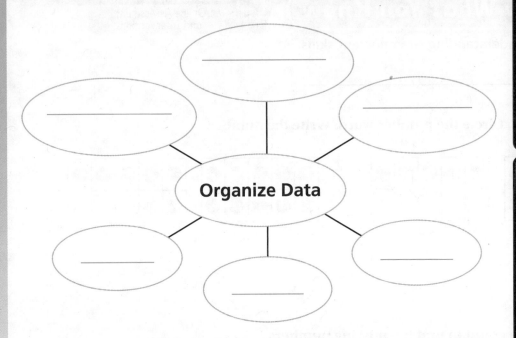

Organize Data

▶ **Understand Vocabulary** ••••••••••••••••••••••••

Write the review word or preview word that answers the riddle.

1. I am a graph that records each piece of data above a number line. _____

2. I am the numbers that are placed at fixed distances on a graph to help label the graph. _____

3. I am the part of a map or graph that explains the symbols. _____

4. I am a graph that uses pictures to show and compare information. _____

5. I am a table that uses numbers to record data. _____

GO DIGITAL
• Interactive Student Edition
• Multimedia eGlossary

Chapter 2 Vocabulary

Frequency Table
tabla de frecuencia

29

Horizontal Bar Graph
gráfica de barras horizontales

33

key
clave

38

line plot
diagrama de puntos

43

Picture Graph
gráfica con dibujos

61

Scale
escala

73

tally table
tabla de conteo

76

Vertical Bar Graph
gráfica de barras verticales

83

A bar graph in which the bars go across from left to right

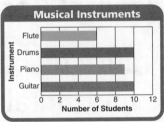

A table that uses numbers to record data

Favorite Color	
Color	Number
Blue	10
Green	8
Red	7
Yellow	4

A graph that records each piece of data on a number line

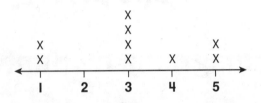

The part of a map or graph that explains the symbols

Fish in Eric's Tank	
Guppies	🐟 🐟
Mollies	🐟 🐟 🐟 🐟 🐟
Neons	🐟 🐟 🐟

Key — Key: Each 🐟 stands for 5 fish.

The numbers placed at fixed distances on a graph to help label the graph

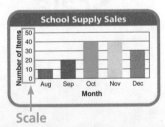

Scale

A graph that uses pictures to show and compare information

Fish in Eric's Tank	
Guppies	🐟 🐟
Mollies	🐟 🐟 🐟 🐟 🐟
Neons	🐟 🐟 🐟

Key: Each 🐟 stands for 5 fish.

A bar graph in which the bars go up from bottom to top

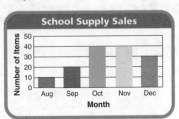

A table that uses tally marks to record data

Favorite Sport	
Sport	Tally
Soccer	卌 |||
Baseball	|||
Football	卌
Basketball	卌	

Going Places with GO MATH! words

Game

Picture It

Word Box

frequency table

horizontal bar
  graph

key

line plot

picture graph

scale

tally table

vertical bar graph

For 3 to 4 players

Materials

- timer
- sketch pad

How to Play

1. Take turns to play.
2. To take a turn, choose a math term but do not say it aloud.
3. Set the timer for 1 minute.
4. Draw pictures and numbers to give clues about the word.
5. The first player to guess the word before time runs out gets
   1 point. If that player can use the word in a sentence, he or she
   gets 1 more point. Then that player gets a turn choosing a word.
6. The first player to score 10 points wins.

The Write Way

Reflect

Choose one idea. Write about it.

- Describe something you know about bar graphs.
- Write two questions you have about how to use a key or scale in graphs.
- Explain how to read a line plot.

Name _____

Problem Solving • Organize Data

Essential Question How can you use the strategy *make a table* to organize data and solve problems?

Learning Objective You will use the strategy *make a table* with tally tables and frequency tables to organize data and solve problems.

🔑 Unlock the Problem

The students in Alicia's class voted for their favorite yogurt flavor. They organized the data in this tally table. How many more students chose chocolate than strawberry?

Another way to show the data is in a frequency table. A **frequency table** uses numbers to record data.

Favorite Yogurt Flavor	
Flavor	**Tally**
Vanilla	卌 ‖
Chocolate	卌 ‖‖
Strawberry	‖‖‖

Read the Problem

What do I need to find?

How many more students chose

_____ than _____ yogurt
as their favorite?

What information do I need to use?

the data about favorite _____
in the tally table

How will I use the information?

I will count the _____. Then I will put the numbers in a frequency table and compare the number of students

who chose _____ to the number of

students who chose _____.

Solve the Problem

Favorite Yogurt Flavor	
Flavor	**Number**
Vanilla	

Count the tally marks. Record _____ for vanilla. Write the other flavors and record the number of tally marks.

To compare the number of students who chose strawberry and the number of students who chose chocolate, subtract.

_____ − _____ = _____

So, _____ more students chose chocolate as their favorite flavor.

Math Processes and Practices ②

Reason Abstractly Why would you record data in a frequency table?

Try Another Problem

Two classes in Carter's school grew bean plants for a science project. The heights of the plants after six weeks are shown in the tally table. The plants were measured to the nearest inch. How many fewer bean plants were 9 inches tall than 7 inches and 8 inches combined?

Bean Plant Heights

Height in Inches	Tally
7	卌 IIII
8	卌 III
9	卌 卌 II
10	卌 IIII

Read the Problem	Solve the Problem
What do I need to find?	**Record the steps you used to solve the problem.**
What information do I need to use?	
How will I use the information?	

- Suppose the number of 3-inch plants was half the number of 8-inch plants. How many 3-inch bean plants were there?

_____

Math Talk

Math Processes and Practices ①

Explain a Method What is another strategy you could use to solve the problem?

Name _____

Share and Show MATH BOARD

Use the Shoe Lengths table for 1–3.

☑ 1. The students in three third-grade classes recorded
   the lengths of their shoes to the nearest centimeter.
   The data are in the tally table. How many more shoes
   were 18 or 22 centimeters long combined than
   20 centimeters long?

   First, count the tally marks and record the data
   in a frequency table.

   To find the number of shoes that were 18 or
   22 centimeters long, add

   6 + _____ + _____ + _____ = _____.

   To find the number of shoes that were

   20 centimeters long, add _____ + _____ = _____.

   To find the difference between the shoes that were
   18 or 22 centimeters long and the shoes that were
   20 centimeters long, subtract the sums.

   _____ − _____ = _____.

   So, _____ more shoes were 18 or 22 centimeters long
   than 20 centimeters long.

Shoe Lengths		
Length in Centimeters	Tally	
	Boys	Girls
18	卌 I	IIII
19	卌	IIII
20	卌 III	卌 IIII
21	卌 II	卌
22	卌 IIII	卌 II

Shoe Lengths		
Length in Centimeters	Number	
	Boys	Girls
18		
19		
20		
21		
22		

☑ 2. How many fewer boys' shoes were 19 cm long than 22 cm long?

   _____

On Your Own

3. _THINK SMARTER_ What if the length of 5 more boys' shoes measured
   21 centimeters? Explain how the table would change.

   _____

   _____

4. **Math Processes and Practices ①** **Analyze** Raj asked his classmates to choose their favorite outdoor game. His results are shown in the frequency table at the right. How many more students chose hide-and-seek than scavenger hunt?

Favorite Outdoor Game	
Game Type	Number
Hide-and-Seek	14
Jump Rope	9
Scavenger Hunt	6
Tag	16

5. **GO DEEPER** How many students in all chose tag, jump rope, or hide-and-seek?

6. **THINK SMARTER** Andrew has 10 more goldfish than Todd. Together, they have 50 goldfish. How many goldfish does each boy have?

7. **THINK SMARTER** Jade made this tally table to record how many students have different types of pets.

Students' Pets	
Type of Pet	Tally
Dog	JHT JHT IIII
Rabbit	III
Hamster	JHT
Cat	JHT II

For numbers 7a–7d, select True or False for each statement.

7a. Nine fewer students have hamsters than have dogs. ○ True   ○ False

7b. Seven students have cats. ○ True   ○ False

7c. Fewer students have cats than hamsters. ○ True   ○ False

7d. More students have dogs than all other animals combined. ○ True   ○ False

Name _____

Problem Solving • Organize Data

Learning Objective You will use the strategy *make a table* with tally tables and frequency tables to organize data and solve problems.

Use the Favorite School Subject tables for 1–3.

1. The students in two third-grade classes recorded their favorite school subject. The data are in the tally table. How many fewer students chose science than chose social studies as their favorite school subject?

   Think: Use the data in the tally table to record the data in the frequency table. Then solve the problem.

   social studies: __12__ students

   science: __5__ students

   $12 - 5 = $ __7__

   So, __7__ fewer students chose science.

2. What subject did the least number of students choose?

   _____

3. How many more students chose math than language arts as their favorite subject?

   _____ more students

Favorite School Subject	
Subject	Tally
Math	‖‖‖ ‖‖‖ │
Science	‖‖‖
Language Arts	‖‖‖ ‖‖
Reading	‖‖‖ ‖‖‖
Social Studies	‖‖‖ ‖‖‖ ‖‖

Favorite School Subject	
Subject	Number
Math	
Science	5
Language Arts	
Reading	
Social Studies	12

4. **WRITE** ▸*Math* Give one example of when you would make a frequency table to solve a problem.

_____

_____

Lesson Check

The tally table shows the cards in Kyle's sports card collection.

1. How many hockey and football cards does Kyle have combined?

Kyle's Sports Cards	
Sport	Tally
Baseball	IIII IIII
Hockey	IIII
Basketball	III
Football	IIII III

_____

Spiral Review

2. There are 472 people in the concert hall. What is 472 rounded to the nearest hundred?

3. Max and Anna played a video game as a team. Max scored 463 points and Anna scored 329 points. How many points did they score?

_____   _____

4. Judy has 573 baseball cards in her collection. Todd has 489 baseball cards in his collection. How many fewer cards does Todd have than Judy?

5. Ms. Westin drove 542 miles last week and 378 miles this week on business. How many miles did she drive on business during the two weeks?

_____   _____

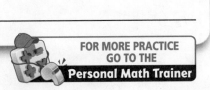

FOR MORE PRACTICE
GO TO THE
Personal Math Trainer

Name _____

Use Picture Graphs

Essential Question How can you read and interpret data in a picture graph?

Learning Objective You will read and interpret data in a picture graph.

Unlock the Problem Real World

A **picture graph** uses small pictures or symbols to show and compare information.

Nick has a picture graph that shows how some students get to school. How many students ride the bus?

- Underline the words that tell you where to find the information to answer the question.
- How many ☺ are shown for Bus?

  _____

Each row has a label that names one way students get to school.

How We Get to School	
Walk	☺ ☺ ☺
Bike	☺ ☺ ☺ ☺
Bus	☺ ☺ ☺ ☺ ☺ ☺ ☺ ☺
Car	☺ ☺ ☺ ☺ ☺ ☺

Key: Each ☺ = 10 students.

The title says that the picture graph is about how some students get to school.

The **key** tells that each picture or symbol stands for the way 10 students get to school.

🔑 To find the number of students who ride the bus, count each ☺ as 10 students.

10, 20, _____, _____, _____, _____, _____, _____

So, _____ students ride the bus to school.

1. How many fewer students walk than ride the bus? _____

2. How many students were surveyed? _____

3. What if the symbol stands for 5 students? How many symbols will you need to show the number of students who walk to school? _____

Use a Half Symbol

🔖 How many students chose an orange as their favorite fruit?

Math Idea

Half of the picture stands for half the value of the whole picture.

☺ = 2 students

◖ = 1 student

Our Favorite Fruit

Banana	☺ ☺ ☺ ☺ ☺
Apple	☺ ☺ ☺
Pear	☺ ☺
Orange	☺ ☺ ☺ ☺ ◖

Key: Each ☺ = 2 students.

Count the ☺ in the orange row by twos. Then add 1 for the half symbol.

2, 4, _____, _____   _____ + _____ = _____

So, _____ students chose an orange as their favorite fruit.

Share and Show MATH BOARD

Use the **Number of Books Students Read** picture graph for 1–3.

Number of Books Students Read

September	📖 📖 📖 📖
October	📖 📖 📖 📖 📖 📖
November	📖 📖 📖 📖

Key: Each 📖 = 2 books.

1. What does  stand for?

   Think: Half of 2 is 1.

   _____

✔ 2. How many books did the students read in September?

   _____

✔ 3. How many more books did the students read in October than in November?

   _____

Math Talk   Math Processes and Practices ❹

Use Graphs How does the graph change if 6 fewer books were read in October and 3 more books were read in September?

Name _____

On Your Own

Use the Favorite Game picture graph for 4–10.

4. How many students chose puzzles?

_____

5. GO DEEPER If 6 more students voted for card games and 4 more students voted for board games, how many more students voted for puzzles and card games than board games?

_____

6. **Math Processes and Practices 8** **Draw Conclusions** Which two types of games did a total of 34 students choose?

_____

7. GO DEEPER How many students were surveyed?

_____

8. How many students did not choose card games?

_____

9. **WRITE** ▸Math **What's the Error?** Jacob said one more student chose board games than puzzles. Explain his error.

_____

_____

_____

10. GO DEEPER What if computer games were added as a choice and more students chose it than puzzles, but fewer students chose it than board games? How many students would choose computer games?

_____

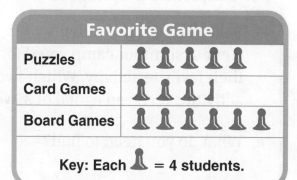

Favorite Game					
Puzzles	♟	♟	♟	♟	♟
Card Games	♟	♟	♟	♩	
Board Games	♟	♟	♟	♟	♟

Key: Each ♟ = 4 students.

Unlock the Problem

Use the picture graph for 11–12.

11. **THINK SMARTER** The students who went to summer camp voted for their favorite activity. Which two activities received a total of 39 votes?

Favorite Camp Activity	
Biking	☀ ☀ ☀ 🌤
Hiking	☀ ☀ ☀ ☀
Boating	☀ ☀ ☀
Fishing	☀ 🌤

Key: Each ☀ = 6 students.

a. What do you need to find?

_____

b. What steps will you use to solve the problem?

_____

c. Show the steps you used to solve the problem.

d. Complete the sentences.

Each ☀ = _____ students.

Each 🌤 = _____ students.

votes for biking + hiking = _____

votes for hiking + boating = _____

votes for biking + boating = _____

votes for fishing + hiking = _____

So, _____ received a total of 39 votes.

Personal Math Trainer

12. **THINK SMARTER +** Choose the word from each box that makes the sentence true.

Fifteen fewer students voted for
| hiking |
| boating |
| fishing |
than for
| hiking |
| boating |
| fishing |
.

Name _____

Use Picture Graphs

Learning Objective You will read and interpret data in a picture graph.

Use the Math Test Scores picture graph for 1–5.

Mrs. Perez made a picture graph of her students' scores on a math test.

Math Test Scores	
100	★★★★★
95	★★★
90	★★★◗
85	★

Key: Each ★ = 4 students.

1. How many students scored 100? How can you find the answer?

   To find the number of students who scored 100, count each star as 4 students. So, 20 students scored 100.

2. What does ◗ stand for?

3. How many students in all scored 100 or 95?

Problem Solving (Real World)

4. Suppose the students who scored 85 and 90 on the math test take the test again and score 95. How many stars would you have to add to the picture graph next to 95?

5. If 2 more students took the math test and both made a score of 80, what would the picture graph look like?

6. **WRITE** ▸Math Explain what you can tell just by comparing the symbols in a picture graph.

Lesson Check

1. Karen asked her friends to name their favorite type of dog.

Favorite Dog

Retriever	🦴 🦴 🦴 🦴 🦴 🦴
Poodle	🦴 🦴 🦴
Terrier	🦴 🦴

Key: Each 🦴 = 2 people.

How many people chose poodles?

_____

2. Henry made a picture graph to show what topping people like on their pizza. This is his key.

Each 🍕 = 6 people.

What does 🍕 🍕 stand for?

_____

Spiral Review

3. Estimate the sum.

$$\begin{array}{r} 523 \\ + 295 \\ \hline \end{array}$$

_____

_____

4. Estimate the difference.

$$\begin{array}{r} 610 \\ - 187 \\ \hline \end{array}$$

_____

_____

5. What is 871 rounded to the nearest ten?

6. What is 473 rounded to the nearest hundred?

© Houghton Mifflin Harcourt Publishing Company

**FOR MORE PRACTICE
GO TO THE
Personal Math Trainer**

Name _____

Make Picture Graphs

Essential Question How can you draw a picture graph to show data in a table?

Learning Objective You will create a scaled picture graph to represent a data set given in a table.

Unlock the Problem Real World

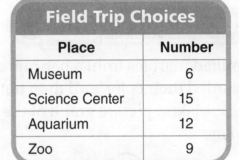

Delia made the table at the right. She used it to record the places the third grade classes would like to go during a field trip. How can you show the data in a picture graph?

Field Trip Choices

Place	Number
Museum	6
Science Center	15
Aquarium	12
Zoo	9

🔑 **Make a picture graph.**

STEP 1

Write the title at the top of the picture graph. Write the name of a place in each row.

STEP 2

Look at the numbers in the table. Choose a picture for the key, and tell how many students each picture represents. Write the key at the bottom of the graph.

STEP 3

Draw the correct number of pictures for each field trip choice.

Museum	

Key: Each ____ = ____ students.

- How did you decide how many pictures to draw for the Science Center?

_____

_____

Try This! Make a picture graph from data you collect. Take a survey or observe a subject that interests you. Collect and record the data in a frequency table. Then make a picture graph. Decide on a symbol and a key. Include a title and labels.

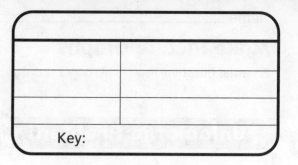

Key:	

Jeremy pulled marbles from a bag one at a time, recorded their color, and then put them back. Make a picture graph of the data. Use this key:

Each ◯ = 2 marbles.

Jeremy's Marble Experiment

Color	Number
Blue	4
Green	11
Red	8

Key:	

Use your picture graph above for 1–2.

☑ **1.** How many more times did Jeremy pull out a red marble than a blue marble?

☑ **2.** How many fewer times did Jeremy pull out green marbles than blue and red marbles combined?

_____

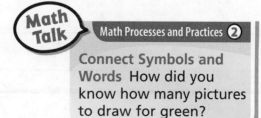

Math Talk

Math Processes and Practices ❷

Connect Symbols and Words How did you know how many pictures to draw for green?

Name _____

3. Two classes from Delia's school visited the Science Center. They recorded their favorite exhibit in the tally table. Use the data in the table to make a picture graph. Use this key:

Each ☼ = 4 votes.

Favorite Exhibit

Exhibit	Tally
Nature	IIII I
Solar System	IIII III
Light and Sound	IIII IIII IIII
Human Body	IIII III

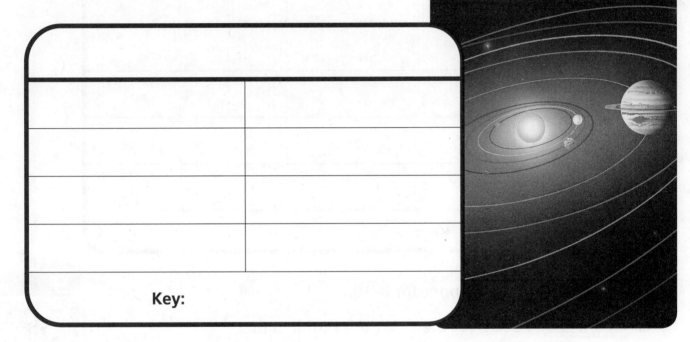

Key:	

Use your picture graph above for 4–6.

4. Which exhibits received the same number of votes?

_____

5. (Math Processes and Practices 4) **Model Mathematics** What if a weather exhibit received 22 votes? Explain how many pictures you would draw.

_____

6. *THINK SMARTER* What if the Solar System exhibit received 15 votes? Would it make sense to use the key Each ☼ = 4 votes to represent 15 votes? Explain.

_____

Problem Solving • Applications

Teeth in Mammals	
Animal	**Number**
Hamster	16
Cat	30
Dog	42
Cow	32

7. While at the Science Center, Delia's classmates learned how many teeth some mammals have. Use the data in the table to make a picture graph. Use this key:

Each △ = 4 teeth.

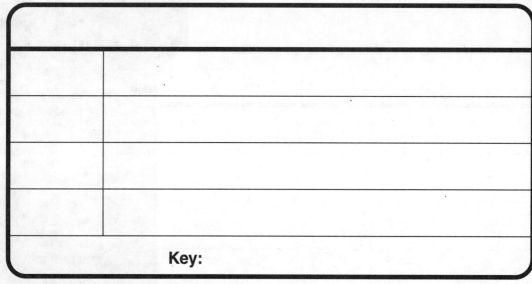

Key:

Use your picture graph above for 8–10.

8. **THINK SMARTER** **Pose a Problem** Write a problem that can be solved by using the data in your picture graph. Then solve the problem.

_____

9. **GO DEEPER** How many fewer teeth do cats and hamsters have combined than dogs and cows combined?

_____

10. **THINK SMARTER** How many pictures would you draw for Cat if each △ = 5 teeth? Explain your reasoning.

_____

_____

Name _____

Make Picture Graphs

Learning Objective You will create a scaled picture graph to represent a data set given in a table.

Ben asked his classmates about their favorite kind of TV show. He recorded their responses in a frequency table. Use the data in the table to make a picture graph.

Follow the steps to make a picture graph.

Step 1 Write the title at the top of the graph

Step 2 Look at the numbers in the table. Tell how many students each picture represents for the key

Step 3 Draw the correct number of pictures for each type of show.

Use your picture graph for 1–4.

1. What title did you give the graph?

   _____

2. What key did you use?

   _____

Favorite TV Show	
Type	Number
Cartoons	9
Sports	6
Movies	3

Cartoons	■ ■ ■
Sports	
Movies	

Key: Each ■ =

Problem Solving Real World

3. How many pictures would you draw if 12 students chose game shows as their favorite kind of TV show?

   _____

4. What key would you use if 10 students chose cartoons?

   _____

5. **WRITE** ▸ *Math* Describe why it might not be a good idea to use a key where each symbol stands for 1 in a picture graph.

   _____

   _____

Lesson Check

1. Sandy made a picture graph to show the sports her classmates like to play. How many fewer students chose baseball than chose soccer?

Favorite Sport	
Basketball	○○○○○○○○
Soccer	○○○○○○○○○◖
Baseball	○○○○○

Key: Each ○ = 2 students.

_____

2. Tommy is making a picture graph to show his friends' favorite kind of music. He plans to use one musical note to represent 2 people. How many notes will he use to represent that 4 people chose country music?

_____

Spiral Review

3. Find the sum.

$$490$$
$$+\ 234$$

_____

_____

4. Sophie wrote odd numbers on her paper. What is a number Sophie did NOT write?

_____

_____

5. Miles ordered 126 books to give away at the store opening. What is 126 rounded to the nearest hundred?

_____

_____

6. Estimate the difference.

$$422$$
$$-\ 284$$

_____

_____

FOR MORE PRACTICE
GO TO THE
Personal Math Trainer

Name _____

Personal Math Trainer
Online Assessment
and Intervention

Vocabulary

Choose the best term from the box.

Vocabulary
frequency table
key
picture graph

1. A _____ uses numbers to record data. (p. 87)

2. A _____ uses small pictures or symbols to show and compare information. (p. 93)

Concepts and Skills

Use the Favorite Season table for 3–6.

Favorite Season	
Season	**Number**
Spring	19
Summer	28
Fall	14
Winter	22

3. Which season got the most votes?

   _____

4. Which season got 3 fewer votes than winter?

   _____

5. How many more students chose summer than fall?

   _____

6. How many students chose a favorite season?

   _____

Use the Our Pets picture graph for 7–9.

7. How many students have cats as pets?

   _____

8. Five more students have dogs than which other pet? _____

9. How many pets in all do students have?

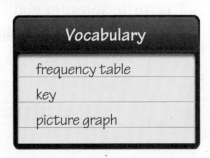

Our Pets	
Bird	🐾 🐾 🐾 🐾
Cat	🐾 🐾 🐾 🐾 🐾
Dog	🐾 🐾 🐾 🐾 🐾 🐾 ◖
Fish	🐾 🐾 🐾
Key: Each 🐾 = 2 students.	

   _____

© Houghton Mifflin Harcourt Publishing Company

Use the Favorite Summer Activity picture graph for 10–14.

10. Some students in Brooke's school chose their favorite summer activity. The results are in the picture graph at the right. How many students chose camping?

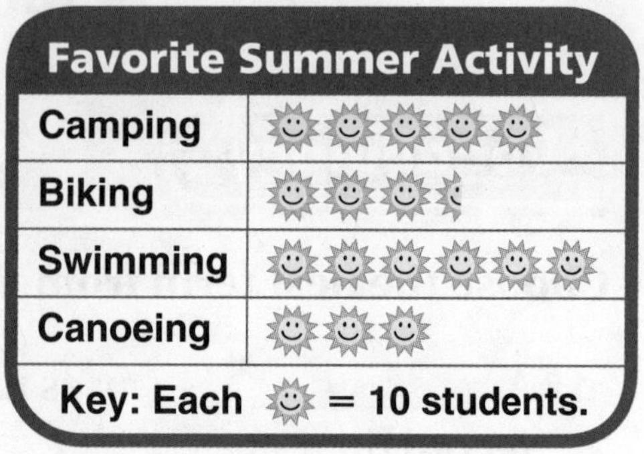

Favorite Summer Activity	
Camping	☀☀☀☀☀
Biking	☀☀☀☀
Swimming	☀☀☀☀☀☀
Canoeing	☀☀☀
Key: Each ☀ = 10 students.	

_____

11. How many more students chose swimming than canoeing?

_____

12. Which activity did 15 fewer students choose than camping?

_____

13. How many pictures would you draw for biking if each ☀ = 5 students?

_____

14. **GO DEEPER** How many more students choose swimming and camping combined than biking and canoeing?

_____

Name _____

Use Bar Graphs

Essential Question How can you read and interpret data in a bar graph?

Learning Objective You will read and interpret data in a bar graph.

Unlock the Problem

A **bar graph** uses bars to show data. A **scale** of equally spaced numbers helps you read the number each bar shows.

The students in the reading group made a bar graph to record the number of books they read in October. How many books did Seth read?

> • Underline the words that tell you where to find the information to answer the question.

The title tells what the bar graph is about.

Books Read in October

The length of a bar tells how many books each student read.

The scale is 0–16 by twos.

Each bar is labeled with a student's name.

Student: Max, Amy, Seth, Kate

Number of Books: 0 2 4 6 8 10 12 14 16

Math Talk

Math Processes and Practices ②

Connect Symbols and Words Explain how to read the bar that tells how many books Amy read.

Find the bar for Seth. It ends at _____.

So, Seth read _____ books in October.

1. How many books did Max read? _____

2. Who read 4 fewer books than Kate? _____

3. What if Amy read 5 more books? How many books did Amy read? _____ Shade the graph to show how many she read.

More Examples These bar graphs show the same data.

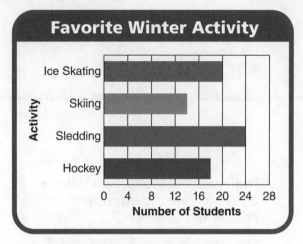

In a **horizontal bar graph**, the bars go across from left to right. The length of the bar shows the number.

In a **vertical bar graph**, the bars go up from the bottom. The height of the bar shows the number.

4. What does each space between two numbers represent?

_____

5. Why do you think the scale in the graphs is 0 to 28 by fours instead of 0 to 28 by ones? What other scale could you use?

_____

_____

Share and Show MATH BOARD

Use the Favorite Way to Exercise bar graph for 1–3.

1. Which activity did the most students choose?

Think: Which bar is the longest?

_____

☑ **2.** How many students answered the survey? _____

☑ **3.** Which activity received 7 fewer votes than soccer? _____

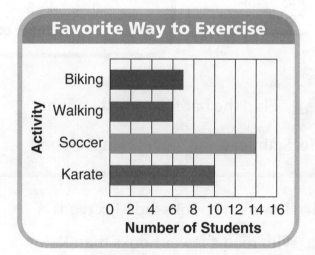

Math Talk

Math Processes and Practices ②

Reason Quantitatively
What can you tell just by comparing the lengths of the bars in the graph?

Name _____

Problem Solving • Applications

Use the Favorite Kind of Book bar graph for 4–8.

Favorite Kind of Book

4. Which kind of book was chosen by half the number of students as books about animals?

_____

5. **GO DEEPER** Which two kinds of books combined were chosen as often as books about sports?

_____

6. **Math Processes and Practices 4** **Use Graphs** Write and solve a problem that matches the data in the graph.

_____

_____

7. **THINK SMARTER** What if 10 more students were asked and they chose books about animals? Describe what the bar graph would look like.

_____

_____

8. **THINK SMARTER** For numbers 8a–8d, select True or False for each statement.

8a. More students chose books about sports than any other kind of book. ○ True ○ False

8b. Five more students chose books about puzzles than books about space. ○ True ○ False

8c. Thirty more students chose books about animals than books about nature. ○ True ○ False

8d. Fifteen fewer students chose books about puzzles than books about sports. ○ True ○ False

Sense or Nonsense?

9. **THINK SMARTER** The table shows data about some students' favorite amusement park rides. Four students graphed the data. Which student's bar graph makes sense?

Favorite Amusement Ride

Ride	Number of Students
Super Slide	11
Ferris Wheel	14
Bumper Cars	18
Roller Coaster	23

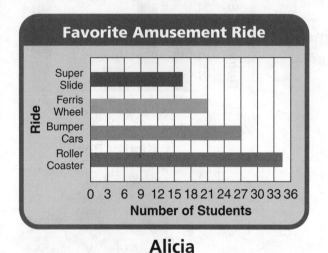

Alicia

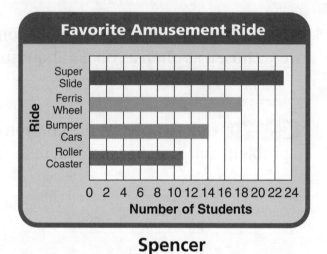

Spencer

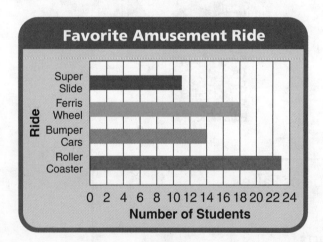

Tyler

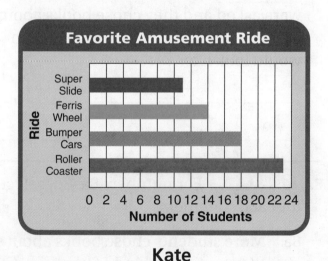

Kate

• Explain why the other bar graphs do not make sense.

_____

_____

Name _____

Use Bar Graphs

Learning Objective You will read and interpret data in a bar graph.

Use the After-Dinner Activities bar graph for 1–6.

The third-grade students at Case Elementary School were asked what they spent the most time doing last week after dinner. The results are shown in the bar graph at the right.

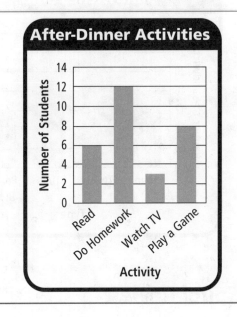

1. How many students spent the most time watching TV after dinner?

   _____3 students_____

2. How many students in all answered the survey?

   _____

3. How many students in all played a game or read?

   _____

4. How many fewer students read than did homework?

   _____

Problem Solving · Real World

5. Suppose 3 students changed their answers to reading instead of doing homework. Where would the bar for reading end?

   _____

6. **WRITE** ▸ *Math* Use After-Dinner Activites bar graph to describe what the bar for Do Homework means.

   _____

   _____

Lesson Check

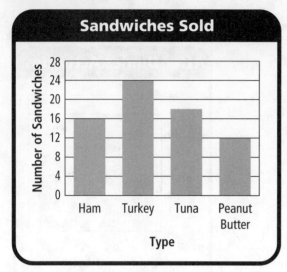

Sandwiches Sold

1. The bar graph shows the number of sandwiches sold at Lisa's sandwich cart yesterday. How many tuna sandwiches were sold?

_____

Spiral Review

2. What is 582 rounded to the nearest ten?

_____

3. Savannah read 178 minutes last week. What is 178 rounded to the nearest hundred?

_____

4. Estimate the difference.

```
  371
-  99
```

5. Estimate the difference.

```
  625
- 248
```

_____

FOR MORE PRACTICE GO TO THE Personal Math Trainer

Name _____

Make Bar Graphs

Essential Question How can you draw a bar graph to show data in a table or picture graph?

Learning Objective You will create a scaled bar graph to represent a data set given in a table or a picture graph.

 Unlock the Problem Real World

Jordan took a survey of his classmates' favorite team sports. He recorded the results in the table at the right. How can he show the results in a bar graph?

Favorite Team Sport

Sport		Tally
Soccer	⚽	IIII IIII II
Basketball	🏀	IIII
Baseball	⚾	IIII IIII IIII
Football	🏈	IIII IIII

🔑 **Make a bar graph.**

STEP 1

Write a title at the top to tell what the graph is about. Label the side of the graph to tell about the bars. Label the bottom of the graph to explain what the numbers tell.

STEP 2

Choose numbers for the bottom of the graph so that most of the bars will end on a line. Since the least number is 4 and the greatest number is 14, make the scale 0–16. Mark the scale by twos.

STEP 3

Draw and shade a bar to show the number for each sport.

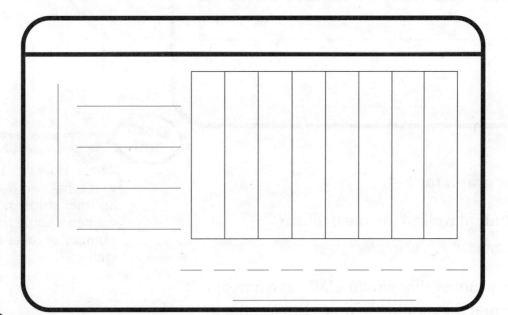

Math Talk

Math Processes and Practices ⑥

Make Connections How did you know how long to draw the bar for all of the sports?

Share and Show

Matt's school is having a walk-a-thon to raise money for the school library. Matt made a picture graph to show the number of miles some students walked. Make a bar graph of Matt's data. Use a scale of 0–_____, and mark the scale by _____.

School Walk-a-Thon					
Sam	👕	👕	👕	👕	👕
Matt	👕	👕	👕		
Ben	👕				
Erica	👕	👕	👕	👕	

Key: Each 👕 = 2 miles.

Use your bar graph for 1–4.

1. Which student walked the most miles? _____

   Think: Which student's bar is the tallest?

2. How many more miles would Matt have had to walk to equal the number of miles Erica walked? _____

3. How many miles did the students walk? _____

4. Write the number of miles the students walked in order from greatest to least. _____

Math Talk

Math Processes and Practices 3

Apply How would the graph have to change if another student, Daniel, walked double the number of miles Erica walked?

114

Name _____

5. Lydia and Joey did an experiment with a spinner. Lydia recorded the result of each spin in the table at the right. Use the data in the table to make a bar graph. Choose numbers and a scale and decide how to mark your graph.

Spinner Results	
Color	Tally
Red	卌 卌 卌 I
Yellow	卌 III
Blue	卌 卌 II
Green	卌 卌

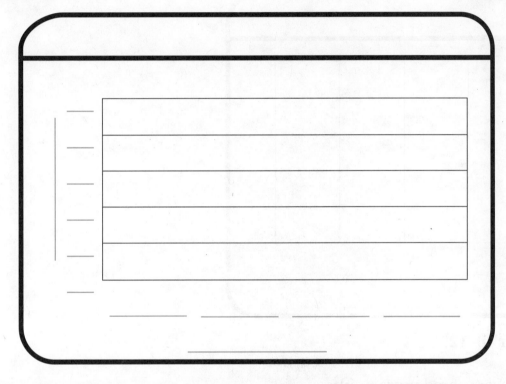

 ERROR Alert
Be sure to draw the bars correctly when you transfer data from a table.

Use your bar graph for 6–8.

6. The pointer stopped on _____ half the number of times that it stopped on _____ .

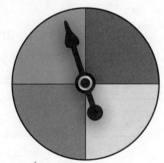

7. GO DEEPER The pointer stopped on green _____ fewer times than it stopped on blue and yellow combined.

8. Math Processes and Practices 6 **Explain** why you chose the scale you did.

_____

_____

Problem Solving • Applications

9. ⟨Math Processes and Practices ④⟩ **Use Graphs** Susie recorded the number of points some basketball players scored. Use the data in the table to make a bar graph. Choose numbers so that most of the bars will end on a line.

Points Scored	
Player	**Number of Points**
Billy	10
Dwight	30
James	15
Raul	25
Sean	10

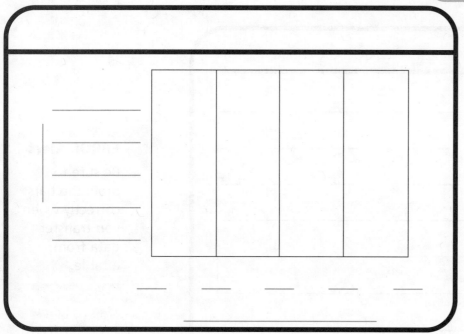

Use your bar graph for 10–12.

10. ⟨GO DEEPER⟩ Which player scored more points than James but fewer points than Dwight? _____

11. ⟨THINK SMARTER⟩ Write and solve a new question that matches the data in your bar graph.

_____

_____

12. ⟨THINK SMARTER⟩ Which player scored 10 more points than James?

_____

Make Bar Graphs

Learning Objective You will create a scaled bar graph to represent a data set given in a table or a picture graph.

Ben asked some friends to name their favorite breakfast food. He recorded their choices in the frequency table at the right.

Favorite Breakfast Food	
Food	Number of Votes
Waffles	8
Cereal	14
Pancakes	12
Oatmeal	4

1. Complete the bar graph by using Ben's data.

Favorite Breakfast Food

Use your bar graph for 2–4.

2. Which food did the most people choose as their favorite breakfast food?

   _____

3. How many people chose waffles as their favorite breakfast food?

   _____

4. Suppose 6 people chose oatmeal as their favorite breakfast food. How would you change the bar graph?

   _____

   _____

   _____

5. **WRITE** ▸ *Math* Have students use the data on page 116 and explain how to draw a bar for a player named Eric who scored 20 points.

   _____

   _____

Lesson Check

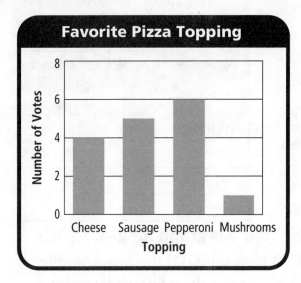

Favorite Pizza Topping

1. Gary asked his friends to name their favorite pizza topping. He recorded the results in a bar graph. How many people chose pepperoni?

   _____

2. Suppose 3 more friends chose mushrooms. Where would the bar for mushrooms end?

   _____

Spiral Review

3. Estimate the sum.

   $$458$$
   $$+\ 214$$

   _____

4. Matt added 14 + 0. What is this sum?

   _____

5. There are 682 runners registered for an upcoming race. What is 682 rounded to the nearest hundred?

   _____

6. There are 187 new students this year at Maple Elementary. What is 187 rounded to the nearest ten?

   _____

FOR MORE PRACTICE GO TO THE
Personal Math Trainer

Name _____

Solve Problems Using Data

Essential Question How can you solve problems using data represented in bar graphs?

Learning Objective You will use bar graphs to solve one- and two-step "how many more" and "how many less" problems.

Unlock the Problem

CONNECT Answering questions about data helps you better understand the information.

Derek's class voted on a topic for the school bulletin board. The bar graph shows the results. How many more votes did computers receive than space?

- How do you know you need to subtract?

_____

_____

One Way Use a model.

Count back along the scale to find the difference between the bars.

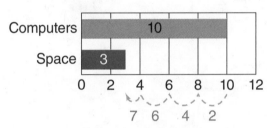

Count back from 10 to 3.
Skip count by twos.

The difference is _____ votes.

Another Way Write a number sentence.

Think: There are 10 votes for computers. There are 3 votes for space. Subtract to compare the number of votes.

_____

So, computers received _____ more votes than space.

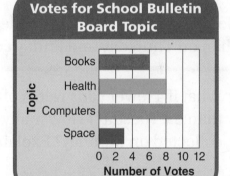

Votes for School Bulletin Board Topic

Topic / Number of Votes

Books, Health, Computers, Space
0 2 4 6 8 10 12

Math Talk

Math Processes and Practices ⑥

Explain another way you can skip count to find the difference.

🔑 Example

Brooke's school collected cans of food. The bar graph at the right shows the number of cans. How many fewer cans were collected on Tuesday than on Thursday and Friday combined?

STEP 1 Find the total for Thursday and Friday.

_____

STEP 2 Subtract to compare the total for Thursday and Friday to Tuesday and to find the difference.

_____

So, _____ fewer cans were collected on Tuesday than on Thursday and Friday combined.

Cans of Food Collected

- What if 4 fewer cans were collected on Monday than on Tuesday? How many cans were collected on Monday? Explain.

Share and Show MATH BOARD

Use the Spinner Results bar graph for 1–3.

1. How many more times did the pointer stop on green than on purple?

   _____ more times

✓ 2. How many fewer times did the pointer stop on blue than on red and green combined?

   _____ fewer times

✓ 3. What if there were 15 more spins and the pointer stopped 10 more times on green and 5 more times on blue? How many more total times did the pointer stop on green than blue?

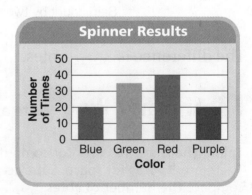

Spinner Results

Math Talk

Math Processes and Practices ②

Use Reasoning What can you tell just by comparing the lengths of the bars in the graphs?

Name _____

On Your Own

Use the Diego's DVDs bar graph for 4–6.

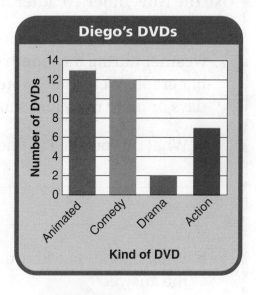

Diego's DVDs

4. Diego has 5 fewer of this kind of DVD than comedy. Which kind of DVD is this?

_____

5. **GO DEEPER** Is the number of comedy and action DVDs greater than or less than the number of animated and drama DVDs? Explain.

_____

_____

6. **THINK SMARTER** How many DVDs does Diego have that are NOT comedy DVDs?

_____

Problem Solving • Applications Real World

Use the Science Fair Projects bar graph for 7–9.

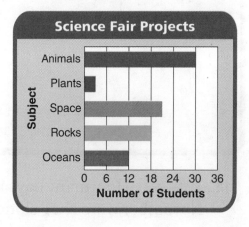

Science Fair Projects

7. How many more students would have to do a project on plants to equal the number of projects on space?

_____

8. **WRITE** *Math* **What's the Question?** The answer is animals, space, rocks, oceans, and plants.

_____

_____

9. **Math Processes and Practices 1** What if 3 fewer students did a project on weather than did a project on rocks? **Describe** what the bar graph would look like.

_____

_____

Unlock the Problem

Use the November Weather bar graph for 10–12.

10. **GO DEEPER** Lacey's class recorded the kinds of weather during the month of November in a bar graph. Were there more cloudy and sunny days or more rainy and snowy days?

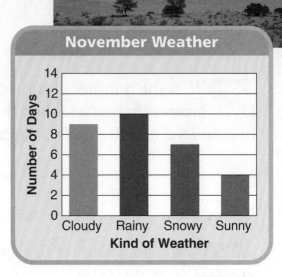

November Weather

Number of Days (y-axis: 0, 2, 4, 6, 8, 10, 12, 14)

Cloudy: 9
Rainy: 10
Snowy: 7
Sunny: 4

Kind of Weather

a. What do you need to find?

_____

_____

b. What operation will you use to find the answer?

_____

c. Show the steps you used to find the answer.

d. Complete the sentences.

_____ cloudy days +

_____ sunny days = _____ days

_____ rainy days +

_____ snowy days = _____ days

_____ > _____

So, there were more _____ days.

11. **GO DEEPER** How many days in November were NOT cloudy?

Think: There are 30 days in November.

_____

12. **THINK SMARTER +** Is the number of cloudy and snowy days greater than or less than the number of rainy and sunny days? Explain.

Personal Math Trainer

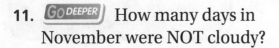

_____

_____

Solve Problems Using Data

Learning Objective You will use bar graphs to solve one- and two-step "how many more" and "how many less" problems.

Use the Favorite Hot Lunch bar graph for 1–2.

1. How many more students chose pizza than chose grilled cheese?

   Think: Subtract the number of students who chose grilled cheese, 2, from the number of students who chose pizza, 11.

   $11 - 2 = 9$ _____ more students

2. How many students did not choose chicken patty? _____ students

Use the Ways to Get to School bar graph for 3–5.

3. How many more students walk than ride in a car to get to school?

   _____ more students

Favorite Hot Lunch

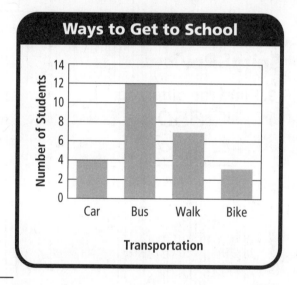

Ways to Get to School

Problem Solving Real World

4. Is the number of students who get to school by car and bus greater than or less than the number of students who get to school by walking and biking? **Explain.**

   _____

   _____

5. What if 5 more students respond that they get to school by biking? Would more students walk or ride a bike to school? **Explain.**

   _____

6. **WRITE** ▸Math Write a word problem that can be solved by using the November Weather bar graph on page 122.

   _____

   _____

Lesson Check

1. How many fewer votes were for bench repair than for food drive?

_____

2. How many votes were there in all?

Community Project

_____

Spiral Review

3. Find the difference.

$$650$$
$$-\ 189$$

4. Greyson has 75 basketball cards. What is 75 rounded to the nearest ten?

_____

5. Sue spent $18 on a shirt, $39 on a jacket, and $12 on a hat. How much did she spend?

6. There are 219 adults and 174 children at a ballet. How many people are at the ballet?

_____

**FOR MORE PRACTICE
GO TO THE
Personal Math Trainer**

Name _____

Use and Make Line Plots

Essential Question How can you read and interpret data in a line plot and use data to make a line plot?

Learning Objective You will read and interpret data in a line plot and use data to make a line plot.

🔑 Unlock the Problem

A **line plot** uses marks to record each piece of data above a number line. It helps you see groups in the data.

Some students took a survey of the number of letters in their first names. Then they recorded the data in a line plot.

How many students have 6 letters in their first names?

> Each ✗ stands for 1 student.

→

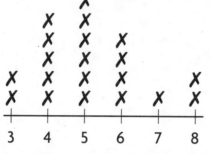

Number of Letters in Our First Names

← The numbers show the number of letters in a name.

🔑 Find 6 on the number line. The 6 stands for 6 _____.

There are _____ ✗s above the 6.

So, _____ students have 6 letters in their first names.

1. Which number of letters was found most often? _____

2. Write a sentence to describe the data. _____

   _____

3. How many letters are in your first name? _____

4. Put an ✗ above the number of letters in your first name.

Math Processes and Practices 8

Generalize What information can the shape of a graph tell you about the data used to create the graph?

Activity Make a line plot.

Materials ■ ruler ■ measuring tape

Measure the height of four classmates to the nearest inch. Combine your data with other groups. Make a line plot to show the data you collected.

STEP 1 Record the heights in the table.

STEP 2 Write a title below the number line to describe your line plot.

STEP 3 Write the number of inches in order from left to right above the title.

STEP 4 Draw Xs above the number line to show each student's height.

Heights in Inches	
Number of Inches	Tally

5. Which height appears most often? _____

   Think: Which height has the most Xs?

6. Which height appears least often? _____

7. Complete the sentence. Most of the students in the class are _____ inches tall or taller.

8. **THINK SMARTER** Is there any height for which there are no data? Explain.

_____

_____

Name _____

Share and Show MATH BOARD

1. Measure the length of three drawing tools from your desk to the nearest inch. Combine your data with several other classmates. Record the lengths in the table.

✓ 2. Make a line plot to show the data you collected.

Lengths in Inches	
Number of Inches	Tally

┼──────┼──────┼──────┼──────┼

____ ____ ____ ____ ____

_____

✓ 3. Which length appears most often? _____

Problem Solving • Applications

Use the line plot at the right for 4–6.

4. **Math Processes and Practices 5** **Use Appropriate Tools** Garden club members recorded the height of their avocado plants to the nearest inch in a line plot. Write a sentence to describe what the line plot shows.

   _____

   _____

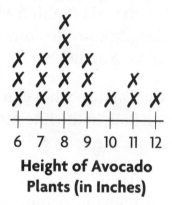

Height of Avocado Plants (in Inches)

5. **THINK SMARTER** How many more plants are 8 or 9 inches tall than are 6 or 7 inches tall? Explain.

   _____

   _____

6. **THINK SMARTER** How many plants are taller than 8 inches?

   _____ plants

© Houghton Mifflin Harcourt Publishing Company

GO DEEPER **Make an Inference**

Addison made the line plot below to show the high temperature every day for one month. What *inference* can you make about what season this is?

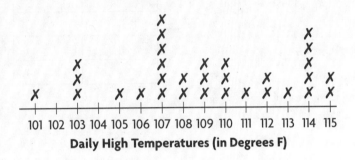

Daily High Temperatures (in Degrees F)

When you combine what you see with what you already know to come up with an idea, you are making an inference.

You can use what you know about weather and the data in the line plot to make an inference about the season.

You know that the numbers in the line plot are the high temperatures recorded during the month.

The highest temperature recorded was _____.

The lowest temperature recorded was _____.

The temperature recorded most often was _____.

Since all the high temperatures are greater than 100, you know the days were hot. This will help you make an inference about the season.

So, you can infer that the season is _____.

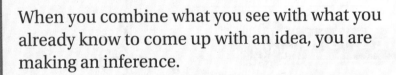

Remember

The Four Seasons

spring

summer

fall

winter

Use and Make Line Plots

Learning Objective You will read and interpret data in a line plot and use data to make a line plot.

Use the data in the table to make a line plot.

How Many Shirts Were Sold at Each Price?	
Price	Number Sold
$11	1
$12	4
$13	6
$14	4
$15	0
$16	2

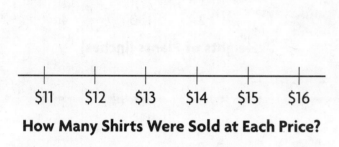

$11 $12 $13 $14 $15 $16

How Many Shirts Were Sold at Each Price?

1. How many shirts sold for $12?

    4 shirts

2. How many shirts were sold for $13 or more?

Problem Solving (Real World)

Use the line plot above for 3–4.

3. Were more shirts sold for less than $13 or more than $13? **Explain**.

    _____

4. Is there any price for which there are no data? **Explain**.

    _____

    _____

5. **WRITE** ▸Math Have students write and solve another problem using the data in the Daily High Temperatures line plot on page 128.

    _____

    _____

Lesson Check

1. Pedro made a line plot to show the heights of the plants in his garden. How many plants are less than 3 inches tall?

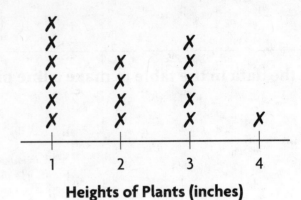

Heights of Plants (inches)

_____

Spiral Review

2. Find the sum.

$$642$$
$$+\ 259$$

_____

3. Find the difference.

$$460$$
$$-\ 309$$

_____

4. There were 262 hamburgers cooked for the school fair. What is 262 rounded to the nearest hundred?

_____

5. Makenzie has 517 stickers in her collection. What is 517 rounded to the nearest ten?

_____

FOR MORE PRACTICE
GO TO THE
Personal Math Trainer

✓ Chapter 2 Review/Test

Personal Math Trainer
Online Assessment and Intervention

1. Mia made a tally table to record the different types of birds she saw at the bird feeder in the garden.

Birds at the Feeder	
Name	**Tally**
Jay	‖‖‖
Sparrow	‖‖‖ ‖‖‖ ‖‖
Finch	‖‖‖ ‖‖‖
Blackbird	‖‖‖ ‖

For numbers 1a–1c, select True or False for each statement.

1a. Mia saw twice as many sparrows as blackbirds.   ○ True   ○ False

1b. Mia saw 8 finches.   ○ True   ○ False

1c. Mia saw 4 fewer jays than blackbirds.   ○ True   ○ False

2. Jake asked 25 students in his class how close they live to school. The frequency table shows the results.

Miles to School		
	Boys	Girls
about 1 mile	4	5
about 2 miles		4
about 3 miles	3	2

Part A

Complete the table and explain how you found the answer.

Part B

How many more students live about 2 miles or less from school than students who live about 3 miles from school? Show your work.

Use the picture graph for 3–6.

Students at Barnes School are performing in a play. The picture graph shows the number of tickets each class has sold so far.

3. How many tickets were sold altogether? Explain how you found the total.

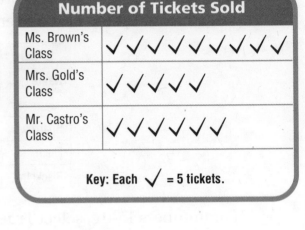

Number of Tickets Sold	
Ms. Brown's Class	✓✓✓✓✓✓✓✓
Mrs. Gold's Class	✓✓✓✓✓
Mr. Castro's Class	✓✓✓✓✓✓

Key: Each ✓ = 5 tickets.

4. Choose the name from each box that makes the sentence true.

Five fewer tickets were sold by
| Ms. Brown's |
| Mrs. Gold's | class
| Mr. Castro's |

than
| Ms. Brown's |
| Mrs. Gold's | class.
| Mr. Castro's |

5. How many more tickets were sold by Ms. Brown's class than Mr. Castro's class?

_____ tickets

6. What if Mrs. Gold's class sold 20 more tickets? Draw a picture to show how the graph would change.

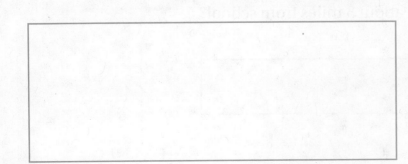

132

Name _____

Use the frequency table for 7–8.

7. GO DEEPER The Pet Shop keeps track of the number of fish it has for sale. The frequency table shows how many fish are in three tanks.

Fish in Tanks	
Tank	Number of Fish
Tank 1	16
Tank 2	9
Tank 3	12

Part A

Use the data in the table to complete the picture graph.

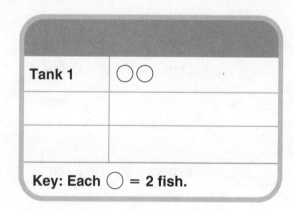

Part B

How many pictures did you draw for Tank 2? Explain.

8. Each tank can hold up to 20 fish. How many more fish can the Pet Shop put in the three tanks?

Ⓐ 60 fish   Ⓒ 20 fish

Ⓑ 23 fish   Ⓓ 33 fish

Use the bar graph for 9–12.

9. Three more students play piano than which other instrument?

_____

10. The same number of students play which two instruments?

_____

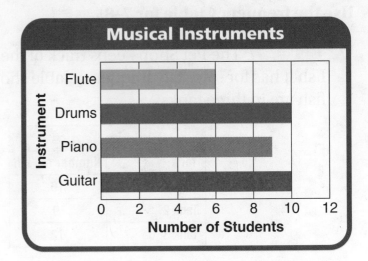

Musical Instruments

11. For numbers 11a–11d, select True or False for each statement.

11a. Ten more students play guitar than play flute. ○ True ○ False

11b. Nine students play piano. ○ True ○ False

11c. Six fewer students play flute and piano combined than play drums and guitar combined. ○ True ○ False

11d. Nine more students play piano and guitar combined than play drums. ○ True ○ False

12. There are more students who play the trumpet than play the flute, but fewer students than play the guitar. Explain how you would change the bar graph to show the number of students who play the trumpet.

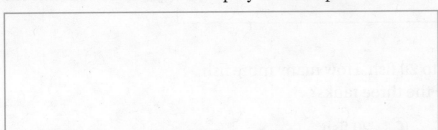

Name _____

Use the frequency table for 13-14.

13. **THINK SMARTER +** Karen asks students what vegetables they would like to have in the school cafeteria. The table shows the results of her survey.

Favorite Vegetables	
Vegetable	**Number of Votes**
broccoli	15
carrots	40
corn	20
green beans	10

Part A

Use the data in the table to complete the bar graph.

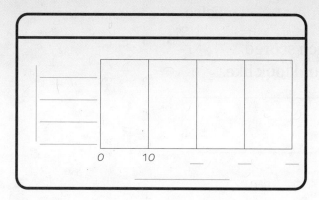

Part B

How do you know how long to make the bars on your graph? How did you show 15 votes for broccoli? Explain.

14. How many more votes did the two most popular vegetables get than the two least popular vegetables? Explain how you solved the problem.

_____

_____

_____

Use the line plot for 15–16.

The line plot shows the number of goals the players on Scot's team scored.

Number of Goals Scored

15. For numbers 15a–15d, select True or False for each statement.

15a. Three players scored 2 goals.   ○ True   ○ False

15b. Six players scored fewer than 2 goals.   ○ True   ○ False

15c. There are 8 players on the team.   ○ True   ○ False

15d. Five players scored more than 1 goal.   ○ True   ○ False

16. What if two more people played and each scored 3 goals? Describe what the line plot would look like.

Use the line plot for 17–18.

Robin collected shells during her vacation. She measured the length of each shell to the nearest inch and recorded the data in a line plot.

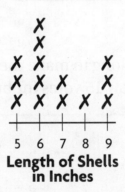

Length of Shells in Inches

17. How many shells were 6 inches long or longer?

_____ shells

18. How many more shells did Robin collect that were 5 inches long than 8 inches long?

_____ shells

Understand Multiplication

Show What You Know

Personal Math Trainer
Online Assessment and Intervention

Check your understanding of important skills.

Name _____

▶ **Count On to Add** Use the number line. Write the sum.

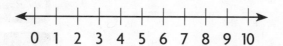

0 1 2 3 4 5 6 7 8 9 10

1. 6 + 2 = _____   **2.** 3 + 7 = _____

▶ **Skip Count by Twos and Fives** Skip count. Write the missing numbers.

3. 2, 4, 6, _____, _____, _____   **4.** 5, 10, 15, _____, _____, _____

▶ **Model with Arrays** Use the array. Complete.

5.

____ + ____ + ____ = ____

6.

____ + ____ = ____

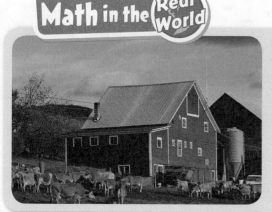

Math in the Real World

Ryan's class went on a field trip to a farm. They saw 5 cows and 6 chickens. Help to find how many legs were on all the animals they saw.

Vocabulary Builder

▶ **Visualize It** ••••••••••••••••••••••••••••••••••••••

Complete the tree map by using the review words.

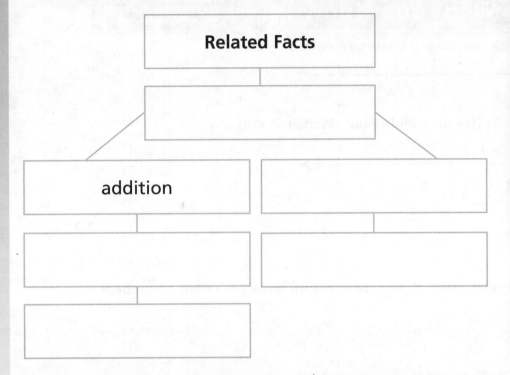

Related Facts

addition

Review Words

addend

addition

difference

number sentences

related facts

subtraction

sum

Preview Words

array

equal groups

factor

multiply

product

▶ **Understand Vocabulary** •••••••••••••••••••••••••••••••

Read the definition. Write the preview word that matches it.

1. A set of objects arranged in rows and columns _____

2. The answer in a multiplication problem _____

3. When you combine equal groups to find how many in all _____

4. A number that is multiplied by another number to find a product _____

GO DIGITAL
• **Interactive Student Edition**
• **Multimedia eGlossary**

Chapter 3 Vocabulary

array

matriz

4

Commutative Property of Multiplication

Propiedad conmutativa de la multiplicación

9

equal groups

grupos iguales

20

factor

factor

25

Identity Property of Multiplication

Propiedad de identidad de la multiplicación

35

multiply

multiplicar

51

product

producto

65

Zero Property of Multiplication

Propiedad del cero de la multiplicación

85

The property that states that you can multiply two factors in any order and get the same product

Example: 4 × 3 = 3 × 4

A set of objects arranged in rows and columns

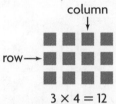

3 × 4 = 12

A number that is multiplied by another number to find a product

Example: 4 × 5 = 20

factor   factor

Groups that have the same number of objects

To combine equal groups to find how many in all; the opposite operation of division

2   ×   2   =   4

factor   factor   product

The property that states that the product of any number and 1 is that number

Example: 17 × 1 = 17

The property that states that the product of zero and any number is zero

Example: 34 × 0 = 0

The answer in a multiplication problem

Example: 4 × 5 = 20

product

Matchup

For 2–3 players

Materials

1 set of word cards

How to Play

1. Put the cards face-down in rows. Take turns to play.

2. Choose two cards and turn them face-up.

   • If the cards show a word and its meaning, it's a match. Keep the pair and take another turn.

   • If the cards do not match, turn them back over.

3. The game is over when all cards have been matched. The players count their pairs. The player with the most pairs wins.

Word Box
array
equal groups
factors
multiply
product
Commutative Property of Multiplication
Identity Property of Multiplication
Zero Property of Multiplication

The Write Way

Reflect

Choose one idea. Write about it.

- Do $4 + 4 + 4$ and 4×3 represent equal groups? Explain why or why not.

- Explain how to use an array to find a product.

- Summarize how to solve 5×0, including any "false starts" or "dead ends" you might take.

_____

_____

_____

_____

_____

_____

_____

_____

_____

_____

_____

_____

_____

_____

Name _____

Count Equal Groups

Essential Question How can you use equal groups to find how many in all?

Learning Objective You will use equal-sized groups to find how many in all.

🔑 Unlock the Problem

Equal groups have the same number of objects in each group.

Tim has 6 toy cars. Each car has 4 wheels. How many wheels are there in all?

- How many wheels are on each car?

  _____

- How many equal groups of wheels are there?

  _____

- How can you find how many wheels in all?

  _____

🔒 Activity Use counters to model the equal groups.

Materials ■ counters

STEP 1 Draw 4 counters in each group.
_____

STEP 2 Skip count to find how many wheels in all.
Skip count by 4s until you say 6 numbers.

number of
equal groups →   1   2   3   4   5   6

4, _____, 12, _____, _____, _____

There are _____ groups with _____ wheels in each group.

So, there are _____ wheels in all.

Math Talk

Math Processes and Practices ②

Reason Quantitatively
What if Tim had 8 cars? How could you find the total number of wheels?

© Houghton Mifflin Harcourt Publishing Company

☐ Example Count equal groups to find the total.

Sam, Kyla, and Tia each have 5 pennies.
How many pennies do they have in all?

How many pennies does each person have? _____

How many equal groups of pennies are there? _____

Draw 5 counters in each group.

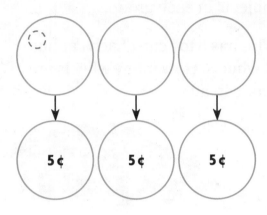

Think: There are _____ groups of 5 pennies.

Think: There are _____ fives.

Skip count to find how many pennies.

So, they have _____ pennies.

_____, _____, _____

- **THINK SMARTER** Explain why you can skip count by 5s to find how many.

Share and Show MATH BOARD

1. Complete. Use the picture. Skip count to find
   how many wheels in all.

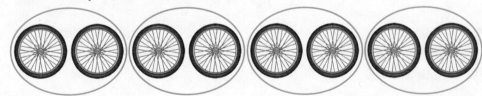

_____ groups of 2

_____ twos

Skip count by 2s.   2, 4, _____, _____

So, there are _____ wheels.

Math Talk Math Processes and Practices ❸

Apply How would your
answer change if 2
more groups of wheels
were added?

Name _____

Draw equal groups. Skip count to find how many.

2. 2 groups of 6 _____

✅ **3.** 3 groups of 2 _____

Count equal groups to find how many.

✅ **4.**

_____ groups of _____

_____ in all

5.

_____ groups of _____

_____ in all

On Your Own

Draw equal groups. Skip count to find how many.

6. 3 groups of 3 _____

7. 2 groups of 9 _____

8. **GO DEEPER** A toy car costs $3. A toy truck costs $4. Which costs more—4 cars or 3 trucks? Explain.

_____

_____

9. **Math Processes and Practices ❸** **Make Arguments** Elliott has a collection of 20 toy cars. Will he be able to put an equal number of toy cars on 3 shelves? Explain your answer.

_____

_____

Unlock the Problem

10. **THINK SMARTER** Tina, Charlie, and Amber have toy cars. Each car has 4 wheels. How many wheels do their cars have altogether?

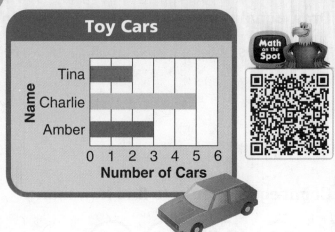

Toy Cars

a. What do you need to find?

_____

b. What information will you use from the graph to solve the problem?

_____

c. Show the steps you used to solve the problem.

d. So, the cars have _____ wheels.

11. **THINK SMARTER** A bookcase has 4 shelves. Each shelf holds 5 books. How many books are in the bookcase?

Draw counters to model the problem. Then explain how you solved the problem.

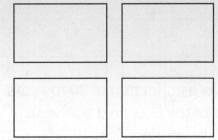

_____

_____

Count Equal Groups

Learning Objective You will use equal-sized groups to find how many in all.

Draw equal groups. Skip count to find how many.

1. 2 groups of 2 ___4___

2. 3 groups of 6 _____

Count equal groups to find how many.

3.

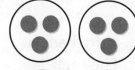

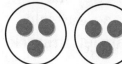

_____ groups of _____

_____ in all

4.

_____ groups of _____

_____ in all

Problem Solving · Real World

5. Marcia puts 2 slices of cheese on each sandwich. She makes 4 cheese sandwiches. How many slices of cheese does Marcia use in all?

_____

6. Tomas works in a cafeteria kitchen. He puts 3 cherry tomatoes on each of 5 salads. How many tomatoes does he use?

_____

7. **WRITE** *Math* Write a problem that can be solved by using equal groups.

_____

_____

Lesson Check

1. Jen makes 3 bracelets. Each bracelet has 3 beads. How many beads does Jen use?

_____

2. Ian has 5 cards to mail. Each card needs 2 stamps. How many stamps does Ian need?

_____

Spiral Review

3. There were 384 people at a play on Friday night. There were 512 people at the play on Saturday night. Estimate the total number of people who attended the play on both nights.

_____

_____

4. Walking the Dog Pet Store has 438 leashes in stock. They sell 79 leashes during a one-day sale. How many leashes are left in stock after the sale?

_____

_____

5. The Lakeside Tour bus traveled 490 miles on Saturday and 225 miles on Sunday. About how many more miles did it travel on Saturday?

_____

_____

6. During one week at Jackson School, 210 students buy milk and 196 students buy juice. How many drinks are sold that week?

_____

_____

FOR MORE PRACTICE
GO TO THE
Personal Math Trainer

Name _____

Relate Addition and Multiplication

Essential Question How is multiplication like addition?
How is it different?

Learning Objective You will represent multiplication with equal-sized groups and write related multiplication and addition sentences.

🔑 Unlock the Problem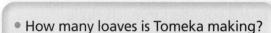

Tomeka needs 3 apples to make one loaf of apple bread. Each loaf has the same number of apples. How many apples does Tomeka need to make 4 loaves?

- How many loaves is Tomeka making?

  _____

- How many apples are in each loaf?

  _____

- How can you solve the problem?

  _____

🔒 One Way Add equal groups.

Use the 4 circles to show the 4 loaves.

Draw 3 counters in each circle to show the apples Tomeka needs for each loaf.

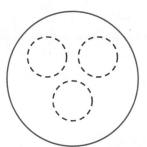 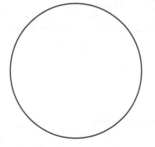

Find the number of counters.
Complete the addition sentence.

3 + _____ + _____ + _____ = _____

So, Tomeka needs _____ apples to

make _____ loaves of apple bread.

Math Talk Math Processes and Practices ④

Use Diagrams How can drawing a picture help you to solve a multiplication problem?

 Another Way Multiply.

When you combine equal groups, you can **multiply** to find how many in all.

Think: 4 groups of 3

Draw 3 counters in each circle.

Since there are the same number of counters in each circle, you can multiply to find how many in all.

Multiplication is another way to find how many there are altogether in equal groups.

Write:

4	×	3	=	12	or	4	← factor
↑		↑		↑		× 3	← factor
factor		factor		product		12	← product

Read: Four times three equals twelve.

The **factors** are the numbers multiplied.

The **product** is the answer to a multiplication problem.

Share and Show

1. Write related addition and multiplication sentences for the model.

____ + ____ + ____ + ____ = ____

____ × ____ = ____

Math Processes and Practices ❹

Use Models How would you change this model so you could write a multiplication sentence to match it?

© Houghton Mifflin Harcourt Publishing Company

146

Draw a quick picture to show the equal groups. Then write related addition and multiplication sentences.

✓**2.** 3 groups of 6

___ + ___ + ___ = ___

___ × ___ = ___

✓**3.** 2 groups of 3

___ + ___ = ___

___ × ___ = ___

On Your Own

Draw a quick picture to show the equal groups. Then write related addition and multiplication sentences.

4. 4 groups of 2

___ + ___ + ___ + ___ = ___

___ × ___ = ___

5. 5 groups of 4

___ + ___ + ___ + ___ + ___ = ____

___ × ___ = ____

Complete. Write a multiplication sentence.

6. Zach buys 4 packs of pens. Each pack has 4 pens. Write a multiplication sentence to show how many pens Zach buys.

___ × ___ = ___

7. Ada has 3 vases. She puts 5 flowers in each vase. Write a multiplication sentence to show how many flowers Ada puts in the vases.

___ × ___ = ___

8. GO DEEPER Mrs. Tomar buys 2 packs of vanilla yogurt and 3 packs of strawberry yogurt. Each pack has 4 yogurts. How many yogurts does Mrs. Tomar buy?

_____

9. GO DEEPER Murray buys 3 packs of red peppers and 4 packs of green peppers. Each pack has 4 peppers. How many peppers does Murray buy?

_____

Problem Solving · Applications

Use the table for 10–11.

Average Weight of Fruits	
Fruit	Weight in Ounces
Apple	6
Orange	5
Peach	3
Banana	4

10. Morris bought 4 peaches. How much do the peaches weigh? Write a multiplication sentence to find the weight of the peaches.

   _____ × _____ = _____ ounces

11. **THINK SMARTER** Thomas bought 2 apples. Sydney bought 4 bananas. Which weighed more—the 2 apples or the 4 bananas? How much more? Explain how you know.

_____

_____

_____

12. **Math Processes and Practices ③ Make Arguments** Shane said that he could write related multiplication and addition sentences for 6 + 4 + 3. Does Shane's statement make sense? Explain.

_____

_____

13. **GO DEEPER** Write a word problem that can be solved using 3 × 4. Solve the problem.

_____

_____

14. **THINK SMARTER** Select the number sentences that represent the model at the right. Mark all that apply.

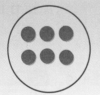

   (A) 3 + 6 = 9   (C) 3 × 6 = 18

   (B) 6 + 6 + 6 = 18   (D) 6 + 3 = 9

Relate Addition and Multiplication

Learning Objective You will represent multiplication with equal-sized groups and write related multiplication and addition sentences.

Draw a quick picture to show the equal groups. Then write related addition and multiplication sentences.

1. 3 groups of 5

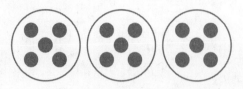

__5__ + __5__ + __5__ = __15__

__3__ × __5__ = __15__

2. 3 groups of 4

___ + ___ + ___ = ___

___ × ___ = ___

3. 5 groups of 2

___ + ___ + ___ + ___ + ___ = ___

___ × ___ = ___

Complete. Write a multiplication sentence.

4. 7 + 7 + 7 = ___

___ × ___ = ___

5. 3 + 3 + 3 = ___

___ × ___ = ___

Problem Solving Real World

6. There are 6 jars of pickles in a box. Ed has 3 boxes of pickles. How many jars of pickles does he have? Write a multiplication sentence to find the answer.

___ × ___ = ___ jars

7. Each day, Jani rides her bike 5 miles. How many miles does Jani ride in 4 days? Write a multiplication sentence to find the answer.

___ × ___ = ___ miles

8. **WRITE** ▸Math Write a word problem that involves combining three equal groups.

_____

_____

Lesson Check

1. What is another way to show

   $3 + 3 + 3 + 3 + 3 + 3$?

2. Use the model. How many counters are there?

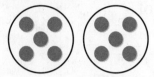

Spiral Review

3. A school gave 884 pencils to students on the first day of school. What is 884 rounded to the nearest hundred?

4. Find the difference.

$$\begin{array}{r} 632 \\ -\ 274 \\ \hline \end{array}$$

5. The line plot below shows how many points Trevor scored in 20 games.

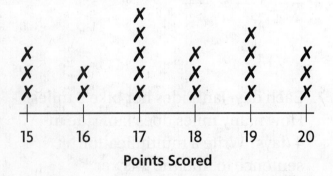

Points Scored

In how many games did Trevor score 18 points or fewer?

6. Darrien read 97 pages last week. Evan read 84 pages last week. How many pages did the boys read?

FOR MORE PRACTICE
GO TO THE
Personal Math Trainer

Name _____

Skip Count on a Number Line

Essential Question How can you use a number line to skip count and find how many in all?

Learning Objective You will use equal "jumps" on a number line to skip count and find how many in all.

🔑 Unlock the Problem

Caleb wants to make 3 balls of yarn for his cat to play with. He uses 6 feet of yarn to make each ball. How many feet of yarn does Caleb need in all?

🔒 **Use a number line to count equal groups.**

- How many equal groups of yarn will Caleb make?

  _____

- How many feet of yarn will be in each group?

  _____

- What do you need to find?

  _____

How many feet of yarn does Caleb

need for each ball? _____

How many equal lengths of yarn does he need? _____

Begin at 0. Skip count by 6s by drawing jumps on the number line.

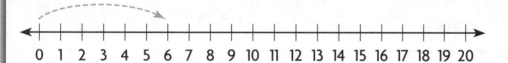

How many jumps did you make? _____

How long is each jump? _____

Multiply. $3 \times 6 =$ _____

So, Caleb needs _____ feet of yarn in all.

Math Talk Math Processes and Practices ❸

Compare Representations How would what you draw on the number line change if instead of 3 balls of yarn made with 6 feet of yarn there were 4 balls of yarn made with 5 feet of yarn?

- **Math Processes and Practices ❶ Analyze** Why did you jump by 6s on the number line?

  _____

1. Skip count by drawing jumps on the number line. Find how many in 5 jumps of 4. Then write the product.

   Think: 1 jump of 4 shows 1 group of 4.

   $5 \times 4 = $ _____

Draw jumps on the number line to show equal groups. Find the product.

2. 3 groups of 8

   $3 \times 8 = $ _____

3. 8 groups of 3

   $8 \times 3 = $ _____

Write the multiplication sentence shown by the number line.

4.

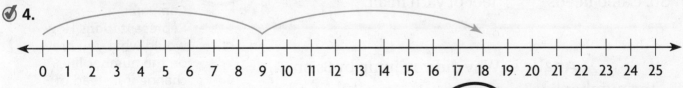

   _____ $\times$ _____ $=$ _____

Math Talk

Math Processes and Practices ④

Model Mathematics
How do equal jumps on the number line show equal groups?

Name _____

On Your Own

Draw jumps on the number line to show equal groups. Find the product.

5. 6 groups of 4

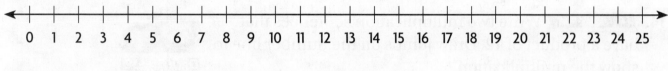

6 × 4 = _____

6. 7 groups of 3

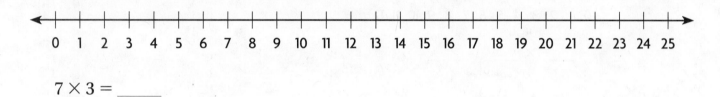

7 × 3 = _____

7. Sam, Kyra, Tia, and Abigail each have 10 pennies. How many pennies do they have in all?

8. Eddie bought snacks for a picnic. He has 3 bags of snacks. Each bag has 4 snacks. How many snacks does Eddie have in all?

9. Ashley digs 7 holes. She puts 2 seeds in each hole. She has 3 seeds left over. How many seeds are there in all?

10. GO DEEPER Carla puts 8 pictures on each page of a photo album. She fills 3 pages. She has 5 pictures left. How many pictures does she have?

11. GO DEEPER A band marches in rows of 5. Each row has 6 people. There are 4 people who carry flags. How many people are in the marching band?

12. GO DEEPER In Mr. Gupta's classroom, there are 4 rows of desks. Each row has 6 desks. Mrs. Loew's classroom has 3 rows of 9 desks. How many desks are in Mr. Gupta's and Mrs. Loew's classrooms?

Problem Solving • Applications

13. **GO DEEPER** Erin displays her toy cat collection on 3 shelves. She puts 8 cats on each shelf. If she collects 3 more cats, how many cats will she have?

_____

14. **THINK SMARTER** Write two multiplication sentences that have a product of 12. Draw jumps on the number line to show the multiplication.

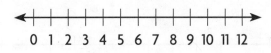

0 1 2 3 4 5 6 7 8 9 10 11 12

____ × ____ = ____

0 1 2 3 4 5 6 7 8 9 10 11 12

____ × ____ = ____

15. **Math Processes and Practices 7** **Identify Relationships** Write a problem that can be solved by finding 8 groups of 5. Write a multiplication sentence to solve the problem. Then solve.

_____

_____

Personal Math Trainer

16. **THINK SMARTER +** Rebecca practices piano for 3 hours each week. How many hours does she practice in 4 weeks?

Draw jumps and label the number line to show your thinking.

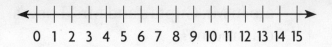

0 1 2 3 4 5 6 7 8 9 10 11 12 13 14 15

_____

Skip Count on a Number Line

Learning Objective You will use equal "jumps" on a number line to skip count and find how many in all.

Draw jumps on the number line to show equal groups. Find the product.

1. 6 groups of 3

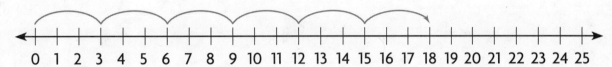

$6 \times 3 = \underline{18}$

Write the multiplication sentence the number line shows.

2. 2 groups of 6

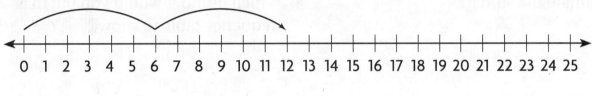

$\underline{} \times \underline{} = \underline{}$

3. Allie is baking muffins for students in her class. There are 6 muffins in each baking tray. She bakes 5 trays of muffins. How many muffins is she baking?

_____

4. A snack package has 4 cheese sticks. How many cheese sticks are in 4 packages?

_____

5. **WRITE** ▸*Math* Write a problem that can be solved by skip counting on a number line.

_____

_____

Lesson Check

1. Louise skip counts by 4 on a number line to find 5×4. How many jumps should she draw on the number line?

2. Theo needs 4 boards that are each 3 feet long to make bookshelves. How many feet of boards does he need altogether?

Spiral Review

3. Estimate the sum.

$$\begin{array}{r} 518 \\ +251 \\ \hline \end{array}$$

4. Which number would you put in a frequency table to show 卌 ||| ?

5. A manager at a shoe store received an order for 346 pairs of shoes. What is 346 rounded to the nearest hundred?

6. Toby is making a picture graph. Each picture of a book is equal to 2 books he has read. The row for Month 1 has 3 pictures of books. How many books did Toby read during Month 1?

FOR MORE PRACTICE
GO TO THE
Personal Math Trainer

Name _____

 **Mid-Chapter Checkpoint**

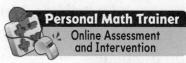
Personal Math Trainer
Online Assessment
and Intervention

Vocabulary

Choose the best term from the box.

Vocabulary
equal groups
factors
multiply
product

1. When you combine equal groups, you can

   _____ to find how many in all. (p. 146)

2. The answer in a multiplication problem is called the

   _____. (p. 146)

3. The numbers you multiply are called the _____. (p. 146)

Concepts and Skills

Count equal groups to find how many.

4.

___ groups of ___

___ in all

5.

___ groups of ___

___ in all

6.

___ groups of ___

___ in all

Write related addition and multiplication sentences.

7. 3 groups of 9

   ___ + ___ + ___ = ___

   ___ × ___ = ___

8. 5 groups of 7

   ___ + ___ + ___ + ___ + ___ = ___

   ___ × ___ = ___

Draw jumps on the number line to show equal groups. Find the product.

9. 6 groups of 3

___ × ___ = ___

10. Beth's mother cut some melons into equal slices. She put 4 slices each on 8 plates. Write a multiplication sentence to show the total number of melon slices she put on the plates.

_____

11. Avery had 125 animal stickers. She gave 5 animal stickers to each of her 10 friends. How many animal stickers did she have left? What number sentences did you use to solve?

_____

12. Matt made 2 equal groups of marbles. Write a multiplication sentence to show the total number of marbles.

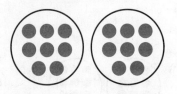

_____

13. 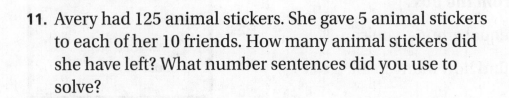 Lindsey has 10 inches of ribbon. She buys another 3 lengths of ribbon, each 5 inches long. How much ribbon does she have now?

_____

14. Jack's birthday is in 4 weeks. How many days is it until Jack's birthday? Describe how you could use a number line to solve.

_____

_____

Name _____

Problem Solving • Model Multiplication

Essential Question How can you use the strategy *draw a diagram* to solve one- and two-step problems?

Learning Objective You will use the strategy *draw a diagram* to solve multiplication problems by drawing bar models.

⚷ Unlock the Problem

Three groups of students are taking drum lessons. There are 8 students in each group. How many students are taking drum lessons?

Read the Problem	**Solve the Problem**
What do I need to find? I need to find how many _____ are taking drum lessons.	Complete the bar model to show the drummers. Write 8 in each box to show the 8 students in each of the 3 groups.
What information do I need to use? There are _____ groups of students taking drum lessons. There are _____ students in each group.	 [8	_____	_____] ▢ students Since there are equal groups, I can multiply to find the number of students taking drum lessons.
How will I use the information? I will draw a bar model to help me see _____ _____ .	_____ × _____ = ▢ _____ = ▢ So, there are _____ students in all.

 Math Talk

Math Processes and Practices ④

Use Models How would the bar model change if there were 6 groups of 4 students?

Try Another Problem

Twelve students in Mrs. Taylor's class want to start a band. Seven students each made a drum. The rest of the students made 2 shakers each. How many shakers were made?

Read the Problem	Solve the Problem
What do I need to find?	**Record the steps you used to solve the problem.**
What information do I need to use?	
How will I use the information?	

Solve the Problem table:

7	_____

12 students

1. How many shakers in all did the students make? _____

2. How do you know your answer is reasonable? _____

© Houghton Mifflin Harcourt Publishing Company

Math Talk

Math Processes and Practices ①

Evaluate Why wouldn't you draw 2 boxes and write 5 in each box?

Name _____

1. There are 6 groups of 4 students who play the trumpet in the marching band. How many students play the trumpet in the band?

   First, draw a bar model to show each group of students.

   Draw _____ boxes and write _____ in each box.

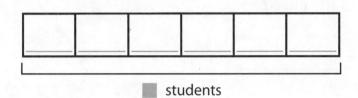

   ■ students

   Then, multiply to find the total number of trumpet players.

   _____ × _____ = ■

   _____ = ■

   So, _____ students play the trumpet in the marching band.

2. What if there are 4 groups of 7 students who play the saxophone? How many students play the saxophone or trumpet?

_____

On Your Own

3. THINK SMARTER Suppose there are 5 groups of 4 trumpet players. In front of the trumpet players are 18 saxophone players. How many students play the trumpet or saxophone?

4. GO DEEPER In a garden there are 3 rows of plants. There are 5 plants in each row. Six of the plants are pumpkin plants and the rest are corn. How many corn plants are in the garden?

_____

Use the picture graph for 5–7.

5. The picture graph shows how students in Jillian's class voted for their favorite instrument. How many students voted for the guitar?

_____

Favorite Instrument Survey	
Flute	☺☺
Trumpet	☺☺☺
Guitar	☺☺☺☺☺
Drum	☺☺☺☺

Key: Each ☺ = 2 votes.

6. **GO DEEPER** On the day of the survey, two students were absent. The picture graph shows the votes of all the other students in the class, including Jillian. How many students are in the class? Explain your answer.

_____

_____

_____

7. **THINK SMARTER** Jillian added the number of votes for two instruments and got a total of 12 votes. For which two instruments did she add the votes?

_____ and _____

8. **Math Processes and Practices 8 Use Repeated Reasoning** The flute was invented 26 years after the harmonica. The electric guitar was invented 84 years after the flute. How many years was the electric guitar invented after the harmonica?

_____

Personal Math Trainer

9. **THINK SMARTER +** Raul buys 4 packages of apple juice and 3 packages of grape juice. There are 6 drink boxes in each package. How many drink boxes does Raul buy? Show your work.

_____

Problem Solving • Model Multiplication

Draw a diagram to solve each problem.

Learning Objective You will use the strategy *draw a diagram* to solve multiplication problems by drawing bar models.

1. Robert put some toy blocks into 3 rows. There are 5 blocks in each row. How many blocks are there?

   _____**15 blocks**_____

2. Mr. Fernandez is putting tiles on his kitchen floor. There are 2 rows with 9 tiles in each row. How many tiles are there?

   _____

3. In Jillian's garden, there are 3 rows of carrots, 2 rows of string beans, and 1 row of peas. There are 8 plants in each row. How many plants are there in the garden?

   _____

4. Maya visits the movie rental store. On one wall, there are 6 DVDs on each of 5 shelves. On another wall, there are 4 DVDs on each of 4 shelves. How many DVDs are there on the shelves?

   _____

5. The media center at Josh's school has a computer area. The first 4 rows have 6 computers each. The fifth row has 4 computers. How many computers are there?

   _____

6. **WRITE** ▸*Math*   Describe one kind of diagram you might draw to help you solve a problem.

   _____

   _____

Lesson Check

1. There are 5 shelves of video games in a video store. There are 6 video games on each shelf. How many video games are there on the shelves?

_____

_____

2. Ken watches a marching band. He sees 2 rows of flute players. Six people are in each row. He sees 8 trombone players. How many flute players and trombone players does Ken see?

_____

_____

Spiral Review

3. What is the sum of 438 and 382?

_____

_____

4. Estimate the sum.

$$
\begin{array}{r}
622 \\
+\ \ 84 \\
\hline
\end{array}
$$

_____

_____

5. Francine uses 167 silver balloons and 182 gold balloons for her store party. How many silver and gold balloons does Francine use?

_____

_____

6. Yoshi is making a picture graph. Each picture of a soccer ball stands for two goals he scored for his team. The row for January has 9 soccer balls. How many goals did Yoshi score during January?

_____

_____

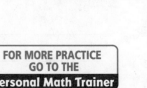

FOR MORE PRACTICE
GO TO THE
Personal Math Trainer

Name _____

Model with Arrays

Essential Question How can you use arrays to model multiplication and find factors?

Learning Objective You will use arrays to model multiplication and find factors.

Unlock the Problem

Many people grow tomatoes in their gardens. Lee plants 3 rows of tomato plants with 6 plants in each row. How many tomato plants are there?

▲ Tomatoes are a great source of vitamins.

Activity 1

Materials ■ square tiles ■ MathBoard

- You make an **array** by placing the same number of tiles in each row. Make an array with 3 rows of 6 tiles to show the tomato plants.

- Now draw the array you made.

- Find the total number of tiles.

  Multiply.   3   ×   6 = _____
                  ↑   ↑
             number   number
             of rows   in each row

So, there are _____ tomato plants.

Math Talk

Math Processes and Practices ②

Reason Abstractly Does the number of tiles change if you turn the array to show 6 rows of 3?

© Houghton Mifflin Harcourt Publishing Company • Image Credits: (cr) ©Getty Images/Photodisc

Activity 2 Materials ■ square tiles ■ MathBoard

Use 8 tiles. Make as many different arrays as you can, using all 8 tiles. Draw the arrays. The first one is done for you.

A

1 row of 8

$1 \times 8 = 8$

B

8 rows of _____

$8 \times$ _____ $= 8$

C

_____ rows of _____

_____ $\times$ _____ $= 8$

D

_____ rows of _____

_____ $\times$ _____ $= 8$

You can make _____ different arrays using 8 tiles.

Share and Show

1. Complete. Use the array.

_____ rows of _____ = _____

_____ $\times$ _____ = _____

Write a multiplication sentence for the array.

2.  _____

3.  _____

Name _____

Write a multiplication sentence for the array.

4.

_____

5.

_____

Draw an array to find the product.

6. $3 \times 6 =$ _____

7. $4 \times 7 =$ _____

8. GO DEEPER   DeShawn makes an array using 3 rows of 5 tiles. How many tiles does Deshawn have if he adds 2 more rows to the array?

_____

9. GO DEEPER   Ming makes an array using 2 rows of 7 tiles. She adds 3 more rows to the array. Write a multiplication sentence that shows Ming's array.

_____

10. GO DEEPER   Use 6 tiles. Make as many different arrays as you can using all the tiles. Draw the arrays. Then write a multiplication sentence for each array.

_____

_____

Problem Solving · Applications (Real World)

Use the table to solve 11–12.

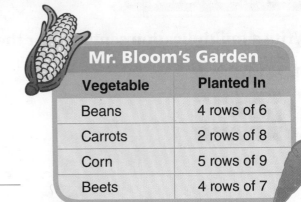

Mr. Bloom's Garden	
Vegetable	**Planted In**
Beans	4 rows of 6
Carrots	2 rows of 8
Corn	5 rows of 9
Beets	4 rows of 7

11. **(Math Processes and Practices 4)** **Use Models** Mr. Bloom grows vegetables in his garden. Draw an array and write the multiplication sentence to show how many corn plants Mr. Bloom has in his garden.

_____

12. **THINK SMARTER** Could Mr. Bloom have planted his carrots in equal rows of 4? If so, how many rows could he have planted? Explain.

_____

_____

_____

13. **(Math Processes and Practices 5)** **Communicate** Mr. Bloom has 12 strawberry plants. Describe all of the different arrays that Mr. Bloom could make using all of his strawberry plants. The first one is done for you.

2 rows of 6; _____

_____

14. **THINK SMARTER** Elizabeth planted 5 rows of pansies with 3 pansies in each row. How many pansies did she plant in all? Draw the rest of the squares to make an array to represent the problem. Then solve.

_____

Name _____

Model with Arrays

Learning Objective You will use arrays to model multiplication and find factors.

Write a multiplication sentence for the array.

1.

$3 \times 7 = \underline{\ 21\ }$

2.

$2 \times 5 = \underline{\qquad}$

Draw an array to find the product.

3. $4 \times 2 = \underline{\qquad}$

4. $2 \times 8 = \underline{\qquad}$

Problem Solving *Real World*

5. Lenny is moving tables in the school cafeteria. He places all the tables in a 7×4 array. How many tables are in the cafeteria?

_____

6. Ms. DiMeo directs the school choir. She has the singers stand in 3 rows. There are 8 singers in each row. How many singers are there?

_____

7. **WRITE** ▸*Math* Write a word problem that can be solved by drawing an array. Then draw the array and solve the problem.

_____

_____

Lesson Check

1. What multiplication sentence does this array show?

_____

2. What multiplication sentence does this array show?

_____

Spiral Review

3. Use the table to find who traveled 700 miles farther than Paul during summer vacation.

Summer Vacations	
Name	**Distance in Miles**
Paul	233
Andrew	380
Bonnie	790
Tara	933
Susan	853

4. Use the bar graph to find what hair color most students have.

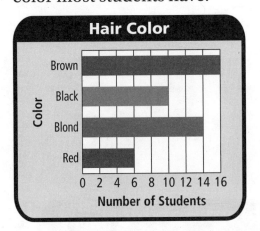

_____

5. Spencer orders 235 cans of tomatoes to make salsa for the festival. What is 235 rounded to the nearest ten?

6. Which bar would be the longest on a bar graph of the data?

Favorite Pizza Topping	
Topping	**Votes**
Cheese	5
Pepperoni	4
Vegetable	1
Sausage	3

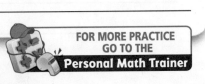

FOR MORE PRACTICE
GO TO THE
Personal Math Trainer

Name _____

Commutative Property of Multiplication

Essential Question How can you use the Commutative Property of Multiplication to find products?

Learning Objective You will use the Commutative Property of Multiplication to find products.

Unlock the Problem

Dave works at the Bird Store. He arranges 15 boxes of birdseed in rows on the shelf. What are two ways he can arrange the boxes in equal rows?

Activity Make an array.

Materials ■ square tiles ■ MathBoard

Arrange 15 tiles in 5 equal rows. Draw a quick picture of your array.

- Circle the number that is the product.

How many tiles are in each row? _____

What multiplication sentence does your array show? _____

_____

Suppose Dave arranges the boxes in 3 equal rows. Draw a quick picture of your array.

How many tiles are in each row? _____

What multiplication sentence does your array show?

_____

So, two ways Dave can arrange the 15 boxes are

in _____ rows of 3 or in 3 rows of _____.

Math Processes and Practices 7

Identify Relationships When using an array to help solve a multiplication problem, why does the answer stay the same when the array is turned?

Multiplication Property The **Commutative Property of Multiplication** states that when you change the order of the factors, the product stays the same. You can think of it as the Order Property of Multiplication.

2 × _____ = _____   3 × _____ = _____

> ## Math Idea
> Facts that show the Commutative Property of Multiplication have the same factors in a different order.
>
> 2 × 3 = 6 and 3 × 2 = 6

So, 2 × _____ = 3 × _____.

- Explain how the models are alike and how they are different.

_____

_____

Try This! Draw a quick picture on the right that shows the Commutative Property of Multiplication. Then complete the multiplication sentences.

_____ × 4 = _____   _____ × 3 = _____

2 × _____ = _____   5 × _____ = _____

172

Name _____

1. Write a multiplication sentence for the array.

Math Talk

Math Processes and Practices ①

Make Sense of Problems Explain what the factor 2 means in each multiplication sentence.

Write a multiplication sentence for the model. Then use the Commutative Property of Multiplication to write a related multiplication sentence.

2.

___ × ___ = ___

___ × ___ = ___

⌖3.

___ × ___ = ___

___ × ___ = ___

⌖4.

___ × ___ = ___

___ × ___ = ___

Write a multiplication sentence for the model. Then use the Commutative Property of Multiplication to write a related multiplication sentence.

5.

___ × ___ = ___

___ × ___ = ___

6.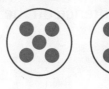

___ × ___ = ___

___ × ___ = ___

7.

___ × ___ = ___

___ × ___ = ___

Math Processes and Practices ② **Use Reasoning Algebra** Write the unknown factor.

8. $3 \times 7 = $ _____ $ \times 3$

9. $4 \times 5 = 10 \times$ _____

10. $3 \times 6 = $ _____ $ \times 9$

11. $6 \times$ _____ $ = 4 \times 9$

12. _____ $ \times 8 = 4 \times 6$

13. $5 \times 8 = 8 \times$ _____

Problem Solving • Applications

14. Jenna used pinecones to make 18 peanut butter bird feeders. She hung the same number of feeders in 6 trees. Draw an array to show how many feeders she put in each tree.

She put _____ bird feeders in each tree.

15. **GO DEEPER**   Mr. Diaz sets out 6 rows of glasses with 3 glasses in each row. Mrs. Diaz sets out 3 rows of glasses with 6 glasses in each row. How many glasses do Mr. and Mrs. Diaz set out in all?

_____

16. **GO DEEPER**   Write two different word problems about 12 birds to show 2×6 and 6×2. Solve each problem.

_____

_____

17. **THINK SMARTER**   There are 4 rows of 6 bird stickers in Don's sticker album. There are 7 rows of 5 bird stickers in Lindsey's album. How many bird stickers do they have?

_____

18. **THINK SMARTER**   Write the letter for each multiplication sentence on the left next to the multiplication sentence on the right that has the same value.

Ⓐ $5 \times 7 = \blacksquare$ ☐ $6 \times 3 = \blacksquare$

Ⓑ $8 \times 2 = \blacksquare$ ☐ $2 \times 8 = \blacksquare$

Ⓒ $3 \times 6 = \blacksquare$ ☐ $4 \times 9 = \blacksquare$

Ⓓ $9 \times 4 = \blacksquare$ ☐ $7 \times 5 = \blacksquare$

Name _____

Commutative Property of Multiplication

Learning Objective You will use the Commutative Property of Multiplication to find products.

Write a multiplication sentence for the model. Then use the Commutative Property of Multiplication to write a related multiplication sentence.

1.

__5__ × __2__ = __10__

__2__ × __5__ = __10__

2.

____ × ____ = ____

____ × ____ = ____

3.

____ × ____ = ____

____ × ____ = ____

4.

____ × ____ = ____

____ × ____ = ____

Problem Solving Real World

5. A garden store sells trays of plants. Each tray holds 2 rows of 8 plants. How many plants are in one tray?

6. Jeff collects toy cars. They are displayed in a case that has 4 rows. There are 6 cars in each row. How many cars does Jeff have?

7. **WRITE** ▸Math How are the Commutative Property of Addition and the Commutative Property of Multiplication alike?

_____

_____

Lesson Check

1. Write a sentence that shows the Commutative Property of Multiplication.

   _____

   _____

   _____

2. What factor makes the number sentence true?

   $7 \times 4 = \blacksquare \times 7$

   _____

   _____

Spiral Review

3. Ms. Williams drove 149 miles on Thursday and 159 miles on Friday. About how many miles did she drive altogether?

   _____

   _____

4. Inez has 699 pennies and 198 nickels. Estimate how many more pennies than nickels she has.

   _____

   _____

5. This year, the parade had 127 floats. That was 34 fewer floats than last year. How many floats were in the parade last year?

   _____

6. Jeremy made a tally table to record how his friends voted for their favorite pet. His table shows ⲩ ⲩ || next to Dog. How many friends voted for dog?

   _____

FOR MORE PRACTICE
GO TO THE
Personal Math Trainer

Name _____

Multiply with 1 and 0

Essential Question What happens when you multiply a number by 0 or 1?

Learning Objective You will understand the properties of 0 and 1 in multiplication.

🔑 Unlock the Problem

Luke sees 4 birdbaths. Each birdbath has 2 birds in it. What multiplication sentence tells how many birds there are?

* How many birdbaths are there?

_____

* How many birds does Luke see in

each birdbath? _____

🔓 **Draw a quick picture to show the birds in the birdbaths.**

_____ × _____ = _____

One bird flies away from each birdbath. Cross out 1 bird in each birdbath above. What multiplication sentence shows the total number of birds now?

_____ × _____ = _____
  ↑   ↑   ↑
birdbaths   bird in each   total number
            birdbath now   of birds

Now cross out another bird in each birdbath. What multiplication sentence shows the total number of birds in the birdbaths now?

_____ × _____ = _____
  ↑   ↑   ↑
birdbaths   birds in each   total number
            birdbath now   of birds

* How do the birdbaths look now? _____

Math Talk Math Processes and Practices ❶

Analyze What if there were 5 birdbaths with 0 birds in each of them? What would be the product? Explain.

🔒 Example

Jenny has 2 pages of bird stickers. There are 4 stickers on each page. How many stickers does she have in all?

$2 \times 4 =$ _____   Think: 2 groups of 4

So, Jenny has _____ stickers in all.

Suppose Jenny uses 1 page of the stickers. What fact shows how many stickers she has now?

_____ $\times$ _____ $=$ _____   Think: 1 group of 4

So, Jenny has _____ stickers now.

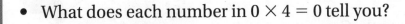

Then, Jenny uses the rest of the stickers. What fact shows how many stickers Jenny has now?

_____ $\times$ _____ $=$ _____   Think: 0 groups of 4

So, Jenny has _____ stickers now.

- What does each number in $0 \times 4 = 0$ tell you?

_____

_____

> **⚠ ERROR Alert**
>
> A 0 in a multiplication sentence means 0 groups or 0 things in a group, so the product is always 0.

1. What pattern do you see when you multiply numbers with 1 as a factor?

   Think: $1 \times 2 = 2$ $1 \times 3 = 3$ $1 \times 4 = 4$

   _____

   _____

The **Identity Property of Multiplication** states that the product of any number and 1 is that number.

$$7 \times 1 = 7 \qquad 6 \times 1 = 6$$
$$1 \times 7 = 7 \qquad 1 \times 6 = 6$$

2. What pattern do you see when you multiply numbers with 0 as a factor?

   Think: $0 \times 1 = 0$ $0 \times 2 = 0$ $0 \times 5 = 0$

   _____

   _____

The **Zero Property of Multiplication** states that the product of zero and any number is zero.

$$0 \times 5 = 0 \qquad 0 \times 8 = 0$$
$$5 \times 0 = 0 \qquad 8 \times 0 = 0$$

Name _____

1. What multiplication sentence matches this picture? Find the product.

   _____

Find the product.

2. $5 \times 1 =$ ____

3. $0 \times 2 =$ ____

4. $4 \times 0 =$ ____

5. $1 \times 6 =$ ____

6. $3 \times 0 =$ ____

7. $1 \times 2 =$ ____

8. $0 \times 6 =$ ____

9. $8 \times 1 =$ ____

Math Talk   Math Processes and Practices 6

Compare Explain how 3×1 and $3 + 1$ are different.

On Your Own

Find the product.

10. $3 \times 1 =$ ____

11. $8 \times 0 =$ ____

12. $1 \times 9 =$ ____

13. $0 \times 7 =$ ____

Math Processes and Practices 2   **Use Reasoning Algebra Complete the multiplication sentence.**

14. ____ $\times 1 = 15$

15. $1 \times 28 =$ ____

16. $0 \times 46 =$ ____

17. $36 \times 0 =$ ____

18. ____ $\times 5 = 5$

19. $19 \times$ ____ $= 0$

20. ____ $\times 0 = 0$

21. $7 \times$ ____ $= 7$

22. Noah sets out 7 baskets at the Farmers' Market. Each basket holds 1 watermelon. How many watermelons does Noah set out?

   _____

23. **GO DEEPER** Mason and Alexis each have 1 bag of marbles. There are 9 marbles in each bag. How many marbles do they have altogether?

   _____

24. **GO DEEPER** Each box holds 6 black markers and 4 red markers. Derek has 0 boxes of markers. Write a number sentence that shows how many markers Derek has. Explain how you found your answer.

   _____

   _____

Problem Solving • Applications

Use the table for 25–27.

25. At the circus Jon saw 5 unicycles. How many wheels are on the 5 unicycles? Write a multiplication sentence.

   _____ × _____ = _____

Circus Vehicles	
Type of Vehicle	**Number of Wheels**
Car	4
Tricycle	3
Bicycle	2
Unicycle	1

26. **What's the Question?** Julia used multiplication with 1 and the information in the table. The answer is 3.

   _____

   _____

27. **THINK SMARTER** Brian saw some circus vehicles. He saw 17 wheels in all. If 2 of the vehicles are cars, how many vehicles are bicycles and tricycles?

   _____

28. **WRITE** ▸*Math* Write a word problem that uses multiplying with 1 or 0. Show how to solve your problem.

   _____

   _____

29. **THINK SMARTER** For numbers 29a–29d, select True or False for each multiplication sentence.

   29a. $6 \times 0 = 0$ ○ True   ○ False

   29b. $0 \times 9 = 9 \times 0$ ○ True   ○ False

   29c. $1 \times 0 = 1$ ○ True   ○ False

   29d. $3 \times 1 = 3$ ○ True   ○ False

Multiply with 1 and 0

Learning Objective You will understand the properties of 0 and 1 in multiplication.

Find the product.

1. $1 \times 4 =$ __4__

2. $0 \times 8 =$ ____

3. $0 \times 4 =$ ____

4. $1 \times 6 =$ ____

5. $3 \times 0 =$ ____

6. $0 \times 9 =$ ____

7. $8 \times 1 =$ ____

8. $1 \times 2 =$ ____

9. $10 \times 1 =$ ____

10. $2 \times 0 =$ ____

11. $5 \times 1 =$ ____

12. $1 \times 0 =$ ____

13. $0 \times 0 =$ ____

14. $1 \times 3 =$ ____

15. $9 \times 0 =$ ____

16. $1 \times 1 =$ ____

Problem Solving Real World

17. Peter is in the school play. His teacher gave 1 copy of the play to each of 6 students. How many copies of the play did the teacher hand out?

_____

18. There are 4 egg cartons on the table. There are 0 eggs in each carton. How many eggs are there in all?

_____

19. **WRITE** ▸*Math* One group has 5 people, and each person has 1 granola bar. Another group has 5 people, and each person has 0 granola bars. Which group has more granola bars? Explain.

_____

_____

_____

Lesson Check

1. There are 0 bicycles in each bicycle rack. If there are 8 bicycle racks, how many bicycles are there in the rack?

   _____

2. What is the product?

   $1 \times 0 = $ ___

   _____

Spiral Review

3. Mr. Ellis drove 197 miles on Monday and 168 miles on Tuesday. How many miles did he drive?

   _____

4. What multiplication sentence does the array show?

   _____

Use the bar graph for 5–6.

5. How many cars were washed on Friday and Saturday combined?

   _____

6. How many more cars were washed on Saturday than on Sunday?

   _____

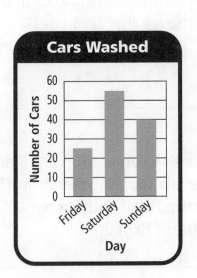

FOR MORE PRACTICE
GO TO THE
Personal Math Trainer

✓ Chapter 3 Review/Test

1. There are 3 boats on the lake. Six people ride in each boat. How many people ride in the boats? Draw equal groups to model the problem and explain how to solve it.

_____ people

2. Nadia has 4 sheets of stickers. There are 8 stickers on each sheet. She wrote this number sentence to represent the total number of stickers.

$$4 \times 8 = 32$$

What is a related number sentence that also represents the total number of stickers she has?

Ⓐ $8 + 4 = \blacksquare$

Ⓑ $4 + 4 + 4 + 4 = \blacksquare$

Ⓒ $8 \times 8 = \blacksquare$

Ⓓ $8 \times 4 = \blacksquare$

3. Lindsay went hiking for two days in Yellowstone National Park. The first jump on the number line shows how many birds she saw the first day. She saw the same number of birds the next day.

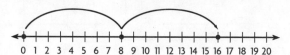

Write the multiplication sentence that is shown on the number line.

_____ × _____ = _____

GO DIGITAL Assessment Options
Chapter Test

4. Paco drew an array to show the number of desks in his classroom.

Write a multiplication sentence for the array.

---

5. Alondra makes 4 necklaces. She uses 5 beads on each necklace.

For numbers 5a–5d, choose Yes or No to tell if the number sentence could be used to find the number of beads Alondra uses.

5a. $4 \times 5 = $ ▦   ○ Yes   ○ No

5b. $4 + 4 + 4 + 4 = $ ▦   ○ Yes   ○ No

5c. $5 + 5 + 5 + 5 = $ ▦   ○ Yes   ○ No

5d. $5 + 4 = $ ▦   ○ Yes   ○ No

6. John sold 3 baskets of apples at the market. Each basket contained 9 apples. How many apples did John sell? Make a bar model to solve the problem.

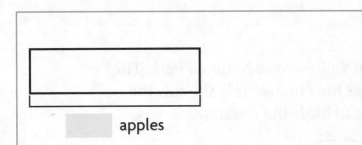

apples

© Houghton Mifflin Harcourt Publishing Company

Name _____

7. Select the number sentences that show the Commutative Property of Multiplication. Mark all that apply.

Ⓐ $3 \times 2 = 2 \times 3$

Ⓑ $4 \times 9 = 4 \times 9$

Ⓒ $5 \times 0 = 0$

Ⓓ $6 \times 1 = 1 \times 6$

Ⓔ $7 \times 2 = 14 \times 1$

8. A waiter carried 6 baskets with 5 dinner rolls in each basket. How many dinner rolls did he carry? Show your work.

_____ dinner rolls

9. Sonya needs 3 equal lengths of wire to make 3 bracelets. The jump on the number line shows the length of one wire in inches. How many inches of wire will Sonya need to make the 3 bracelets?

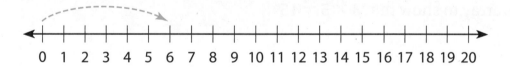

0 1 2 3 4 5 6 7 8 9 10 11 12 13 14 15 16 17 18 19 20

_____ inches

10. Josh has 4 dogs. Each dog gets 2 dog biscuits every day. How many biscuits will Josh need for all of his dogs for Saturday and Sunday?

_____ biscuits

11. GO DEEPER Jorge displayed 28 cans of paint on a shelf in his store.

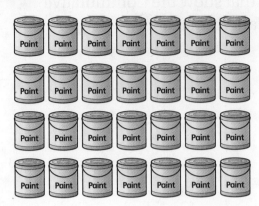

Select other ways Jorge could arrange the same number of cans.
Mark all that apply.

(A) 2 rows of 14   (D) 8 rows of 3

(B) 1 row of 28   (E) 7 rows of 4

(C) 6 rows of 5

12. Choose the number that makes the statement true.

The product of any number and $\boxed{\begin{array}{c} 0 \\ 1 \\ 10 \end{array}}$ is zero.

13. James made this array to show that $3 \times 5 = 15$.

Part A

James says that $5 \times 3 = 15$. Is James correct? Draw an array to
explain your answer.

_____

Part B

Which number property supports your answer?

_____

_____

186

Name _____

14. Julio has a collection of coins. He puts the coins in 2 equal groups. There are 6 coins in each group. How many coins does Julio have? Use the number line to show your work.

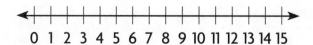

0 1 2 3 4 5 6 7 8 9 10 11 12 13 14 15

_____ coins

15. GO DEEPER Landon collects trading cards.

Part A

Yesterday, Landon sorted his trading cards into 4 groups. Each group had 7 cards. Draw a bar model to show Landon's cards. How many cards does he have?

_____ trading cards

Part B

Landon buys 3 more packs of trading cards today. Each pack has 8 cards. Write a multiplication sentence to show how many cards Landon buys today. Then find how many cards Landon has now. Show your work.

_____

16. A unicycle has only 1 wheel. Write a multiplication sentence to show how many wheels there are on 9 unicycles.

_____ × _____ = _____

17. Carlos spent 5 minutes working on each of 8 math problems. He can use 8×5 to find the total amount of time he spent on the problems.

For numbers 17a–17d, choose Yes or No to show which are equal to 8×5.

17a. $8 + 5$ ○ Yes   ○ No

17b. $5 + 5 + 5 + 5 + 5$ ○ Yes   ○ No

17c. $8 + 8 + 8 + 8 + 8$ ○ Yes   ○ No

17d. $5 + 5 + 5 + 5 + 5 + 5 + 5 + 5$ ○ Yes   ○ No

18. Lucy and her mother made tacos. They put 2 tacos on each of 7 plates.

Select the number sentences that show all the tacos Lucy and her mother made. Mark all that apply.

(A) $2 + 2 + 2 + 2 + 2 + 2 + 2 = 14$

(B) $2 + 7 = 9$

(C) $7 + 7 = 14$

(D) $8 + 6 = 14$

(E) $2 \times 7 = 14$

Personal Math Trainer

19. **THINK SMARTER +** Jayson is making 5 sock puppets. He glues 2 buttons on each puppet for its eyes. He glues 1 pompom on each puppet for its nose.

Part A

Write the total number of buttons and pompoms he uses. Write a multiplication sentence for each.

Eyes   **Noses**

_____ buttons   _____ pompoms

_____ × _____ = _____   _____ × _____ = _____

Part B

After making 5 puppets, Jayson has 4 buttons and 3 pompoms left. What is the greatest number of puppets he can make with those items if he wants all his puppets to look the same? Draw models and use them to explain.

At most, he can make _____ more puppets.

_____

_____

_____

_____

Chapter 4

Multiplication Facts and Strategies

✓ Show What You Know

Personal Math Trainer
Online Assessment and Intervention

Check your understanding of important skills.

Name _____

▶ **Doubles and Doubles Plus One** Write the doubles and doubles plus one facts.

1.

___ + ___ = ___   ___ + ___ = ___

2.

___ + ___ = ___   ___ + ___ = ___

▶ **Equal Groups** Complete.

3.

___ groups of ___

___ in all

4.

___ groups of ___

___ in all

Math in the Real World

Stephen needs to use these clues to find a buried time capsule.

- Start with a number that is the product of 3 and 4.
- Double the product and go to that number.
- Add 2 tens and find the number that is 1 less than the sum.

Help Stephen find the time capsule. At what number is the time capsule buried?

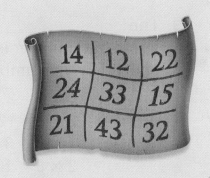

14	12	22
24	33	15
21	43	32

Vocabulary Builder

▶ **Visualize It** ••••••••••••••••••••••••••••••••••••••

Complete the tree map by using the words with a ✓.

Multiplication Properties

_____ Property of Multiplication	_____ Property of Multiplication	_____ Property of Multiplication
$1 \times 4 = 4$ 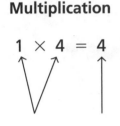 _____ _____	$(4 \times 2) \times 3 = 4 \times (2 \times 3)$	$3 \times 2 = 2 \times 3$ :: ::: _____

▶ **Understand Vocabulary** ••••••••••••••••••••••••••••

Complete the sentences by using the preview words.

1. The _____ Property of Multiplication states that when the grouping of factors is changed, the product is the same.

2. A _____ of 5 is any product that has 5 as one of its factors.

3. The _____ Property states that multiplying a sum by a number is the same as multiplying each addend by the number and then adding the products.

    Example: $2 \times 8 = 2 \times (4 + 4)$
                $2 \times 8 = (2 \times 4) + (2 \times 4)$
                $2 \times 8 = 8 + 8$
                $2 \times 8 = 16$

GO DIGITAL
• Interactive Student Edition
• Multimedia eGlossary

array

matriz

4

**Associative Property
of Multiplication**

Propiedad asociativa
de la multiplicación

6

**Commutative Property
of Multiplication**

Propiedad conmutativa
de la multiplicación

9

Distributive Property

Propiedad distributiva

13

factor

factor

25

**Identity Property
of Multiplication**

Propiedad de identidad
de la multiplicación

35

multiple

múltiplo

50

product

producto

65

The property that states that when the grouping of factors is changed, the product remains the same

Example: $(5 \times 4) \times 3 = 5 \times (4 \times 3)$

A set of objects arranged in rows and columns

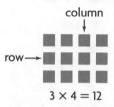

$3 \times 4 = 12$

The property that states that multiplying a sum by a number is the same as multiplying each addend by the number and then adding the products

Example: $5 \times 8 = 5 \times (4 + 4)$
$5 \times 8 = (5 \times 4) + (5 \times 4)$
$5 \times 8 = 20 + 20$
$5 \times 8 = 40$

The property that states that you can multiply two factors in any order and get the same product

Example: $4 \times 3 = 3 \times 4$

The property that states that the product of any number and 1 is that number

Example: $17 \times 1 = 17$

A number that is multiplied by another number to find a product

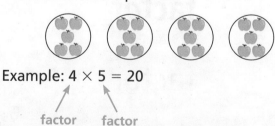

Example: $4 \times 5 = 20$

factor   factor

The answer in a multiplication problem

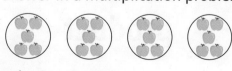

Example: $4 \times 5 = 20$

product

A number that is the product of two counting numbers

6	6	6	6	counting
$\times 1$	$\times 2$	$\times 3$	$\times 4$	← numbers
6	12	18	24	← multiples of 6

© Houghton Mifflin Harcourt Publishing Company

Guess the Word

Word Box

arrays

Associative Property of Multiplication

Commutative Property of Multiplication

Distributive Property

Identity Property of Multiplication

factors

multiple

product

For 3 to 4 players

Materials

• timer

How to Play

1. Take turns to play.

2. Choose a math term, but do not say it aloud.

3. Set the timer for 1 minute.

4. Give a one-word clue about your term. Give each player one chance to guess the term.

5. If nobody guesses correctly, repeat Step 4 with a different clue. Repeat until a player guesses the term or time runs out.

6. The player who guesses the term gets 1 point. If the player can use the word in a sentence, he or she gets 1 more point. Then that player gets a turn choosing a word.

7. The first player to score 10 points wins.

The Write Way

Reflect

Choose one idea. Write about it.

- Tell how to solve this problem: $4 \times 6 = $ _____.
- Explain the Distributive Property.
- Write about a topic in Chapter 4 that was hard to learn. Tell how you figured out how to learn it.

Name _____

Multiply with 2 and 4

Essential Question How can you multiply with 2 and 4?

Learning Objective You will use equal-sized groups, equal "jumps" on a number line, and doubles to multiply with 2 and 4.

Unlock the Problem

Two students are in a play. Each of the students has 3 costumes. How many costumes do they have in all?

Multiplying when there are two equal groups is like adding doubles.

- What does the word "each" tell you?

  _____

- How can you find the number of costumes the 2 students have?

  _____

Find 2 × 3.

MODEL	THINK	RECORD
Draw counters to show the costumes.  	2 groups of 3 3 + 3 6	2 × 3 = 6 ↑ ↑ ↑ how many groups — how many in each group — how many in all

So, the 2 students have _____ costumes in all.

Try This!

2 × 1 = 1 + 1 = 2

2 × 2 = 2 + 2 = 4

2 × _____ = 3 + _____ = 6

2 × _____ = 4 + _____ = 8

2 × _____ = 5 + _____ = _____

2 × _____ = 6 + _____ = _____

2 × _____ = 7 + _____ = _____

2 × _____ = 8 + _____ = _____

2 × _____ = 9 + _____ = _____

 Math Talk

Math Processes and Practices ❷

Reason Abstractly What do you notice about the product when you multiply by 2?

🔑 Count by 2s.

When there are 2 in each group, you can count by 2s to find how many there are in all.

There are 4 students with 2 costumes each. How many costumes do they have in all?

Skip count by drawing the jumps on the number line.

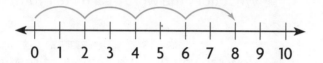

So, the 4 students have _____ in all.

- How can you decide whether to count by 2s or double?

_____

🔑 Example Use doubles to find 4 × 5.

When you multiply with 4, you can multiply with 2 and then double the product.

| **MULTIPLY WITH 2** | **DOUBLE THE PRODUCT** |

4 × 5 | $2 \times 5 = 10$ | $10 + 10 = 20$

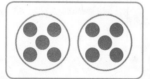 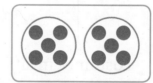 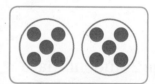

So, $4 \times 5 =$ ____.

Share and Show MATH BOARD

1. Double 2 × 7 to find 4 × 7.

   Multiply with 2. $2 \times 7 =$ ____

   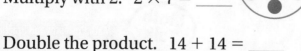

   Double the product. $14 + 14 =$ ____

   So, $4 \times 7 =$ ____.

Math Talk

Math Processes and Practices ⑦

Identify Relationships Explain how knowing the product for 2 × 8 helps you find the product for 4 × 8.

Name _____

Write a multiplication sentence for the model.

2.

___ × ___ = ___

✓3.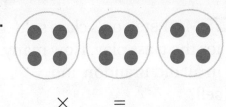

___ × ___ = ___

Find the product.

4. 6	**5.** 9	**6.** 2	**7.** 8	**✓8.** 5
×2	×4	×7	×4	×2

On Your Own

Find the product. Use your MathBoard.

9. 10	**10.** 2	**11.** 4	**12.** 7	**13.** 2
× 4	×9	×6	×2	×0

14. 4	**15.** 2	**16.** 4	**17.** 10	**18.** 4
×3	×8	×4	× 2	×5

Math Processes and Practices 7 **Look for Structure Algebra** Complete the table for the factors 2 and 4.

×	1	2	3	4	5	6	7	8	9	10
19. 2										
20. 4										

Math Processes and Practices 2 **Reason Quantitatively Algebra** Write the unknown number.

21. 4 × 8 = 16 + ____   **22.** 20 = 2 × ____   **23.** 8 × 2 = 10 + ____

24. **THINK SMARTER** Lindsey, Louis, Sally, and Matt each bring 5 guests to the school play. How many guests in all did they bring to the school play? Explain.

_____

Unlock the Problem

25. **GO DEEPER** Ms. Peterson's class sold tickets for the class play. How many tickets in all did Brandon and Haylie sell?

Play Tickets	
Brandon	🎟🎟🎟🎟
Haylie	🎟🎟🎟🎟🎟🎟
Elizabeth	🎟🎟🎟🎟🎟🎟🎟

Key: Each 🎟 = 2 tickets sold.

a. What do you need to find?

_____

_____

b. Why should you multiply to find the number of tickets shown? Explain.

_____

_____

c. Show the steps you used to solve the problem.

d. Complete the sentences.

Brandon sold ____ tickets. Haylie sold

____ tickets. So, Brandon and Haylie

sold ____ tickets.

26. **Math Processes and Practices ❶** **Analyze** Suppose Sam sold 20 tickets to the school play. How many pictures of tickets should be on the picture graph above to show his sales? Explain.

_____

_____

27. **THINK SMARTER** Alex exchanges some dollar bills for quarters at the bank. He receives 4 quarters for each dollar bill. Select the numbers of quarters that Alex could receive. Mark all that apply.

Ⓐ 16   Ⓓ 32

Ⓑ 18   Ⓔ 50

Ⓒ 24

Multiply with 2 and 4

Learning Objective You will use equal-sized groups, equal "jumps" on a number line, and doubles to multiply with 2 and 4.

Write a multiplication sentence for the model.

1.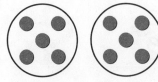

   Think: There are 2 groups of 5 counters.

   $\underline{\ 2\ } \times \underline{\ 5\ } = \underline{\ 10\ }$

2.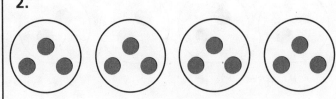

   $\underline{\ \ \ } \times \underline{\ \ \ } = \underline{\ \ \ }$

Find the product.

3. $\begin{array}{r} 2 \\ \times\ 6 \\ \hline \end{array}$

4. $\begin{array}{r} 4 \\ \times\ 8 \\ \hline \end{array}$

5. $\begin{array}{r} 2 \\ \times\ 3 \\ \hline \end{array}$

6. $\begin{array}{r} 4 \\ \times\ 6 \\ \hline \end{array}$

Problem Solving

7. On Monday, Steven read 9 pages of his new book. To finish the first chapter on Tuesday, he needs to read double the number of pages he read on Monday. How many pages does he need to read on Tuesday?

   _____

8. Courtney's school is having a family game night. Each table has 4 players. There are 7 tables in all. How many players are at the game night?

   _____

9. **WRITE** *Math* Explain how you can use doubles when multiplying with 4 to find 4×8.

   _____

   _____

Lesson Check

1. What multiplication sentence matches the model?

_____

_____

2. Find the product.

$$\begin{array}{r} 2 \\ \times\ 8 \\ \hline \end{array}$$

Spiral Review

3. Sean made a picture graph to show his friends' favorite colors.

This is the key for the graph.
Each 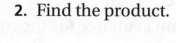 = 2 friends.

How many friends does
🔵🔵🔵🔵 stand for?

_____

4. The table shows the lengths of some walking trails.

Walking Trails	
Name	Length (in feet)
Mountain Trail	844
Lake Trail	792
Harmony Trail	528

How many feet longer is Mountain Trail than Harmony Trail?

_____

5. Find the sum.

$$\begin{array}{r} 527 \\ +\ 154 \\ \hline \end{array}$$

6. A bar graph shows that sports books received 9 votes. If the scale is 0 to 20 by twos, where should the bar end for the sports books?

_____

FOR MORE PRACTICE
GO TO THE
Personal Math Trainer

Name _____

Multiply with 5 and 10

Essential Question How can you multiply with 5 and 10?

Learning Objective You will use equal "jumps" on a number line and models to multiply with 5 and 10.

Unlock the Problem

Marcel is making 6 toy banjos. He needs 5 strings for each banjo. How many strings does he need in all?

 Use skip counting.

Skip count by 5s until you say 6 numbers.

5, _____, _____, _____, _____, _____

6 × 5 = _____

So, Marcel needs _____ strings in all.

- How many banjos is Marcel making? _____
- How many strings does each banjo have? _____

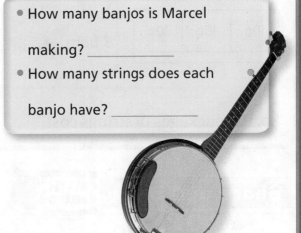

Example 1 Use a number line.

Each string is 10 inches long. How many inches of string will Marcel use for each banjo?

Think: 1 jump = 10 inches

- Draw 5 jumps for the 5 strings. Jump 10 spaces at a time for the length of each string.

- You land on 10, _____, _____, _____, and _____.   5 × 10 = _____

The numbers 10, 20, 30, 40, and 50 are multiples of 10.

So, Marcel will use _____ inches of string for each banjo.

A **multiple** of 10 is any product that has 10 as one of its factors.

 Math Talk

Math Processes and Practices ①

Analyze What do you notice about the multiples of 10?

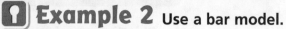 **Example 2** Use a bar model.

Marcel bought 3 packages of strings. Each package cost 10¢. How much did the packages cost in all?

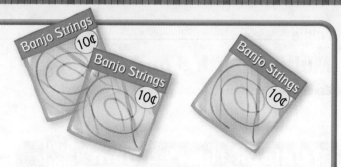

MODEL	THINK	RECORD
	1 unit → 10¢	
10¢ | 10¢ | 10¢	3 units → ____ × ____	____ × ____ = ____

So, the packages of strings cost _____ in all.

Share and Show

1. How can you use this number line to find 8×5?

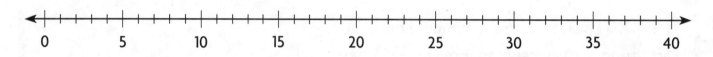

0   5   10   15   20   25   30   35   40

_____

_____

Math Talk Math Processes and Practices ③

Apply How can knowing 4×5 help you find 4×10?

Find the product.

2. $2 \times 5 =$ ____

3. ____ $= 6 \times 10$

4. ____ $= 5 \times 5$

✓5. $10 \times 7 =$ ____

6. $\begin{array}{r} 10 \\ \times\ 4 \\ \hline \end{array}$

7. $\begin{array}{r} 5 \\ \times 6 \\ \hline \end{array}$

8. $\begin{array}{r} 10 \\ \times\ 0 \\ \hline \end{array}$

✓9. $\begin{array}{r} 5 \\ \times 3 \\ \hline \end{array}$

10. $\begin{array}{r} 7 \\ \times 5 \\ \hline \end{array}$

11. $\begin{array}{r} 5 \\ \times 10 \\ \hline \end{array}$

12. $\begin{array}{r} 4 \\ \times 5 \\ \hline \end{array}$

13. $\begin{array}{r} 9 \\ \times 10 \\ \hline \end{array}$

Name _____

On Your Own

Find the product.

14. $5 \times 1 =$ _____

15. _____ $= 10 \times 2$

16. _____ $= 4 \times 5$

17. $10 \times 10 =$ _____

18. $10 \times 0 =$ _____

19. $10 \times 5 =$ _____

20. _____ $= 1 \times 5$

21. _____ $= 5 \times 9$

22.
$$\begin{array}{r} 3 \\ \times\, 4 \\ \hline \end{array}$$

23.
$$\begin{array}{r} 5 \\ \times\, 0 \\ \hline \end{array}$$

24.
$$\begin{array}{r} 4 \\ \times\, 8 \\ \hline \end{array}$$

25.
$$\begin{array}{r} 10 \\ \times\, 5 \\ \hline \end{array}$$

Identify Relationships Algebra **Use the pictures to find the unknown numbers.**

26.

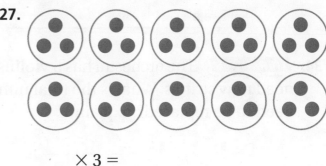

$3 \times$ _____ $=$ _____

27.

_____ $\times 3 =$ _____

Use a Diagram **Complete the bar model to solve.**

28. Marcel played 5 songs on the banjo. If each song lasted 8 minutes, how long did he play?

_____ minutes

29. There are 6 banjo players. If each player needs 10 sheets of music, how many sheets of music are needed?

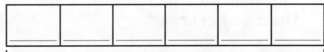

_____ sheets

30. GODEEPER Chris has 5 stacks of DVDs on a shelf. Each stack has 10 DVDs. If Chris adds 2 more identical stacks of DVDs to the shelves, how many DVDs will Chris have?

31. GODEEPER Mark is making 10 kites. He uses 5 yards of ribbon for each kite. He has already made 2 of the kites. How many yards of ribbon will Mark need to make the rest of the kites?

Problem Solving • Applications

Use the table for 32–34.

32. John and his dad own 7 banjos. They want to replace the strings on all of them. How many strings should they buy? Write a multiplication sentence to solve.

_____

Stringed Instruments	
Instrument	**Strings**
Guitar	6
Banjo	5
Mandolin	8
Violin	4

33. **GO DEEPER** Mr. Lemke has 5 guitars, 4 banjos, and 2 mandolins. What is the total number of strings on Mr. Lemke's instruments?

_____

34. **THINK SMARTER** The orchestra has 5 violins and 3 guitars that need new strings. What is the total number of strings that need to be replaced? Explain.

_____

_____

_____

35. **WRITE** ▸ Math **What's the Error?** Mr. James has 3 banjos. Mr. Lewis has 5 times the number of banjos Mr. James has. Riley says Mr. Lewis has 12 banjos. Describe her error.

_____

_____

36. **THINK SMARTER** Circle the number that makes the multiplication sentence true.

$$5 \times \boxed{\begin{matrix} 7 \\ 8 \\ 9 \end{matrix}} = 45$$

Name _____

Multiply with 5 and 10

Learning Objective You will use equal "jumps" on a number line and models to multiply with 5 and 10.

Find the product.

1. $5 \times 7 =$ __35__   2. $5 \times 1 =$ _____   3. $2 \times 10 =$ _____   4. _____ $= 8 \times 5$

5. $1 \times 10 =$ _____   6. _____ $= 4 \times 5$ 7. $5 \times 10 =$ _____   8. $7 \times 5 =$ _____

9. $\begin{array}{r} 5 \\ \times\ 6 \\ \hline \end{array}$ 10. $\begin{array}{r} 10 \\ \times\ 7 \\ \hline \end{array}$ 11. $\begin{array}{r} 5 \\ \times\ 3 \\ \hline \end{array}$ 12. $\begin{array}{r} 10 \\ \times\ 4 \\ \hline \end{array}$

13. $\begin{array}{r} 5 \\ \times\ 0 \\ \hline \end{array}$ 14. $\begin{array}{r} 10 \\ \times\ 8 \\ \hline \end{array}$ 15. $\begin{array}{r} 5 \\ \times\ 2 \\ \hline \end{array}$ 16. $\begin{array}{r} 10 \\ \times\ 6 \\ \hline \end{array}$

Problem Solving Real World

17. Ginger takes 10 nickels to buy some pencils at the school store. How many cents does Ginger have to spend?

18. The gym at Evergreen School has three basketball courts. There are 5 players on each of the courts. How many players are there?

_____   _____

19. **WRITE** ▸*Math* Michelle bought some pinwheels for a dollar and paid in dimes. How many dimes did she use? Explain.

_____

_____

Lesson Check

1. Mrs. Hinely grows roses. There are 6 roses on each of her 10 rose bushes. How many roses in all are on Mrs. Hinely's rose bushes?

_____

2. Find the product.

$$\begin{array}{r} 5 \\ \times\ 8 \\ \hline \end{array}$$

Spiral Review

3. Mr. Miller's class voted on where to go for a field trip. Use the picture graph to find which choice had the most votes.

Field Trip Choices

Science Center	★★
Aquarium	★★★★
Zoo	★★★★★
Museum	★★

Key: Each ★ = 2 votes.

_____

4. Zack made this table for his survey.

Favorite Juice

Flavor	Votes
Grape	16
Orange	10
Berry	9
Apple	12

How many votes were cast?

_____

5. Which of the following is an even number?

25, 28, 31, 37

_____

6. Estimate the sum.

$$\begin{array}{r} 479 \\ +\ 89 \\ \hline \end{array}$$

_____

© Houghton Mifflin Harcourt Publishing Company

FOR MORE PRACTICE
GO TO THE
Personal Math Trainer

Name _____

Multiply with 3 and 6

Essential Question What are some ways to multiply with 3 and 6?

🔑 Unlock the Problem

Sabrina is making triangles with toothpicks. She uses 3 toothpicks for each triangle. She makes 4 triangles. How many toothpicks does Sabrina use?

- Why does Sabrina need 3 toothpicks for each triangle?

  _____

  _____

 Draw a picture.

STEP 1

Complete the 4 triangles.

STEP 2

Skip count by the number of sides. _____, _____, _____, _____

How many triangles are there in all? _____

How many toothpicks are in each triangle? _____

How many toothpicks are there in all?

$4 \times$ _____ = _____

4 triangles have _____ toothpicks.

So, Sabrina uses _____ toothpicks.

Math Talk

Math Processes and Practices ②

Reason Abstractly How can you use what you know about the number of toothpicks needed for 4 triangles to find the number of toothpicks needed for 8 triangles?

Try This! Find the number of toothpicks needed for 6 triangles.

Draw a quick picture to help you. How did you find the answer?

_____

_____

_____

Jessica is using craft sticks to make 6 octagons.
How many craft sticks will she use?

1 One Way Use 5s facts and addition.

▲ An octagon has 8 sides.

To multiply a factor by 6, multiply the factor
by 5, and then add the factor.

$6 \times 7 = 5 \times 7 + 7 = 42$

$6 \times 6 = 5 \times 6 + \underline{\hspace{1cm}} = \underline{\hspace{1cm}}$

$6 \times 8 = 5 \times \underline{\hspace{1cm}} + \underline{\hspace{1cm}} = \underline{\hspace{1cm}}$

$6 \times 9 = \underline{\hspace{1cm}} \times \underline{\hspace{1cm}} + \underline{\hspace{1cm}} = \underline{\hspace{1cm}}$

So, Jessica will use \underline{\hspace{1cm}} craft sticks.

5×8

$+ 8$

2 Other Ways

Ⓐ Use doubles.

When at least one factor is an even number,
you can use doubles.

$6 \times 8 = \blacksquare$

First multiply with half of an even number.

$3 \times 8 = \underline{\hspace{1cm}}$

After you multiply, double the product.

$\underline{\hspace{1cm}} + 24 = \underline{\hspace{1cm}}$

$6 \times 8 = \underline{\hspace{1cm}}$

Ⓑ Use a multiplication table.

Hands On

Find the product 6×8 where
row 6 and column 8 meet.

$6 \times 8 = \underline{\hspace{1cm}}$

• Shade the row for 3 in the table. Then,
compare the rows for 3 and 6. What do
you notice about their products?

\underline{\hspace{5cm}}

\underline{\hspace{5cm}}

×	0	1	2	3	4	5	6	7	8	9	10
0	0	0	0	0	0	0	0	0	0	0	0
1	0	1	2	3	4	5	6	7	8	9	10
2	0	2	4	6	8	10	12	14	16	18	20
3	0	3	6	9	12	15	18	21	24	27	30
4	0	4	8	12	16	20	24	28	32	36	40
5	0	5	10	15	20	25	30	35	40	45	50
6	0	6	12	18	24	30	36	42	48	54	60
7	0	7	14	21	28	35	42	49	56	63	70
8	0	8	16	24	32	40	48	56	64	72	80
9	0	9	18	27	36	45	54	63	72	81	90
10	0	10	20	30	40	50	60	70	80	90	100

Name _____

1. Use 5s facts and addition to find $6 \times 4 =$ ■.

$6 \times 4 =$ _____ $\times$ _____ $+$ _____ $=$ _____

$6 \times 4 =$ _____

Math Talk Math Processes and Practices ⑥

Explain how you would use 5s facts and addition to find 6×3.

Find the product.

2. $6 \times 1 =$ _____   **3.** _____ $= 3 \times 7$ ✔ **4.** _____ $= 6 \times 5$ ✔ **5.** $3 \times 9 =$ _____

On Your Own

Find the product.

6. $2 \times 3 =$ _____   **7.** _____ $= 3 \times 6$ **8.** _____ $= 3 \times 0$ **9.** $1 \times 6 =$ _____

10. $\begin{array}{r} 3 \\ \times 6 \\ \hline \end{array}$ **11.** $\begin{array}{r} 8 \\ \times 3 \\ \hline \end{array}$ **12.** $\begin{array}{r} 6 \\ \times 7 \\ \hline \end{array}$ **13.** $\begin{array}{r} 3 \\ \times 3 \\ \hline \end{array}$ **14.** $\begin{array}{r} 10 \\ \times\ 6 \\ \hline \end{array}$

Math Processes and Practices ② **Use Reasoning Algebra** Complete the table.

Multiply by 3.	
Factor	Product
15. 4	
16.	18

Multiply by 6.	
Factor	Product
17. 5	
18. 7	

19. | Multiply by ▢. | |
|---|---|
| Factor | Product |
| 3 | 15 |
| **20.** 2 | |

Problem Solving • Applications Real World

Use the table for 21–22.

Quilt Pieces	
Shape	**Number in One Quilt Piece**
Square	6
Triangle	4
Circle	4

21. **GO DEEPER** The table tells about quilt pieces Jenna has made. How many squares and circles are there in 6 of Jenna's quilt pieces?

_____

22. **GO DEEPER** How many more squares than triangles are in 3 of Jenna's quilt pieces?

_____

23. **THINK SMARTER** Alli used some craft sticks to make shapes. If she used one craft stick for each side of the shape, would Alli use more craft sticks for 5 squares or 6 triangles? Explain.

_____

_____

_____

24. **Math Processes and Practices 3** **Apply** Draw a picture and use words to explain the Commutative Property of Multiplication with the factors 3 and 4.

_____

_____

25. **THINK SMARTER** Omar reads 6 pages in his book each night. How many pages does Omar read in 7 nights?

Use the array to explain how you know your answer is correct.

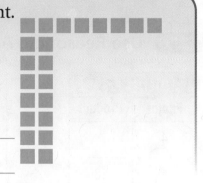

_____

Name _____

Multiply with 3 and 6

Learning Objective You will use strategies to multiply with 3 and 6.

Find the product.

1. $6 \times 4 =$ <u>24</u>   2. $3 \times 7 =$ _____   3. _____ $= 2 \times 6$ 4. _____ $= 3 \times 5$

Think: You can use doubles.

$3 \times 4 = 12$

$12 + 12 = 24$

5. $1 \times 3 =$ _____   6. _____ $= 6 \times 8$ 7. $3 \times 9 =$ _____   8. _____ $= 6 \times 6$

9. $\begin{array}{r} 4 \\ \times\ 3 \\ \hline \end{array}$
10. $\begin{array}{r} 6 \\ \times\ 5 \\ \hline \end{array}$
11. $\begin{array}{r} 2 \\ \times\ 3 \\ \hline \end{array}$
12. $\begin{array}{r} 6 \\ \times\ 3 \\ \hline \end{array}$

13. $\begin{array}{r} 10 \\ \times\ 6 \\ \hline \end{array}$
14. $\begin{array}{r} 3 \\ \times\ 6 \\ \hline \end{array}$
15. $\begin{array}{r} 7 \\ \times\ 6 \\ \hline \end{array}$
16. $\begin{array}{r} 3 \\ \times\ 0 \\ \hline \end{array}$

 Problem Solving Real World

17. James got 3 hits in each of his baseball games. He has played 4 baseball games. How many hits has he had?

18. Mrs. Burns is buying muffins. There are 6 muffins in each box. If she buys 5 boxes, how many muffins will she buy?

_____

19. **WRITE** ▸ *Math* Explain how multiplying with 6 is like multiplying with 3.

_____

_____

Lesson Check

1. Paco buys a carton of eggs. The carton has 2 rows of eggs. There are 6 eggs in each row. How many eggs are in the carton?

_____

2. Find the product.

$$\begin{array}{r} 9 \\ \times\ 3 \\ \hline \end{array}$$

Spiral Review

3. Find the difference.

$$\begin{array}{r} 568 \\ -\ 283 \\ \hline \end{array}$$

4. Dwight made double the number of baskets in the second half of the basketball game than in the first half. He made 5 baskets in the first half. How many baskets did he make in the second half?

_____

5. In Jane's picture graph, the symbol ☺ represents two students. One row in the picture graph has 8 symbols. How many students does that represent?

_____

6. What multiplication sentence does this array show?

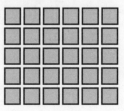

_____

208

FOR MORE PRACTICE
GO TO THE
Personal Math Trainer

Distributive Property

Essential Question How can you use the Distributive Property to find products?

Learning Objective You will use arrays and the Distributive Property to represent products.

⚷ Unlock the Problem

Mark bought 6 new fish for his aquarium. He paid $7 for each fish. How much money did he spend in all?

Find 6 × $7.

You can use the Distributive Property to solve the problem.

The **Distributive Property** states that multiplying a sum by a number is the same as multiplying each addend by the number and then adding the products.

- Describe the groups in this problem.

_____

- Circle the numbers you will use to solve the problem.

Remember

sum—the answer to an addition problem

addends—the numbers being added

🔑 Activity **Materials** ■ square tiles

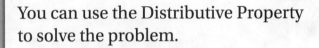

Make an array with tiles to show 6 rows of 7.

$6 \times 7 =$ ■

Break apart the array to make two smaller arrays for facts you know.

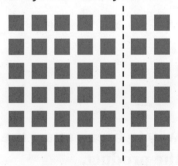

6×5 6×2

$6 \times 7 =$ ■
$6 \times 7 = 6 \times (5 + 2)$ Think: $7 = 5 + 2$
$6 \times 7 = (6 \times 5) + (6 \times 2)$ Multiply each addend by 6.

$6 \times 7 =$ _____ + _____   Add the products.

$6 \times 7 =$ _____

So, Mark spent $_____ for his new fish.

Math Talk   Math Processes and Practices ②

Reason Quantitatively What other ways could you break apart the 6 × 7 array?

Try This!

Suppose Mark bought 9 fish for $6 each.

You can break apart a 9 × 6 array into two smaller arrays for facts you know. One way is to think of 9 as 5 + 4. Draw a line to show this way. Then find the product.

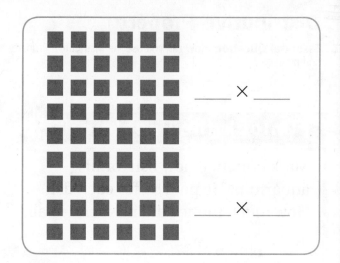

$9 \times 6 = (\underline{\quad} \times \underline{\quad}) + (\underline{\quad} \times \underline{\quad})$

$9 \times 6 = \underline{\quad} + \underline{\quad}$

So, Mark spent $\underline{\quad}$ for 9 fish.

Share and Show MATH BOARD

1. Draw a line to show how you could break apart this 6 × 8 array into two smaller arrays for facts you know.

• What numbers do you multiply? $\underline{\quad}$ and $\underline{\quad}$

$\underline{\quad}$ and $\underline{\quad}$

• What numbers do you add? $\underline{\quad} + \underline{\quad}$

$6 \times 8 = 6 \times (\underline{\quad} + \underline{\quad})$

$6 \times 8 = (\underline{\quad} \times \underline{\quad}) + (\underline{\quad} \times \underline{\quad})$

$6 \times 8 = \underline{\quad} + \underline{\quad}$

$6 \times 8 = \underline{\quad}$

Math Talk Math Processes and Practices ⑦

Look for Structure Why do you have to add to find the total product when you use the Distributive Property?

Write one way to break apart the array. Then find the product.

 2.

_____

_____

 3.

_____

_____

210

© Houghton Mifflin Harcourt Publishing Company

On Your Own

4. **GO DEEPER** Shade tiles to make an array that shows a fact with 7, 8, or 9 as a factor. Write the fact. Explain how you found the product.

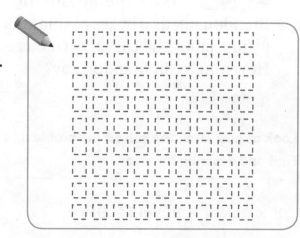

_____

_____

_____

_____

5. **THINK SMARTER** Robin says, "I can find 8×7 by multiplying 3×7 and doubling it." Does her statement make sense? Justify your answer.

_____

_____

6. **GO DEEPER** Kent buys 5 bags of potatoes that cost $7 each. He gives the clerk $40. How much change should Kent receive?

_____

7. **THINK SMARTER** For numbers 7a–7d, choose Yes or No to indicate whether the sum or product is equal to 7×5.

7a. $7 + (3 + 2) = $ ▮   ○ Yes   ○ No

7b. $7 \times (3 + 2) = $ ▮   ○ Yes   ○ No

7c. $(5 \times 4) + (5 \times 3) = $ ▮   ○ Yes   ○ No

7d. $(7 \times 2) + (7 \times 5) = $ ▮   ○ Yes   ○ No

Problem Solving • Applications

What's the Error?

8. **(Math Processes and Practices 3)** **Verify the Reasoning of Others**
Brandon needs 8 boxes of spinners for his
fishing club. The cost of each box is $9.
How much will Brandon pay?

$8 \times \$9 = \blacksquare$

Look at how Brandon solved the problem.
Find and describe his error.

$8 \times 9 = (4 \times 9) + (5 \times 9)$

$8 \times 9 = 36 + 45$

$8 \times 9 = 81$

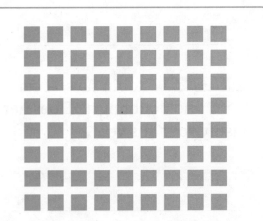

_____

_____

Use the array to help solve the problem
and correct his error.

$8 \times 9 = (4 + 4) \times 9$

$8 \times 9 = (\underline{} \times \underline{}) + (\underline{} \times \underline{})$

$8 \times 9 = \underline{} + \underline{}$

$8 \times 9 = \underline{}$

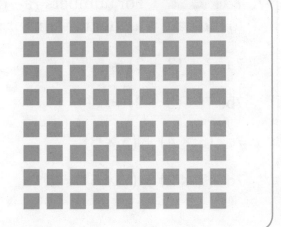

So, Brandon will pay $ _____ for the spinners.

Distributive Property

Learning Objective You will use arrays and the Distributive Property to represent products.

**Write one way to break apart the array.
Then find the product.**

1.

(3 × 7) + (3 × 7)
_____

42
_____

2.

_____

_____

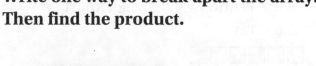

Problem Solving Real World

3. There are 2 rows of 8 chairs set up in the library for a puppet show. How many chairs are set up? Use the Distributive Property to solve.

_____

4. A marching band has 4 rows of trumpeters with 10 trumpeters in each row. How many trumpeters are in the marching band? Use the Distributive Property to solve.

_____

5. **WRITE** ▸*Math* What are some ways you could break apart 7 × 9 using the Distributive Property?

_____

_____

Lesson Check

1. Complete the number sentence to show the Distributive Property.

    $7 \times 6 =$

    _____

    _____

    _____

2. What is one way to break apart the array?

    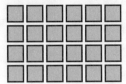

    _____

    _____

Spiral Review

3. The school auditorium has 448 chairs set out for the third-grade performance. What is 448 rounded to the nearest ten?

    _____

4. Find the difference.

    $$\begin{array}{r} 400 \\ -\ 296 \\ \hline \end{array}$$

5. There are 622 fruit snacks in one crate and 186 in another crate. How many fruit snacks are there?

    $$\begin{array}{r} 622 \\ +\ 186 \\ \hline \end{array}$$

6. Which sport do exactly 6 students play?

    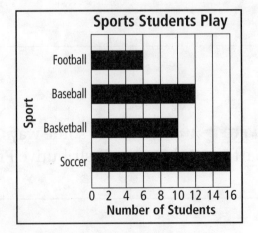

    _____

FOR MORE PRACTICE
GO TO THE
Personal Math Trainer

Multiply with 7

Essential Question What strategies can you use to multiply with 7?

Learning Objective You will use arrays and properties of operations to multiply with 7.

Unlock the Problem

Jason's family has a new puppy. Jason takes a turn walking the puppy once a day. How many times will Jason walk the puppy in 4 weeks?

Find 4 × 7.

- How often does Jason walk the puppy?

  _____

- How many days are in 1 week?

  _____

One Way Use the Commutative Property of Multiplication.

If you know 7 × 4, you can use that fact to find 4 × 7.

You can change the order of the factors and the product is the same.

7 × 4 = _____, so 4 × 7 = _____.

So, Jason will walk the puppy _____ times in 4 weeks.

Other Ways

A Use the Distributive Property.

STEP 1 Complete the array to show 4 rows of 7.

STEP 2 Draw a line to break the array into two smaller arrays for facts you know.

STEP 3 Multiply the facts for the smaller arrays. Add the products.

So, 4 × 7 = _____.

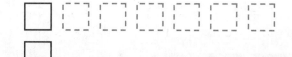

4 × _____ = _____   4 × _____ = _____

_____ + _____ = _____

Math Talk

Math Processes and Practices ⑧

Generalize Why would you use the Distributive Property as a strategy to multiply?

B **Use a fact you know.**

Multiply. $4 \times 7 =$ ■

- Start with a fact you know.

  $2 \times 7 = \underline{\quad}$

- Add a group of 7 for 3×7.

  $2 \times 7 + 7 = \underline{\quad}$

- Then add 7 more for 4×7.

  $3 \times 7 + 7 = \underline{\quad}$

  So, $4 \times 7 = \underline{\quad}$.

Share and Show MATH BOARD

1. **Explain** how you could break apart an array to find 6×7. Draw an array to show your work.

   _____

   _____

Math Talk Math Processes and Practices ➊

Apply How can you use doubles to find 8×7?

Find the product.

2. $9 \times 7 = \underline{\quad}$ 3. $\underline{\quad} = 5 \times 7$ ✓ 4. $\underline{\quad} = 7 \times 3$ ✓ 5. $1 \times 7 = \underline{\quad}$

On Your Own

Find the product.

6. $\underline{\quad} = 7 \times 7$ 7. $6 \times 7 = \underline{\quad}$ 8. $\underline{\quad} = 7 \times 10$ 9. $\underline{\quad} = 7 \times 2$

10.	11.	12.	13.	14.	15.
7	6	9	8	1	4
$\times 3$	$\times 7$	$\times 7$	$\times 7$	$\times 7$	$\times 7$

16. **GO DEEPER** Anders makes 7 fruit cups. He puts 2 green grapes, 2 red grapes, and 2 black grapes in each fruit cup. How many grapes does Anders use for the fruit cups?

Problem Solving • Applications

Use the table for 17–19.

Rusty's Care	
Food	3 cups a day
Water	4 cups a day
Bath	2 times a month

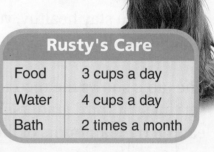

17. Lori has a dog named Rusty. How many baths will Rusty have in 7 months?

_____

18. *THINK SMARTER* How many more cups of water than food will Rusty get in 1 week?

_____

19. *GO DEEPER* Tim's dog, Midnight, eats 28 cups of food in a week. Midnight eats the same amount each day. In one day, how many more cups of food will Midnight eat than Rusty? Explain.

WRITE ▸ *Math* • **Show Your Work**

_____

_____

_____

20. José walks his dog 10 miles every week. How many miles do they walk in 7 weeks?

_____

21. *Math Processes and Practices ⑦* **Look for Structure** Dave takes Zoey, his dog, for a 3-mile walk twice a day. How many miles do they walk in one week?

_____

22. *THINK SMARTER* Alia arranges some playing cards in 7 equal rows with 7 cards in each row. How many cards does Alia arrange?

_____

Connect to Reading

Summarize

To help you stay healthy, you should eat a balanced diet and exercise every day.

The table shows the recommended daily servings for third graders. You should eat the right amounts of the food groups.

Suppose you want to share with your friends what you learned about healthy eating. How could you summarize what you learned?

When you *summarize*, you restate the most important information in a shorter way to help you understand what you have read.

Recommended Daily Servings	
Food Group	**Servings**
Whole Grains (bread, cereal)	6 ounces
Vegetables (carrot, corn)	2 cups
Fruits (apples, oranges)	1 cup
Dairy Products (milk, cheese)	3 cups
Meat, Beans, Fish, Eggs, Nuts	5 ounces
8 ounces = 1 cup	

- To stay healthy, you should eat a balanced

   _____ and _____ every day.

- A third grader should eat 3 cups of _____,
   such as milk and cheese, each day.

- A third grader should eat _____ of
   vegetables and fruits each day.

   How many cups of vegetables and fruits should a third

   grader eat in 1 week? _____

   Remember: 1 week = 7 days

- A third grader should eat _____ of whole
   grains, such as bread and cereal, each day.

   How many ounces of whole grains should a third grader

   eat in 1 week? _____

Name _____

Multiply with 7

Learning Objective You will use arrays and properties of operations to multiply with 7.

Find the product.

1. $6 \times 7 = \underline{\ 42\ }$ 2. $\underline{\quad} = 7 \times 9$ 3. $\underline{\quad} = 1 \times 7$ 4. $3 \times 7 = \underline{\quad}$

5. $7 \times 7 = \underline{\quad}$ 6. $\underline{\quad} = 2 \times 7$ 7. $7 \times 8 = \underline{\quad}$ 8. $\underline{\quad} = 4 \times 7$

9. $\quad 7$ 10. $\quad 7$ 11. $\quad 6$ 12. $\quad 7$ 13. $\quad 2$
$\underline{\times\ 5}$ $\underline{\times\ 1}$ $\underline{\times\ 7}$ $\underline{\times\ 4}$ $\underline{\times\ 7}$

14. $\quad 10$ 15. $\quad 3$ 16. $\quad 7$ 17. $\quad 8$ 18. $\quad 7$
$\underline{\times\ 7}$ $\underline{\times\ 7}$ $\underline{\times\ 9}$ $\underline{\times\ 7}$ $\underline{\times\ 0}$

Problem Solving Real World

19. Julie buys a pair of earrings for $7. Now she would like to buy the same earrings for 2 of her friends. How much will she spend for all 3 pairs of earrings?

_____

20. Owen and his family will go camping in 8 weeks. There are 7 days in 1 week. How many days are in 8 weeks?

_____

21. **WRITE** ▸ *Math* Explain how you would use the Commutative Property of Multiplication to answer 7×3.

_____

_____

Lesson Check

1. Find the product.

$$\begin{array}{r} 7 \\ \times\ 8 \\ \hline \end{array}$$

2. What product does the array show?

_____

Spiral Review

3. Which numbers below are even?

6, 12, 15, 24, 30

4. How many more people chose retriever than poodle?

Favorite Breed of Dog	
Dog	**Number**
Shepherd	58
Retriever	65
Poodle	26

_____

5. What is 94 rounded to the nearest ten?

6. Jack has 5 craft sticks. He needs 4 times that number for a project. How many craft sticks does Jack need altogether?

_____

_____

© Houghton Mifflin Harcourt Publishing Company

FOR MORE PRACTICE
GO TO THE
Personal Math Trainer

 Mid-Chapter Checkpoint

Personal Math Trainer
Online Assessment
and Intervention

Vocabulary

Choose the best term from the box to complete the sentence.

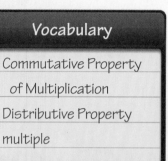

Vocabulary
Commutative Property of Multiplication
Distributive Property
multiple

1. A _____ of 4 is any product that has 4 as one of its factors. (p. 197)

2. This is an example of the _____ Property.

$$3 \times 8 = (3 \times 6) + (3 \times 2)$$

This property states that multiplying a sum by a number is the same as multiplying each addend by the number and then adding the products. (p. 209)

Concepts and Skills

Write one way to break apart the array. Then find the product.

3.

_____

_____

4.

_____

_____

Find the product.

5. $3 \times 1 =$ ____   6. $5 \times 6 =$ ____   7. ____ $= 7 \times 7$ 8. $2 \times 10 =$ ____

9. $\begin{array}{r} 2 \\ \times 1 \\ \hline \end{array}$ 10. $\begin{array}{r} 6 \\ \times 6 \\ \hline \end{array}$ 11. $\begin{array}{r} 8 \\ \times 7 \\ \hline \end{array}$ 12. $\begin{array}{r} 6 \\ \times 0 \\ \hline \end{array}$ 13. $\begin{array}{r} 3 \\ \times 8 \\ \hline \end{array}$

14. Lori saw 6 lightning bugs. They each had 6 legs. How many legs did the lightning bugs have in all?

_____

15. `GO DEEPER` Zach walked his dog twice a day, for 7 days. Moira walked her dog three times a day for 5 days. Whose dog was walked more times? How many more?

_____

16. `GO DEEPER` Annette buys 4 boxes of pencils. There are 8 pencils in each box. Jordan buys 3 boxes of pencils with 10 pencils in each box. Who buys more pencils? How many more?

_____

17. Shelly can paint 4 pictures in a day. How many pictures can she paint in 7 days?

_____

Associative Property of Multiplication

Essential Question How can you use the Associative Property of Multiplication to find products?

Learning Objective You will use the Associative Property of Multiplication to find products.

CONNECT You have learned the Associative Property of Addition. When the grouping of the addends is changed, the sum stays the same.

$$(2 + 3) + 4 = 2 + (3 + 4)$$

The **Associative Property of Multiplication** states that when the grouping of the factors is changed, the product is the same. It is also called the Grouping Property of Multiplication.

$$2 \times (3 \times 4) = (2 \times 3) \times 4$$

> **Math Idea**
> Always multiply the numbers inside the parentheses first.

Unlock the Problem (Real World)

Each car on the roller coaster has 2 rows of seats. Each row has 2 seats. There are 3 cars in each train. How many seats are on each train?

- Underline what you need to find.
- Describe the grouping of the seats.

_____

Use an array.

You can use an array to show $3 \times (2 \times 2)$.

$3 \times (2 \times 2) = $ ▨

$3 \times $ _____ = _____

So, there are 3 cars with 4 seats in each car.

There are _____ seats on each roller coaster train.

You can change the grouping with parentheses and the product is the same.

$(3 \times 2) \times 2 = $ ▨

_____ $\times 2 = $ _____

Math Talk

Math Processes and Practices 8

Generalize Why does changing the placement of the parentheses not change the answer when multiplying 3 numbers together?

© Houghton Mifflin Harcourt Publishing Company

Example Use the Commutative and Associative Properties.

You can also change the order of the factors.
The product is the same.

$(4 \times 3) \times 2 =$

$4 \times (3 \times 2) =$ ◻   Associative Property

$4 \times$ _____ = _____

$4 \times (3 \times 2) =$ ◻

$4 \times (2 \times 3) =$ ◻   Commutative Property

$(4 \times 2) \times 3 =$ ◻   Associative Property

_____ $\times 3 =$ _____

Share and Show MATH BOARD

1. Find the product of 5, 2, and 3. Write another way to group the factors. Is the product the same? Why?

_____

_____

Write another way to group the factors. Then find the product.

2. $(2 \times 1) \times 7$

_____

_____

3. $3 \times (3 \times 4)$

_____

_____

✓ 4. $5 \times (2 \times 5)$

_____

_____

✓ 5. $3 \times (2 \times 6)$

_____

_____

6. $2 \times (2 \times 5)$

_____

_____

7. $(1 \times 3) \times 6$

_____

_____

Math Talk   Math Processes and Practices ②

Use Reasoning Why would you use both the Commutative and Associative Properties when solving a multiplication problem?

Name _____

On Your Own

Write another way to group the factors. Then find the product.

8. $(2 \times 3) \times 3$

_____

_____

9. $(8 \times 3) \times 2$

_____

_____

10. $2 \times (5 \times 5)$

_____

_____

11. $(3 \times 2) \times 4$

_____

_____

12. $(6 \times 1) \times 4$

_____

_____

13. $2 \times (2 \times 6)$

_____

_____

Practice: Copy and Solve Use parentheses and multiplication properties. Then, find the product.

14. $6 \times 5 \times 2$

15. $2 \times 3 \times 5$

16. $3 \times 1 \times 6$

17. $2 \times 5 \times 6$

18. $2 \times 0 \times 8$

19. $1 \times 9 \times 4$

THINK SMARTER **Algebra** Find the unknown factor.

20. $7 \times (2 \times \underline{\quad}) = 56$

21. $30 = 6 \times (5 \times \underline{\quad})$

22. $\underline{\quad} \times (2 \times 2) = 32$

23. $42 = 7 \times (2 \times \underline{\quad})$

24. $8 \times (5 \times \underline{\quad}) = 40$

25. $0 = \underline{\quad} \times (25 \times 1)$

26. **GO DEEPER** What number sentence does this array represent? Write another way to group the factors.

_____

_____

27. **GO DEEPER** Jamal has 65 quilt patches. He makes 2 quilts with 5 rows of 6 patches in each quilt. How many quilt patches will be left over?

_____

_____

Problem Solving • Applications

Use the graph for 28–29.

28. **Math Processes and Practices ②** **Represent a Problem**
Each car on the Steel Force train has 3 rows with 2 seats in each row. How many seats are on the train? Draw a quick picture.

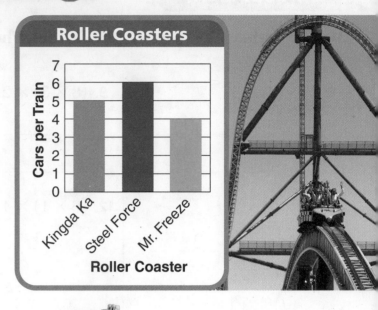

Roller Coasters

29. **THINK SMARTER** A Kingda Ka train has 4 seats per car, but the last car has only 2 seats. How many seats are on one Kingda Ka train?

WRITE ▸ *Math*
Show Your Work

30. **GO DEEPER** **Sense or Nonsense?** Each week, Kelly works 2 days for 4 hours each day and earns $5 an hour. Len works 5 days for 2 hours each day and earns $4 an hour. Kelly says they both earn the same amount. Does this statement make sense? Explain.

31. **THINK SMARTER** Clayton packs 3 boxes. He puts 3 lunch bags in each box. There are 4 sandwiches in each lunch bag. How many sandwiches does Clayton pack? Show your work.

Associative Property of Multiplication

Learning Objective You will use the Associative Property of Multiplication to find products.

**Write another way to group the factors.
Then find the product.**

1. $(3 \times 2) \times 5$

$\underline{\qquad 3 \times (2 \times 5) \qquad}$

$\underline{\qquad 30 \qquad}$

2. $(4 \times 3) \times 2$

$\underline{\qquad\qquad}$

$\underline{\qquad\qquad}$

3. $2 \times (2 \times 8)$

$\underline{\qquad\qquad}$

$\underline{\qquad\qquad}$

4. $9 \times (2 \times 1)$

$\underline{\qquad\qquad}$

$\underline{\qquad\qquad}$

5. $2 \times (3 \times 6)$

$\underline{\qquad\qquad}$

$\underline{\qquad\qquad}$

6. $(2 \times 4) \times 5$

$\underline{\qquad\qquad}$

$\underline{\qquad\qquad}$

**Use parentheses and multiplication properties.
Then, find the product.**

7. $9 \times 1 \times 5 = \underline{\qquad}$

8. $3 \times 3 \times 2 = \underline{\qquad}$

9. $2 \times 4 \times 3 = \underline{\qquad}$

10. $7 \times 2 \times 3 = \underline{\qquad}$

11. $4 \times 1 \times 3 = \underline{\qquad}$

12. $10 \times 2 \times 4 = \underline{\qquad}$

 **Problem Solving** *Real World*

13. Beth and Maria are going to the county fair. Admission costs $4 per person for each day. They plan to go for 3 days. How much will the girls pay for all 3 days?

$\underline{\qquad\qquad\qquad\qquad}$

14. Randy's garden has 3 rows of carrots with 3 plants in each row. Next year, he plans to plant 4 times the number of rows. How many plants will he have next year?

$\underline{\qquad\qquad\qquad\qquad}$

15. **WRITE** ▸ *Math* Why would you use the Associative Property of Multiplication to solve $(10 \times 4) \times 2$? How would you regroup the factors?

$\underline{\qquad\qquad\qquad\qquad\qquad\qquad\qquad\qquad\qquad\qquad\qquad}$

Lesson Check

1. There are 2 benches in each car of a train ride. Two people ride on each bench. If a train has 5 cars, how many people can be on a train?

2. Crystal has 2 CDs in each box. She has 3 boxes on each of her 6 shelves. How many CDs does Crystal have?

Spiral Review

3. Find the sum.

$$\begin{array}{r} 472 \\ + \ 186 \\ \hline \end{array}$$

4. Trevor made a picture graph to show how many minutes each student biked last week. This is his key.

Each  = 10 minutes.

What does ⊛⊛◖ stand for?

5. Madison has 142 stickers in her collection. What is 142 rounded to the nearest ten?

6. There are 5 pages of photos. Each page has 6 photos. How many photos are there?

FOR MORE PRACTICE
GO TO THE
Personal Math Trainer

Patterns on the Multiplication Table

Essential Question How can you use properties to explain patterns on the multiplication table?

Learning Objective You will create and extend number patterns using the multiplication table.

🔑 Unlock the Problem

You can use a multiplication table to explore number patterns.

🔓 Activity 1

Materials ■ MathBoard

- Write the products for the green squares. What do you notice about the products?

_____

_____

_____

Write the multiplication sentences for the products on your MathBoard. What do you notice about the factors?

_____

- Will this be true in the yellow squares? **Explain** using a property you know.

_____

Write the products for the yellow squares.

- Complete the columns for 1, 5, and 6. Look across each row and compare the products. What do you notice?

_____

What property does this show?

_____

×	0	1	2	3	4	5	6	7	8	9	10
0											
1											
2											
3											
4											
5											
6											
7											
8											
9											
10											

Math Talk Math Processes and Practices ❼

Look for a Pattern How can you use patterns on a multiplication chart to find other products?

🔓 Activity 2

Materials ■ yellow and blue crayons

- Shade the rows for 0, 2, 4, 6, 8, and 10 yellow.

- What pattern do you notice about each shaded row? _____

_____

- Compare the rows for 2 and 4. What do you notice about the products?

_____

- Shade the columns for 1, 3, 5, 7, and 9 blue.

- What do you notice about the products for each shaded column?

_____

- Compare the products for the green squares. What do you notice? What do you notice about the factors?

_____

- What other patterns do you see?

_____

×	0	1	2	3	4	5	6	7	8	9	10
0	0	0	0	0	0	0	0	0	0	0	0
1	0	1	2	3	4	5	6	7	8	9	10
2	0	2	4	6	8	10	12	14	16	18	20
3	0	3	6	9	12	15	18	21	24	27	30
4	0	4	8	12	16	20	24	28	32	36	40
5	0	5	10	15	20	25	30	35	40	45	50
6	0	6	12	18	24	30	36	42	48	54	60
7	0	7	14	21	28	35	42	49	56	63	70
8	0	8	16	24	32	40	48	56	64	72	80
9	0	9	18	27	36	45	54	63	72	81	90
10	0	10	20	30	40	50	60	70	80	90	100

Share and Show MATH BOARD

1. Use the table to write the products for the row for 2.

_____, _____, _____, _____, _____,

_____, _____, _____, _____, _____, _____

Describe a pattern you see.

_____

Math Talk Math Processes and Practices ❶

Analyze What do you notice about the product of any number and 2?

Is the product even or odd? Write *even* or *odd*.

2. 5 × 8 _____   **3.** 6 × 3 _____   **4.** 3 × 5 _____   ✅ **5.** 4 × 4 _____

Name _____

Use the multiplication table. Describe a pattern you see.

6. in the column for 10

_____

_____

 **7.** in the column for 8

_____

_____

On Your Own

Is the product even or odd? Write _even_ or _odd_.

8. 4×8 _____

9. 5×5 _____

10. 7×4 _____

11. 2×9 _____

12. Use the multiplication table. Rewrite the correct pattern.

6, 12, 18, 22, 30, 36 _____

Problem Solving • Applications 🌍

Complete the table. Then describe a pattern you see in the products.

13.

×	2	4	6	8	10
5					

_____

_____

14.

×	1	3	5	7	9
5					

_____

_____

15. *THINK SMARTER* **Explain** how patterns of the ones digits in the products relate to the factors in Exercises 13 and 14.

_____

_____

_____

Personal Math Trainer

16. *THINK SMARTER +* Helene selected an odd number to multiply by the factors in this table. Write *even* or *odd* to describe each product.

×	1	2	3	4	5
odd number					

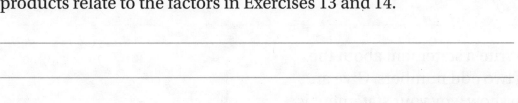

Sense or Nonsense?

17. **(Math Processes and Practices 3) Make Arguments** Whose statement makes sense? Whose statement is nonsense? Explain your reasoning.

The product of an odd number and an even number is even.

The product of two even numbers is even.

Gunter's Work

odd   even   even
3 × 4 = 12

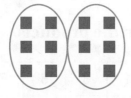

I can circle 2 equal groups of 6 with no tiles left over. So, the product is even.

Giselle's Work

even   even   even
2 × 6 = 12

I can circle 6 pairs with no tiles left over. So, the product is even.

18. **GO DEEPER** Write a statement about the product of two odd numbers. Give an example to show why your statement is true.

Patterns on the Multiplication Table

Learning Objective You will create and extend number patterns using the multiplication table.

Is the product even or odd? Write *even* or *odd*.

1. $2 \times 7 =$ __even__   Think: Products with 2 as a factor are even.

2. $4 \times 6 =$ _____

3. $8 \times 3 =$ _____

Use the multiplication table. Describe a pattern you see.

4. in the column for 5

_____

_____

×	0	1	2	3	4	5	6	7	8	9	10
0	0	0	0	0	0	0	0	0	0	0	0
1	0	1	2	3	4	5	6	7	8	9	10
2	0	2	4	6	8	10	12	14	16	18	20
3	0	3	6	9	12	15	18	21	24	27	30
4	0	4	8	12	16	20	24	28	32	36	40
5	0	5	10	15	20	25	30	35	40	45	50
6	0	6	12	18	24	30	36	42	48	54	60
7	0	7	14	21	28	35	42	49	56	63	70
8	0	8	16	24	32	40	48	56	64	72	80
9	0	9	18	27	36	45	54	63	72	81	90
10	0	10	20	30	40	50	60	70	80	90	100

5. in the row for 10

_____

_____

6. in the rows for 3 and 6

_____

_____

Problem Solving *Real World*

7. Carl shades a row in the multiplication table. The products in the row are all even. The ones digits in the products repeat 0, 4, 8, 2, 6. What row does Carl shade?

_____

8. Jenna says that no row or column contains products with only odd numbers. Do you agree? Explain.

_____

_____

_____

9. **WRITE** ▸*Math* Draw a picture that shows an example of a product of two even numbers. Write the matching multiplication sentence.

_____

Lesson Check

1. Is the product of 4×9 even or odd?

_____

_____

2. Describe a pattern you see.

10, 15, 20, 25, 30

_____

_____

Spiral Review

3. Lexi has 2 cans of tennis balls. There are 3 tennis balls in each can. She buys 2 more cans. How many tennis balls does she now have?

4. Use the picture graph.

Color of Eyes					
Blue	⬤	⬤	⬤		
Green	⬤	⬤	⬤	⬤	
Brown	⬤	⬤	⬤	⬤	⬤

Key: Each ⬤ = 4 students.

How many students have green eyes?

_____

_____

5. Sasha bought 3 boxes of pencils. If each box has 6 pencils, how many pencils did Sasha buy?

6. Find the sum.

$$\begin{array}{r} 219 \\ + 763 \\ \hline \end{array}$$

_____

FOR MORE PRACTICE
GO TO THE
Personal Math Trainer

Name _____

Multiply with 8

Essential Question What strategies can you use to multiply with 8?

Learning Objective You will use strategies and the Associative Property of Multiplication to multiply with 8.

🔑 Unlock the Problem

A scorpion has 8 legs. How many legs do 5 scorpions have?

Find 5×8.

🔓 One Way Use doubles.

$5 \times 8 = \blacksquare$

$\swarrow \searrow$

$4 + 4$

Think: The factor 8 is an even number. $4 + 4 = 8$

$5 \times 4 =$ _____

20 doubled is _____.

$5 \times 8 =$ _____

So, 5 scorpions have _____ legs.

🔓 Another Way Use a number line.

Use the number line to show 5 jumps of 8.

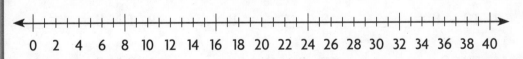

0 2 4 6 8 10 12 14 16 18 20 22 24 26 28 30 32 34 36 38 40

So, 5 jumps of 8 is _____.   _____ × _____ = _____

- **Describe** two different ways you can use doubles to find 6×8.

_____

_____

• How many legs does one scorpion have?

_____

• What are you asked to find?

_____

_____

ERROR Alert

Be sure to count the spaces between the tick marks, not the tick marks.

🔑 Example Use the Associative Property of Multiplication.

Scorpions have two eyes on the top of the head, and usually two to five pairs along the front corners of the head. If each scorpion has 6 eyes, how many eyes would 8 scorpions have?

$8 \times 6 = $ ■

$8 \times 6 = (2 \times 4) \times 6$ Think: $8 = 2 \times 4$

$8 \times 6 = 2 \times (4 \times 6)$ Use the Associative Property.

$8 \times 6 = 2 \times$ _____   Multiply. 4×6

$8 \times 6 = $ _____ + _____   Double the product.

$8 \times 6 = $ _____

Math Talk   Math Processes and Practices ③

Apply When you multiply with 8, will the product always be even?

Share and Show

1. **Explain** one way you can find 4×8.

_____

Find the product.

2. $3 \times 8 = $ _____   3. _____ $= 8 \times 2$ ✅ 4. _____ $= 7 \times 8$ ✅ 5. $9 \times 8 = $ _____

On Your Own

Find the product.

6. _____ $= 6 \times 8$ 7. $10 \times 8 = $ _____   8. _____ $= 8 \times 3$ 9. $1 \times 8 = $ _____

10. $4 \times 8 = $ _____   11. $5 \times 8 = $ _____   12. $0 \times 8 = $ _____   13. $8 \times 8 = $ _____

14.
$\begin{array}{r} 6 \\ \times 8 \\ \hline \end{array}$
   15.
$\begin{array}{r} 8 \\ \times 2 \\ \hline \end{array}$
   16.
$\begin{array}{r} 5 \\ \times 8 \\ \hline \end{array}$
   17.
$\begin{array}{r} 3 \\ \times 8 \\ \hline \end{array}$
   18.
$\begin{array}{r} 10 \\ \times 8 \\ \hline \end{array}$
   19.
$\begin{array}{r} 7 \\ \times 8 \\ \hline \end{array}$

20. **GO DEEPER** Jamal buys 4 sets of animal postcards and 5 sets of nature postcards. Each set has 6 cards. How many postcards does Jamal buy?

_____

Name _____

Use the table for 21–24.

21. About how much rain falls in the Chihuahuan Desert in 6 years? **Explain** how you can use doubles to find the answer.

_____

_____

Average Yearly Rainfall in North American Deserts	
Desert	**Inches**
Chihuahuan	8
Great Basin	9
Mojave	4
Sonoran	9

22. **GO DEEPER** In 2 years, about how many more inches of rain will fall in the Sonoran Desert than in the Chihuahuan Desert? **Explain**.

_____

_____

23. **Math Processes and Practices 6** **Describe a Method** Look back at Exercise 22. Write and show how to solve a similar problem by comparing two different deserts.

_____

_____

24. **THINK SMARTER** How can you find about how many inches of rain will fall in the Mojave Desert in 20 years?

_____

_____

25. **THINK SMARTER** For numbers 25a–25d, select True or False for each multiplication sentence.

25a. $3 \times (2 \times 4) = 24$ ○ True ○ False

25b. $4 \times 8 = 32$ ○ True ○ False

25c. $7 \times 8 = 72$ ○ True ○ False

25d. $2 \times (5 \times 8) = 80$ ○ True ○ False

There are 90 species of scorpions that live in the United States. Only 3 species of scorpions live in Arizona. They are the Arizona bark scorpion, the Desert hairy scorpion, and the Stripe-tailed scorpion.

Facts About Scorpions

Scorpions:

- are between 1 and 4 inches long
- mostly eat insects
- glow under ultraviolet light

They have:

- 8 legs for walking
- 2 long, claw-like pincers used to hold their food
- a curled tail held over their body with a stinger on the tip

▲ Scorpions glow under ultraviolet light.

26. How many species of scorpions do *not* live in Arizona?

_____

27. Students saw 8 scorpions. What multiplication sentences can help you find how many pincers and legs the 8 scorpions had?

_____

28. **GO DEEPER** Three scorpions were in a display with ultraviolet light. Eight groups of 4 students saw the display. How many students saw the glowing scorpions?

_____

Multiply with 8

Learning Objective You will use strategies and the Associative Property of Multiplication to multiply with 8.

Find the product.

1. $8 \times 10 =$ __80__

2. $8 \times 8 =$ _____

3. $8 \times 5 =$ _____

4. $3 \times 8 =$ _____

5. _____ $= 4 \times 8$

6. $8 \times 7 =$ _____

7. $6 \times 8 =$ _____

8. _____ $= 9 \times 8$

9. $\begin{array}{r} 8 \\ \times\ 8 \\ \hline \end{array}$

10. $\begin{array}{r} 9 \\ \times\ 8 \\ \hline \end{array}$

11. $\begin{array}{r} 8 \\ \times\ 3 \\ \hline \end{array}$

12. $\begin{array}{r} 8 \\ \times\ 1 \\ \hline \end{array}$

13. $\begin{array}{r} 4 \\ \times\ 8 \\ \hline \end{array}$

 Problem Solving Real World

14. There are 6 teams in the basketball league. Each team has 8 players. How many players are there?

_____

15. Lynn has 4 stacks of quarters. There are 8 quarters in each stack. How many quarters does Lynn have?

_____

16. Tomas is packing 7 baskets for a fair. He is placing 8 apples in each basket. How many apples are there in the baskets?

_____

17. There are 10 pencils in each box. If Jenna buys 8 boxes, how many pencils will she buy?

_____

18. **WRITE** ▸Math   What two facts can you double to find 8×4? Explain.

_____

_____

Lesson Check

1. Find the product.

$$5 \times 8 =$$

2. There are 7 tarantulas in the spider exhibit at the zoo. Each tarantula has 8 legs. How many legs do the 7 tarantulas have?

Spiral Review

3. Find the difference.

$$
\begin{array}{r}
652 \\
- 99 \\
\hline
\end{array}
$$

4. The school library received an order of 232 new books. What is 232 rounded to the nearest ten?

5. Sam's picture graph shows that 8 students chose pizza as their favorite lunch. This is the key for the graph.

Each ☺ = 2 students.

How many ☺ should be next to pizza on Sam's graph?

6. Tashia buys 5 packages of oranges. Each package has 4 oranges. How many oranges does Tashia buy?

FOR MORE PRACTICE
GO TO THE
Personal Math Trainer

Name _____

Multiply with 9

Essential Question What strategies can you use to multiply with 9?

Learning Objective You will use the Distributive Property and patterns to multiply with 9.

Unlock the Problem

Olivia's class is studying the solar system. Seven students are making models of the solar system. Each model has 9 spheres (eight for the planets and one for Pluto, a dwarf planet). How many spheres do the 7 students need for all the models?

• What are you asked to find?

_____

_____

• How many students are making

models? _____

Find 7×9.

One Way Use the Distributive Property.

A With multiplication and addition

$$7 \times 9 = \blacksquare$$

Think: $9 = 3 + 6$ $7 \times 9 = 7 \times (3 + 6)$

Multiply each addend by 7. $7 \times 9 = (7 \times 3) + (7 \times 6)$

Add the products. $7 \times 9 = $ _____ + _____

$7 \times 9 = $ _____

B With multiplication and subtraction

$$7 \times 9 = \blacksquare$$

Think: $9 = 10 - 1$ $7 \times 9 = 7 \times (10 - 1)$

Multiply each number by 7. $7 \times 9 = (7 \times 10) - (7 \times 1)$

Subtract the products. $7 \times 9 = $ _____ − _____

$7 \times 9 = $ _____

So, 7 students need _____ spheres for all the models.

🔒 Another Way Use patterns of 9.

The table shows the 9s facts.

- What do you notice about the tens digit in the product?

  The tens digit is _____ less than the factor that is multiplied with 9.

- What do you notice about the sum of the digits in the product?

  The sum of the digits in the product is always _____.

  So, to multiply 7 × 9, think the tens digit is _____

  and the ones digit is _____. The product is _____.

Multiply by 9.	
Factors	Product
1 × 9	9
2 × 9	18
3 × 9	27
4 × 9	36
5 × 9	45
6 × 9	54
7 × 9	
8 × 9	
9 × 9	

Try This! Complete the table above.

Use the patterns to find 8 × 9 and 9 × 9.

Share and Show

Math Talk

Math Processes and Practices ⑤

Use Patterns Explain how you can easily find the product of 3 × 9.

1. What is the tens digit in the product

   3 × 9? _____

   Think: What number is 1 less than 3?

Find the product.

2. 9 × 8 = _____   **3.** _____ = 2 × 9   ✓**4.** _____ = 6 × 9   ✓**5.** 9 × 1 = _____

On Your Own

Find the product.

6. 4 × 9 = _____   **7.** 5 × 9 = _____   **8.** 10 × 9 = _____   **9.** 1 × 9 = _____

10. 9
    × 5

11. 9
    × 3

12. 6
    × 9

13. 7
    × 9

14. 4
    × 9

Name _____

15. $2 \times 9 \bigcirc 3 \times 6$ **16.** $5 \times 9 \bigcirc 6 \times 7$ **17.** $1 \times 9 \bigcirc 3 \times 3$

18. $9 \times 4 \bigcirc 7 \times 5$ **19.** $9 \times 0 \bigcirc 2 \times 3$ **20.** $5 \times 8 \bigcirc 3 \times 9$

Problem Solving • Applications

Use the table for 21–24.

21. The number of moons for one of the planets can be found by multiplying 7×9. Which planet is it?

_____

22. **GO DEEPER** This planet has 9 times the number of moons that Mars and Earth have together. Which planet is it? **Explain** your answer.

_____

_____

_____

Moons	
Planet	**Number of Moons**
Earth	1
Mars	2
Jupiter	63
Saturn	47
Uranus	27
Neptune	13

23. **THINK SMARTER** Uranus has 27 moons. What multiplication fact with 9 can be used to find the number of moons Uranus has? Describe how you can find the fact.

_____

_____

_____

24. **Math Processes and Practices ②** **Use Reasoning** Nine students made models of Mars and its moons. The answer is 18. What's the question?

_____

Unlock the Problem (Real World)

25. The school library has 97 books about space. John and 3 of his friends each check out 9 books. How many space books are still in the school library?

a. What do you need to find? _____

_____

b. Describe one way you can find the answer. _____

_____

c. Show the steps you used to solve the problem.

d. Complete the sentences.

The library has _____ space books.

Multiply _____ × _____ to find how many books John and his 3 friends check out in all.

After you find the number of books

they check out, _____

to find the number of books still in the library.

So, there are _____ space books still in the library.

26. THINK SMARTER Circle the symbol that makes the multiplication sentence true.

$$9 \times 7 \quad \boxed{\begin{array}{c} > \\ < \\ = \end{array}} \quad 3 \times (3 \times 7)$$

Multiply with 9

Learning Objective You will use the Distributive Property and patterns to multiply with 9.

Find the product.

1. $10 \times 9 =$ __90__   **2.** $2 \times 9 =$ _____   **3.** $9 \times 4 =$ _____   **4.** $0 \times 9 =$ _____

5. $1 \times 9 =$ _____   **6.** $8 \times 9 =$ _____   **7.** $9 \times 5 =$ _____   **8.** $6 \times 9 =$ _____

9. 10   **10.**   3   **11.**   9   **12.**   6   **13.**   9
    $\times\ 9$ $\times\ 9$ $\times\ 8$ $\times\ 9$ $\times\ 1$

Problem Solving

14. There are 9 positions on the softball team. Three people are trying out for each position. How many people are trying out?

15. Carlos bought a book for $9. Now he would like to buy 4 other books for the same price. How much will he have to pay for the other 4 books?

_____

_____

16. WRITE ▸ *Math* Explain how you know whether to add or subtract when you use the Distributive Property to multiply.

_____

_____

Lesson Check

1. Find the product.

$$7 \times 9 =$$

_____

2. Clare buys 5 tickets for the high school musical. Each ticket costs $9. How much do the tickets cost?

_____

Spiral Review

3. The table shows the hair color of girls in Kim's class. How many girls have brown hair?

Kim's Class	
Hair Color	Number of Girls
Brown	⊬⊬	
Black	|||
Blonde	||||
Red		

_____

4. Miles picked up 9 shirts from the dry cleaners. It costs $4 to clean each shirt. How much did Miles spend to have all the shirts cleaned?

_____

5. In a picture graph, each picture of a baseball is equal to 5 games won by a team. The row for the Falcons has 7 baseballs. How many games have the Falcons won?

_____

6. An array has 8 rows with 4 circles in each row. How many circles are in the array?

_____

FOR MORE PRACTICE
GO TO THE
Personal Math Trainer

Name _____

Problem Solving • Multiplication

Essential Question How can you use the strategy *make a table* to solve multiplication problems?

Learning Objective You will use the strategy *make a table* to organize information and find patterns to solve multiplication problems.

Unlock the Problem

Scott has a stamp album. Some pages have 1 stamp on them, and other pages have 2 stamps on them. If Scott has 18 stamps, show how many different ways he could put them in the album. Use the graphic organizer below to solve the problem.

Read the Problem	Solve the Problem
What do I need to find? _____ _____ _____	Make a table to show the number of pages with 1 stamp and with 2 stamps. Each row must equal _____, the total number of stamps.

Solve the Problem

Pages with 2 Stamps	Pages with 1 Stamp	Total Stamps
8	2	18
7	4	18
6	6	18
5		18
	10	18
3	12	
2		

What information do I need to use?

Scott has _____ stamps. Some of the

pages have _____ stamp on them, and

the other pages have _____ stamps.

How will I use the information?

I will make a _____ showing all the different ways of arranging the stamps in the album.

So, there are _____ different ways.

1. What number patterns do you see in the table?

_____

_____

🔒 Try Another Problem

What if Scott bought 3 more stamps and now has 21 stamps? Some album pages have 1 stamp and some pages have 2 stamps. Show how many different ways he could put the odd number of stamps in the album.

Read the Problem	Solve the Problem
What do I need to find?	
What information do I need to use?	
How will I use the information?	
	So, there are _____ different ways.

2. What patterns do you see in this table? _____

_____

3. How are these patterns different from the patterns in

the table on page 247? _____

_____

248

Name _____

1. Aaron's mother is making lemonade. For each pitcher, she uses 1 cup of lemon juice, 1 cup of sugar, and 6 cups of water. What is the total number of cups of ingredients she will use to make 5 pitchers of lemonade?

   First, make a table to show the number of cups of lemon juice, sugar, and water that are in 1 pitcher of lemonade.

   Next, multiply to find the number of cups of water needed for each pitcher of lemonade.

   Think: For every pitcher, the number of cups of water increases by 6.

   Last, use the table to solve the problem.

Number of Pitchers	1	2	3		5
Cups of Lemon Juice	1		3		
Cups of Sugar	1	2			
Cups of Water	6	12		24	
Total Number of Cups of Ingredients	8				

So, in 5 pitchers of lemonade, there are _____ cups of

lemon juice, _____ cups of sugar, and _____ cups of water.

This makes a total of _____ cups of ingredients.

2. What if it takes 4 lemons to make 1 cup of lemon juice? How many lemons would it take to make 5 pitchers? Explain how you can use the table to help you find the answer.

   _____

   _____

3. What pattern do you see in the total number of cups of ingredients?

   _____

   _____

On Your Own

4. Julie saw 3 eagles each day she went bird-watching. How many eagles did Julie see in 6 days?

_____

5. **Math Processes and Practices 2** **Use Reasoning** Greg has a dollar bill, quarters, and dimes. How many ways can he make $1.75?

Name the ways. _____

_____

_____

6. **THINK SMARTER** Cammi needs 36 postcards. She buys 4 packages of 10 postcards. How many postcards will Cammi have left over? Explain.

_____

_____

_____

7. **GO DEEPER** Phillip has 8 books on each of 3 bookshelves. His aunt gives him 3 new books. How many books does Phillip have now?

_____

Personal Math Trainer

8. **THINK SMARTER +** Stuart has some 2-ounce, 3-ounce, and 4-ounce weights. How many different ways can Stuart combine the weights to make a total of 12 ounces? List the ways.

_____

_____

_____

Problem Solving • Multiplication

Learning Objective You will use the strategy *make a table* to organize information and find patterns to solve multiplication problems.

Solve.

1. Henry has a new album for his baseball cards. He uses pages that hold 6 cards and pages that hold 3 cards. If Henry has 36 cards, how many different ways can he put them in his album?

Pages with 6 Cards	1	2	3	4	5
Pages with 3 Cards	10	8	6	4	2
Total Cards	36	36	36	36	36

Henry can put the cards in his album __5__ ways.

2. Ms. Hernandez has 17 tomato plants that she wants to plant in rows. She will put 2 plants in some rows and 1 plant in the others. How many different ways can she plant the tomato plants? Make a table to solve.

Rows with 2 Plants	
Rows with 1 Plant	
Total Plants	

Ms. Hernandez can plant the tomato plants _____ ways.

3. **WRITE** ▸ *Math* Write a problem you can use the *make a table* strategy to solve. Then solve the problem.

_____

_____

Lesson Check

1. The table shows different ways that Cameron can display his 12 model cars on shelves. How many shelves will display 2 cars if 8 of the shelves each display 1 car?

Shelves with 1 Car	2	4	6	8	10
Shelves with 2 Cars	5	4	3	■	■
Total cars	12	12	12	12	12

_____

Spiral Review

2. Find the sum.

$$317$$
$$+\ 151$$

3. The school cafeteria has an order for 238 hot lunches. What is 238 rounded to the nearest ten?

_____

4. Tyler made a picture graph to show students' favorite colors. This is the key for his graph.

Each 🔵 = 3 votes.

If 12 students voted for green, how many 🔵 should there be in the green row of the graph?

5. There are 5 bikes in each bike rack at the school. There are 6 bike racks. How many bikes are in the bike racks?

_____

_____

FOR MORE PRACTICE
GO TO THE
Personal Math Trainer

Name _____

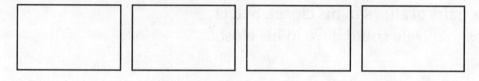
1. Mrs. Ruiz sorted spools of thread into 4 boxes.
   Each box holds 5 spools. How many spools of thread
   does Mrs. Ruiz have?

   Draw circles to model the problem. Then solve.

   ┌──────────┐ ┌──────────┐ ┌──────────┐ ┌──────────┐
   │   │ │   │ │   │ │   │
   │   │ │   │ │   │ │   │
   └──────────┘ └──────────┘ └──────────┘ └──────────┘

   _____

   _____

2. For numbers 2a–2d, select True or False for each
   multiplication sentence.

   2a. $2 \times 8 = 16$ ○ True   ○ False

   2b. $5 \times 8 = 40$ ○ True   ○ False

   2c. $6 \times 8 = 56$ ○ True   ○ False

   2d. $8 \times 8 = 64$ ○ True   ○ False

3. Bella is planning to write in a journal. Some pages will have
   one journal entry on them, and other pages will have two
   journal entries on them. If Bella wants to make 10 entries,
   how many different ways can she write them in her journal?

   ┌───┐
   │   │
   │   │
   │   │
   └───┘

4. There are 7 days in 1 week. How many days are there
   in 4 weeks?

   _____ days

5. Circle groups to show $3 \times (2 \times 3)$.

6. Dale keeps all of his pairs of shoes in his closet. Select the number of shoes that Dale could have in his closet. Mark all that apply.

(A) 3

(D) 7

(B) 4

(E) 8

(C) 6

7. **GO DEEPER** Lisa completed the table to describe the product of a mystery one-digit factor and each number.

×	1	2	3	4	5
?	even	even	even	even	even

Part A

Give all of the possible numbers that could be Lisa's mystery one-digit factor.

_____

Part B

Explain how you know that you have selected all of the correct possibilities.

_____

_____

_____

Name _____

8. Kate drew 7 octagons. An octagon has 8 sides.
   How many sides did Kate draw?

_____ sides

9. José buys 6 bags of flour. Each bag weighs 5 pounds.
   How many pounds of flour did José buy?

_____ pounds

10. Break apart the array to show $8 \times 6 = (4 \times 6) + (4 \times 6)$.

11. Circle the symbol that makes the multiplication sentence
    true.

$$9 \times 6 \quad \boxed{\begin{array}{c} > \\ < \\ = \end{array}} \quad 3 \times (3 \times 9)$$

12. Roberto wants to display his 18 sports cards in an album.
    Some pages hold 2 cards and others hold 3 cards. How
    many different ways can Roberto display his figures?

_____ different ways

13. A carpenter builds stools that have 3 legs each. How many legs does the carpenter use to build 5 stools? Use the array to explain how you know your answer is correct.

_____

_____

14. Etta buys some ribbon and cuts it into 7 pieces that are the same length. Each piece is 9 inches long. How long was the ribbon that Etta bought?

_____ inches

15. Antoine and 3 friends divide some pennies evenly among themselves. Each friend separates his pennies into 3 equal stacks with 5 pennies in each stack.

Write a multiplication sentence that shows the total number of pennies.

_____

16. Luke is making 4 first-aid kits. He wants to put 3 large and 4 small bandages in each kit. How many bandages does he need for the kits? Show your work.

_____ bandages

Name _____

17. For numbers 17a–17d, select True or False for each equation.

17a. $3 \times 7 = 21$　　　　○ True　　○ False

17b. $5 \times 7 = 28$　　　　○ True　　○ False

17c. $8 \times 7 = 49$　　　　○ True　　○ False

17d. $9 \times 7 = 63$　　　　○ True　　○ False

18. Circle the number that makes the multiplication sentence true.

$$10 \times \boxed{\begin{array}{c} 4 \\ 5 \\ 8 \end{array}} = 40$$

19. For numbers 19a–19d, select Yes or No to indicate whether the sum or product is equal to 8×6.

19a. $8 + (4 \times 2) = \blacksquare$　　　○ Yes　　○ No

19b. $(8 \times 4) + (8 \times 2) = \blacksquare$　　○ Yes　　○ No

19c. $(6 \times 4) + (6 \times 2) = \blacksquare$　　○ Yes　　○ No

19d. $6 \times (4 + 4) = \blacksquare$　　　○ Yes　　○ No

20. Chloe bought 4 movie tickets. Each ticket cost $6. What was the total cost of the movie tickets?

$ _____

21. Write a multiplication sentence using the following numbers and symbols.

| 6 | 60 | 5 | 2 | ( ) | = |

_____

22. THINKSMARTER ✚ Louis started a table showing a multiplication pattern.

Part A

Complete the table. Describe a pattern you see in the products.

×	1	2	3	4	5	6	7	8	9	10
3	3	6	9							

_____

_____

Part B

If you multiplied 3 × 37, would the product be an even number or an odd number? Use the table to explain your reasoning.

_____

_____

_____

_____

_____

23. Use the number line to show the product of 4 × 8.

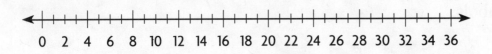

0 2 4 6 8 10 12 14 16 18 20 22 24 26 28 30 32 34 36

4 × 8 = _____

5 Use Multiplication Facts

Show What You Know

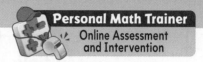

Personal Math Trainer
Online Assessment
and Intervention

Check your understanding of important skills.

Name _____

▶ **Add Tens** Write how many tens. Then add.

1. $30 + 30 =$ ■

____ tens + ____ tens =

____ tens

$30 + 30 =$ ____

2. $40 + 50 =$ ■

____ tens + ____ tens =

____ tens

$40 + 50 =$ ____

▶ **Regroup Tens as Hundreds** Write the missing numbers.

3. 35 tens = ____ hundreds ____ tens

4. 52 tens = ____ hundreds ____ tens

5. 97 tens = ____ hundreds ____ tens

▶ **Multiplication Facts Through 9** Find the product.

6. $3 \times 9 =$ ____   **7.** $4 \times 5 =$ ____   **8.** $7 \times 6 =$ ____   **9.** $8 \times 2 =$ ____

The butterfly exhibit at the museum will display 60 different butterfly species arranged in an array. Each row has 6 butterflies. How many rows are in the butterfly exhibit?

The butterfly exhibit will open soon.

Vocabulary Builder

▶ **Visualize It** •••

Complete the tree map by using the words with a ✓.

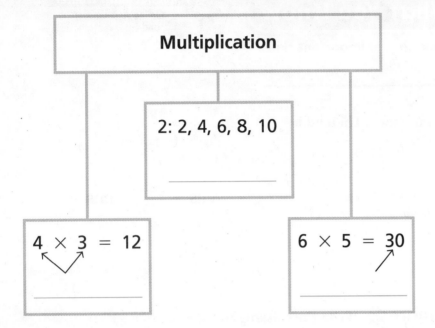

Multiplication

2: 2, 4, 6, 8, 10

_____

4 × 3 = 12

_____

6 × 5 = 30

_____

Review Words
array
Commutative Property of Multiplication
Distributive Property
✓ factors
hundreds
✓ multiples
ones
pattern
place value
✓ product
tens

Preview Words
equation

▶ **Understand Vocabulary** •••••••••••••••••••••••••••

**Read the definition. Write the preview word
or review word that matches it.**

1. An ordered set of numbers or objects
   in which the order helps you predict
   what will come next.   _____

2. A set of objects arranged in rows
   and columns.   _____

3. A number sentence that uses the equal
   sign to show that two amounts are equal.   _____

4. The property that states that multiplying
   a sum by a number is the same as
   multiplying each addend by the number
   and then adding the products.   _____

5. The value of each digit in a number, based
   on the location of the digit.   _____

GO DIGITAL
• Interactive Student Edition
• Multimedia eGlossary

array

matriz

4

Commutative Property of Multiplication

Propiedad conmutativa de la multiplicación

9

Distributive Property

Propiedad distributiva

13

equation

ecuación

22

factor

factor

25

Pattern

patrón

57

place value

valor posicional

62

product

producto

65

The property that states that you can multiply two factors in any order and get the same product

Example: $4 \times 3 = 3 \times 4$

A set of objects arranged in rows and columns

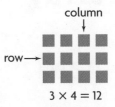

$3 \times 4 = 12$

A number sentence that uses the equal sign to show that two amounts are equal

Example: $9 \times 2 = 18$ is an equation

The property that states that multiplying a sum by a number is the same as multiplying each addend by the number and then adding the products

Example: $5 \times 8 = 5 \times (4 + 4)$
$5 \times 8 = (5 \times 4) + (5 \times 4)$
$5 \times 8 = 20 + 20$
$5 \times 8 = 40$

An ordered set of numbers or objects in which the order helps you predict what will come next

Examples: 2, 4, 6, 8, 10, 2, 4, 6, 8, 10

A number that is multiplied by another number to find a product

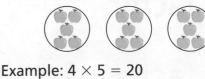

Example: $4 \times 5 = 20$

factor   factor

The answer in a multiplication problem

Example: $4 \times 5 = 20$

product

The value of each digit in a number, based on the location of the digit

MILLIONS			THOUSANDS			ONES		
Hundreds	Tens	Ones	Hundreds	Tens	Ones	Hundreds	Tens	Ones
		1,	3	9	2,	0	0	0
		$1 \times 1{,}000{,}000$	$3 \times 100{,}000$	$9 \times 10{,}000$	$2 \times 1{,}000$	0×100	0×10	0×1
		1,000,000	300,000	90,000	2,000	0	0	0

Pick It

For 3 players

Materials
- 4 sets of word cards

How to Play

1. Each player is dealt 5 cards. The remaining cards are a draw pile.

2. To take a turn, ask any player if he or she has a word that matches one of your word cards.

3. If the player has the word, he or she gives the word card to you.
   - If you are correct, keep the card and put the matching pair in front of you. Take another turn.
   - If you are wrong, return the card. Your turn is over.

4. If the player does not have the word, he or she answers, "Pick it." Then you take a card from the draw pile.

5. If the card you draw matches one of your word cards, follow the directions for Step 3 above. If it does not, your turn is over.

6. The game is over when one player has no cards left. The player with the most pairs wins.

Word Box

array

Commutative
 Property of
 Multiplication

Distributive
 Property

equation

factors

pattern

place value

product

The Write Way

Reflect

Choose one idea. Write about it.

- Work with a partner to explain and illustrate two ways to multiply with multiples of 10. Use a separate piece of paper for your drawing.

- Write a paragraph that uses at least three of these words.

  equation   factors   pattern   place value   product

- Think about what you learned in class today. Complete one of these sentences.

  I learned that I _____.

  I was surprised that I _____.

  I noticed that I _____.

  I discovered that I _____.

  I was pleased that I _____.

260B

Name _____

Describe Patterns

Essential Question What are some ways you can describe a pattern in a table?

Learning Objective You will extend and describe rules for patterns in tables and explain them using properties of operations.

🔑 Unlock the Problem

The outdoor club is planning a camping trip. Each camper will need a flashlight. One flashlight uses 4 batteries. How many batteries are needed for 8 flashlights?

You can describe a pattern in a table.

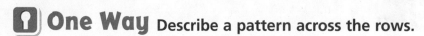

Flashlights	1	2	3	4	5	6	7	8
Batteries	4	8	12	16	20	24	28	■

Think: Count by 1s.

Think: Count by 4s.

🔓 One Way Describe a pattern across the rows.

STEP 1 Look for a pattern to complete the table. As you look across the rows, you can see that the number of batteries increases by 4 for each flashlight.

So, for every flashlight add _____ batteries.

STEP 2 Use the pattern to find the number of batteries in 8 flashlights.

Add _____ to 28 batteries. $28 + 4 =$ _____

So, _____ batteries are needed for 8 flashlights.

🔓 Another Way Describe a pattern in the columns.

STEP 1 Look for a pattern by comparing the columns in the table. You can multiply the number of flashlights by 4 to find the number of batteries that are needed.

STEP 2 Use the pattern to find how many batteries are needed for 8 flashlights.

$8 \times 4 =$ _____

> **! ERROR Alert**
> Check that your pattern will work for all the numbers in the table.

 Math Talk

 Math Processes and Practices ⑦

Look for a Pattern Do you notice any other patterns in the Flashlights/Batteries table?

Try This! Describe a pattern. Then complete the table.

The campers need 5 packs of batteries. If there are 8 batteries in each pack, how many batteries will be in 5 packs?

Packs of Batteries	Number of Batteries
1	8
2	16
3	
4	32
5	

Use addition.

Describe a pattern.

Add _____ batteries for each pack.

Use multiplication.

Describe a pattern.

Multiply the number of packs of batteries

by _____.

So, there will be _____ batteries in 5 packs.

Share and Show

1. How can you describe a pattern to find the cost of 4 packs of batteries?

_____

Packs of Batteries	1	2	3	4
Cost	$3	$6	$9	

Describe a pattern in the table. Then complete the table.

2.

Tents	Lanterns
2	4
3	6
4	8
5	10
6	
7	

_____

3.

Adults	1	2	3	4	5
Campers	6	12	18		

_____

Math Talk

Math Processes and Practices ①

Describe how you use your description for a pattern to complete a table.

© Houghton Mifflin Harcourt Publishing Company

On Your Own

Describe a pattern in the table. Then complete the table.

4.

Hours	1	2	3	4	5
Miles Hiked	2	4	6		

5.

Cabins	3	4	5	6	7
Campers	27	36	45		

6.

Cabins	Beds
1	5
2	10
3	
4	20
5	
6	

7.

Adults	Students
2	12
3	18
4	
5	30
6	
7	

8. THINK SMARTER   Students made a craft project at camp. They used 2 small pine cone patterns and 1 large pine cone pattern. Complete the table to find how many patterns were used for the different numbers of projects.

Math on the Spot

Projects	1	2	3						
Small Pattern	2								
Large Pattern	1								

9. GO DEEPER   Isaac uses 4 red beads and 3 blue beads to make a belt. How many beads will Isaac use to make 4 belts?

10. GO DEEPER   Corey uses 5 yellow tiles and 4 green tiles to make a design. How many tiles will he need to repeat the design 5 times?

Problem Solving • Applications (Real World)

Math Processes and Practices ④ Use Graphs **Use the picture graph for 11–13.**

11. Jena bought 3 fishing poles. How much money did she spend?

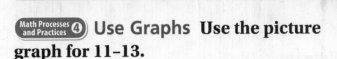

Cost of Fishing Supplies	
Corks	🐟 🐟
Poles	🐟 🐟 🐟 🐟 🐟
Worms	🐟 🐟 🐟 🐟

Key: Each 🐟 = $2.

WORMS

12. **GO DEEPER** Noah bought 1 fishing pole, 2 corks, and 1 carton of worms. What was the total cost?

13. **WRITE ▸ Math** Ryan bought 8 corks. Explain how you can use the Commutative Property to find the cost.

14. **GO DEEPER** The cost to rent a raft is $7 per person. A raft can hold up to 6 people. There is a $3 launch fee per raft. What is the total cost for a group of 6? Explain.

15. A group of students and adults are going on a field trip in vans. In each van, there will be 8 students and 2 adults. How many people will be in 4 vans?

Personal Math Trainer

16. **THINK SMARTER +** Complete the table. Amir said a rule for the pattern shown in this table is "Multiply by 4." Is he correct? Explain how you know your answer is reasonable.

Cans	2	3	4		6
Peaches	8	12		20	

Describe Patterns

Learning Objective You will extend and describe rules for patterns in tables and explain them using properties of operations.

Describe a pattern for the table. Then complete the table.

1.

Pans	1	2	3	4	5
Muffins	6	12	18	24	30

Add 6 muffins for each pan;

Multiply the number of pans by 6.

2.

Wagons	2	3	4	5	6
Wheels	8	12	16		

3.

Vases	2	3	4	5	6
Flowers	14		28		42

4.

Spiders	1	2	3	4	5
Legs	8		24		40

Problem Solving (Real World)

5. Caleb buys 5 cartons of yogurt. Each carton has 8 yogurt cups. How many yogurt cups does Caleb buy?

6. Libby bought 4 packages of pencils. Each package has 6 pencils. How many pencils did Libby buy?

7. **WRITE** *Math* How does finding a pattern help you complete a table?

Lesson Check

1. Describe a pattern in the table.

Tables	1	2	3	4	5
Chairs	5	10	15	20	25

_____

2. What number completes this table?

Butterflies	3	4	5	6	7
Wings	12	16	20	■	28

_____

Spiral Review

3. Jennilee buys 7 packs of crayons. There are 6 crayons in each pack. How many crayons does Jennilee buy?

_____

4. Maverick has 5 books of circus tickets. Each book has 5 tickets. How many tickets does Maverick have?

_____

5. Bailey walked his dog 2 times each day for 9 days. How many times did Bailey walk his dog?

_____

6. Drew's Tree Company delivers pear trees in groups of 4. Yesterday, the company delivered 8 groups of pear trees. How many pear trees were delivered?

_____

FOR MORE PRACTICE
GO TO THE
Personal Math Trainer

Name _____

Find Unknown Numbers

Essential Question How can you use an array or a multiplication table to find an unknown factor or product?

Learning Objective You will use an array or a multiplication table to find an unknown factor or product.

⚷ Unlock the Problem

Tanisha plans to invite 24 people to a picnic. The invitations come in packs of 8. How many packs of invitations does Tanisha need to buy?

An **equation** is a number sentence that uses the equal sign to show that two amounts are equal.

A symbol or letter can stand for an unknown number. You can write the equation, $n \times 8 = 24$, to find how many packs of invitations Tanisha needs. Find the number, n, that makes the equation true.

- How many people is Tanisha inviting? _____
- How many invitations are in 1 pack? _____

🔒 Use an array.

- Show an array of 24 tiles with 8 tiles in each row by completing the drawing.

Math Talk Math Processes and Practices ⑥

Explain how the array represents the problem. How do the factors relate to the array?

$$n \quad \times \quad 8 \quad = \quad 24$$
$$\uparrow \qquad \uparrow \qquad \quad \uparrow$$
factor   factor   product
number of   number in   total
rows   each row   number

- Count how many rows of 8 tiles there are.   **Think:** What number times 8 equals 24?

There are _____ rows of 8 tiles. The unknown factor is _____. $n =$ _____

      _____ $\times 8 = 24$ Check.

      _____ $= 24$ ✓ The equation is true.

So, Tanisha needs _____ packs of invitations.

Use a multiplication table.

$3 \times 8 = $ ▨

Think: The symbol, ▨, stands for the unknown product.

Find the product 3×8 where row 3 and column 8 meet.

The unknown product is _____.

▨ = _____

$3 \times 8 = $ _____   Check.

$24 = $ _____ ✓ The equation is true.

×	0	1	2	3	4	5	6	7	8	9	10
0	0	0	0	0	0	0	0	0	0	0	0
1	0	1	2	3	4	5	6	7	8	9	10
2	0	2	4	6	8	10	12	14	16	18	20
3	0	3	6	9	12	15	18	21	24	27	30
4	0	4	8	12	16	20	24	28	32	36	40
5	0	5	10	15	20	25	30	35	40	45	50
6	0	6	12	18	24	30	36	42	48	54	60
7	0	7	14	21	28	35	42	49	56	63	70
8	0	8	16	24	32	40	48	56	64	72	80
9	0	9	18	27	36	45	54	63	72	81	90
10	0	10	20	30	40	50	60	70	80	90	100

Share and Show MATH BOARD

1. What is the unknown factor shown by this array?

$5 \times $ ▨ $ = 35$

▨ = _____

Find the unknown number.

2. $d \times 3 = 27$

$d = $ _____

3. $6 \times 5 = $ ▲

▲ = _____

✓ 4. $c = 5 \times 4$

$c = $ _____

✓ 5. ▨ $\times 2 = 14$

▨ = _____

6. $b = 4 \times 9$

$b = $ _____

7. $8 \times e = 64$

$e = $ _____

8. $7 \times $ ★ $ = 42$

★ = _____

9. $8 \times 9 = z$

$z = $ _____

Math Talk

Math Processes and Practices ②

Use Reasoning How do you know if you are looking for the number of rows or the number in each row when you make an array to find an unknown factor?

Name _____

Find the unknown number.

10. $\blacksquare = 9 \times 2$

$\blacksquare = $ ____

11. $28 = 4 \times m$

$m = $ ____

12. $y \times 3 = 9$

$y = $ ____

13. $7 \times 9 = g$

$g = $ ____

14. $a = 6 \times 4$

$a = $ ____

15. $7 = 7 \times n$

$n = $ ____

16. $w \times 3 = 15$

$w = $ ____

17. $\bigstar = 8 \times 6$

$\bigstar = $ ____

Math Processes and Practices ② **Reason Quantitatively** **Algebra** **Find the unknown number.**

18. $3 \times 6 = k \times 9$

$k = $ ____

19. $4 \times y = 2 \times 6$

$y = $ ____

20. $5 \times g = 36 - 6$

$g = $ ____

21. $6 \times 4 = \blacksquare \times 3$

$\blacksquare = $ ____

22. $9 \times d = 70 + 2$

$d = $ ____

23. $8 \times h = 60 - 4$

$h = $ ____

24. GODEEPER Invitations cost $3 for a pack of 8. Lori gives the cashier $20 to buy invitations and gets $11 in change. How many packs of invitations does Lori buy? Explain.

_____

_____

25. GODEEPER Coz and Amelia each make a tile design with 36 tiles. Coz puts his in rows of 4. Amelia puts hers in rows of 6. How many more tiles are in each of Coz's rows than Amelia's?

_____

Problem Solving • Applications

Use the table for 26–29.

Picnic Supplies		
Item	Number in 1 Pack	Cost
Bowls	6	$10
Cups	8	$3
Tablecloth	1	$2
Napkins	36	$2
Forks	50	$3

26. Tanisha needs 40 cups for the picnic. How many packs of cups should she buy?

_____

27. GO DEEPER   Ms. Hill buys 3 tablecloths and 2 packs of napkins. How much money does she spend?

_____

28. THINK SMARTER   What if Tanisha needs 40 bowls for the picnic? Explain how to write an equation with a letter for an unknown factor to find the number of packs she should buy. Then find the unknown factor.

_____

_____

_____

29. Math Processes and Practices ➊ **Analyze**   What if Randy needs an equal number of bowls and cups for his picnic? How many packs of each will he need to buy?

_____

_____

30. THINK SMARTER   For numbers 30a–30d, choose Yes or No to show whether the unknown factor is 8.

30a. $8 \times \boxed{} = 64$ ○ Yes   ○ No

30b. $\boxed{} \times 3 = 27$ ○ Yes   ○ No

30c. $6 \times \boxed{} = 42$ ○ Yes   ○ No

30d. $\boxed{} \times 7 = 56$ ○ Yes   ○ No

Name _____

Find Unknown Numbers

Learning Objective You will use an array or a multiplication table to find an unknown factor or product.

Find the unknown number.

1. $n \times 3 = 12$

Think: How many groups of 3 equal 12?

$n = \underline{\quad 4 \quad}$

2. $s \times 8 = 64$

$s = \underline{\qquad}$

3. $21 = 7 \times n$

$n = \underline{\qquad}$

4. $y \times 2 = 18$

$y = \underline{\qquad}$

5. $5 \times p = 10$

$p = \underline{\qquad}$

6. $56 = 8 \times t$

$t = \underline{\qquad}$

7. $m \times 4 = 28$

$m = \underline{\qquad}$

8. $\bigstar \times 1 = 9$

$\bigstar = \underline{\qquad}$

9. $b \times 6 = 54$

$b = \underline{\qquad}$

10. $5 \times \blacktriangle = 40$

$\blacktriangle = \underline{\qquad}$

11. $30 = d \times 3$

$d = \underline{\qquad}$

12. $7 \times k = 42$

$k = \underline{\qquad}$

Problem Solving Real World

13. Carmen spent $42 for 6 hats. How much did each hat cost?

_____

14. Mark has a baking tray with 24 muffins. The muffins are arranged in 4 equal rows. How many muffins are in each row?

_____

15. **WRITE** ▸*Math* Explain why it does not matter what letter or symbol is used to find an unknown number.

_____

_____

Lesson Check

1. What is the unknown number?

$$b \times 7 = 56$$

_____

2. What is the unknown number shown by this array?

$$3 \times \blacksquare = 24$$

_____

Spiral Review

3. The number sentence $4 \times 6 = 6 \times 4$ is an example of what property?

_____

_____

_____

4. Find the product.

$$5 \times (4 \times 2)$$

_____

_____

_____

5. The number sentence $4 \times 7 = (4 \times 3) + (4 \times 4)$ is an example of what property?

6. In a group of 10 boys, each boy had 2 hats. How many hats did they have?

_____

_____

FOR MORE PRACTICE
GO TO THE
Personal Math Trainer

272

Name _____

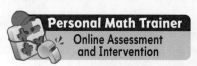

Vocabulary

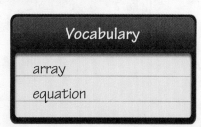

Vocabulary
array
equation

Choose the best term from the box.

1. An _____ is a number sentence that uses the equal sign to show that two amounts are equal. (p. 267)

Concepts and Skills

Describe a pattern in the table. Then complete the table.

2.

Weeks	1	2	3	4	5
Days	7	14	21		

_____

3.

Tickets	2	3	4	5	6
Cost	$8	$12	$16		

_____

4.

Project Teams	Members
3	9
4	12
5	
6	18
7	

5.

Tables	Chairs
1	8
2	16
3	
4	32
5	

Find the unknown number.

6. $m \times 5 = 30$

   $m =$ _____

7. $\blacksquare \times 6 = 48$

   $\blacksquare =$ _____

8. $n = 2 \times 10$

   $n =$ _____

9. $4 \times 8 = p$

   $p =$ _____

10. $25 = y \times 5$

    $y =$ _____

11. $\blacklozenge \times 10 = 10$

    $\blacklozenge =$ _____

12. Describe a pattern in the table.

Packages	1	2	3	4	5
Stickers	6	12	18	24	30

_____

13. What number makes the equation true?

$$a \times 8 = 72$$

_____

14. Mia bought 2 copies of the same book. She spent $18. What was the cost of one book?

_____

15. Kyle saves $10 every week for 6 weeks. How much money will Kyle have in Week 6?

Weeks	1	2	3	4	5	6
Amount	$10	$20	$30	■	■	■

_____

16. GO DEEPER Tennis balls cost $7 for a can of 3. Steve gives the cashier $40 to buy balls and receives $12 in change. How many tennis balls did Steve buy?

_____

Name _____

Problem Solving •
Use the Distributive Property

Essential Question How can you use the strategy *draw a diagram* to multiply with multiples of 10?

Learning Objective You will use the strategy *draw a diagram* and the Distributive Property to multiply with multiples of 10.

Unlock the Problem

The school assembly room has 5 rows of chairs with 20 chairs in each row. If the third-grade classes fill 3 rows of chairs, how many third graders are at the assembly?

Read the Problem	**Solve the Problem**
What do I need to find? I need to find how many _____ are at the assembly.	Draw a diagram. Finish the shading to show 3 rows of 20 chairs. 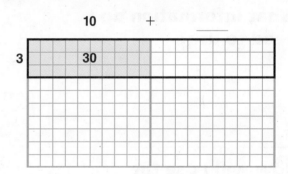
What information do I need to use? There are _____ chairs in each row. The third graders fill _____ rows of chairs.	I can use the sum of the products of the smaller rectangles to find how many third graders are at the assembly. $3 \times 10 =$ _____ $3 \times 10 =$ _____ _____ + _____ = _____ $3 \times 20 =$ _____
How will I use the information? The Distributive Property tells me I can _____ the factor 20 to multiply. $3 \times 20 = 3 \times (10 +$ _____$)$	So, _____ third graders are at the assembly.

1. Explain how breaking apart the factor 20 makes finding the

   product easier. _____

Try Another Problem

Megan is watching a marching band practice. The band marches by with 4 rows of people playing instruments. She counts 30 people in each row. How many people march in the band?

Read the Problem	Solve the Problem
What do I need to find?	**Record the steps you used to solve the problem.**
What information do I need to use?	
How will I use the information?	

2. How can you check to see if your answer is reasonable?

_____

_____

3. Explain how you can use the Distributive Property to help you find a product.

_____

_____

Name _____

Unlock the Problem

√ Circle the numbers you will use.

√ Use the Distributive Property and break apart a greater factor to use facts you know.

√ Draw a diagram to help you solve the problem.

Share and Show

1. People filled all the seats in the front section of the theater. The front section has 6 rows with 40 seats in each row. How many people are in the front section of the theater?

   First, draw and label a diagram to break apart the problem into easier parts to solve.

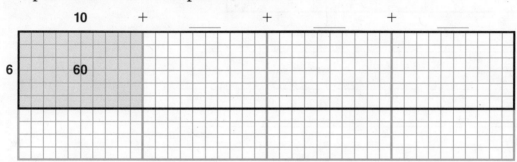

   Next, find the products of the smaller rectangles.

   6 × 10 = _____   _____ × _____ = _____

   _____ × _____ = _____   _____ × _____ = _____

   Then, find the sum of the products.

   _____ + _____ + _____ + _____ = _____

   So, there are _____ people in the front section of the theater.

2. What if seats are added to the front section of the theater so that there are 6 rows with 50 seats in each row? How many seats are in the front section?

   _____

On Your Own

3. *THINK SMARTER* Tova sewed 60 pieces of blue ribbon together to make a costume. Each piece of ribbon was 2 meters long. She also sewed 40 pieces of red ribbon together that were each 3 meters long. Did Tova use more blue ribbon or red ribbon? Explain.

4. **Math Processes and Practices ③** Verify the Reasoning of Others

Carina draws this diagram to show that $8 \times 30 = 210$. Explain her error.

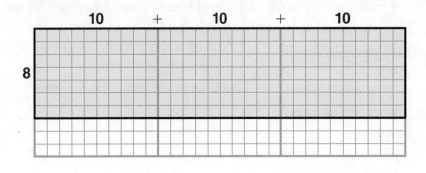

_____

_____

_____

_____

5. **WRITE** ▸*Math* Tamika wants to display 10 trophies on a table in a rectangular array. How many different ways can Tamika arrange the trophies? Explain your answer.

_____

_____

6. **GO DEEPER** The drama club has 350 tickets to sell. They sell 124 tickets on Monday and 98 tickets on Tuesday. How many tickets does the drama club have left to sell?

_____

7. **THINK SMARTER** Select the equations that show the Distributive Property. Mark all that apply.

Ⓐ $3 \times 20 = (3 \times 10) + (3 \times 10)$

Ⓑ $(7 + 3) + 8 = 7 + (3 + 8)$

Ⓒ $(5 \times 10) + (5 \times 10) = 5 \times 20$

Ⓓ $(9 \times 2) + (9 \times 4) = 9 \times 6$

Name _____

Problem Solving • Use the Distributive Property

Learning Objective You will use the strategy *draw a diagram* and the Distributive Property to multiply with multiples of 10.

Read each problem and solve.

1. Each time a student turns in a perfect spelling test, Ms. Ricks puts an achievement square on the bulletin board. There are 6 rows of squares on the bulletin board. Each row has 30 squares. How many perfect spelling tests have been turned in?

   Think: $6 \times 30 = 6 \times (10 + 10 + 10)$

   $= 60 + 60 + 60 = 180$

   180 spelling tests

2. Norma practices violin for 50 minutes every day. How many minutes does Norma practice violin in 7 days?

   _____

3. A kitchen designer is creating a new backsplash for the wall behind a kitchen sink. The backsplash will have 5 rows of tiles. Each row will have 20 tiles. How many tiles are needed for the entire backsplash?

   _____

4. A bowling alley keeps shoes in rows of cubbyholes. There are 9 rows of cubbyholes, with 20 cubbyholes in each row. If there is a pair of shoes in every cubbyhole, how many pairs of shoes are there?

   _____

5. **WRITE** ▸*Math* Write a description of how a diagram can help you solve 2×40.

   _____

   _____

Lesson Check

1. Each snack pack holds 20 crackers. How many crackers in all are there in 4 snack packs?

   _____

2. A machine makes 70 springs each hour. How many springs will the machine make in 8 hours?

   _____

Spiral Review

3. Lila read 142 pages on Friday and 168 pages on Saturday. Estimate how many pages Lila read on Friday and Saturday combined.

   _____

   _____

4. Jessica wrote 6 + 6 + 6 + 6 on the board. What is another way to show 6 + 6 + 6 + 6?

   _____

   _____

Use the line plot for 5–6.

5. Eliot made a line plot to record the number of birds he saw at his bird feeder. How many more sparrows than blue jays did he see?

   _____

6. How many robins and cardinals combined did Eliot see?

   _____

   _____

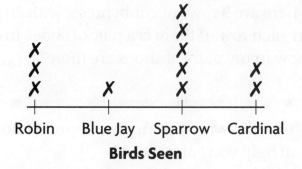

Birds Seen

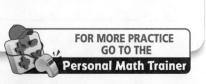

FOR MORE PRACTICE
GO TO THE
Personal Math Trainer

Multiplication Strategies with Multiples of 10

Essential Question What strategies can you use to multiply with multiples of 10?

Learning Objective You will use base-ten blocks and strategies based on place value to multiply with multiples of 10.

Unlock the Problem

You can use models and place value to multiply with multiples of 10.

- What is a product of 10 and the counting numbers 1, 2, 3, and so on?

_____

Activity Model multiples of 10.

Materials ■ base-ten blocks

Model the first nine multiples of 10.

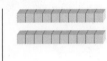 1 × 10
1 × 1 ten
1 ten
10

2 × 10
2 × 1 ten
2 tens
20

 3 × 10
3 × 1 ten
3 tens
30

What are the first nine multiples of 10?

10, 20, 30, _____ , _____ , _____ , _____ , _____ , _____

Best Care Veterinary Clinic offered free pet care classes for 5 days. Erin attended the pet care class for 30 minutes each day. How many minutes did Erin attend the class?

One Way Use a number line.

5 × 30 = ■   **Think:** 30 = 3 tens

STEP 1 Complete the number line. Write the labels for the multiples of 10.

STEP 2 Draw jumps on the number line to show 5 groups of 3 tens.

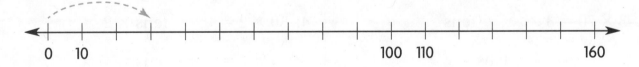

0 10   100 110   160

5 × 30 = _____

So, Erin attended the pet care class for _____ minutes.

Another Way Use place value.

MODEL

So, 5 × 30 = _____.

THINK

5 × 30 = 5 × _____ tens

= _____ tens = _____

Try This!

4 × 50 = _____ × _____ tens

= _____ tens = _____

Math Talk

Math Processes and Practices ①

Make Sense of Problems Why does 5 × 30 have one zero in the product and 4 × 50 has two zeros in the product?

Share and Show MATH BOARD

Use a number line to find the product.

1. 3 × 40 = _____   Think: There are 3 jumps of 40.

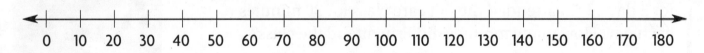

2. 8 × 20 = _____

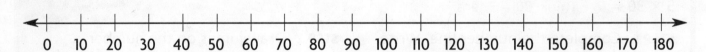

Use place value to find the product.

3. 3 × 70 = 3 × _____ tens

= _____ tens = _____

4. 50 × 2 = _____ tens × 2

= _____ tens = _____

Math Talk

Math Processes and Practices ⑧

Use Repeated Reasoning Why will the product of a multiplication problem be the same when the factors are reversed?

Name _____

Use a number line to find the product.

5. $7 \times 20 =$ _____

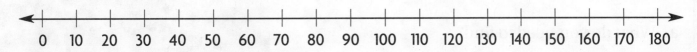

6. $3 \times 50 =$ _____

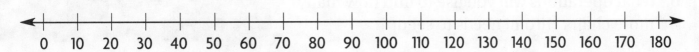

Use place value to find the product.

7. $6 \times 60 = 6 \times$ _____ tens

     $=$ _____ tens $=$ _____

8. $50 \times 7 =$ _____ tens $\times 7$

     $=$ _____ tens $=$ _____

Problem Solving • Applications

Use the table for 9–11.

9. GO DEEPER A bottle of shampoo costs \$8 and a package of cat toys costs \$7. If the clinic sells its entire supply of shampoo and cat toys, how much money will it receive?

_____

10. What's the Question? Each bag of treats has 30 treats. The answer is 240.

_____

Best Care Clinic Pet Supplies	
Item	**Amount**
Cat toys	10 packs
Treats	8 bags
Shampoo	20 bottles
Vitamins	3 boxes

11. THINK SMARTER There are 4 bottles of vitamins in each box of vitamins. Each bottle of vitamins has 20 vitamins. If the clinic wants to have a supply of 400 vitamins, how many more boxes should it order?

_____

⚷ Unlock the Problem Real World

12. **Math Processes and Practices ❶ Make Sense of Problems** Hiromi needs to set up chairs for 155 people to attend the school career day program. So far she has set up 6 rows with 20 chairs in each row. How many more chairs does Hiromi need to set up?

a. What do you need to find?

_____

b. What operations will you use to find how many more chairs Hiromi needs to set up?

_____

c. Write the steps you will use to solve the problem.

d. Complete the sentences.

Hiromi needs to set up _____ chairs for people to attend the program.

She has set up _____ rows with _____ chairs in each row.

So, Hiromi needs to set up _____ more chairs.

13. **Go DEEPER** Last week, Dr. Newman examined the paws of 30 dogs at her clinic. She examined the paws of 20 cats. What is the total number of paws Dr. Newman examined last week?

_____

14. **THINK SMARTER** Nick made this multiplication model. Complete the equation that represents the model.

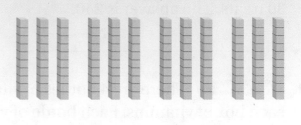

_____ × _____ = _____

Name _____

Multiplication Strategies with Multiples of 10

Learning Objective You will use base-ten blocks and strategies based on place value to multiply with multiples of 10.

Use a number line to find the product.

1. $2 \times 40 =$ ___80___

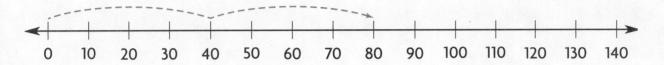

2. $4 \times 30 =$ _____

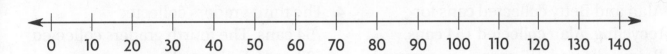

Use place value to find the product.

3. $5 \times 70 = 5 \times$ _____ tens

       $=$ _____ tens $=$ _____

4. $60 \times 4 =$ _____ tens $\times 4$

       $=$ _____ tens $=$ _____

Problem Solving Real World

5. One exhibit at the aquarium has 5 fish tanks. Each fish tank holds 50 gallons of water. How much water do the 5 tanks hold?

_____

6. In another aquarium display, there are 40 fish in each of 7 large tanks. How many fish are in the display?

_____

7. **WRITE** ▸*Math* Which strategy do you prefer to use to multiply with multiples of 10: base ten blocks, a number line, or place value? Explain why.

_____

_____

Lesson Check

1. Each bag of pattern blocks contains 50 blocks. To make a class pattern, the teacher combines 4 bags of blocks. How many pattern blocks are there?

   _____

2. A deli received 8 blocks of cheese. Each block of cheese weighs 60 ounces. What is the total weight of the cheeses?

   _____

Spiral Review

3. Alan and Betty collected cans for recycling. Alan collected 154 cans. Betty collected 215 cans. How many cans did they collect?

   _____

   _____

4. The third graders collected 754 cans. The fourth graders collected 592 cans. Estimate how many more cans the third graders collected.

   _____

   _____

Use the bar graph for 5–6.

5. How many more books did Ed read than Bob?

   _____

6. How many books did the four students read in June?

   _____

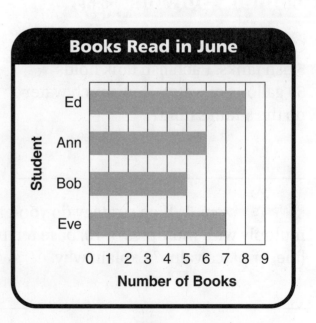

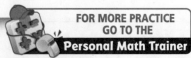

FOR MORE PRACTICE
GO TO THE
Personal Math Trainer

Name _____

Multiply 1-Digit Numbers by Multiples of 10

Essential Question How can you model and record multiplying 1-digit whole numbers by multiples of 10?

Learning Objective You will use base-ten blocks and draw quick pictures to model and record multiplying 1-digit whole numbers by multiples of 10.

Unlock the Problem

The community center offers 4 dance classes. If 30 students sign up for each class, how many students sign up for dance class?

- How many equal groups are there? _____
- How many are in each group? _____

Activity Use base-ten blocks to model 4 × 30.

Materials ■ base-ten blocks

STEP 1 Model 4 groups of 30.

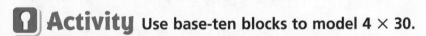

STEP 2 Combine the tens. Regroup 12 tens as 1 hundred 2 tens.

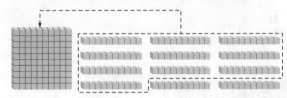

4 × 30 = _____

So, _____ students sign up for dance class.

> **Math Idea**
> If one factor is a multiple of 10, then the product will also be a multiple of 10.

Try This! Find 7 × 40.

Use a quick picture to record your model. Draw a stick for each ten. Draw a square for each hundred.

STEP 1 Model _____ groups of _____.

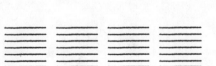

STEP 2 Combine the tens. Regroup 28 tens as _____ hundreds _____ tens.

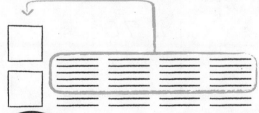

So, 7 × 40 = _____.

Math Processes and Practices ⑦

Look for Structure Why will the product of 7 × 40 be the same as 4 × 70?

🔑 **Example** Use place value and regrouping.

Find 9 × 50.

MODEL	THINK	RECORD
STEP 1 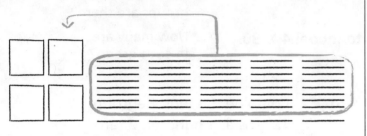	Multiply the ones. 9×0 ones = _____ ones	5 0 × 9 ‾‾‾ 0
STEP 2 	Multiply the tens. 9×5 tens = 45 tens Regroup the _____ tens as _____ hundreds _____ tens.	5 0 × 9 ‾‾‾ 4 5 0

So, 9 × 50 = _____.

Share and Show 🖊️ MATH BOARD

1. Use the quick picture to find 5 × 40.

   5 × 40 = _____

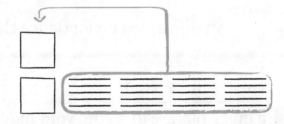

Find the product. Use base-ten blocks or draw a quick picture on your MathBoard.

✓ **2.** 7 × 30 = _____   **3.** _____ = 2 × 90   **4.** 8 × 40 = _____   **5.** _____ = 4 × 60

Find the product.

✓ **6.** 80
        × 9
     ‾‾‾‾‾

7. 70
      × 7
    ‾‾‾‾‾

8. 90
      × 4
    ‾‾‾‾‾

9. 60
      × 8
    ‾‾‾‾‾

Math Talk

Math Processes and Practices ①

Analyze Explain why a 1-digit number multiplied by a multiple of 10 is easily computed mentally.

Name _____

Find the product. Use base-ten blocks or draw a quick picture on your MathBoard.

10. $2 \times 70 =$ _____   **11.** $8 \times 50 =$ _____   **12.** _____ $= 3 \times 90$ **13.** $2 \times 80 =$ _____

Find the product.

14.
$$\begin{array}{r} 80 \\ \times\ 3 \\ \hline \end{array}$$

15.
$$\begin{array}{r} 60 \\ \times\ 9 \\ \hline \end{array}$$

16.
$$\begin{array}{r} 90 \\ \times\ 8 \\ \hline \end{array}$$

17.
$$\begin{array}{r} 80 \\ \times\ 8 \\ \hline \end{array}$$

Practice: Copy and Solve Find the product.

18. 6×70 **19.** 9×90 **20.** 70×8 **21.** 90×7

Math Processes and Practices ② Reason Quantitatively **Algebra** Find the unknown factor.

22. $a \times 80 = 480$

$a =$ _____

23. $b \times 30 = 30$

$b =$ _____

24. $7 \times$ $= 420$

■ $=$ _____

25. $50 \times$ ▲ $= 0$

▲ $=$ _____

Problem Solving • Applications (Real World)

26. (THINK SMARTER) Ava's class bought 6 packages of balloons for a school celebration. Each package had 30 balloons. If 17 balloons were left over, how many balloons were used for the party?

_____

27. Sense or Nonsense? Lori says that 8 is not a factor of 80 because 8 does not end in zero. Does Lori's statement make sense? Explain.

_____

28. **Math Processes and Practices ④** Model Mathematics The book club members read 200 books in all. Each member read 5 books. Write an equation to find the number of members in the book club. Use a letter to stand for the unknown factor.

_____

Unlock the Problem

29. GO DEEPER   Frank has a 2-digit number on his baseball uniform. The number is a multiple of 10 and has 3 for one of its factors. What three numbers could Frank have on his uniform?

a. What do you need to find?

_____

b. What information do you need to use?

_____

c. How can you solve the problem?

d. Complete the sentences.

Frank has a _____ on his uniform.

The number is a multiple of _____.

One factor of the number is _____.

Frank could have _____, _____, or

_____ on his uniform.

Personal Math Trainer

30. THINK SMARTER +   Baker Farm grows and sells carrots to local grocery stores. The stores bundle the carrots to sell. Which grocery store bought the greatest number of carrots from Baker Farm? How many carrots did the store buy?

Grocery Store	Number of Carrots in 1 Bundle	Number of Bundles
Buy–More Foods	6	90
Lower Price Foods	8	60
Yummy Foods	7	80
Healthy Foods	9	70

_____

Name _____

Multiply 1-Digit Numbers by Multiples of 10

Learning Objective You will use base-ten blocks and draw quick pictures to model and record multiplying 1-digit whole numbers by multiples of 10.

Find the product. Use base-ten blocks or draw a quick picture.

1. $4 \times 50 = \underline{200}$

2. $60 \times 3 = \underline{}$

3. $\underline{} = 60 \times 5$

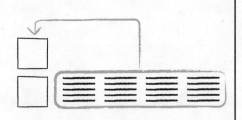

Find the product.

4. $\begin{array}{r} 80 \\ \times\ 3 \\ \hline \end{array}$

5. $\begin{array}{r} 50 \\ \times\ 2 \\ \hline \end{array}$

6. $\begin{array}{r} 60 \\ \times\ 7 \\ \hline \end{array}$

7. $\begin{array}{r} 70 \\ \times\ 4 \\ \hline \end{array}$

8. $6 \times 90 = \underline{}$

9. $9 \times 70 = \underline{}$

10. $8 \times 90 = \underline{}$

11. $\underline{} = 6 \times 80$

Problem Solving Real World

12. Each model car in a set costs $4. There are 30 different model cars in the set. How much would it cost to buy all the model cars in the set?

13. Amanda exercises for 50 minutes each day. How many minutes will she exercise in 7 days?

_____

_____

14. **WRITE** ▸*Math* Explain how to find 4×80. Show your work.

_____

_____

Lesson Check

1. Each shelf in one section of the library holds 30 books. There are 9 shelves in that section. How many books will these shelves hold?

   _____

2. One can of juice mix makes 30 ounces of juice. How many ounces of juice can be made from 6 cans of juice mix?

   _____

Spiral Review

3. Sue bought 7 cans of tennis balls. There are 3 balls in each can. How many balls did Sue buy?

   _____

4. Use the Commutative Property of Multiplication to write a related multiplication sentence.

   $$3 \times 4 = 12$$

   _____

5. Lyn drew this bar model to solve a problem. What operation should she use to find the unknown number?

   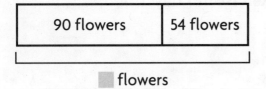

   ▮ flowers

   _____

6. Joe drew this bar model to find the unknown number of balls. Find the unknown number.

   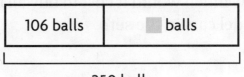

   250 balls

   _____

FOR MORE PRACTICE
GO TO THE
Personal Math Trainer

✓ Chapter 5 Review/Test

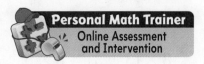

Personal Math Trainer
Online Assessment
and Intervention

1. The camping club wants to rent rafts. Each raft can hold
   8 people. Which equation could be used to find how
   many rafts are needed for 32 people?

   Ⓐ $8 \times 32 = $ ■

   Ⓑ $32 \times $ ■ $= 8$

   Ⓒ   ■ $\times 8 = 32$

   Ⓓ $32 \times 8 = $ ■

2. Select the equations that show the Distributive Property.
   Mark all that apply.

   Ⓐ $8 \times 20 = 8 \times (10 + 10)$

   Ⓑ $5 \times 60 = 5 \times (20 + 40)$

   Ⓒ $30 \times 6 = 6 \times 30$

   Ⓓ $9 \times (4 + 3) = 9 \times 7$

3. Choose the number from the box that makes the
   sentence true.

   A library has 48 shelves of fiction books. There are
   6 shelves in each cabinet.

   There are | 7
 8
 9 | cabinets of fiction books in the library.

GO DIGITAL   **Assessment Options**
Chapter Test

4. For numbers 4a–4d, choose True or False for each equation.

4a. $5 \times (4 + 4) = 8 \times 5$ ○ True   ○ False

4b. $8 \times (3 + 3) = 8 \times 5$ ○ True   ○ False

4c. $(3 \times 5) + (5 \times 5) = 8 \times 5$ ○ True   ○ False

4d. $(3 \times 2) + (8 \times 3) = 8 \times 5$ ○ True   ○ False

5. Alya planted 30 trays of flowers. Each tray held 8 flowers. Javon planted 230 flowers. Did Alya plant more flowers than Javon, the same number of flowers as Javon, or fewer flowers than Javon?

Ⓐ   She planted more flowers than Javon.

Ⓑ   She planted the exact same number of flowers as Javon.

Ⓒ   She planted fewer flowers than Javon.

6. For numbers 6a–6d, choose Yes or No to show whether the unknown number is 6.

6a. $4 \times \blacksquare = 32$ ○ Yes   ○ No

6b. $\blacksquare \times 6 = 36$ ○ Yes   ○ No

6c. $8 \times \blacksquare = 49$ ○ Yes   ○ No

6d. $\blacksquare \times 30 = 180$ ○ Yes   ○ No

7. Each train can carry 20 cars. Use the number line to find how many cars 6 trains can carry.

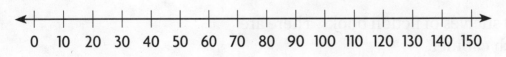

_____ cars

Name _____

8. Samantha made this multiplication model. Complete the equation that represents the model.

_____ × _____ = _____

9. A printer prints newsletters for many groups every month. Which group uses the greatest number of pieces of paper?

Group	Number of pieces of paper in newsletter	Number of copies of newsletter printed
Garden Ladies	5	70
Book Lovers Club	6	80
Model Train Fans	7	60
Travel Club	8	50

_____

10. GO DEEPER   A store has 30 boxes of melons. Each box holds 4 bags. Each bag holds 2 melons. What is the total number of melons in the store?

_____ melons

11. Heather's puppy weighs 23 pounds. He has been gaining 3 pounds every month as he grows. If this pattern continues, how much will the puppy weigh 5 months from now?

_____

12. Tim describes a pattern. He says the pattern shown in the table is "Add 3." Is Tim correct? Explain how you know.

Packages	1	2	3	4	5
Markers	4	8	12	16	20

_____

_____

_____

13. This shows a part of a multiplication table. Find the missing numbers. Explain how you found the numbers.

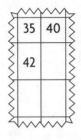

_____

_____

_____

_____

14. Describe a pattern for this table.

Tanks	3	4	5	6	7
Fish	240	320	400	480	560

Pattern: _____

How would the table change if the pattern was "Multiply the number of tanks by 8"? Explain.

_____

_____

296

15. Devon has 80 books to pack in boxes. She packs 20 books in each box. How many boxes does she need?

Write an equation using the letter n to stand for the unknown factor. Explain how to find the unknown factor.

_____

_____

_____

16. **THINK SMARTER +** The bookstore has 6 shelves of books about animals. There are 30 books on each shelf. How many books about animals does the bookstore have?

Shade squares to make a diagram to show how you can use the Distributive Property to find the number of books about animals in the bookstore.

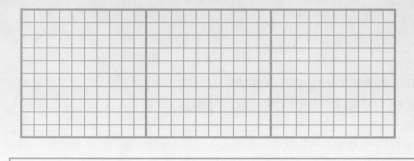

_____ animal books

17. Cody saves all his nickels. Today he is getting them out of his piggy bank and wrapping them to take to the bank. He finds he has 360 nickels. It takes 40 nickels to fill each paper wrapper and make a roll. How many wrappers does he need?

Part A

Write an equation using *n* for the unknown number. Find the number of wrappers needed.

_____ × _____ = _____

Part B

Explain how you solved this problem and how you know your answer is correct.

_____

_____

_____

_____

18. Ruben is collecting cans for the recycling contest at school. He makes two plans to try to collect the most cans.

Plan A: Collect 20 cans each week for 9 weeks.

Plan B: Collect 30 cans each week for 7 weeks.

Part A

Which plan should Ruben choose? _____

Part B

Explain how you made your choice.

_____

_____

_____

_____

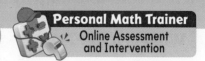

✓ Show What You Know

Personal Math Trainer
Online Assessment
and Intervention

Check your understanding of important skills.

Name _____

▶ **Count Back to Subtract** **Use the number line. Write the difference.**

1. $8 - 5 =$ _____

2. $9 - 4 =$ _____

▶ **Count Equal Groups** **Complete.**

3.

_____ groups

_____ in each group

4.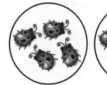

_____ groups

_____ in each group

▶ **Multiplication Facts Through 9** **Find the product.**

5. $8 \times 5 =$ _____   **6.** _____ $= 7 \times 7$ **7.** $3 \times 9 =$ _____

The table shows 3 different ways to score points in basketball. Corina scored 12 points in a basketball game. Find the greatest number of field goals she could have scored. Then find the greatest number of 3-pointers she could have scored.

Scoring Points in Basketball	
free throw	1 point
field goal	2 points
3-pointer	3 points

Vocabulary Builder

▶ **Visualize It**

Complete the bubble map by using the words with a ✓ .

What is it like?   What are some examples?

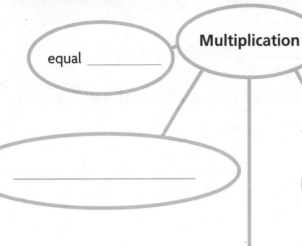

equal _____   **Multiplication**   4 groups with 3 in each group

_____

6	×	3	=	18
6	×	4	=	24
↑		↑		↑
factor	×	____	=	____

$5 + 5 + 5 = 3 \times 5 = 15$

▶ **Understand Vocabulary** •

Draw a line to match each word or term with its definition.

Preview Words   **Definitions**

1. dividend   A set of related multiplication and division equations

2. related facts   The number that divides the dividend

3. divisor   The number that is to be divided in a division problem

Review Words

array

✓ equal groups

equation

✓ factor

Identity Property of Multiplication

✓ product

✓ repeated addition

Preview Words

divide

dividend

divisor

inverse operations

quotient

related facts

• Interactive Student Edition
• Multimedia eGlossary

Chapter 6 Vocabulary

divide

dividir

14

dividend

dividendo

15

divisor

divisor

16

equal groups

grupos iguales

20

factor

factor

25

inverse operations

operaciones inversas

37

quotient

cociente

67

related facts

operaciones
relacionadas

70

The number that is to be divided in a division problem

Examples: $32 \div 4 = 8$ $4\overline{)32}^{\,8}$
          ↑   ↑
       dividend   dividend

To separate into equal groups; the opposite operation of multiplication

$8 \div 4 = 2$ $4\overline{)8}^{\,2}$

Groups that have the same number of objects

The number that divides the dividend

Examples: $32 \div 4 = 8$ $4\overline{)32}^{\,8}$
                  ↑   ↑
               divisor   divisor

Opposite operations, or operations that undo one another, such as addition and subtraction or multiplication and division

Examples: $16 + 8 = 24$; $24 - 8 = 16$
          $4 \times 3 = 12$; $12 \div 4 = 3$

A number that is multiplied by another number to find a product

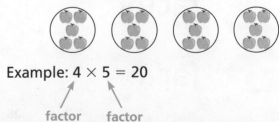

Example: $4 \times 5 = 20$
              ↑   ↑
           factor   factor

A set of related addition and subtraction, or multiplication and division, number sentences

Examples: $4 \times 7 = 28$ $28 \div 4 = 7$
          $7 \times 4 = 28$ $28 \div 7 = 4$

The number, not including the remainder, that results from division

Example: $35 \div 7 = 5$
                     ↑
                  quotient

Going Places with GO MATH! words

Game

Bingo

> **Word Box**
> divide
> dividend
> divisor
> equal groups
> inverse operations
> factors
> quotient
> related facts

For 3–6 players

Materials

- 1 set of word cards
- 1 Bingo board for each player
- counters, paperclips, or coins for game markers

How to Play

1. The caller chooses a card and reads the definition.
   Then the caller puts the card in a second pile.
2. Players put a marker on the word that matches the definition
   each time they find it on their Bingo boards.
3. Repeat Steps 1 and 2 until a player marks 5 boxes in a line
   going down, across, or on a slant and calls "Bingo."
4. Check the answers. Have the player who said "Bingo" read the
   words aloud while the caller checks the definitions on the
   cards in the second pile.

The Write Way

Reflect

Choose one idea. Write about it.

- Explain equal groups and how they relate to division.
- Write a division word problem using the numbers 24 and 6.

Suppose that you write a math advice column, and a reader needs help understanding the division rules for 1. Write a response that explains the rules.

Name _____

Problem Solving • Model Division

Essential Question How can you use the strategy *act it out* to solve problems with equal groups?

Learning Objective You will use counters and the strategy *act it out* to solve problems with equal groups.

🔑 Unlock the Problem

Stacy has 16 flowers. She puts an equal number of flowers in each of 4 vases. How many flowers does Stacy put in each vase?

Use the graphic organizer below to solve the problem.

Read the Problem

What do I need to find?

I need to find the number

of _____ Stacy puts in

each _____.

What information do I need to use?

Stacy has _____ flowers. She puts an equal number of flowers in each of

_____ vases.

How will I use the information?

I will act out the problem

by making equal _____ with counters.

Solve the Problem

Describe how to act out the problem to solve.

First, count out _____ counters.

Next, make _____ equal groups. Place 1 counter at a time in each group until all 16 counters are used.

Last, draw the equal groups by completing the picture below.

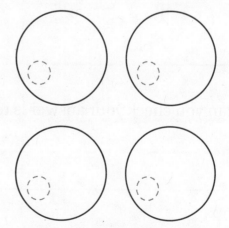

So, Stacy puts _____ flowers in each vase.

❶ Try Another Problem

Jamal is at the pet store. He buys 21 dog treats. If he plans to give each dog 3 treats, how many dogs does he feed?

Read the Problem	Solve the Problem
What do I need to find?	**Describe how to act out the problem to solve.**
What information do I need to use?	
How will I use the information?	

- How can you check your answer is reasonable? _____

_____

_____

Math Talk

Math Processes and Practices ❽

Generalize How does a strategy like *acting it out* help you solve a problem?

Name _____

Unlock the Problem

√ Use the Problem Solving MathBoard
√ Underline important facts.
√ Choose a strategy you know.

Share and Show

1. Mariana is having a party. She has 16 cups. She puts them in 2 equal stacks. How many cups are in each stack?

First, decide how to act out the problem.
You can use counters to represent the _____.

You can draw _____ to represent the stacks.

Then, draw to find the number of _____ in each stack.

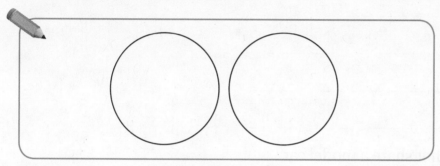

There are _____ groups. There are _____ counters in each group.

So, there are _____ cups in each stack.

2. **Math Processes and Practices 1** **Make Sense of Problems** What if Mariana has 24 cups and puts 4 cups in each stack? If she already made 4 stacks, how many more stacks can she make with the remaining cups?

_____

On Your Own

3. *THINK SMARTER* At Luke's school party, the children make teams of 5 to play a game. If there are 20 boys and 15 girls, how many teams are there?

_____

4. *GO DEEPER* Anne put 20 party hats and 20 balloons on 4 tables. She put an equal number of hats and an equal number of balloons on each table. How many hats and how many balloons did she put on each table?

_____

Use the table for 5–6.

5. Sadie's plates came in packages of 5 plates. How many packages of plates did she buy?

_____

6. (Math Processes and Practices ⑥) **Explain a Method** Sadie bought 4 packages of napkins and 3 packages of cups. Which type of package had more items in it? How many more items are in each package? Explain.

_____

_____

_____

_____

Sadie's Party Supplies

Item	Number
Plates	30
Napkins	28
Cups	24

7. GO DEEPER   Ira and his brother share a model car collection. Ira has 25 cars, and his brother has 15 cars. They store the model cars on a bookshelf and place the same number of cars on each shelf. There are 5 shelves. How many model cars are on each shelf?

_____

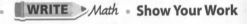

WRITE ▸ Math · Show Your Work

Personal Math Trainer

8. THINK SMARTER ➕ Miguel gave 2 party favors to each of the children at his party. He gave away 18 party favors. How many children were at Miguel's party?

Circle equal groups to model the problem.

_____ children

Name _____

Problem Solving • Model Division

Learning Objective You will use counters and the strategy *act it out* to solve problems with equal groups.

Solve each problem.

1. Six customers at a toy store bought 18 jump ropes. Each customer bought the same number of jump ropes. How many jump ropes did each customer buy?

   _____3 jump ropes_____

2. Hiro has 36 pictures of his summer trip. He wants to put them in an album. Each page of the album holds 4 pictures. How many pages will Hiro need for his pictures?

   _____

3. Katia has 42 crayons in a box. She buys a storage bin that has 6 sections. She puts the same number of crayons in each section. How many crayons does Katia put in each section of the storage bin?

   _____

4. Ms. Taylor's students give cards to each of the 3 class parent helpers. There are 24 cards. How many cards will each helper get if the students give an equal number of cards to each helper?

   _____

5. **WRITE** ▸*Math* Write a word problem about equal groups and act it out to solve.

   _____

   _____

Lesson Check

1. Maria buys 15 apples at the store and places them into bags. She puts 5 apples into each bag. How many bags does Maria use for all the apples?

_____

2. Tom's neighbor is fixing a section of his walkway. He has 32 bricks that he is placing in 8 equal rows. How many bricks will Tom's neighbor place in each row?

_____

Spiral Review

3. Find the unknown factor.

$$7 \times \blacksquare = 56$$

4. How many students practiced the piano more than 3 hours?

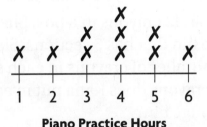

Piano Practice Hours

_____

5. Count equal groups to find how many counters there are.

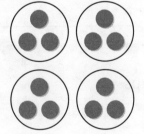

6. What is another way to group the factors?

$$(3 \times 2) \times 5$$

_____

_____

FOR MORE PRACTICE GO TO THE
Personal Math Trainer

Name _____

Size of Equal Groups

Essential Question How can you model a division problem to find how many in each group?

Learning Objective You will use counters and draw quick pictures to model sharing and find how many in each group.

🔑 Unlock the Problem

Hector has 12 rocks from a nearby state park. He puts an equal number of his rocks in each of 3 boxes. How many rocks are in each box?

When you multiply, you put equal groups together. When you **divide**, you separate into equal groups.

You can divide to find the number in each group.

- What do you need to find?

_____

- Circle the numbers you need to use.

🔓 Activity Use counters to model the problem.

Materials ■ counters ■ MathBoard

STEP 1

Use 12 counters.

STEP 2

Draw 3 circles on your MathBoard. Place 1 counter at a time in each circle until all 12 counters are used. Draw the rest of the counters to show your work.

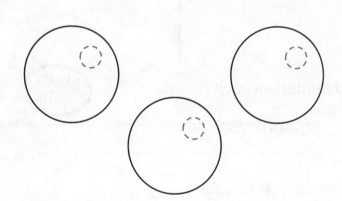

There are _____ counters in each group.

So, there are _____ rocks in each box.

Try This!

Madison has 15 rocks. She puts an equal number of rocks in each of 5 boxes. How many rocks are in each box?

STEP 1

Draw 5 squares to show 5 boxes.

_____

STEP 2

Draw 1 counter in each square to show the rocks. Continue drawing 1 counter at a time in each box until all 15 counters are drawn.

There are _____ counters in each group.

So, there are _____ rocks in each box.

Math Talk

Math Processes and Practices ❶

Describe another way to arrange 15 counters to make equal groups.

1. How many counters did you draw? _____

2. How many equal groups did you make? _____

3. How many counters are in each group? _____

Name _____

1. Jon has 8 counters. He makes 4 equal groups.
   Draw a picture to show the number of counters
   in each group.

Math Talk

Math Processes and Practices ④

Use Models Explain how you made the groups equal.

Use counters or draw a quick picture on your MathBoard. Make equal groups. Complete the table.

	Counters	Number of Equal Groups	Number in Each Group
✓2.	10	2	
✓3.	24	6	

On Your Own

Use counters or draw a quick picture on your MathBoard. Make equal groups. Complete the table.

	Counters	Number of Equal Groups	Number in Each Group
4.	14	7	
5.	21	3	

6. **GO DEEPER** Cameron and Jody collected 20 stamps. Cameron says
   they can put an equal number of stamps on each of 5 pages of
   their album. Jody says they can put an equal number on each of
   4 pages. Whose statement makes sense? Explain.

   _____

   _____

Problem Solving • Applications

Use the table for 7–8.

Photos	
Name	**Number of Photos**
Madison	28
Joe	25
Ella	15

7. Madison puts all of her photos in a photo album. She puts an equal number of photos on each of 4 pages in her album. How many photos are on each page?

_____

8. **THINK SMARTER** Joe and Ella combine their photos. Then they put an equal number on each page of an 8-page photo album. How many photos are on each page?

_____

9. **Math Processes and Practices ③ Make Arguments** Rebekah found 28 seashells. Can she share all the seashells equally among the 6 people in her family? Explain.

_____

_____

_____

10. **THINK SMARTER** Zana has 9 rocks from a trip. She puts an equal number of rocks in each of 3 bags. How many rocks are in each bag?

Circle the amount to complete the sentence.

There are
| 3 |
| 6 |
| 12 |
| 27 |
rocks in each bag.

Name _____

Size of Equal Groups

Learning Objective You will use counters and draw quick pictures to model sharing and find how many in each group.

Use counters or draw a quick picture. Make equal groups. Complete the table.

	Counters	Number of Equal Groups	Number in Each Group
1.	15	3	5
2.	21	7	
3.	28	7	
4.	32	4	
5.	9	3	
6.	35	5	
7.	24	3	

 Problem Solving Real World

8. Alicia has 12 eggs that she will use to make 4 different cookie recipes. If each recipe calls for the same number of eggs, how many eggs will she use in each recipe?

9. Brett picked 27 flowers from the garden. He plans to give an equal number of flowers to each of 3 people. How many flowers will each person get?

_____

_____

10. **WRITE** ▸*Math* Describe how to divide 18 strawberries equally between 2 of your friends.

_____

_____

Lesson Check

1. Ryan has 21 pencils. He wants to put the same number of pencils in each of 3 pencil holders. How many pencils will he put in each pencil holder?

2. Corrine is setting out 24 plates on 6 tables for a dinner. She sets the same number of plates on each table. How many plates does Corrine set on each table?

Spiral Review

3. Each table has 4 legs. How many legs do 4 tables have?

4. Tina has 3 stacks of 5 CDs on each of 3 shelves. How many CDs does she have?

5. What is the unknown factor?

$$7 \times \blacksquare = 35$$

6. Describe a pattern in the table.

Number of packs	1	2	3	4	5
Number of yo-yos	3	6	9	12	?

© Houghton Mifflin Harcourt Publishing Company

FOR MORE PRACTICE
GO TO THE
Personal Math Trainer

Name _____

Number of Equal Groups

Essential Question How can you model a division problem to find how many equal groups?

Learning Objective You will use counters and draw quick pictures to find how many equal groups.

CONNECT You have learned how to divide to find the number in each group. Now you will learn how to divide to find the number of equal groups.

Unlock the Problem

Juan has 12 shells and some boxes. He wants to put each group of 3 shells in a box. How many boxes does he need for his shells?

- Underline what you need to find.
- How many shells does Juan want to put in each box?

_____

🔑 **Make equal groups.**

- Look at the 12 counters.
- Circle a group of 3 counters.
- Continue circling groups of 3 until all 12 counters are in groups.

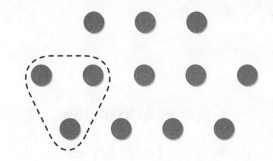

There are _____ groups of counters.

So, Juan needs _____ boxes for his shells.

Math Processes and Practices ⑥

Compare How would the drawing change if Juan wanted to put his shells in groups of 4?

Try This!

Sarah has 15 shells. She wants to put each group of 5 shells in a box.
How many boxes does she need for her shells?

STEP 1

Draw 15 counters.

STEP 2

Make a group of 5 counters by
drawing a circle around them.
Continue circling groups of 5
until all 15 counters are in groups.

There are _____ groups of 5 counters.

So, Sarah needs _____ boxes for her shells.

- **THINK SMARTER** What if Sarah puts her 15 shells in
groups of 3?

How many boxes does she need? _____
Draw a quick picture to show your work.

Name _____

1. Tamika has 12 counters. She puts them in groups of 2. Draw a picture to show the number of groups.

Math Talk Math Processes and Practices ③

Apply How do you find the number of equal groups when you divide?

Draw counters on your MathBoard. Then circle equal groups. Complete the table.

	Counters	Number of Equal Groups	Number in Each Group
✓**2.**	20		4
✓**3.**	24		3

On Your Own

Draw counters on your MathBoard. Then circle equal groups. Complete the table.

	Counters	Number of Equal Groups	Number in Each Group
4.	18		2
5.	16		8

6. **THINK SMARTER** A store has 18 red beach balls and 17 green beach balls in boxes of 5 beach balls each. How many boxes of beach balls are at the store?

? Unlock the Problem Real World

7. **Math Processes and Practices ①** **Make Sense of Problems** A store has 24 beach towels in stacks of 6 towels each. How many stacks of beach towels are at the store?

a. What do you need to find? _____

_____

b. How will you use what you know about making equal groups

to solve the problem? _____

_____

c. Draw equal groups to find how many stacks of beach towels there are at the store.

d. Complete the sentences.

The store has _____ beach towels.

There are _____ towels in each stack.

So, there are _____ stacks of beach towels at the store.

8. **GO DEEPER** Write a problem about dividing beach toys into equal groups. Then solve the problem.

_____

_____

_____

9. **THINK SMARTER** Dan's train is 27 inches long. If each train car is 3 inches long, how many train cars are there?

Choose a number from the box to complete the sentence.

| 6 |
| 7 |
| 8 |
| 9 |

There are _____ train cars.

Number of Equal Groups

Learning Objective You will use counters and draw quick pictures to find how many equal groups.

Draw counters on your MathBoard. Then circle equal groups. Complete the table.

	Counters	Number of Equal Groups	Number in Each Group
1.	24	3	8
2.	35		7
3.	30		5
4.	16		4
5.	12		6
6.	36		9
7.	18		3

Problem Solving · Real World

8. In his bookstore, Toby places 21 books on shelves, with 7 books on each shelf. How many shelves does Toby need?

9. Mr. Holden has 32 quarters in stacks of 4 on his desk. How many stacks of quarters are on his desk?

10. **WRITE** ▸ Math Write and solve a math problem in which you need to find how many equal groups.

Lesson Check

1. Ramon works at a clothing store. He puts 24 pairs of jeans into stacks of 8. How many stacks does Ramon make?

2. There are 36 people waiting in line for a hay ride. Only 6 people can ride on each wagon. If each wagon is full, how many wagons are needed for all 36 people?

Spiral Review

3. What multiplication sentence does the array show?

4. Austin buys 4 boxes of nails for his project. There are 30 nails in each box. How many nails does Austin buy in all?

5. What property does the number sentence show?

$$8 + 0 = 8$$

6. Each month for 6 months, Kelsey completes 5 paintings. How many more paintings does she need to complete before she has completed 38 paintings?

© Houghton Mifflin Harcourt Publishing Company

FOR MORE PRACTICE
GO TO THE
Personal Math Trainer

Model with Bar Models

Essential Question How can you use bar models to solve division problems?

Learning Objective You will use bar models to find how many in each group and find how many equal groups and write a division equation.

🔑 Unlock the Problem

A dog trainer has 20 dog treats for 5 dogs in his class. If each dog gets the same number of treats, how many treats will each dog get?

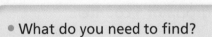

• What do you need to find?

_____

🔑 Activity 1 Use counters to find how many in each group.

Materials ■ counters ■ MathBoard

• Use 20 counters.

• Draw 5 circles on your MathBoard.

• Place 1 counter at a time in each circle until all 20 counters are used.

• Draw the rest of the counters to show your work.

There are _____ counters in each of the 5 groups.

A bar model can show how the parts of a problem are related.

• Complete the bar model to show 20 dog treats divided into 5 equal groups.

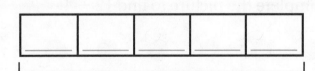

20 dog treats

So, each dog will get _____ treats.

⓵ Activity 2 Draw to find how many equal groups.

A dog trainer has 20 dog treats. If the dog trainer gives 5 treats to each dog in the class, how many dogs are in the class?

- Look at the 20 counters.
- Circle a group of 5 counters.
- Continue circling groups of 5 until all 20 counters are in groups.

There are _____ groups of 5 counters.

- Complete the bar model to show 20 treats divided into groups of 5 treats.

So, there are _____ dogs in the class.

_____ dogs

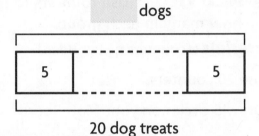

20 dog treats

Here are two ways to record division.

Write: 20   ÷   5   =   4
            ↑   ↑   ↑
      dividend divisor quotient

$$\begin{array}{r} 4 \leftarrow \text{quotient} \\ \text{divisor} \rightarrow 5\overline{)20} \\ \uparrow \\ \text{dividend} \end{array}$$

Read: Twenty divided by five equals four.

Math Talk — Math Processes and Practices ⑥

Use Math Vocabulary Describe how you solved the problem in Activity 2. Use the terms *dividend*, *divisor*, and *quotient* in your explanation.

Share and Show

1. Complete the picture to find $12 \div 4$. _____

Math Talk — Math Processes and Practices ②

Reason Quantitatively How do you know how many groups to make?

320

Name _____

Write a division equation for the picture.

2.

_____

3.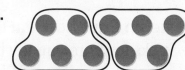

_____

On Your Own

Write a division equation for the picture.

4.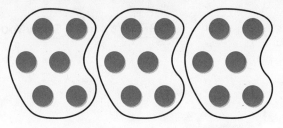

_____

5.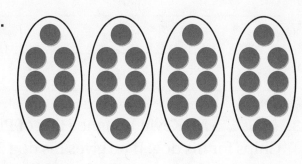

_____

Practice: Copy and Solve Make equal groups to find the quotient. Draw a quick picture to show your work.

6. 20 ÷ 2

7. 27 ÷ 9

8. 20 ÷ 5

9. 18 ÷ 3

Complete the bar model to solve. Then write a division equation for the bar model.

10. There are 24 books in 4 equal stacks. How many books are in each stack?

24 books

_____

11. There are 8 matching socks. How many pairs of socks can you make?

[   ] pairs

| 2 | - - - - - - - - | 2 |

8 socks

_____

Problem Solving • Applications

Use the table for 12–13.

12. **Math Processes and Practices 4** **Write an Equation** Pat bought one box of Chew Sticks to share equally between his 2 dogs. Mia bought one box of Chewies to share equally among her 5 dogs. How many more treats will each of Pat's dogs get than each of Mia's dogs? Explain.

_____

_____

_____

_____

Dog Treats	
Type	**Number in Box**
Chew Sticks	14
Chewies	25
Dog Bites	30
Puppy Chips	45

WRITE ▶ _Math_ • **Show Your Work**

13. **THINK SMARTER** Kevin bought a box of Puppy Chips for his dog. If he gives his dog 5 treats each day, for how many days will one box of treats last?

_____

_____

14. **GO DEEPER** Write and solve a problem for $42 \div 7$ in which the quotient is the number of groups.

_____

_____

_____

15. **THINK SMARTER** Ed buys 5 bags of treats. He buys 15 treats in all. How many treats are in each bag?

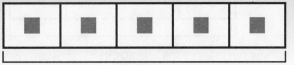

15 treats

_____ treats

Model with Bar Models

Learning Objective You will use bar models to find how many in each group and find how many equal groups and write a division equation.

Write a division equation for the picture.

1.

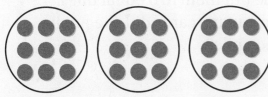

$27 \div 3 = 9$ or $27 \div 9 = 3$

2.

Complete the bar model to solve. Then write a division equation for the bar model.

3. There are 15 postcards in 3 equal stacks. How many postcards are in each stack?

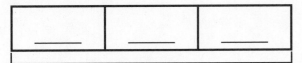

15 postcards

_____

4. There are 21 key rings. How many groups of 3 key rings can you make?

[____] groups

| 3 | | 3 |

21 key rings

_____

5. Jalyn collected 24 stones. She put them in 4 equal piles. How many stones are in each pile?

_____

6. Tanner has 30 stickers. He puts 6 stickers on each page. On how many pages does he put stickers?

_____

7. **WRITE** *Math* Describe how to find the number of $4 train tickets you can buy with $32.

_____

_____

Lesson Check

1. Jack and his little sister are stacking 24 blocks. They put the blocks in 3 equal stacks. How many blocks are in each stack?

_____

2. Melissa made 45 greeting cards. She put them in 5 equal piles. How many cards did she put in each pile?

_____

Spiral Review

3. Angie puts 1 stamp on each envelope. She puts stamps on 7 envelopes. How many stamps does Angie use?

_____

4. A carnival ride has 8 cars. Each car holds 4 people. How many people are on the ride if all the cars are full?

_____

Use the line plot for 5–6.

5. How many families have exactly 1 computer at home?

_____

6. How many families have more than 1 computer at home?

_____

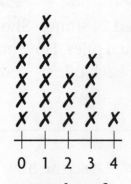

Number of Computers at Home

FOR MORE PRACTICE
GO TO THE
Personal Math Trainer

Name _____

Relate Subtraction and Division

Essential Question How is division related to subtraction?

Learning Objective You will use repeated subtraction and count back on a number line to show how subtraction relates to division.

⚿ Unlock the Problem

Serena and Mandy brought a total of 12 newspapers to school for the recycling program. Each girl brought in one newspaper each day. For how many days did the girls bring in newspapers?

- How many newspapers were brought in altogether?

  _____

- How many newspapers did the two girls bring in altogether each day?

  _____

🔓 One Way Use repeated subtraction.

- Start with 12.

- Subtract 2 until you reach 0.

- Count the number of times you subtract 2.

$$
\begin{array}{cccccc}
12 & 10 & 8 & 6 & 4 & 2 \\
-\,2 & -\,2 & -\,2 & -\,2 & -\,2 & -\,2 \\
\hline
10 & 8 & & & &
\end{array}
$$

Number of times you subtract 2: 1 2 3 4 5 6

 ERROR Alert

Be sure to keep subtracting 2 until you are unable to subtract 2 anymore.

Since you subtract 2 six times,

there are _____ groups of 2 in 12.

So, Serena and Mandy brought in

newspapers for _____ days.

Write: $12 \div 2 = 6$ or $2\overline{)12}^{\,6}$

Read: Twelve divided by two equals six.

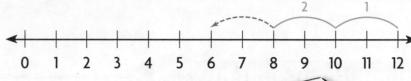
Another Way Count back on a number line.

- Start at 12.
- Count back by 2s as many times as you can. Draw the rest of the jumps on the number line.
- Count the number of times you jumped back 2.

You jumped back by 2 six times.

There are _____ jumps of 2 in 12.

$12 \div 2 = $ _____

Math Talk   Math Processes and Practices 4

Use Diagrams How does using a number line make solving a division problem easier?

- What do your jumps of 2 represent? _____

Share and Show   MATH BOARD

1. Draw the rest of the jumps on the number line to complete the division equation. $12 \div 4 = $ _____

Math Talk   Math Processes and Practices 7

Identify Relationships How is counting back on a number line like using repeated subtraction to solve a division problem?

Write a division equation.

2.
$$\begin{array}{r} 10 \\ -\ 5 \\ \hline 5 \end{array} \qquad \begin{array}{r} 5 \\ -\ 5 \\ \hline 0 \end{array}$$

_____

3.
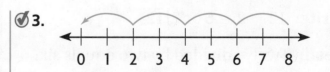

_____

On Your Own

Write a division equation.

4.
$$
\begin{array}{cccc}
28 & 21 & 14 & 7 \\
-\ 7 & -\ 7 & -\ 7 & -\ 7 \\
\hline
21 & 14 & 7 & 0
\end{array}
$$

_____

5.

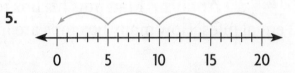

_____

Use repeated subtraction or a number line to solve.

6. $18 \div 6 =$ _____

7. $9\overline{)27}$

8. [THINK SMARTER] Write a word problem that can be solved by using one of the division equations above.

_____

_____

9. Jeff has a booklet of 30 stickers. He uses one page of stickers. If there are 6 stickers on each page, how many pages are left?

_____

10. Tara has 32 beads. She takes out 4 red beads, then sorts the rest into 4 equal groups. How many beads are in each group?

_____

11. [GO DEEPER] Tim has 30 grapes. He keeps 9 grapes for himself. Then he gives 7 grapes each to some of his friends. To how many friends does Tim give grapes?

12. [GO DEEPER] There are 16 dolphins in a pod. Each pod has the same number of males and females. The female dolphins are swimming in pairs. How many pairs of female dolphins are there?

Problem Solving • Applications

Use the graph for 13–15.

13. **Math Processes and Practices 1** **Analyze** Matt puts his box tops in 2 equal piles. How many box tops are in each pile?

_____

14. **THINK SMARTER** Paige brought an equal number of box tops to school each day for 5 days. Alma also brought an equal number of box tops each day for 5 days. How many box tops did the two students bring in altogether each day? Explain.

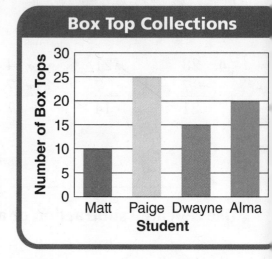

Box Top Collections

_____

_____

_____

15. **GO DEEPER** Dwayne collects another 15 box tops and puts all his box tops into bins. He puts an equal number in each bin. The answer is 5. What's the question?

_____

_____

_____

Personal Math Trainer

16. **THINK SMARTER+** Maya collected 4 box tops each day. She collected 20 box tops in all. For how many days did Maya collect box tops?

Draw jumps on the number line to model the problem.

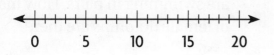

0   5   10   15   20   _____ days

Name _____

Relate Subtraction and Division

Learning Objective You will use repeated subtraction and count back on a number line to show how subtraction relates to division.

Write a division equation.

1.

$$\begin{array}{cccc} 16 & 12 & 8 & 4 \\ -\ 4 & -\ 4 & -\ 4 & -\ 4 \\ \hline 12 & 8 & 4 & 0 \end{array}$$

$$16 \div 4 = 4$$

2.

$$\begin{array}{cccc} 20 & 15 & 10 & 5 \\ -\ 5 & -\ 5 & -\ 5 & -\ 5 \\ \hline 15 & 10 & 5 & 0 \end{array}$$

_____

Use repeated subtraction or a number line to solve.

3. $28 \div 7 =$ _____

4. $18 \div 6 =$ _____

5. $8\overline{)40}$

6. $9\overline{)36}$

Problem Solving Real World

7. Mrs. Costa has 18 pencils. She gives 9 pencils to each of her children for school. How many children does Mrs. Costa have?

_____

8. Boël decides to plant rose bushes in her garden. She has 24 bushes. She places 6 bushes in each row. How many rows of rose bushes does she plant in her garden?

_____

9. **WRITE** ▸ *Math* Explain why you can use subtraction to solve a division problem.

_____

_____

Lesson Check

1. What division equation is shown?

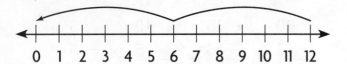

2. Isabella has 35 cups of dog food. She feeds her dogs 5 cups of food each day. For how many days will the dog food last?

_____

_____

_____

_____

Spiral Review

3. Ellen buys 4 bags of oranges. There are 6 oranges in each bag. How many oranges does Ellen buy?

4. Each month for 7 months, Samuel mows 3 lawns. How many more lawns does he need to mow before he has mowed 29 lawns?

_____

_____

Use the graph for 5–6.

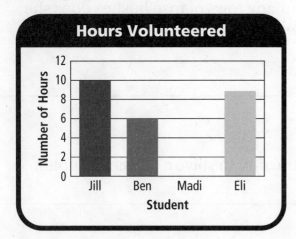

5. How many hours did Eli volunteer?

_____

6. Madi volunteered 2 hours less than Jill. At what number should the bar for Madi end?

_____

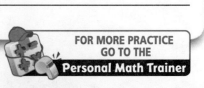

FOR MORE PRACTICE
GO TO THE
Personal Math Trainer

Name _____

Personal Math Trainer
Online Assessment
and Intervention

Vocabulary

Choose the best term from the box to complete
the sentence.

Vocabulary
divide
divisor

1. You _____ when you separate into equal
groups. (p. 307)

Concepts and Skills

Use counters or draw a quick picture on your MathBoard.
Make or circle equal groups. Complete the table.

	Counters	Number of Equal Groups	Number in Each Group
2.	6	2	
3.	30		5
4.	28	7	

Write a division equation for the picture.

5.

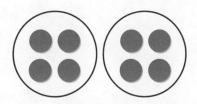

_____

6.

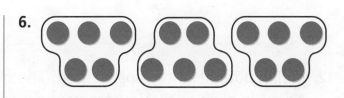

_____

Write a division equation.

7.
$$\begin{array}{r} 36 \\ -\ 9 \\ \hline 27 \end{array} \quad \begin{array}{r} 27 \\ -\ 9 \\ \hline 18 \end{array} \quad \begin{array}{r} 18 \\ -\ 9 \\ \hline 9 \end{array} \quad \begin{array}{r} 9 \\ -\ 9 \\ \hline 0 \end{array}$$

_____

8.

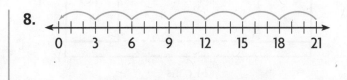

_____

9. Victor plants 14 seeds in some flowerpots. If he puts 2 seeds in each pot, how many flowerpots does he use?

_____

10. 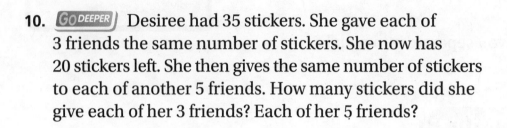 Desiree had 35 stickers. She gave each of 3 friends the same number of stickers. She now has 20 stickers left. She then gives the same number of stickers to each of another 5 friends. How many stickers did she give each of her 3 friends? Each of her 5 friends?

_____

11. Jayden modeled a division equation with some counters. What division equation could Jayden have modeled?

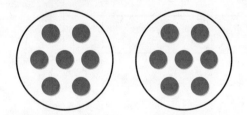

_____

12. Lillian bought 24 cans of cat food. There were 4 cans in each pack. How many packs of cat food did Lillian buy?

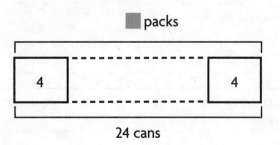

_____

Name _____

Model with Arrays

Learning Objective You will make arrays using square tiles to model division, find equal groups, and write a division equation.

Essential Question How can you use arrays to solve division problems?

Investigate

Materials ■ square tiles

You can use arrays to model division and find equal groups.

A. Count out 30 tiles. Make an array to find how many rows of 5 are in 30.

B. Make a row of 5 tiles.

C. Continue to make as many rows of 5 tiles as you can.

How many rows of 5 did you make? _____

Draw Conclusions

1. Explain how you used the tiles to find the number of rows of 5 in 30.

_____

_____

2. What multiplication equation could you write for the array? Explain.

_____

_____

3. Tell how to use an array to find how many rows of 6 are in 30.

_____

_____

Chapter 6 333

Make Connections

You can write a division equation to show how many rows of 5 are in 30. Show the array you made in Investigate by completing the drawing below.

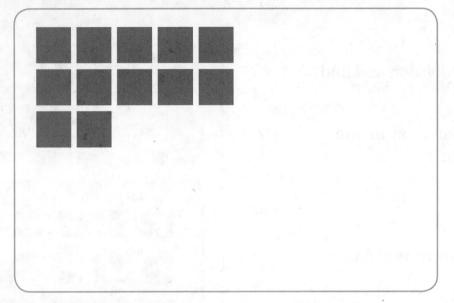

Math Idea
You can divide to find the number of equal rows or to find the number in each row.

$30 \div 5 = $ ▪

There are _____ rows of 5 tiles in 30.

So, $30 \div 5 = $ _____.

Try This!

Count out 24 tiles. Make an array with the same number of tiles in 4 rows. Place 1 tile in each of the 4 rows. Then continue placing 1 tile in each row until you use all the tiles. Draw your array below.

Math Talk

Math Processes and Practices ④

Use Models How does making an array help you divide?

- How many tiles are in each row? _____

- What division equation can you write for your array? _____

© Houghton Mifflin Harcourt Publishing Company

334

Name _____

Share and Show

Use square tiles to make an array. Solve.

1. How many rows of 3 are in 18?

   _____

2. How many rows of 6 are in 12?

   _____

3. How many rows of 7 are in 21?

   _____

4. How many rows of 8 are in 32?

   _____

Make an array. Then write a division equation.

5. 25 tiles in 5 rows

   _____

6. 14 tiles in 2 rows

   _____

7. 28 tiles in 4 rows

   _____

8. 27 tiles in 9 rows

   _____

Problem Solving • Applications

9. **THINK SMARTER** Tell how to use an array to find how many rows of 8 are in 40.

   _____

   _____

10. **Math Processes and Practices 4** **Model Mathematics** Show two ways you could make an array with tiles for 18 ÷ 6. Shade squares on the grid to record the arrays.

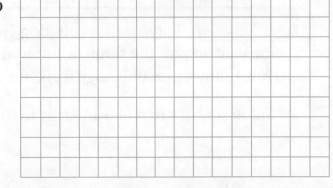

Unlock the Problem

11. **Math Processes and Practices 7** **Look for Structure** Thomas has 28 tomato seedlings to plant in his garden. He wants to plant 4 seedlings in each row. How many rows of tomato seedlings will Thomas plant?

a. What do you need to find? _____

_____

b. What operation could you use to solve the problem? _____

_____

c. Draw an array to find the number of rows of tomato seedlings.

e. Complete the sentences.

Thomas has _____ tomato seedlings.

He wants to plant _____ seedlings in each row.

So, Thomas will plant _____ rows of tomato seedlings.

d. What is another way you could have solved the problem?

_____

_____

12. **GO DEEPER** There were 20 plants sold at a store on Saturday, and 30 plants sold at the store on Sunday. Customers bought 5 plants each. How many customers in all bought the plants?

_____

13. **THINK SMARTER** Paige walked her dog 15 times in 5 days. She walked him the same number of times each day. How many times did Paige walk her dog each day?

Shade squares to make an array to model the problem.

_____ times

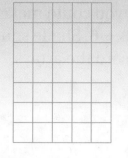

Model with Arrays

Learning Objective You will make arrays using square tiles to model division, find equal groups, and write a division equation.

Use square tiles to make an array. Solve.

1. How many rows of 4 are in 12?

    _____3 rows_____

2. How many rows of 3 are in 21?

    _____

Make an array. Then write a division equation.

3. 20 tiles in 5 rows

    _____

4. 28 tiles in 7 rows

    _____

 Problem Solving *Real World*

5. A dressmaker has 24 buttons. He needs 3 buttons to make one dress. How many dresses can he make with 24 buttons?

    _____

6. Liana buys 36 party favors for her 9 guests. She gives an equal number of favors to each guest. How many party favors does each guest get?

    _____

7. **WRITE** ▶*Math* Draw an array to show how to arrange 20 chairs into 5 equal rows. Explain what each part of the array represents.

    _____

    _____

Lesson Check

1. Mr. Canton places 24 desks in 6 equal rows. How many desks are in each row?

_____

_____

2. Which division equation is shown by the array?

_____

_____

Spiral Review

3. Amy has 2 rows of 4 sports trophies on each of her 3 shelves. How many sports trophies does Amy have?

_____

4. What is the unknown factor?

$$9 \times p = 45$$

_____

5. Sam has 7 stacks with 4 quarters each. How many quarters does Sam have?

_____

6. Skip count. How many counters are there in all?

_____

FOR MORE PRACTICE
GO TO THE
Personal Math Trainer

Name _____

Relate Multiplication and Division

Essential Question How can you use multiplication to divide?

ALGEBRA
Lesson 6.7

Learning Objective You will use bar models and arrays to show the relationship between multiplication and division.

Unlock the Problem (Real World)

Pam went to the fair. She went on the same ride 6 times and used the same number of tickets each time. She used 18 tickets. How many tickets did she use each time she went on the ride?

- **What do you need to find?**

_____

_____

- **Circle the numbers you need to use.**

One Way Use bar models.

You can use bar models to understand how multiplication and division are related.

Complete the bar model to show 18 tickets divided into 6 equal groups.

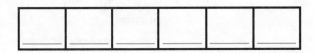

18 tickets

Write: 18 ÷ 6 = _____

So, Pam used _____ tickets each time she went on the ride.

What if the problem said Pam went on the ride 6 times and used 3 tickets each time? How many tickets did Pam use in all?

Complete the bar model to show 6 groups of 3 tickets.

3	3	3	3	3	3

[   ] tickets

Write: 6 × 3 = _____

Multiplication and division are opposite operations, or **inverse operations**.

You can think about multiplication to solve a division problem.

To solve 18 ÷ 6 = ■, think 6 × ■ = 18.

Since 6 × 3 = 18, then 18 ÷ 6 = 3.

Math Talk Math Processes and Practices ⑤

Use a Concrete Model What information is given in each of the bar models?

Chapter 6 339

© Houghton Mifflin Harcourt Publishing Company • Image Credits: ©kali9/Getty Images

1 Another Way Use an array.

You can use an array to see how multiplication and division are related.

Show an array with 18 counters in 3 equal rows by completing the drawing.

There are _____ counters in each row.

Write: 18 ÷ 3 = _____

The same array can be used to find the total number if you know there are 3 rows with 6 counters in each row.

Write: 3 × 6 = _____

Share and Show MATH BOARD

1. Use the array to complete the equation.

   Think: There are 3 counters in each row.

   6 ÷ 2 = _____

Math Talk Math Processes and Practices 3

Apply What is another way to find the quotient for 6 ÷ 2?

Complete.

2.

   3 rows of ____ = 15

   3 × ____ = 15

   15 ÷ 3 = ____

3.

   2 rows of ____ = 12

   2 × ____ = 12

   12 ÷ 2 = ____

4.

   3 rows of ____ = 21

   3 × ____ = 21

   21 ÷ 3 = ____

Complete the equations.

5. 5 × ____ = 40   40 ÷ 5 = ____

6. 6 × ____ = 18   18 ÷ 6 = ____

340

© Houghton Mifflin Harcourt Publishing Company

Name _____

Complete.

7.

5 rows of _____ = 30

5 × _____ = 30

30 ÷ 5 = _____

8.

4 rows of _____ = 20

4 × _____ = 20

20 ÷ 4 = _____

9.

4 rows of _____ = 28

4 × _____ = 28

28 ÷ 4 = _____

Complete the equations.

10. 7 × _____ = 21   21 ÷ 7 = _____

11. 8 × _____ = 16   16 ÷ 8 = _____

Math Processes and Practices 6 **Attend to Precision** **Algebra** **Complete.**

12. 3 × 3 = 27 ÷ _____

13. 16 ÷ 2 = _____ × 2

14. 9 = _____ ÷ 4

15. Justin and Ivan went to the fair when all rides were $2 each. They each went on the same number of rides. Each boy spent $10. How many rides did each boy go on?

_____

16. **GO DEEPER** Roshan has 18 crackers. He shares the crackers equally with his brother. Then Roshan eats 3 crackers. How many crackers does Roshan have left?

_____

17. **GO DEEPER** Paul is in charge of the egg toss at the World Egg Day fair. There are 48 people participating in teams of 8 people. Each team needs 1 egg. Paul is buying eggs in cartons that each have 6 eggs. How many cartons does Paul need?

_____

Problem Solving • Applications

Use the table for 18–19.

<table>
<tr><td colspan="2" align="center">Ventura County Fair</td></tr>
<tr><td colspan="2" align="center">Price of Admission</td></tr>
<tr><td>Adults</td><td>$6</td></tr>
<tr><td>Students</td><td>$3</td></tr>
<tr><td colspan="2" align="center">Children 5 and under free</td></tr>
</table>

18. Mr. Jerome paid $24 for some students to get into the fair. How many students did Mr. Jerome pay for?

_____

19. **THINK SMARTER**   Garrett is 8 years old. He and his family are going to the county fair. What is the price of admission for Garrett, his 2 parents, and baby sister?

_____

20. **Math Processes and Practices 4** **Use a Diagram** There are 20 seats on the Wildcat ride. The number of seats in each car is the same. If there are 5 cars on the ride, how many seats are in each car? Complete the bar model to show the problem. Then answer the question.

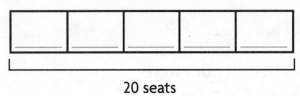

20 seats

21. **GO DEEPER** How many days are there in 2 weeks? Write and solve a related word problem to represent the inverse operation.

_____

22. **THINK SMARTER**   There are 35 prizes in 5 equal rows. How many prizes are in each row?

Complete each equation to represent the problem.

$5 \times \underline{\quad} = 35$ $35 \div 5 = \underline{\quad}$

_____ prizes

342

Relate Multiplication and Division

Learning Objective You will use bar models and arrays to show the relationship between multiplication and division.

Complete.

1.

5 rows of __4__ = 20

5 × __4__ = 20

20 ÷ 5 = __4__

2.

4 rows of _____ = 24

4 × _____ = 24

24 ÷ 4 = _____

3.

3 rows of _____ = 24

3 × _____ = 24

24 ÷ 3 = _____

Complete the equations.

4. 4 × _____ = 28   28 ÷ 4 = _____

5. 6 × _____ = 36   36 ÷ 6 = _____

6. 4 × _____ = 36   36 ÷ 4 = _____

7. 8 × _____ = 40   40 ÷ 8 = _____

 Problem Solving ⟨Real World⟩

8. Mr. Martin buys 36 muffins for a class breakfast. He places them on plates for his students. If he places 9 muffins on each plate, how many plates does Mr. Martin use?

9. Ralph read 18 books during his summer vacation. He read the same number of books each month for 3 months. How many books did he read each month?

_____

_____

10. **WRITE** ▸ *Math* Use examples to show that multiplication and division are inverse operations.

_____

_____

Lesson Check

1. What number will complete the equations?

$$6 \times \blacksquare = 24$$

$$24 \div 6 = \blacksquare$$

_____

2. Alice has 14 seashells. She divides them equally between her 2 sisters. How many seashells does each sister get?

_____

Spiral Review

3. Sam and Jesse can wash 5 cars each hour. They work for 7 hours each day over 2 days. How many cars did Sam and Jesse wash?

_____

4. Keisha skip counted to find how many counters in all. How many equal groups are there?

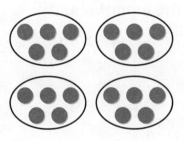

_____ groups of 5

5. The key for a picture graph showing the number of books students read is: Each ▱ = 2 books. How many books did Nancy read if she has ▱▱▱ by her name?

_____

6. Jan surveyed her friends to find their favorite season. She recorded ⅢⅢ for summer. How many people chose summer as their favorite season?

_____

FOR MORE PRACTICE
GO TO THE
Personal Math Trainer

Name _____

Write Related Facts

Essential Question How can you write a set of related multiplication and division facts?

Learning Objective You will make arrays using square tiles then write sets of related multiplication and division facts.

🔑 Unlock the Problem

Related facts are a set of related multiplication and division equations. What related facts can you write for 2, 4, and 8?

 **Activity**

Materials ■ square tiles

> • What model can you use to show how multiplication and division are related?
>
> _____

STEP 1

Use 8 tiles to make an array with 2 equal rows.

Draw the rest of the tiles.

How many tiles are in each row? _____

Write a division equation for the array using the total number of tiles as the dividend and the number of rows as the divisor.

_____ ÷ _____ = _____

Write a multiplication equation for the array.

_____ × _____ = _____

STEP 2

Now, use 8 tiles to make an array with 4 equal rows.

Draw the rest of the tiles.

How many tiles are in each row? _____

Write a division equation for the array using the total number of tiles as the dividend and the number of rows as the divisor.

_____ ÷ _____ = _____

Write a multiplication equation for the array.

_____ × _____ = _____

So, 8 ÷ 2 = _____, 2 × 4 = _____, 8 ÷ 4 = _____,

and 4 × 2 = _____ are related facts.

Try This! Draw an array with 4 rows of 4 tiles.

Your array shows the related facts for 4, 4, and 16.

$4 \times 4 =$ _____ $16 \div 4 =$ _____

Since both factors are the same, there are only two equations in this set of related facts.

• **Math Processes and Practices 6** **Attend to Precision** Write another set of related facts that has only two equations.

_____

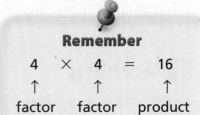
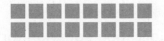 **Share and Show**

1. Complete the related facts for this array.

$2 \times 8 = 16$ $16 \div 2 = 8$

_____   _____

Math Talk   **Math Processes and Practices 7**

Identify Relationships Look at the multiplication and division equations in a set of related facts. What do you notice about the products and dividends?

Write the related facts for the array.

2.

_____

_____

_____

_____

⊘ 3.

_____

_____

_____

_____

⊘ 4.

_____

_____

_____

_____

5. Why do the related facts for the array in Exercise 2 have only two equations?

_____

Name _____

Write the related facts for the array.

6.

_____

_____

_____

7.

_____

_____

_____

8.

_____

_____

_____

Write the related facts for the set of numbers.

9. 2, 5, 10

_____

_____

_____

10. 3, 8, 24

_____

_____

_____

11. 6, 6, 36

_____

_____

_____

Complete the related facts.

12. $4 \times 7 =$ _____

   $7 \times$ _____ $= 28$

   $28 \div$ _____ $= 4$

   $28 \div 4 =$ _____

13. $5 \times$ _____ $= 30$

   $6 \times$ _____ $= 30$

   $30 \div 6 =$ _____

   $30 \div 5 =$ _____

14. _____ $\times 9 = 27$

   _____ $\times 3 = 27$

   _____ $\div 9 = 3$

   $27 \div$ _____ $= 9$

15. Write a set of related facts that has only two equations. Draw an array to show the facts.

_____

16.  Maria has an array with 4 rows of 5 tiles. She wants an array that shows the related facts for 5, 5, and 25. What can she do to change her array?

_____

Problem Solving • Applications

Use the table for 17–18.

Clay Supplies	
Item	**Number in Package**
Clay	12 sections
Clay tool set	11 tools
Glitter dough	36 sections

17. **Math Processes and Practices 3 Verify the Reasoning of Others** Ty has a package of glitter dough. He says he can give each of 9 friends 5 equal sections. Describe his error.

_____

_____

_____

WRITE ▸ Math
Show Your Work

18. **THINK SMARTER** Mr. Lee divides 1 package of clay and 1 package of glitter dough equally among 4 students. How many more glitter dough sections than clay sections does each student get?

_____

19. **GO DEEPER** Ms. Cohn divides 21 markers equally among 7 students. Write an equation to show how many markers each student gets. Then write a related fact.

_____

_____

20. **THINK SMARTER** Select the equations that the array represents. Mark all that apply.

(A) $2 \times 10 = 20$ (D) $20 \div 2 = 10$

(B) $20 \div 4 = 5$ (E) $4 \times 5 = 20$

(C) $5 \times 4 = 20$ (F) $20 \div 5 = 4$

Write Related Facts

Learning Objective You will make arrays using square tiles then write sets of related multiplication and division facts.

Write the related facts for the array.

1.

      $2 \times 6 = 12$

      $6 \times 2 = 12$

      $12 \div 2 = 6$

      $12 \div 6 = 2$

2.

      _____

      _____

      _____

      _____

3.

      _____

      _____

      _____

      _____

Write the related facts for the set of numbers.

4. 3, 7, 21

5. 2, 9, 18

6. 4, 8, 32

7. CDs are on sale for $5 each. Jennifer has $45 and wants to buy as many as she can. How many CDs can Jennifer buy?

    _____

8. Mr. Moore has 21 feet of wallpaper. He cuts it into sections that are each 3 feet long. How many sections does Mr. Moore have?

    _____

9. **WRITE** ▸*Math* Write a division fact. Write the rest of the related facts.

_____

_____

Lesson Check

1. What number completes the set of related facts?

$5 \times \blacksquare = 40$ $40 \div \blacksquare = 5$

$\blacksquare \times 5 = 40$ $40 \div 5 = \blacksquare$

_____

_____

2. Write the related facts for the set of numbers.

4, 7, 28

_____

_____

Spiral Review

3. Beth runs 20 miles each week for 8 weeks. How many miles does Beth run in 8 weeks?

_____

4. Find the product.

5×0

_____

5. Uri's bookcase has 5 shelves. There are 9 books on each shelf. How many books are in Uri's bookcase?

_____

6. There are 6 batteries in one package. How many batteries will 6 packages have?

_____

FOR MORE PRACTICE
GO TO THE
Personal Math Trainer

Name _____

Division Rules for 1 and 0

Essential Question What are the rules for dividing with 1 and 0?

Unlock the Problem

What rules for division can help you divide with 1 and 0?

If there is only 1 fishbowl, then all the fish must go in that fishbowl.

$$4 \div 1 = 4$$

number of fish   number of bowls   number in each bowl

Rule A: Any number divided by 1 equals that number.

Try This! There are 3 fish and 1 fishbowl. Draw a quick picture to show the fish in the fishbowl.

Write the equation your picture shows.

_____ ÷ _____ = _____

Math Talk

Math Processes and Practices ⑦

Identify Relationships Explain how Rule A is related to the Identity Property of Multiplication.

If there is the same number of fish and fishbowls, then 1 fish goes in each fishbowl.

$$4 \div 4 = 1$$

number of fish   number of bowls   number in each bowl

Rule B: Any number (except 0) divided by itself equals 1.

Try This! There are 3 fish and 3 fishbowls. Draw a quick picture to show the fish divided equally among the fishbowls.

Write the equation your picture shows.

_____ ÷ _____ = _____

If there are 0 fish and 4 fishbowls, there will not be any fish in the fishbowls.

$$0 \div 4 = 0$$

number of fish   number of bowls   number in each bowl

Try This! There are 0 fish and 3 fishbowls. Draw a quick picture to show the fishbowls.

Write the equation your picture shows.

_____ ÷ _____ = _____

> **Rule C:** Zero divided by any number (except 0) equals 0.

If there are 0 fishbowls, then you cannot separate the fish equally into fishbowls. Dividing by 0 is not possible.

> **Rule D:** You cannot divide by 0.

Share and Show MATH BOARD

1. Use the picture to find 2 ÷ 2. _____

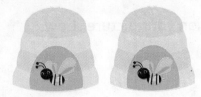

Math Talk   Math Processes and Practices ⑧

Generalize What happens when you divide a number (except 0) by itself?

Find the quotient.

2. $7 \div 1 =$ _____   3. $8 \div 8 =$ _____   ✔4. $0 \div 5 =$ _____   ✔5. _____ $= 6 \div 6$

Name _____

On Your Own

Find the quotient.

6. $0 \div 8 =$ _____   **7.** $5 \div 5 =$ _____   **8.** $2 \div 1 =$ _____   **9.** $0 \div 7 =$ _____

10. $5\overline{)0}$ **11.** $1\overline{)9}$ **12.** $7\overline{)7}$ **13.** $10\overline{)10}$

Practice: Copy and Solve Find the quotient.

14. $6 \div 1$ **15.** $25 \div 5$ **16.** $0 \div 6$ **17.** $18 \div 3$

18. $14 \div 2$ **19.** $9 \div 9$ **20.** $28 \div 4$ **21.** $8 \div 1$

22. $3\overline{)27}$ **23.** $5\overline{)10}$ **24.** $3\overline{)0}$ **25.** $1\overline{)0}$

Problem Solving • Applications

26. *THINK SMARTER* Claire has 7 parakeets. She puts 4 of them in a cage. She divides the other parakeets equally among 3 friends to hold. How many parakeets does each friend get to hold?

_____

27. *GO DEEPER* Lena has 5 parrots. She gives each parrot 1 grape in the morning and 1 grape in the evening. How many grapes does she give to her parrots each day?

_____

28. *Math Processes and Practices 6* Suppose a pet store has 21 birds that are in 21 cages. Use what you know about division rules to find the number of birds in each cage. **Explain** your answer.

_____

_____

29. **THINK SMARTER** For numbers 29a–29c, select True or False for each equation.

29a. $4 \div 4 = 1$ ○ True   ○ False

29b. $6 \div 1 = 1$ ○ True   ○ False

29c. $1 \div 5 = 1$ ○ True   ○ False

Connect to Reading

Compare and Contrast

You have learned the rules for division with 1. Compare and contrast them to help you learn how to use the rules to solve problems.

Compare the rules. Think about how they are *alike*.

Contrast the rules. Think about how they are *different*.

Read: Rule A: Any number divided by 1 equals that number.

Rule B: Any number (except 0) divided by itself equals 1.

Compare: How are the rules alike?

• Both are division rules for 1.

Contrast: How are the rules different?

• Rule A is about dividing a number by 1.
The quotient is that number.

• Rule B is about dividing a number (except 0) by itself.
The quotient is always 1.

Read the problem. Write an equation. Solve.
Write *Rule A* or *Rule B* to tell which rule you used.

30. Jamal bought 7 goldfish at the pet store. He put them in 1 fishbowl. How many goldfish did he put in the fishbowl?

31. Ava has 6 turtles. She divides them equally among 6 aquariums. How many turtles does she put in each aquarium?

Division Rules for 1 and 0

Learning Objective You will use rules and strategies to understand the properties of 0 and 1 in division.

Find the quotient.

1. $3 \div 1 = \underline{\quad 3 \quad}$ 2. $8 \div 8 = \underline{\quad\quad}$ 3. $\underline{\quad\quad} = 0 \div 6$ 4. $2 \div 2 = \underline{\quad\quad}$

5. $\underline{\quad\quad} = 9 \div 1$ 6. $0 \div 2 = \underline{\quad\quad}$ 7. $0 \div 3 = \underline{\quad\quad}$ 8. $\underline{\quad\quad} = 0 \div 4$

9. $7\overline{)7}$ 10. $1\overline{)6}$ 11. $9\overline{)0}$ 12. $1\overline{)5}$

13. $1\overline{)0}$ 14. $4\overline{)4}$ 15. $1\overline{)10}$ 16. $2\overline{)2}$

Problem Solving

17. There are no horses in the stables. There are 3 stables in all. How many horses are in each stable?

    _____

18. Jon has 6 kites. He and his friends will each fly 1 kite. How many people in all will fly a kite?

    _____

19. **WRITE** ▸*Math* Compare and contrast the multiplication rules for 1 and 0 with the division rules for 1 and 0.

_____

_____

Lesson Check

1. Candace has 6 pairs of jeans. She places each pair on its own hanger. How many hangers does Candace use?

   _____

2. There are 0 birds and 4 bird cages. What division equation describes how many birds are in each cage?

   _____

Spiral Review

3. There are 7 plates on the table. There are 0 sandwiches on each plate. How many sandwiches are on the plates?

   $$7 \times 0$$

   _____

   _____

   _____

4. Write one way to break apart the array to find the product.

   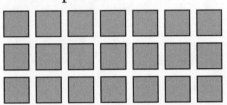

   _____

   _____

   _____

5. Describe a pattern in the table.

Vans	1	2	3	4	5
Students	6	12	18	24	30

   _____

   _____

6. Use the graph.

   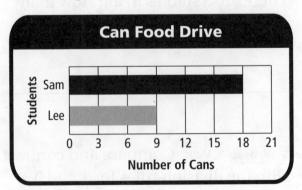

   How many more cans did Sam bring in than Lee?

   _____

   _____

FOR MORE PRACTICE
GO TO THE
Personal Math Trainer

Name _____

✓ Chapter 6 Review/Test

1. For numbers 1a–1d, select True or False for each equation.

    1a. $3 \div 1 = 1$ ○ True   ○ False

    1b. $0 \div 4 = 0$ ○ True   ○ False

    1c. $7 \div 7 = 1$ ○ True   ○ False

    1d. $6 \div 1 = 6$ ○ True   ○ False

2. Elizabeth has 12 horses on her farm. She puts an equal number of horses in each of 3 pens. How many horses are in each pen?

Circle a number that makes the sentence true.

There are
4
9
36
horses in each pen.

3. Chris plants 25 pumpkin seeds in 5 equal rows. How many seeds does Chris plant in each row?

Make an array to represent the problem. Then solve the problem.

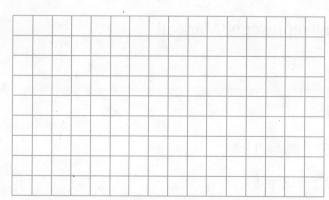

_____ seeds

GO
DIGITAL **Assessment Options**
Chapter Test

© Houghton Mifflin Harcourt Publishing Company

4. Becca spent 24 minutes walking around a track. It took her 3 minutes to walk each time around the track. How many times did Becca walk around the track?

Make equal groups to model the problem. Then explain how you solved the problem.

_____

_____

5. There are 7 cars in an amusement park ride. There are 42 people in the cars. An equal number of people ride in each car. How many people ride in one car?

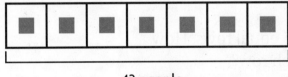

42 people

_____ people

6. Select the equations that the array represents. Mark all that apply.

(A) $3 \times 5 = \blacksquare$

(B) $2 \times \blacksquare = 12$

(C) $\blacksquare \div 3 = 5$

(D) $5 \times \blacksquare = 15$

(E) $12 \div 3 = \blacksquare$

(F) $15 \div 5 = \blacksquare$

Name _____

7. **GO DEEPER** Eduardo visited his cousin for 28 days over the summer. There are 7 days in each week. How long, in weeks, was Eduardo's visit?

Part A
Draw jumps on the number line to model the problem.

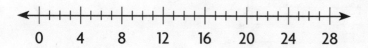

0   4   8   12   16   20   24   28

Part B
Write a division equation to represent the model.

_____

_____ weeks

8. A workbook is 64 pages long. If each chapter is 8 pages long, how many chapters are there?

_____ chapters

9. There are 56 apples packed in 7 baskets with the same number of apples in each basket. How many apples are in each basket?

For numbers 9a–9d, choose Yes or No to tell whether the equation represents the problem.

9a. $56 + 7 = \blacksquare$ ○ Yes   ○ No

9b. $7 \times \blacksquare = 56$ ○ Yes   ○ No

9c. $56 \div \blacksquare = 8$ ○ Yes   ○ No

9d. $56 - \blacksquare = 8$ ○ Yes   ○ No

10. Stefan has 24 photos to display on some posters. Select a way that he could display all of the photos in equal groups on the posters. Mark all that apply.

(A) 6 photos on each of 4 posters   (D) 5 photos on each of 5 posters

(B) 7 photos on each of 3 posters   (E) 3 photos on each of 8 posters

(C) 4 photos on each of 6 posters   (F) 7 photos on each of 4 posters

11. Debbie made this array to model a division equation. Which equation could Debbie have modeled? Mark all that apply.

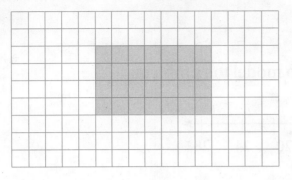

(A) $14 \div 7 = 2$ (C) $28 \div 7 = 4$

(B) $28 \div 4 = 7$ (D) $14 \div 2 = 7$

12. Mrs. Edwards knitted some gloves. Each glove had 5 fingers. She knitted a total of 40 fingers. How many gloves did Mrs. Edwards knit?

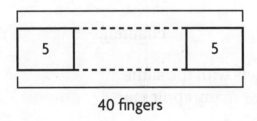

40 fingers

_____ gloves

13. Select a number to complete each equation.

| 0 | 1 | 7 |

$7 \div 7 =$ _____ $7 \div 1 =$ _____ $0 \div 7 =$ _____

14. The coach separated the 18 players at lacrosse practice into 3 equal groups. How many players were in each group?

_____ players

15. Write a division equation to represent the repeated subtraction.

$$\begin{array}{cccc} 32 & 24 & 16 & 8 \\ -\ 8 & -\ 8 & -\ 8 & -\ 8 \\ \hline 24 & 16 & 8 & 0 \end{array}$$

_____

16. Write related facts for the array. Explain why there are not more related facts.

_____

_____

Personal Math Trainer

17. **THINK SMARTER +** Darius bakes 18 muffins for his friends. He gives each of his friends an equal number of muffins and has none left over.

Part A

Draw a picture to show how Darius divided the muffins and complete the sentence.

Darius gave muffins to _____

_____ friends.

Part B

Could Darius have given 4 of his friends an equal number of muffins and have none left over? Explain why or why not.

_____

_____

18. Circle numbers to complete the related facts.

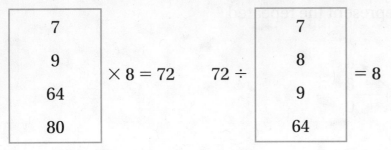

| 7 |
| 9 |
| 64 |
| 80 |

$\times\, 8 = 72$ $\qquad$ $72 \div$

| 7 |
| 8 |
| 9 |
| 64 |

$= 8$

19. Use the numbers to write related multiplication and division facts.

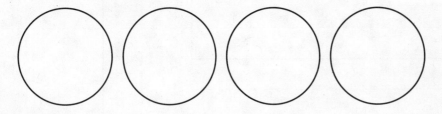

9 $\qquad$ 45 $\qquad$ 5

_____

_____

20. Tyrone took 16 pennies from his bank and put them in 4 equal stacks. How many pennies did Tyrone put in each stack? Show your work.

◯ ◯ ◯ ◯

_____ pennies

Personal Math Trainer
Online Assessment
and Intervention

Chapter 7 Division Facts and Strategies

✓ Show What You Know

Check your understanding of important skills.

Name _____

▶ **Think Addition to Subtract** Write the missing numbers.

1. $10 - 3 = \blacksquare$

Think: $3 + \blacksquare = 10$

$3 + \underline{} = 10$

So, $10 - 3 = \underline{}$.

2. $12 - 8 = \blacksquare$

Think: $8 + \blacksquare = 12$

$8 + \underline{} = 12$

So, $12 - 8 = \underline{}$.

▶ **Missing Factors** Write the missing factor.

3. $2 \times \underline{} = 10$

4. $42 = \underline{} \times 7$

5. $\underline{} \times 6 = 18$

▶ **Multiplication Facts Through 9** Find the product.

6. $\underline{} = 6 \times 9$

7. $3 \times 8 = \underline{}$

8. $4 \times 4 = \underline{}$

Math in the Real World

On Monday, the students in Mr. Carson's class worked in pairs. On Tuesday, the students worked in groups of 3. On Wednesday, the students worked in groups of 4. Each day the students made equal groups with no student left out of a group. How many students could be in Mr. Carson's class?

© Houghton Mifflin Harcourt Publishing Company • Image Credits: ©Radius Images/Alamy Images

Chapter 7 363

Vocabulary Builder

▶ **Visualize It** ••

Sort the review words into the Venn diagram.

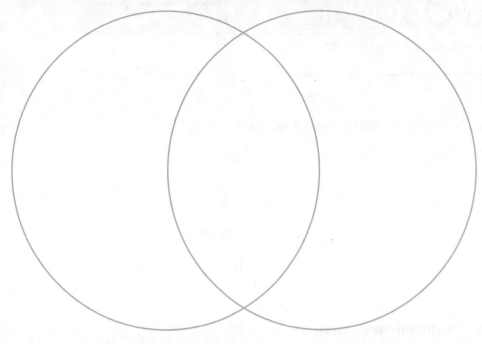

Multiplication Words   **Division Words**

Review Words
divide
dividend
divisor
equation
factor
inverse operations
multiply
product
quotient
related facts

Preview Words
order of operations

▶ **Understand Vocabulary** •••••••••••••••••••••••••••••••

Complete the sentences by using the review and preview words.

1. An _____ is a number sentence that uses the equal sign to show that two amounts are equal.

2. The _____ is a special set of rules that gives the order in which calculations are done to solve a problem.

3. _____ are a set of related multiplication and division equations.

GO DIGITAL
• **Interactive Student Edition**
• **Multimedia eGlossary**

dividend

dividendo

15

divisor

divisor

16

equation

ecuación

22

inverse operations

operaciones inversas

37

order of operations

orden de las
operaciones

55

product

producto

65

quotient

cociente

67

related facts

operaciones
relacionadas

70

The number that divides the dividend

Examples: $32 \div 4 = 8$ $4\overline{)32}$ with quotient 8

↑ divisor   ↑ divisor

The number that is to be divided in a division problem

Examples: $32 \div 4 = 8$ $4\overline{)32}$ with quotient 8

↑ dividend   ↑ dividend

Opposite operations, or operations that undo one another, such as addition and subtraction or multiplication and division

Examples: $16 + 8 = 24$; $24 - 8 = 16$
$4 \times 3 = 12$; $12 \div 4 = 3$

A number sentence that uses the equal sign to show that two amounts are equal

Example: $9 \times 2 = 18$ is an equation

The answer in a multiplication problem

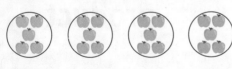

Example: $4 \times 5 = 20$

↑ product

A special set of rules that gives the order in which calculations are done

A set of related addition and subtraction, or multiplication and division, number sentences

Examples: $4 \times 7 = 28$ $28 \div 4 = 7$
$7 \times 4 = 28$ $28 \div 7 = 4$

The number, not including the remainder, that results from division

Example: $35 \div 7 = 5$

↑ quotient

Matchup

For 2–3 players

Materials

- 1 set of word cards

How to Play

1. Put the cards face-down in rows. Take turns to play.
2. Choose two cards and turn them face-up.
   - If the cards show a word and its meaning. it's a match. Keep the pair and take another turn.
   - If the cards do not match, turn them back over.
3. The game is over when all cards have been matched. The players count their pairs. The player with the most pairs wins.

Word Box
dividend
divisor
equation
inverse operations
order of operations
product
quotient
related facts

The Write Way

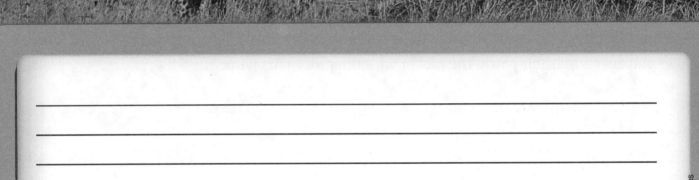

Reflect

Choose one idea. Write about it.

- Do 16 ÷ 8 and 8 ÷ 16 have the same quotient? Explain why or why not.
- Explain the Order of Operations in your own words.
- Write a creative story that includes division by 2, 5, or 10.

_____
_____
_____
_____
_____
_____
_____
_____
_____
_____
_____
_____
_____
_____
_____
_____

Name _____

Divide by 2

Essential Question What does dividing by 2 mean?

Learning Objective You will use counters to model dividing by 2 and write a division equation.

Unlock the Problem

There are 10 hummingbirds and 2 feeders in Marissa's backyard. If there are an equal number of birds at each feeder, how many birds are at each one?

Activity 1

Use counters to find how many in each group.

Materials ■ counters ■ MathBoard

- What do you need to find?

  _____

- Circle the numbers you need to use.
- What can you use to help solve the

  problem? _____

MODEL

- Use 10 counters.
- Draw 2 circles on your MathBoard.
- Place 1 counter at a time in each circle until all 10 counters are used.
- Draw the rest of the counters to show your work.

THINK

_____ in all

_____ equal groups

_____ in each group

RECORD

$$10 \div 2 = 5 \text{ or } 2)\overline{10}^{\,5}$$

Read: Ten divided by two equals five.

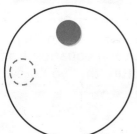 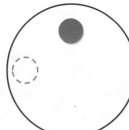

There are _____ counters in each of the 2 groups.

So, there are _____ hummingbirds at each feeder.

► A hummingbird can fly right, left, up, down, forward, backward, and even upside down!

Math Talk

Math Processes and Practices ①

Analyze What does each number in $10 \div 2 = 5$ represent from the word problem?

Chapter 7 365

Activity 2 Draw to find how many equal groups.

There are 10 hummingbirds in Tyler's backyard. If there are 2 hummingbirds at each feeder, how many feeders are there?

MODEL

- Look at the 10 counters.
- Circle a group of 2 counters.
- Continue circling groups of 2 until all 10 counters are in groups.

There are _____ groups of 2 counters.

So, there are _____ feeders.

THINK

_____ in all

_____ in each group

_____ equal groups

RECORD

$$10 \div 2 = 5 \text{ or } 2\overline{)10}^{\,5}$$

Read: Ten divided by two equals five.

Share and Show MATH BOARD

Math Talk

Math Processes and Practices ②

Use Reasoning Explain why you can write more than one division equation from the picture that you drew.

1. Complete the picture to find $6 \div 2$. _____

Write a division equation for the picture.

2.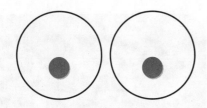

_____

✓3.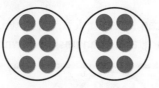

_____

✓4.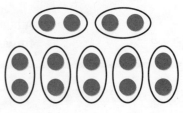

_____

366

Name _____

Write a division equation for the picture.

5.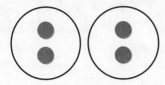

_____

6.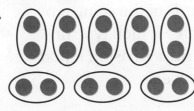

_____

7.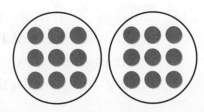

_____

Find the quotient. You may want to draw a quick picture to help.

8. $2 \div 2 = $ ____

9. $16 \div 2 = $ ____

10.
$$2\overline{)20}$$

Math Processes and Practices 2 **Reason Abstractly** **Algebra** **Find the unknown number.**

11. ____ $\div 2 = 5$

12. ____ $\div 2 = 2$

13. ____ $\div 2 = 3$

14. ____ $\div 2 = 8$

15. Lin makes a tile design with 16 tiles. Half of the tiles are red, and half of the tiles are blue. He takes away 4 red tiles. How many red tiles are in the design now?

_____

_____

16. **GO DEEPER** Becky made 2 video tapes while a giant hummingbird fed 4 times and a ruby throated hummingbird fed 8 times from her new feeder. Each video tape caught the same number of feedings by the hummingbirds. How many feedings were shown on each video tape? Justify your answer.

_____

_____

Problem Solving • Applications

Use the table for 17–18.

17. **GO DEEPER** Two hummingbirds of the same type have a total mass of 10 grams. Which type of hummingbird are they? Write a division equation to show how to find the answer.

_____

Hummingbirds	
Type	Mass (in grams)
Magnificent	7
Ruby-throated	3
Violet-crowned	5

18. **THINK SMARTER** There are 3 ruby-throated hummingbirds and 2 of another type of hummingbird at a feeder. The birds have a mass of 23 grams in all. What other type of hummingbird is at the feeder? **Explain**.

WRITE ✏ *Math* • **Show Your Work**

_____

_____

_____

_____

19. **THINK SMARTER** Ryan has 18 socks.

Divisor	Quotient
○ 1	○ 1
○ 2	○ 3
○ 6	○ 9
○ 18	○ 18

Select one number from each column to show the division equation represented by the picture.

$$18 \div \underset{\text{(divisor)}}{\underline{\quad ? \quad}} = \underset{\text{(quotient)}}{\underline{\quad ? \quad}}$$

Name _____

Divide by 2

Learning Objective You will use counters to model dividing by 2 and write a division equation.

Write a division equation for the picture.

1.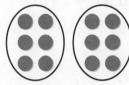

$12 \div 2 = 6$ or _____

$12 \div 6 = 2$ _____

2.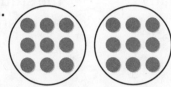

_____

_____

3.

_____

_____

Find the quotient. You may want to draw a quick picture to help.

4. _____ $= 14 \div 2$

5.

6. $16 \div 2 =$ _____

Problem Solving Real World

7. Mr. Reynolds, the gym teacher, divided a class of 16 students into 2 equal teams. How many students were on each team?

_____

8. Sandra has 10 books. She divides them into groups of 2 each. How many groups can she make?

_____

9. **WRITE** ▸Math Explain how to divide an amount by 2. Use the terms *dividend*, *divisor*, and *quotient*.

_____

_____

Lesson Check

1. Ava has 12 apples and 2 baskets. She puts an equal number of apples in each basket. How many apples are in a basket?

2. There are 8 students singing a song in the school musical. Ms. Lang put the students in 2 equal rows. How many students are in each row?

Spiral Review

3. Find the product.

$$2 \times 6$$

4. Jayden plants 24 trees. He plants the trees in 3 equal rows. How many trees are in each row?

5. Describe a pattern in the numbers.

9, 12, 15, 18, 21, 24

6. A tricycle has 3 wheels. How many wheels are there on 4 tricycles?

© Houghton Mifflin Harcourt Publishing Company

FOR MORE PRACTICE
GO TO THE
Personal Math Trainer

Name _____

Divide by 10

Essential Question What strategies can you use to divide by 10?

Learning Objective You will use repeated subtraction, number lines, and the relationship between multiplication and division to divide by 10.

🔑 Unlock the Problem

There are 50 students going on a field trip to the Philadelphia Zoo. The students are separated into equal groups of 10 students each. How many groups of students are there?

- What do you need to find?

  _____

- Circle the numbers you need to use.

🔒 One Way Use repeated subtraction.

- Start with 50.
- Subtract 10 until you reach 0.
- Count the number of times you subtract 10.

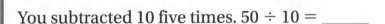

$$\begin{array}{ccccc} 50 & 40 & 30 & 20 & 10 \\ -10 & -10 & -10 & -10 & -10 \\ \hline 40 & 30 & & & \end{array}$$

  1   2   3   4   5

You subtracted 10 five times. $50 \div 10 =$ _____

So, there are _____ groups of 10 students.

🔒 Other Ways

A Use a number line.

- Start at 50 and count back by 10s until you reach 0.
- Count the number of times you jumped back 10.

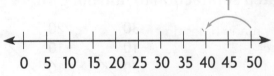

0 5 10 15 20 25 30 35 40 45 50

You jumped back by 10 five times.

$50 \div 10 =$ _____

Math Talk   Math Processes and Practices ③

Compare Representations How is counting on a number line to divide by 10 different from counting on a number line to multiply by 10?

B Use a multiplication table.

Divide. 50 ÷ 10 = ▣

×	0	1	2	3	4	5	6	7	8	9	10
0	0	0	0	0	0	0	0	0	0	0	0
1	0	1	2	3	4	5	6	7	8	9	10
2	0	2	4	6	8	10	12	14	16	18	20
3	0	3	6	9	12	15	18	21	24	27	30
4	0	4	8	12	16	20	24	28	32	36	40
5	0	5	10	15	20	25	30	35	40	45	50
6	0	6	12	18	24	30	36	42	48	54	60
7	0	7	14	21	28	35	42	49	56	63	70
8	0	8	16	24	32	40	48	56	64	72	80
9	0	9	18	27	36	45	54	63	72	81	90
10	0	10	20	30	40	50	60	70	80	90	100

Since division is the opposite of multiplication, you can use a multiplication table to find a quotient.

Think of a related multiplication fact.

▣ × 10 = 50

STEP 1 Find the factor, 10, in the top row.

STEP 2 Look down to find the product, 50.

STEP 3 Look left to find the unknown

factor, _____.

Since _____ × 10 = 50, then 50 ÷ 10 = _____.

In Step 1, is the divisor or the dividend the given factor in the related multiplication fact?

_____

In Step 2, is the divisor or the dividend the product in the related multiplication fact?

_____

The quotient is the unknown factor.

Share and Show MATH BOARD

Math Talk Math Processes and Practices ③

Compare Strategies What are some other strategies besides repeated subtraction to solve 30 ÷ 10?

1. Use repeated subtraction to find 30 ÷ 10. _____

Think: How many times do you subtract 10?

$$\begin{array}{c} 30 \\ -10 \\ \hline 20 \end{array}$$
$$\begin{array}{c} 20 \\ -10 \\ \hline 10 \end{array}$$
$$\begin{array}{c} 10 \\ -10 \\ \hline \blacksquare \end{array}$$

Find the unknown factor and quotient.

2. 10 × ____ = 40   ____ = 40 ÷ 10

3. 10 × ____ = 60   60 ÷ 10 = ____

Find the quotient.

4. ____ = 20 ÷ 10

5. 10)‾5‾0‾

6. 10)‾7‾0‾

7. 90 ÷ 10 = ____

On Your Own

Find the unknown factor and quotient.

8. $10 \times$ ___ $= 70$ $70 \div 10 =$ ___

9. $10 \times$ ___ $= 10$ $10 \div 10 =$ ___

Find the quotient.

10. $50 \div 10 =$ ___

11. ___ $= 60 \div 10$

12. $10\overline{)40}$

13. $10\overline{)80}$

Math Processes and Practices (2) Reason Quantitatively **Algebra** Write $<$, $>$, or $=$.

14. $10 \div 1 \bigcirc 4 \times 10$

15. $17 - 6 \bigcirc 18 \div 2$

16. $4 \times 4 \bigcirc 8 + 8$

17. $23 + 14 \bigcirc 5 \times 8$

18. $70 \div 10 \bigcirc 23 - 16$

19. $9 \times 0 \bigcirc 9 + 0$

20. **GO DEEPER** There are 70 pieces of chalk in a box. If each of 10 students gets an equal number of chalk pieces, how many pieces of chalk does each student get?

_____

21. **GO DEEPER** Elijah wrote his name in 15 school shirts. Cora wrote her name in 15 school shirts. Together they labeled 10 shirts each day. On how many days did Elijah and Cora label shirts?

_____

22. **GO DEEPER** Peyton has 32 cubes. Myra has 18 cubes. If both students use all of the cubes to make trains with 10 cubes, how many trains can they make?

_____

Problem Solving · Applications

Use the picture graph for 23–25.

23. Lyle wants to add penguins to the picture graph. There are 30 stickers of penguins. How many symbols should Lyle draw for penguins?

_____

24. **GO DEEPER** Write a word problem using information from the picture graph. Then solve your problem.

_____

_____

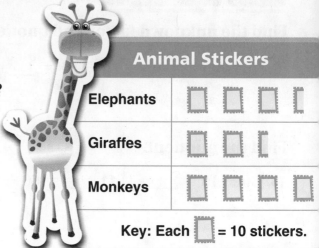

Animal Stickers

Elephants	☐ ☐ ☐ ☐
Giraffes	☐ ☐ ☐
Monkeys	☐ ☐ ☐ ☐

Key: Each ☐ = 10 stickers.

25. **THINK SMARTER** **Sense or Nonsense?** Lena wants to put the monkey stickers in an album. She says she will use more pages if she puts 5 stickers on a page instead of 10 stickers on a page. Is she correct? Explain.

_____

_____

_____

WRITE Math · **Show Your Work**

26. **Math Processes and Practices 6** **Explain** how a division problem is like an unknown factor problem.

_____

_____

_____

27. **THINK SMARTER** Lilly found 40 seashells. She put 10 seashells in each bucket. How many buckets did Lilly use? Show your work.

_____ buckets

Divide by 10

Learning Objective You will use repeated subtraction, number lines, and the relationship between multiplication and division to divide by 10.

Find the unknown factor and quotient.

1. $10 \times \underline{\ 2\ } = 20$ $20 \div 10 = \underline{\ 2\ }$

2. $10 \times \underline{\quad} = 70$ $70 \div 10 = \underline{\quad}$

3. $10 \times \underline{\quad} = 80$ $80 \div 10 = \underline{\quad}$

4. $10 \times \underline{\quad} = 30$ $30 \div 10 = \underline{\quad}$

Find the quotient.

5. $60 \div 10 = \underline{\quad}$

6. $\underline{\quad} = 40 \div 4$

7. $20 \div 2 = \underline{\quad}$

8. $50 \div 10 = \underline{\quad}$

9. $10\overline{)40}$

10. $10\overline{)70}$

11. $10\overline{)100}$

12. $10\overline{)20}$

Problem Solving

13. Pencils cost 10¢ each. How many pencils can Brent buy with 90¢?

14. Mrs. Marks wants to buy 80 pens. If the pens come in packs of 10, how many packs does she need to buy?

_____

_____

15. **WRITE** ▸*Math* Write and solve a word problem that involves dividing by 10.

_____

_____

Lesson Check

1. Gracie uses 10 beads on each necklace she makes. She has 60 beads to use. How many necklaces can Gracie make?

   _____

2. A florist arranges 10 flowers in each vase. How many vases does the florist need to arrange 40 flowers?

   _____

Spiral Review

3. What is the unknown factor?

   $$7 \times p = 14$$

   _____

4. Aspen Bakery sold 40 boxes of rolls in one day. Each box holds 6 rolls. How many rolls did the bakery sell?

   _____

5. Mr. Samuels buys a sheet of stamps. There are 4 rows with 7 stamps in each row. How many stamps does Mr. Samuels buy?

   _____

6. There are 56 students going on a field trip to the science center. The students tour the center in groups of 8. How many groups of students are there?

   _____

FOR MORE PRACTICE
GO TO THE
Personal Math Trainer

Name _____

Divide by 5

Essential Question What does dividing by 5 mean?

Learning Objective You will use counting up and counting back on a number line as strategies to divide by 5.

🔑 Unlock the Problem

Kaley wants to buy a new cage for Coconut, her guinea pig. She has saved 35¢. If she saved a nickel each day, for how many days has she been saving?

> • How much is a nickel worth?
>
> _____

🔒 One Way Count up by 5s.

• Begin at 0.

• Count up by 5s until you reach 35.   0, 5, 10, _____, _____, _____, _____

• Count the number of times you count up.

      1   2   3   4   5   6   7

You counted up by 5 seven times. 35 ÷ 5 = _____

So, Kaley has been saving for _____ days.

🔒 Another Way

Count back on a number line.

• Start at 35.

• Count back by 5s until you reach 0. Complete the jumps on the number line.

• Count the number of times you jumped back 5.

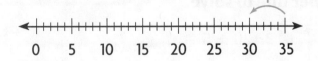

0   5   10   15   20   25   30   35

You jumped back by 5 _____ times.

35 ÷ 5 = _____

Math Talk

Math Processes and Practices ②

Reason Abstractly What if Kaley saved 7¢ each day instead of a nickel? What would you do differently to find how many days she has saved?

Strategies for Multiplying and Dividing with 5

You have learned how to use doubles to multiply. Now you will learn how to use doubles to divide by 5.

Use 10s facts, and then take half to multiply with 5.

When one factor is 5, you can use a 10s fact.

$5 \times 2 = $ ■

First, multiply by 10.

$10 \times 2 = $ _____

After you multiply, take half of the product.

$20 \div 2 = $ _____

So, $5 \times 2 = $ _____ .

Divide by 10, and then double to divide by 5.

When the divisor is 5 and the dividend is even, you can use a 10s fact.

$30 \div 5 = $ ■

First, divide by 10.

$30 \div 10 = $ _____

After you divide, double the quotient.

$3 + $ _____ $ = $ _____

So, $30 \div 5 = $ _____ .

Share and Show MATH BOARD

1. Count back on the number line to find $15 \div 5$. _____

Math Talk   Math Processes and Practices ⑥

Explain how counting up to solve a division problem is like counting back on a number line.

Use count up or count back on a number line to solve.

2. $10 \div 2 = $ _____

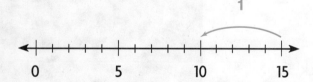

③ 3. $20 \div 5 = $ _____

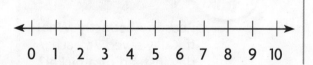

Find the quotient.

4. $50 \div 5 = $ _____   **5.** $5 \div 5 = $ _____   **③ 6.** $45 \div 5 = $ _____

On Your Own

Use count up or count back on a number line to solve.

7. $30 \div 5 =$ _____

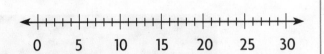

0   5   10   15   20   25   30

8. $25 \div 5 =$ _____

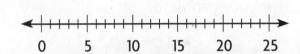

0   5   10   15   20   25

Find the quotient.

9. ____ $= 20 \div 5$ **10.** $40 \div 5 =$ ____   **11.** ____ $= 18 \div 2$ **12.** $0 \div 5 =$ ____

13. $35 \div 5 =$ ____   **14.** ____ $= 10 \div 5$ **15.** $40 \div 10 =$ ____   **16.** ____ $= 4 \div 2$

17. $10\overline{)30}$ **18.** $2\overline{)16}$ **19.** $5\overline{)45}$ **20.** $5\overline{)15}$

Math Processes and Practices ⑦ Look for a Pattern Algebra Complete the table.

21.

×	1	2	3	4	5
10					
5					

22.

÷	10	20	30	40	50
10					
5					

Problem Solving • Applications Real World

23. **Math Processes and Practices ①** **Evaluate** Guinea pigs eat hay, pellets, and vegetables. If Wonder Hay comes in a 5-pound bag and costs \$15, how much does 1 pound of hay cost?

_____

24. **GO DEEPER** Ana picks 25 apples. Pedro picks 20 apples. Ana and Pedro use the apples to make apple pies. They put 5 apples in each pie. How many apple pies can they make?

_____

25. **GO DEEPER** The clerk at a store worked 45 hours one week. He worked an equal number of hours each day on Monday through Friday. He worked an extra 5 hours on Saturday. How many hours did he work on each weekday?

_____

26. **THINK SMARTER** **Pose a Problem** Maddie went to a veterinary clinic. She saw the vet preparing some carrots for the guinea pigs.

Write a division problem that can be solved using the picture of carrots. Draw circles to group the carrots for your problem.

Pose a problem.

Solve your problem.

- Group the carrots in a different way. Then write a problem for the new groups. Solve your problem.

_____

_____

_____

27. **THINK SMARTER** Circle the unknown factor and quotient.

$$5 \times \boxed{\begin{matrix} 5 \\ 6 \\ 7 \end{matrix}} = 35 \qquad \boxed{\begin{matrix} 5 \\ 6 \\ 7 \end{matrix}} = 35 \div 5$$

Divide by 5

Learning Objective You will use counting up and counting back on a number line as strategies to divide by 5.

Use count up or count back on a number line to solve.

1. $40 \div 5 =$ __8__

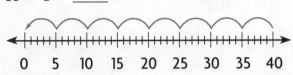

```
0   5   10  15  20  25  30  35  40
```

2. $25 \div 5 =$ ____

```
0     5     10     15     20     25
```

Find the quotient.

3. ____ $= 10 \div 5$

4. ____ $= 30 \div 5$

5. $14 \div 2 =$ ____

6. $5 \div 5 =$ ____

7. ____ $= 0 \div 5$

8. $20 \div 5 =$ ____

9. $25 \div 5 =$ ____

10. ____ $= 35 \div 5$

11. $5\overline{)20}$

12. $10\overline{)70}$

13. $5\overline{)15}$

14. $5\overline{)40}$

Problem Solving Real World

15. A model car maker puts 5 wheels in each kit. A machine makes 30 wheels at a time. How many packages of 5 wheels can be made from the 30 wheels?

_____

16. A doll maker puts a small bag with 5 hair ribbons inside each box with a doll. How many bags of 5 hair ribbons can be made from 45 hair ribbons?

_____

17. **WRITE** ▸ *Math* Write about which method you prefer to use to divide by 5—counting up, counting back on a number line, or dividing by 10, and then doubling the quotient. Explain why.

_____

_____

Lesson Check

1. A model train company puts 5 boxcars with each train set. How many sets can be completed using 35 boxcars?

_____

2. A machine makes 5 buttons at a time. Each doll shirt gets 5 buttons. How many doll shirts can be finished with 5 buttons?

_____

Spiral Review

3. Julia earns $5 each day running errands for a neighbor. How much will Julia earn if she runs errands for 6 days in one month?

_____

4. Marcus has 12 slices of bread. He uses 2 slices of bread for each sandwich. How many sandwiches can Marcus make?

_____

Use the line plot for 5–6.

5. How many students have no pets?

_____

6. How many students answered the question "How many pets do you have?"

_____

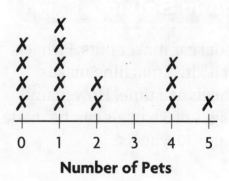

Number of Pets

FOR MORE PRACTICE
GO TO THE
Personal Math Trainer

Name _____

Divide by 3

Essential Question What strategies can you use to divide by 3?

Learning Objective You will use counters to make equal-sized groups and count back on a number line to divide by 3.

Unlock the Problem

For field day, 18 students have signed up for the relay race. Each relay team needs 3 students. How many teams can be made?

- What do you need to find?

  _____

  _____

- Circle the numbers you need to use.

One Way Make equal groups.

- Look at the 18 counters below.

- Circle as many groups of 3 as you can.

- Count the number of groups.

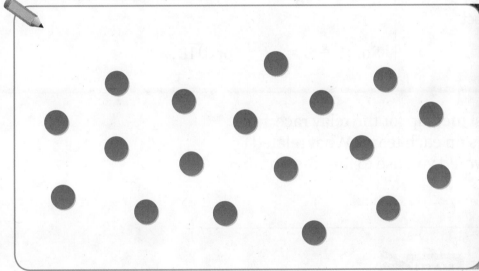

There are _____ groups of 3.

So, _____ teams can be made.

You can write $18 \div 3 =$ _____ or $3)\overline{18}$.

Math Talk

Math Processes and Practices ①

Make Sense of Problems Suppose the question asked how many students would be on 3 equal teams. How would you model 3 equal teams? Would the quotient be the same?

Other Ways

A Count back on a number line.

- Start at 18.

- Count back by 3s as many times as you can. Complete the jumps on the number line.

- Count the number of times you jumped back 3.

ERROR Alert

Be sure to count back the same number of spaces each time you jump back on the number line.

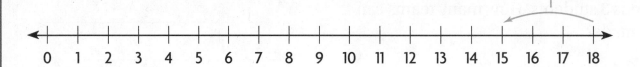

You jumped back by 3 _____ times.

B Use a related multiplication fact.

Since division is the opposite of multiplication, think of a related multiplication fact to find $18 \div 3$.

⬛ × 3 = 18
6 × 3 = 18

Think: What number completes the multiplication fact?

So, $18 \div 3 =$ _____ or $3\overline{)18}$.

- What if 24 students signed up for the relay race and there were 3 students on each team? What related multiplication fact would you use to find the number of teams?

_____

Share and Show MATH BOARD

1. Circle groups of 3 to find $12 \div 3$. _____

Math Talk Math Processes and Practices ④

Model Mathematics What does the number of groups that you circled represent?

Find the quotient.

✓ 2. $6 \div 3 =$ ___   3. ___ $= 14 \div 2$ ✓ 4. $21 \div 3 =$ ___   5. ___ $= 30 \div 5$

On Your Own

Practice: Copy and Solve Find the quotient. Draw a quick picture to help.

6. $9 \div 3$ **7.** $10 \div 5$ **8.** $18 \div 2$ **9.** $24 \div 3$

Find the quotient.

10. ___ $= 12 \div 2$ **11.** $40 \div 5 =$ ___ **12.** $60 \div 10 =$ ___ **13.** ___ $= 20 \div 10$

14. $3\overline{)15}$ **15.** $2\overline{)4}$ **16.** $5\overline{)20}$ **17.** $3\overline{)18}$

Math Processes and Practices ② Use Reasoning **Algebra** Write $+$, $-$, $\times$, or $\div$.

18. $25 \bigcirc 5 = 10 \div 2$

19. $3 \times 3 = 6 \bigcirc 3$

20. $16 \bigcirc 2 = 24 - 16$

21. $13 + 19 = 8 \bigcirc 4$

22. $14 \bigcirc 2 = 6 \times 2$

23. $21 \div 3 = 5 \bigcirc 2$

24. Jem pastes 21 photos and 15 postcards in a scrap album. She puts 3 items on each page. How many pages does Jem fill in the scrap album?

_____

25. GO DEEPER Sue plants 18 pink flowers and 9 yellow flowers in flowerpots. She plants 3 flowers in each flowerpot. How many flowerpots does Sue use?

_____

26. GO DEEPER Blaine makes an array of 12 red squares and 18 blue squares. She puts 3 squares in each row. How many rows does Blaine have in the array?

_____

Problem Solving • Applications

Use the table for 27–28.

Field Day Events	
Activity	Number of Students
Relay race	25
Beanbag toss	18
Jump-rope race	27

27. **GO DEEPER** There are 5 equal teams in the relay race. How many students are on each team? Write a division equation that shows the number of students on each team.

_____

28. **THINK SMARTER** Students doing the jump-rope race and the beanbag toss compete in teams of 3. How many more teams participate in the jump-rope race than in the beanbag toss? **Explain** how you know.

WRITE ▸ *Math*
Show Your Work

_____

29. **Math Processes and Practices ①** **Make Sense of Problems** Michael puts 21 sports cards into stacks of 3. The answer is 7 stacks. What's the question?

_____

30. **THINK SMARTER** Jorge made $24 selling water at a baseball game. He wants to know how many bottles of water he sold. Jorge used this number line to help him.

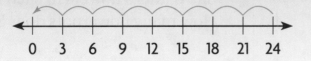

Write the division equation that the number line represents.

_____ ÷ _____ = _____

Divide by 3

Learning Objective You will use counters to make equal-sized groups and count back on a number line to divide by 3.

Find the quotient. Draw a quick picture to help.

1. $12 \div 3 = \underline{\ 4\ }$

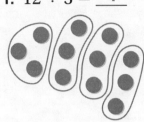

2. $24 \div 3 = \underline{\quad}$

3. $\underline{\quad} = 6 \div 3$

4. $40 \div 5 = \underline{\quad}$

Find the quotient.

5. $\underline{\quad} = 15 \div 3$

6. $\underline{\quad} = 21 \div 3$

7. $16 \div 2 = \underline{\quad}$

8. $27 \div 3 = \underline{\quad}$

9. $0 \div 3 = \underline{\quad}$

10. $9 \div 3 = \underline{\quad}$

11. $\underline{\quad} = 30 \div 3$

12. $\underline{\quad} = 12 \div 4$

13. $3\overline{)12}$

14. $3\overline{)15}$

15. $3\overline{)24}$

16. $3\overline{)9}$

Problem Solving

17. The principal at Miller Street School has 12 packs of new pencils. She will give 3 packs to each third-grade class. How many third-grade classes are there?

_____

18. Mike has $21 to spend at the mall. He spends all of his money on bracelets for his sisters. Bracelets cost $3 each. How many bracelets does he buy?

_____

19. [WRITE] ▶ *Math* Explain how to divide an amount by 3.

_____

_____

Lesson Check

1. There are 18 counters divided equally among 3 groups. How many counters are in each group?

   _____

2. Josh has 27 signed baseballs. He places the baseballs equally on 3 shelves. How many baseballs are on each shelf?

   _____

Spiral Review

3. Each bicycle has 2 wheels. How many wheels do 8 bicycles have?

   _____

4. How many students watch less than 3 hours of TV a day?

   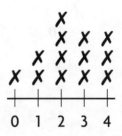

   Hours Watching TV

   _____

5. Complete the number sentence to show an example of the Distributive Property.

   $$3 \times 6 =$$

   _____

   _____

6. What unknown number completes the equations?

   $$3 \times \blacksquare = 21 \qquad 21 \div 3 = \blacksquare$$

   _____

   _____

   _____

   _____

FOR MORE PRACTICE
GO TO THE
Personal Math Trainer

Name _____

Divide by 4

Essential Question What strategies can you use to divide by 4?

Learning Objective You will make arrays using square tiles and make equal-sized groups using counters as strategies to divide by 4.

Unlock the Problem

A tree farmer plants 12 red maple trees in 4 equal rows. How many trees are in each row?

• What strategy could you use to solve the problem?

_____

🔑 One Way Make an array.

• Look at the array.

• Continue the array by drawing 1 tile in each of the 4 rows until all 12 tiles are drawn.

• Count the number of tiles in each row.

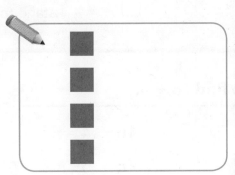

There are _____ tiles in each row.

So, there are _____ trees in each row.

Write: _____ ÷ _____ = _____ or 4)$\overline{12}$

Read: Twelve divided by four equals three.

🔑 Other Ways

Ⓐ **Make equal groups.**

• Draw 1 counter in each group.

• Continue drawing 1 counter at a time until all 12 counters are drawn.

There are _____ counters in each group.

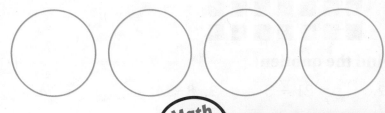

Math Talk Math Processes and Practices ⑥

Compare How is making an array to solve the problem like making equal groups?

B Use factors to find 12 ÷ 4.

The factors of 4 are 2 and 2.

$$2 \times 2 = 4$$

factors   product

To divide by 4, use the factors.

$12 \div 4 = n$

Divide by 2. $12 \div 2 = 6$

Then divide by 2 again. $6 \div 2 = 3$

$12 \div 4 =$ _____

C Use a related multiplication fact.

$12 \div 4 = n$

$4 \times n = 12$

$4 \times 3 = 12$

Think: What number completes the multiplication fact?

$12 \div 4 =$ _____ or $4 \overline{)12}$

Remember

A letter or symbol, like n, can stand for an unknown number.

Try This! Use factors of 4 to find 16 ÷ 4.

The factors of 4 are 2 and 2. $16 \div 4 = $ ■

Divide by 2. $16 \div 2 = $ _____

Then divide by 2 again. $8 \div 2 = $ _____

Think: Dividing by the factors of the divisor is the same as dividing by the divisor.

So, $16 \div 4 = $ _____.

Share and Show   MATH BOARD

1. Use the array to find 28 ÷ 4. _____

Math Talk   Math Processes and Practices ④

Use Models How does using an array help you to find a quotient?

Find the quotient.

2. _____ $= 21 \div 3$ 3. $8 \div 4 = $ _____   4. _____ $= 40 \div 5$ ⊘ 5. $24 \div 4 = $ _____

Find the unknown number.

6. $20 \div 4 = a$ 7. $12 \div 2 = p$ 8. $27 \div 3 = $ ▲   ⊘ 9. $12 \div 4 = t$

$a = $ _____ $p = $ _____   ▲ $= $ _____ $t = $ _____

Name _____

Practice: Copy and Solve Draw tiles to make an array.
Find the quotient.

10. $30 \div 10$ **11.** $15 \div 5$ **12.** $40 \div 4$ **13.** $16 \div 2$

Find the quotient.

14. $12 \div 3 =$ ___   **15.** $20 \div 4 =$ ___   **16.** $4\overline{)16}$ **17.** $5\overline{)25}$

Find the unknown number.

18. $45 \div 5 = b$ **19.** $20 \div 10 = e$ **20.** $8 \div 2 = \blacksquare$ **21.** $24 \div 3 = h$

$b =$ ___ $e =$ ___ $\blacksquare =$ ___ $h =$ ___

Algebra Complete the table.

22.

÷	9	12	15	18
3				

23.

÷	20	24	28	32
4				

Math Processes and Practices 2   **Use Reasoning** **Algebra** Find the unknown number.

24. $14 \div$ ___ $= 7$ **25.** $30 \div$ ___ $= 6$ **26.** $8 \div$ ___ $= 2$ **27.** $24 \div$ ___ $= 8$

28. $36 \div$ ___ $= 9$ **29.** $40 \div$ ___ $= 4$ **30.** $3 \div$ ___ $= 1$ **31.** $35 \div$ ___ $= 7$

32. Mr. Benz arranges 24 music stands in class. He puts the stands in 4 equal rows. How many music stands are in each row?

33. **GO DEEPER** Monty has 16 toy cars in 4 equal groups and 24 toy boats in 3 equal groups. How many more toy boats are in each group than toy cars?

34. **GO DEEPER** Mia puts 15 animal stickers in 3 equal rows in her sticker book. She puts 28 flower stickers in 4 equal rows. How many more flower stickers than animal stickers are in each row?

Problem Solving • Applications

Use the table for 35–36.

35. **GO DEEPER** Douglas planted the birch trees in 4 equal rows. Then he added 2 maple trees to each row. How many trees did he plant in each row?

_____

36. **THINK SMARTER** Mrs. Banks planted the oak trees in 4 equal rows. Mr. Webb planted the dogwood trees in 3 equal rows. Who planted more trees in each row? How many more? Explain how you know.

_____

_____

Trees Planted

Type	Number Planted
Dogwood	24
Oak	28
Birch	16

WRITE ▸ *Math*
Show Your Work

37. **Math Processes and Practices 6** **Use Math Vocabulary** Bryan earns $40 mowing lawns each week. He earns the same amount of money for each lawn. If he mows 4 lawns, how much does Bryan earn for each lawn? Explain how you found your answer.

_____

_____

_____

Personal Math Trainer

38. **THINK SMARTER +** For numbers 38a–38d, select True or False for each equation.

38a. $0 \div 4 = 4$ ○ True   ○ False

38b. $4 \div 4 = 1$ ○ True   ○ False

38c. $20 \div 4 = 6$ ○ True   ○ False

38d. $24 \div 4 = 8$ ○ True   ○ False

Name _____

Divide by 4

Learning Objective You will make arrays using square tiles and make equal-sized groups using counters as strategies to divide by 4.

Draw tiles to make an array. Find the quotient.

1. ___4___ $= 16 \div 4$

2. $20 \div 4 =$ _____

3. $12 \div 4 =$ _____

4. $10 \div 2 =$ _____

Find the quotient.

5. $24 \div 3 =$ _____

6. _____ $= 8 \div 2$

7. $32 \div 4 =$ _____

8. _____ $= 28 \div 4$

9. $4\overline{)36}$

10. $4\overline{)8}$

11. $4\overline{)24}$

12. $3\overline{)30}$

Find the unknown number.

13. $20 \div 5 = a$

14. $32 \div 4 = p$

15. $40 \div 10 = \blacksquare$

16. $18 \div 3 = x$

$a =$ _____

$p =$ _____

$\blacksquare =$ _____

$x =$ _____

Problem Solving Real World

17. Ms. Higgins has 28 students in her gym class. She puts them in 4 equal groups. How many students are in each group?

18. Andy has 36 CDs. He buys a case that holds 4 CDs in each section. How many sections can he fill?

_____

_____

19. **WRITE** ▸*Math* Write and solve a word problem that involves dividing by 4.

_____

_____

Lesson Check

1. Darion picks 16 grapefruits off a tree in his backyard. He puts 4 grapefruits in each bag. How many bags does he need?

2. Tori has a bag of 32 markers to share equally among 3 friends and herself. How many markers will Tori and each of her friends get?

Spiral Review

3. Find the product.

$$3 \times 7$$

4. Describe a pattern below.

8, 12, 16, 20, 24, 28

5. Use the Commutative Property of Multiplication to write a related number sentence.

$$4 \times 5 = 20$$

6. Jasmine has 18 model horses. She places the model horses equally on 3 shelves. How many model horses are on each shelf?

FOR MORE PRACTICE
GO TO THE
Personal Math Trainer

Name _____

Divide by 6

Essential Question What strategies can you use to divide by 6?

Learning Objective You will draw counters to make equal-sized groups and use the relationship between multiplication and division to divide by 6.

 Unlock the Problem

Ms. Sing needs to buy 24 juice boxes for the class picnic. Juice boxes come in packs of 6. How many packs does Ms. Sing need to buy?

- Circle the number that tells you how many juice boxes come in a pack.

- How can you use the information to solve the problem?

_____

_____

_____

One Way Make equal groups.

- Draw 24 counters.

- Circle as many groups of 6 as you can.

- Count the number of groups.

There are _____ groups of 6.

So, Ms. Sing needs to buy _____ packs of juice boxes.

You can write _____ ÷ _____ = _____ or $6\overline{)24}$.

Math Talk Math Processes and Practices ①

Make Sense of Problems If you divided the 24 counters into groups of 4, how many groups would there be?

Chapter 7 395

🔑 Other Ways

Ⓐ Use a related multiplication fact.

dividend divisor quotient

$24 \div 6 = \blacksquare$

$\blacksquare \times 6 = 24$ Think: What number completes the multiplication fact?

$4 \times 6 = 24$

$24 \div 6 = \underline{\quad}$ or $6\overline{)24}$

Ⓑ Use factors to find $24 \div 6$.

The factors of 6 are 3 and 2.

$3 \times 2 = 6$

factors product

To divide by 6, use the factors.

$24 \div 6 = \blacksquare$

Divide by 3. $24 \div 3 = 8$

Then divide by 2. $8 \div 2 = 4$

$24 \div 6 = \underline{\quad}$

- How does knowing $6 \times 9 = 54$ help you find $54 \div 6$?

_____

_____

Share and Show 📝 MATH BOARD

1. Continue making equal groups to find $18 \div 6$. ____

Find the unknown factor and quotient.

Math Talk

Math Processes and Practices ②

Use Reasoning How can you use factors to find $18 \div 6$?

2. ___ $\times 6 = 36$ $36 \div 6 =$ ___

✅**3.** $6 \times$ ___ $= 12$ $12 \div 6 =$ ___

Find the quotient.

4. ___ $= 0 \div 2$ **5.** $6 \div 6 =$ ___   **6.** ___ $= 28 \div 4$ ✅**7.** $42 \div 6 =$ ___

396

On Your Own

Find the unknown factor and quotient.

8. $6 \times$ ____ $= 30$ $30 \div 6 =$ ____

9. ____ $\times 6 = 48$ $48 \div 6 =$ ____

Find the quotient.

10. $12 \div 6 =$ ____

11. ____ $= 6 \div 1$

12. $6\overline{)6}$

13. $2\overline{)10}$

Find the unknown number.

14. $24 \div 6 = n$

$n =$ ____

15. $40 \div 5 = \blacktriangle$

$\blacktriangle =$ ____

16. $60 \div 10 = m$

$m =$ ____

17. $18 \div 6 = \blacksquare$

$\blacksquare =$ ____

Math Processes and Practices ② **Use Reasoning** **Algebra** **Find the unknown number.**

18. $20 \div$ ____ $= 4$

19. $24 \div$ ____ $= 8$

20. $16 \div$ ____ $= 4$

21. $3 \div$ ____ $= 3$

22. $42 \div$ ____ $= 7$

23. $30 \div$ ____ $= 10$

24. $10 \div$ ____ $= 2$

25. $32 \div$ ____ $= 4$

26. Mr. Brooks has 36 students in his gym class. He makes 6 teams. If each team has the same number of students, how many students are on each team?

_____

27. _GO DEEPER_ Sandy bakes 18 pies. She keeps 2 of the pies. She sells the rest of the pies to 4 people at a bake sale. If each person buys the same number of pies, how many pies does Sandy sell to each person?

_____

28. _THINK SMARTER_ Derek has 2 boxes of fruit snacks. There are 12 fruit snacks in each box. If he eats 6 fruit snacks each day, how many days will the fruit snacks last? Explain.

_____

_____

Problem Solving • Applications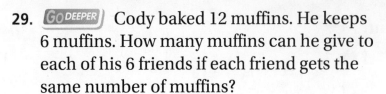

29. **GO DEEPER** Cody baked 12 muffins. He keeps 6 muffins. How many muffins can he give to each of his 6 friends if each friend gets the same number of muffins?

_____

30. **Math Processes and Practices ③** **Make Arguments** Mary has 36 stickers to give to 6 friends. She says she can give each friend only 5 stickers. Use a division equation to describe Mary's error.

_____

_____

_____

WRITE ▸*Math* • **Show Your Work**

31. **WRITE** ▸*Math* **Pose a Problem** Write and solve a word problem for the bar model.

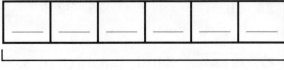

30

_____

_____

_____

_____

Personal Math Trainer

32. **THINK SMARTER +** Each van can transport 6 people. How many vans are needed to transport 48 people to an event? Explain the strategy you used to solve the problem.

_____ vans

Divide by 6

Learning Objective You will draw counters to make equal-sized groups and use the relationship between multiplication and division to divide by 6.

Find the unknown factor and quotient.

1. $6 \times \underline{\ 7\ } = 42$ $42 \div 6 = \underline{\ 7\ }$

2. $6 \times \underline{\ \ \ } = 18$ $18 \div 6 = \underline{\ \ \ }$

3. $4 \times \underline{\ \ \ } = 24$ $24 \div 4 = \underline{\ \ \ }$

4. $6 \times \underline{\ \ \ } = 54$ $54 \div 6 = \underline{\ \ \ }$

Find the quotient.

5. $\underline{\ \ \ } = 24 \div 6$

6. $48 \div 6 = \underline{\ \ \ }$

7. $\underline{\ \ \ } = 6 \div 6$

8. $12 \div 6 = \underline{\ \ \ }$

9. $6\overline{)36}$

10. $6\overline{)54}$

11. $6\overline{)30}$

12. $1\overline{)6}$

Find the unknown number.

13. $p = 42 \div 6$

14. $18 \div 3 = q$

15. $r = 30 \div 6$

16. $60 \div 6 = s$

$p = \underline{\ \ \ }$

$q = \underline{\ \ \ }$

$r = \underline{\ \ \ }$

$s = \underline{\ \ \ }$

Problem Solving

17. Lucas has 36 pages of a book left to read. If he reads 6 pages a day, how many days will it take Lucas to finish the book?

_____

18. Juan has $24 to spend at the bookstore. If books cost $6 each, how many books can he buy?

_____

19. **WRITE** ▸*Math* Which strategy would you use to divide $36 \div 6$? Explain why you chose that strategy.

_____

_____

Lesson Check

1. Ella earned $54 last week babysitting. She earns $6 an hour. How many hours did Ella babysit last week?

_____

2. What is the unknown factor and quotient?

$$6 \times \blacksquare = 42 \qquad 42 \div 6 = \blacksquare$$

_____

Spiral Review

3. Coach Clarke has 48 students in his P.E. class. He places the students in teams of 6 for an activity. How many teams can Coach Clarke make?

_____

4. Each month for 7 months, Eva reads 3 books. How many more books does she need to read before she has read 30 books?

_____

5. Each cow has 4 legs. How many legs do 5 cows have?

_____

6. Find the product.

$$3 \times 9$$

_____

© Houghton Mifflin Harcourt Publishing Company

FOR MORE PRACTICE
GO TO THE
Personal Math Trainer

Name _____

✓ Mid-Chapter Checkpoint

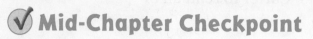

Personal Math Trainer
Online Assessment
and Intervention

Concepts and Skills

1. **Explain** how to find 20 ÷ 4 by making an array.

   _____

   _____

   _____

2. **Explain** how to find 30 ÷ 6 by making equal groups.

   _____

   _____

   _____

   _____

Find the unknown factor and quotient.

3. $10 \times$ ___ $= 50$ ___ $= 50 \div 10$

4. $2 \times$ ___ $= 16$ ___ $= 16 \div 2$

5. $2 \times$ ___ $= 20$ ___ $= 20 \div 2$

6. $5 \times$ ___ $= 20$ ___ $= 20 \div 5$

Find the quotient.

7. ___ $= 6 \div 6$

8. $21 \div 3 =$ ___

9. ___ $= 0 \div 3$

10. $36 \div 4 =$ ___

11. $5\overline{)35}$ 12. $4\overline{)24}$ 13. $6\overline{)54}$ 14. $3\overline{)9}$

15. Carter has 18 new books. He plans to read 3 of them each week. How many weeks will it take Carter to read all of his new books?

_____

16. GO DEEPER Gabriella made 5 waffles for breakfast. She has 25 strawberries and 15 blueberries to put on top of the waffles. She will put an equal number of berries on each waffle. How many berries will Gabriella put on each waffle?

_____

17. There are 60 people at the fair waiting in line for a ride. Each car in the ride can hold 10 people. Write an equation that could be used to find the number of cars needed to hold all 60 people.

_____

18. Alyssa has 4 cupcakes. She gives 2 cupcakes to each of her cousins. How many cousins does Alyssa have?

_____

Name _____

Divide by 7

Essential Question What strategies can you use to divide by 7?

Learning Objective You will make arrays using square tiles, use the relationship between multiplication and division, and draw counters to make equal-sized groups to divide by 7.

🔑 Unlock the Problem Real World

 Hands On

Yasmin used 28 large apples to make 7 loaves of apple bread. She used the same number of apples for each loaf. How many apples did Yasmin use for each loaf?

- Do you need to find the number of equal groups or the number in each group?

  _____

- What label will your answer have?

  _____

🔒 One Way Make an array.

- Draw 1 tile in each of 7 rows.

- Continue drawing 1 tile in each of the 7 rows until all 28 tiles are drawn.

- Count the number of tiles in each row.

There are _____ tiles in each row.

So, Yasmin used _____ for each loaf.

You can write $28 \div 7 =$ _____ or $7\overline{)28}$.

 Math Talk Math Processes and Practices ①

Make Sense of Problems Why can you use division to solve the problem?

🚀 Other Ways

Ⓐ Use a related multiplication fact.

$28 \div 7 = a$ $7 \times a = 28$ **Think:** What number $28 \div 7 =$ _____ or $7\overline{)28}$
                            $7 \times 4 = 28$ completes the
                                                        multiplication fact?

Ⓑ Make equal groups.

- Draw 7 circles to
  show 7 groups.

- Draw 1 counter in
  each group.

- Continue drawing
  1 counter at a time
  until all 28 counters
  are drawn.

There are _____ counters in each group.

Share and Show

1. Use the related multiplication fact to find $42 \div 7$.
   $6 \times 7 = 42$

   $42 \div 7 =$ _____

Math Talk   **Math Processes and Practices ⑧**

Generalize Why can
you use a related
multiplication fact
to solve a division
problem?

Find the unknown factor and quotient.

2. $7 \times$ _____ $= 7$ $7 \div 7 =$ _____   ✓ 3. $7 \times$ _____ $= 35$ $35 \div 7 =$ _____

Find the quotient.

4. $4 \div 2 =$ _____   5. $56 \div 7 =$ _____   6. _____ $= 20 \div 5$ ✓ 7. _____ $= 21 \div 7$

Name _____

Find the unknown factor and quotient.

8. $3 \times$ _____ $= 9$ _____ $= 9 \div 3$

9. $7 \times$ _____ $= 49$ $49 \div 7 =$ _____

Find the quotient.

10. $48 \div 6 =$ _____ **11.** $7 \div 1 =$ _____ **12.** $7\overline{)21}$ **13.** $2\overline{)8}$

Find the unknown number.

14. $60 \div 10 = \blacksquare$ **15.** $70 \div 7 = k$ **16.** $m = 63 \div 9$ **17.** $r = 12 \div 6$

$\blacksquare =$ _____ $k =$ _____ $m =$ _____ $r =$ _____

Math Processes and Practices 6 **Make Connections** **Algebra** **Complete the table.**

18.

÷	18	30	24	36
6				

19.

÷	56	42	49	35
7				

20. Clare bought 35 peaches to make peach jam. She uses 7 peaches for each jar of jam. How many jars can Clare make?

21. There are 49 jars of peach salsa packed into 7 gift boxes. If each box has the same number of jars of salsa, how many jars are in each box?

_____

_____

22. **GO DEEPER** There are 31 girls and 25 boys in the marching band. When the band marches, they are in 7 rows. How many people are in each row?

23. **GO DEEPER** Ed has 42 red beads and 28 blue beads. He uses an equal number of all the beads to decorate each of 7 clay sculptures. How many beads are on each sculpture?

_____

_____

Unlock the Problem

24. THINK SMARTER Gavin sold 21 bagels to 7 different people. Each person bought the same number of bagels. How many bagels did Gavin sell to each person?

a. What do you need to find? _____

_____

b. How can you use a bar model to help you decide which

operation to use to solve the problem? _____

_____

_____

c. Complete the bar model to help you find the number of bagels Gavin sold to each person.

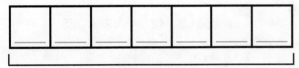

21 bagels

d. What is another way you could have solved the problem?

_____

_____

e. Complete the sentences.

Gavin sold _____ bagels to _____ different people.

Each person bought the same number

of _____.

So, Gavin sold _____ bagels to each person.

---

25. GO DEEPER There are 35 plain bagels and 42 wheat bagels on 7 shelves in the bakery. Each shelf has the same number of plain bagels and the same number of wheat bagels. How many bagels are on each shelf?

_____

26. THINK SMARTER Write the correct symbol that makes the equations true.

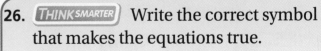

$28 = 7\ \boxed{}\ 4$ $42\ \boxed{}\ 7 = 35$

$7 = 49\ \boxed{}\ 7$

Name _____

Divide by 7

Learning Objective You will make arrays using square tiles, use the relationship between multiplication and division, and draw counters to make equal-sized groups to divide by 7.

Find the unknown factor and quotient.

1. $7 \times \underline{\quad 6 \quad} = 42$ $42 \div 7 = \underline{\quad 6 \quad}$

2. $7 \times \underline{\qquad} = 35$ $35 \div 7 = \underline{\qquad}$

3. $7 \times \underline{\qquad} = 7$ $7 \div 7 = \underline{\qquad}$

4. $5 \times \underline{\qquad} = 20$ $20 \div 5 = \underline{\qquad}$

Find the quotient.

5. $7\overline{)21}$

6. $7\overline{)14}$

7. $6\overline{)48}$

8. $7\overline{)63}$

9. $\underline{\qquad} = 35 \div 7$

10. $0 \div 7 = \underline{\qquad}$

11. $\underline{\qquad} = 56 \div 7$

12. $32 \div 8 = \underline{\qquad}$

Find the unknown number.

13. $56 \div 7 = e$

$e = \underline{\qquad}$

14. $k = 32 \div 4$

$k = \underline{\qquad}$

15. $g = 49 \div 7$

$g = \underline{\qquad}$

16. $28 \div 7 = s$

$s = \underline{\qquad}$

 Problem Solving *Real World*

17. Twenty-eight players sign up for basketball. The coach puts 7 players on each team. How many teams are there?

18. Roberto read 42 books over 7 months. He read the same number of books each month. How many books did Roberto read each month?

_____

_____

19. **WRITE** ▸*Math* Describe how to find the number of weeks equal to 56 days.

_____

_____

Lesson Check

1. Elliot earned $49 last month walking his neighbor's dog. He earns $7 each time he walks the dog. How many times did Elliot walk his neighbor's dog last month?

_____

2. What is the unknown factor and quotient?

$$7 \times \blacksquare = 63$$

$$63 \div 7 = \blacksquare$$

_____

Spiral Review

3. Maria puts 6 strawberries in each smoothie she makes. She makes 3 smoothies. Altogether, how many strawberries does Maria use in the smoothies?

_____

4. Kaitlyn makes 4 bracelets. She uses 8 beads for each bracelet. How many beads does she use?

_____

5. What is the unknown factor?

$$2 \times 5 = 5 \times \blacksquare$$

_____

_____

6. What division equation is related to the following multiplication equation?

$$3 \times 4 = 12$$

_____

_____

FOR MORE PRACTICE
GO TO THE
Personal Math Trainer

Name ______________________________

Lesson 7.8

Divide by 8

Essential Question What strategies can you use to divide by 8?

Learning Objective You will use repeated subtraction and the relationship between multiplication and division to divide by 8.

Unlock the Problem (Real World)

At Stephen's camping store, firewood is sold in bundles of 8 logs. He has 32 logs to put in bundles. How many bundles of firewood can he make?

- What will Stephen do with the 32 logs?

____

____

One Way Use repeated subtraction.

- Start with 32.
- Subtract 8 until you reach 0.
- Count the number of times you subtract 8.

$$\begin{array}{r} 32 \\ -\ 8 \\ \hline 24 \end{array} \quad \begin{array}{r} 24 \\ -\ 8 \\ \hline \square \end{array} \quad \begin{array}{r} \square \\ -\ 8 \\ \hline \square \end{array} \quad \begin{array}{r} \square \\ -\ 8 \\ \hline \square \end{array}$$

Number of times you subtract 8: 1 2 3 4

ERROR Alert

Continue to subtract the divisor, 8, until the difference is less than 8.

You subtracted 8 _____ times.

So, Stephen can make _____ bundles of firewood.

You can write 32 ÷ 8 = _____ or 8)32.

Another Way Use a related multiplication fact.

32 ÷ 8 = ▢ ▢ × 8 = 32

4 × 8 = 32

Think: What number completes the multiplication fact?

32 ÷ 8 = _____ or 8)32

Math Talk Math Processes and Practices 1

Make Sense of Problems How does knowing 4 × 8 = 32 help you find 32 ÷ 8?

Example Find the unknown divisor.

Stephen has a log that is 16 feet long. If he cuts the log into pieces that are 2 feet long, how many pieces will Stephen have?

Divide. 16 ÷ ▨ = 2

You can also use a multiplication table to find the divisor in a division problem.

Think: ▨ × 2 = 16

STEP 1 Find the factor, 2, in the top row.

STEP 2 Look down to find the product, 16.

STEP 3 Look left to find the unknown factor.

The unknown factor is _____.

▨ = _____

_____ × 2 = 16   Check.

_____ = 16 ✓   The equation is true.

So, Stephen will have _____ pieces.

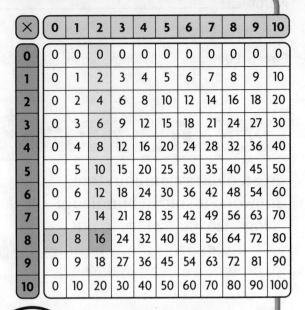

×	0	1	2	3	4	5	6	7	8	9	10
0	0	0	0	0	0	0	0	0	0	0	0
1	0	1	2	3	4	5	6	7	8	9	10
2	0	2	4	6	8	10	12	14	16	18	20
3	0	3	6	9	12	15	18	21	24	27	30
4	0	4	8	12	16	20	24	28	32	36	40
5	0	5	10	15	20	25	30	35	40	45	50
6	0	6	12	18	24	30	36	42	48	54	60
7	0	7	14	21	28	35	42	49	56	63	70
8	0	8	16	24	32	40	48	56	64	72	80
9	0	9	18	27	36	45	54	63	72	81	90
10	0	10	20	30	40	50	60	70	80	90	100

Math Talk   Math Processes and Practices ⑤

Use Patterns How do you know how to use the multiplication table to find the unknown dividend for ▨ ÷ 8 = 5?

Share and Show MATH BOARD

Math Talk   Math Processes and Practices ⑥

Describe why you subtract 8 from 24 to find 24 ÷ 8.

1. Use repeated subtraction to find 24 ÷ 8. _____

$$\begin{array}{ccc} 24 & 16 & 8 \\ -\ 8 & -\ 8 & -\ 8 \\ \hline 16 & 8 & 0 \end{array}$$

Think: How many times do you subtract 8?

Find the unknown factor and quotient.

2. 8 × _____ = 56   56 ÷ 8 = _____   ✓3. _____ × 8 = 40   40 ÷ 8 = _____

Find the quotient.

4. 18 ÷ 3 = _____   5. _____ = 48 ÷ 8   6. 56 ÷ 7 = _____   ✓7. _____ = 32 ÷ 8

Name _____

Find the unknown factor and quotient.

8. $6 \times$ ____ $= 18$ $18 \div 6 =$ ____ | 9. $8 \times$ ____ $= 72$ ____ $= 72 \div 8$

Find the quotient.

10. $28 \div 4 =$ ____   11. $42 \div 7 =$ ____   12. $8\overline{)64}$ 13. $1\overline{)8}$

Find the unknown number.

14. $16 \div p = 8$ 15. $t \div 8 = 2$ 16. $64 \div \triangle = 8$ 17. $m \div 8 = 10$

$p =$ ____ $t =$ ____ $\triangle =$ ____ $m =$ ____

18. $\triangle \div 2 = 10$ 19. $40 \div \blacksquare = 8$ 20. $25 \div k = 5$ 21. $54 \div n = 9$

$\triangle =$ ____ $\blacksquare =$ ____ $k =$ ____ $n =$ ____

22. **Math Processes and Practices 2** **Connect Symbols and Words** Write a word problem that can be solved by using one of the division facts above.

_____

_____

Math Processes and Practices 4 **Use Symbols** **Algebra** Write $+$, $-$, $\times$, or $\div$.

23. $6 \times 6 = 32 \bigcirc 4$ | 24. $12 \bigcirc 3 = 19 - 15$ | 25. $40 \div 8 = 35 \bigcirc 7$

26. **GO DEEPER** Kyle has 4 packs of baseball cards. Each pack has 12 cards. If Kyle wants to share the cards equally among himself and his 7 friends, how many baseball cards will each person get?

_____

Problem Solving • Applications

Use the table for 27–28.

Tent Sizes	
Type	**Number of People**
Cabin	10
Vista	8
Trail	4

27. **GO DEEPER** There are 32 people who plan to camp over the weekend. Describe two different ways the campers can sleep using 4 tents.

_____

_____

_____

WRITE Math · **Show Your Work** · · ·

28. **THINK SMARTER** There are 36 people camping at Max's family reunion. They have cabin tents and vista tents. How many of each type of tent do they need to sleep exactly 36 people if each tent is filled? Explain.

_____

_____

_____

29. Josh is dividing 64 bags of trail mix equally among 8 campers. How many bags of trail mix will each camper get?

_____

30. **THINK SMARTER** Circle the unknown factor and quotient.

$$8 \times \boxed{\begin{array}{c} 6 \\ 7 \\ 8 \end{array}} = 48 \qquad \boxed{\begin{array}{c} 6 \\ 7 \\ 8 \end{array}} = 48 \div 8$$

Name _____

Divide by 8

Learning Objective You will use repeated subtraction and the relationship between multiplication and division to divide by 8.

Find the unknown factor and quotient.

1. $8 \times \underline{\ 4\ } = 32$ $32 \div 8 = \underline{\ \ \ \ }$

2. $3 \times \underline{\ \ \ \ } = 27$ $27 \div 3 = \underline{\ \ \ \ }$

3. $8 \times \underline{\ \ \ \ } = 8$ $8 \div 8 = \underline{\ \ \ \ }$

4. $8 \times \underline{\ \ \ \ } = 72$ $72 \div 8 = \underline{\ \ \ \ }$

Find the quotient.

5. $\underline{\ \ \ \ } = 24 \div 8$

6. $40 \div 8 = \underline{\ \ \ \ }$

7. $\underline{\ \ \ \ } = 56 \div 8$

8. $14 \div 2 = \underline{\ \ \ \ }$

9. $8\overline{)64}$

10. $7\overline{)28}$

11. $8\overline{)16}$

12. $8\overline{)48}$

Find the unknown number.

13. $72 \div \blacksquare = 9$

14. $25 \div \blacksquare = 5$

15. $24 \div a = 3$

16. $k \div 10 = 8$

$\blacksquare = \underline{\ \ \ \ }$

$\blacksquare = \underline{\ \ \ \ }$

$a = \underline{\ \ \ \ }$

$k = \underline{\ \ \ \ }$

Problem Solving Real World

17. Sixty-four students are going on a field trip. There is 1 adult for every 8 students. How many adults are there?

_____

18. Mr. Chen spends $32 for tickets to a play. If the tickets cost $8 each, how many tickets does Mr. Chen buy?

_____

19. **WRITE** ▸Math Describe which strategy you would use to divide 48 by 8.

_____

_____

Lesson Check

1. Mrs. Wilke spends $72 on pies for the school fair. Each pie costs $8. How many pies does Mrs. Wilke buy for the school fair?

_____

2. Find the unknown factor and quotient.

$$8 \times \blacksquare = 40$$

$$40 \div 8 = \blacksquare$$

_____

Spiral Review

3. Find the product.

$$(3 \times 2) \times 5$$

_____

4. Use the Commutative Property of Multiplication to write a related multiplication sentence.

$$9 \times 4 = 36$$

_____

5. Find the unknown factor.

$$8 \times \blacksquare = 32$$

_____

6. What multiplication sentence represents the array?

_____

_____

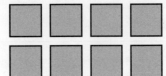

© Houghton Mifflin Harcourt Publishing Company

FOR MORE PRACTICE
GO TO THE
Personal Math Trainer

Divide by 9

Essential Question What strategies can you use to divide by 9?

Lesson 7.9

Learning Objective You will use equal-sized groups and the relationship between multiplication and division to divide by 9.

Unlock the Problem

Becket's class goes to the aquarium. The 27 students from the class are separated into 9 equal groups. How many students are in each group?

• Do you need to find the number of equal groups or the number in each group?

_____

🔑 One Way Make equal groups.

• Draw 9 circles to show 9 groups.

• Draw 1 counter in each group.

• Continue drawing 1 counter at a time until all 27 counters are drawn.

There are _____ counters in each group.

So, there are _____ in each group.

You can write $27 \div 9 =$ _____ or $9\overline{)27}$.

Math Processes and Practices ②

Reason Quantitatively
What is another way you could solve the problem?

🔓 Other Ways

A Use factors to find 27 ÷ 9.

The factors of 9 are 3 and 3.

$$3 \ \times \ 3 \ = \ 9$$

factors product

To divide by 9, use the factors.

27 ÷ 9 = s

Divide by 3.   27 ÷ 3 = 9

Then divide by 3 again.   9 ÷ 3 = 3

27 ÷ 9 = _____

B Use a related multiplication fact.

27 ÷ 9 = s

9 × s = 27   **Think:** What number completes the multiplication fact?

9 × 3 = 27

27 ÷ 9 = _____ or 9)27

• What multiplication fact can you use to find 63 ÷ 9? _____

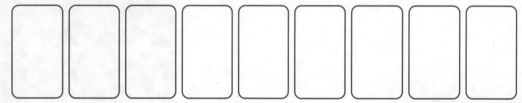
Share and Show MATH BOARD

1. Draw counters in the groups to find 18 ÷ 9. _____

Math Talk   Math Processes and Practices ❸

Apply How would you use factors to find 18 ÷ 9?

Find the quotient.

2. ____ = 45 ÷ 9   **3.** 36 ÷ 6 = ____   **4.** 9 ÷ 1 = ____   ✅**5.** ____ = 54 ÷ 9

6. 7)28   **7.** 9)9   **8.** 5)40   ✅**9.** 9)36

Name _____

10. ____ = 36 ÷ 4   **11.** ____ = 72 ÷ 9   **12.** 81 ÷ 9 = ____   **13.** ____ = 27 ÷ 9

14. 4)‾12‾   **15.** 9)‾63‾   **16.** 2)‾16‾   **17.** 5)‾25‾

Find the unknown number.

18. 64 ÷ 8 = e   **19.** 0 ÷ 9 = g   **20.** ■ = 20 ÷ 4   **21.** s = 9 ÷ 9

e = ____   g = ____   ■ = ____   s = ____

Math Processes and Practices ② Use Reasoning **Algebra** Complete the table.

22.

÷	24	40	32	48
8				

23.

÷	54	45	72	63
9				

24. Baseball games have 9 innings. The Little Tigers played 72 innings last season. How many games did the Little Tigers play last year?

_____

25. **GO DEEPER** Sophie has two new fish. She feeds one fish 4 pellets and the other fish 5 pellets each day. If Sophie has fed her fish 72 pellets, for how many days has she had her fish? Explain.

_____

_____

26. **Math Processes and Practices ④** Write an Equation Each van going to the aquarium carries 9 students. If 63 third-grade students go to the aquarium, what multiplication fact can you use to find the number of vans that will be needed?

_____

Unlock the Problem ⓇWorld

27. **THINK SMARTER** Carlos has 28 blue tang fish and 17 yellow tang fish in one large fish tank. He wants to separate the fish so that there are the same number of fish in each of 9 smaller tanks. How many tang fish will Carlos put in each smaller tank?

a. What do you need to find? _____

_____

b. Why do you need to use two operations to solve the problem? _____

_____

c. Write the steps to find how many tang fish Carlos will put in each smaller tank.

d. Complete the sentences.

Carlos has ____ blue tang fish

and ____ yellow tang fish in one large fish tank.

He wants to separate the fish so that there are the same number

of fish in each of ____ smaller tanks.

So, Carlos will put ____ fish in each smaller tank.

28. **THINK SMARTER** Complete the chart to show the quotients.

÷	27	18	45	36
9				

Divide by 9

Learning Objective You will use equal-sized groups and the relationship between multiplication and division to divide by 9.

Find the quotient.

1. __4__ = 36 ÷ 9   **2.** 30 ÷ 6 = _____   **3.** _____ = 81 ÷ 9   **4.** 27 ÷ 9 = _____

5. 9 ÷ 9 = _____   **6.** _____ = 63 ÷ 7   **7.** 36 ÷ 6 = _____   **8.** _____ = 90 ÷ 9

9. $9\overline{)63}$ **10.** $9\overline{)18}$ **11.** $7\overline{)49}$ **12.** $9\overline{)45}$

Find the unknown number.

13. 48 ÷ 8 = g   **14.** s = 72 ÷ 9   **15.** m = 0 ÷ 9   **16.** 54 ÷ 9 = n

g = _____   s = _____   m = _____   n = _____

Problem Solving

17. A crate of oranges has trays inside that hold 9 oranges each. There are 72 oranges in the crate. If all trays are filled, how many trays are there?

18. Van has 45 new baseball cards. He puts them in a binder that holds 9 cards on each page. How many pages does he fill?

_____   _____

19. WRITE ▸ *Math* Explain which division facts were the easiest for you to learn.

_____

_____

Lesson Check

1. Darci sets up a room for a banquet. She has 54 chairs. She places 9 chairs at each table. How many tables have 9 chairs?

2. Mr. Robinson sets 36 glasses on a table. He puts the same number of glasses in each of 9 rows. How many glasses does he put in each row?

Spiral Review

3. Each month for 9 months, Jordan buys 2 sports books. How many more sports books does he need to buy before he has bought 25 sports books?

4. Find the product.

$$\begin{array}{r} 8 \\ \times\, 7 \\ \hline \end{array}$$

5. Adriana made 30 pet collars to bring to the pet fair. She wants to display 3 pet collars on each hook. How many hooks will Adriana need to display all 30 pet collars?

6. Carla packs 4 boxes of books. Each box has 9 books. How many books does Carla pack?

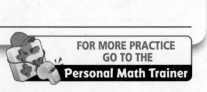

FOR MORE PRACTICE
GO TO THE
Personal Math Trainer

Name _____

Problem Solving • Two-Step Problems

Essential Question How can you use the strategy *act it out* to solve two-step problems?

Learning Objective You will use the strategy *act it out* by writing an equation using an unknown number to solve two-step problems.

🔑 Unlock the Problem

Madilyn bought 2 packs of pens and a notebook for $11. The notebook cost $3. Each pack of pens cost the same amount. What is the price of 1 pack of pens?

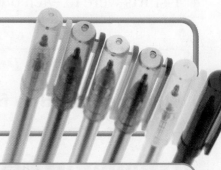

Read the Problem	**Solve the Problem**

Read the Problem

What do I need to find?

I need to find the price of

1 pack of _____ .

What information do I need to use?

Madilyn spent _____ in all.

She bought _____ packs of

pens and _____ notebook.

The notebook cost _____ .

How will I use the information?

I will use the information to

_____ out the problem.

Solve the Problem

Describe how to act out the problem.

Start with 11 counters. Take away 3 counters.

total cost	cost of notebook	p, cost of 2 packs of pens
↓	↓	↓

$$ \_\_\_\_ - \_\_\_\_ = p $$

$$ \_\_\_\_ = p $$

Now I know that 2 packs of pens cost _____ .

Next, make _____ equal groups with the 8 remaining counters.

p, cost of 2 packs of pens	number of packs	c, cost of 1 pack of pens
↓	↓	↓

$$ \$8 \div \_\_\_\_ = c $$

$$ \_\_\_\_ = c $$

So, the price of 1 pack of pens is _____ .

Math Talk

Math Processes and Practices ①

Make Sense of Problems Why do you need to use two operations to solve the problem?

🔑 Try Another Problem

Chad bought 4 packs of T-shirts. He gave 5 T-shirts to his brother. Now Chad has 19 shirts. How many T-shirts were in each pack?

Read the Problem	Solve the Problem
What do I need to find?	**Describe how to act out the problem.**
What information do I need to use?	
How will I use the information?	

- How can you use multiplication and subtraction to check your answer?

_____

_____

_____

Math Talk

Math Processes and Practices ③

Apply What is another strategy you could use to solve this problem?

Name _____

Unlock the Problem

√ Circle the question.
√ Underline the important facts.
√ Choose a strategy you know.

✓ **1.** Mac bought 4 packs of toy cars. Then his friend gave him 9 cars. Now Mac has 21 cars. How many cars were in each pack?

Act out the problem by using counters or the picture and by writing equations.

First, subtract the cars Mac's friend gave him.

total cars		cars given to Mac		c, cars in 4 packs
↓		↓		↓
21	−	_____	=	c
		_____	=	c

Then, divide to find the number of cars in each pack.

c, cars in 4 packs		number of packs		p, number in each pack
↓		↓		↓
12	÷	_____	=	p
		_____	=	p

So, there were _____ cars in each pack.

✓ **2.** THINK SMARTER What if Mac bought 8 packs of toy boats, and then he gave his friend 3 boats? If Mac has 13 boats now, how many boats were in each pack?

_____

3. THINK SMARTER Ryan gave 7 of his model cars to a friend. Then he bought 6 more cars. Now Ryan has 13 cars. How many cars did Ryan start with?

4. **GO DEEPER** Chloe bought 5 sets of books. Each set has the same number of books. She donated 9 of her books to her school. Now she has 26 books. How many books were in each set?

_____

5. Hilda cuts a ribbon into 2 equal pieces. Then she cuts 4 inches off one piece. That piece is now 5 inches long. What was the length of the original ribbon?

_____

6. **GO DEEPER** Teanna has 2 boxes of color pencils. One box has 20 color pencils and the other box has 16 color pencils. She gives her brother 3 of the color pencils. She wants to put the color pencils that she has left into 3 equal groups. How many color pencils will Teanna put in each group?

_____

WRITE ▸ *Math*
Show Your Work

7. **Math Processes and Practices 6** Rose saw a movie, shopped, and ate at a restaurant. She did not see the movie first. She shopped right after she ate. In what order did Rose do these activities? **Explain** how you know.

_____

_____

_____

Personal Math Trainer

8. **THINK SMARTER +** Eleni bought 3 packs of crayons. Each pack contains the same number of crayons. She then found 3 crayons in her desk. Eleni now has 24 crayons. How many crayons were in each pack she bought? Explain how you solved the problem.

_____

Problem Solving • Two-Step Problems

Learning Objective You will use the strategy *act it out* by writing an equation using an unknown number to solve two-step problems.

Solve the problem.

1. Jack has 3 boxes of pencils with the same number of pencils in each box. His mother gives him 4 more pencils. Now Jack has 28 pencils. How many pencils are in each box?

   Think: I can start with 28 counters and act out the problem.

   _____**8 pencils**_____

2. The art teacher has 48 paintbrushes. She puts 8 paintbrushes on each table in her classroom. How many tables are in her classroom?

   _____

3. Ricardo has 2 cases of video games with the same number of games in each case. He gives 4 games to his brother. Ricardo has 10 games left. How many video games were in each case?

   _____

4. Patty has $20 to spend on gifts for her friends. Her mother gives her $5 more. If each gift costs $5, how many gifts can she buy?

   _____

5. Joe has a collection of 35 DVD movies. He received 8 of them as gifts. Joe bought the rest of his movies over 3 years. If he bought the same number of movies each year, how many movies did Joe buy last year?

   _____

6. **WRITE** ▶*Math* Write a division word problem and explain how to solve it by *acting it out*.

   _____

   _____

Lesson Check

1. Gavin saved $16 to buy packs of baseball cards. His father gives him $4 more. If each pack of cards costs $5, how many packs can Gavin buy?

2. Chelsea buys 8 packs of markers. Each pack contains the same number of markers. Chelsea gives 10 markers to her brother. Then, she has 54 markers left. How many markers were in each pack?

Spiral Review

3. Each foot has 5 toes. How many toes do 6 feet have?

4. Each month for 5 months, Sophie makes 2 quilts. How many more quilts does she need to make before she has made 16 quilts?

5. Meredith practices the piano for 3 hours each week. How many hours will she practice in 8 weeks?

6. Find the unknown factor.

$$9 \times \blacksquare = 36$$

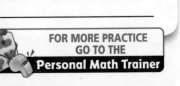

FOR MORE PRACTICE
GO TO THE
Personal Math Trainer

Name _____

Order of Operations

Essential Question Why are there rules such as the order of operations?

Learning Objective You will use the order of operations to solve problems.

Investigate

CONNECT You can use what you know about acting out a two-step problem to write one equation to describe and solve a two-step problem.

- If you solved a two-step problem in a different order, what do you think might happen?

_____

Use different orders to find 4 + 16 ÷ 2.

A. Make a list of all the possible orders you can use to find the answer to 4 + 16 ÷ 2.

_____

B. Use each order in your list to find the answer. Show the steps you used.

_____

_____

Draw Conclusions

1. Did following different orders change the answer? _____

2. (Math Processes and Practices 8) **Draw Conclusions** If a problem has more than one type of operation, how does the order in which you perform the operations affect the answer?

_____

_____

3. Explain the need for setting an order of operations that everyone follows.

_____

_____

Make Connections

When solving problems with more than one type of operation, you need to know which operation to do first. A special set of rules, called the **order of operations**, gives the order in which calculations are done in a problem.

First, multiply and divide from left to right.

Then, add and subtract from left to right.

Meghan buys 2 books for $4 each. She pays with a $10 bill. How much money does she have left?

You can write $\$10 - 2 \times \$4 = c$ to describe and solve the problem.

Use the order of operations to solve $\$10 - 2 \times \$4 = c$.

STEP 1

Multiply from left to right.
$$\$10 - 2 \times \$4 = c$$
$$\$10 - \quad \$8 \quad = c$$

STEP 2

Subtract from left to right.
$$\$10 - \$8 = c$$
$$\$2 \quad = c$$

So, Meghan has _____ left.

- Does your answer make sense? Explain.

_____

_____

_____

> **Math Talk**
>
> Math Processes and Practices ⑦
>
> **Identify Relationships**
> What operation should you do first to find:
> $12 - 6 \div 2$ and
> $12 \div 6 - 2$? What is the answer to each problem?

Share and Show

Write *correct* if the operations are listed in the correct order. If not correct, write the correct order of operations.

1. $4 + 5 \times 2$ multiply, add

_____

✓ 2. $8 \div 4 \times 2$ multiply, divide

_____

3. $12 + 16 \div 4$ add, divide

_____

4. $9 + 2 \times 3$ add, multiply

_____

5. $4 + 6 \div 3$ divide, add

_____

6. $36 - 7 \times 3$ multiply, subtract

_____

Name _____

**Follow the order of operations to find the unknown number.
Use your MathBoard.**

7. $63 \div 9 - 2 = f$

$f =$ _____

8. $7 - 5 + 8 = y$

$y =$ _____

☑**9.** $3 \times 6 - 2 = h$

$h =$ _____

10. $80 - 64 \div 8 = n$

$n =$ _____

11. $3 \times 4 + 6 = a$

$a =$ _____

12. $2 \times 7 \div 7 = c$

$c =$ _____

Problem Solving • Applications

Math Processes and Practices ④ **Write an Equation** **Algebra** **Use the numbers listed to make the equation true.**

13. 2, 6, and 5

_____ + _____ × _____ = 16

14. 4, 12, and 18

_____ − _____ ÷ _____ = 15

15. 8, 9, and 7

_____ × _____ − _____ = 47

16. 2, 4, and 9

_____ ÷ _____ + _____ = 11

17. **WRITE** ▸Math **Pose a Problem** Write a word problem
that can be solved by using $2 \times 5 \div 5$. Solve your problem.

_____

_____

_____

_____

18. *THINK SMARTER* Is $4 + 8 \times 3$ equal to $4 + 3 \times 8$? Explain
how you know without finding the answers.

_____

_____

19. **THINK SMARTER** For numbers 19a–19d, select True or False for each equation.

19a. $24 \div 3 + 5 = 13$ ○ True   ○ False

19b. $5 + 2 \times 3 = 21$ ○ True   ○ False

19c. $15 - 3 \div 3 = 14$ ○ True   ○ False

19d. $18 \div 3 \times 2 = 12$ ○ True   ○ False

Connect to Social Studies

Picture Book Art

The Eric Carle Museum of Picture Book Art in Amherst, Massachusetts, is the first museum in the United States that is devoted to picture book art. Picture books introduce literature to young readers.

The museum has 3 galleries, a reading library, a café, an art studio, an auditorium, and a museum shop. The exhibits change every 3 to 6 months, depending on the length of time the picture art is on loan and how fragile it is.

The table shows prices for some souvenirs in the bookstore in the museum.

Souvenir Prices	
Souvenir	**Price**
Firefly Picture Frame	$25
Exhibition Posters	$10
Caterpillar Note Cards	$8
Caterpillar Pens	$4
Sun Note Pads	$3

20. Kallon bought 3 Caterpillar note cards and 1 Caterpillar pen. How much did he spend on souvenirs?

_____

21. **GO DEEPER** Raya and 4 friends bought their teacher 1 Firefly picture frame. They shared the cost equally. Then Raya bought an Exhibition poster. How much money did Raya spend in all? Explain.

_____

_____

_____

Order of Operations

Learning Objective You will use the order of operations to solve problems.

Write *correct* if the operations are listed in the correct order. If not correct, write the correct order of operations.

1. $45 - 3 \times 5$ subtract, multiply

2. $3 \times 4 \div 2$ divide, multiply

_____ **multiply, subtract** _____

3. $5 + 12 \div 2$ divide, add

4. $7 \times 10 + 3$ add, multiply

Follow the order of operations to find the unknown number.

5. $6 + 4 \times 3 = n$

6. $8 - 3 + 2 = k$

7. $24 \div 3 + 5 = p$

$n =$ _____

$k =$ _____

$p =$ _____

 Problem Solving *Real World*

8. Shelley bought 3 kites for $6 each. She gave the clerk $20. How much change should Shelley get?

9. Tim has 5 apples and 3 bags with 8 apples in each bag. How many apples does Tim have in all?

_____

_____

10. **WRITE** ▸*Math* Give a description of the rules for the order of operations in your own words.

_____

_____

Lesson Check

1. Natalie is making doll costumes. Each costume has 4 buttons that cost 3¢ each and a zipper that costs 7¢. How much does she spend on buttons and a zipper for each costume?

2. Leonardo's mother gave him 5 bags with 6 flower bulbs in each bag to plant. He has planted all except 3 bulbs. How many flower bulbs has Leonardo planted?

Spiral Review

3. Each story in Will's apartment building is 9 feet tall. There are 10 stories in the building. How tall is the apartment building?

4. Describe a pattern in the table.

Tables	1	2	3	4
Chairs	4	8	12	16

5. For decorations, Meg cut out 8 groups of 7 snowflakes each. How many snowflakes did Meg cut out in all?

6. A small van can hold 6 students. How many small vans are needed to take 36 students on a field trip to the music museum?

FOR MORE PRACTICE
GO TO THE
Personal Math Trainer

✓ Chapter 7 Review/Test

Personal Math Trainer
Online Assessment
and Intervention

1. Ming shared 35 marbles among 7 different friends. Each friend received the same number of marbles. How many marbles did Ming give to each friend?

$$35 \div 7 = a$$
$$7 \times a = 35$$

(A) 4   (C) 6

(B) 5   (D) 7

2. Mrs. Conner has 16 shoes.

Select one number from each column to show the division equation represented by the picture.

$$16 \div \frac{?}{\text{(divisor)}} = \frac{?}{\text{(quotient)}}$$

Divisor	Quotient
○ 1	○ 1
○ 2	○ 4
○ 4	○ 8
○ 16	○ 16

3. Twenty boys are going camping. They brought 5 tents. An equal number of boys sleep in each tent. How many boys will sleep in each tent?

_____ boys

GO DIGITAL   Assessment Options
Chapter Test

4. Circle a number for the unknown factor and quotient that makes the equation true.

$4 \times \boxed{\begin{matrix} 6 \\ 7 \\ 8 \end{matrix}} = 28$

$\boxed{\begin{matrix} 6 \\ 7 \\ 8 \end{matrix}} = 28 \div 4$

5. Mrs. Walters has 30 markers. She gives each student 10 markers. How many students received the markers?

$$\begin{matrix} 30 \\ -10 \\ \hline 20 \end{matrix} \quad \begin{matrix} 20 \\ -10 \\ \hline 10 \end{matrix} \quad \begin{matrix} 10 \\ -10 \\ \hline 0 \end{matrix}$$

Write a division equation to represent the repeated subtraction.

_____ ÷ _____ = _____

6. Complete the chart to show the quotients.

÷	27	36	45	54
9				

7. For numbers 7a–7e, select True or False for each equation.

7a. $12 \div 6 = 2$ ○ True   ○ False

7b. $24 \div 6 = 3$ ○ True   ○ False

7c. $30 \div 6 = 6$ ○ True   ○ False

7d. $42 \div 6 = 7$ ○ True   ○ False

7e. $48 \div 6 = 8$ ○ True   ○ False

Name _____

8. Alicia says that $6 \div 2 + 5$ is the same as $5 + 6 \div 2$.
Is Alicia correct or incorrect? Explain.

_____

_____

_____

_____

9. Keith arranged 40 toy cars in 8 equal rows. How many
toy cars are in each row?

_____ toy cars

10. Bella made $21 selling bracelets. She wants to know how
many bracelets she sold. Bella used this number line.

Write the division equation that the number
line represents.

_____ $\div$ _____ $=$ _____

11. Each picnic table seats 6 people. How many picnic tables
are needed to seat 24 people? Explain the strategy you
used to solve the problem.

_____

_____

_____

12. Finn bought 2 packs of stickers. Each pack had the same number of stickers. A friend gave him 4 more stickers. Now he has 24 stickers in all. How many stickers were in each pack? Explain how you solved the problem.

_____

_____

_____

13. Ana used 49 strawberries to make 7 strawberry smoothies. She used the same number of strawberries in each smoothie. How many strawberries did Ana use in each smoothie?

_____ strawberries

14. For numbers 14a–14e, use the order of operations. Select True or False for each equation.

14a. $81 \div 9 + 2 = 11$ ○ True ○ False

14b. $6 + 4 \times 5 = 50$ ○ True ○ False

14c. $10 + 10 \div 2 = 15$ ○ True ○ False

14d. $12 - 3 \times 2 = 6$ ○ True ○ False

14e. $20 \div 4 \times 5 = 1$ ○ True ○ False

15. A flower shop sells daffodils in bunches of 9 daffodils. The shop sells 27 daffodils. How many bunches of daffodils does the shop sell?

_____ bunches

Name _____

16. THINK SMARTER + Aviva started a table showing a
division pattern.

÷	20	30	40	50
10				
5				

Part A

Complete the table.

Compare the quotients when dividing by 10 and
when dividing by 5. Describe a pattern you see in
the quotients.

_____

_____

Part B

Find the quotient, a.

$70 \div 10 = a$

$a =$ _____

How could you use a to find the value of n? Find the
value of n.

$70 \div 5 = n$

$n =$ _____

_____

_____

17. Ben needs 2 oranges to make a glass of orange juice.
If oranges come in bags of 10, how many glasses of
orange juice can he make using one bag of oranges?

_____ glasses

© Houghton Mifflin Harcourt Publishing Company

Chapter 7 437

18. For numbers 18a–18e, select True or False for
each equation.

18a. $0 \div 9 = 0$ ○ True   ○ False

18b. $9 \div 9 = 1$ ○ True   ○ False

18c. $27 \div 9 = 4$ ○ True   ○ False

18d. $54 \div 9 = 6$ ○ True   ○ False

18e. $90 \div 9 = 9$ ○ True   ○ False

19. Ellen is making gift baskets for four friends. She has
16 prizes she wants to divide equally among the baskets.
How many prizes should she put in each basket?

_____ prizes

20. GO DEEPER   Emily is buying a pet rabbit. She needs to buy
items for her rabbit at the pet store.

Part A

Emily buys a cage and 2 bowls for $54. The cage costs
$40. Each bowl costs the same amount. What is the
price of 1 bowl? Explain the steps you used to solve
the problem.

_____

_____

_____

Part B

Emily also buys food and toys for her rabbit. She buys
a bag of food for $20. She buys 2 toys for $3 each. Write
one equation to describe the total amount Emily spends
on food and toys. Explain how to use the order of
operations to solve the equation.

_____

_____

_____

Glossary

A

addend [aˈdend] **sumando** Any of the numbers that are added in addition
Examples: 2 + 3 = 5
         ↑   ↑
      addend   addend

addition [ə•dishˈən] **suma** The process of finding the total number of items when two or more groups of items are joined; the opposite operation of subtraction

A.M. [āˈ•em] **a.m.** The time after midnight and before noon

analog clock [anˈə•log kläk] **reloj analógico** A tool for measuring time, in which hands move around a circle to show hours and minutes
Example:

angle [angˈgəl] **ángulo** A shape formed by two rays that share an endpoint
Example:

Word History

When the letter *g* is replaced with the letter *k* in the word *angle*, the word becomes *ankle*. Both words come from the same Latin root, *angulus*, which means "a sharp bend."

area [ârˈē•ə] **área** The measure of the number of unit squares needed to cover a surface
Example:

Area = 6 square units

array [ə•rā′] **matriz** A set of objects
arranged in rows and columns
Example:

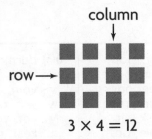

$$3 \times 4 = 12$$

Associative Property of Addition [ə•sō′shē•āt•iv
präp′ər•tē əv ə•dish′ən] **propiedad asociativa
de la suma** The property that states that you
can group addends in different ways and still
get the same sum
Example:
$$4 + (2 + 5) = 11$$
$$(4 + 2) + 5 = 11$$

Associative Property of Multiplication
[ə•sō′shē•āt•iv präp′ər•tē əv mul•tə•pli•kā′shən]
propiedad asociativa de la multiplicación
The property that states that when the
grouping of factors is changed, the product
remains the same
Example:
$$(3 \times 2) \times 4 = 24$$
$$3 \times (2 \times 4) = 24$$

bar graph [bär graf] **gráfica de barras** A graph
that uses bars to show data
Example:

capacity [kə•pas′i•tē] **capacidad** The amount
a container can hold
Example:
1 liter = 1,000 milliliters

cent sign (¢) [sent sīn] **símbolo de centavo**
A symbol that stands for *cent* or *cents*
Example: 53¢

centimeter (cm) [sen′tə•mēt•ər] **centímetro (cm)**
A metric unit that is used to measure length
or distance
Example:

circle [sûr′kəl] **círculo** A round closed
plane shape
Example:

closed shape [klōzd shāp] **figura cerrada** A shape
that begins and ends at the same point
Examples:

Commutative Property of Addition
[kə•myōōt′ə•tiv präp′ər•tē əv ə•dish′ən]
propiedad conmutativa de la suma
The property that states that you can add
two or more numbers in any order and get
the same sum
Example: $6 + 7 = 13$
$7 + 6 = 13$

Commutative Property of Multiplication
[kə•myōōt′ə•tiv präp′ər•tē əv mul•tə•pli•kā′shən]
propiedad conmutativa de la multiplicación
The property that states that you can multiply
two factors in any order and get the same
product
Example: $2 \times 4 = 8$
$4 \times 2 = 8$

compare [kəm•pâr′] **comparar** To describe
whether numbers are equal to, less than,
or greater than each other

compatible numbers [kəm•pat′ə•bəl num′bərz]
números compatibles Numbers that are
easy to compute with mentally

H2 **Glossary**

cone [kōn] **cono** A three-dimensional, pointed shape that has a flat, round base
Example:

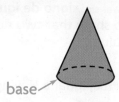

base

counting number [kount´ing num´bər] **número natural** A whole number that can be used to count a set of objects (1, 2, 3, 4 . . .)

cube [kyo͞ob] **cubo** A three-dimensional shape with six square faces of the same size
Example:

cylinder [sil´ən•dər] **cilindro** A three-dimensional object that is shaped like a can
Example:

data [dāt´ə] **datos** Information collected about people or things

decagon [dek´ə•gän] **decágono** A polygon with ten sides and ten angles
Example:

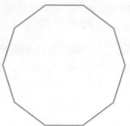

decimal point [des´ə•məl point] **punto decimal** A symbol used to separate dollars from cents in money
Example: $4.52

∟ decimal point

denominator [dē•näm´ə•nāt•ər] **denominador** The part of a fraction below the line, which tells how many equal parts there are in the whole or in the group
Example: $\frac{3}{4}$ ← denominator

difference [dif´ər•əns] **diferencia** The answer to a subtraction problem
Example: $6 - 4 = 2$

∟difference

digital clock [dij´i•təl kläk] **reloj digital** A clock that shows time to the minute, using digits
Example:

digits [dij´its] **dígitos** The symbols 0, 1, 2, 3, 4, 5, 6, 7, 8, and 9

dime [dīm] **moneda de 10¢** A coin worth 10 cents and with a value equal to that of 10 pennies; 10¢
Example:

Distributive Property [di•strib´yo͞o•tiv präp´ər•tē] **propiedad distributiva** The property that states that multiplying a sum by a number is the same as multiplying each addend by the number and then adding the products
Example: $5 \times 8 = 5 \times (4 + 4)$
   $5 \times 8 = (5 \times 4) + (5 \times 4)$
   $5 \times 8 = 20 + 20$
   $5 \times 8 = 40$

divide [də•vīd´] **dividir** To separate into equal groups; the opposite operation of multiplication

dividend [div´ə•dend] **dividendo** The number that is to be divided in a division problem
Example: $35 \div 5 = 7$

∟dividend

division [də•vizh′ən] **división** The process of sharing a number of items to find how many groups can be made or how many items will be in a group; the opposite operation of multiplication

divisor [de•vī′zər] **divisor** The number that divides the dividend
Example: 35 ÷ 5 = 7
⤒___divisor

dollar [däl′ər] **dólar** Paper money worth 100 cents and equal to 100 pennies; $1.00
Example:

edge [ej] **arista** A line segment formed where two faces meet

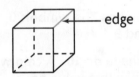
edge

eighths [ātths] **octavos**

These are eighths

elapsed time [ē•lapst′ tīm] **tiempo transcurrido** The time that passes from the start of an activity to the end of that activity

endpoint [end′point] **extremo** The point at either end of a line segment

equal groups [ē′kwəl gro͞opz] **grupos iguales** Groups that have the same number of objects

equal parts [ē′kwəl pärts] **partes iguales** Parts that are exactly the same size

equal sign (=) [ē′kwəl sīn] **signo de igualdad** A symbol used to show that two numbers have the same value
Example: 384 = 384

equal to (=) [ē′kwəl to͞o] **igual a** Having the same value
Example: 4 + 4 is equal to 3 + 5.

equation [ē•kwā′zhən] **ecuación** A number sentence that uses the equal sign to show that two amounts are equal
Examples:
3 + 7 = 10
4 − 1 = 3
6 × 7 = 42
8 ÷ 2 = 4

equivalent [ē•kwiv′ə•lənt] **equivalente** Two or more sets that name the same amount

equivalent fractions [ē•kwiv′ə•lənt frak′shənz] **fracciones equivalentes** Two or more fractions that name the same amount
Example:

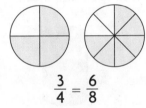

$$\frac{3}{4} = \frac{6}{8}$$

estimate [es′tə•māt] *verb* **estimar** To find about how many or how much

estimate [es′tə•mit] *noun* **estimación** A number close to an exact amount

even [ē′vən] **par** A whole number that has a 0, 2, 4, 6, or 8 in the ones place

expanded form [ek•span′did fôrm] **forma desarrollada** A way to write numbers by showing the value of each digit
Example: 721 = 700 + 20 + 1

experiment [ek•sper′ə•mənt] **experimento** A test that is done in order to find out something

© Houghton Mifflin Harcourt Publishing Company

F

face [fās] **cara** A polygon that is a flat surface of a solid shape

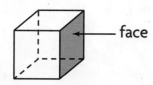

factor [fak'tər] **factor** A number that is multiplied by another number to find a product
Examples: 3 × 8 = 24
      ↑   ↑
   factor factor

foot (ft) [fŏŏt] **pie** A customary unit used to measure length or distance;
1 foot = 12 inches

fourths [fôrths] **cuartos**

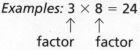

These are fourths

fraction [frak'shən] **fracción** A number that names part of a whole or part of a group
Examples:

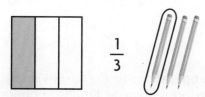

$\frac{1}{3}$

Word History

Often, a *fraction* is a part of a whole that is broken into pieces. *Fraction* comes from the Latin word *frangere*, which means "to break."

fraction greater than 1 [frak'shən grāt'ər <u>than</u> wun] **fracción mayor que 1** A number which has a numerator that is greater than its denominator
Examples:

$\frac{6}{3}$ $\frac{2}{1}$

frequency table [frē'kwən•sē tā'bəl] **tabla de frecuencia** A table that uses numbers to record data
Example:

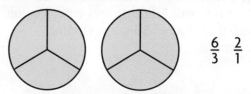

Favorite Color	
Color	Number
Blue	10
Green	8
Red	7
Yellow	4

G

gram (g) [gram] **gramo (g)** A metric unit that is used to measure mass;
1 kilogram = 1,000 grams

greater than (>) [grāt'ər <u>than</u>] **mayor que** A symbol used to compare two numbers when the greater number is given first
Example:
Read 6 > 4 as "six is greater than four."

Grouping Property of Addition [grōŏp'ing präp'ər•tē əv ə•dish'ən] **propiedad de agrupación de la suma** *See* Associative Property of Addition.

Grouping Property of Multiplication [grōŏp'ing präp'ər•tē əv mul•tə•pli•kā'shən] **propiedad de agrupación de la multiplicación** *See* Associative Property of Multiplication.

half dollar [haf dol'ər] **moneda de 50¢**
A coin worth 50 cents and with a value equal to that of 50 pennies; 50¢
Example:

half hour [haf our] **media hora** 30 minutes
Example: Between 4:00 and 4:30 is one half hour.

halves [havz] **mitades**

These are halves

hexagon [hek'sə•gän] **hexágono** A polygon with six sides and six angles
Examples:

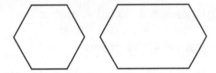

horizontal bar graph [hôr•i•zänt'l bär graf] **gráfica de barras horizontales** A bar graph in which the bars go from left to right
Examples:

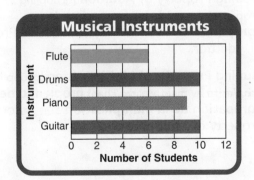

hour (hr) [our] **hora (h)** A unit used to measure time; in one hour, the hour hand on an analog clock moves from one number to the next; 1 hour = 60 minutes

hour hand [our hand] **horario** The short hand on an analog clock

Identity Property of Addition [ī•den'tə•tē präp'ər•tē əv ə•dish'ən] **propiedad de identidad de la suma** The property that states that when you add zero to a number, the result is that number
Example: 24 + 0 = 24

Identity Property of Multiplication [ī•den'tə•tē präp'ər•tē əv mul•tə•pli•kā'shən] **propiedad de identidad de la multiplicación** The property that states that the product of any number and 1 is that number
Examples: 5 × 1 = 5
1 × 8 = 8

inch (in.) [inch] **pulgada (pulg.)** A customary unit used to measure length or distance
Example:

intersecting lines [in•tər•sekt'ing līnz] **líneas secantes** Lines that meet or cross
Example:

inverse operations [in'vûrs äp•ə•rā'shənz] **operaciones inversas** Opposite operations, or operations that undo one another, such as addition and subtraction or multiplication and division

key [kē] **clave** The part of a map or graph that explains the symbols

kilogram (kg) [kil'ō•gram] **kilogramo (kg)** A metric unit used to measure mass; 1 kilogram = 1,000 grams

length [lengkth] **longitud** The measurement of the distance between two points

less than (<) [les <u>th</u>an] **menor que** A symbol used to compare two numbers when the lesser number is given first
Example:
Read 3 < 7 as "three is less than seven."

line [līn] **línea** A straight path extending in both directions with no endpoints
Example:

⟷

Word History

The word *line* comes from *linen*, a thread spun from the fibers of the flax plant. In early times, thread was held tight to mark a straight line between two points.

line plot [līn plät] **diagrama de puntos** A graph that records each piece of data on a number line
Example:

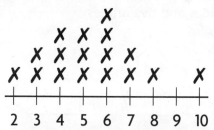

Height of Bean Seedlings to the Nearest Centimeter

line segment [līn seg'mənt] **segmento** A part of a line that includes two points, called endpoints, and all of the points between them
Example:

•————————•

liquid volume [lik'wid väl'yoom] **volumen de un líquido** The amount of liquid in a container

liter (L) [lēt'ər] **litro (L)** A metric unit used to measure capacity and liquid volume; 1 liter = 1,000 milliliters

mass [mas] **masa** The amount of matter in an object

meter (m) [mēt'ər] **metro (m)** A metric unit used to measure length or distance; 1 meter = 100 centimeters

midnight [mid'nīt] **medianoche** 12:00 at night

milliliter (mL) [mil'i•lēt•ər] **mililitro (mL)** A metric unit used to measure capacity and liquid volume

minute (min) [min'it] **minuto (min)** A unit used to measure short amounts of time; in one minute, the minute hand on an analog clock moves from one mark to the next

minute hand [min'it hand] **minutero** The long hand on an analog clock

multiple [mul'tə•pəl] **múltiplo** A number that is the product of two counting numbers
Examples:

6	6	6	6	counting
× 1	× 2	× 3	× 4	← numbers
6	12	18	24	← multiples of 6

multiplication [mul•tə•pli•kā'shən] **multiplicación** The process of finding the total number of items in two or more equal groups; the opposite operation of division

multiply [mul'tə•plī] **multiplicar** To combine equal groups to find how many in all; the opposite operation of division

nickel [nik'əl] **moneda de 5¢** A coin worth 5 cents and with a value equal to that of 5 pennies; 5¢
Example:

noon [noon] **mediodía** 12:00 in the day

Glossary **H7**

© Houghton Mifflin Harcourt Publishing Company

number line [num′bər līn] **recta numérica**
A line on which numbers can be located
Example:

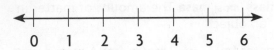

number sentence [num′bər sent′ns] **enunciado numérico** A sentence that includes numbers, operation symbols, and a greater than symbol, a less than symbol, or an equal sign
Example: 5 + 3 = 8

numerator [nōō′mər•āt•ər] **numerador** The part of a fraction above the line, which tells how many parts are being counted
Example: $\frac{3}{4}$ ← numerator

octagon [äk′tə•gän] **octágono** A polygon with eight sides and eight angles
Examples:

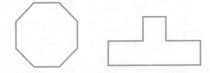

odd [od] **impar** A whole number that has a 1, 3, 5, 7, or 9 in the ones place

open shape [ō′pən shāp] **figura abierta** A shape that does not begin and end at the same point
Examples:

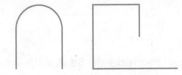

order [ôr′dər] **orden** A particular arrangement or placement of numbers or things, one after another

order of operations [ôr′dər əv äp•ə•rā′shənz] **orden de las operaciones** A special set of rules that gives the order in which calculations are done

Order Property of Addition [ôr′dər präp′ər•tē əv ə•dish′ən] **propiedad de orden de la suma** *See* Commutative Property of Addition.

Order Property of Multiplication [ôr′dər präp′ər•tē əv mul•tə•pli•kā′shən] **propiedad de orden de la multiplicación** *See* Commutative Property of Multiplication.

parallel lines [pâr′ə•lel līnz] **líneas paralelas** Lines in the same plane that never cross and are always the same distance apart
Example:

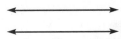

pattern [pat′ərn] **patrón** An ordered set of numbers or objects in which the order helps you predict what will come next
Examples:
  2, 4, 6, 8, 10

pentagon [pen′tə•gän] **pentágono** A polygon with five sides and five angles
Examples:

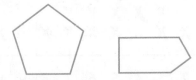

perimeter [pə•rim′ə•tər] **perímetro** The distance around a figure
Example:

perpendicular lines [pər•pən•dik′yōō•lər līnz] **líneas perpendiculares** Lines that intersect to form right angles
Example:

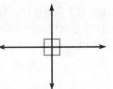

picture graph [pik'chər graf] **gráfica con dibujos** A graph that uses pictures to show and compare information
Example:

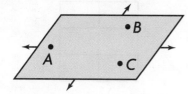

How We Get to School	
Walk	✳ ✳ ✳
Ride a Bike	✳ ✳ ✳ ✳
Ride a Bus	✳ ✳ ✳ ✳ ✳ ✳
Ride in a Car	✳ ✳
Key: Each ✳ = 10 students.	

place value [plās val'yoo] **valor posicional** The value of each digit in a number, based on the location of the digit

plane [plān] **plano** A flat surface that extends without end in all directions
Example:

plane shape [plān shāp] **figura plana** A shape in a plane that is formed by curves, line segments, or both
Example:

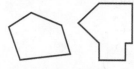

P.M. [pē•em] **p.m.** The time after noon and before midnight

point [point] **punto** An exact position or location

polygon [päl'i•gän] **polígono** A closed plane shape with straight sides that are line segments
Examples:

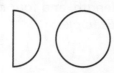

polygons   not polygons

© Houghton Mifflin Harcourt Publishing Company

---

product [präd'əkt] **producto** The answer in a multiplication problem
Example: $3 \times 8 = 24$
product

Q

quadrilateral [kwäd•ri•lat'ər•əl] **cuadrilátero** A polygon with four sides and four angles
Example:

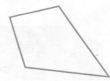

quarter [kwôrt'ər] **moneda de 25¢** A coin worth 25 cents and with a value equal to that of 25 pennies; 25¢
Example:

quarter hour [kwôrt'ər our] **cuarto de hora** 15 minutes
Example: Between 4:00 and 4:15 is one quarter hour.

quotient [kwō'shənt] **cociente** The number, not including the remainder, that results from division
Example: $8 \div 4 = 2$
quotient

ray [rā] **semirrecta** A part of a line, with one endpoint, that is straight and continues in one direction
Example:

rectangle [rek′tang•gəl] **rectángulo** A quadrilateral with two pairs of parallel sides, two pairs of sides of equal length, and four right angles
Example:

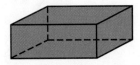

rectangular prism [rek•tang′gyə•lər priz′əm] **prisma rectangular** A three-dimensional shape with six faces that are all rectangles
Example:

regroup [rē•grōōp′] **reagrupar** To exchange amounts of equal value to rename a number
Example: 5 + 8 = 13 ones or 1 ten 3 ones

related facts [ri•lāt′id fakts] **operaciones relacionadas** A set of related addition and subtraction, or multiplication and division, number sentences
Examples: $4 \times 7 = 28$ $28 \div 4 = 7$
$7 \times 4 = 28$ $28 \div 7 = 4$

remainder [ri•mān′dər] **residuo** The amount left over when a number cannot be divided evenly

results [ri•zults′] **resultados** The answers from a survey

rhombus [räm′bəs] **rombo** A quadrilateral with two pairs of parallel sides and four sides of equal length
Example:

right angle [rīt ang′gəl] **ángulo recto** An angle that forms a square corner
Example:

round [round] **redondear** To replace a number with another number that tells about how many or how much

scale [skāl] **escala** The numbers placed at fixed distances on a graph to help label the graph

side [sīd] **lado** A straight line segment in a polygon

sixths [siksths] **sextos**

These are sixths

skip count [skip kount] **contar salteado** A pattern of counting forward or backward
Example: 5, 10, 15, 20, 25, 30, . . .

solid shape [sä′lid shāp] **cuerpo geométrico** *See* three-dimensional shape.

sphere [sfir] **esfera** A three-dimensional shape that has the shape of a round ball
Example:

square [skwâr] **cuadrado** A quadrilateral with two pairs of parallel sides, four sides of equal length, and four right angles
Example:

square unit [skwâr yōō′nit] **unidad cuadrada**
A unit used to measure area such as square
foot, square meter, and so on

standard form [stan′dərd fôrm] **forma normal**
A way to write numbers by using the digits
0–9, with each digit having a place value
Example: 345 ← standard form

subtraction [səb•trak′shən] **resta** The process of
finding how many are left when a number of
items are taken away from a group of items;
the process of finding the difference when two
groups are compared; the opposite operation
of addition

sum [sum] **suma o total** The answer to an
addition problem
Example: 6 + 4 = 10
                    └─sum

survey [sûr′vā] **encuesta** A method of gathering
information

tally table [tal′ē tā′bəl] **tabla de conteo** A table
that uses tally marks to record data
Example:

Favorite Sport	
Sport	**Tally**
Soccer	JHJ III
Baseball	III
Football	JHJ
Basketball	JHJ I

thirds [thûrdz] **tercios**

These are thirds

three-dimensional shape [thrē də•men′shə•nəl shāp]
figura tridimensional A shape that has length,
width, and height
Example:

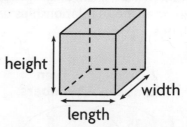

time line [tīm līn] **línea cronológica**
A drawing that shows when and in what
order events took place

trapezoid [trap′i•zoid] **trapecio**
A quadrilateral with at least one pair of
parallel sides
Example:

triangle [trī′ang•gəl] **triángulo** A polygon with
three sides and three angles
Examples:

two-dimensional shape [tōō də•men′shə•nəl shāp]
figura bidimensional A shape that has only
length and width
Example:

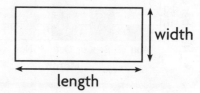

unit fraction [yōō′nit frak′shən] **fracción
unitaria** A fraction that has 1 as its top
number, or numerator
Examples: $\frac{1}{2}$ $\frac{1}{3}$ $\frac{1}{4}$

unit square [yōō′nit skwâr] **cuadrado de una unidad**
A square with a side length of 1 unit, used to
measure area

Venn diagram [ven dī'ə•gram] **diagrama de Venn**
A diagram that shows relationships among
sets of things
Example:

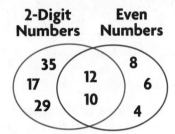

vertex [vûr'teks] **vértice** The point at which
two rays of an angle or two (or more) line
segments meet in a plane shape or where
three or more edges meet in a solid shape
Examples:

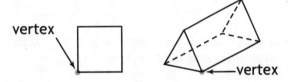

vertical bar graph [vûr'ti•kəl bär graf] **gráfica
de barras verticales** A bar graph in which the
bars go up from bottom to top

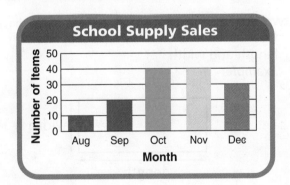

whole [hōl] **entero** All of the parts of a shape
or group
Example:

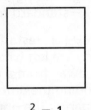

$$\frac{2}{2} = 1$$

This is one whole.

whole number [hōl num'bər] **número entero**
One of the numbers 0, 1, 2, 3, 4, . . .
The set of whole numbers goes on
without end

word form [wûrd fôrm] **en palabras** A way
to write numbers by using words
Example: The word form of 212 is
two hundred twelve.

Zero Property of Multiplication [zē'rō
präp'ər•tē əv mul•tə•pli•kā'shən] **propiedad
del cero de la multiplicación** The property
that states that the product of zero and
any number is zero
Example: $0 \times 6 = 0$

Index

A

Act It Out, 301–304, 421–424, 507–510

Activities

Activity, 5, 6, 126, 139, 165, 166, 171, 209, 229, 230, 281, 287, 307, 319, 320, 345, 365, 366, 467, 487, 533, 534, 594, 599, 600, 605, 606, 612, 631, 643, 649, 650, 669, 675, 681, 704, 729, 735

Cross-Curricular Activities and Connections. *See Cross-Curricular Activities and Connections*

Investigate, 301–304, 421–424, 507–510

Math in the Real World, 3, 85, 137, 189, 259, 299, 363, 441, 505, 559, 623, 695

Addition

with addition tables, 5–6

bar models, 73–76

break apart strategy, 25, 35–38, 42, 56

with compatible numbers, 17–20, 24–25

draw a diagram, 73–76

elapsed time, 573–576

estimate sums, 17–20

with friendly numbers, 24–26

as inverse operations, 61, 637

of liquid volume, 611–614

of mass, 612–614

mental math strategies, 23–26

on number lines, 23–26, 573–574, 579–581, 585–587

place value strategy, 41–44

properties of

Associative, 29–32, 223

Commutative, 6, 29–32

Identity, 5, 29–32

regrouping, 41–43

related to area, 655–658, 669–672

related to multiplication, 145–148

rounding and, 17–20

three-digit numbers, 17–20, 23–26, 35–38, 41–44

of time intervals, 573–576, 579–582, 585–587

two-digit numbers, 23–26, 29–32

Addition tables, 5, 6

Algebra

addition

Associative Property of Addition, 29–32, 223

Commutative Property of Addition, 6, 29–32

describe a number pattern, 5–8, 261–264

Identity Property of Addition, 5, 29–32

patterns on the addition table, 5–8

related to area, 655–658, 669–672

related to multiplication, 145–148

unknown digits, 43

area, 275–278, 643–646, 655–658

division

factors, 389–392, 396–397, 415–418

related facts, 345–348

related to subtraction, 325–328

relate multiplication to division, 339–342, 345–348, 372–374, 384–386, 390–392, 396–398, 404–406, 409–412, 416–418

rules for one and zero, 351–354

unknown divisor, 410

equations, 267–270, 585

input/output tables, 261–264

inverse operations, 61, 339–342

multiplication

area models, 275–278, 655–658, 663–666

arrays, 165–168, 209–212, 223, 267–268, 340–342

Associative Property of Multiplication, 223–226, 236

Commutative Property of Multiplication, 171–174, 215, 224

describe a number pattern, 229–232, 261–264

Distributive Property, 209–212, 215, 241, 275–278, 669–672

factors, 145–148, 267–270

Identity Property of Multiplication, 177–180

number pattern, 229–232, 261–264

with one and zero, 177–180

order of operations, 427–430

patterns on a multiplication table, 229–232

Division
- act it out, 301–304, 421–424
- with arrays, 333–336, 340–341, 345–348, 389–391, 403–406
- bar models, 319–322, 339–342
- count back on number line, 326–328, 371, 377, 384
- dividend, 320
- dividing by
    - eight, 409–412
    - five, 377–380
    - four, 389–392
    - nine, 415–418
    - one, 351–354
    - seven, 403–406
    - six, 395–398
    - ten, 371–374
    - three, 383–386
    - two, 365–368
- dividing with zero, 351–354
- divisors, 320, 410
- doubles, 378
- equal groups, 301–304, 307–310, 313–316, 319–322, 333–336, 365–368, 383–386, 389, 395–398, 403–406, 415–418
- equations, 320–322, 325–328, 334–335, 339–342, 345–348, 351–354, 365–368, 391
- as inverse operation, 339–342
- of liquid volume, 611–614
- of mass, 611–614
- with measurement quantities, 316, 410, 611–614
- modeling, 301–304, 319–322
- number lines, 326–328, 371, 384
- quotients, 320
- related facts, 345–348
- related to multiplication, 339–342, 345–348, 372–374, 384–386, 390–392, 396–398, 404–406, 409–412, 416–418
- repeated (successive) subtraction as, 325–328, 371–374, 409–412
- rules for one and zero, 351–354
- unknown factor problem, 372–374, 384, 390, 396, 404, 409, 416
- using factors, 410
- using related multiplication fact, 345–348, 372–378, 384, 390, 396, 404, 409, 416

Divisors, 320, 410

Doubles, 191–194, 204, 235

Draw a bar graph, 113–116

Draw a Diagram, 73–76, 159–162, 275–278, 493–496, 585–588, 741–744

Draw a picture graph, 99–102

Drawing
- bar models, 73–75, 198–200, 319–322, 611–614
- draw a bar graph, 113–116
- draw a diagram, 73–76, 159–162, 275–278, 493–496, 741–744
- draw a picture graph, 99–102
- number lines, 23–26, 55–58, 147, 281–284
- quadrilaterals, 697–700, 729–732
- quick pictures, 147, 171–174, 177–180, 287–288, 309, 314, 351–354, 367, 445, 449, 452
- shapes, 203, 698, 712, 716, 729–732, 747–750
- solving problems, 73–76, 159–162, 475, 493–496

E

Eighths, 443

Elapsed time, 573–576, 579–582, 585–588
- on clocks, 573–576, 579–582
- defined, 573
- find end time, 579–582, 585–588
- find start time (begin), 579–582, 585–588
- on number lines, 573–576, 579–582, 585–587
- using subtraction, 574

Endpoints, defined 697

Equal groups
- counting, 139–142, 145–148, 191–194, 301–304, 307–310, 313–316, 319–322, 333–336, 365–368, 383–386, 389–392, 395–398, 403–406, 415–418
- defined, 139
- division and, 301–304, 307–310, 313–316, 319–322, 333–336, 365–368, 383–386, 389–392, 395–398, 403–406, 415–418
- multiplication and, 139–142, 145–148, 151–154, 339–342
- number of, 313–316
- size of, 307–310
- skip counting, 139–142, 151–154

Equal parts, 443–446, 747–750

Equal parts of a whole, 443–446

© Houghton Mifflin Harcourt Publishing Company

problem solving, 73–74, 87–88, 159–160,
247–248, 275–276, 301–302, 421–424,
493–494, 507–508, 585–586, 663–664,
741–742
Tree Map, 138, 190, 260, 696
Venn diagram, 4, 364, 624

Graphs
bar graphs
analyzing and constructing, 107–110,
113–116
defined, 107
horizontal bar graphs, 107–108,
110–113, 116–121
scale, 107–110, 113–116
vertical bar graphs, 108–109, 114–115,
120–121, 122
key, 93–96, 99–102, 114, 162, 374
line plots
analyzing and constructing, 125–128
defined, 125
generating measurement data, 126,
593–596
picture graphs
analyzing and constructing, 93–96,
99–102, 113–116
defined, 93
key, 93
solving problems, 119–122

Greater than (>)
angles and, 703–706
fractions and, 507–510, 513–516,
519–522, 525–528

Grouping Property of Multiplication,
223–226

Groups
equal groups. *See* Equal groups
fractions of, 481–484, 487–490, 493–496

Half hours, 579, 585

Half symbol, 94

Halves, 443–446
measure to the nearest half inch, 593–596

Hexagons
angles of, 710–712
sides of, 710–712

Horizontal bar graphs, 107–108, 110–113,
116–121

Hour hand, 561–564

Hours
half, 559, 567–570, 579, 585
minutes after hour, 562
minutes before hour, 562

Hundreds
place value, 11–14, 18–20, 41–44, 50–52,
61–64, 67–70, 282–284, 288
round to nearest, 11–14

Identity Property
Addition, 5, 29–32
Multiplication, 177–180

Inches
as customary unit, 593–596
generating data in, 126, 593–596
measure to nearest fourth inch, 593–596
measure to nearest half inch, 593–596
measure to nearest inch, 126

Intersecting lines, 715–718

Inverse operations, 61, 339

Investigate, 333–336, 427–430, 539–542,
625–628, 747–750

Keys, 93–96, 99–102, 114, 162, 374

Kilograms
defined, 605
as metric unit, 605–608
solving problems in, 605–608, 611–614

Length
customary units for
feet, 151, 633, 637–640
inches, 593–596, 633
measure in centimeters, 631–634
measure to nearest fourth inch, 593–596
measure to nearest half inch, 593–596
measure to nearest inch, 126
metric units for
centimeters, 89, 631–634

Less than (<)
    angles and, 703–706
    comparing with greater than and equal
       to, 243, 507
    fractions and, 507–510, 513–516,
       519–522, 525–528

Line plots
    defined, 125
    generating measurement data for, 126,
       593–596
    making, 125–128
    read and interpret data in, 125–128

Lines
    defined, 697
    intersecting, 715–718
    parallel, 715–718
    perpendicular, 715–718

Line segments, 697
    describing, 699, 715–718

Liquid volume. *See also* Measurement;
    Units
    defined, 599
    estimating and measuring, 599–602
    liters, 599–602
    metric units for, 599–602
    solving problems, 599–602, 611–614

Liters
    defined, 599
    estimating and measuring, 599–602
    as metric unit, 599–602
    solving problems in, 599–602, 611–614

Make a table, 247–250
Make Connections, 334, 428, 540, 626, 748
Manipulatives and materials
    addition tables, 5, 6
    base-ten blocks, 281, 287
    beakers, 599, 600
    clock faces, 561–562, 567–570
    containers, 599, 600
    counters, 139, 307, 319, 365, 487
    crayons, 5–6, 230, 539, 594
    dot paper, 625
    fraction strips, 467, 489, 507
    geoboards, 625, 643
    glue stick, 613
    gram masses, 605, 606, 612
    1inch grid paper, 649

    kilogram masses, 605, 606
    MathBoard. *See* MathBoard
    measuring tape, 126
    multiplication table, 229
    number lines, 11–14, 25, 55, 281–283,
       467–470, 475–478, 514–515, 540–541,
       546, 573–576
    pan balance, 605, 606, 612
    pattern blocks, 747
    pitchers. *See* Beakers
    rubber bands, 625, 643
    rulers, 126, 594, 631, 729, 747
       centimeter, 631–634
       inch, 593–596, 631–634
    square tiles, 165, 166, 171, 173, 209, 333,
       345, 669, 675, 681
    straws, 704, 735
    two-color counters, 487

Mass. *See also* Measurement; Units
    defined, 605
    estimating and measuring, 605–608
    metric units for, 605–608
    solving problems, 605–608, 611–614

MathBoard, In every lesson. Some examples
    are: 43, 378, 410, 731, 748

Math Idea, 23, 29, 61, 94, 172, 223, 287, 334,
    366, 461, 467, 475, 513, 540, 593, 637,
    643, 709, 747

Math Processes and Practices
    1. Problem Solving. In many lessons.
       Some examples are: 11, 24, 90, 160,
       173, 216, 230, 631, 724
    2. Abstract and Quantitative Reasoning.
       In many lessons. Some examples are: 7,
       29, 87, 100, 209, 226, 651, 704, 735
    3. Use and Evaluate Logical Reasoning. In
       many lessons. Some examples are: 8,
       50, 57, 114, 151, 198, 626, 699, 718
    4. Mathematical Modeling. In many
       lessons. Some examples are: 23, 94,
       116, 145, 152, 168, 633, 652, 681
    5. Use Mathematical Tools. In many
       lessons. Some examples are: 38, 64,
       127, 168, 242, 535, 596, 646, 710
    6. Use Precise Mathematical Language.
       In many lessons. Some examples are:
       6, 25, 51, 113, 179, 237, 656, 716, 725
    7. See Structure. In many lessons. Some
       examples are: 5, 154, 171, 199, 217,
       326, 428, 650, 655
    8. Generalize. In many lessons. Some
       examples are: 25, 95, 125, 215, 427,
       599, 644, 710, 737

© Houghton Mifflin Harcourt Publishing Company

counting back on, 55, 326–328, 371–374, 377–380, 384
counting up on, 55, 378–379
dividing with, 325–328, 371, 377–380, 384
elapsed time. *See* Time
fractions greater than 1, 495–501
fractions on, 467–470
multiplying with, 151–154, 197–200, 235, 281–284
number line for hours in a day, 567
round numbers and, 11–14
skip counting, 151–154
    by eights, 235
    by fives, 197–198
    by sixes, 151
    by tens, 197–198
    time intervals. *See* Time
    by twos, 192
subtracting with, 55–58
take away tens and ones, 55–58
use to represent
    distances, 467–470
    elapsed time, 573–575, 579–582, 585–588
whole numbers on, 467–470, 475–478

Number patterns, 5–8, 229–232, 242, 261–264

Numbers
compatible, 17–20, 24–25, 49–52
counting, 281, 562, 438, 625
even, 5–8, 229–232, 235–236
expanded form of, 24, 35–38, 42, 56
fractions, 443–446, 449–452, 437–440, 455–458, 467–470, 475–478, 481–484, 487–490, 493–496, 507–510, 513–516, 519–522, 525–528, 533–536, 539–542, 545–548
hundreds, 11–14, 18–20, 35–38, 41–44, 50–52, 56–57, 61–64, 67–70, 281–284, 287–290
odd, 5–8, 229–232, 235–238
ones, 23–26, 29–32, 35–38, 41–44, 50–52, 55–58, 61–64, 67–70, 177–180, 351–354
ordering, 533–536
rounding, 11–14, 17–20
standard form of, 36
tens, 11–14, 23–26, 29–32, 35–38, 41–44, 55–58, 61–64, 67–70, 197–200, 287–290
unknown, 63, 193, 199, 225, 267–270, 367, 390–391, 396–397, 404–405, 410–411, 417, 429
zero, 177–180, 351–354

Numerators, 461
comparing fractions with same, 519–522, 525–528
defined, 461
fractions greater than 1, 476–478
ordering fractions with same, 533–536

Octagons
angles of, 709–712
sides of, 709–712

Odd numbers, 5–8, 229–232, 235–236

Ones, 12–14, 23–26, 29–32, 35–38, 41–44, 50–52, 55–58, 61–64, 67–70, 177–180, 287–290

On Your Own, In most lessons. Some examples are: 7, 43, 379, 411, 731, 744

Open shapes, 698–700

Ordering
fractions, 533–536
fraction strips, 533–536
liquid volume, 600
mass, 606

Order of operations, 427–430

Organize data, 87–90

Parallel lines, 715–718

Partitioning
fractions, 443–446, 449–452
shapes, 747–750

Patterns
addition, 5–8, 261–264
on the addition table, 5–8
arithmetic, 5–8, 229–232, 261–264
defined, 5
describing, 261–264
explaining using properties, 5–8, 229–232, 236
finding, 663–666
multiplication, 229–232, 242, 261–264
on the multiplication table, 229–232
with nine, 241–244
number, 5–8, 229–232
in a table, 261–264

© Houghton Mifflin Harcourt Publishing Company

Table of Measures

METRIC	CUSTOMARY
Length	

1 centimeter (cm) = 10 millimeters (mm)

1 decimeter (dm) = 10 centimeters (cm)   1 foot (ft) = 12 inches (in.)

1 meter (m) = 100 centimeters   1 yard (yd) = 3 feet, or 36 inches

1 meter (m) = 10 decimeters   1 mile (mi) = 1,760 yards, or 5,280 feet

1 kilometer (km) = 1,000 meters

Capacity and Liquid Volume

1 liter (L) = 1,000 milliliters (mL)   1 pint (pt) = 2 cups (c)

1 quart (qt) = 2 pints

1 gallon (gal) = 4 quarts

Mass/Weight

1 kilogram (kg) = 1,000 grams (g)   1 pound (lb) = 16 ounces (oz)

TIME

1 minute (min) = 60 seconds (sec)   1 year (yr) = 12 months (mo), or

1 hour (hr) = 60 minutes   about 52 weeks

1 day = 24 hours   1 year = 365 days

1 week (wk) = 7 days   1 leap year = 366 days

1 decade = 10 years

1 century = 100 years

MONEY

1 penny = 1 cent (¢)

1 nickel = 5 cents

1 dime = 10 cents

1 quarter = 25 cents

1 half dollar = 50 cents

1 dollar ($) = 100 cents

SYMBOLS

< is less than

> is greater than

= is equal to

Houghton
Mifflin
Harcourt

Volume 2

Houghton
Mifflin
Harcourt

2017 Edition

Copyright © by Houghton Mifflin Harcourt Publishing Company

Printed in the U.S.A.

ISBN 978-0-544-71059-7

12 0877 20

4500789750   D E F G

on a number line, 573–576, 579–582, 585–588
    subtracting, 573–576, 579–582, 585–588
measure in minutes, 561–564
to minute, 561–564, 567–570
number line, 567, 573–576, 579–582
P.M., 567–570
reading time, 561–564
time lines, 567
telling time, 561–564, 567–570
writing time, 561–564, 567–570

Time intervals. *See* Elapsed time; Time

Trapezoids
    angles of, 723–726
    drawing, 729–732
    sides of, 723–726

Triangles
    angles of, 698–699, 736–738
    classifying, 735–738
    comparing, 736–738
    describing, 735–738
    drawing, 735–738
    modeling, 735
    sides of, 710–711, 735–738

Try Another Problem, 74, 88, 160, 248, 276, 302, 422, 494, 508, 586, 664, 742

Try This!, In some lessons. Some examples are: 12, 42, 390, 444, 709, 716

Two-digit numbers
    addition, 18–20, 23–26, 29–32
    subtraction, 49–52, 55–58

Two-dimensional shapes
    angles. *See* Angles
    area. *See* Area
    attributes of, 697–700, 703–706, 709–712, 715–718, 723–726, 729–732, 735–738, 741–744, 747–755
    classifying, 697–700, 723–726, 741–744
    comparing, 695–700, 723–726
    defined, 698
    describing, 697–700
    draw a diagram, 741–744
    drawing, 698, 712, 716, 729–732
    partitioning shapes to make equal areas, 747–750
    perimeter. *See* Perimeter
    plane shapes, 697–700, 703–706, 741–747
        circles, 698, 709, 712
        decagons, 709–712
        hexagons, 709–712

octagons, 709–712
open or closed shapes, 698–700, 709–712
pentagons, 709–712
polygons, 709–712
quadrilaterals, 709–712, 723–726
rectangles, 723–726
rhombuses, 723–726
squares, 723–726
trapezoids, 723–726
triangles, 709–712, 735–738
polygons. *See* Polygons
quadrilaterals, 709
    angles of, 723–726
    classifying, 723–726
    drawing, 729–732
    rectangles, 723–726, 729–732
    rhombuses, 723–726, 729–732
    sides of, 723–726
    squares, 723–726, 729–732
    trapezoids, 723–726, 729–732
sides
    defined, 709
    describing, 715–718
    of polygons, 710–712
    of quadrilaterals, 710–711, 723–726
    of triangles, 710–711, 735–738
vertex, 703

Two-step problems, 73–76, 159–162, 421–424, 427–430

U

Understand Vocabulary, 4, 86, 138, 190, 260, 300, 364, 442, 506, 560, 624, 696

Unit fractions, 455–458, 461, 467–470, 487–490, 493–496, 747–750

Unit squares, 643

Units
    customary units
        for area
            square feet, 656–658, 663–666, 669
            square inches, 649, 651
        for length
            feet, 151, 634, 638, 664
            inches, 593–596, 631–633
        for liquid volume and capacity, cups, 217
        for mass, grams, 605–608
        for weight, ounces, 148

Dear Students and Families,

Welcome to **Go Math!**, Grade 3! In this exciting mathematics program, there are hands-on activities to do and real-world problems to solve. Best of all, you will write your ideas and answers right in your book. In **Go Math!**, writing and drawing on the pages helps you think deeply about what you are learning, and you will really understand math!

By the way, all of the pages in your **Go Math!** book are made using recycled paper. We wanted you to know that you can Go Green with **Go Math!**

Sincerely,

The Authors

Made in the United States
Text printed on 100% recycled paper

Authors

Juli K. Dixon, Ph.D.
Professor, Mathematics Education
University of Central Florida
Orlando, Florida

Edward B. Burger, Ph.D.
President, Southwestern University
Georgetown, Texas

Steven J. Leinwand
Principal Research Analyst
American Institutes for
 Research (AIR)
Washington, D.C.

Contributor

Rena Petrello
Professor, Mathematics
Moorpark College
Moorpark, CA

Matthew R. Larson, Ph.D.
K-12 Curriculum Specialist for
 Mathematics
Lincoln Public Schools
Lincoln, Nebraska

Martha E. Sandoval-Martinez
Math Instructor
El Camino College
Torrance, California

English Language Learners Consultant

Elizabeth Jiménez
CEO, GEMAS Consulting
Professional Expert on English
 Learner Education
Bilingual Education and
 Dual Language
Pomona, California

VOLUME 1
Whole Number Operations

Big Idea Develop a conceptual understanding of whole number operations and data. Use strategies for addition and subtraction within 1,000 and multiplication and division within 100.

Big Idea

GO DIGITAL

Go online! Your math lessons are interactive. Use *i*Tools, Animated Math Models, the Multimedia eGlossary, and more.

Chapter 1 Overview

In this chapter, you will explore and discover answers to the following **Essential Questions**:

- How can you add and subtract whole numbers and decide if an answer is reasonable?
- How do you know when an estimate will be close to an exact answer?
- When do you regroup to add or subtract whole numbers?
- How might you decide which strategy to use to add or subtract?

Chapter 2 Overview

In this chapter, you will explore and discover answers to the following **Essential Questions**:

- How can you represent and interpret data?
- What are some ways to organize data so it is easy to use?
- How can analyzing data in graphs help you solve problems?

③ Understand Multiplication 137

Chapter 3 Overview

In this chapter, you will explore and discover answers to the following **Essential Questions**:

- How can you use multiplication to find how many in all?
- What models can help you multiply?
- How can you use skip counting to help you multiply?
- How can multiplication properties help you find products?
- What types of problems can be solved by using multiplication?

Practice and Homework

Lesson Check and Spiral Review in every lesson

④ Multiplication Facts and Strategies 189

Chapter 4 Overview

In this chapter, you will explore and discover answers to the following **Essential Questions**:

- What strategies can you use to multiply?
- How are patterns and multiplication related?
- How can multiplication properties help you find products?
- What types of problems can be solved by using multiplication?

Chapter 5 Overview

In this chapter, you will explore and discover answers to the following **Essential Questions**:

• How can you use multiplication facts, place value, and properties to solve multiplication problems?

• How are patterns and multiplication related?

• How can multiplication properties help you find products?

• What types of problems can be solved by using multiplication?

Chapter 6 Overview

In this chapter, you will explore and discover answers to the following **Essential Questions**:

• How can you use division to find how many in each group or how many equal groups?

• How are multiplication and division related?

• What models can help you divide?

• How can subtraction help you divide?

Chapter 7 Overview

In this chapter, you will explore and discover answers to the following **Essential Questions**:

- What strategies can you use to divide?
- How can you use a related multiplication fact to divide?
- How can you use factors to divide?
- What types of problems can be solved by using division?

7 Division Facts and Strategies — 363

VOLUME 2
Fractions

Big Idea Develop a conceptual understanding of fractions and fraction concepts, including fraction comparisons and equivalence.

Big Idea

GO DIGITAL

Go online! Your math lessons are interactive. Use *i*Tools, Animated Math Models, the Multimedia *e*Glossary, and more.

Essential Question
What are equal parts of a whole?
Start

Chapter 8 Overview

In this chapter, you will explore and discover answers to the following **Essential Questions**:

• How can you use fractions to describe how much or how many?

• Why do you need to have equal parts for fractions?

• How can you solve problems that involve fractions?

Chapter 9 Overview

In this chapter, you will explore and discover answers to the following **Essential Questions**:

• How can you compare fractions?

• What models can help you compare and order fractions?

• How can you use the size of the pieces to help you compare and order fractions?

• How can you find equivalent fractions?

GO DIGITAL

Go online! Your math lessons are interactive. Use *i*Tools, Animated Math Models, the Multimedia *e*Glossary, and more.

Chapter 10 Overview

In this chapter, you will explore and discover answers to the following **Essential Questions**:

• How can you tell time and use measurement to describe the size of something?

• How can you tell time and find the elapsed time, starting time, or ending time of an event?

• How can you measure the length of an object to the nearest half or fourth inch?

Chapter 11 Overview

In this chapter, you will explore and discover answers to the following **Essential Questions**:

• How can you solve problems involving perimeter and area?

• How can you find perimeter?

• How can you find area?

• What might you need to estimate or measure perimeter and area?

Measurement

Big Idea Develop a conceptual understanding of measurement, including time, linear, and liquid measures. Develop concepts of area and perimeter.

Geometry

Big Idea Describe, analyze, and compare two-dimensional shapes. Develop a conceptual understanding of dividing shapes into equal areas and writing the area as a fraction.

GO DIGITAL

Go online! Your math lessons are interactive. Use *i*Tools, Animated Math Models, the Multimedia eGlossary, and more.

Chapter 12 Overview

In this chapter, you will explore and discover answers to the following **Essential Questions**:

- What are some ways to describe and classify two-dimensional shapes?
- How can you describe the angles and sides in polygons?
- How can you use sides and angles to describe quadrilaterals and triangles?
- How can you use properties of shapes to classify them?
- How can you divide shapes into equal parts and use unit fractions to describe the parts?

Personal Math Trainer
Online Assessment and Intervention

Big Idea Fractions

BIG IDEA Develop a conceptual understanding of fractions and fraction concepts, including fraction comparisons and equivalence.

The Missouri quarter shows explorers Lewis and Clark traveling down the Missouri River. The Gateway Arch is in the background.

Real World Project

Coins in the U.S.

Many years ago, a coin called a *piece of eight* was sometimes cut into 8 equal parts. Each part was equal to one eighth ($\frac{1}{8}$) of the whole. Now, U.S. coin values are based on the dollar. Four quarters are equal in value to 1 dollar. So, 1 quarter is equal to one fourth ($\frac{1}{4}$) of a dollar.

Get Started

 WRITE ► Math

Work with a partner. In which year were the Missouri state quarters minted? Use the Important Facts to help you. Then write fractions to answer these questions:

1. 2 quarters are equal to what part of a dollar?
2. 1 nickel is equal to what part of a dime?
3. 2 nickels are equal to what part of a dime?

Important Facts

- The U.S. government minted state quarters every year from 1999 to 2008 in the order that the states became part of the United States.
- 1999—Delaware, Pennsylvania, New Jersey, Georgia, Connecticut
- 2000—Massachusetts, Maryland, South Carolina, New Hampshire, Virginia
- 2001—New York, North Carolina, Rhode Island, Vermont, Kentucky
- 2002—Tennessee, Ohio, Louisiana, Indiana, Mississippi
- 2003—Illinois, Alabama, Maine, Missouri, Arkansas
- 2004—Michigan, Florida, Texas, Iowa, Wisconsin
- 2005—California, Minnesota, Oregon, Kansas, West Virginia
- 2006—Nevada, Nebraska, Colorado, North Dakota, South Dakota
- 2007—Montana, Washington, Idaho, Wyoming, Utah
- 2008—Oklahoma, New Mexico, Arizona, Alaska, Hawaii

Completed by _____

Understand Fractions

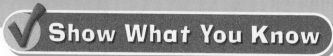 Show What You Know

 **Personal Math Trainer**
Online Assessment
and Intervention

Check your understanding of important skills.

Name _____

▶ **Equal Parts** Circle the shape that has equal parts.

1.

2.

▶ **Combine Plane Shapes** Write the number of ▲ needed to cover the shape.

3.

_____ triangles

4.

_____ triangles

5.

_____ triangles

▶ **Count Equal Groups** Complete.

6.

_____ groups

_____ in each group

7.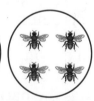

_____ groups

_____ in each group

 **Math in the Real World**

Casey shared a pizza with some friends. They each ate $\frac{1}{3}$ of the pizza. How many people shared the pizza?

▶ **Visualize It** ••

Complete the bubble map by using the words with a ✓.

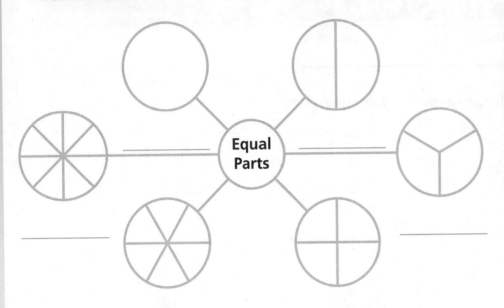

Preview Words

denominator

✓ eighths

   equal parts

✓ fourths

   fraction

   fraction greater than 1

✓ halves

   numerator

✓ sixths

✓ thirds

   unit fraction

✓ whole

▶ **Understand Vocabulary** ••••••••••••••••••••••••••••••••

Read the description. Write the preview word.

1. It is a number that names part of a whole or part

   of a group. _____

2. It is the part of a fraction above the line, which tells
   how many parts are being counted.

   _____

3. It is the part of a fraction below the line, which tells
   how many equal parts there are in the whole or in the

   group. _____

4. It is a number that names 1 equal part of a whole and

   has 1 as its numerator. _____

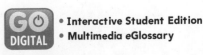

• **Interactive Student Edition**
• **Multimedia eGlossary**

Chapter 8 Vocabulary

denominator

denominador

11

Eighths

octavos

17

Equal Parts

partes iguales

21

Fourths

cuartos

26

fraction

fracción

27

Fraction Greater than 1

fraccíon mayor que 1

28

Halves

mitades

32

numerator

numerador

53

These are eighths

The part of a fraction below the line, which tells how many equal parts there are in the whole or in the group

Example: $\frac{1}{5}$ ← denominator

These are fourths

Parts that are exactly the same size

6 equal parts

A number which has a numerator that is greater than its denominator

Examples:

  $\frac{6}{3}$ $\frac{2}{1}$

A number that names part of a whole or part of a group

Examples:

 $\frac{1}{3}$

The part of a fraction above the line, which tells how many parts are being counted

Example: $\frac{1}{5}$ ← numerator

These are halves

Sixths

sextos

74

Thirds

tercios

77

unit fraction

fraccíon unitaria

79

Whole

entero

84

These are thirds

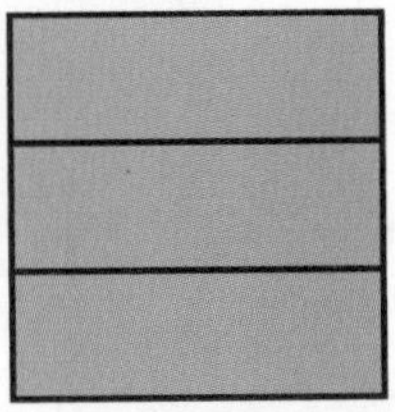

© Houghton Mifflin Harcourt Publishing Company

These are sixths

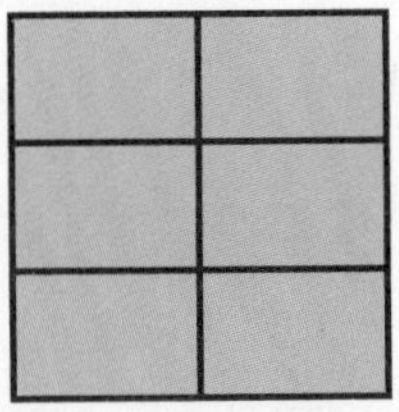

© Houghton Mifflin Harcourt Publishing Company

All of the parts of a shape or group

Example:

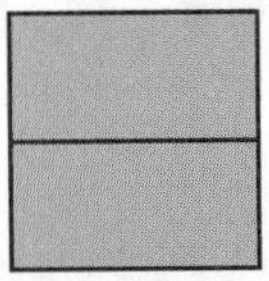

$\frac{2}{2} = 1$

This is one whole.

© Houghton Mifflin Harcourt Publishing Company

A fraction that has 1 as its top number, or numerator

Example: $\frac{1}{3}$ is a unit fraction

Going to the Mint

For 2 to 4 players

Word Box
denominator
eighths
equal parts
fourths
fraction
fraction greater than 1
halves
numerator
sixths
thirds
unit fraction
whole

Materials

- 3 red playing pieces
- 3 blue playing pieces
- 3 green playing pieces
- 3 yellow playing pieces
- 1 number cube

How to Play

1. Put your 3 playing pieces in the START circle of the same color.

2. To get a playing piece out of START, you must toss a 6 on the number cube.
   - If you toss a 6, move 1 of your playing pieces to the same colored circle on the path.
   - If you do not toss a 6, wait until your next turn.

3. Once you have a playing piece on the path, toss the number cube to take a turn. Move the playing pieces that many tan spaces. You must get all 3 of your playing pieces on the path.

4. If you land on a space with a question, answer it. If you are correct, move ahead 1 space.

5. To reach FINISH, move your playing pieces up the path that is the same color as your playing pieces. The first player to get all three playing pieces on FINISH wins.

START

What is the name of the part of a fraction above the line?

Why is $\frac{1}{4}$ a unit fraction?

How many fourths are in a whole?

What is a fraction?

FINISH

What is the meaning of a whole?

How many sixths does three thirds equal?

START

Why is $\frac{4}{3}$ a fraction greater than 1?

Which is a whole: $\frac{3}{8}$ or $\frac{8}{8}$?

442B

START

What are sixths?

What kind of number has a numerator greater than its denominator?

FINISH

What kind of fraction is $\frac{1}{3}$?

If a whole has two equal parts, what are the equal parts called?

How many equal parts called thirds are in a whole?

What are equal parts?

If there are 8 equal parts in a whole, what are the equal parts called?

What is the meaning of denominator?

START

Journal

The Write Way

Reflect

Choose one idea. Write about it.

- Draw and explain the ideas of *equal* and *unequal parts*. Use a separate piece of paper for your drawing.
- Tell the most important idea to understand about fractions.
- Define *numerator and denominator* so that a younger child would understand.

Equal Parts of a Whole

Essential Question What are equal parts of a whole?

Learning Objective You will describe equal parts of a whole.

 Unlock the Problem Real World

Lauren shares a sandwich with her brother. They each get an equal part. How many equal parts are there?

Each whole shape below is divided into equal parts. A **whole** is all of the parts of one shape or group. **Equal parts** are exactly the same size.

• What do you need to find?

_____

_____

• How many people share the

sandwich? _____

2 **halves**

3 **thirds**

4 **fourths**

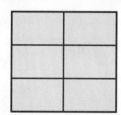

_____ **sixths**

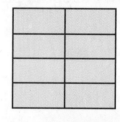

_____ **eighths**

Lauren's sandwich is divided into halves.

So, there are _____ equal parts.

• Draw a picture to show a different way Lauren's sandwich could have been divided into halves.

 Math Talk

Math Processes and Practices ③

Verify the Reasoning of Others Are your halves the same shape as your classmates' halves? Explain why both halves represent the same size.

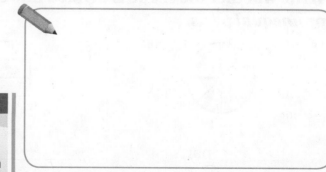

Try This! Write whether the shape is divided into *equal* parts or *unequal* parts.

A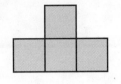

4 _____ parts
fourths

B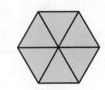

6 _____ parts
sixths

C

2 _____ parts
These are not halves.

⚠ **ERROR Alert**

Be sure the parts are equal in size.

equal   unequal

Share and Show MATH BOARD

1. This shape is divided into 3 equal parts. What is the name for the parts?

_____

Math Talk Math Processes and Practices ❸

Apply How do you determine if the shapes are divided into equal parts?

Write the number of equal parts. Then write the name for the parts.

2.

_____ equal parts

_____

3.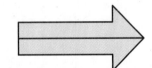

_____ equal parts

_____

✓4.

_____ equal parts

_____

Write whether the shape is divided into *equal* parts or *unequal* parts.

5.

_____ parts

6.

_____ parts

✓7.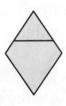

_____ parts

444

© Houghton Mifflin Harcourt Publishing Company

Name _____

On Your Own

Write the number of equal parts. Then write the name for the parts.

8.

_____ equal parts

_____

9.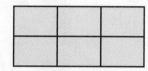

_____ equal parts

_____

10.

_____ equal parts

_____

11.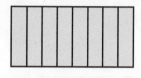

_____ equal parts

_____

12.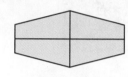

_____ equal parts

_____

13.

_____ equal parts

_____

Write whether the shape is divided into *equal* parts or *unequal* parts.

14.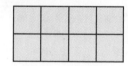

_____ parts

15.

_____ parts

16.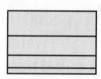

_____ parts

17. Draw lines to divide the circle into 8 eighths.

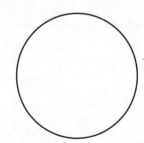

18. **Go DEEPER** Thomas wants to divide a square piece of paper into 4 equal parts. Draw two different quick pictures to show what his paper could look like.

Problem Solving • Applications

Use the pictures for 19–20.

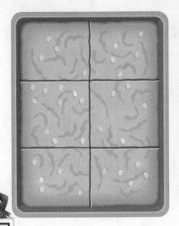

19. Mrs. Rivera made 2 pans of corn casserole for a large family dinner. She cut each pan into parts. What is the name of the parts in A?

_____

20. THINK SMARTER Alex said his mom divided Pan B into eighths. Does his statement make sense? Explain.

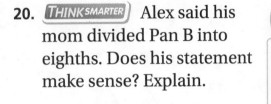

Pan A   **Pan B**

_____

_____

21. Math Processes and Practices ⑥ **Explain** why the rectangle is divided into 4 equal parts.

_____

_____

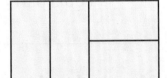

22. GO DEEPER Shakira cut a triangle out of paper. She wants to divide the triangle into 2 equal parts. Draw a quick picture to show what her triangle could look like.

23. THINK SMARTER Parker divides a fruit bar into 3 equal parts. Circle the word that makes the sentence true.

The fruit bar is divided into | thirds |
                               | halves |
                               | fourths | .

Name _____

Equal Parts of a Whole

Learning Objective You will describe equal parts of a whole.

Write the number of equal parts.
Then write the name for the parts.

1.

___4___ equal parts

___fourths___

2.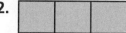

_____ equal parts

_____

Write whether the shape is divided into *equal* parts or *unequal* parts.

3.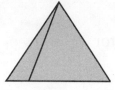

_____ parts

4.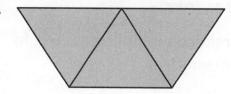

_____ parts

 Problem Solving *Real World*

5. Diego cuts a round pizza into eight equal slices. What is the name for the parts?

_____

6. Madison is making a place mat. She divides it into 6 equal parts to color. What is the name for the parts?

_____

7. **WRITE** ▸*Math* Describe how 4 friends could share a sandwich equally.

_____

_____

Lesson Check

1. How many equal parts are in this shape?

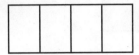

_____

2. What is the name for the equal parts of the whole?

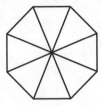

_____

Spiral Review

3. Use a related multiplication fact to find the quotient.

$$49 \div 7 =$$

_____

4. Find the unknown factor and quotient.

$$9 \times \boxed{} = 45$$

$$45 \div 9 = \boxed{}$$

_____

5. There are 5 pairs of socks in one package. Matt buys 3 packages of socks. How many pairs of socks does Matt buy?

_____

6. Mrs. McCarr buys 9 packages of markers for an art project. Each package has 10 markers. How many markers does Mrs. McCarr buy?

_____

FOR MORE PRACTICE
GO TO THE
Personal Math Trainer

Name _____

Equal Shares

Essential Question Why do you need to know how to make equal shares?

Learning Objective You will draw models to make equal shares.

Unlock the Problem

Four friends share 2 small pizzas equally. What are two ways the pizza could be divided equally? How much pizza will each friend get?

- How might the two ways be different?

_____

_____

 Draw to model the problem.

Draw 2 circles to show the pizzas.

One Way

There are _____ friends.

So, divide each pizza into 4 slices.

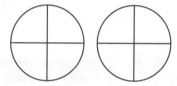

There are _____ equal parts.

Each friend can have 2 equal parts. Each friend will get 2 eighths of all the pizza.

Another Way

There are _____ friends.

So, divide all the pizza into 4 slices.

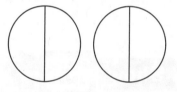

There are _____ equal parts.

Each friend can have 1 equal part. Each friend will get 1 half of a pizza.

Math Talk

Math Processes and Practices ②

Use Reasoning Why does dividing the pizza into different size slices still allow the friends to have an equal share?

Try This! Four girls share 3 oranges equally. Draw a quick picture to find out how much each girl gets.

- Draw 3 circles to show the oranges.
- Draw lines to divide the circles equally.
- Shade the part 1 girl gets.
- Describe what part of an orange each girl gets.

_____

🔑 Example

Melissa and Kyle are planning to share one pan of lasagna with 6 friends. They do not agree on the way to cut the pan into equal parts. Will each friend get an equal share using Melissa's way? Using Kyle's way?

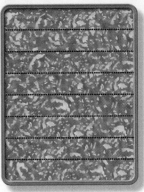 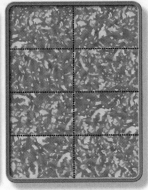

Melissa's Way　　**Kyle's Way**

- Will Melissa's shares and Kyle's shares have the same shape? _____

- Will their shares using either way be the same size? _____

So, each friend will get an _____ share using either way.

- Explain why both ways let the friends have the same amount.

_____

_____

Share and Show 🖊 MATH BOARD

1. Two friends share 4 oranges equally. Use the picture to find how much each friend gets.

Think: There are more oranges than friends.

Math Talk　Math Processes and Practices ⑥

Explain another way the oranges could have been divided. Tell how much each friend will get.

_____

Draw lines to show how much each person gets.
Write the answer.

✅ 2. 8 sisters share 3 eggrolls equally.

✅ 3. 6 students share 4 bagels equally.

_____

Name _____

Draw lines to show how much each person gets. Write the answer.

4. 3 classmates share 2 granola bars equally.

_____

5. 4 brothers share 2 sandwiches equally.

_____

Draw to show how much each person gets. Shade the amount that one person gets. Write the answer.

6. 8 friends share 4 sheets of construction paper equally.

_____

7. (Math Processes and Practices 4) **Model Mathematics** 4 sisters share 3 muffins equally.

_____

8. (GO DEEPER) Maria prepared 5 quesadillas. She wants to share them equally among 8 of her neighbors. How much of a quesadilla will each neighbor get?

_____

© Houghton Mifflin Harcourt Publishing Company

Chapter 8 • Lesson 2 451

🔑 Unlock the Problem

9. **THINK SMARTER** Julia holds a bread-baking class. She has 4 adults and 3 children in the class. The class will make 2 round loaves of bread. If Julia plans to give each person, including herself, an equal part of the baked breads, how much bread will each person get?

a. What do you need to find? _____

_____

b. How will you use what you know about drawing equal

   shares to solve the problem? _____

_____

c. Draw a quick picture to find the share
   of bread each person will get.

d. So, each person will get

   _____ of a loaf of bread.

10. **THINK SMARTER** Lara and three girl friends share three
    sandwiches equally.

How much does each girl get? Mark all that apply.

Ⓐ 3 fifths of a sandwich   Ⓒ 1 whole sandwich

Ⓑ 3 fourths of a sandwich   Ⓓ one half and 1 fourth of a sandwich

Equal Shares

Learning Objective You will draw models to make equal shares.

Draw lines to show how much each person gets. Write the answer.

1. 6 friends share 3 sandwiches equally.

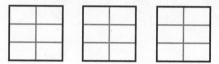

3 sixths of a sandwich
_____
_____

2. 4 teammates share 5 granola bars equally. Draw to show how much each person gets. Shade the amount that one person gets. Write the answer.

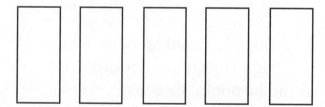

_____

Problem Solving *Real World*

3. Three brothers share 2 sandwiches equally. How much of a sandwich does each brother get?

_____

_____

4. Six neighbors share 4 pies equally. How much of a pie does each neighbor get?

_____

_____

5. **WRITE** *Math* Draw a diagram to show 3 pizzas shared equally among 6 friends.

_____

_____

Lesson Check

1. Two friends share 3 fruit bars equally. How much does each friend get?

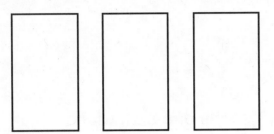

_____

2. Four brothers share 3 pizzas equally. How much of a pizza does each brother get?

_____

Spiral Review

3. Find the quotient.

$$3\overline{)27}$$

_____

4. Tyrice put 4 cookies in each of 7 bags. How many cookies in all did he put in the bags?

_____

5. Ryan earned $5 per hour raking leaves. He earned $35. How many hours did he rake leaves?

_____

6. Hannah has 229 horse stickers and 164 kitten stickers. How many more horse stickers than kitten stickers does Hannah have?

_____

FOR MORE PRACTICE
GO TO THE
Personal Math Trainer

Name _____

Unit Fractions of a Whole

Essential Question What do the top and bottom numbers of a fraction tell?

Learning Objective You will use fraction models to recognize and name the quantity formed by one part when a whole is divided into equal parts.

A **fraction** is a number that names part of a whole or part of a group.

In a fraction, the top number tells how many equal parts are being counted.

The bottom number tells how many equal parts are in the whole or in the group.

$\longrightarrow \dfrac{1}{6}$

A **unit fraction** names 1 equal part of a whole. It has 1 as its top number. $\frac{1}{6}$ is a unit fraction.

Unlock the Problem Real World

Luke's family picked strawberries. They put the washed strawberries in one part of a fruit platter. The platter had 6 equal parts. What fraction of the fruit platter had strawberries?

Find part of a whole.

Shade 1 of the 6 equal parts.

Read: one sixth   **Write:** $\frac{1}{6}$

So, _____ of the platter had strawberries.

Use a fraction to find a whole.

This shape ☐ is $\frac{1}{4}$ of the whole. Here are examples of what the whole could look like.

Math Talk

Math Processes and Practices ②

Reason Abstractly How can you make a whole if you know what one equal part looks like?

Ⓐ 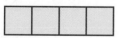   Ⓑ   Ⓒ

© Houghton Mifflin Harcourt Publishing Company

Try This! Look again at the examples at the bottom of page 455.
Draw two other pictures of how the whole might look.

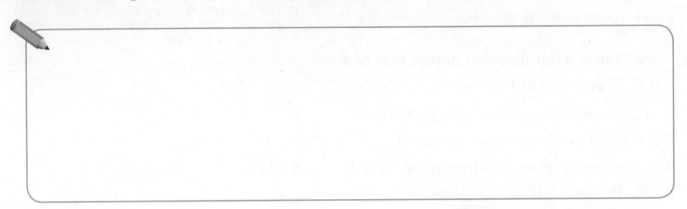

Share and Show

Math Talk

Math Processes and Practices ④

Use Models When using a fraction model, how do you know what the denominator of the fraction will be?

1. What fraction names the shaded part? _____

   Think: 1 out of 3 equal parts is shaded.

Write the number of equal parts in the whole.
Then write the fraction that names the shaded part.

2.

   _____ equal parts

   _____

3.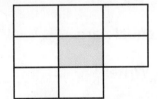

   _____ equal parts

   _____

✓ 4.

   _____ equal parts

   _____

5.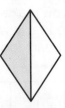

   _____ equal parts

   _____

6.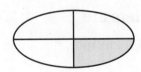

   _____ equal parts

   _____

✓ 7.

   _____ equal parts

   _____

Name _____

On Your Own

Write the number of equal parts in the whole.
Then write the fraction that names the shaded part.

8.

_____ equal parts

_____

9.
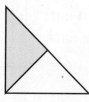
_____ equal parts

_____

10.

_____ equal parts

_____

11.
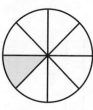
_____ equal parts

_____

12.

_____ equal parts

_____

13. GO DEEPER
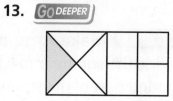
_____ equal parts

_____

Math Processes and Practices 4 **Use Diagrams** **Draw a picture of the whole.**

14. $\frac{1}{2}$ is

15. $\frac{1}{3}$ is

16. $\frac{1}{6}$ is

17. $\frac{1}{4}$ is

Problem Solving • Applications

Use the pictures for 18–19.

Kylie's Lunch	Dylan's Lunch
sandwich	pizza
apple	fruit bar

18. The missing parts of the pictures show what Kylie and Dylan ate for lunch. What fraction of the pizza did Dylan eat? What fraction of the fruit bar did he eat?

_____

19. What fraction of the apple did Kylie eat? Write the fraction in numbers and in words.

_____ _____

20. **Math Processes and Practices 3** **Make Arguments** Diego drew lines to divide the square into 6 pieces as shown. Then he shaded part of the square. Diego says he shaded $\frac{1}{6}$ of the square. Is he correct? Explain how you know.

_____

_____

21. *THINK SMARTER* Riley and Chad each have a granola bar broken into equal pieces. They each eat one piece, or $\frac{1}{4}$, of their granola bar. How many more pieces do Riley and Chad need to eat to finish both granola bars? Draw a picture to justify your answer.

22. *THINK SMARTER* What fraction names the shaded part? Explain how you know how to write the fraction.

_____

_____

Name _____

Unit Fractions of a Whole

Learning Objective You will use fraction models to recognize and name the quantity formed by one part when a whole is divided into equal parts.

**Write the number of equal parts in the whole.
Then write the fraction that names the shaded part.**

1.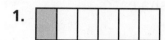

____6____ equal parts

____$\frac{1}{6}$____

2.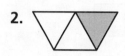

_____ equal parts

_____

Draw a picture of the whole.

3. $\frac{1}{3}$ is

4. $\frac{1}{8}$ is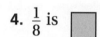

Problem Solving ·Real· World

5. Tyler made a pan of cornbread. He cut it into 8 equal pieces and ate 1 piece. What fraction of the cornbread did Tyler eat?

_____

6. Anna cut an apple into 4 equal pieces. She gave 1 piece to her sister. What fraction of the apple did Anna give to her sister?

_____

7. ▌**WRITE** ▸*Math* Draw a picture to show what 1 out of 3 equal parts looks like. Then write the fraction.

_____

_____

Lesson Check

1. What fraction names the shaded part?

2. Tasha cut a fruit bar into 3 equal parts. She ate 1 part. What fraction of the fruit bar did Tasha eat?

Spiral Review

3. Alex has 5 lizards. He divides them equally among 5 cages. How many lizards does Alex put in each cage?

4. Find the product.

$$8 \times 1 = \boxed{}$$

5. Leo bought 6 chew toys for his new puppy. Each chew toy cost $4. How much did Leo spend for the chew toys?

6. Lilly is making a picture graph. Each picture of a star is equal to two books she has read. The row for the month of December has 3 stars. How many books did Lilly read during the month of December?

FOR MORE PRACTICE
GO TO THE
Personal Math Trainer

Fractions of a Whole

Essential Question How does a fraction name part of a whole?

Learning Objective You will use fraction models to name equal parts of a whole.

Unlock the Problem

The first pizzeria in America opened in New York in 1905. The pizza recipe came from Italy. Look at Italy's flag. What fraction of the flag is not red?

 Name equal parts of a whole.

A fraction can name more than 1 equal part of a whole.

The flag is divided into 3 equal parts, and 2 parts are not red.

2 parts not red   → $\frac{2}{3}$ ←   numerator
3 equal parts in all → $\frac{2}{3}$ ←   denominator

Read: two thirds or two parts out of three equal parts

Write: $\frac{2}{3}$

So, _____ of the flag is not red.

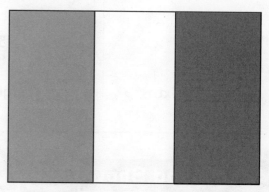

▲ Italy's flag has three equal parts.

> **Math Idea**
> When all the parts are shaded, one whole shape is equal to all of its parts. It represents the whole number 1.
> $$\frac{3}{3} = 1$$

The **numerator** tells how many parts are being counted.

The **denominator** tells how many equal parts are in the whole or in the group.

You can count equal parts, such as sixths, to make a whole.

One $\frac{1}{6}$ part	Two $\frac{1}{6}$ parts	Three $\frac{1}{6}$ parts	Four $\frac{1}{6}$ parts	Five $\frac{1}{6}$ parts	Six $\frac{1}{6}$ parts
$\frac{1}{6}$	$\frac{2}{6}$	$\frac{3}{6}$	$\frac{}{6}$	$\frac{}{6}$	$\frac{}{6}$

For example, $\frac{6}{6}$ = one whole, or 1.

Try This! Write the missing word or number to name the shaded part.

A

$\frac{2}{6}$

_____ sixths

B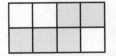

$\frac{5}{8}$

_____ eighths

C

$\frac{}{3}$

two thirds

D

$\frac{}{6}$, or 1

six sixths, or one whole

Share and Show MATH BOARD

Math Talk Math Processes and Practices ⑧

Generalize What do the numerator and denominator of a fraction tell you?

1. Shade two parts out of eight equal parts. Write a fraction in words and in numbers to name the shaded part.

   Think: Each part is $\frac{1}{8}$.

   Read: _____ eighths   **Write:** _____

Write the fraction that names each part. Write a fraction in words and in numbers to name the shaded part.

2.

   Each part is ____.

   _____ fourths

   _____

3.

   Each part is ____.

   _____ sixths

   _____

4.

   Each part is ____.

   _____ fourths

   _____

462

Name _____

Write the fraction that names each part. Write a fraction in words and in numbers to name the shaded part.

5.

Each part is ____.

_____ eighths

_____

6.

Each part is ____.

_____ thirds

_____

7.

Each part is ____.

_____ sixths

_____

Shade the fraction circle to model the fraction. Then write the fraction in numbers.

8. six out of eight

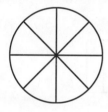

_____

9. three fourths

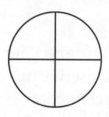

_____

10. three out of three

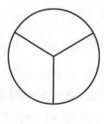

_____

11. A flag is divided into four equal sections. One section is white. What fraction of the flag is not white?

_____

12. A garden has six sections. Two sections are planted with tomatoes. Which fraction represents the part of the garden without tomatoes?

_____

13. Jane is making a memory quilt from some of her old favorite clothes that are too small. She will use T-shirts for the shaded squares in the pattern. What names the part of the quilt that will be made of T-shirts?

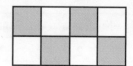

_____

Problem Solving • Applications

Use the diagrams for 14–15.

14. GO DEEPER Mrs. Ormond ordered pizza. Each pizza had 8 equal slices. What fraction of the pepperoni pizza was eaten? What fraction of the cheese pizza is left?

Pepperoni   Cheese   Veggie

_____

15. THINK SMARTER **Pose a Problem** Use the picture of the veggie pizza to write a problem that includes a fraction. Solve your problem.

_____

_____

_____

16. Math Processes and Practices ③ **Verify the Reasoning of Others** Kate says that $\frac{2}{4}$ of the rectangle is shaded. Describe her error. Use the model to write the correct fraction for the shaded part.

_____

_____

_____

17. THINK SMARTER Select a numerator and a denominator for the fraction that names the shaded part of the shape.

Numerator	Denominator
○ 2	○ 3
○ 3	○ 5
○ 5	○ 6
○ 6	○ 8

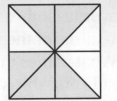

Fractions of a Whole

Learning Objective You will use fraction models to name equal parts of a whole.

Write the fraction that names each part. Write a fraction in words and in numbers to name the shaded part.

1.

Each part is _____$\frac{1}{6}$_____.

_____three_____ sixths

_____$\frac{3}{6}$_____

2.

Each part is _____.

_____ eighths

_____

Shade the fraction circle to model the fraction. Then write the fraction in numbers.

3. four out of six

_____

4. eight out of eight

_____

Problem Solving Real World

5. Emma makes a poster for the school's spring concert. She divides the poster into 8 equal parts. She uses two of the parts for the title. What fraction of the poster does Emma use for the title?

_____

6. Lucas makes a flag. It has 6 equal parts. Five of the parts are red. What fraction of the flag is red?

_____

7. **WRITE** ▸Math Draw a rectangle and divide it into 4 equal parts. Shade 3 parts. Then write the fraction that names the shaded part.

_____

_____

Lesson Check

1. What fraction names the shaded part?

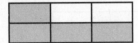

_____

2. What fraction names the shaded part?

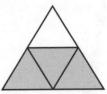

_____

Spiral Review

3. Sarah biked for 115 minutes last week. Jennie biked for 89 minutes last week. How many minutes did the girls bike?

_____

4. Harrison made a building using 124 blocks. Greyson made a building using 78 blocks. How many more blocks did Harrison use than Greyson?

_____

5. Von buys a bag of 24 dog treats. He gives his puppy 3 treats a day. How many days will the bag of dog treats last?

6. How many students chose swimming?

Favorite Activity	
Skating	☺ ☺
Swimming	☺ ☺ ☺ ☺ ☺
Biking	☺ ☺ ☺ ☺
Key: Each ☺ = 5 votes.	

_____

FOR MORE PRACTICE
GO TO THE
Personal Math Trainer

Name _____

Fractions on a Number Line

Essential Question How can you represent and locate fractions on a number line?

Learning Objective You will use fraction strips to represent fractions and recognize fractions as points on a number line.

Unlock the Problem

Billy's family is traveling from his house to his grandma's house. They stop at gas stations when they are $\frac{1}{4}$ and $\frac{3}{4}$ of the way there. How can you represent those distances on a number line?

You can use a number line to show fractions. The length from one whole number to the next whole number represents one whole. The line can be divided into any number of equal parts, or lengths.

Math Idea

A point on a number line shows the endpoint of a length, or distance, from zero. A number or fraction can name the distance.

Activity Locate fractions on a number line.

Materials ■ fraction strips

Billy's House 0   Grandma's House 1

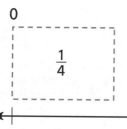
$\frac{1}{4}$

$\frac{0}{4}$ $\frac{4}{4}$

STEP 1 Divide the line into four equal lengths, or fourths.
Place four $\frac{1}{4}$-fraction strips end-to-end above the line to help.

STEP 2 At the end of each strip, draw a mark on the line.

STEP 3 Count the fourths from zero to 1 to label the distances from zero.

STEP 4 Think: $\frac{1}{4}$ is 1 out of 4 equal lengths.
Draw a point at $\frac{1}{4}$ to represent the distance from 0 to $\frac{1}{4}$.
Label the point *G1*.

STEP 5 Think: $\frac{3}{4}$ is 3 out of 4 equal lengths.
Draw a point at $\frac{3}{4}$ to represent the distance from 0 to $\frac{3}{4}$.
Label the point *G2*.

🔑 Example Complete the number line to name the point.

Materials ■ color pencils

Write the fraction that names the point on the number line.

Think: This number line is divided into six equal lengths, or sixths.

The length of one equal part is _____.

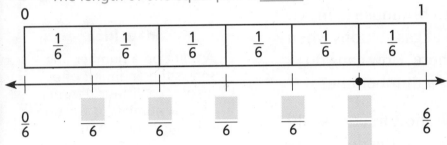

Shade the fraction strips to show the location of the point.

There are _____ out of _____ equal lengths shaded.
The shaded length shows $\frac{5}{6}$.

So, _____ names the point.

Share and Show

1. Complete the number line. Draw a point to show $\frac{2}{3}$.

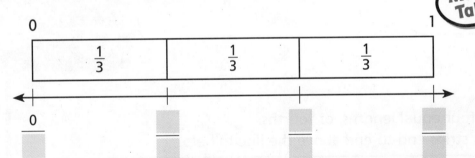

Math Talk Math Processes and Practices ④

Use Models What does the length between each mark on this number line represent?

Write the fraction that names the point.

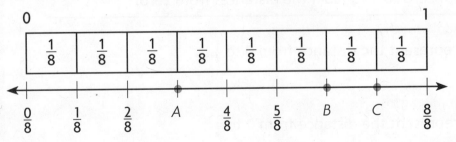

2. point A _____   ✅ 3. point B _____   ✅ 4. point C _____

468

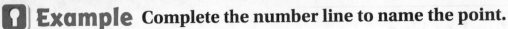

© Houghton Mifflin Harcourt Publishing Company

Name _____

On Your Own

Use fraction strips to help you complete the number line. Then locate and draw a point for the fraction.

5. $\frac{2}{6}$

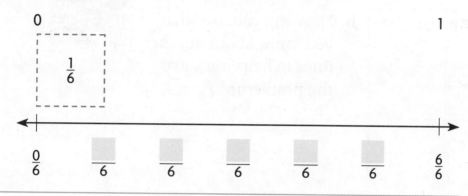

6. $\frac{2}{3}$

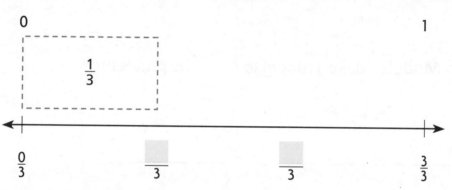

Write the fraction that names the point.

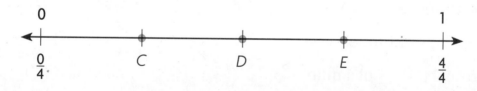

7. point C _____   8. point D _____   9. point E _____

10. There is a walking trail at the park. Four laps around the trail is a distance of 1 mile. How many laps does it take to walk $\frac{3}{4}$ mile?

11. GO DEEPER A recipe for pasta makes enough for eight servings. How many servings can be made using $\frac{4}{8}$ of each ingredient in the recipe?

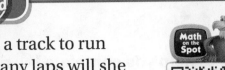

Unlock the Problem

12. **THINK SMARTER**   Javia ran 8 laps around a track to run a total of 1 mile on Monday. How many laps will she need to run on Tuesday to run $\frac{3}{8}$ of a mile?

a. What do you need to find?

_____

_____

_____

b. How will you use what you know about number lines to help you solve the problem?

_____

_____

_____

_____

c. **Math Processes and Practices ④** **Use Models** Make a model to solve the problem.

⟵————————————————————⟶

d. Complete the sentences.

There are _____ laps in 1 mile.

Each lap represents _____ of a mile.

_____ laps represent the distance of three eighths of a mile.

So, Javia will need to run _____ laps to run $\frac{3}{8}$ of a mile.

Personal Math Trainer

13. **THINK SMARTER +**   Locate and draw point F on the number line to represent the fraction $\frac{2}{4}$.

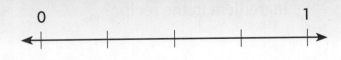

Name _____

Fractions on a Number Line

Learning Objective You will use fraction strips to represent fractions and recognize fractions as points on a number line.

Use fraction strips to help you complete the number line. Then locate and draw a point for the fraction.

1. $\frac{1}{3}$

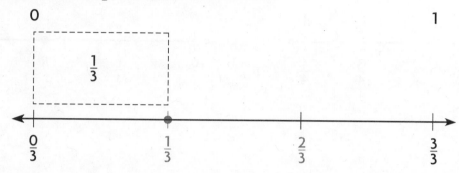

Write the fraction that names the point.

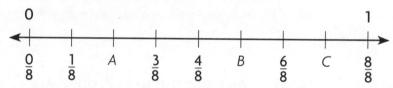

2. point A _____

3. point B _____

4. point C _____

Problem Solving (Real World)

5. Jade ran 6 times around her neighborhood to complete a total of 1 mile. How many times will she need to run to complete $\frac{5}{6}$ of a mile?

_____

6. A missing fraction on a number line is located exactly halfway between $\frac{3}{6}$ and $\frac{5}{6}$. What is the missing fraction?

_____

7. **WRITE** ▸*Math* Explain how showing fractions with models and a number line are alike and different.

_____

_____

Lesson Check

1. What fraction names point *G* on the number line?

2. What fraction names point *R* on the number line?

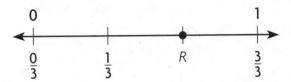

Spiral Review

3. Each table in the cafeteria can seat 10 students. How many tables are needed to seat 40 students?

4. Use the Commutative Property of Multiplication to write a related number sentence.

$$4 \times 9 = 36$$

5. Pedro shaded part of a circle. What fraction names the shaded part?

6. Find the quotient.

$$8 \div 1 = \boxed{}$$

FOR MORE PRACTICE
GO TO THE
Personal Math Trainer

✓Mid-Chapter Checkpoint

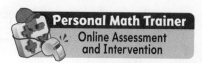

Personal Math Trainer
Online Assessment
and Intervention

Vocabulary

Choose the best term from the box to complete the sentence.

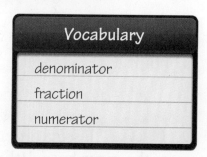

Vocabulary
denominator
fraction
numerator

1. A _____ is a number that names part of a whole or part of a group. (p. 455)

2. The _____ tells how many equal parts are in the whole or in the group. (p. 461)

Concepts and Skills

Write the number of equal parts. Then write the name for the parts.

3.

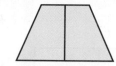

_____ equal parts

_____

4.

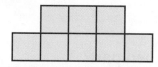

_____ equal parts

_____

5.

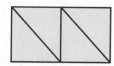

_____ equal parts

_____

Write the number of equal parts in the whole. Then write the fraction that names the shaded part.

6.

_____ equal parts

_____

7.

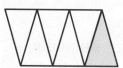

_____ equal parts

_____

8.

_____ equal parts

_____

Write the fraction that names the point.

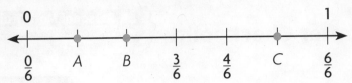

9. point A _____   **10.** point B _____   **11.** point C _____

12. GO DEEPER Jessica ordered a pizza. What fraction of the pizza has mushrooms? What fraction of the pizza does not have mushrooms?

_____

13. Which fraction names the shaded part?

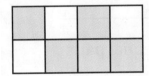

_____

14. Six friends share 3 oatmeal squares equally. How much of an oatmeal square does each friend get?

Name _____

Relate Fractions and Whole Numbers

Essential Question When might you use a fraction greater than 1 or a whole number?

Learning Objective You will locate and draw points as fractions and whole numbers on a number line and then use models to write fractions greater than 1.

🔑 Unlock the Problem · Real World

Steve ran 1 mile and Jenna ran $\frac{4}{4}$ of a mile. Did Steve and Jenna run the same distance?

🔑 **Locate 1 and $\frac{4}{4}$ on a number line.**

- Shade 4 lengths of $\frac{1}{4}$ and label the number line.

- Draw a point at 1 and $\frac{4}{4}$.

> **Math Idea**
> If two numbers are located at the same point on a number line, then they are equal and represent the same distance.

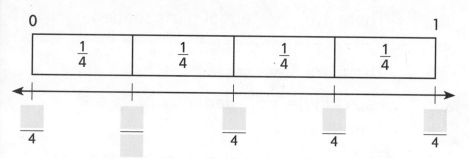

Since the distance _____ and _____ end at the same point, they are equal.

So, Steve and Jenna ran the _____ distance.

Try This! Complete the number line. Locate and draw points at $\frac{3}{6}$, $\frac{6}{6}$, and 1.

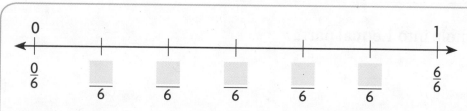

A Are $\frac{3}{6}$ and 1 equal? Explain.

Think: Do the distances end at the same point?

_____

_____

So, $\frac{3}{6}$ and 1 are _____.

B Are $\frac{6}{6}$ and 1 equal? Explain.

Think: Do the distances end at the same point?

_____

_____

So, $\frac{6}{6}$ and 1 are _____.

CONNECT The number of equal parts the whole is divided into is the denominator of a fraction. The number of parts being counted is the numerator. A **fraction greater than 1** has a numerator greater than its denominator.

🔒 Examples

Each shape is 1 whole. Write a whole number and a fraction greater than 1 for the parts that are shaded.

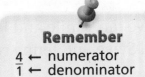

Remember

$$\frac{4}{1} \leftarrow \text{numerator} \\ \leftarrow \text{denominator}$$

A

There are 2 wholes.

Each whole is divided into 4 equal parts, or fourths.

$2 = \frac{8}{4}$

There are _____ equal parts shaded.

B

There are 3 wholes.

Each whole is divided into 1 equal part.

$3 = \frac{3}{1}$

There are _____ equal parts shaded.

1. Explain what *each whole is divided into 1 equal part* means in Example B.

   _____

   _____

Read Math

Read $\frac{3}{1}$ as *three ones*.

2. How do you divide a whole into 1 equal part?

   _____

   _____

Try This!

Each shape is 1 whole. Write a whole number and a fraction greater than 1 for the parts that are shaded.

Name _____

1. Each shape is 1 whole. Write a whole number and a fraction greater than 1 for the parts that are shaded.

There are _____ wholes.

Each whole is divided into _____ equal parts.

There are _____ equal parts shaded.

$\boxed{} = \dfrac{}{}$

Use the number line to find whether the two numbers are equal. Write *equal* or *not equal*.

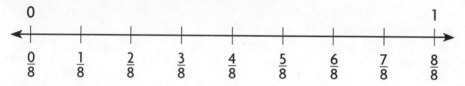

2. $\frac{1}{8}$ and $\frac{8}{8}$ _____

☑ **3.** $\frac{8}{8}$ and 1 _____

☑ **4.** 1 and $\frac{4}{8}$ _____

On Your Own

Use the number line to find whether the two numbers are equal. Write *equal* or *not equal*.

> **Math Talk**
>
> Math Processes and Practices ①
>
> **Evaluate** How do you know whether the two fractions are equal or not equal when using a number line?

5. $\frac{0}{3}$ and 1 _____

6. 1 and $\frac{2}{3}$ _____

7. $\frac{3}{3}$ and 1 _____

Each shape is 1 whole. Write a fraction for the parts that are shaded.

8.

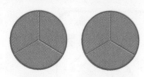

$2 =$ _____

9.

$1 =$ _____

10.

$3 =$ _____

11.

$2 =$ _____

Math Processes and Practices ⑥ **Make Connections** Draw a model of the fraction or fraction greater than 1. Then write it as a whole number.

12. $\frac{8}{4} =$ _____

13. $\frac{6}{6} =$ _____

14. $\frac{5}{1} =$ _____

Problem Solving · Applications Real World

15. GO DEEPER Jeff rode his bike around a bike trail that was $\frac{1}{3}$ of a mile long. He rode around the trail 9 times. Write a fraction greater than 1 for the distance. How many miles did Jeff ride?

_____

16. THINK SMARTER **What's the Error?** Andrea drew the number line below. She said that $\frac{9}{8}$ and 1 are equal. Explain her error.

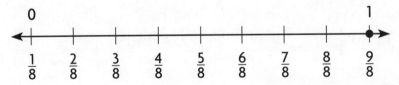

_____

17. THINK SMARTER Each shape is 1 whole. Which numbers name the parts that are shaded? Mark all that apply.

Ⓐ 4   Ⓒ $\frac{26}{6}$ Ⓔ $\frac{6}{4}$

Ⓑ 6   Ⓓ $\frac{24}{6}$

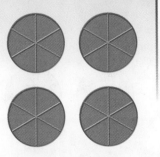

Learning Objective You will locate and draw points as fractions and whole numbers on a number line and then use models to write fractions greater than 1.

Use the number line to find whether the two numbers are equal. Write *equal* or *not equal*.

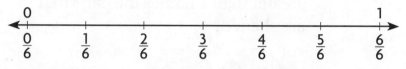

1. $\frac{0}{6}$ and 1

2. 1 and $\frac{6}{6}$

3. $\frac{1}{6}$ and $\frac{6}{6}$

_____not equal_____   _____   _____

Each shape is 1 whole. Write a fraction for the parts that are shaded.

4.

$1 = $ _____

5.

$4 = $ _____

 Problem Solving *Real World*

6. Rachel jogged along a trail that was $\frac{1}{4}$ of a mile long. She jogged along the trail 8 times. How many miles did Rachel jog?

_____

7. Jon ran around a track that was $\frac{1}{8}$ of a mile long. He ran around the track 24 times. How many miles did Jon run?

_____

8. **WRITE** ▸*Math* Write a problem that uses a fraction greater than 1.

_____

_____

Lesson Check

1. Each shape is 1 whole. What fraction greater than 1 names the parts that are shaded?

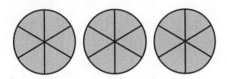

_____

2. Each shape is 1 whole. What fraction greater than 1 names the parts that are shaded?

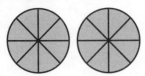

_____

Spiral Review

3. Tara has 598 pennies and 231 nickels. How many pennies and nickels does she have?

$$\begin{array}{r} 598 \\ + \ 231 \\ \hline \end{array}$$

_____
_____

4. Dylan read 6 books. Kylie read double the number of books that Dylan read. How many books did Kylie read?

_____
_____

5. Alyssa divides a granola bar into halves. How many equal parts are there?

_____
_____

6. There are 4 students in each small reading group. If there are 24 students in all, how many reading groups are there?

_____
_____

FOR MORE PRACTICE
GO TO THE
Personal Math Trainer

Name _____

Fractions of a Group

Essential Question How can a fraction name part of a group?

Learning Objective You will use fractions to name parts of a group.

Unlock the Problem

Jake and Emma each have a collection of marbles.
What fraction of each collection is blue?

 You can use a fraction to name part of a group.

Jake's Marbles

number of
blue marbles → [ ] ← numerator
total number → $\overline{8}$ ← denominator
of marbles

Read: three eighths, or three out of eight

Write: $\frac{3}{8}$

So, ____ of Jake's marbles
are blue.

Emma's Marbles

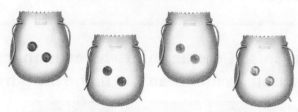

bags of
blue marbles → [ ] ← numerator
total number → $\overline{4}$ ← denominator
of bags

Read: one fourth, or one out of four

Write: $\frac{1}{4}$

So, ____ of Emma's marbles
are blue.

Try This! **Name part of a group.**

Draw 2 red counters and 6 yellow counters.

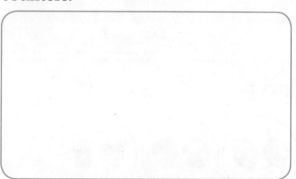

Write the fraction of counters that are red.

[ ] ← number of red counters
___
[ ] ← total number of counters

Write the fraction of counters that are not red.

[ ] ← number of yellow counters
___
[ ] ← total number of counters

So, ____ of the counters are red and ____ are not red.

Fractions Greater Than 1

Sometimes a fraction can name more than a whole group.

Daniel collects baseballs. He has collected 8 so far. He puts them in cases that hold 4 baseballs each. What part of the baseball cases has Daniel filled?

Think: 1 case = 1

Daniel has two full cases of 4 baseballs each.

So, 2, or $\frac{8}{4}$, baseball cases are filled.

Try This! Complete the whole number and the fraction greater than 1 to name the part filled.

A

Think: 1 pan = 1

_____, or $\dfrac{}{6}$

B

Think: 1 box = 1

_____, or $\dfrac{}{8}$

Share and Show MATH BOARD

1. What fraction of the counters are red? _____

Think: How many red counters are there? How many counters are there in all?

Write a fraction to name the red part of each group.

2.   _____

✓ 3.  _____

Math Talk Math Processes and Practices ⑥

Explain another way to name the fraction for Exercise 3.

Name _____

Write a whole number and a fraction greater than 1 to name the part filled.

4.

Think: 1 carton = 1

_____ _____

5.

Think: 1 container = 1

_____ _____

On Your Own

Write a fraction to name the blue part of each group.

6.

_____

7.

_____

8.

_____

9.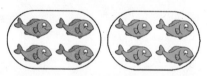

_____

Write a whole number and a fraction greater than 1 to name the part filled.

10.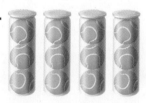

Think: 1 container = 1

_____ _____

11. THINK SMARTER

Think: 1 carton = 1

_____ _____

Draw a quick picture on your MathBoard. Then write a fraction to name the shaded part of the group.

12. Draw 8 circles.
Shade 8 circles.

_____

13. Draw 8 triangles.
Make 4 groups.
Shade 1 group.

_____

14. Draw 4 rectangles.
Shade 2 rectangles.

_____

Problem Solving • Applications

School Marble Tournament

Use the graph for 15–16.

15. **GO DEEPER** The bar graph shows the winners of the Smith Elementary School Marble Tournament. How many games were played? What fraction of the games did Scott win?

_____   _____

16. **Math Processes and Practices ❶ Analyze** What fraction of the games did Robyn NOT win?

_____

WRITE ▸ *Math*
Show Your Work

17. **THINK SMARTER** Li has 6 marbles. Of them, $\frac{1}{3}$ are blue. The rest are red. Draw a picture to show Li's marbles.

18. **WRITE** ▸ *Math* **What's the Question?** A bag has 2 yellow cubes, 3 blue cubes, and 1 white cube. The answer is $\frac{1}{6}$.

_____

19. **THINK SMARTER** Makayla picked some flowers. What fraction of flowers are yellow or red? What fraction of the flowers are NOT yellow or red? Show your work.

Fractions of a Group

Learning Objective You will use fractions to name parts of a group.

Write a fraction to name the shaded part of each group.

1. $\frac{6}{8}$ or $\frac{3}{4}$

2.   _____

Write a whole number and a fraction greater than 1 to name the part filled. Think: 1 container = 1

3.

   _____   _____

4.

   _____   _____

Draw a quick picture. Then, write a fraction to name the shaded part of the group.

5. Draw 4 circles.
   Shade 2 circles.

6. Draw 6 circles.
   Make 3 groups.
   Shade 1 group.

_____   _____

Problem Solving · Real World

7. Brian has 3 basketball cards and 5 baseball cards. What fraction of Brian's cards are baseball cards?

8. **WRITE** ▶ *Math* Draw a set of objects where you can find a fractional part of the group using the total number of objects and by using subgroups.

_____   _____

Lesson Check

1. What fraction of the group is shaded?

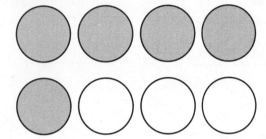

_____

2. What fraction of the group is shaded?

_____

Spiral Review

3. What multiplication number sentence does the array represent?

_____

_____

4. Juan has 436 baseball cards and 189 football cards. How many more baseball cards than football cards does Juan have?

_____

_____

5. Sydney bought 3 bottles of glitter. Each bottle of glitter cost $6. How much did Sydney spend on the bottles of glitter?

_____

6. Add.

$$\begin{array}{r} 262 \\ +\ 119 \\ \hline \end{array}$$

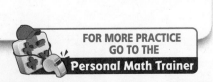

FOR MORE PRACTICE
GO TO THE
Personal Math Trainer

Name _____

Find Part of a Group Using Unit Fractions

Essential Question How can a fraction tell how many are in part of a group?

Learning Objective You will use two-color counters to model and find parts of a group.

Unlock the Problem

Audrey buys a bouquet of 12 flowers. One third of them are red. How many of the flowers are red?

- How many flowers does Audrey buy in all? _____
- What fraction of the flowers are red? _____

Activity

Materials ■ two-color counters ■ MathBoard

- Put 12 counters on your MathBoard.

- Since you want to find $\frac{1}{3}$ of the group, there should

  be _____ equal groups. Draw the counters below.

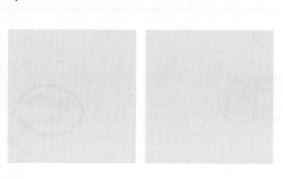

- Circle one of the groups to show _____.

  Then count the number of counters in that group.

There are _____ counters in 1 group. $\frac{1}{3}$ of 12 = _____

So, _____ of the flowers are red.

- What if Audrey buys a bouquet of 9 flowers and one third of them are yellow? Use your MathBoard and counters to find how many of the flowers are yellow.

  _____

Math Talk

Math Processes and Practices ❸

Apply How can you use the numerator and denominator in a fraction to find part of a group?

Try This! Find part of a group.

Raul picks 20 flowers from his mother's garden. One fourth of them are purple. How many of the flowers are purple?

STEP 1 Draw a row of 4 counters.

Think: To find $\frac{1}{4}$, make 4 equal groups.

_____

STEP 2 Continue to draw as many rows of 4 counters as you can until you have 20 counters.

_____

STEP 3 Then circle _____ equal groups.

Think: Each group represents $\frac{1}{4}$ of the flowers.

There are _____ counters in 1 group.

$\frac{1}{4}$ of 20 = _____

$\frac{1}{4}$ $\frac{1}{4}$ $\frac{1}{4}$ $\frac{1}{4}$

So, _____ of the flowers are purple.

Share and Show

1. Use the model to find $\frac{1}{2}$ of 8. _____

Think: How many counters are in 1 of the 2 equal groups?

> **Math Talk** Math Processes and Practices ⑥
>
> Describe why you count the number of counters in just one of the groups when finding $\frac{1}{2}$ of any number.

Circle equal groups to solve. Count the number of flowers in 1 group.

2. $\frac{1}{4}$ of 8 = _____

✓**3.** $\frac{1}{3}$ of 6 = _____

✓**4.** $\frac{1}{6}$ of 12 = _____

Name _____

**Circle equal groups to solve. Count the number
of flowers in 1 group.**

5. $\frac{1}{4}$ of 12 = _____

6. $\frac{1}{3}$ of 15 = _____

7. $\frac{1}{4}$ of 16 = _____

8. $\frac{1}{6}$ of 30 = _____

9. $\frac{1}{3}$ of 12 = _____

10. THINK SMARTER

$\frac{1}{2}$ of 6 = _____

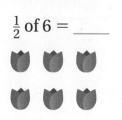

THINK SMARTER **Draw counters. Then circle equal groups to solve.**

11. $\frac{1}{8}$ of 16 = _____

12. $\frac{1}{6}$ of 24 = _____

13. GO DEEPER Gerry has 50 sports trading
cards. Of those cards, $\frac{1}{5}$ of them are
baseball cards, $\frac{1}{10}$ of them are football
cards, and the rest are basketball cards.
How many more basketball cards than
baseball cards does Gerry have?

14. GO DEEPER Barbara has a mixed garden
that has 16 rows of different flowers
and vegetables. One-fourth of the rows
are lettuce, $\frac{1}{8}$ of the rows are pumpkins,
and $\frac{1}{2}$ of the rows are red tulips. The
other rows are carrots. How many rows
of carrots are in Barbara's garden?

Problem Solving · Applications

Use the table for 15–16.

| Flower Seeds Bought | |
Name	Number of Packs
Ryan	8
Brooke	12
Cole	20

15. **Math Processes and Practices 4** **Use Diagrams** One fourth of the seed packs Ryan bought are violet seeds. How many packs of violet seeds did Ryan buy? Draw counters to solve.

_____

16. **GO DEEPER** One third of Brooke's seed packs and one fourth of Cole's seed packs are daisy seeds. How many packs of daisy seeds did they buy altogether? Explain how you know.

_____

_____

_____

WRITE ▸ Math
Show Your Work

17. **THINK SMARTER** **Sense or Nonsense?** Sophia bought 12 pots. One sixth of them are green. Sophia said she bought 2 green pots. Does her answer make sense? Explain how you know.

_____

_____

_____

18. **THINK SMARTER +** A florist has 24 sunflowers in a container. Mrs. Mason buys $\frac{1}{4}$ of the flowers. Mr. Kim buys $\frac{1}{3}$ of the flowers. How many sunflowers are left? Explain how you solved the problem.

_____

_____

_____

Name _____

Find Part of a Group Using Unit Fractions

Learning Objective You will use two-color counters to model and find parts of a group.

Circle equal groups to solve. Count the number of items in 1 group.

1. $\frac{1}{4}$ of 12 = __3__

2. $\frac{1}{8}$ of 16 = _____

○ ○ ○ ○ ○ ○ ○ ○
○ ○ ○ ○ ○ ○ ○ ○

3. $\frac{1}{3}$ of 12 = _____

○ ○ ○
○ ○ ○
○ ○ ○
○ ○ ○

4. $\frac{1}{3}$ of 9 = _____

○ ○ ○
○ ○ ○
○ ○ ○

Problem Solving

5. Marco drew 24 pictures. He drew $\frac{1}{6}$ of them in art class. How many pictures did Marco draw in art class?

_____

6. Caroline has 16 marbles. One eighth of them are blue. How many of Caroline's marbles are blue?

_____

7. **WRITE** *Math* Explain how to find which is greater: $\frac{1}{4}$ of 12 or $\frac{1}{3}$ of 12.

_____

_____

© Houghton Mifflin Harcourt Publishing Company

Lesson Check

1. Ms. Davis made 12 blankets for her grandchildren. One third of the blankets are blue. How many blue blankets did she make?

_____

2. Jackson mowed 16 lawns. One fourth of the lawns are on Main Street. How many lawns on Main Street did Jackson mow?

_____

Spiral Review

3. Find the difference.

$$509$$
$$-175$$

4. Find the quotient.

$$6\overline{)54}$$

_____

5. There are 226 pets entered in the pet show. What is 226 rounded to the nearest hundred?

6. Ladonne made 36 muffins. She put the same number of muffins on each of 4 plates. How many muffins did she put on each plate?

_____

_____

FOR MORE PRACTICE
GO TO THE
Personal Math Trainer

Name _____

Problem Solving • Find the Whole Group Using Unit Fractions

Essential Question How can you use the strategy *draw a diagram* to solve fraction problems?

Learning Objective You will use the strategy *draw a diagram* to find parts of a group by drawing counters.

Unlock the Problem

Cameron has 4 clown fish in his fish tank. One third of the fish in the tank are clown fish. How many fish does Cameron have in his tank?

Use the graphic organizer to help you solve the problem.

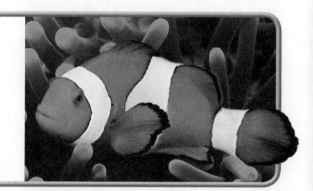

Read the Problem	Solve the Problem
What do I need to find? I need to find _____ are in Cameron's fish tank.	**Describe how to draw a diagram to solve.** The denominator in $\frac{1}{3}$ tells you that there are _____ equal parts in the whole group. Draw 3 circles to show _____ equal parts. Since 4 fish are $\frac{1}{3}$ of the whole group, draw _____ counters in the first circle.
What information do I need to use? Cameron has _____ clown fish. _____ of the fish in the tank are clown fish.	Since there are _____ counters in the first circle, draw _____ counters in each of the remaining circles. Then find the total number of counters.
How will I use the information? I will use the information in the problem to draw a _____.	So, Cameron has _____ fish in his tank.

🔑 Try Another Problem

A pet store has 2 gray rabbits. One eighth of the rabbits at the pet store are gray. How many rabbits does the pet store have?

Read the Problem	Solve the Problem
What do I need to find?	
What information do I need to use?	
How will I use the information?	

1. (Math Processes and Practices 8) **Draw Conclusions** How do you know that your answer is reasonable?

_____

_____

2. How did your diagram help you solve the problem? _____

_____

© Houghton Mifflin Harcourt Publishing Company • Image Credits: (tr) ©Getty Images

Math Processes and Practices ❶

Make Sense of Problems Suppose $\frac{1}{2}$ of the rabbits are gray. How can you find the number of rabbits at the pet store?

Name _____

Share and Show [MATH BOARD]

Unlock the Problem
✓ Circle the question.
✓ Underline important facts.
✓ Put the problem in your own words.
✓ Choose a strategy you know.

1. Lily has 3 dog toys that are red. One fourth of all her dog toys are red. How many dog toys does Lily have?

    First, draw _____ circles to show _____ equal parts.

    Next, draw _____ toys in _____ circle since

    _____ circle represents the number of red toys.

    Last, draw _____ toys in each of the remaining circles. Find the total number of toys.

    So, Lily has _____ dog toys.

2. **THINK SMARTER** What if Lily has 4 toys that are red? How many dog toys would she have?

    _____

3. The pet store sells bags of pet food. There are 4 bags of cat food. One sixth of the bags of food are cat food. How many bags of pet food does the pet store have?

    _____

4. Rachel owns 2 parakeets. One fourth of all her birds are parakeets. How many birds does Rachel own?

    _____

On Your Own

5. **THINK SMARTER** Before lunchtime, Abigail and Teresa each read some pages from different books. Abigail read 5, or one fifth, of the pages in her book. Teresa read 6, or one sixth, of the pages in her book. Whose book had more pages? How many more pages?

· · · · **WRITE** ▸ *Math* · **Show Your Work** · · · ·

_____

6. **Math Processes and Practices ②** **Represent a Problem** Six friends share 5 meat pies. Each friend first eats half of a meat pie. How much more meat pie does each friend need to eat to finish all the meat pies and share them equally? Draw a quick picture to solve.

_____

7. **GO DEEPER** Braden bought 4 packs of dog treats. He gave 4 treats to his neighbor's dog. Now Braden has 24 treats left for his dog. How many dog treats were in each pack? Explain how you know.

_____

_____

_____

_____

_____

8. **THINK SMARTER** Two hats are $\frac{1}{3}$ of the group. How many hats are in the whole group?

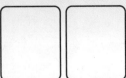

_____ hats

Problem Solving • Find the Whole Group Using Unit Fractions

Learning Objective You will use the strategy *draw a diagram* to find parts of a group by drawing counters.

Draw a quick picture to solve.

1. Katrina has 2 blue ribbons for her hair. One fourth of all her ribbons are blue. How many ribbons does Katrina have in all?

   8 ribbons

2. One eighth of Tony's books are mystery books. He has 3 mystery books. How many books does Tony have in all?

   _____

3. Brianna has 4 pink bracelets. One third of all her bracelets are pink. How many bracelets does Brianna have?

   _____

4. Ramal filled 3 pages in a stamp album. This is one sixth of the pages in the album. How many pages are there in Ramal's stamp album?

   _____

5. Jeff helped repair one half of the bicycles in a bike shop last week. If Jeff worked on 5 bicycles, how many bicycles did the shop repair last week?

   _____

6. **WRITE** ▸*Math* Write a problem about a group of objects in your classroom. Tell how many are in one equal part of the group. Solve your problem. Draw a diagram to help you.

   _____

   _____

Lesson Check

1. A zoo has 2 male lions. One sixth of the lions are male lions. How many lions are there at the zoo?

_____

2. Max has 5 red model cars. One third of his model cars are red. How many model cars does Max have?

_____

Spiral Review

3. There are 382 trees in the local park. What is the number of trees rounded to the nearest hundred?

_____

4. The Jones family is driving 458 miles on their vacation. So far, they have driven 267 miles. How many miles do they have left to drive?

$$458$$
$$- 267$$

_____

5. Ken has 6 different colors of marbles. He has 9 marbles of each color. How many marbles does Ken have in all?

_____

6. Eight friends share two pizzas equally. How much of a pizza does each friend get?

_____

FOR MORE PRACTICE
GO TO THE
Personal Math Trainer

Name _____

1. Each shape is divided into equal parts. Select the shapes that show thirds. Mark all that apply.

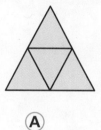   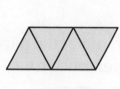   

Ⓐ   Ⓑ   Ⓒ   Ⓓ

2. What fraction names the shaded part of the shape?

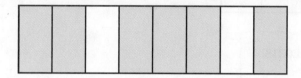

Ⓐ   8 sixths

Ⓑ   8 eighths

Ⓒ   6 eighths

Ⓓ   2 sixths

3. Omar shaded a model to show the part of the lawn that he finished mowing. What fraction names the shaded part? Explain how you know how to write the fraction.

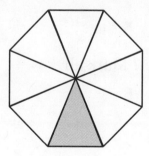

_____

_____

GO DIGITAL   Assessment Options
Chapter Test

4. What fraction names point *A* on the number line?

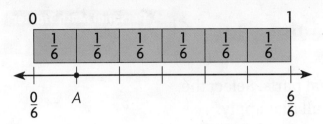

_____

5. Jamal folded this piece of paper into equal parts. Circle the word that makes the sentence true.

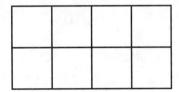

The paper is folded into

sixths
eighths
fourths

.

6. Caleb took 18 photos at the zoo. One sixth of his photos are of giraffes. How many of Caleb's photos are of giraffes?

_____ photos

7. Three teachers share 2 packs of paper equally.

How much paper does each teacher get? Mark all that apply.

Ⓐ 3 halves of a pack

Ⓑ 2 thirds of a pack

Ⓒ 3 sixths of a pack

Ⓓ 1 half of a pack

Ⓔ 1 third of a pack

Name _____

8. Lilly shaded this design.

Select one number from each column to show
the part of the design that Lilly shaded.

Numerator	Denominator
○ 1	○ 3
○ 3	○ 4
○ 5	○ 5
○ 6	○ 6

9. Marcus baked a loaf of banana bread for a party.
He cut the loaf into equal size pieces. At the end of the
party, there were 6 pieces left. Explain how you can find
the number of pieces in the whole loaf if Marcus told you
that $\frac{1}{3}$ of the loaf was left. Use a drawing to show your
work.

_____

_____

_____

_____

10. The model shows one whole. What fraction of the model is NOT shaded?

_____

11. Together, Amy and Thea make up $\frac{1}{4}$ of the midfielders on the soccer team. How many midfielders are on the team? Show your work.

_____ midfielders

12. Six friends share 4 apples equally. How much apple does each friend get?

_____

13. Each shape is 1 whole.

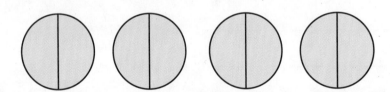

For numbers 13a–13e, choose Yes or No to show whether the number names the parts that are shaded.

13a. 4   ○ Yes   ○ No

13b. 8   ○ Yes   ○ No

13c. $\frac{8}{2}$ ○ Yes   ○ No

13d. $\frac{8}{4}$ ○ Yes   ○ No

13e. $\frac{2}{8}$ ○ Yes   ○ No

14. Alex has 3 baseballs. He brings 2 baseballs to school. What fraction of his baseballs does Alex bring to school?

_____

15. GO DEEPER Janeen and Nicole each made fruit salad for a school event.

Part A

Janeen used 16 pieces of fruit to make her salad. If $\frac{1}{4}$ of the fruits were peaches, how many peaches did she use? Make a drawing to show your work.

_____ peaches

Part B

Nicole used 24 pieces of fruit. If $\frac{1}{6}$ of them were peaches, how many peaches in all did Janeen and Nicole use to make their fruit salads? Explain how you found your answer.

_____

_____

16. There are 8 rows of chairs in the auditorium. Three of the rows are empty. What fraction of the rows are empty?

_____

17. Tara ran 3 laps around her neighborhood for a total of 1 mile yesterday. Today she wants to run $\frac{2}{3}$ of a mile. How many laps will she need to run around her neighborhood?

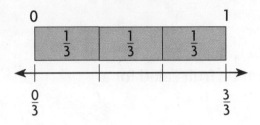

_____ laps

18. Gary painted some shapes.

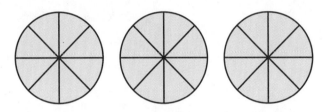

Select one number from each column to show a fraction greater than 1 that names the parts Gary painted.

Numerator	Denominator
○ 3	○ 3
○ 4	○ 4
○ 8	○ 8
○ 24	○ 24

Personal Math Trainer

19. THINK SMARTER ✚ Angelo rode his bike around a bike trail that was $\frac{1}{4}$ of a mile long. He rode his bike around the trail 8 times. Angelo says he rode a total of $\frac{8}{4}$ miles. Teresa says he is wrong and that he actually rode 2 miles. Who is correct? Use words and drawings to explain how you know.

_____

_____

_____

_____

Compare Fractions

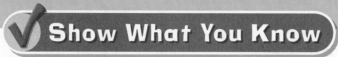

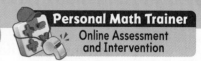

Personal Math Trainer
Online Assessment
and Intervention

Show What You Know

Check your understanding of important skills.

Name _____

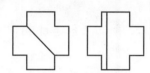

▶ Halves and Fourths

1. Find the shape that is divided into 2 equal parts. Color $\frac{1}{2}$.

2. Find the shape that is divided into 4 equal parts. Color $\frac{1}{4}$.

▶ Parts of a Whole   Write the number of shaded parts and the number of equal parts.

3. ____ shaded parts

   ____ equal parts

4. ____ shaded parts

   ____ equal parts

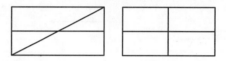

▶ Fractions of a Whole

Write the fraction that names the shaded part of each shape.

5. _____

6. _____

7. _____

Hannah keeps her marbles in bags with 4 marbles in each bag. She writes $\frac{3}{4}$ to show the number of red marbles in each bag. Find another fraction to name the number of red marbles in 2 bags.

Vocabulary Builder

▶ **Visualize It** •

Complete the flow map by using the words with a ✓.

Fractions and Whole Numbers

What is it?		What are some examples?
_____	→	$\frac{2}{3} > \frac{1}{3}$
_____	→	$\frac{1}{4} < \frac{2}{4}$
_____	→	$\frac{1}{2} = \frac{2}{4}$
_____	→	$\frac{1}{3}, \frac{1}{4}$
_____	→	$\frac{2}{2}, \frac{4}{2}$

Review Words

compare
denominator
eighths
equal parts
equal to (=)
fourths
fraction
✓ greater than (>)
halves
✓ less than (<)
numerator
order
sixths
thirds
✓ unit fractions
✓ whole numbers

Preview Word

✓ equivalent
fractions

▶ **Understand Vocabulary** • • • • • • • • • • • • • • •

Write the review word or preview word that answers the riddle.

1. We are two fractions that name the same amount.

   _____

2. I am the part of a fraction above the line. I tell how many parts are being counted.

   _____

3. I am the part of a fraction below the line. I tell how many equal parts are in the whole or in the group.

   _____

506

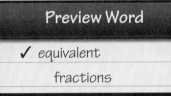
• Interactive Student Edition
• Multimedia eGlossary

© Houghton Mifflin Harcourt Publishing Company

denominator

denominator

11

Eighths

octavos

17

Equal Parts

partes iguales

21

equivalent fractions

fracciones equivalentes

23

greater than (>)

mayor que

31

less than (<)

menor que

41

numerator

numerador

53

unit fraction

fracción unitaria

79

These are eighths

The part of a fraction below the line, which tells how many equal parts there are in the whole or in the group

Example: $\frac{1}{5}$ ← denominator

Two or more fractions that name the same amount

Example: $\frac{1}{2}$ and $\frac{3}{6}$ are equivalent fractions

Parts that are exactly the same size

6 equal parts

A symbol used to compare two numbers when the lesser number is given first

Example:
Read 3 < 7 as "three is less than seven."

A symbol used to compare two numbers when the greater number is given first

Example:
Read 6 > 4 as "six is greater than four."

A fraction that has 1 as its top number, or numerator

Example: $\frac{1}{3}$ is a unit fraction

The part of a fraction above the line, which tells how many parts are being counted

Example: $\frac{1}{5}$ ← numerator

Game

Pick It

For 3 players

Materials

- 4 sets of word cards

How to Play

1. Each player is dealt 5 cards. The remaining cards are a draw pile.

2. To take a turn, ask any player if he or she has a word that matches one of your word cards.

3. If the player has the word, he or she gives the card to you, and you must define the word.
   - If you are correct, keep the card and put the matching pair in front of you. Take another turn.
   - If you are wrong, return the card. Your turn is over.

4. If the player does not have the word, he or she answers, "Pick it." Then you take a card from the draw pile.

5. If the card you draw matches one of your word cards, follow the directions for Step 3 above. If it does not, your turn is over.

6. The game is over when one player has no cards left. The player with the most pairs wins.

The Write Way

Reflect

Choose one idea. Write about it.

- Juan swam $\frac{3}{5}$ of a mile, and Greg swam $\frac{3}{8}$ of a mile. Explain how you know who swam farther.
- Explain how to compare two fractions.
- Write two examples of equivalent fractions and explain how you know they are equivalent.

Name _____

Problem Solving • Compare Fractions

Essential Question How can you use the strategy *act it out* to solve comparison problems?

Learning Objective You will use the strategy *act it out* to solve comparison problems by modeling and comparing with fraction strips or fraction circles.

Unlock the Problem

Mary and Vincent climbed up a rock wall at the park. Mary climbed $\frac{3}{4}$ of the way up the wall. Vincent climbed $\frac{3}{8}$ of the way up the wall. Who climbed higher?

You can act out the problem by using manipulatives to help you compare fractions.

Remember
$<$ is less than
$>$ is greater than
$=$ is equal to

Read the Problem

What do I need to find?

_____

What information do I need to use?

Mary climbed _____ of the way.

Vincent climbed _____ of the way.

How will I use the information?

I will use _____

and _____ the lengths of

the models to find who climbed

_____ .

Solve the Problem

Record the steps you used to solve the problem.

Compare the lengths.

_____ ◯ _____

The length of the $\frac{3}{4}$ model is _____

than the length of the $\frac{3}{8}$ model.

So, _____ climbed higher on the rock wall.

Math Processes and Practices ④

Use Models When comparing fractions using fraction strips, how do you know which fraction is the lesser fraction?

Chapter 9   507

🔑 Try Another Problem

Students at day camp are decorating paper circles for placemats. Tracy finished $\frac{3}{6}$ of her placemat. Kim finished $\frac{5}{6}$ of her placemat. Who finished more of her placemat?

Read the Problem	**Solve the Problem**
What do I need to find?	**Record the steps you used to solve the problem.**
What information do I need to use?	
How will I use the information?	

Math Talk

Math Processes and Practices ②

Use Reasoning How do you know that $\frac{5}{6}$ is greater than $\frac{3}{6}$ without using models?

1. How did your model help you solve the problem? _____

_____

2. Tracy and Kim each had a carton of milk with lunch. Tracy drank $\frac{5}{8}$ of her milk. Kim drank $\frac{7}{8}$ of her milk. Who drank more of her milk? Explain.

_____

_____

Name _____

Share and Show

✓ Circle the question.
✓ Underline important facts.
✓ Act out the problem using
   manipulatives.

✓ **1.** At the park, people can climb a rope ladder
to its top. Rosa climbed $\frac{2}{8}$ of the way up the
ladder. Justin climbed $\frac{2}{6}$ of the way up the ladder.
Who climbed higher on the rope ladder?

First, what are you asked to find?

_____

Then, model and compare the fractions. **Think:** Compare $\frac{2}{8}$ and $\frac{2}{6}$.

Last, find the greater fraction.

____ ◯ ____

So, _____ climbed higher on the rope ladder.

✓ **2.** What if Cara also tried the rope ladder and climbed
$\frac{2}{4}$ of the way up? Who climbed highest on the rope
ladder: Rosa, Justin, or Cara? Explain how you know.

_____

_____

_____

_____

On Your Own

3. **Math Processes and Practices ⑤ Use a Concrete Model** Ted walked $\frac{2}{3}$ mile
to his soccer game. Then he walked $\frac{1}{3}$ mile to his
friend's house. Which distance is shorter? Explain
how you know.

_____

_____

© Houghton Mifflin Harcourt Publishing Company

Use the table for 4–5.

4. **GO DEEPER** Suri is spreading jam on 8 biscuits for breakfast. The table shows the fraction of biscuits spread with each jam flavor. Which flavor did Suri use on the most biscuits?

   Hint: Use 8 counters to model the biscuits.

   _____

Suri's Biscuits	
Jam Flavor	**Fraction of Biscuits**
Peach	$\frac{3}{8}$
Raspberry	$\frac{4}{8}$
Strawberry	$\frac{1}{8}$

5. **WRITE** ▸ *Math* **What's the Question?** The answer is strawberry.

   _____

   _____

WRITE ▸ *Math* · **Show Your Work** ·

6. **THINK SMARTER** Suppose Suri had also used plum jam on the biscuits. She frosted $\frac{1}{2}$ of the biscuits with peach jam, $\frac{1}{4}$ with raspberry jam, $\frac{1}{8}$ with strawberry jam, and $\frac{1}{8}$ with plum jam. Which flavor of jam did Suri use on the most biscuits?

   _____

7. Ms. Gordon has many snack bar recipes. One recipe uses $\frac{1}{3}$ cup oatmeal, $\frac{1}{4}$ cup of milk, and $\frac{1}{2}$ cup flour. Which ingredient will Ms. Gordon use the most of?

   _____

8. **THINK SMARTER** Rick lives $\frac{4}{6}$ mile from school. Noah lives $\frac{3}{6}$ mile from school.

   Use the fractions and symbols to show which distance is longer.

   $\frac{3}{6}$, $\frac{4}{6}$, < and >   ☐ ◯ ☐

Problem Solving • Compare Fractions

Learning Objective You will use the strategy *act it out* to solve comparison problems by modeling and comparing with fraction strips or fraction circles.

Solve.

1. Luis skates $\frac{2}{3}$ mile from his home to school. Isabella skates $\frac{2}{4}$ mile to get to school. Who skates farther?

   Think: Use fraction strips to act it out.

   _____ Luis _____

2. Sandra makes a pizza. She puts mushrooms on $\frac{2}{8}$ of the pizza. She adds green peppers to $\frac{5}{8}$ of the pizza. Which topping covers more of the pizza?

   _____

3. The jars of paint in the art room have different amounts of paint. The green paint jar is $\frac{4}{8}$ full. The purple paint jar is $\frac{4}{6}$ full. Which paint jar is less full?

   _____

4. Jan has a recipe for bread. She uses $\frac{2}{3}$ cup of flour and $\frac{1}{3}$ cup of chopped onion. Which ingredient does she use more of, flour or onion?

   _____

5. **WRITE** ▸ *Math* Explain how you can find whether $\frac{5}{6}$ or $\frac{5}{8}$ is greater.

   _____

   _____

Lesson Check

1. Ali and Jonah collect seashells in identical buckets. When they are finished, Ali's bucket is $\frac{2}{6}$ full and Jonah's bucket is $\frac{3}{6}$ full. Compare the fractions using >, < or =.

$\frac{3}{6} \bigcirc \frac{2}{6}$

2. Rosa paints a wall in her bedroom. She puts green paint on $\frac{5}{8}$ of the wall and blue paint on $\frac{3}{8}$ of the wall. Compare the fractions using >, < or =.

$\frac{5}{8} \bigcirc \frac{3}{8}$

Spiral Review

3. Dan divides a pie into eighths. How many equal parts are there?

4. Draw lines to divide the circle into 4 equal parts.

5. Charles places 30 pictures on his bulletin board in 6 equal rows. How many pictures are in each row?

6. Describe a pattern in the table.

Tables	1	2	3	4	5
Chairs	5	10	15	20	25

FOR MORE PRACTICE
GO TO THE
Personal Math Trainer

Compare Fractions with the Same Denominator

Learning Objective You will use visual fraction models and reasoning strategies to compare fractions of a whole and fractions of a group with the same denominator.

Essential Question How can you compare fractions with the same denominator?

Unlock the Problem

Jeremy and Christina are each making a quilt block. Both blocks are the same size and both are made of 4 equal-size squares. $\frac{2}{4}$ of Jeremy's squares are green. $\frac{1}{4}$ of Christina's squares are green. Whose quilt block has more green squares?

- Circle the two fractions you need to compare.
- How are the two fractions alike?

_____

 Compare fractions of a whole.

- Shade $\frac{2}{4}$ of Jeremy's quilt block.

- Shade $\frac{1}{4}$ of Christina's quilt block.

- Compare $\frac{2}{4}$ and $\frac{1}{4}$.

The greater fraction will have the larger amount of the whole shaded.

$$\frac{2}{4} \bigcirc \frac{1}{4}$$

Jeremy's Quilt Block   **Christina's Quilt Block**

Math Idea
You can compare two fractions when they refer to the same whole or to groups that are the same size.

So, _____ quilt block has more green squares.

 Compare fractions of a group.

Jen and Maggie each have 6 buttons.

- Shade 3 of Jen's buttons to show the number of buttons that are red. Shade 5 of Maggie's buttons to show the number that are red.

- Write a fraction to show the number of red buttons in each group. Compare the fractions.

Jen's Buttons

Maggie's Buttons

There are the same number of buttons in each group, so you can count the number of red buttons to compare the fractions.

$$3 < \underline{\quad}, \text{ so } \frac{}{6} < \frac{}{6}.$$

So, _____ has a greater fraction of red buttons.

Use fraction strips and a number line.

At the craft store, one piece of ribbon is $\frac{2}{8}$ yard long. Another piece of ribbon is $\frac{7}{8}$ yard long. If Sean wants to buy the longer piece of ribbon, which piece should he buy?

Compare $\frac{2}{8}$ and $\frac{7}{8}$.

- Shade the fraction strips to show the locations of $\frac{2}{8}$ and $\frac{7}{8}$.

- Draw and label points on the number line to represent the distances $\frac{2}{8}$ and $\frac{7}{8}$.

- Compare the lengths.

  $\frac{2}{8}$ is to the left of $\frac{7}{8}$. It is closer to $\frac{0}{8}$, or _____.

  $\frac{7}{8}$ is to the _____ of $\frac{2}{8}$. It is closer to ─, or _____.

  $\dfrac{\ }{\ } < \dfrac{\ }{\ }$ and $\dfrac{\ }{\ } > \dfrac{\ }{\ }$

So, Sean should buy the piece of ribbon that is $\dfrac{\ }{\ }$ yard long.

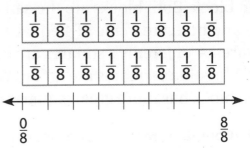

$$\begin{array}{|c|c|c|c|c|c|c|c|}\hline \frac18 & \frac18 & \frac18 & \frac18 & \frac18 & \frac18 & \frac18 & \frac18 \\\hline\end{array}$$

$$\begin{array}{|c|c|c|c|c|c|c|c|}\hline \frac18 & \frac18 & \frac18 & \frac18 & \frac18 & \frac18 & \frac18 & \frac18 \\\hline\end{array}$$

$\frac{0}{8}$ ← · · · · · · · → $\frac{8}{8}$

- On a number line, a fraction farther to the right is greater than a fraction to its left.

- On a number line, a fraction farther to the left is _____ a fraction to its right.

Use reasoning.

Ana and Omar are decorating same-size bookmarks. Ana covers $\frac{3}{3}$ of her bookmark with glitter. Omar covers $\frac{1}{3}$ of his bookmark with glitter. Whose bookmark is covered with more glitter?

Compare $\frac{3}{3}$ and $\frac{1}{3}$.

- When the denominators are the same, the whole is divided

  into same-size pieces. You can look at the _____ to compare the number of pieces.

- Both fractions involve third-size pieces. _____ pieces

  are more than _____ piece. 3 > _____, so $\dfrac{\ }{\ } > \dfrac{\ }{\ }$.

So, _____ bookmark is covered with more glitter.

Math Talk

Math Processes and Practices ⑥

Explain how you can use reasoning to compare fractions with the same denominator.

514

Name _____

1. Draw points on the number line to show $\frac{1}{6}$ and $\frac{5}{6}$. Then compare the fractions.

Math Processes and Practices ②

Reason Abstractly Why do fractions increase in size as you move right on the number line?

←———+——+——+——+——+——+——→
$\frac{0}{6}$ $\frac{1}{6}$ $\frac{2}{6}$ $\frac{3}{6}$ $\frac{4}{6}$ $\frac{5}{6}$ $\frac{6}{6}$

Think: $\frac{1}{6}$ is to the left of $\frac{5}{6}$ on the number line.

$$\frac{1}{6} \bigcirc \frac{5}{6}$$

Compare. Write <, >, or =.

2. $\frac{4}{8} \bigcirc \frac{3}{8}$ ✓**3.** $\frac{1}{4} \bigcirc \frac{4}{4}$ **4.** $\frac{1}{2} \bigcirc \frac{1}{2}$ ✓**5.** $\frac{3}{6} \bigcirc \frac{2}{6}$

Compare. Write <, >, or =.

6. $\frac{2}{4} \bigcirc \frac{3}{4}$ **7.** $\frac{2}{3} \bigcirc \frac{2}{3}$ **8.** $\frac{4}{6} \bigcirc \frac{2}{6}$ **9.** $\frac{0}{8} \bigcirc \frac{2}{8}$

THINK SMARTER Write a fraction less than, greater than, or equal to the given fraction.

10. $\frac{1}{2} < \frac{\ \square\ }{\square}$ **11.** $\frac{\ \square\ }{\square} < \frac{12}{6}$ **12.** $\frac{8}{8} = \frac{\ \square\ }{\square}$ **13.** $\frac{\ \square\ }{\square} > \frac{2}{4}$

Problem Solving • Applications

14. Carlos finished $\frac{5}{8}$ of his art project on Monday. Tyler finished $\frac{7}{8}$ of his art project on Monday. Who finished more of his art project on Monday?

15. **Math Processes and Practices ②** **Use Reasoning** Ms. Endo made two loaves of bread that are the same size. Her family ate $\frac{1}{4}$ of the banana bread and $\frac{3}{4}$ of the cinnamon bread. Which loaf of bread had less left over?

16. **THINK SMARTER** Todd and Lisa are comparing fraction strips. Which statements are correct? Mark all that apply.

Ⓐ $\frac{1}{4} < \frac{4}{4}$ Ⓑ $\frac{5}{6} < \frac{4}{6}$ Ⓒ $\frac{2}{3} > \frac{1}{3}$ Ⓓ $\frac{5}{8} > \frac{4}{8}$

THINK SMARTER **What's the Error?**

17. Gary and Vanessa are comparing fractions. Vanessa models $\frac{2}{4}$ and Gary models $\frac{3}{4}$. Vanessa writes $\frac{3}{4} < \frac{2}{4}$. Look at Gary's model and Vanessa's model and describe her error.

Vanessa's Model

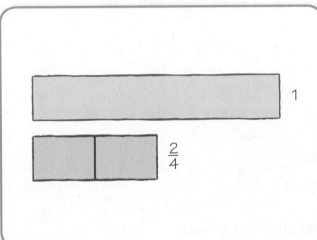

Gary's Model

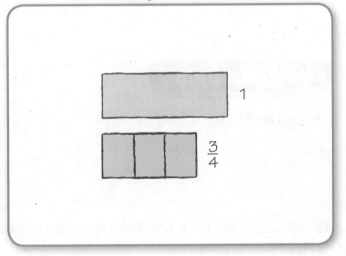

- Describe Vanessa's error.

_____

_____

18. **GO DEEPER** Explain how to correct Vanessa's error. Then show the correct model.

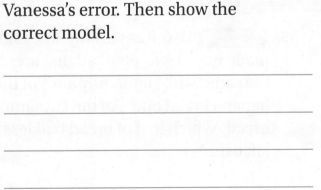

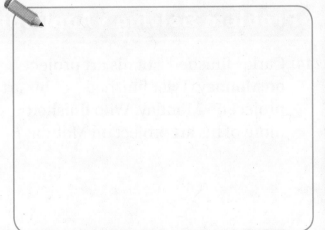

_____

_____

_____

Compare Fractions with the Same Denominator

Learning Objective You will use visual fraction models and reasoning strategies to compare fractions of a whole and fractions of a group with the same denominator.

Compare. Write $<$, $>$, or $=$.

1. $\frac{3}{4} \; \boxed{>} \; \frac{1}{4}$

2. $\frac{3}{6} \; \bigcirc \; \frac{0}{6}$

3. $\frac{1}{2} \; \bigcirc \; \frac{1}{2}$

4. $\frac{5}{6} \; \bigcirc \; \frac{6}{6}$

5. $\frac{7}{8} \; \bigcirc \; \frac{5}{8}$

6. $\frac{2}{3} \; \bigcirc \; \frac{3}{3}$

7. $\frac{8}{8} \; \bigcirc \; \frac{0}{8}$

8. $\frac{1}{6} \; \bigcirc \; \frac{1}{6}$

9. $\frac{3}{4} \; \bigcirc \; \frac{2}{4}$

10. $\frac{1}{6} \; \bigcirc \; \frac{2}{6}$

11. $\frac{1}{2} \; \bigcirc \; \frac{0}{2}$

12. $\frac{3}{8} \; \bigcirc \; \frac{3}{8}$

13. $\frac{1}{4} \; \bigcirc \; \frac{4}{4}$

14. $\frac{5}{8} \; \bigcirc \; \frac{4}{8}$

15. $\frac{4}{6} \; \bigcirc \; \frac{6}{6}$

Problem Solving · Real World

16. Ben mowed $\frac{5}{6}$ of his lawn in one hour. John mowed $\frac{4}{6}$ of his lawn in one hour. Who mowed less of his lawn in one hour?

17. Darcy baked 8 muffins. She put blueberries in $\frac{5}{8}$ of the muffins. She put raspberries in $\frac{3}{8}$ of the muffins. Did more muffins have blueberries or raspberries?

_____

_____

18. **WRITE** ▸*Math* Explain how you can use reasoning to compare two fractions with the same denominator.

_____

_____

Lesson Check

1. Julia paints $\frac{2}{6}$ of a wall in her room white. She paints more of the wall green than white. What fraction could show the part of the wall that is green?

_____

2. Compare. Write <, >, or =.

$$\frac{2}{8} \bigcirc \frac{3}{8}$$

Spiral Review

3. Mr. Edwards buys 2 new knobs for each of his kitchen cabinets. The kitchen has 9 cabinets. How many knobs does he buy?

_____

4. Allie builds a new bookcase with 8 shelves. She can put 30 books on each shelf. How many books can the bookcase hold?

_____

5. The Good Morning Café has 28 customers for breakfast. There are 4 people sitting at each table. How many tables are filled?

_____

6. Ella wants to use the Commutative Property of Multiplication to help find the product 5 × 4. What number sentence can she use?

_____

FOR MORE PRACTICE
GO TO THE
Personal Math Trainer

Name _____

Compare Fractions with the Same Numerator

Learning Objective You will use visual fraction models and reasoning strategies to compare fractions with the same numerator.

Essential Question How can you compare fractions with the same numerator?

Unlock the Problem

Markos is at Athena's Cafe. He can sit at a table with 5 of his friends or at a different table with 7 of his friends. The same-size spinach pie is shared equally among the people at each table. At which table should Markos sit to get more pie?

- Including Markos, how many friends will be sharing pie at each table?

  _____

- What will you compare?

  _____

  _____

Model the problem.

There will be 6 friends sharing Pie A or 8 friends sharing Pie B.

So, Markos will get either $\frac{1}{6}$ or $\frac{1}{8}$ of a pie.

- Shade $\frac{1}{6}$ of Pie A.

- Shade $\frac{1}{8}$ of Pie B.

- Which piece of pie is larger?

- Compare $\frac{1}{6}$ and $\frac{1}{8}$.

$$\frac{1}{6} \bigcirc \frac{1}{8}$$

So, Markos should sit at the table with _____ friends to get more pie.

Pie A

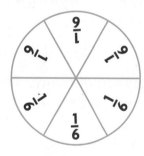

Pie B

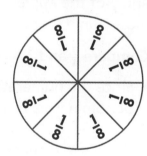

---

1. Which pie has more pieces? _____
   The *more* pieces a whole is divided into,

   the _____ the pieces are.

2. Which pie has fewer pieces? _____
   The *fewer* pieces a whole is divided into,

   the _____ the pieces are.

Math Talk

Math Processes and Practices ①

Make Sense of Problems Suppose Markos wants two pieces of one of the pies above. Is $\frac{2}{6}$ or $\frac{2}{8}$ of the pie a greater amount? Explain how you know.

Use fraction strips.

On Saturday, the campers paddled $\frac{2}{8}$ of their planned route down the river. On Sunday, they paddled $\frac{2}{3}$ of their route down the river. On which day did the campers paddle farther?

Compare $\frac{2}{8}$ and $\frac{2}{3}$.

- Place a ✓ next to the fraction strips that show more parts in the whole.

- Shade $\frac{2}{8}$. Then shade $\frac{2}{3}$. Compare the shaded parts.

- $\frac{2}{8}$ ◯ $\frac{2}{3}$

1							
$\frac{1}{8}$	$\frac{1}{8}$	$\frac{1}{8}$	$\frac{1}{8}$	$\frac{1}{8}$	$\frac{1}{8}$	$\frac{1}{8}$	$\frac{1}{8}$

$\frac{1}{3}$	$\frac{1}{3}$	$\frac{1}{3}$

Think: $\frac{1}{8}$ is less than $\frac{1}{3}$, so $\frac{2}{8}$ is less than $\frac{2}{3}$.

So, the campers paddled farther on _____.

Use reasoning.

For her class party, Felicia baked two trays of snacks that were the same size. After the party, she had $\frac{3}{4}$ of the carrot snack and $\frac{3}{6}$ of the apple snack left over. Was more carrot snack or more apple snack left over?

Compare $\frac{3}{4}$ and $\frac{3}{6}$.

- Since the numerators are the same, look at the denominators to compare the size of the pieces. $\frac{3}{4}$ $\frac{3}{6}$

  - The *more* pieces a whole is divided into, the _____ the pieces are.
  - The *fewer* pieces a whole is divided into, the _____ the pieces are.

- $\frac{1}{4}$ is _____ than $\frac{1}{6}$ because there are _____ pieces.

- $\frac{3}{4}$ ◯ $\frac{3}{6}$

> **ERROR Alert**
> When comparing fractions with the same numerator, be sure the symbol shows that the fraction with fewer pieces in the whole is the greater fraction.

So, there was more of the _____ snack left over.

Name _____

1. Shade the models to show $\frac{1}{6}$ and $\frac{1}{4}$.

   Then compare the fractions.

   $\frac{1}{6}$ ◯ $\frac{1}{4}$

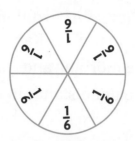

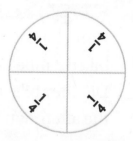

Compare. Write <, >, or =.

✓2. $\frac{1}{8}$ ◯ $\frac{1}{3}$

✓3. $\frac{3}{4}$ ◯ $\frac{3}{8}$

4. $\frac{2}{6}$ ◯ $\frac{2}{3}$

5. $\frac{4}{8}$ ◯ $\frac{4}{4}$

6. $\frac{3}{6}$ ◯ $\frac{3}{6}$

7. $\frac{8}{4}$ ◯ $\frac{8}{8}$

Math Talk Math Processes and Practices ①

Evaluate Why is $\frac{1}{2}$ greater than $\frac{1}{4}$?

On Your Own

Compare. Write <, >, or =.

8. $\frac{1}{3}$ ◯ $\frac{1}{4}$

9. $\frac{2}{3}$ ◯ $\frac{2}{6}$

10. $\frac{4}{8}$ ◯ $\frac{4}{2}$

11. $\frac{6}{8}$ ◯ $\frac{6}{6}$

12. $\frac{1}{6}$ ◯ $\frac{1}{2}$

13. $\frac{7}{8}$ ◯ $\frac{7}{8}$

14. **GO DEEPER** James ate $\frac{3}{4}$ of his quesadilla. David ate $\frac{2}{3}$ of his quesadilla. Both are the same size. Who ate more of his quesadilla?

James said he knows he ate more because he looked at the amounts left. Does his answer make sense? Shade the models. Explain.

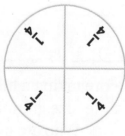

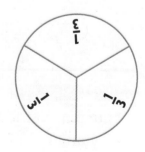

James   David

_____

_____

Unlock the Problem (Real World)

15. **Math Processes and Practices 1** **Make Sense of Problems** Quinton and Hunter are biking on trails in Katy Trail State Park. They biked $\frac{5}{6}$ mile in the morning and $\frac{5}{8}$ mile in the afternoon. Did they bike a greater distance in the morning or in the afternoon?

a. What do you need to know? _____

b. The numerator is 5 in both fractions, so compare $\frac{1}{6}$ and $\frac{1}{8}$. Explain.

_____

c. How can you solve the problem?

d. Complete the sentences.

   In the morning, the boys biked

   _____ mile. In the afternoon, they biked _____ mile.

   So, the boys biked a greater distance

   in the _____. $\frac{5}{6}$ ◯ $\frac{5}{8}$

16. **THINK SMARTER** Zach has a piece of pie that is $\frac{1}{4}$ of a pie. Max has a piece of pie that is $\frac{1}{2}$ of a pie. Max's piece is smaller than Zach's piece. Explain how this could happen. Draw a picture to show your answer.

_____

_____

17. **THINK SMARTER +** Before taking a hike, Kate and Dylan each ate part of their same-size granola bars. Kate ate $\frac{1}{3}$ of her bar. Dylan ate $\frac{1}{2}$ of his bar. Who ate more of the granola bar? Explain how you solved the problem.

_____

_____

Compare Fractions with the Same Numerator

Learning Objective You will use visual fraction models and reasoning strategies to compare fractions with the same numerator.

Compare. Write <, >, or =.

1. $\frac{1}{8}$ $\boxed{<}$ $\frac{1}{2}$

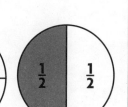

2. $\frac{3}{8}$ ◯ $\frac{3}{6}$

3. $\frac{2}{3}$ ◯ $\frac{2}{4}$

4. $\frac{2}{8}$ ◯ $\frac{2}{3}$

5. $\frac{3}{6}$ ◯ $\frac{3}{4}$

6. $\frac{1}{2}$ ◯ $\frac{1}{6}$

7. $\frac{5}{6}$ ◯ $\frac{5}{8}$

8. $\frac{4}{8}$ ◯ $\frac{4}{8}$

9. $\frac{6}{8}$ ◯ $\frac{6}{6}$

Problem Solving

10. Javier is buying food in the lunch line. The tray of salad plates is $\frac{3}{8}$ full. The tray of fruit plates is $\frac{3}{4}$ full. Which tray is more full?

_____

11. Rachel bought some buttons. Of the buttons, $\frac{2}{4}$ are yellow and $\frac{2}{8}$ are red. Rachel bought more of which color buttons?

_____

12. **WRITE** ▸*Math* Explain how the number of pieces in a whole relates to the size of each piece.

_____

_____

Lesson Check

1. What symbol makes the statement true? Write <, >, or =.

   $\frac{3}{4}$ ◯ $\frac{3}{8}$

2. What symbol makes the statement true? Write <, >, or =.

   $\frac{2}{4}$ ◯ $\frac{2}{3}$

Spiral Review

3. Anita divided a circle into 6 equal parts and shaded 1 of the parts. What fraction names the part she shaded?

4. What fraction names the shaded part of the rectangle?

   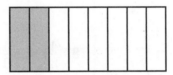

5. Chip worked at the animal shelter for 6 hours each week for several weeks. He worked for a total of 42 hours. How many weeks did Chip work at the animal shelter?

6. Mr. Jackson has 20 quarters. If he gives 4 quarters to each of his children, how many children does Mr. Jackson have?

© Houghton Mifflin Harcourt Publishing Company

FOR MORE PRACTICE
GO TO THE
Personal Math Trainer

Name _____

Compare Fractions

Essential Question What strategies can you use to compare fractions?

Learning Objective You will use models and strategies involving the sizes of the pieces in the whole to compare fractions of the same whole.

Unlock the Problem

Luka and Ann are eating the same-size small pizzas. One plate has $\frac{3}{4}$ of Luka's cheese pizza. Another plate has $\frac{5}{6}$ of Ann's mushroom pizza. Whose plate has more pizza?

- Circle the numbers you need to compare.
- How many pieces make up each whole pizza?

_____

 Compare $\frac{3}{4}$ and $\frac{5}{6}$.

Missing Pieces Strategy

- You can compare fractions by comparing pieces missing from a whole.

- Shade $\frac{3}{4}$ of Luka's pizza and $\frac{5}{6}$ of Ann's pizza. Each fraction represents a whole that is missing one piece.

- Since $\frac{1}{6}$ ◯ $\frac{1}{4}$, a smaller piece is missing from Ann's pizza.

- If a smaller piece is missing from Ann's pizza, she must have more pizza.

So, _____ plate has more pizza.

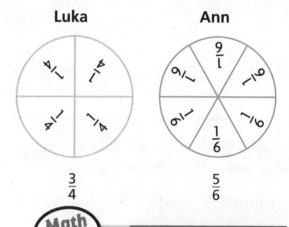

Luka

Ann

$\frac{3}{4}$

$\frac{5}{6}$

Math Talk Math Processes and Practices ②

Reason Abstractly How does knowing that $\frac{1}{4}$ is less than $\frac{1}{3}$ help you compare $\frac{3}{4}$ and $\frac{2}{3}$?

Morgan ran $\frac{2}{3}$ mile. Alexa ran $\frac{1}{3}$ mile. Who ran farther?

 Compare $\frac{2}{3}$ and $\frac{1}{3}$.

Same Denominator Strategy

- When the denominators are the same, you can compare only the number of pieces, or the numerators.

So, _____ ran farther.

Ms. Davis is making a fruit salad with $\frac{3}{4}$ pound of cherries and $\frac{3}{8}$ pound of strawberries. Which weighs less, the cherries or the strawberries?

 Compare $\frac{3}{4}$ and $\frac{3}{8}$.

Same Numerator Strategy

• When the numerators are the same, look at the denominators to compare the size of the pieces.

Think: $\frac{1}{8}$ is smaller than $\frac{1}{4}$ because there are more pieces.

$$\frac{3}{\boxed{}} < \frac{3}{\boxed{}}$$

So, the _____ weigh less.

Share and Show

1. Compare $\frac{7}{8}$ and $\frac{5}{6}$.

   Think: What is missing from each whole?

   Write <, >, or =. $\frac{7}{8} \bigcirc \frac{5}{6}$

Compare. Write <, >, or =. Write the strategy you used.

2. $\frac{1}{2} \bigcirc \frac{2}{3}$

_____

✓ 3. $\frac{3}{4} \bigcirc \frac{2}{4}$

_____

✓ 4. $\frac{3}{8} \bigcirc \frac{3}{6}$

_____

5. $\frac{3}{4} \bigcirc \frac{7}{8}$

_____

Math Talk — Math Processes and Practices ❶

Make Sense of Problems
How do the missing pieces in Exercise 1 help you compare $\frac{7}{8}$ and $\frac{5}{6}$?

Name _____

Compare. Write <, >, or =. Write the strategy you used.

6. $\frac{1}{2}$ ◯ $\frac{2}{2}$

_____

7. $\frac{1}{3}$ ◯ $\frac{1}{4}$

_____

8. $\frac{2}{3}$ ◯ $\frac{5}{6}$

_____

9. $\frac{4}{6}$ ◯ $\frac{4}{2}$

_____

Name a fraction that is less than or greater than the given fraction. Draw to justify your answer.

10. less than $\frac{5}{6}$ _____

11. greater than $\frac{3}{8}$ _____

12. **GO DEEPER** Luke, Seth, and Anja have empty glasses. Mr. Gabel pours $\frac{3}{6}$ cup of orange juice in Seth's glass. Then he pours $\frac{1}{6}$ cup of orange juice in Luke's glass and $\frac{2}{6}$ cup of orange juice in Anja's glass. Who gets the most orange juice?

_____

13. **THINK SMARTER** **What's the Error?** Jack says that $\frac{5}{8}$ is greater than $\frac{5}{6}$ because the denominator 8 is greater than the denominator 6. Describe Jack's error. Draw a picture to explain your answer.

_____

_____

_____

Unlock the Problem

14. **Math Processes and Practices ❶** **Analyze** Tracy is making blueberry muffins. She is using $\frac{4}{4}$ cup of honey and $\frac{4}{2}$ cups of flour. Does Tracy use more honey or more flour?

a. What do you need to know?

_____

b. What strategy will you use to compare the fractions?

_____

c. Show the steps you used to solve the problem.

d. Complete the comparison.

___ > ___

So, Tracy uses more _____.

15. **THINK SMARTER**   Compare the fractions. Circle a symbol that makes the statement true.

$$\frac{2}{8} \begin{array}{c} > \\ < \\ = \end{array} \frac{2}{4} \qquad \frac{1}{4} \begin{array}{c} > \\ < \\ = \end{array} \frac{4}{8}$$

Compare Fractions

Learning Objective You will use models and strategies involving the sizes of the pieces in the whole to compare fractions of the same whole.

Compare. Write <, >, or =. Write the strategy you used.

1. $\frac{3}{8}$ ⃝< $\frac{3}{4}$

   Think: The numerators are the same. Compare the denominators. The greater fraction will have the lesser denominator.

   __same numerator__

2. $\frac{2}{3}$ ⃝ $\frac{7}{8}$

   _____

3. $\frac{3}{4}$ ⃝ $\frac{1}{4}$

   _____

Name a fraction that is less than or greater than the given fraction. Draw to justify your answer.

4. greater than $\frac{1}{3}$ —

5. less than $\frac{3}{4}$ —

Problem Solving · Real World

6. At the third-grade party, two groups each had their own pizza. The blue group ate $\frac{7}{8}$ pizza. The green group ate $\frac{2}{8}$ pizza. Which group ate more of their pizza?

   _____

7. Ben and Antonio both take the same bus to school. Ben's ride is $\frac{7}{8}$ mile. Antonio's ride is $\frac{3}{4}$ mile. Who has a longer bus ride?

   _____

8. **WRITE** ▸*Math* Explain how to use the missing pieces strategy to compare two fractions. Include a diagram with your explanation.

_____

Lesson Check

1. Compare $\frac{2}{3}$ and $\frac{7}{8}$. Write <, >, or =.

2. What symbol makes the statement true? Write <, >, or =.

Spiral Review

3. Cam, Stella, and Rose each picked 40 apples. They put all their apples in one crate. How many apples are in the crate?

4. Each shape is 1 whole. What fraction is represented by the shaded part of the model?

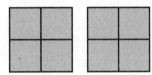

5. What related multiplication fact can you use to find $16 \div \blacksquare = 2$?

6. What is the unknown factor?

$$9 \times \blacksquare = 36$$

FOR MORE PRACTICE
GO TO THE
Personal Math Trainer

Name _____

Concepts and Skills

1. When two fractions refer to the same whole, explain why the fraction with a lesser denominator has larger pieces than the fraction with a greater denominator.

_____

_____

_____

2. When two fractions refer to the same whole and have the same denominators, explain why you can compare only the numerators.

_____

_____

_____

Compare. Write <, >, or =.

3. $\frac{1}{6} \bigcirc \frac{1}{4}$

4. $\frac{1}{8} \bigcirc \frac{1}{8}$

5. $\frac{2}{8} \bigcirc \frac{2}{3}$

6. $\frac{4}{2} \bigcirc \frac{1}{2}$

7. $\frac{7}{8} \bigcirc \frac{3}{8}$

8. $\frac{5}{6} \bigcirc \frac{2}{3}$

9. $\frac{2}{4} \bigcirc \frac{3}{4}$

10. $\frac{6}{6} \bigcirc \frac{6}{8}$

11. $\frac{3}{4} \bigcirc \frac{7}{8}$

Name a fraction that is less than or greater than the given fraction. Draw to justify your answer.

12. greater than $\frac{2}{6}$ _____

13. less than $\frac{2}{3}$ _____

© Houghton Mifflin Harcourt Publishing Company

14. Two walls in Tiffany's room are the same size. Tiffany paints $\frac{1}{4}$ of one wall. Roberto paints $\frac{1}{8}$ of the other wall. Who painted a greater amount in Tiffany's room?

_____

15. Matthew ran $\frac{5}{8}$ mile during track practice. Pablo ran $\frac{5}{6}$ mile. Who ran farther?

_____

16. Mallory bought 6 roses for her mother. Two-sixths of the roses are red and $\frac{4}{6}$ are yellow. Did Mallory buy fewer red roses or yellow roses?

_____

17. GO DEEPER Lani used $\frac{2}{3}$ cup of raisins, $\frac{3}{8}$ cup of cranberries, and $\frac{3}{4}$ cup of oatmeal to bake cookies. Which ingredient did Lani use the least amount of?

_____

Name _____

Compare and Order Fractions

Essential Question How can you compare and order fractions?

Learning Objective You will use visual fraction models and strategies to compare and order fractions with the same numerator or the same denominator.

🔑 Unlock the Problem

Sierra, Tad, and Dale ride their bikes to school. Sierra rides $\frac{3}{4}$ mile, Tad rides $\frac{3}{8}$ mile, and Dale rides $\frac{3}{6}$ mile. Compare and order the distances from least to greatest.

- Circle the fractions you need to use.
- Underline the sentence that tells you what you need to do.

🔓 Activity 1 Order fractions with the same numerator.

Materials ■ color pencil

You can order fractions by reasoning about the size of unit fractions.

1

$\frac{1}{4}$	$\frac{1}{4}$	$\frac{1}{4}$	$\frac{1}{4}$

$\frac{1}{8}$	$\frac{1}{8}$	$\frac{1}{8}$	$\frac{1}{8}$	$\frac{1}{8}$	$\frac{1}{8}$	$\frac{1}{8}$	$\frac{1}{8}$

$\frac{1}{6}$	$\frac{1}{6}$	$\frac{1}{6}$	$\frac{1}{6}$	$\frac{1}{6}$	$\frac{1}{6}$

Remember
- The *more* pieces a whole is divided into, the smaller the pieces are.
- The *fewer* pieces a whole is divided into, the larger the pieces are.

STEP 1 Shade one unit fraction for each fraction strip.

_____ is the longest unit fraction.

_____ is the shortest unit fraction.

STEP 2 Shade one more unit fraction for each fraction strip.

Are the shaded fourths still the longest? _____

Are the shaded eighths still the shortest? _____

STEP 3 Continue shading the fraction strips so that three unit fractions are shaded for each strip.

Are the shaded fourths still the longest? _____

Are the shaded eighths still the shortest? _____

$\frac{3}{4}$ mile is the _____ distance. $\frac{3}{8}$ mile is the _____ distance. $\frac{3}{6}$ mile is *between* the other two distances.

So, the distances in order from least to greatest are

_____ mile, _____ mile, _____ mile.

Try This! Order $\frac{2}{6}$, $\frac{2}{3}$, and $\frac{2}{4}$ from greatest to least.

Order the fractions $\frac{2}{6}$, $\frac{2}{3}$, and $\frac{2}{4}$ by thinking about the length of the unit fraction strip. Then label the fractions *shortest*, *between*, or *longest*.

Fraction	Unit Fraction	Length
$\frac{2}{6}$		
$\frac{2}{3}$		
$\frac{2}{4}$		

Math Talk   Math Processes and Practices ⑧

Generalize When ordering three fractions, what do you know about the third fraction when you know which fraction is the shortest and which fraction is the longest? Explain your answer.

• When the numerators are the same, think about the

_____ of the pieces to compare and order fractions.

So, the order from greatest to least is _____ , _____ , _____ .

🔓 Activity 2 Order fractions with the same denominator.

Materials ■ color pencil

Shade fraction strips to order $\frac{5}{8}$, $\frac{8}{8}$, and $\frac{3}{8}$ from least to greatest.

1

| $\frac{1}{8}$ | $\frac{1}{8}$ | $\frac{1}{8}$ | $\frac{1}{8}$ | $\frac{1}{8}$ | $\frac{1}{8}$ | $\frac{1}{8}$ | $\frac{1}{8}$ | Shade $\frac{5}{8}$. |

| $\frac{1}{8}$ | $\frac{1}{8}$ | $\frac{1}{8}$ | $\frac{1}{8}$ | $\frac{1}{8}$ | $\frac{1}{8}$ | $\frac{1}{8}$ | $\frac{1}{8}$ | Shade $\frac{8}{8}$. |

| $\frac{1}{8}$ | $\frac{1}{8}$ | $\frac{1}{8}$ | $\frac{1}{8}$ | $\frac{1}{8}$ | $\frac{1}{8}$ | $\frac{1}{8}$ | $\frac{1}{8}$ | Shade $\frac{3}{8}$. |

• When the denominators are the same, the size of the pieces is the _____ .

So, think about the _____ of pieces to compare and order fractions.

_____ is the shortest. _____ is the longest.

_____ is between the other two fractions.

So, the order from least to greatest is _____ , _____ , _____ .

Name _____

1. Shade the fraction strips to order $\frac{4}{6}$, $\frac{4}{4}$, and $\frac{4}{8}$ from least to greatest.

Use a Concrete Model Why does using fraction strips help you order fractions with unlike denominators?

1					
$\frac{1}{6}$	$\frac{1}{6}$	$\frac{1}{6}$	$\frac{1}{6}$	$\frac{1}{6}$	$\frac{1}{6}$

$\frac{1}{4}$	$\frac{1}{4}$	$\frac{1}{4}$	$\frac{1}{4}$

$\frac{1}{8}$	$\frac{1}{8}$	$\frac{1}{8}$	$\frac{1}{8}$	$\frac{1}{8}$	$\frac{1}{8}$	$\frac{1}{8}$	$\frac{1}{8}$

_____ is the shortest. _____ is the longest.

_____ is between the other two lengths. _____, _____, _____

Write the fractions in order from least to greatest.

2. $\frac{1}{2}$, $\frac{0}{2}$, $\frac{2}{2}$ _____, _____, _____

3. $\frac{1}{6}$, $\frac{1}{2}$, $\frac{1}{3}$ _____, _____, _____

On Your Own

Write the fractions in order from greatest to least.

4. $\frac{6}{6}$, $\frac{2}{6}$, $\frac{5}{6}$ _____, _____, _____

5. $\frac{1}{8}$, $\frac{1}{4}$, $\frac{1}{2}$ _____, _____, _____

Write the fractions in order from least to greatest.

6. THINK SMARTER
$\frac{6}{3}$, $\frac{6}{2}$, $\frac{6}{8}$ _____, _____, _____

7. THINK SMARTER
$\frac{4}{2}$, $\frac{2}{2}$, $\frac{8}{2}$ _____, _____, _____

8. Math Processes and Practices 6 **Compare** Pam is making biscuits. She needs $\frac{2}{6}$ cup of oil, $\frac{2}{3}$ cup of water, and $\frac{2}{4}$ cup of milk. Write the ingredients from greatest to least amount.

_____, _____, _____

Problem Solving • Applications

9. In fifteen minutes, Greg's sailboat went $\frac{3}{6}$ mile, Gina's sailboat went $\frac{6}{6}$ mile, and Stuart's sailboat went $\frac{4}{6}$ mile. Whose sailboat went the longest distance in fifteen minutes?

   _____

   Whose sailboat went the shortest distance?

   _____

10. **GO DEEPER** Look back at Problem 9. Write a similar problem by changing the fraction of a mile each sailboat traveled, so the answers are different from Problem 9. Then solve the problem.

   _____

   _____

   _____

   _____

WRITE ▸ *Math* • **Show Your Work**

11. **THINK SMARTER** Tom has three pieces of wood. The length of the longest piece is $\frac{3}{4}$ foot. The length of the shortest piece is $\frac{3}{8}$ foot. What might be the length of the third piece of wood?

   _____

12. **THINK SMARTER** Jesse ran $\frac{2}{4}$ mile on Monday, $\frac{2}{3}$ mile on Tuesday, and $\frac{2}{8}$ mile on Wednesday. Order the fractions from least to greatest.

   $\frac{2}{4}$, $\frac{2}{3}$ and $\frac{2}{8}$ ☐ ☐ ☐

Name _____

Compare and Order Fractions

Learning Objective You will use visual fraction models and strategies to compare and order fractions with the same numerator or the same denominator.

Write the fractions in order from greatest to least.

1. $\frac{4}{4}, \frac{1}{4}, \frac{3}{4}$ $\frac{4}{4}$, $\frac{3}{4}$, $\frac{1}{4}$

Think: The denominators are the same, so compare the numerators: $4 > 3 > 1$.

2. $\frac{2}{8}, \frac{5}{8}, \frac{1}{8}$ _____, _____, _____

3. $\frac{1}{3}, \frac{1}{6}, \frac{1}{2}$ _____, _____, _____

4. $\frac{2}{3}, \frac{2}{6}, \frac{2}{8}$ _____, _____, _____

Write the fractions in order from least to greatest.

5. $\frac{2}{4}, \frac{4}{4}, \frac{3}{4}$ _____, _____, _____

6. $\frac{4}{6}, \frac{5}{6}, \frac{2}{6}$ _____, _____, _____

 Problem Solving *Real World*

7. Mr. Jackson ran $\frac{7}{8}$ mile on Monday. He ran $\frac{3}{8}$ mile on Wednesday and $\frac{5}{8}$ mile on Friday. On which day did Mr. Jackson run the shortest distance?

_____

8. Delia has three pieces of ribbon. Her red ribbon is $\frac{2}{4}$ foot long. Her green ribbon is $\frac{2}{3}$ foot long. Her yellow ribbon is $\frac{2}{6}$ foot long. She wants to use the longest piece for a project. Which color ribbon should Delia use?

_____

9. **WRITE** ▸*Math* Describe how fraction strips can help you order fractions.

_____

_____

_____

Lesson Check

1. Write the fractions in order from least to greatest.

$$\frac{1}{8}, \frac{1}{3}, \frac{1}{6}$$

_____

2. Write the fractions in order from greatest to least.

$$\frac{3}{6}, \frac{3}{4}, \frac{3}{8}$$

_____

Spiral Review

3. What fraction of the group of cars is shaded?

_____

4. Wendy has 6 pieces of fruit. Of these, 2 pieces are bananas. What fraction of Wendy's fruit is bananas?

_____

5. Toby collects data and makes a bar graph about his classmates' pets. He finds that 9 classmates have dogs, 2 classmates have fish, 6 classmates have cats, and 3 classmates have gerbils. What pet will have the longest bar on the bar graph?

_____

6. The number sentence is an example of which multiplication property?

$$6 \times 7 = (6 \times 5) + (6 \times 2)$$

_____

FOR MORE PRACTICE
GO TO THE
Personal Math Trainer

Model Equivalent Fractions

Essential Question How can you use models to find equivalent fractions?

Learning Objective You will use area models and number lines to recognize and generate equivalent fractions.

Investigate
Hands On

Materials ■ sheet of paper ■ crayon or color pencil

Two or more fractions that name the same amount are called **equivalent fractions**. You can use a sheet of paper to model fractions equivalent to $\frac{1}{2}$.

A. First, fold a sheet of paper into two equal parts. Open the paper and count the parts.

There are _____ equal parts. Each part is _____ of the paper.

Shade one of the halves. Write $\frac{1}{2}$ on each of the halves.

B. Next, fold the paper in half two times. Open the paper.

Now there are _____ equal parts. Each part is

_____ of the paper.

Write $\frac{1}{4}$ on each of the fourths.

Look at the shaded parts. $\frac{1}{2} = \frac{}{4}$

C. Last, fold the paper in half three times.

Now there are _____ equal parts. Each part is

_____ of the paper.

Write $\frac{1}{8}$ on each of the eighths.

Find the fractions equivalent to $\frac{1}{2}$ on your paper.

So, $\frac{1}{2}$, $\dfrac{}{}$, and $\dfrac{}{}$ are equivalent.

Draw Conclusions

1. Explain how many $\frac{1}{8}$ parts are equivalent to one $\frac{1}{4}$ part on your paper.

_____

_____

2. *THINK SMARTER* What do you notice about how the numerators changed for the shaded part as you folded the paper? _____

   What does this tell you about the change in the number of parts? _____

   How did the denominators change for the shaded part as you folded? _____

   What does this tell you about the change in the size of the parts? _____

Make Connections

You can use a number line to find equivalent fractions.

Find a fraction equivalent to $\frac{2}{3}$.

Materials ■ fraction strips

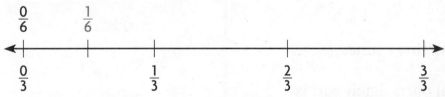

STEP 1 Draw a point on the number line to represent the distance $\frac{2}{3}$.

_____

STEP 2 Use fraction strips to divide the number line into sixths. At the end of each strip, draw a mark on the number line and label the marks to show sixths.

_____

STEP 3 Identify the fraction that names the same point as $\frac{2}{3}$. _____

So, $\frac{2}{3} = \frac{}{6}$.

Name _____

Shade the model. Then divide the pieces to find the equivalent fraction.

1.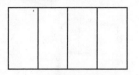

$$\frac{1}{4} = \frac{}{8}$$

2.

$$\frac{2}{3} = \frac{}{6}$$

Use the number line to find the equivalent fraction.

3.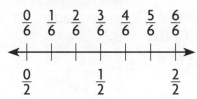

$$\frac{1}{2} = \frac{}{6}$$

4.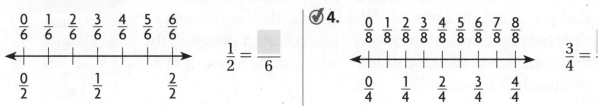

$$\frac{3}{4} = \frac{}{8}$$

Problem Solving • Applications

5. **Math Processes and Practices 6** **Explain** why $\frac{2}{2} = 1$. Write another fraction that is equal to 1. Draw to justify your answer.

_____

_____

_____

Personal Math Trainer

6. **THINK SMARTER +** For numbers 6a–6d, select True or False to tell whether the fractions are equivalent.

6a. $\frac{6}{6}$ and $\frac{3}{3}$ ○ True ○ False

6b. $\frac{4}{6}$ and $\frac{1}{3}$ ○ True ○ False

6c. $\frac{2}{3}$ and $\frac{3}{6}$ ○ True ○ False

6d. $\frac{1}{3}$ and $\frac{2}{6}$ ○ True ○ False

Summarize

You can *summarize* the information in a problem by underlining it or writing the information needed to answer a question.

Read the problem. Underline the important information.

7. **THINK SMARTER** Mrs. Akers bought three sandwiches that were the same size. She cut the first one into thirds. She cut the second one into fourths and the third one into sixths. Marian ate 2 pieces of the first sandwich. Jason ate 2 pieces of the second sandwich. Marcos ate 3 pieces of the third sandwich. Which children ate the same amount of a sandwich? Explain.

The first sandwich was cut into _____.	The second sandwich was cut into _____.	The third sandwich was cut into _____.
Marian ate _____ pieces of the sandwich. Shade the part Marian ate.	Jason ate _____ pieces of the sandwich. Shade the part Jason ate.	Marcos ate _____ pieces of the sandwich. Shade the part Marcos ate.
Marian ate — of the first sandwich.	Jason ate — of the second sandwich.	Marcos ate — of the third sandwich.

Are all the fractions equivalent? _____

Which fractions are equivalent? — = —

So, _____ and _____ ate the same amount of a sandwich.

Name _____

Model Equivalent Fractions

Learning Objective You will use area models and number lines to recognize and generate equivalent fractions.

Shade the model. Then divide the pieces to find the equivalent fraction.

1.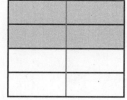

$$\frac{2}{4} = \frac{4}{8}$$

Use the number line to find the equivalent fraction.

2.
```
0   1   2   3   4   5   6   7   8
8   8   8   8   8   8   8   8   8
```

```
0       1       2       3       4
4       4       4       4       4
```

$$\frac{3}{4} = \frac{\boxed{\ }}{8}$$

Problem Solving · Real World

3. Mike says that $\frac{3}{3}$ of his fraction model is shaded blue. Ryan says that $\frac{6}{6}$ of the same model is shaded blue. Are the two fractions equivalent? If so, what is another equivalent fraction?

_____

4. Brett shaded $\frac{4}{8}$ of a sheet of notebook paper. Aisha says he shaded $\frac{1}{2}$ of the paper. Are the two fractions equivalent? If so, what is another equivalent fraction?

_____

5. **WRITE** ▸*Math* Draw a number line that shows two equivalent fractions. Label your number line and explain how you know the fractions are equivalent.

_____

Lesson Check

1. Name a fraction equivalent to $\frac{2}{3}$.

_____

2. Find the fraction equivalent to $\frac{1}{4}$.

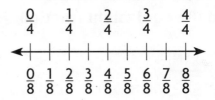

_____

Spiral Review

3. Eric practiced piano and guitar for a total of 8 hours this week. He practiced the piano for $\frac{1}{4}$ of that time. How many hours did Eric practice the piano this week?

_____

4. Kylee bought a pack of 12 cookies. One-third of the cookies are peanut butter. How many of the cookies in the pack are peanut butter?

_____

5. There are 56 students going to the game. The coach puts 7 students in each van. How many vans are needed to take the students to the game?

_____

6. Write a division equation for the picture.

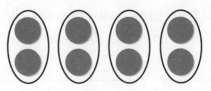

_____

_____

FOR MORE PRACTICE GO TO THE
Personal Math Trainer

Name _____

Equivalent Fractions

Essential Question How can you use models to name equivalent fractions?

Learning Objective You will draw circles and shade area models to show equal groups and to find equivalent fractions.

Unlock the Problem

Cole brought a submarine sandwich to the picnic. He shared the sandwich equally with 3 friends. The sandwich was cut into eighths. What are two ways to describe the part of the sandwich each friend ate?

Cole grouped the smaller pieces into twos. Draw circles to show equal groups of two pieces to show what each friend ate.

- How many people shared the sandwich?

_____

There are 4 equal groups. Each group is $\frac{1}{4}$ of the whole sandwich. So, each friend ate $\frac{1}{4}$ of the whole sandwich.

How many eighths did each friend eat? _____

$\frac{1}{4}$ and _____ are equivalent fractions since they both name

the _____ amount of the sandwich.

So, $\frac{1}{4}$ and _____ of the sandwich are two ways to describe the part of the sandwich each friend ate.

Try This! Circle equal groups. Write an equivalent fraction for the shaded part of the whole.

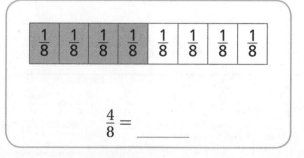

$$\frac{4}{8} = \underline{\quad}$$

Math Processes and Practices ❸

Apply What is a different way you could have circled the equal groups?

🔑 Example Model the problem.

Heidi ate $\frac{3}{6}$ of her fruit bar. Molly ate $\frac{4}{8}$ of her fruit bar, which is the same size. Which girl ate more of her fruit bar?

Shade $\frac{3}{6}$ of Heidi's fruit bar and $\frac{4}{8}$ of Molly's fruit bar.

- Is $\frac{3}{6}$ greater than, less than, or equal to $\frac{4}{8}$? _____

So, both girls ate the _____ amount.

Heidi

$\frac{1}{6}$	$\frac{1}{6}$	$\frac{1}{6}$
$\frac{1}{6}$	$\frac{1}{6}$	$\frac{1}{6}$

Molly

$\frac{1}{8}$	$\frac{1}{8}$	$\frac{1}{8}$	$\frac{1}{8}$
$\frac{1}{8}$	$\frac{1}{8}$	$\frac{1}{8}$	$\frac{1}{8}$

Try This! Each shape is 1 whole. Write an equivalent fraction for the shaded part of the models.

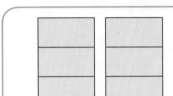 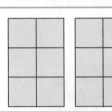

$$\frac{6}{3} = \frac{\boxed{}}{6}$$

Share and Show MATH BOARD

1. Each shape is 1 whole. Use the model to find the equivalent fraction.

$$\frac{2}{4} = \frac{\boxed{}}{2}$$

> **Math Talk** Math Processes and Practices ②
>
> **Use Reasoning** Explain why equivalent fractions name the same amount.

Each shape is 1 whole. Shade the model to find the equivalent fraction.

 2.

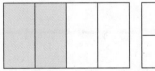

$$\frac{2}{4} = \frac{\boxed{}}{8}$$

3.

$$\frac{12}{6} = \frac{\boxed{}}{3}$$

4. Andy swam $\frac{8}{8}$ mile in a race. Use the number line to find a fraction that is equivalent to $\frac{8}{8}$.

$$\frac{8}{8} = \frac{\boxed{}}{}$$

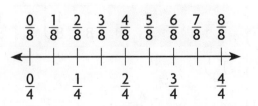

Name _____

Circle equal groups to find the equivalent fraction.

5.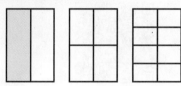

$$\frac{3}{6} = \frac{\boxed{}}{2}$$

6.

$$\frac{6}{6} = \frac{\boxed{}}{3}$$

On Your Own

Each shape is 1 whole. Shade the model to find the equivalent fraction.

7.

$$\frac{1}{2} = \frac{2}{\boxed{}} = \frac{\boxed{}}{8}$$

8.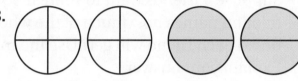

$$\frac{8}{\boxed{}} = \frac{4}{2}$$

Circle equal groups to find the equivalent fraction.

9.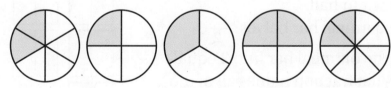

$$\frac{6}{8} = \frac{\boxed{}}{4}$$

10.

$$\frac{2}{6} = \frac{\boxed{}}{3}$$

11. Write the fraction that names the shaded part of each circle.

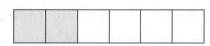

_____   _____   _____   _____   _____

Which pairs of fractions are equivalent? _____

12. (Math Processes and Practices ③) **Apply** Matt cut his small pizza into 6 equal pieces and ate 4 of them. Josh cut his small pizza, which is the same size, into 3 equal pieces and ate 2 of them. Write fractions for the amount they each ate. Are the fractions equivalent? Draw to explain.

_____

Problem Solving • Applications

13. **GO DEEPER** Christy bought 8 muffins. She chose 2 apple, 2 banana, and 4 blueberry. She and her family ate the apple and banana muffins for breakfast. What fraction of the muffins did they eat? Write an equivalent fraction. Draw a picture.

_____

14. **THINK SMARTER** After dinner, $\frac{2}{3}$ of the corn bread is left. Suppose 4 friends want to share it equally. What fraction names how much of the whole pan of corn bread each friend will get? Use the model on the right. Explain your answer.

_____

_____

15. There are 16 people having lunch. Each person wants $\frac{1}{4}$ of a pizza. How many whole pizzas are needed? Draw a picture to show your answer.

_____

16. Lucy has 5 oatmeal bars, each cut in half. What fraction names all of the oatmeal bar halves? $\frac{\ }{2}$

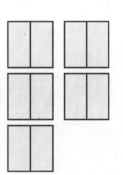

What if Lucy cuts each part of the oatmeal bar into 2 equal pieces to share with friends? What fraction names all of the oatmeal bar pieces now? $\frac{\ }{4}$

$\frac{\ }{2}$ and $\frac{\ }{4}$ are equivalent fractions.

17. **THINK SMARTER** Mr. Peters made a pizza. There is $\frac{4}{8}$ of the pizza left over. Select the fractions that are equivalent to the part of the pizza that is left over. Mark all that apply.

(A) $\frac{5}{8}$ (B) $\frac{3}{4}$ (C) $\frac{2}{4}$ (D) $\frac{1}{2}$

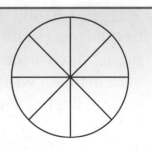

Name _____

Equivalent Fractions

Learning Objective You will draw circles and shade area models to show equal groups and to find equivalent fractions.

Each shape is 1 whole. Shade the model to find the equivalent fraction.

1.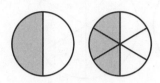

$$\frac{1}{2} = \frac{3}{6}$$

2.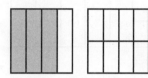

$$\frac{3}{4} = \frac{6}{\square}$$

Circle equal groups to find the equivalent fraction.

3.

$$\frac{2}{4} = \frac{\square}{2}$$

4.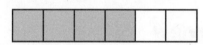

$$\frac{4}{6} = \frac{\square}{3}$$

Problem Solving Real World

5. May painted 4 out of 8 equal parts of a poster board blue. Jared painted 2 out of 4 equal parts of a same-size poster board red. Write fractions to show which part of the poster board each person painted.

_____

6. **WRITE** ▸ *Math* Explain how you can find a fraction that is equivalent to $\frac{1}{4}$.

_____

_____

Lesson Check

1. What fraction is equivalent to $\frac{6}{8}$?

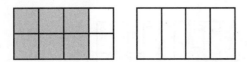

_____

2. What fraction is equivalent to $\frac{1}{3}$?

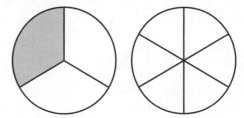

_____

Spiral Review

3. What division number sentence is shown by the array?

_____

_____

4. Cody put 4 plates on the table. He put 1 apple on each plate. What number sentence can be used to find the total number of apples on the table?

_____

_____

5. Write a division number sentence that is a related fact to $7 \times 3 = 21$.

_____

_____

6. Find the quotient.

$$4\overline{)36}$$

_____

_____

FOR MORE PRACTICE
GO TO THE
Personal Math Trainer

✅ Chapter 9 Review/Test

Personal Math Trainer
Online Assessment
and Intervention

1. Alexa and Rose read books that have the same number of pages. Alexa's book is divided into 8 equal chapters. Rose's book is divided into 6 equal chapters. Each girl has read 3 chapters of her book.

   Write a fraction to describe what part of the book each girl read. Then tell who read more pages. Explain.

   _____

   _____

   _____

2. David, Maria, and Simone are shading same-sized index cards for a science project. David shaded $\frac{2}{4}$ of his index card. Maria shaded $\frac{2}{8}$ of her index card and Simone shaded $\frac{2}{6}$ of her index card.

   For 2a–2d, choose Yes or No to indicate whether the comparisons are correct.

   2a. $\frac{2}{4} > \frac{2}{8}$ ○ Yes   ○ No

   2b. $\frac{2}{8} > \frac{2}{6}$ ○ Yes   ○ No

   2c. $\frac{2}{6} < \frac{2}{4}$ ○ Yes   ○ No

   2d. $\frac{2}{8} = \frac{2}{4}$ ○ Yes   ○ No

3. Dan and Miguel are working on the same homework assignment. Dan has finished $\frac{1}{4}$ of the assignment. Miguel has finished $\frac{3}{4}$ of the assignment. Which statement is correct? Mark all that apply.

   Ⓐ Miguel has completed the entire assignment.

   Ⓑ Dan has not completed the entire assignment.

   Ⓒ Miguel has finished more of the assignment than Dan.

   Ⓓ Dan and Miguel have completed equal parts of the assignment.

Assessment Options
Chapter Test

4. Bryan cut two peaches that were the same size for lunch. He cut one peach into fourths and the other into sixths. Bryan ate $\frac{3}{4}$ of the first peach. His brother ate $\frac{5}{6}$ of the second peach. Who ate more peach? Explain the strategy you used to solve the problem.

_____

_____

_____

5. A nature center offers 2 guided walks. The morning walk is $\frac{2}{3}$ mile. The evening walk is $\frac{3}{6}$ mile. Which walk is shorter? Explain how you can use the model to find the answer.

$\frac{1}{3}$		$\frac{1}{3}$		$\frac{1}{3}$	
$\frac{1}{6}$	$\frac{1}{6}$	$\frac{1}{6}$	$\frac{1}{6}$	$\frac{1}{6}$	$\frac{1}{6}$

_____

_____

6. Chun lives $\frac{3}{8}$ mile from school. Gail lives $\frac{5}{8}$ mile from school.

Use the fractions and symbols to show which distance is longer.

| $\frac{3}{8}$ | $\frac{5}{8}$ | $<$ | $>$ |

▢ ◯ ▢

Name _____

7. THINK SMARTER ➕ Mrs. Reed baked four pans of lasagna for a family party. Use the rectangles to represent the pans.

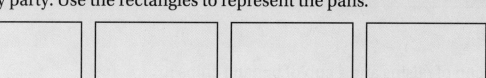

Part A

Draw lines to show how Mrs. Reed could cut one pan of lasagna into thirds, one into fourths, one into sixths, and one into eighths.

Part B

At the end of the dinner, equivalent amounts of lasagna in two pans were left. Use the models to show the lasagna that might have been left over. Write two pairs of equivalent fractions to represent the models.

_____

8. Tom rode his horse for $\frac{4}{6}$ mile. Liz rode her horse for an equal distance. What is an equivalent fraction that describes how far Liz rode? Use the models to show your work.

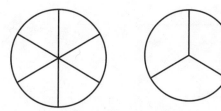

_____

9. Avery prepares 2 equal-size oranges for the bats at the zoo. One dish has $\frac{3}{8}$ of an orange. Another dish has $\frac{2}{8}$ of an orange. Which dish has more orange? Show your work.

_____

10. Jenna painted $\frac{1}{8}$ of one side of a fence. Mark painted $\frac{1}{6}$ of the other side of the same fence. Use >, =, or < to compare the parts that they painted.

_____

11. Bill used $\frac{1}{3}$ cup of raisins and $\frac{2}{3}$ cup of banana chips to make a snack.

For 11a–11d, select True or False for each comparison.

11a. $\frac{1}{3} > \frac{2}{3}$ ○ True   ○ False

11b. $\frac{2}{3} = \frac{1}{3}$ ○ True   ○ False

11c. $\frac{1}{3} < \frac{2}{3}$ ○ True   ○ False

11d. $\frac{2}{3} > \frac{1}{3}$ ○ True   ○ False

12. **GO DEEPER** Jorge, Lynne, and Crosby meet at the playground. Jorge lives $\frac{5}{6}$ mile from the playground. Lynne lives $\frac{4}{6}$ mile from the playground. Crosby lives $\frac{7}{8}$ mile from the playground.

Part A

Who lives closer to the playground, Jorge or Lynne? Explain how you know.

_____

_____

_____

Part B

Who lives closer to the playground, Jorge or Crosby? Explain how you know.

_____

_____

_____

554

Name _____

13. Ming needs $\frac{1}{2}$ pint of red paint for an art project. He has 6 jars that have the following amounts of red paint in them. He wants to use only 1 jar of paint. Mark all of the jars of paints that Ming could use.

(A) $\frac{2}{3}$ pint   (D) $\frac{3}{4}$ pint

(B) $\frac{1}{4}$ pint   (E) $\frac{3}{8}$ pint

(C) $\frac{4}{6}$ pint   (F) $\frac{2}{6}$ pint

14. There are 12 people having lunch. Each person wants $\frac{1}{3}$ of a sub sandwich. How many whole sub sandwiches are needed? Use the models to show your answer.

[ ]   [ ]   [ ]

[ ]   [ ]   [ ]

_____ sub sandwiches

15. Mavis mixed $\frac{2}{4}$ quart of apple juice with $\frac{1}{2}$ quart of cranberry juice. Compare the fractions. Choose the symbol that makes the statement true.

$$\frac{2}{4} \quad \begin{array}{c} < \\ = \\ > \end{array} \quad \frac{1}{2}$$

16. Pat has three pieces of fabric that measure $\frac{3}{6}$, $\frac{5}{6}$, and $\frac{2}{6}$ yards long. Write the lengths in order from least to greatest.

_____

17. Cora measures the heights of three plants. Draw a line to match each height on the left to the word on the right that describes its place in the order of heights.

$\frac{4}{6}$ foot •   • least

$\frac{4}{4}$ foot •   • between

$\frac{4}{8}$ foot •   • greatest

18. Danielle drew a model to show equivalent fractions.

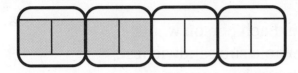

Use the model to complete the number sentence.

$\frac{1}{2} =$ _____ $=$ _____

19. Floyd caught a fish that weighed $\frac{2}{3}$ pound. Kira caught a fish that weighed $\frac{7}{8}$ pound. Whose fish weighed more? Explain the strategy you used to solve the problem.

_____

_____

_____

_____

20. Sam went for a ride on a sailboat. The ride lasted $\frac{3}{4}$ hour.

What fraction is equivalent to $\frac{3}{4}$?

_____

556

Big Idea Measurement

BIG IDEA Develop a conceptual understanding of measurement, including time, linear, and liquid measures. Develop concepts of area and perimeter.

Measurement tools and data are used to design and build a safe and enjoyable playground.

557

Plan a Playground

Is there a playground at your school, in your neighborhood, or in a nearby park? Playgrounds provide a fun and safe outdoor space for you to climb, swing, slide, and play.

Get Started

Suppose you want to help plan a playground for a block in your neighborhood.

- Draw a large rectangle on the grid paper to show a fence around your playground. Find the distance around your playground by counting the number of units on each side. Record the distance.

- Use the Important Facts to help you decide on features to have in your playground. Shade parts of your playground to show each feature's location. Then find the number of unit squares the feature covers and record it on your plan.

Important Facts
Playground Features

- Bench
- Jungle Gym
- Playhouse
- Sandbox
- Seesaw
- Slide
- Swing Set
- Water Fountain

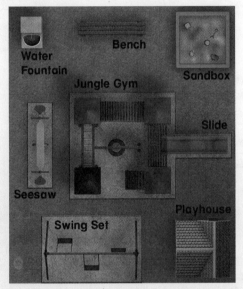

▲ This drawing shows a plan for a playground.

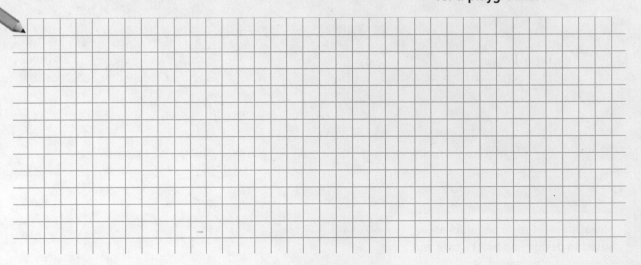

Completed by _____

Chapter 10
Time, Length, Liquid Volume, and Mass

✓ Show What You Know

Personal Math Trainer
Online Assessment
and Intervention

Check your understanding of important skills.

Name _____

▶ **Time to the Half Hour** Read the clock. Write the time.

1.   _____

2.   _____

▶ **Skip Count by Fives**

Skip count by fives. Write the missing numbers.

3. 5, 10, 15, ____, 25, ____, 35

4. 55, 60, ____, 70, ____, ____, 85

▶ **Inches** Use a ruler to measure the length to the nearest inch.

5.

about _____ inches

6.

about _____ inch

Math in the Real World

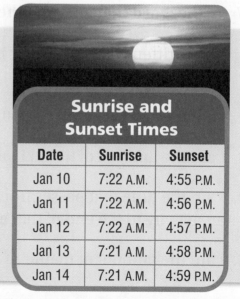

You can look at the time the sun rises and sets to find the amount of daylight each day. The table shows the time the sun rose and set from January 10 to January 14 in Philadelphia, Pennsylvania. Find which day had the least daylight and which day had the most daylight.

Sunrise and Sunset Times

Date	Sunrise	Sunset
Jan 10	7:22 A.M.	4:55 P.M.
Jan 11	7:22 A.M.	4:56 P.M.
Jan 12	7:22 A.M.	4:57 P.M.
Jan 13	7:21 A.M.	4:58 P.M.
Jan 14	7:21 A.M.	4:59 P.M.

Vocabulary Builder

▶ **Visualize It** ••••••••••••••••••••••••••••••••••••••

Complete the graphic organizer by using the words with a ✓. Write the words in order from the greatest to the least length of time.

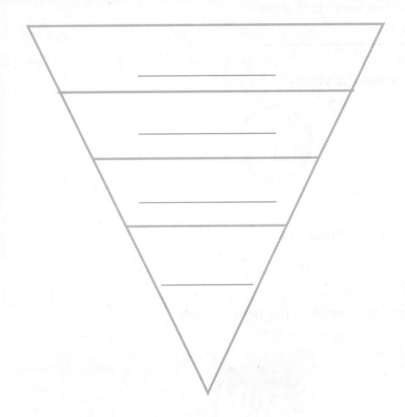

Review Words

analog clock
digital clock
fourth
half
✓ half hour
✓ hour (hr)
inch (in.)
✓ quarter hour

Preview Words

A.M.
elapsed time
gram (g)
kilogram (kg)
liquid volume
liter (L)
mass
midnight
✓ minute (min)
noon
P.M.

▶ **Understand Vocabulary** •••••••••••••••••••••••••••

Write the word that answers the riddle.

1. I am written with times after midnight and before noon. _____

2. I am the time when it is 12:00 in the daytime. _____

3. I am the amount of liquid in a container. _____

4. I am the time that passes from the start of an activity to the end of that activity. _____

5. I am the amount of matter in an object. _____

• **Interactive Student Edition**
• **Multimedia eGlossary**

Chapter 10 Vocabulary

A.M.

A.M.

1

Elapsed Time

tiempo transcurrido

18

gram (g)

gramo (g)

30

Halves

mitades

32

kilogram (kg)

kilogramo (kg)

39

liquid volume

volumen de un líquido

45

liter (L)

litro (L)

46

mass

masa

47

The time that passes from the start of an activity to the end of that activity

So, the elapsed time is 43 minutes.

The time after midnight and before noon

After Midnight and Before Noon

These are halves

A metric unit used to measure mass
1 kilogram = 1,000 grams

A small paper clip has a mass of about 1 gram.

The amount of liquid in a container

A metric unit used to measure mass
1 kilogram = 1,000 grams

1,000 Paper clips

A box of 1,000 paper clips has a mass of about 1 kilogram.

The amount of matter in an object

A metric unit used to measure liquid volume

1 liter

Midnight

medianoche

48

minute

minuto

49

Noon

mediadía

52

P.M.

P.M.

63

A unit used to measure short amounts of time; in one minute, the minute hand on an analog clock moves from one mark to the next

minute

12:00 at night

Midnight

The time after noon and before midnight

P.M.

12:00 in the day

Noon

Game

Going to the Playground

© Houghton Mifflin Harcourt Publishing Company • Image Credits: (bg) ©PhotoDisc/Getty Images

For 2 players

Materials

- 1 red playing piece
- 1 blue playing piece
- 1 number cube

How to Play

1. Each player chooses a playing piece and puts it on START.
2. Toss the number cube to take a turn. Move your playing piece that many spaces.
3. If you land on these spaces, follow the instructions.

   White Space Tell the meaning of the math term, or use it in a sentence. If your answer is correct, jump to the next space with the same term. If your answer is not correct, stay where you are.

   Green Space Follow the directions printed in the space. If there are no directions, stay where you are.
4. The first player to reach FINISH wins.

Word Box
A.M.
elapsed time
gram (g)
kilogram (kg)
liquid volume
liter (L)
mass
midnight
minute
noon
P.M.

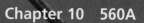

Game

HOW TO PLAY

1. Each player chooses a playing piece and puts it on START.
2. Toss the number cube to take a turn. Move your playing piece that many spaces.
3. If you land on these spaces, follow the instructions.
   - White Space: Tell the meaning of the math term, or use it in a sentence. If your answer is correct, jump to the next space with the same term. If your answer is not correct, stay where you are.
   - Green Space: Follow the directions printed in the space. If there are no directions, stay where you are.
4. The first player to reach FINISH wins.

MATERIALS
- 1 red playing piece
- 1 blue playing piece
- 1 number cube

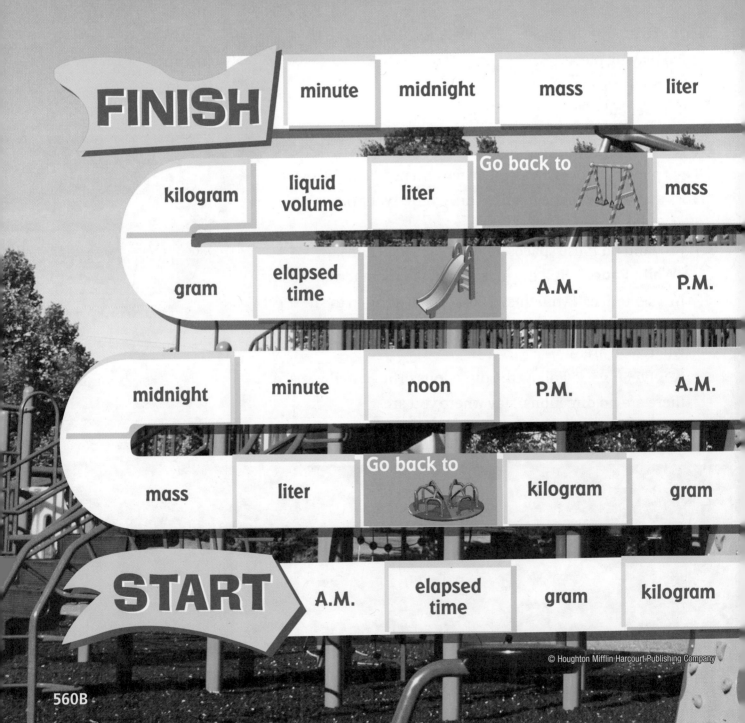

FINISH | minute | midnight | mass | liter

kilogram | liquid volume | liter | Go back to | mass

gram | elapsed time | | A.M. | P.M.

midnight | minute | noon | P.M. | A.M.

mass | liter | Go back to | kilogram | gram

START | A.M. | elapsed time | gram | kilogram

Game

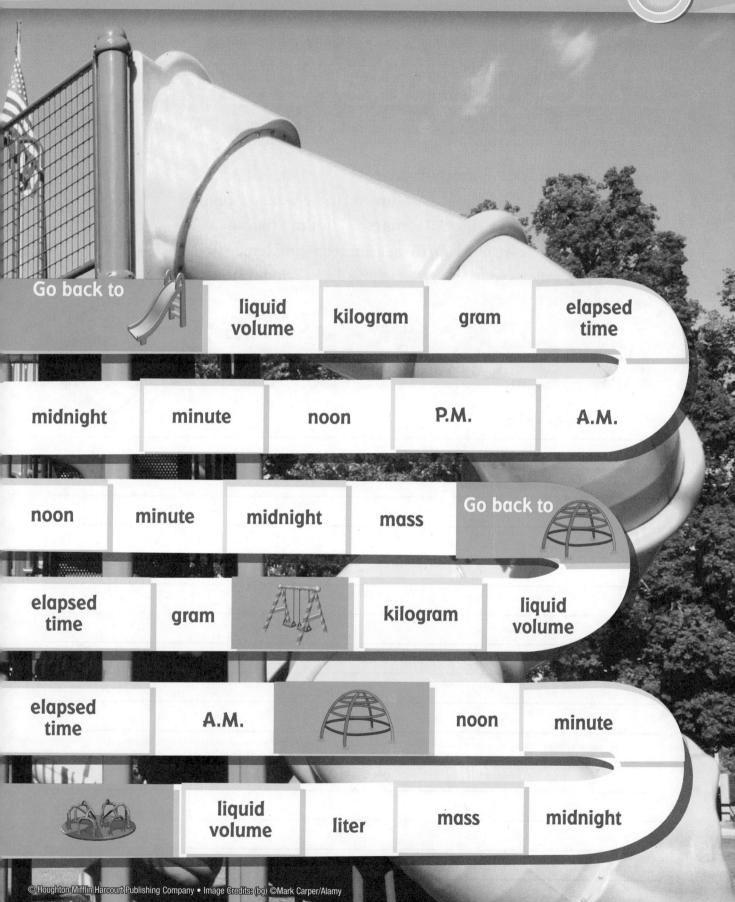

Go back to

liquid volume

kilogram

gram

elapsed time

midnight

minute

noon

P.M.

A.M.

noon

minute

midnight

mass

Go back to

elapsed time

gram

kilogram

liquid volume

elapsed time

A.M.

noon

minute

liquid volume

liter

mass

midnight

The Write Way

Reflect

Choose one idea. Write about it.

- Write a paragraph that uses at least **three** of these words or phrases.

  gram   kilogram   liter   mass   liquid volume

- Explain how you solve one kind of measurement problem.

- Write two questions you have about telling time or finding time intervals.

Name _____

Time to the Minute

Essential Question How can you tell time to the nearest minute?

Learning Objective You will tell and write time to the nearest minute by using analog and digital clocks to write one way you can read the time.

Unlock the Problem

Groundhog Day is February 2. People say that if a groundhog can see its shadow on that morning, winter will last another 6 weeks. The clock shows the time when the groundhog saw its shadow. What time was it?

> • Underline the question.
> • Where will you look to find the time?
> _____

🔒 Example

Look at the time on this clock face.

• What does the hour hand tell you?

_____

• What does the minute hand tell you?

_____

In 1 **minute**, the minute hand moves from one mark to the next on a clock. It takes 5 minutes for the minute hand to move from one number to the next on a clock.

You can count on by fives to tell time to five minutes. Count zero at the 12.

0, 5, 10, 15, _____, _____, _____, _____

So, the groundhog saw its shadow at _____.

Write: 7:35

Read:

• seven _____

• thirty-five minutes after _____

 Math Talk Math Processes and Practices ②

Reason Abstractly How does skip counting by fives help you tell the time when the minute hand points to a number?

• Is 7:35 a reasonable answer? Explain. _____

_____

Time to the Minute

Count by fives and ones to help you.

🔓 One Way Find minutes after the hour.

Look at the time on this clock face.

- What does the hour hand tell you?

  _____

- What does the minute hand tell you?

  _____

Count on by fives and ones from the 12 on the clock to where the minute hand is pointing. Write the missing counting numbers next to the clock.

When a clock shows 30 or fewer minutes after the hour, you can read the time as a number of minutes *after* the hour.

Write: _____

Read:

- twenty-three minutes after _____

- one _____

🔓 Another Way Find minutes before the hour.

Look at the time on this clock face.

- What does the hour hand tell you?

  _____

- What does the minute hand tell you?

  _____

Now count by fives and ones from the 12 on the clock back to where the minute hand is pointing. Write the missing counting numbers next to the clock.

When a clock shows 31 or more minutes after the hour, you can read the time as a number of minutes *before* the next hour.

Write: 2:43

Read:

- seventeen _____ before three

- two _____

 ERROR Alert

Remember that time *after* the hour uses the previous hour, and time *before* the hour uses the next hour.

Name _____

1. How would you use counting and the minute hand to find the time shown on this clock? Write the time.

_____

Write the time. Write one way you can read the time.

2.

_____

_____

☑ 3.

_____

_____

☑ 4.

_____

_____

Math Talk

Math Processes and Practices ❸

Apply How do you know when to stop counting by fives and start counting by ones when counting minutes after an hour?

On Your Own

Write the time. Write one way you can read the time.

5.

_____

_____

6.

_____

_____

7.

_____

_____

Math Processes and Practices ❷ **Represent a Problem** **Write the time another way.**

8. 34 minutes after 5

_____

9. 11 minutes before 6

_____

10. 22 minutes after 11

_____

11. 5 minutes before 12

_____

Problem Solving • Applications

Use the clocks for 12–13.

Time of Day the Groundhog Saw Its Shadow

NY   PA

12. How many minutes later in the day did the groundhog in Pennsylvania see its shadow than the groundhog in New York?

_____

13. **GO DEEPER** What if the groundhog in Pennsylvania saw its shadow 5 minutes later? What time would this be?

_____

14. If you look at your watch and the hour hand is between the 8 and the 9 and the minute hand is on the 11, what time is it?

_____

15. **THINK SMARTER** What time is it when the hour hand and the minute hand are both pointing to the same number? Aiden says it is 6:30. Camilla says it is 12:00. Who is correct? Explain.

_____

_____

16. **Math Processes and Practices ③ Verify the Reasoning of Others** Lucy said the time is 4:46 on her digital watch. Explain where the hands on an analog clock are pointing when it is 4:46.

_____

_____

17. **THINK SMARTER** Write the time that is shown on the clock. Then write the time another way.

_____

Name _____

Time to the Minute

Learning Objective You will tell and write time to the nearest minute by using analog and digital clocks to write one way you can read the time.

Write the time. Write one way you can read the time.

1.

1:16; sixteen minutes

after one

2.

_____

_____

3.

_____

_____

4.

_____

_____

5.

_____

_____

6.

_____

_____

Write the time another way.

7. 23 minutes after 4

_____

8. 18 minutes before 11

_____

Problem Solving

9. What time is it when the hour hand is a little past the 3 and the minute hand is pointing to the 3?

_____

10. Pete began practicing at twenty-five minutes before eight. What is another way to write this time?

_____

11. **WRITE** ▸*Math* Draw a clock showing a time to the nearest minute. Write the time as many different ways you can.

_____

_____

Lesson Check

1. What is another way to write 13 minutes before 10?

2. What time does the clock show?

Spiral Review

3. Each bird has 2 wings. How many wings do 5 birds have?

4. Find the unknown factor.

$$8 \times \blacksquare = 56$$

5. Mr. Wren has 56 paintbrushes. He places 8 paintbrushes on each of the tables in the art room. How many tables are in the art room?

6. What number completes the equations?

$$4 \times \blacktriangle = 20 \quad 20 \div 4 = \blacktriangle$$

FOR MORE PRACTICE
GO TO THE
Personal Math Trainer

Name _____

A.M. and P.M.

Essential Question How can you tell when to use A.M. and P.M. with time?

Learning Objective You will decide when to use A.M. or P.M. with times by using a number line to show order of events.

Unlock the Problem

Lauren's family is going hiking tomorrow at 7:00. How should Lauren write the time to show that they are going in the morning, not in the evening?

You can use a number line to show the sequence or order of events. It can help you understand the number of hours in a day.

Think: The distance from one mark to the next mark represents one hour.

- Circle the helpful information that tells about the hiking time.
- What do you need to find?

_____

_____

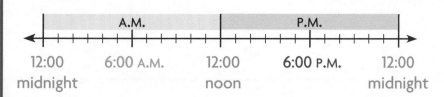

A.M.	P.M.

12:00 midnight   6:00 A.M.   12:00 noon   6:00 P.M.   12:00 midnight

Tell time after midnight.

Midnight is 12:00 at night.

The times after midnight and before noon are written with **A.M.**

7:00 in the morning is written as

7:00 _____

So, Lauren should write the hiking time as 7:00 _____

After Midnight and Before Noon

A.M.

- Find the mark that shows 7:00 A.M. on the number line above. Circle the mark.

Math Talk

Math Processes and Practices 3

Compare Representations How are the number line on this page and the clock face alike? How are they different?

© Houghton Mifflin Harcourt Publishing Company • Image Credits: ©Michael Halbersta ©Steve Mason/Photodisc/Getty Images

Chapter 10 567

🔑 Tell time after noon.

Callie's family is going for a canoe ride at 3:00 in the afternoon. How should Callie write the time?

Noon is 12:00 in the daytime.

The times after noon and before midnight are written with **P.M.**

3:00 in the afternoon is written as 3:00 _____

After Noon and Before Midnight

P.M.

So, Callie should write the time as 3:00 _____

Share and Show MATH BOARD

1. Name two things you do in the A.M. hours.
   Name two things you do in the P.M. hours.

_____

_____

Write the time for the activity. Use A.M. or P.M.

2. ride a bicycle

_____

☑ 3. make a sandwich

_____

☑ 4. get ready for bed

5. This morning Sam woke up at the time shown on this
   clock. Write the time using A.M. or P.M. _____

 Math Talk Math Processes and Practices ③

Apply How do you decide whether to use A.M. or P.M. when you write the time?

Name _____

Write the time for the activity. Use A.M. or P.M.

6. eat breakfast

_____

7. have science class

_____

8. play softball

_____

Write the time. Use A.M. or P.M.

9. quarter after 9:00 in the morning

_____

10. 6 minutes after 7:00 in the morning

_____

11. Mark is taking a trip on an airplane. His flight leaves at 24 minutes before 9 in the morning. Using A.M. or P.M., at what time does Mark's flight leave?

_____

12. Jennie's class ate lunch at 18 minutes before noon each day. Using A.M. or P.M., write the time that Jennie's class ate lunch.

_____

13. Daylight saving time begins on the second Sunday in March at 2:00 in the morning. Write the time.

Use A.M. or P.M. _____

14. GO DEEPER Jane and her dad are using their new telescope to look at the stars. They start looking at the stars at 23 minutes after 9 and stopped looking at the stars at 10 minutes after 10. Using A.M. or P.M., at what time did they start and stop looking at the stars?

_____

15. THINK SMARTER From midnight to noon each day, how many times does the minute hand on a clock pass 6? Explain how you found your answer.

_____

_____

Unlock the Problem

16. Lea and her father arrived at the scenic overlook 15 minutes before noon and left 12 minutes after noon. Using A.M. or P.M., write the time when Lea and her father arrived at the scenic overlook and the time when they left.

a. What do you need to find? _____

_____

_____

b. What do you need to find first? _____

c. **Math Processes and Practices** ⑥ **Describe a Method** Show the steps you used to solve the problem.

d. They arrived at _____ _____.M.

They left at _____ _____.M.

---

17. **THINK SMARTER**   The Davis family spent the day at the lake. Write the letter for each activity next to the time they did it.

Ⓐ Went swimming soon after lunch.   ☐ 9:50 A.M.

Ⓑ Ate breakfast at home.   ☐ 7:00 P.M.

Ⓒ Watched the sunset over the lake.   ☐ 12:15 P.M.

Ⓓ Got to the lake cabin in the morning.   ☐ 1:30 P.M.

Ⓔ Had sandwiches for lunch.   ☐ 7:00 A.M.

Name _____

A.M. and P.M.

Learning Objective You will decide when to use A.M. or P.M. with times by using a number line to show order of events.

Write the time for the activity. Use A.M. or P.M.

1. eat lunch

12:20 P.M.

2. go home after school

_____

3. see the sunrise

_____

4. go for a walk

_____

5. go to school

_____

6. get ready for art class

_____

Write the time. Use A.M. or P.M.

7. one half hour past midnight

_____

8. one-half hour after 4:00 in the morning

_____

Problem Solving Real World

9. Jaime is in math class. What time is it? Use A.M. or P.M.

_____

10. Pete began practicing his trumpet at fifteen minutes past three. Write this time using A.M. or P.M.

_____

11. **WRITE** ▸*Math* Write your schedule for today. List each activity with its starting time. Write A.M. or P.M. for each time.

_____

_____

Lesson Check

1. Steven is doing his homework. What time is it? Use A.M. or P.M.

_____

2. After he finished breakfast, Mr. Edwards left for work at fifteen minutes after seven. What time is this? Use A.M. or P.M.

_____

Spiral Review

3. What division equation is related to the multiplication equation

$$4 \times 6 = 24?$$

_____

_____

4. There are 50 toothpicks in each box. Jaime buys 4 boxes for her party platter. How many toothpicks does Jaime buy?

_____

_____

5. A pet store sold 145 bags of beef-flavored dog food and 263 bags of cheese-flavored dog food. How many bags of dog food were sold?

_____

6. Compare. Write <, >, or =.

$$\frac{3}{6} \bigcirc \frac{4}{6}$$

© Houghton Mifflin Harcourt Publishing Company

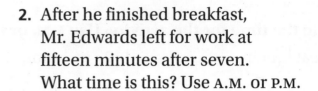

FOR MORE PRACTICE
GO TO THE
Personal Math Trainer

Name _____

Measure Time Intervals

Essential Question How can you measure elapsed time in minutes?

Learning Objective You will measure time intervals in minutes by drawing jumps on a number line or using an analog clock.

🗝️ Unlock the Problem

Alicia and her family visited the Kennedy Space Center. They watched a movie that began at 4:10 P.M. and ended at 4:53 P.M. How long did the movie last?

- Circle the times the movie began and ended.
- Underline the question.

To find **elapsed time**, find the amount of time that passes from the start of an activity to the end of the activity.

🔑 One Way Use a number line.

STEP 1 Find the time on the number line that the movie began.

STEP 2 Count on to the ending time, 4:53. Count on by tens for each 10 minutes. Count on by ones for each minute. Write the times below the number line.

STEP 3 Draw the jumps on the number line to show the minutes from 4:10 to 4:53. Record the minutes. Then add them.

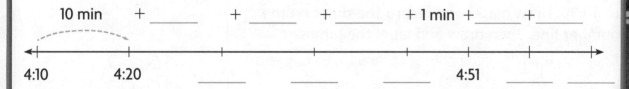

10 min   +_____   +_____   +_____   + 1 min   +_____   +_____

4:10   4:20   _____   _____   4:51   _____   _____

10 + 10 + 10 + 10 + 1 + 1 + 1 = _____

The elapsed time from 4:10 P.M. to

4:53 P.M. is _____ minutes.

So, the movie lasted _____ minutes.

Math Talk

Math Processes and Practices ④

Use Models What is another way you can use jumps on the number line to find the elapsed time from 4:10 P.M. to 4:53 P.M?

Chapter 10 573

🔟 Other Ways

Start time: 4:10 P.M. End time: 4:53 P.M.

Ⓐ Use an analog clock.

STEP 1 Find the starting time on the clock.

STEP 2 Count the minutes by counting on by fives and ones to 4:53 P.M. Write the missing counting numbers next to the clock.

So, the elapsed time is _____ minutes.

Ⓑ Use subtraction.

STEP 1 Write the ending time. Then write the starting time so that the hours and minutes line up.

STEP 2 The hours are the same, so subtract the minutes.

$$4:\boxed{} \leftarrow \text{end time}$$
$$-4:\boxed{} \leftarrow \text{start time}$$
$$\overline{} \leftarrow \text{elapsed time}$$

Try This! Find the elapsed time in minutes two ways.

Start time: 10:05 A.M. End time: 10:30 A.M.

Ⓐ Use a number line.

STEP 1 Find 10:05 on the number line. Count on from 10:05 to 10:30. Draw marks and record the times on the number line. Then draw and label the jumps.

Think: Count on using longer amounts of time that make sense.

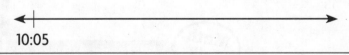

10:05

STEP 2 Add to find the total minutes from 10:05 to 10:30.

From 10:05 A.M. to _____ is _____ minutes.

So, the elapsed time is _____ minutes.

Ⓑ Use subtraction.

Think: The hours are the same, so subtract the minutes.

$$\begin{array}{r} 10:30 \\ -10:05 \\ \hline \boxed{} \end{array}$$

Math Talk

© Houghton Mifflin Harcourt Publishing Company

Math Processes and Practices ❸

Compare Strategies Which method do you prefer to use to find elapsed time?

Name _____

1. Use the number line to find the elapsed time

   from 1:15 P.M. to 1:40 P.M. _____

Find the elapsed time.

2. Start: 11:35 A.M. End: 11:54 A.M.

_____

3. Start: 4:20 P.M. End: 5:00 P.M.

_____

Math Talk

Math Processes and Practices ④

Use a Model How would you use a number line to find the elapsed time from 11:10 A.M. until noon?

Math Processes and Practices ⑤ **Use Appropriate Tools** **Find the elapsed time.**

4. Start: 8:35 P.M. End: 8:55 P.M.

_____

5. Start: 10:10 A.M. End: 10:41 A.M.

_____

6. Start: 9:25 A.M. End: 9:43 A.M.

7. Start: 2:15 P.M. End: 2:52 P.M.

Problem Solving • Applications (Real World)

8. John started reading his book about outer space at quarter after nine in the morning. He read until quarter to ten in the morning. How long did John read his book?

_____

WRITE ▸ *Math* • **Show Your Work**

9. **Math Processes and Practices ②) Use Reasoning** Tim and Alicia arrived at the rocket display at 3:40 P.M. Alicia left the display at 3:56 P.M. Tim left at 3:49 P.M. If the answer is Alicia, what is the question?

_____

_____

10. **GO DEEPER** At the space center, Karen bought a model of a shuttle. She started working on the model the next day at 11:13 A.M. She worked until leaving for lunch at 11:51 A.M. After lunch, she worked on the model again from 1:29 P.M. until 1:48 P.M. How long did Karen work on the model?

_____

11. **THINK SMARTER** Aiden arrived at the rocket display at 3:35 P.M. and left at 3:49 P.M. Ava arrived at the rocket display at 3:30 P.M. and left at 3:56 P.M. Ava spent how many more minutes at the rocket display than Aiden?

_____

12. **THINK SMARTER** Kira got on the tour bus at 5:15 P.M. She got off the bus at 5:37 P.M. How long was Kira on the bus?

Select the number to make the sentence true.

Kira was on the bus for _____ minutes.

15
22
37
52

Name _____

Measure Time Intervals

Learning Objective You will measure time intervals in minutes by drawing jumps on a number line or using an analog clock.

Find the elapsed time.

1. Start: 8:10 A.M. End: 8:45 A.M.

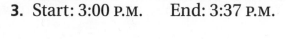

35 minutes

2. Start: 6:45 P.M. End: 6:54 P.M.

_____

3. Start: 3:00 P.M. End: 3:37 P.M.

_____

4. Start: 5:20 A.M. End: 5:47 A.M.

_____

 Problem Solving *Real World*

5. A show at the museum starts at 7:40 P.M. and ends at 7:57 P.M. How long is the show?

_____

6. The first train leaves the station at 6:15 A.M. The second train leaves at 6:55 A.M. How much later does the second train leave the station?

_____

7. **WRITE** ▸*Math* Describe two different methods to find the elapsed time from 2:30 P.M. to 2:58 P.M.

_____

_____

Lesson Check

1. Marcus began playing basketball at 3:30 P.M. and stopped playing at 3:55 P.M. For how many minutes did he play basketball?

2. The school play started at 8:15 P.M. and ended at 8:56 P.M. How long was the school play?

Spiral Review

3. Each car has 4 wheels. How many wheels do 7 cars have?

4. What number completes the equations?

$$3 \times \blacksquare = 27 \quad 27 \div 3 = \blacksquare$$

5. There are 20 napkins in each package. Kelli bought 8 packages for her party. How many napkins did Kelli buy in all?

6. Mr. Martin drove 290 miles last week. This week he drove 125 miles more than last week. How many miles did Mr. Martin drive this week?

FOR MORE PRACTICE
GO TO THE
Personal Math Trainer

Name _____

Use Time Intervals

Essential Question How can you find a starting time or an ending time when you know the elapsed time?

Learning Objective You will use a number line or a clock to find a starting time or ending time when you know the elapsed time.

⚿ Unlock the Problem

Javier begins working on his oceans project at 1:30 P.M. He spends 42 minutes painting a model of Earth and labeling the oceans. At what time does Javier finish working on his project?

- Circle the information you need.
- What time do you need to find?

_____

_____

🔓 One Way Use a number line to find the ending time.

STEP 1 Find the time on the number line when Javier started working on the project.

_____

STEP 2 Count forward on the number line to add the elapsed time. Draw and label the jumps to show the minutes.

> Think: I can break apart 42 minutes into shorter amounts of time.

_____

STEP 3 Write the times below the number line.

Math Talk Math Processes and Practices ④

Model Mathematics When finding times on the number line, how do you know what size jumps to make?

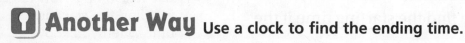

1:30 P.M.

The jumps end at _____

So, Javier finishes working on his project at _____

🔓 Another Way Use a clock to find the ending time.

STEP 1 Find the starting time on the clock.

_____

STEP 2 Count on by fives and ones for the elapsed time of 42 minutes. Write the missing counting numbers next to the clock.

So, the ending time is _____

Find Starting Times

Whitney went swimming in the ocean for
25 minutes. She finished swimming at 11:15 A.M.
At what time did Whitney start swimming?

🔓 One Way Use a number line to find the starting time.

STEP 1 Find the time on the number line when Whitney finished swimming in the ocean.

STEP 2 Count back on the number line to subtract the elapsed time. Draw and label the jumps to show the minutes.

STEP 3 Write the times below the number line.

```
←————————————————————————————|——→
                          11:15 A.M.
```

You jumped back to _____

So, Whitney started swimming at _____

🔓 Another Way Use a clock to find the starting time.

STEP 1 Find the ending time on the clock.

STEP 2 Count back by fives for the elapsed time of 25 minutes. Write the missing counting numbers next to the clock.

So, the starting time is _____

Share and Show  MATH BOARD

Math Talk

Math Processes and Practices ②

Use Reasoning How do you find the starting time when you know the ending time and the elapsed time?

1. Use the number line to find the starting time if the elapsed time is 35 minutes. _____

```
←————————————————————————————|——→
                          5:10 P.M.
```

580

Name _____

Find the ending time.

2. Starting time: 1:40 P.M.
   Elapsed time: 33 minutes

   ⟵————————————————————⟶

3. Starting time: 9:55 A.M.
   Elapsed time: 27 minutes

Find the starting time.

4. Ending time: 3:05 P.M.
   Elapsed time: 40 minutes

   ⟵————————————————————⟶

5. Ending time: 8:06 A.M.
   Elapsed time: 16 minutes

Problem Solving • Applications

6. THINK SMARTER Suzi began fishing at 10:30 A.M.
   and fished until 11:10 A.M. James finished fishing
   at 11:45 A.M. He fished for the same length of time
   as Suzi. At what time did James start fishing? **Explain.**

   _____

   _____

7. GO DEEPER Jessica starts cleaning her room at 5:50 P.M. and
   finishes at 6:44 P.M. Her sister Norah finishes cleaning her
   room at 7:12 P.M. She cleans for the same amount of time as
   Jessica. At what time does Norah start cleaning?

   _____

8. **THINK SMARTER +** Dante's surfing lesson began at 2:35 P.M. His lesson lasted 45 minutes.

Draw hands on the clock to show the time Dante's surfing lesson ended.

Connect to Science

Tides

If you have ever been to the beach, you have seen the water rise and fall along the shore every day. This change in water level is called the tide. Ocean tides are mostly caused by the pull of the moon and the sun's gravity. High tide is when the water is at its highest level. Low tide is when the water is at its lowest level. In most places on Earth, high tide and low tide each occur about twice a day.

Use the table for 9–10.

9. **GO DEEPER** The first morning, Courtney walked on the beach for 20 minutes. She finished her walk 30 minutes before high tide. At what time did Courtney start her walk?

_____

10. **Math Processes and Practices 2** **Use Reasoning** The third afternoon, Courtney started collecting shells at low tide. She collected shells for 35 minutes. At what time did Courtney finish collecting shells?

_____

Tide Times Atlantic City, NJ		
	Low Tide	High Tide
Day 1	2:12 A.M.	9:00 A.M.
	2:54 P.M.	9:00 P.M.
Day 2	3:06 A.M.	9:36 A.M.
	3:36 P.M.	9:54 P.M.
Day 3	4:00 A.M.	10:12 A.M.
	4:30 P.M.	10:36 P.M.

Name _____

Use Time Intervals

Learning Objective You will use a number line or a clock to find a starting time or ending time when you know the elapsed time.

Find the starting time.

1. Ending time: 4:29 P.M.
Elapsed time: 55 minutes

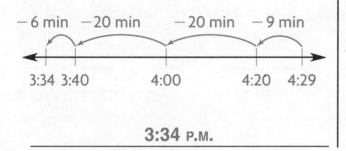

3:34 P.M.

2. Ending time: 10:08 A.M.
Elapsed time: 30 minutes

_____

Find the ending time.

3. Starting time: 2:15 A.M.
Elapsed time: 45 minutes

4. Starting time: 6:57 P.M.
Elapsed time: 47 minutes

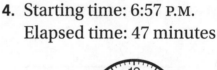

_____

Problem Solving *Real World*

5. Jenny spent 35 minutes doing research on the Internet. She finished at 7:10 P.M. At what time did Jenny start her research?

6. Clark left for school at 7:43 A.M. He got to school 36 minutes later. At what time did Clark get to school?

_____   _____

7. **WRITE** ▸*Math* Describe a situation in your life when you need to know how to find a starting time.

_____

_____

Lesson Check

1. Cody and his friends started playing a game at 6:30 P.M. It took them 37 minutes to finish the game. At what time did they finish?

_____

2. Delia worked for 45 minutes on her oil painting. She took a break at 10:35 A.M. At what time did Delia start working on the painting?

_____

Spiral Review

3. Sierra has 30 collector's pins. She wants to put an equal number of pins in each of 5 boxes. How many pins should she put in each box?

?	?	?	?	?

30 pins

_____

4. What time is shown on the clock?

_____

5. Ricardo has 32 books to put on 4 shelves. He puts the same number of books on each shelf. How many books does Ricardo put on each shelf?

_____

6. Jon started playing a computer game at 5:35 P.M. He finished the game at 5:52 P.M. How long did Jon play the game?

_____

FOR MORE PRACTICE
GO TO THE
Personal Math Trainer

Name _____

Problem Solving • Time Intervals

Essential Question How can you use the strategy *draw a diagram* to solve problems about time?

Learning Objective You will use the strategy *draw a diagram* to solve problems about time by drawing jumps on number lines to show the elapsed time.

Unlock the Problem

Zach and his family are going to New York City. Their airplane leaves at 9:15 A.M. They need to arrive at the airport 60 minutes before their flight. It takes 15 minutes to get to the airport. The family needs 30 minutes to get ready to leave. At what time should Zach's family start getting ready?

Read the Problem

What do I need to find?	**What information do I need to use?**	**How will I use the information?**
I need to find what _____ Zach's family should start _____.	the time the _____ leaves; the time the family needs to arrive at the _____; the time it takes to get to the _____; and the time the family needs to _____	I will use a number line to find the answer.

Solve the Problem

• Find 9:15 A.M. on the number line. Draw the jumps to show the time.

• Count back _____ minutes to find the time they need to arrive at the airport.

◄──────────────────────────────────┤──►
                                                                    9:15 A.M.

• Count back _____ minutes to find the time they need to leave for the airport.

• Count back _____ minutes to find the time they need to start getting ready.

So, Zach's family should start getting ready at _____ _____.M.

Math Processes and Practices ①

Analyze How can you check your answer by starting with the time the family starts getting ready?

© Houghton Mifflin Harcourt Publishing Company • Image Credits: © PhotoDisc/Getty Images

🔓 Try Another Problem

Bradley gets out of school at 2:45 P.M. It takes him
10 minutes to walk home. Then he spends 10 minutes
eating a snack. He spends 8 minutes putting on his
soccer uniform. It takes 20 minutes for Bradley's father to
drive him to soccer practice. At what time does Bradley
arrive at soccer practice?

Read the Problem

What do I need to find?	What information do I need to use?	How will I use the information?

Solve the Problem

Draw a diagram to help you explain your answer.

⟵—————————————⟶

1. At what time does Bradley arrive at soccer practice? _____

2. How do you know your answer is reasonable?

_____

_____

Math Processes and Practices ①

Analyze Do you need
to draw jumps on the
number line in the
same order as the times
in the problem?

Name _____

Unlock the Problem
✓ Circle the question.
✓ Underline important facts.
✓ Choose a strategy you know.

Share and Show MATH BOARD

1. Patty went to the shopping mall at 11:30 A.M.
She shopped for 25 minutes. She spent 40 minutes
eating lunch. Then she met a friend at a movie.
At what time did Patty meet her friend?

First, begin with _____ on the number line.

Then, count forward _____ and _____.

Think: I can break apart the times into shorter amounts of time
that make sense.

$\longleftarrow\!\!\!\!\!|\!\!\!\!\rule{5cm}{0.4pt}\!\!\!\longrightarrow$

11:30 A.M.

So, Patty met her friend at _____ _____ M.

2. What if Patty goes to the mall at 11:30 A.M. and meets a
friend at a movie at 1:15 P.M.? Patty wants to shop and have
45 minutes for lunch before meeting her friend. How much
time can Patty spend shopping?

_____

3. Avery got on the bus at 1:10 P.M. The trip took 90 minutes.
Then she walked for 32 minutes to get home. At what time
did Avery arrive at home?

_____

On Your Own

4. GO DEEPER Kyle and Josh have a total of 64 CDs. Kyle has
12 more CDs than Josh. How many CDs does each boy
have?

_____

5. Jamal spent 60 minutes using the computer. He spent a half hour of the time playing games and the rest of the time researching his report. How many minutes did Jamal spend researching his report?

_____

6. **THINK SMARTER** When Caleb got home from school, he worked on his science project for 20 minutes. Then he studied for a test for 30 minutes. He finished at 4:35 P.M. At what time did Caleb get home from school?

_____

7. **Math Processes and Practices 6** Miguel played video games each day for a week. On Monday, he scored 83 points. His score went up 5 points each day. On what day did Miguel score 103 points? **Explain** how you found your answer.

_____

_____

8. **THINK SMARTER** When Laura arrived at the library, she spent 40 minutes reading a book. Then she spent 15 minutes reading a magazine. She left the library at 4:15 P.M.

Circle the time that makes the sentence true.

Laura arrived at the library at

3:20 P.M.
3:35 P.M.
5:10 P.M.

Problem Solving • Time Intervals

Learning Objective You will use the strategy *draw a diagram* to solve problems about time by drawing jumps on number lines to show the elapsed time.

Solve each problem. Show your work.

1. Hannah wants to meet her friends downtown. Before leaving home, she does chores for 60 minutes and eats lunch for 20 minutes. The walk downtown takes 15 minutes. Hannah starts her chores at 11:45 A.M. At what time does she meet her friends?

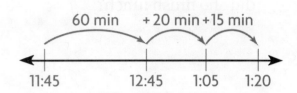

_____ **1:20** P.M.

2. Katie practiced the flute for 45 minutes. Then she ate a snack for 15 minutes. Next, she watched television for 30 minutes, until 6:00 P.M. At what time did Katie start practicing the flute?

_____

3. Nick gets out of school at 2:25 P.M. He has a 15-minute ride home on the bus. Next, he goes on a 30-minute bike ride. Then he spends 55 minutes doing homework. At what time does Nick finish his homework?

_____

4. [WRITE] ▸*Math* Write a multistep word problem that has at least two amounts of elapsed time. The problem may require finding a starting time or ending time. Include a solution.

_____

_____

Lesson Check

1. Gloria went to the mall and spent 50 minutes shopping. Then she had lunch for 30 minutes. If Gloria arrived at the mall at 11:00 A.M., at what time did she finish lunch?

   _____

2. The ball game begins at 2:00 P.M. It takes Ying 30 minutes to get to the ballpark. At what time should Ying leave home to get to the game 30 minutes before it starts?

   _____

Spiral Review

3. Write the fractions $\frac{2}{4}$, $\frac{2}{8}$, and $\frac{2}{6}$ in order from least to greatest.

   _____

4. Find the unknown factor.

   $$6 \times \blacksquare = 36$$

   _____

5. There were 405 books on the library shelf. Some books were checked out. Now there are 215 books left on the shelf. How many books were checked out?

   _____

6. Savannah has 48 photos. She places 8 photos on each page of her photo album. How many pages in the album does she use?

   _____

© Houghton Mifflin Harcourt Publishing Company

FOR MORE PRACTICE
GO TO THE
Personal Math Trainer

Name _____

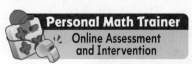

Personal Math Trainer
Online Assessment
and Intervention

Vocabulary

Choose the best term from the box.

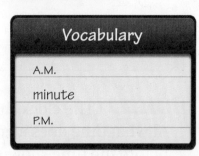

Vocabulary
A.M.
minute
P.M.

1. In one _____, the minute hand moves from one mark to the next on a clock. (p. 561)

2. The times after noon and before midnight are written

   with _____ . (p. 568)

Concepts and Skills

Write the time for the activity. Use A.M. or P.M.

3. play ball

_____

4. eat breakfast

_____

5. do homework

_____

6. sleep

_____

Find the elapsed time.

7. Start: 10:05 A.M.   End: 10:50 A.M.

⟵|————————————————————⟶

10:05

_____

8. Start: 5:30 P.M.
   End: 5:49 P.M.

_____

Find the starting time or the ending time.

9. Starting time: _____
   Elapsed time: 50 minutes
   Ending time: 9:05 A.M.

⟵————————————————————|⟶

9:05 A.M.

10. Starting time: 2:46 P.M.
    Elapsed time: 15 minutes

    Ending time: _____

11. Veronica started walking to school at 7:45 A.M. She arrived at school 23 minutes later. At what time did Veronica arrive at school?

_____

12. **GO DEEPER** The clock shows the time the art class ends. At what time does it end? If the class started 37 minutes before the time shown, at what time did the class start?

_____

13. Matt went to his friend's house. He arrived at 5:10 P.M. He left at 5:37 P.M. How long was Matt at his friend's house?

_____

14. Brenda's train leaves at 7:30 A.M. She needs to arrive 10 minutes early to buy her ticket. It takes her 20 minutes to get to the train station. At what time should Brenda leave her house?

_____

15. Write the time you get home from school.

_____

Name _____

Measure Length

Essential Question How can you generate measurement data and show the data on a line plot?

Learning Objective You will generate measurement data by measuring lengths to the nearest half or fourth inch and display the measurement data in a line plot.

CONNECT You have learned how to measure length to the nearest inch. Sometimes the length of an object is not a whole unit. For example, a paper clip is more than 1 inch but less than 2 inches.

You can measure length to the nearest half inch or fourth inch. The half-inch markings on a ruler divide each inch into two equal parts. The fourth-inch markings divide each inch into four equal parts.

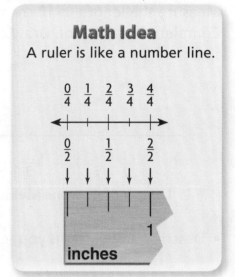

Math Idea
A ruler is like a number line.

🔑 Unlock the Problem

🔑 Example 1 Use a ruler to measure the glue stick to the nearest half inch.

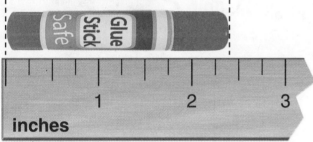

- Line up the left end of the glue stick with the zero mark on the ruler.

- The right end of the glue stick is between the half-inch marks for

  _____ and _____.

- The mark that is closest to the right end

  of the glue stick is for _____ inches.

So, the length of the glue stick to the

nearest half inch is _____ inches.

🔑 Example 2 Use a ruler to measure the paper clip to the nearest fourth inch.

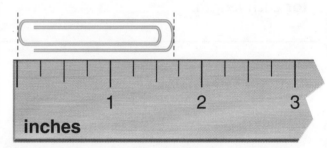

- Line up the left end of the paper clip with the zero mark on the ruler.

- The right end of the paper clip is between the fourth-inch marks for

  _____ and _____.

- The mark that is closest to the right end

  of the paper clip is for _____ inches.

So, the length of the paper clip to the

nearest fourth inch is _____ inches.

Activity Make a line plot to show measurement data.

Materials ■ inch ruler ■ 10 crayons

Measure the length of 10 crayons to the nearest half inch.
Complete the line plot. Draw an ✗ for each length.

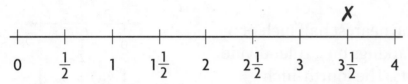

Length of Crayons Measured to the Nearest Half Inch

• Describe any patterns you see in your line plot.

_____

_____

Try This! Measure the length of your fingers to the nearest fourth inch. Complete the line plot. Draw an ✗ for each length.

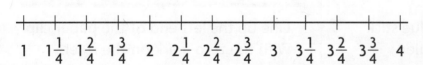

Length of Fingers Measured to the Nearest Fourth Inch

Share and Show MATH BOARD

☑ 1. Measure the length to the nearest half inch. Is the key closest to $1\frac{1}{2}$ inches, 2 inches, or $2\frac{1}{2}$ inches?

_____ inches

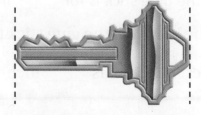

Name _____

Measure the length to the nearest fourth inch.

✓**2.**

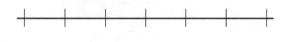

_____ inches

Use the lines for 3–4.

3. Measure the length of the lines to the nearest half inch
   and make a line plot.

   ┼———┼———┼———┼———┼———┼———┼

   ─ ── ── ── ── ─

   _____

4. Measure the length of the lines to the nearest fourth inch
   and make a line plot.

   ┼——┼——┼——┼——┼——┼——┼——┼——┼——┼——┼

   ─ ── ── ── ── ── ─

   _____

Problem Solving • Applications

Use the line plot for 5–7.

5. **GO DEEPER** Tara has a magnet collection from places she visited. She measures the length of the magnets to the nearest half inch and records the data in a line plot. Are more magnets longer than $2\frac{1}{2}$ inches or shorter than $2\frac{1}{2}$ inches? Explain.

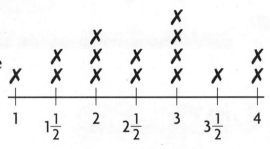

Length of Magnets

_____

_____

_____

6. **THINK SMARTER** How many magnets measure a whole number of inches? How many magnets have a length between two whole numbers?

_____

_____

7. **Math Processes and Practices ⑥** **Explain** why you think the line plot starts at 1 and stops at 4.

_____

_____

_____

8. **THINK SMARTER** What is the length of the pencil to the nearest half inch?

_____ inches

Explain how you measured the pencil.

_____

_____

Measure Length

Learning Objective You will generate measurement data by measuring lengths to the nearest half or fourth inch and display the measurement data in a line plot.

Measure the length to the nearest half inch.

1.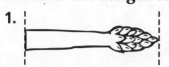

$1\frac{1}{2}$ _____ inches

2.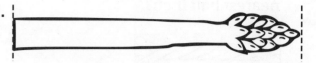

_____ inches

3.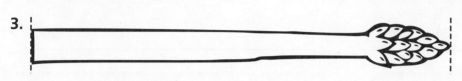

_____ inches

Measure the length to the nearest fourth inch.

4.

_____ inches

5.

_____ inches

Problem Solving

Use a separate sheet of paper for 6.

6. Draw 8 lines that are between 1 inch and 3 inches long. Measure each line to the nearest fourth inch, and make a line plot.

7. Alex's dog has a tail that is $5\frac{1}{4}$ inches long. On a ruler, what inch marks are closest to $5\frac{1}{4}$ inches? Name two inch marks.

_____

8. **WRITE** ▶ *Math* Measure the lengths of 10 color pencils to the nearest fourth inch. Then make a line plot of the data.

_____

_____

Lesson Check

1. What is the length of the string to the nearest half inch?

_____

2. What is the length of the leaf to the nearest fourth inch?

_____

Spiral Review

3. Write the equations included in the same set of related facts as $6 \times 8 = 48$.

_____

_____

_____

4. Brooke says there are 49 days until July 4. There are 7 days in a week. In how many weeks will it be July 4?

_____

_____

_____

5. It is 20 minutes before 8:00 in the morning. What time is this? Use A.M. or P.M.

6. Marcy played the piano for 45 minutes. She stopped playing at 4:15 P.M. At what time did she start playing the piano?

_____

_____

FOR MORE PRACTICE
GO TO THE
Personal Math Trainer

Estimate and Measure Liquid Volume

Essential Question How can you estimate and measure liquid volume in metric units?

Learning Objective You will estimate and measure liquid volume by writing more than 1 liter, about 1 liter, or less than 1 liter.

 Unlock the Problem Real World

 Hands On

Liquid volume is the amount of liquid in a container. The **liter (L)** is the basic metric unit for measuring liquid volume.

Activity 1

Materials ■ 1-L beaker ■ 4 containers ■ water ■ tape

STEP 1 Fill a 1-liter beaker with water to the 1-liter mark.

STEP 2 Pour 1 liter of water into a container. Mark the level of the water with a piece of tape. Draw the container below and name the container.

STEP 3 Repeat Steps 1 and 2 with three different-sized containers.

Container 1

Container 2

 Math Talk

Math Processes and Practices ⑧

Draw Conclusions
What happens to the liquid volume when you pour the same amount of liquid into different sized containers?

Container 3

Container 4

1. How much water did you pour into each container? _____

2. Which containers are mostly full? Describe them.

_____

3. Which containers are mostly empty? Describe them.

_____

Compare Liquid Volumes

A full glass holds less than 1 liter.

A water bottle holds about 1 liter.

A fish bowl holds more than 1 liter.

Activity 2 Materials ■ 1-L beaker ■ 5 different containers ■ water

STEP 1 Write the containers in order from the one you think will hold the least water to the one you think will hold the most water.

_____, _____, _____,

_____, _____

STEP 2 Estimate how much each container will hold. Write _more than 1 liter_, _about 1 liter_, or _less than 1 liter_ in the table.

STEP 3 Pour 1 liter of water into one of the containers. Repeat until the container is full. Record the number of liters you poured. Repeat for each container.

Container	Estimate	Number of Liters

STEP 4 Write the containers in order from the least to the greatest liquid volume.

_____, _____, _____,

_____, _____

Math Talk

Math Processes and Practices ❶

Evaluate Was the order in Step 1 different than the order in Step 4? Explain why they may be different.

Name _____

Share and Show  MATH BOARD

1. The beaker is filled with water. Is the amount *more than 1 liter*, *about 1 liter*, or *less than 1 liter*?

_____

Estimate how much liquid volume there will be when the container is filled. Write *more than 1 liter*, *about 1 liter*, or *less than 1 liter*.

2. cup of tea	✓ 3. kitchen sink	✓ 4. teapot

_____	_____	_____

On Your Own

Estimate how much liquid volume there will be when the container is filled. Write *more than 1 liter*, *about 1 liter*, or *less than 1 liter*.

Math Talk — Math Processes and Practices 8

Generalize How can you estimate the liquid volume in a container?

5. pitcher	6. juice box	7. punch bowl

_____	_____	_____

Use the pictures for 8–10. Rosario pours juice into four bottles that are the same size.

8. Did Rosario pour the same amount into each bottle? _____

9. Which bottle has the least amount of juice? _____

10. Which bottle has the most juice? _____

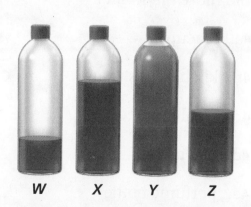

W   X   Y   Z

Problem Solving • Applications

Use the containers for 11–13. Container A is full when 1 liter of water is poured into it.

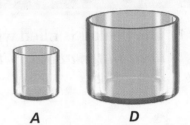

A   D

11. **GO DEEPER** Estimate how many liters will fill Container *C* and how many liters will fill Container *E*. Which container will hold more water when filled?

B

_____

_____

12. **Math Processes and Practices 6** Name two containers that will be filled with about the same number of liters of water. **Explain**.

_____

_____

_____

C   E

13. **THINK SMARTER** **What's the Error?** Samuel says that you can pour more liters of water into Container *B* than into Container *D*. Is he correct? Explain.

_____

_____

_____

_____

Personal Math Trainer

14. **THINK SMARTER +** The bottle of tea holds about 1 liter. For numbers 14a–14e, choose Yes or No to tell whether it will hold more than 1 liter.

14a. teacup   ○ Yes   ○ No

14b. kitchen trash can   ○ Yes   ○ No

14c. small pool   ○ Yes   ○ No

14d. fish tank   ○ Yes   ○ No

14e. perfume bottle   ○ Yes   ○ No

602

Estimate and Measure Liquid Volume

Learning Objective You will estimate and measure liquid volume by writing more than 1 liter, about 1 liter, or less than 1 liter.

Estimate how much liquid volume there will be when the container is filled. Write *more than 1 liter, about 1 liter,* or *less than 1 liter.*

1. large milk container

more than 1 liter

2. small milk container

3. water bottle

4. spoonful of water

5. bathtub

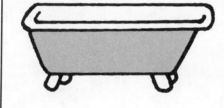

6. eyedropper

Problem Solving *Real World*

Use the pictures for 7. Alan pours water into four glasses that are the same size.

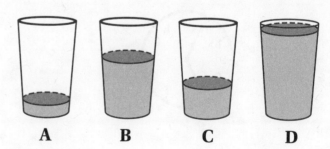

7. Which glass has the most amount

of water? _____

A   B   C   D

8. WRITE ▸Math Name a container that you see at home that when filled has a liquid volume of about 1 liter.

_____

_____

Lesson Check

1. Felicia filled the bathroom sink with water. Is the amount more than 1 liter, about 1 liter, or less than 1 liter?

2. Kyle needed about 1 liter of water to fill a container. Did Kyle most likely fill a small glass, a spoon, or a vase?

Spiral Review

3. Cecil had 6 ice cubes. He put 1 ice cube in each glass. In how many glasses did Cecil put ice cubes?

4. Juan has 12 muffins. He puts $\frac{1}{4}$ of the muffins in a bag. How many muffins does Juan put in the bag?

5. What time is shown on the clock?

6. Julianne drew the line segment below. Use your ruler to measure the segment to the nearest fourth inch.

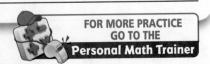

FOR MORE PRACTICE
GO TO THE
Personal Math Trainer

Name _____

Estimate and Measure Mass

Essential Question How can you estimate and measure mass in metric units?

Learning Objective You will choose the unit to measure mass as grams or kilograms and compare masses of objects as less than, same as, or more than one to the other.

Unlock the Problem

 Pedro has a dollar bill in his pocket. Should Pedro measure the mass of the dollar bill in grams or kilograms?

The **gram (g)** is the basic metric unit for measuring **mass**, or the amount of matter in an object. Mass can also be measured by using the metric unit **kilogram (kg)**.

A small paper clip has a mass of about 1 gram.	A box of 1,000 paper clips has a mass of about 1 kilogram.

Think: The mass of a dollar bill is closer to the mass of a small paper clip than it is to a box of 1,000 paper clips.

So, Pedro should measure the mass of the dollar bill in _____.

Activity 1

Materials ■ pan balance ■ gram and kilogram masses

You can use a pan balance to measure mass.

Do 10 grams have the same mass as 1 kilogram?

- Place 10 gram masses on one side of the balance.

- Place a 1-kilogram mass on the other side of the balance.

Think: If it is balanced, then the objects have the same mass. If it is not balanced, the objects do not have the same mass.

- Complete the picture of the balance above by drawing masses to show your balance.

   The pan balance is _____.

So, 10 grams and 1 kilogram _____ the same mass.

Math Talk

Math Processes and Practices ❹

Use Models How do you tell from the balance which side has greater mass?

Activity 2

Materials ■ pan balance ■ gram and kilogram masses ■ classroom objects

STEP 1 Use the objects in the table. Decide if the object should be measured in grams or kilograms.

STEP 2 Estimate the mass of each object. Record your estimates in the table.

STEP 3 Find the mass of each object to the nearest gram or kilogram. Place the object on one side of the balance. Place gram or kilogram masses on the other side until both sides are balanced.

STEP 4 Add the measures of the gram or kilogram masses. This is the mass of the object. Record the mass in the table.

▲ 189 marbles have a mass of 1 kilogram.

Mass		
Object	**Estimate**	**Mass**
crayon		
stapler		
eraser		
marker		
small notepad		
scissors		

Math Talk

Math Processes and Practices ⑥

Compare How did your estimates compare with the actual measurements?

• Write the objects in order from greatest mass to least mass.

_____ , _____ , _____ ,

_____ , _____ , _____

Share and Show MATH BOARD

1. Five bananas have a mass of about _____ .

Think: The pan balance is balanced, so the objects on both sides have the same mass.

© Houghton Mifflin Harcourt Publishing Company

Name _____

Choose the unit you would use to measure the mass.
Write *gram* or *kilogram*.

2. strawberry

_____

☑ 3. dog

_____

Math Talk

Math Processes and Practices ②

Use Reasoning How do you decide which unit to use when measuring the mass of different objects?

Compare the masses of the objects. Write
is less than, is the same as,* or *is more than.

4.

The mass of the bowling pin

_____ the mass of
the chess piece.

☑ 5.

The mass of the erasers

_____ the mass of
the clips.

On Your Own

Choose the unit you would use to measure the mass.
Write *gram* or *kilogram*.

6. chair

_____

7. sunglasses

_____

8. watermelon

_____

Compare the masses of the objects. Write
is less than, is the same as,* or *is more than.

9.

The mass of the pen _____
the mass of the paper clips.

10.

The mass of the straws _____
the mass of the blocks.

Problem Solving • Applications (Real World)

11. **GO DEEPER** Put the sports balls shown at the right in order from greatest mass to least mass.

_____

_____

Golf ball

12. **Math Processes and Practices ④ Use Diagrams** Choose two objects that have about the same mass. Draw a balance with one of these objects on each side.

Table tennis ball

Bowling ball

13. **Math Processes and Practices ④ Use Diagrams** Choose two objects that have different masses. Draw a balance with one of these objects on each side.

Baseball

Tennis ball

14. **THINK SMARTER Pose a Problem** Write a problem about the objects you chose in Exercise 13. Then solve your problem.

_____

_____

15. **THINK SMARTER Sense or Nonsense?** Amber is buying produce at the grocery store. She says that a Fuji apple and a green bell pepper would have the same mass because they are the same size. Does her statement make sense? Explain.

_____

_____

_____

16. **THINK SMARTER** Select the objects with a mass greater than 1 kilogram. Mark all that apply.

Ⓐ skateboard

Ⓓ egg

Ⓑ laptop computer

Ⓔ desk

Ⓒ cell phone

Ⓕ pencil

Name _____

Estimate and Measure Mass

Learning Objective You will choose the unit to measure mass as grams or kilograms and compare masses of objects as less than, same as, or more than one to the other.

Choose the unit you would use to measure the mass. Write *gram* or *kilogram*.

1. CD  gram	2. boy 	3. bag of sugar 

Compare the masses of the objects. Write *is less than*, *is the same as*, or *is more than*.

4.

The mass of the candle _____ the mass of the light bulb.

5.

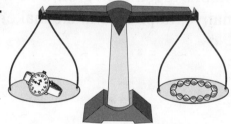

The mass of the watch _____ the mass of the necklace.

Problem Solving Real World

6. A red ball has a mass that is less than 1 kilogram. A blue ball has a mass of 1 kilogram. Is the mass of the blue ball more than or less than the mass of the red ball?

_____

7. Brock's dog is a collie. To find the mass of his dog, should Brock use *grams* or *kilograms*?

_____

8. **WRITE** ▸ *Math* Name an object in your home that has a mass of about 1 kg.

_____

_____

Lesson Check

1. Which unit of measure would you use to measure the mass of a grape? Write *gram* or *kilogram*.

2. Elsie wants to find the mass of her pony. Which unit should she use? Write *gram* or *kilogram*.

Spiral Review

3. Marsie blew up 24 balloons. She tied the balloons together in groups of 4. How many groups did Marsie make?

4. Clark used the order of operations to find the unknown number in $15 - 12 \div 3 = n$. What is the value of the unknown number?

Use the pictures for 5–6. Ralph pours juice into four bottles that are the same size.

5. Which bottle has the most amount of juice?

6. Which bottle has the least amount of juice?

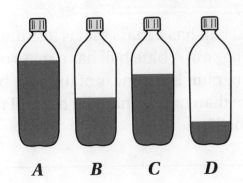

A   B   C   D

FOR MORE PRACTICE
GO TO THE
Personal Math Trainer

Name _____

Solve Problems About Liquid Volume and Mass

Learning Objective You will use bar models then write an equation to solve liquid volume and mass problems.

Essential Question How can you use models to solve liquid volume and mass problems?

Unlock the Problem

A restaurant serves iced tea from a large container that can hold 24 liters. Sadie will fill the container with the pitchers of tea shown below. Will Sadie have tea left over after filling the container?

Example 1 Solve a problem about liquid volume.

_____ L   _____ L   _____ L   _____ L

Since there are _____ equal groups of _____ liters, you can multiply.

_____ ◯ _____ = _____

Circle the correct words to complete the sentences.

_____ liters is *greater than* / *less than* 24 liters.

So, Sadie *will* / *will not* have tea left over.

Try This! Use a bar model to solve.

Raul's fish tank contains 32 liters of water. He empties it with a bucket that holds 4 liters of water. How many times will Raul have to fill the bucket?

_____ ◯ _____ = _____

So, Raul will have to fill the bucket _____ times.

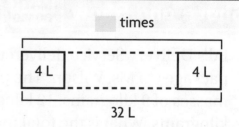

_____ times

| 4 L | - - - - - - - - | 4 L |

32 L

© Houghton Mifflin Harcourt Publishing Company • Image Credits: ©Ted Foxx/Alamy Images

🔒 Activity Solve a problem about mass.

Materials ■ pan balance ■ glue stick ■ gram masses

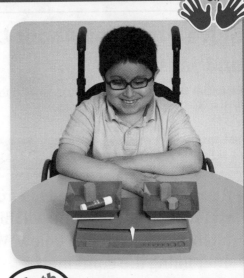

Jeff has a glue stick and a 20-gram mass on one side of a balance and gram masses on the other side. The pan balance is balanced. What is the mass of the glue stick?

STEP 1 Place a glue stick and a 20-gram mass on one side of the balance.

STEP 2 Place gram masses on the other side until the pans are balanced.

STEP 3 To find the mass of the glue stick, remove 20 grams from each side.

  Think: I can remove 20 grams from both sides and the pan balance will still be balanced.

STEP 4 Then add the measures of the gram masses on the balance.

The gram masses have a measure of _____ grams.

So, the glue stick has a mass of _____ .

Math Talk   Math Processes and Practices ④

Write an Equation
What equation can you write to find the mass of the glue stick?

Try This! Use a bar model to solve.

A bag of peas has a mass of 432 grams.
A bag of carrots has a mass of 263 grams.
What is the total mass of both bags?

_____ g	_____ g

_____ g

_____ ◯ _____ = _____

So, both bags have a total mass of _____ grams.

Share and Show   MATH BOARD

1. Ed's Delivery Service delivered three packages to Ms. Wilson. The packages have masses of 9 kilograms, 12 kilograms, and 5 kilograms. What is the total mass of the three packages? Use the bar model to help you solve.

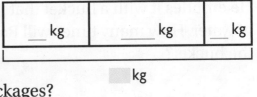

_____

Name _____

Write an equation and solve the problem.

2. Ariel's recipe calls for 64 grams of apples and 86 grams of oranges. How many more grams of oranges than apples does the recipe call for?

_____ ◯ _____ = _____ _____

3. Dan's Clams restaurant sold 45 liters of lemonade. If it sold the same amount each hour for 9 hours, how many liters of lemonade did Dan's Clams sell each hour?

_____ ◯ _____ = _____ _____

Math Talk Math Processes and Practices ④
Use Models How could you use a model to solve Exercise 2?

On Your Own

Math Processes and Practices ④ **Write an Equation** Write an equation and solve the problem.

4. Sasha's box holds 4 kilograms of napkins and 29 kilograms of napkin rings. What is the total mass of the napkins and napkin rings?

_____ ◯ _____ = _____ _____

5. Josh has 6 buckets for cleaning a restaurant. He fills each bucket with 4 liters of water. How many liters of water are in the buckets?

_____ ◯ _____ = _____ _____

6. **THINK SMARTER** Ellen will pour water into Pitcher B until it has 1 more liter of water than Pitcher A. How many liters of water will she pour into Pitcher B? Explain how you found your answer.

Pitcher **A**   Pitcher **B**

_____

_____

7. **Practice: Copy and Solve** Use the pictures to write two problems. Then solve your problems.

Grape Juice   Apple Juice   Cereal   Coffee

© Houghton Mifflin Harcourt Publishing Company

Chapter 10 • Lesson 9   613

Unlock the Problem (Real World)

8. Ken's Café serves fruit smoothies. Each smoothie has 9 grams of fresh strawberries. How many grams of strawberries are in 8 smoothies?

a. What do you need to find? _____

b. What operation will you use to find the answer? _____

c. (Math Processes and Practices ④) **Use Diagrams** Draw a diagram to solve the problem.

d. Complete the sentences.

There are _____ smoothies with _____ grams of strawberries in each.

Since each smoothie is an _____ group, you can _____.

_____ ◯ _____ = _____

So, there are _____ grams of strawberries in 8 smoothies.

9. GO DEEPER Arturo has two containers, each filled with 12 liters of water. Daniel has two containers, each filled with 16 liters of water. What is the total liquid volume of the boys' containers?

_____

10. THINK SMARTER A deli makes its own salad dressing. A small jar has 3 grams of spices. A large jar has 5 grams of spices. Will 25 grams of spices be enough to make 3 small jars and 3 large jars? Show your work.

© Houghton Mifflin Harcourt Publishing Company

Solve Problems About Liquid Volume and Mass

Learning Objective You will use bar models then write an equation to solve liquid volume and mass problems.

Write an equation and solve the problem.

1. Luis was served 145 grams of meat and 217 grams of vegetables at a meal. What was the total mass of the meat and the vegetables?

   Think: Add to find how much in all.

   $\underline{\hspace{0.4cm}145\hspace{0.4cm}} \oplus \underline{\hspace{0.4cm}217\hspace{0.4cm}} = \underline{\hspace{1cm}}\ \underline{\hspace{1.5cm}}$

2. The gas tank of a riding mower holds 5 liters of gas. How many 5-liter gas tanks can you fill from a full 20-liter gas can?

   $\underline{\hspace{1cm}}\bigcirc\underline{\hspace{1cm}} = \underline{\hspace{1cm}}\ \underline{\hspace{1.5cm}}$

3. To make a lemon-lime drink, Mac mixed 4 liters of lemonade with 2 liters of limeade. How much lemon-lime drink did Mac make?

   $\underline{\hspace{1cm}}\bigcirc\underline{\hspace{1cm}} = \underline{\hspace{1cm}}\ \underline{\hspace{1.5cm}}$

4. A nickel has a mass of 5 grams. There are 40 nickels in a roll of nickels. What is the mass of a roll of nickels?

   $\underline{\hspace{1cm}}\bigcirc\underline{\hspace{1cm}} = \underline{\hspace{1cm}}\ \underline{\hspace{1.5cm}}$

Problem Solving · Real World

5. Zoe's fish tank holds 27 liters of water. She uses a 3-liter container to fill the tank. How many times does she have to fill the 3-liter container in order to fill her fish tank?

   _____

6. Adrian's backpack has a mass of 15 kilograms. Theresa's backpack has a mass of 8 kilograms. What is the total mass of both backpacks?

   _____

7. **WRITE** ▸*Math* Write a problem that can be solved with a bar model that shows equal groups of liters. Then solve the problem.

   _____

   _____

Lesson Check

1. Mickey's beagle has a mass of 15 kilograms. His dachshund has a mass of 13 kilograms. What is the combined mass of the two dogs?

2. Lois put 8 liters of water in a bucket for her pony. At the end of the day, there were 2 liters of water left. How much water did the pony drink?

Spiral Review

3. Josiah has 3 packs of toy animals. Each pack has the same number of animals. Josiah gives 6 animals to his sister Stephanie. Then Josiah has 9 animals left. How many animals were in each pack?

4. Tom jogged $\frac{3}{10}$ mile, Betsy jogged $\frac{5}{10}$ mile, and Sue jogged $\frac{2}{10}$ mile. Who jogged a distance longer than $\frac{4}{10}$ mile?

5. Bob started mowing at 9:55 A.M. It took him 25 minutes to mow the front yard and 45 minutes to mow the back yard. At what time did Bob finish mowing?

6. Juliana wants to find the mass of a watermelon. What unit should she use?

FOR MORE PRACTICE
GO TO THE
Personal Math Trainer

✓ Chapter 10 Review/Test

Personal Math Trainer
Online Assessment
and Intervention

1. Yul and Sarah's art class started at 11:25 A.M. The class lasted 30 minutes. Yul left when the class was done. Sarah stayed an extra 5 minutes to talk with the teacher and then left.

   Write the time that each student left. Explain how you found each time.

   _____

   _____

2. Julio measured an object that he found. It was about $\frac{3}{4}$ inch wide.

   For numbers 2a–2d, choose Yes or No to tell whether the object could be the one Julio measured.

2a.    ○ Yes   ○ No

2b.    ○ Yes   ○ No

2c.    ○ Yes   ○ No

2d. 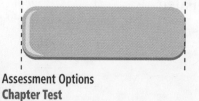   ○ Yes   ○ No

GO DIGITAL

Assessment Options
Chapter Test

3. Dina started swimming at 3:38 P.M. She swam until 4:15 P.M. How long did Dina swim?

_____ minutes

4. Rita's class begins social studies at ten minutes before one in the afternoon. At what time does Rita's class begin social studies? Circle a time that makes the sentence true.

Rita's class begins social studies at

| 1:10 A.M. |
| 1:10 P.M. |
| 12:50 A.M. |
| 12:50 P.M. |

5. Select the objects with a mass greater than 1 kilogram. Mark all that apply.

Ⓐ bicycle   Ⓒ eraser

Ⓑ pen   Ⓓ math book

6. A chicken dish needs to bake in the oven for 35 minutes. The dish needs to cool for at least 8 minutes before serving. Scott puts the chicken dish in the oven at 5:14 P.M.

For numbers 6a–6d, select True or False for each statement.

6a. Scott can serve the
      dish at 5:51 P.M.   ○ True   ○ False

6b. Scott can serve the
      dish at 5:58 P.M.   ○ True   ○ False

6c. Scott should take the
      dish out of the oven
      at 5:51 A.M.   ○ True   ○ False

6d. Scott should take the
      dish out of the oven
      at 5:49 P.M.   ○ True   ○ False

Name _____

7. Anthony read a book to his little brother. He started reading at the time shown on the clock. He stopped reading at 5:45 P.M.

Part A

How long did Anthony read to his little brother?

_____ minutes

Part B

Explain how you found your answer.

_____

_____

_____

8. Tran checked the time on his watch after he finished his daily run.

Select the time that Tran finished running. Mark all that apply.

Ⓐ 14 minutes before nine   Ⓒ quarter to nine

Ⓑ eight forty-six   Ⓓ nine forty-six

9. Cara uses a balance scale to compare mass.

Circle a symbol that makes the comparison true.

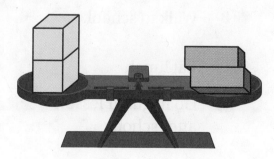

The mass of the blocks

the mass of the erasers.

<
>
=

10. A large bottle of water holds about 2 liters.

For numbers 10a–10e, choose Yes or No to tell whether the container will hold all of the water.

10a.	kitchen sink	○ Yes	○ No
10b.	water glass	○ Yes	○ No
10c.	ice cube tray	○ Yes	○ No
10d.	large soup pot	○ Yes	○ No
10e.	lunchbox thermos	○ Yes	○ No

11. Select the items that would be best measured in grams. Mark all that apply.

Ⓐ watermelon

Ⓑ lettuce leaf

Ⓒ grape

Ⓓ onion

12. Samir made a list of what he did on Tuesday. Write the letter for each activity next to the time he did it.

Ⓐ Get out of bed. ☐ 8:05 A.M.

Ⓑ Walk to school. ☐ 6:25 P.M.

Ⓒ Eat lunch. ☐ 3:50 P.M.

Ⓓ Go to guitar lesson after school. ☐ 11:48 A.M.

Ⓔ Eat dinner at home. ☐ 6:25 A.M.

13. Amy has 30 grams of flour. She puts 4 grams of flour in each pot of chowder that she makes. She puts 5 grams of flour in each pot of potato soup that she makes. She makes 4 pots of chowder. Does Amy have enough flour left over to make 3 pots of potato soup?

14. GO DEEPER Use an inch ruler to measure.

Part A

What is the length of the leaf to the nearest fourth inch?

Part B

Explain what happens if you line up the left side of the object with the 1 on the ruler.

15. Mrs. Park takes the 9:38 A.M. train to the city. The trip takes 3 hours and 20 minutes. What time does Mrs. Park arrive in the city?

16. Hector buys two bags of gravel for his driveway. He buys a total of 35 kilograms of gravel. Select the bags he buys.

15 kg	17 kg	18 kg	19 kg
○	○	○	○

17.  Ashley measures the shells she collects. She records the measurements in a chart.

Number of Shells	Length in Inches
1	1
2	$2\frac{1}{2}$
3	$1\frac{1}{2}$
1	2

Part A

Ashley found a razor clam shell this long. Use an inch ruler to measure. Record the measurement in the chart.

_____ inches

Part B

Complete the line plot to show the data in the chart. How many shells are longer than 2 inches? Tell how you know.

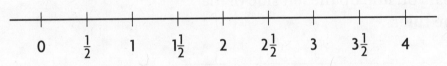

0    $\frac{1}{2}$ 1 $1\frac{1}{2}$ 2 $2\frac{1}{2}$ 3 $3\frac{1}{2}$ 4

Length of Shells Measured to the Nearest Half Inch

_____

_____

18. Lucy fills a bathroom sink with water. Is the amount of water *more than 1 liter, about 1 liter, or less than 1 liter*? Explain how you know.

_____

_____

_____

Perimeter and Area

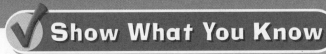

Show What You Know

Personal Math Trainer
Online Assessment and Intervention

Check your understanding of important skills.

Name _____

▶ **Use Nonstandard Units to Measure Length**

Use paper clips to measure the object.

1.

about ____

2.

about ____

▶ **Add 3 Numbers** **Write the sum.**

3. $2 + 7 + 3 =$ ____   **4.** $3 + 5 + 2 =$ ____   **5.** $6 + 1 + 9 =$ ____

▶ **Model with Arrays** **Use the array. Complete.**

6. 3 rows of 4

____ × ____ = ____

7. 4 rows of 2

____ × ____ = ____

Julia has a picture frame with side lengths of 12 inches
and 24 inches. She wants to cut and glue one color
of ribbon that will fit exactly around the edge. The
green ribbon is 72 inches long. The red ribbon is
48 inches long. Find which ribbon she should use
to glue around the picture frame.

Vocabulary Builder

▶ **Visualize It** ••••••••••••••••••••••••••••••••••••

Sort the words with a ✔ into the Venn diagram.

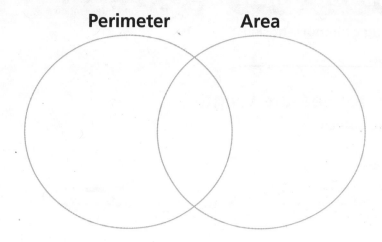

Perimeter   Area

▶ **Understand Vocabulary** •••••••••••••••••••••••••••

Complete the sentences by using the review and preview words.

1. The distance around a figure is the
   _____.

2. The _____ is the measure of the number of unit squares needed to cover a surface.

3. You can count, use _____, or multiply to find the area of a rectangle.

4. A _____ is a square with a side length of 1 unit and is used to measure area.

5. The _____ shows that you can break apart a rectangle into smaller rectangles and add the area of each smaller rectangle to find the total area.

Review Words

addition
array
centimeter (cm)
Distributive Property
foot (ft)
inch (in.)
inverse operations
✓ length
meter (m)
multiplication
pattern
rectangle
repeated addition
✓ unit
✓ width

Preview Words

area
perimeter
✓ square unit
✓ unit square

GO DIGITAL
• Interactive Student Edition
• Multimedia eGlossary

Chapter 11 Vocabulary

area

área

3

centimeter (cm)

centímetro (cm)

7

inverse operation

operaciones inversas

37

length

longitud

40

perimeter

perímetro

59

rectangle

rectángulo

69

square unit

unidad cuadrada

75

unit square

caudrado de una unidad

80

A metric unit used to measure length or distance
100 centimeters = 1 meter

The measure of the number of unit squares needed to cover a surface

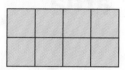

Area = 8 square units

The measurement of the distance between two points

Opposite operations, or operations that undo one another, such as addition and subtraction or multiplication and division

Examples: 16 + 8 = 24; 24 − 8 = 16
4 × 3 = 12; 12 ÷ 4 = 3

A quadrilateral with two pairs of parallel sides, two pairs of sides of equal length, and four right angles

  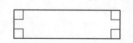

The distance around a figure

Example: The perimeter of this rectangle is 20 inches.

6 in.

4 in.   4 in.

6 in.

A square with a side length of 1 unit, used to measure area

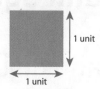

1 unit

1 unit

A unit used to measure area such as square foot, square meter, and so on

Going Places with GO MATH! words

Picture It

For 3 to 4 players

Materials

- timer
- sketch pad

How to Play

1. Take turns to play.
2. To take a turn, choose a word from the Word Box, but do not say the word aloud.
3. Set the timer for 1 minute.
4. Draw pictures and numbers to give clues about the word.
5. The first player to guess the word before time runs out gets 1 point. If that player can use the word in a sentence, he or she gets 1 more point. Then that player gets a turn choosing a word.
6. The first player to score 10 points wins.

Word Box
area
centimeter (cm)
inverse operations
length
perimeter
rectangle
square unit
unit square

Game

The Write Way

Reflect

Choose one idea. Write about it.

- Define perimeter in your own words.
- Write two things you know about area.
- Explain how two rectangles can have the same area, but different perimeter. Give an example.

Name _____

Model Perimeter

Essential Question How can you find perimeter?

Learning Objective You will use dot paper and grid paper to find the perimeter of figures by counting the number of units on each side.

Investigate

Perimeter is the distance around a figure.

Materials ■ geoboard ■ rubber bands

You can find the perimeter of a rectangle on a geoboard or on dot paper by counting the number of units on each side.

A. Make a rectangle on the geoboard that is 3 units on two sides and 2 units on the other two sides.

B. Draw your rectangle on this dot paper.

← 1 Unit

C. Write the length next to each side of your rectangle.

D. Add the number of units on each side.

_____ + _____ + _____ + _____ = _____

E. So, the perimeter of the rectangle

is _____ units.

• How would the perimeter of the rectangle change if the length of two of the sides was 4 units instead of 3 units?

_____

_____

Draw Conclusions

1. Describe how you would find the perimeter of a rectangle that is 5 units wide and 6 units long.

   _____

2. **THINK SMARTER** A rectangle has two pairs of sides of equal length. Explain how you can find the unknown length of two sides when the length of one side is 4 units, and the perimeter is 14 units.

   _____

   _____

   _____

3. **Math Processes and Practices 1** **Evaluate** Jill says that finding the perimeter of a figure with all sides of equal length is easier than finding the perimeter of other figures. Do you agree? Explain.

   _____

   _____

Make Connections

 Hands On

 Math Talk

Math Processes and Practices 3

Apply If a rectangle has a perimeter of 12 units, how many units wide and how many units long could it be?

You can also use grid paper to find the perimeter of figures by counting the number of units on each side.

Start at the arrow and trace the perimeter. Begin counting with 1. Continue counting each unit around the figure until you have counted each unit.

A

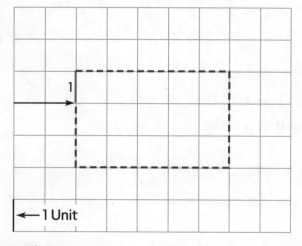

1 Unit

Perimeter = _____ units

B

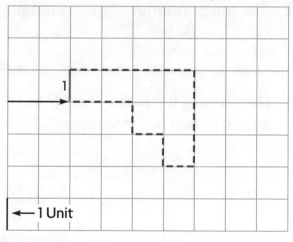

1 Unit

Perimeter = _____ units

Name _____

Find the perimeter of the figure. Each unit is 1 centimeter.

1.

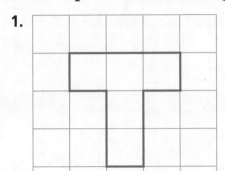

_____ centimeters

✓ 2.

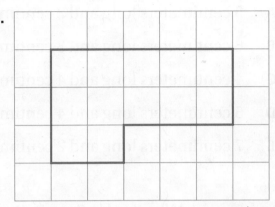

_____ centimeters

3.

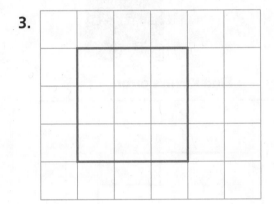

_____ centimeters

4.

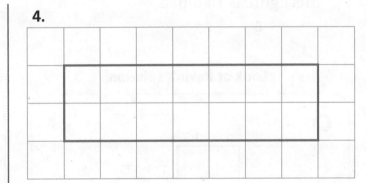

_____ centimeters

Find the perimeter.

5. A figure with four sides that measure
4 centimeters, 6 centimeters,
5 centimeters, and 1 centimeter

_____ centimeters

✓ 6. A figure with two sides that measure
10 inches, one side that measures
8 inches, and one side that measures
4 inches

_____ inches

Problem Solving • Applications (Real World)

7. (Math Processes and Practices **6**) **Explain** how to find the length of each side of
a triangle with sides of equal length and a perimeter of 27 inches.

_____

_____

8. **THINK SMARTER** Luisa drew a rectangle with a perimeter of 18 centimeters. Select the rectangles that Luisa could have drawn. Mark all that apply. Use the grid to help you.

(A) 9 centimeters long and 2 centimeters wide

(B) 6 centimeters long and 3 centimeters wide

(C) 4 centimeters long and 4 centimeters wide

(D) 5 centimeters long and 4 centimeters wide

(E) 7 centimeters long and 2 centimeters wide

9. **THINK SMARTER** **What's the Error?** Kevin is solving perimeter problems. He counts the units and says that the perimeter of this figure is 18 units.

Look at Kevin's solution.

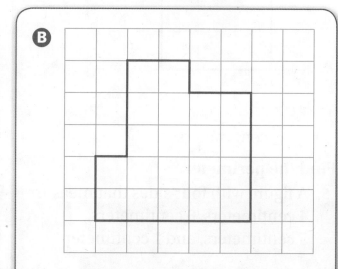

Perimeter = _____ units

Find Kevin's error.

Perimeter = _____ units

• **GO DEEPER** Describe the error Kevin made. Circle the places in the drawing of Kevin's solution where he made an error.

_____

_____

Name _____

Model Perimeter

Learning Objective You will use dot paper and grid paper to find the perimeter of figures by counting the number of units on each side.

Find the perimeter of the figure. Each unit is 1 centimeter.

1.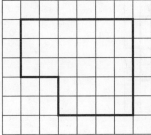

___22___ centimeters

2.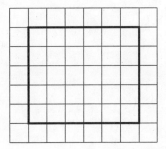

_____ centimeters

Problem Solving Real World

Use the drawing for 3–4. Each unit is 1 centimeter.

3. What is the perimeter of Patrick's figure?

_____

4. How much greater is the perimeter of Jillian's shape than the perimeter of Patrick's figure?

_____

Patrick's Figure

Jillian's Figure

5. **WRITE** ▸*Math* Draw a rectangle and another figure that is not a rectangle by tracing lines on grid paper. Describe how to find the perimeter of both figures.

_____

_____

_____

Lesson Check

1. Find the perimeter of the figure. Each unit is 1 centimeter.

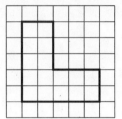

_____

2. Find the perimeter of the figure. Each unit is 1 centimeter.

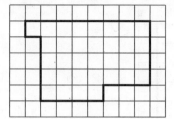

_____

Spiral Review

3. Order the fractions from least to greatest.

$$\frac{2}{4}, \frac{2}{3}, \frac{2}{6}$$

_____

4. Kasey's school starts at the time shown on the clock. What time does Kasey's school start?

_____

5. Compare. Write $<$, $>$, or $=$.

$$\frac{4}{8} \bigcirc \frac{3}{8}$$

6. Aiden wants to find the mass of a bowling ball. Which unit should he use?

_____

© Houghton Mifflin Harcourt Publishing Company

FOR MORE PRACTICE
GO TO THE
Personal Math Trainer

Name _____

Find Perimeter

Essential Question How can you measure perimeter?

Learning Objective You will use rulers to estimate and measure the perimeter of figures in inches and centimeters.

You can estimate and measure perimeter in standard units, such as inches and centimeters.

  Unlock the Problem Real World · Hands On

Find the perimeter of the cover of a notebook.

Activity Materials ■ inch ruler

STEP 1 Estimate the perimeter of a notebook in inches. Record your estimate. _____ inches

STEP 2 Use an inch ruler to measure the length of each side of the notebook to the nearest inch.

STEP 3 Record and add the lengths of the sides measured to the nearest inch.

_____ + _____ + _____ + _____ = _____

So, the perimeter of the notebook cover measured

to the nearest inch is _____ inches.

Math Talk Math Processes and Practices ①

Evaluate How does your estimate compare with your measurement?

Try This! Find the perimeter.

Use an inch ruler to find the length of each side.

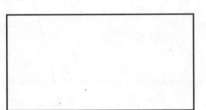

Add the lengths of the sides:

_____ + _____ + _____ + _____ = _____

The perimeter is _____ inches.

Use a centimeter ruler to find the length of each side.

Add the lengths of the sides:

_____ + _____ + _____ + _____ = _____

The perimeter is _____ centimeters.

Share and Show

1. Find the perimeter of the triangle in inches.

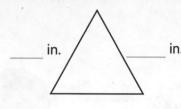

_____ in.   _____ in.   **Think:** How long is
                                  each side?

_____ in.

_____ inches

Math Talk Math Processes and Practices ②

Reason Abstractly How do you use addition to find the perimeter of a figure?

Use a centimeter ruler to find the perimeter.

2.

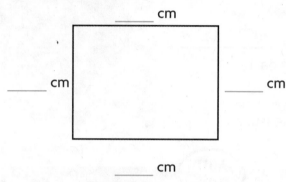

_____ cm

_____ cm   _____ cm

_____ cm

_____ centimeters

☑3.

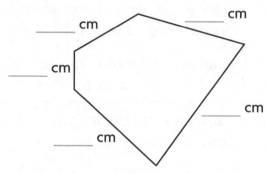

_____ cm   _____ cm

_____ cm

_____ cm

_____ cm

_____ centimeters

Use an inch ruler to find the perimeter.

4.

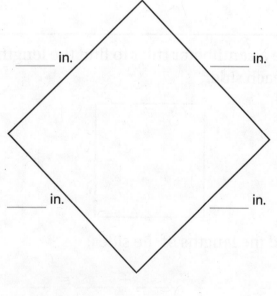

_____ in.   _____ in.

_____ in.   _____ in.

_____ inches

☑5.

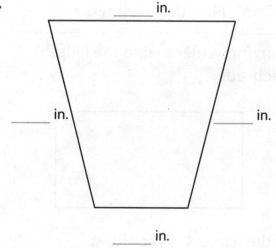

_____ in.

_____ in.   _____ in.

_____ in.

_____ inches

Name _____

Use a ruler to find the perimeter.

6.

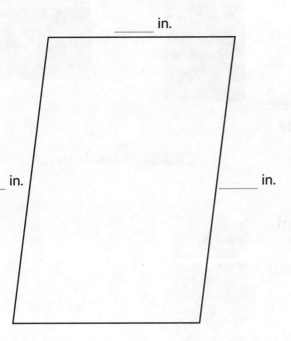

_____ in.

_____ in.   _____ in.

_____ in.

_____ inches

7.

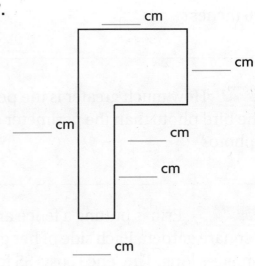

_____ cm

_____ cm

_____ cm

_____ cm

_____ cm

_____ cm

_____ centimeters

8. **Math Processes and Practices ④** **Model Mathematics** Use the grid paper to draw a figure that has a perimeter of 24 centimeters. Label the length of each side.

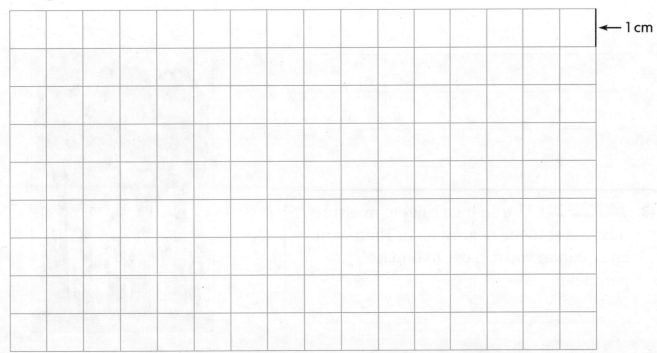

← 1 cm

Problem Solving • Applications Real World

Use the photos for 9–10.

5 in.

8 in.

5 in.

7 in.

8 in.   4 in.   4 in.

7 in.

9. Which of the animal photos has a perimeter of 26 inches?

_____

10. **GO DEEPER** How much greater is the perimeter of the bird photo than the perimeter of the cat photo?

WRITE *Math* • **Show Your Work**

_____

11. **THINK SMARTER** Erin is putting a fence around her square garden. Each side of her garden is 3 meters long. The fence costs $5 for each meter. How much will the fence cost?

_____

12. **WRITE** *Math* Gary's garden is shaped like a rectangle with two pairs of sides of equal length, and it has a perimeter of 28 feet. Explain how to find the lengths of the other sides if one side measures 10 feet.

_____

_____

_____

_____

13. **THINK SMARTER** Use an inch ruler to measure this sticker to the nearest inch. Then write an equation you can use to find its perimeter.

_____

Name _____

Find Perimeter

Learning Objective You will use rulers to estimate and measure the perimeter of figures in inches and centimeters.

Use a ruler to find the perimeter.

1.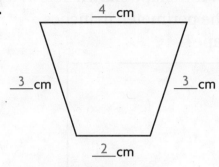
   4 cm

   3 cm   3 cm

   2 cm

   ___12___ centimeters

2.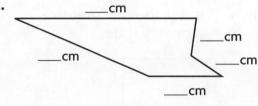
   ___cm

   ___cm   ___cm

   ___cm

   ___cm

   _____ centimeters

Problem Solving Real World

Draw a picture to solve 3–4.

3. Evan has a square sticker that measures 5 inches on each side. What is the perimeter of the sticker?

   _____

4. Sophie draws a shape that has 6 sides. Each side is 3 centimeters. What is the perimeter of the shape?

   _____

5. **WRITE** ▸ Math Draw two different figures that each have a perimeter of 20 units.

   _____

Lesson Check

Use an inch ruler for 1–2.

1. Ty cut a label the size of the shape shown. What is the perimeter, in inches, of Ty's label?

_____

2. Julie drew the shape shown below. What is the perimeter, in inches, of the shape?

_____

Spiral Review

3. What is the perimeter of the shape below?

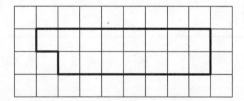

_____

4. Vince arrives for his trumpet lesson after school at the time shown on the clock. What time does Vince arrive for his trumpet lesson?

_____

5. Matthew's small fish tank holds 12 liters. His large fish tank holds 25 liters. How many more liters does his large fish tank hold?

_____

6. Compare. Write $<$, $>$, or $=$.

$$\frac{1}{6} \bigcirc \frac{1}{4}$$

FOR MORE PRACTICE GO TO THE Personal Math Trainer

Name _____

Algebra • Find Unknown Side Lengths

Essential Question How can you find the unknown length of a side in a plane figure when you know its perimeter?

Learning Objective You will find an unknown side length when you know the perimeter of a figure.

 Unlock the Problem

Chen has 27 feet of fencing to put around his garden. He has already used the lengths of fencing shown. How much fencing does he have left for the last side?

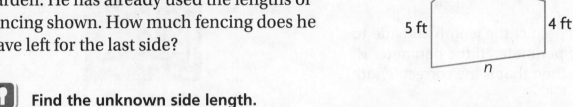

🔑 **Find the unknown side length.**

Write an equation for the perimeter.

Think: If I knew the length *n*, I would add all the side lengths to find the perimeter.

Add the lengths of the sides you know.

Think: Addition and subtraction are inverse operations.

Write a related equation.

So, Chen has _____ feet of fencing left.

$5 + 3 + \underline{} + \underline{} + n = 27$

$5 + 3 + 7 + \underbrace{ 4 } + n = 27$

$\underline{} + n = 27$

$n = 27 - 19$

$\underline{} = 27 - 19$

Math Idea
A symbol or letter can stand for an unknown side length.

Try This!

The perimeter of the figure is 24 meters.
Find the unknown side length, *w*.

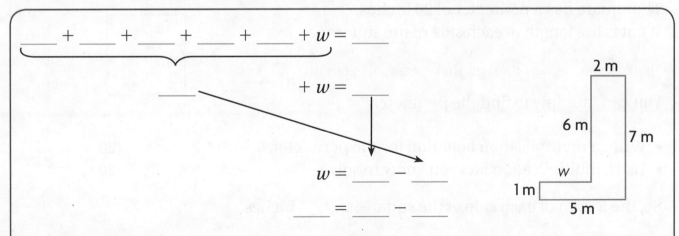

$\underline{} + \underline{} + \underline{} + \underline{} + \underline{} + w = \underline{}$

$\underline{} + w = \underline{}$

$w = \underline{} - \underline{}$

$\underline{} = \underline{} - \underline{}$

So, the unknown side length, *w*, is _____ meters.

🔎 Example Find unknown side lengths of a rectangle.

Lauren has a rectangular blanket. The perimeter is 28 feet. The width of the blanket is 5 feet. What is the length of the blanket?

5 ft

Hint: A rectangle has two pairs of opposite sides that are equal in length.

You can predict the length and add to find the perimeter. If the perimeter is 28 feet, then that is the correct length.

l l

5 ft

Predict	Check	Does it check?
l = 7 feet	5 + ____ + 5 + ____ = ____	**Think:** Perimeter is not 28 feet, so the length does not check.
l = 8 feet	5 + ____ + 5 + ____ = ____	**Think:** Perimeter is not 28 feet, so the length does not check.
l = 9 feet	5 + ____ + 5 + ____ = ____	**Think:** Perimeter is 28 feet, so the length is correct. ✓

So, the length of the blanket is _____ feet.

Try This! Find unknown side lengths of a square.

The square has a perimeter of 20 inches.
What is the length of each side of the square?

Think: A square has four sides that are equal in length.

You can multiply to find the perimeter.

s

s s

s

- Write a multiplication equation for the perimeter. $4 \times s = 20$
- Use a multiplication fact you know to solve. $4 \times$ _____ $= 20$

So, the length of each side of the square is _____ inches.

Name _____

Find the unknown side lengths.

1. Perimeter = 25 centimeters

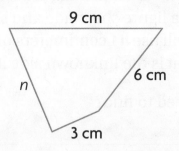

9 cm

6 cm

n

3 cm

$9 +$ _____ $+$ _____ $+ n = 25$

_____ $+ n = 25$

_____ $=$ _____ $-$ _____

$n =$ _____ centimeters

2. Perimeter = 34 meters

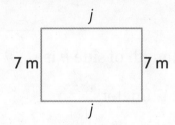

j

7 m   7 m

j

$j =$ _____ meters

3. Perimeter = 12 feet

r

r r

r

$r =$ _____ feet

On Your Own

Find the unknown side lengths.

4. Perimeter = 32 centimeters

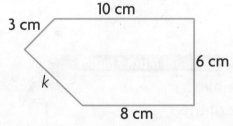

10 cm

3 cm

6 cm

k

8 cm

$k =$ _____ centimeters

5. **THINK SMARTER** Perimeter = 42 feet

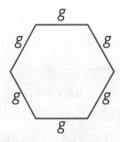

g

g g

g g

g

$g =$ _____ feet

6. **Math Processes and Practices** ④ **Use a Diagram** Eleni wants to put up a fence around her square garden. The garden has a perimeter of 28 meters. How long will each side of the fence be? Explain.

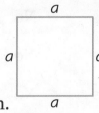

a

a a

a

_____

_____

Math Talk Math Processes and Practices ③

Apply How can you use division to find the length of a side of a square?

© Houghton Mifflin Harcourt Publishing Company

Chapter 11 • Lesson 3 639

Unlock the Problem

7. **GO DEEPER** Latesha wants to make a border with ribbon around a figure she made and sketched at the right. She will use 44 centimeters of ribbon for the border. What is the unknown side length?

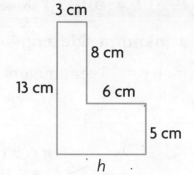

3 cm

8 cm

13 cm   6 cm

5 cm

h

a. What do you need to find?

_____

b. How will you use what you know about perimeter to help you solve the problem?

_____

_____

c. Write an equation to solve the problem.

_____

d. So, the length of side *h* is

_____ centimeters.

8. **THINK SMARTER** A rectangle has a perimeter of 34 inches. The left side is 6 inches long. What is the length of the top side?

_____

Personal Math Trainer

9. **THINK SMARTER +** Michael has 40 feet of fencing to make a rectangular dog run for his dog, Buddy. One side of the run will be 5 feet long. For numbers 9a–9d, choose Yes or No to show what the length of another side will be.

9a. 20 feet   ○ Yes   ○ No

9b. 15 feet   ○ Yes   ○ No

9c. 10 feet   ○ Yes   ○ No

9d.   8 feet   ○ Yes   ○ No

Name _____

Find Unknown Side Lengths

Learning Objective You will find an unknown side length when you know the perimeter of a figure.

Find the unknown side lengths.

1. Perimeter = 33 centimeters

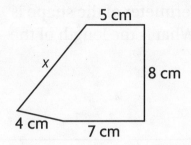

$$5 + 8 + 7 + 4 + x = 33$$
$$24 + x = 33$$
$$x = 9$$

$x =$ _____ **9** _____ centimeters

2. Perimeter = 92 inches

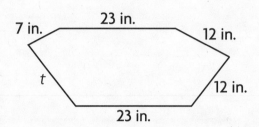

$t =$ _____ inches

Problem Solving Real World

3. Steven has a rectangular rug with a perimeter of 16 feet. The width of the rug is 5 feet. What is the length of the rug?

    _____

4. Kerstin has a square tile. The perimeter of the tile is 32 inches. What is the length of each side of the tile?

    _____

5. **WRITE** ▸*Math* Explain how to write and solve an equation to find an unknown side length of a rectangle when given the perimeter.

    _____

    _____

    _____

Lesson Check

1. Jesse is putting a ribbon around a square frame. He uses 24 inches of ribbon. How long is each side of the frame?

   _____

2. Davia draws a shape with 5 sides. Two sides are each 5 inches long. Two other sides are each 4 inches long. The perimeter of the shape is 27 inches. What is the length of the fifth side?

   _____

Spiral Review

3. What multiplication expression represents 7 + 7 + 7 + 7?

   _____

4. Bob bought 3 packs of model cars. He gave 4 cars to Ann. Bob has 11 cars left. How many model cars were in each pack?

   _____

5. Randy read a book in the afternoon. He looked at his watch when he started and finished reading. How long did Randy read?

   Start   **End**

   _____

6. What fraction and whole number does the model represent?

   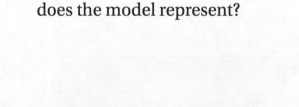

   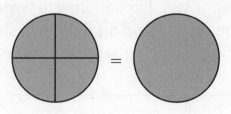

   _____ = _____

FOR MORE PRACTICE
GO TO THE
Personal Math Trainer

Understand Area

Essential Question How is finding the area of a figure different from finding the perimeter of a figure?

Learning Objective You will use dot paper to find the areas of figures by counting the number of unit squares inside a figure and decide when to find area or perimeter for a situation.

🔑 Unlock the Problem

CONNECT You learned that perimeter is the distance around a figure. It is measured in linear units, or units that are used to measure the distance between two points.

Area is the measure of the number of unit squares needed to cover a flat surface. A **unit square** is a square with a side length of 1 unit. It has an area of 1 **square unit**.

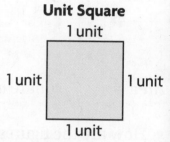

Unit Square

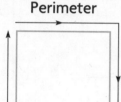

Perimeter

1 unit + 1 unit + 1 unit + 1 unit = 4 units

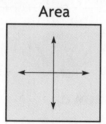

Area

1 square unit

Math Idea

You can count the number of units on each side of a figure to find its perimeter. You can count the number of unit squares inside a figure to find its area in square units.

🔓 Activity Materials ▪ geoboard ▪ rubber bands Hands On

A Use your geoboard to form a figure made from 2 unit squares. Record the figure on this dot paper.

What is the area of this figure?

Area = _____ square units

B Change the rubber band so that the figure is made from 3 unit squares. Record the figure on this dot paper.

What is the area of this figure?

Area = _____ square units

Math Talk

Math Processes and Practices ③

Compare Representations
For B, did your figure look like your classmate's figure?

Try This! Draw three different figures that are each made from 4 unit squares. Find the area of each figure.

Figure 1	Figure 2	Figure 3

Area = _____ square units | Area = _____ square units | Area = _____ square units

- How are the figures the same? How are the figures different?

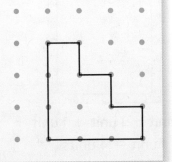

Share and Show MATH BOARD

1. Shade each unit square in the figure shown. Count the unit squares to find the area.

   Area = _____ square units

Count to find the area of the figure.

2.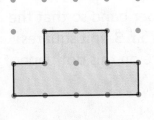

Area = _____ square units

3.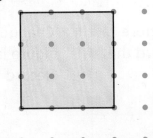

Area = _____ square units

4.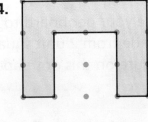

Area = _____ square units

Write *area* or *perimeter* for the situation.

5. buying a rug for a room

_____

6. putting a fence around a garden

_____

Math Talk   Math Processes and Practices ⑧

Generalize What are other situations where you need to find area?

Name _____

Count to find the area of the figure.

7.
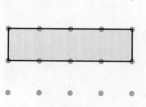

Area = _____ square units

8.
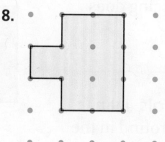

Area = _____ square units

9.
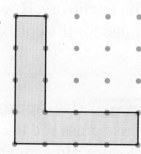

Area = _____ square units

10.
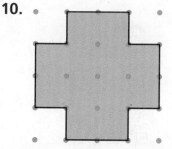

Area = _____ square units

11.
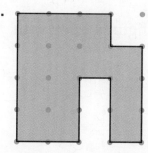

Area = _____ square units

12.
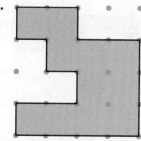

Area = _____ square units

Write *area* or *perimeter* for the situation.

13. painting a wall

_____

14. covering a patio with tiles

_____

15. putting a wallpaper border around a room

_____

16. gluing a ribbon around a picture frame

_____

17. **GO DEEPER** Nicole's mother put tiles on a section of their kitchen floor. The section included 5 rows with 4 tiles in each row. Each tile cost $2. How much money did Nicole's mother spend on the tiles?

_____

Problem Solving · Applications

Juan is building an enclosure for his small dog, Eli. Use the diagram for 18–19.

Eli's Enclosure

18. Juan will put fencing around the outside of the enclosure. How much fencing does he need for the enclosure?

_____

19.  **Use Appropriate Tools** Juan will use grass sod to cover the ground in the enclosure. How much grass sod does Juan need?

_____

20. **THINK SMARTER** Draw two different figures, each with an area of 10 square units.

21. **THINK SMARTER** What is the perimeter and area of this figure? Explain how you found the answer.

Perimeter _____ units

Area _____ square units

_____

_____

_____

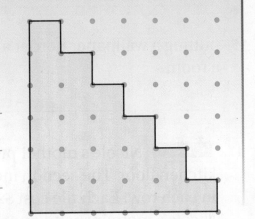

Understand Area

Learning Objective You will use dot paper to find the areas of figures by counting the number of unit squares inside a figure and decide when to find area or perimeter for a situation.

Count to find the area for the shape.

1.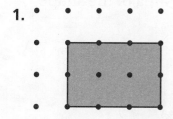

Area = ___6___ square units

2.

Area = _____ square units

3.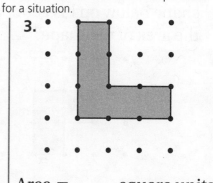

Area = _____ square units

Write *area* or *perimeter* for each situation.

4. carpeting a floor

5. fencing a garden

_____

_____

Problem Solving

Use the diagram for 6–7.

6. Roberto is building a platform for his model railroad. What is the area of the platform?

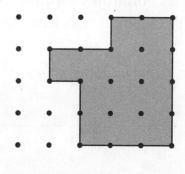

_____

7. Roberto will put a border around the edges of the platform. How much border will he need?

_____

8. [WRITE ▸*Math*] Draw a rectangle using dot paper. Find the area, and explain how you found your answer.

_____

Lesson Check

1. Josh used rubber bands to make the shape below on his geoboard. What is the area of the shape?

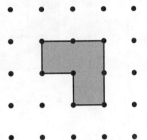

_____

2. Wilma drew the shape below on dot paper. What is the area of the shape she drew?

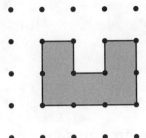

_____

Spiral Review

3. Leonardo knows it is 42 days until summer break. How many weeks is it until Leonardo's summer break? (Hint: There are 7 days in a week.)

4. Nan cut a submarine sandwich into 4 equal parts and ate one part. What fraction represents the part of the sandwich Nan ate?

_____

5. Wanda is eating breakfast at fifteen minutes before eight. What time is this? Use A.M. or P.M.

6. Dick has 2 bags of dog food. Each bag contains 5 kilograms of food. How many kilograms of food does Dick have in all?

_____

FOR MORE PRACTICE
GO TO THE
Personal Math Trainer

Name _____

Measure Area

Essential Question How can you find the area of a plane figure?

Learning Objective You will use square tiles to measure then count unit squares to find the areas of figures.

🔑 Unlock the Problem

Jaime is measuring the area of the rectangles with 1-inch square tiles.

🔒 Activity 1 Materials ▪ 1-inch grid paper ▪ scissors

Cut out eight 1-inch squares. Use the dashed lines as guides to place tiles for A–C.

Ⓐ Place 4 tiles on Rectangle A.

• Are there any gaps? _____

• Are there any overlaps? _____

• Jaime says that the area is 4 square inches. Is Jaime's measurement correct? _____

So, when you measure area, there can be no space between the tiles, or no gaps.

Ⓑ Place 8 tiles on Rectangle B.

• Are there any gaps? _____

• Are there any overlaps? _____

• Jaime says that the area is 8 square inches. Is Jaime's measurement correct? _____

So, when you measure the area, the tiles cannot overlap.

Ⓒ Place 6 tiles on Rectangle C.

• Are there any gaps? _____

• Are there any overlaps? _____

• Jaime says that the area is 6 square inches. Is Jaime's measurement correct? _____

So, the area of the rectangles is

_____ square inches.

1 square inch

Rectangle A

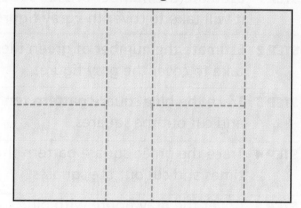

Rectangle B

Rectangle C

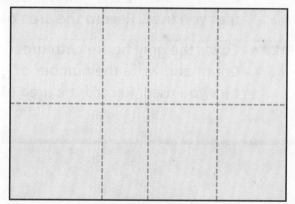

⭕ Activity 2 Materials ■ green and blue paper ■ scissors

STEP 1 Estimate the number of blue square tiles it will take to cover the gray figure.

_____ blue square tiles

STEP 2 Estimate the number of green tiles it will take to cover the gray figure.

_____ green square tiles

STEP 3 Trace the blue square pattern ten times and cut out the squares.

STEP 4 Trace the green square pattern thirty-six times and cut out the squares.

STEP 5 Cover the gray figure with blue square tiles. Count and write the number of blue square tiles you used. Record the area of the figure.

_____ blue square tiles

Area = _____ blue square units

STEP 6 Cover the gray figure with green square tiles. Count and write the number of green square tiles you used. Record the area of the figure.

_____ green square tiles

Area = _____ green square units

Math Talk

Math Processes and Practices ⑦

Identify Relationships Explain why the number of green square tiles needed to cover the figure is different than the number of blue square tiles needed.

Try This! Count to find the area of the figure.

☐ is 1 square centimeter.

There are _____ unit squares in the figure.

So, the area is _____ square centimeters.

650

Name _____

1. Count to find the area of the figure. Each unit square is 1 square centimeter.

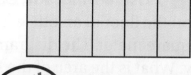

Think: Are there any gaps? Are there any overlaps?

There are _____ unit squares in the figure.

So, the area is _____ square centimeters.

Math Talk Math Processes and Practices ②

Use Reasoning How can you use square centimeters to find the area of different figures?

Count to find the area of the figure.
Each unit square is 1 square centimeter.

✓ 2.
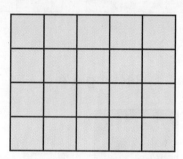

Area = _____ square centimeters

✓ 3.
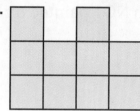

Area = _____ square centimeters

Count to find the area of the figure.
Each unit square is 1 square inch.

4.
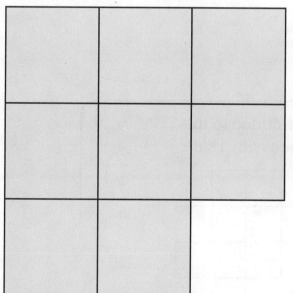

Area = _____ square inches

5.
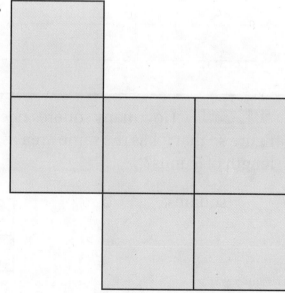

Area = _____ square inches

© Houghton Mifflin Harcourt Publishing Company

Problem Solving • Applications

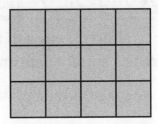

6. **Math Processes and Practices ④ Use a Diagram** Danny is placing tiles on the floor of an office lobby. Each tile is 1 square meter. The diagram shows the lobby. What is the area of the lobby?

_____

7. **GO DEEPER** Angie is painting a space shuttle mural on a wall. Each section is one square foot. The diagram shows the unfinished mural. How many more square feet has Angie painted than NOT painted on her mural?

_____

Rectangle A

8. **THINK SMARTER** You measure the area of a table top with blue unit squares and green unit squares. Which unit square will give you a greater number of square units for area? **Explain.**

_____

_____

_____

9. **THINK SMARTER** How many squares need to be added to this figure so that it has the same area as a square with a side length of 5 units?

_____ squares

Name _____

Measure Area

Learning Objective You will use square tiles to measure then count unit squares to find the areas of figures.

Count to find the area of the shape.
Each unit square is 1 square centimeter.

1.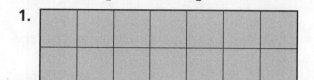

Area = ___14___ square centimeters

2.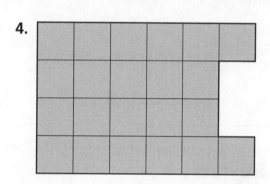

Area = _____ square centimeters

3.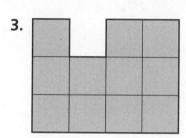

Area = _____ square centimeters

4.

Area = _____ square centimeters

Problem Solving Real World

Alan is painting his deck gray. Use the diagram at the right for 5. Each unit square is 1 square meter.

Alan's Deck

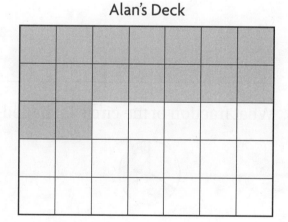

5. What is the area of the deck that Alan has already painted gray?

_____

6. **WRITE** ▸*Math* Explain how to find the area of a figure using square tiles.

_____
_____

Lesson Check

Each unit square in the diagram is 1 square foot.

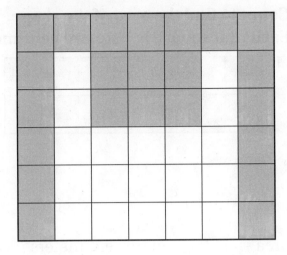

1. How many square feet are shaded?

_____

2. What is the area that has NOT been shaded?

_____

Spiral Review

3. Sonya buys 6 packages of rolls. There are 6 rolls in each package. How many rolls does Sonya buy?

_____

4. Charlie mixed 6 liters of juice with 2 liters of soda to make fruit punch. How many liters of fruit punch did Charlie make?

_____

5. What fraction of the circle is shaded?

_____

6. Use the model on the right to name a fraction that is equivalent to $\frac{1}{2}$.

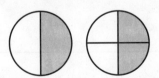

_____

FOR MORE PRACTICE GO TO THE Personal Math Trainer

Name _____

Use Area Models

Essential Question Why can you multiply to find the area of a rectangle?

Learning Objective You will find the area of a rectangle with whole-number side lengths by modeling with unit squares and by multiplying side lengths.

Unlock the Problem

Cristina has a garden that is shaped like the rectangle below. Each unit square represents 1 square meter. What is the area of her garden?

• Circle the shape of the garden.

🔑 One Way Count unit squares.

Count the number of unit squares in all.

There are _____ unit squares.

So, the area is _____ square meters.

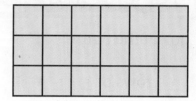

🔑 Other Ways

A Use repeated addition.

Count the number of rows. Count the number of unit squares in each row.

_____ rows of _____ = ▪

Write an addition equation.

So, the area is _____ square meters.

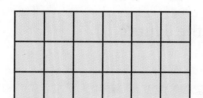

_____ unit squares

_____ unit squares

_____ unit squares

_____ + _____ + _____ = _____

B Use multiplication.

Count the number of rows. Count the number of unit squares in each row.

_____ rows of _____ = ▪

This rectangle is like an array. How do you find the total number of squares in an array?

_____

Write a multiplication equation.

So, the area is _____ square meters.

_____ unit squares in each row

_____ rows

_____ × _____ = _____

 Math Talk **Math Processes and Practices** ❶

Analyze Can you use all 3 methods mentioned to find the area of all figures?

Try This!

Find the area of the figure.
Each unit square is 1 square foot.

Think: There are 4 rows of 10 unit squares.

_____ × _____ = _____

So, the area is _____ square feet.

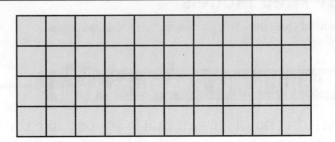

Share and Show MATH BOARD

1. Look at the figure.

   _____ rows of _____ =

   Add. _____ + _____ + _____ = _____

   Multiply. _____ × _____ = _____

   What is the area of the figure?

   _____ square units

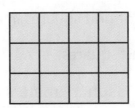

Math Talk

Math Processes and Practices 6

Compare Which method do you prefer using?

Find the area of the figure.
Each unit square is 1 square foot.

2.

_____

✓ 3.

_____

Find the area of the figure.
Each unit square is 1 square meter.

4.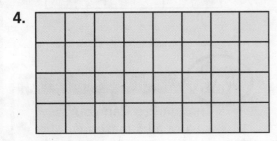

_____

✓ 5.

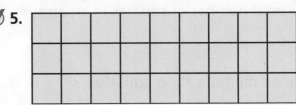

_____

Name _____

On Your Own

Find the area of the figure.
Each unit square is 1 square foot.

6.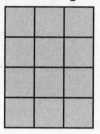

_____

7.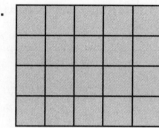

_____

Find the area of the figure.
Each unit square is 1 square meter.

8.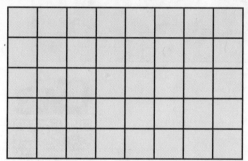

_____

9.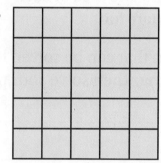

_____

10. **Math Processes and Practices ④** **Use Diagrams** Draw and shade three
rectangles with an area of 24 square units. Then write an
addition or multiplication equation for each.

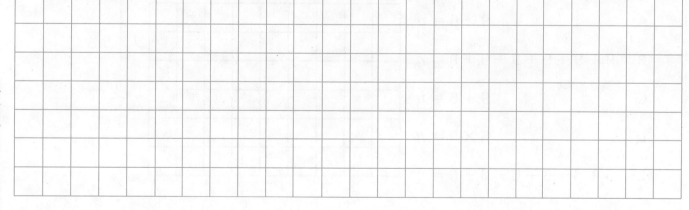

_____

_____

Problem Solving • Applications

11. **GO DEEPER** Compare the areas of the two rugs at the right. Each unit square represents 1 square foot. Which rug has the greater area? Explain.

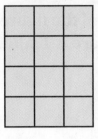 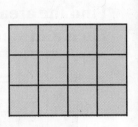

_____

_____

_____

12. **THINK SMARTER** A tile company tiled a wall using square tiles. A mural is painted in the center. The drawing shows the design. The area of each tile used is 1 square foot.

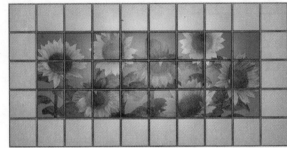

Write a problem that can be solved by using the drawing. Then solve your problem.

_____

_____

_____

13. **THINK SMARTER** Colleen drew this rectangle. Select the equation that can be used to find the area of the rectangle. Mark all that apply.

(A) $9 \times 6 = n$

(B) $9 + 9 + 9 + 9 + 9 + 9 = n$

(C) $9 + 6 = n$

(D) $6 \times 9 = n$

(E) $6 + 6 + 6 + 6 + 6 + 6 = n$

Name _____

Use Area Models

Learning Objective You will find the area of a rectangle with whole-number side lengths by modeling with unit squares and by multiplying side lengths.

Find the area of each shape. Each unit square is 1 square foot.

1.

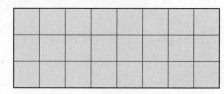

There are 3 rows of 8 unit squares.

$3 \times 8 = 24$

_____**24 square feet**_____

2.

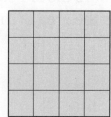

_____

Find the area of each shape.
Each unit square is 1 square meter.

3.

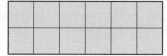

_____

4.

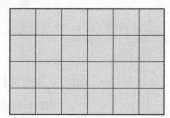

_____

5.

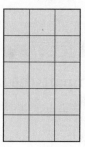

_____

Problem Solving (Real World)

6. Landon made a rug for the hallway. Each unit square is 1 square foot. What is the area of the rug?

_____

7. Eva makes a border at the top of a picture frame. Each unit square is 1 square inch. What is the area of the border?

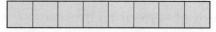

_____

8. **WRITE** ▸ *Math* Describe each of the three methods you can use to find the area of a rectangle.

_____

_____

Lesson Check

1. The entrance to an office has a tiled floor. Each square tile is 1 square meter. What is the area of the floor?

_____

2. Ms. Burns buys a new rug. Each unit square is 1 square foot. What is the area of the rug?

_____

Spiral Review

3. Compare the fractions. Write <, >, or =.

4. Claire bought 6 packs of baseball cards. Each pack had the same number of cards. If Claire bought 48 baseball cards in all, how many cards were in each pack?

_____

5. Austin left for school at 7:35 A.M. He arrived at school 15 minutes later. What time did Austin arrive at school?

6. Wyatt's room is a rectangle with a perimeter of 40 feet. The width of the room is 8 feet. What is the length of the room?

_____

FOR MORE PRACTICE
GO TO THE
Personal Math Trainer

Name _____

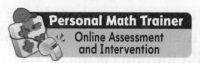
Vocabulary

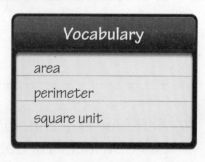

Vocabulary
area
perimeter
square unit

Choose the best term from the box.

1. The distance around a figure is the _____. (p. 625)

2. The measure of the number of unit squares needed to cover a figure with no gaps or overlaps is the _____. (p. 643)

Concepts and Skills

Find the perimeter of the figure. Each unit is 1 centimeter.

3.

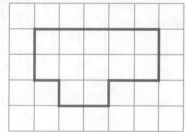

_____ centimeters

4.

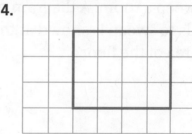

_____ centimeters

Find the unknown side lengths.

5. Perimeter = 33 centimeters

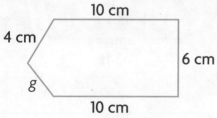

$g =$ _____ centimeters

6. Perimeter = 32 feet

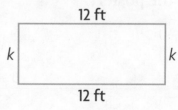

$k =$ _____ feet

Find the area of the figure. Each unit square is 1 square meter.

7.

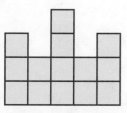

_____ square meters

8.

_____ square meters **Chapter 11 661**

© Houghton Mifflin Harcourt Publishing Company

9. Ramona is making a lid for her rectangular jewelry box. The jewelry box has side lengths of 6 centimeters and 4 centimeters. What is the area of the lid Ramona is making?

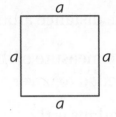

6 cm

4 cm

_____

10. Adrienne is decorating a square picture frame. She glued 36 inches of ribbon around the edge of the frame. What is the length of each side of the picture frame?

a

a   a

a

_____

11. Margo will sweep a room. A diagram of the floor that she needs to sweep is shown at the right. What is the area of the floor?

_____

12. Jeff is making a poster for a car wash for the Campout Club. What is the perimeter of the poster?

3 ft

1 ft 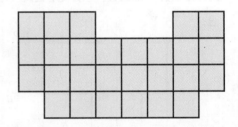 1 ft

CAMPOUT CLUB
CAR WASH

3 ft

_____

13. Go DEEPER A rectangle has two side lengths of 8 inches and two side lengths of 10 inches. What is the perimeter of the rectangle? What is the area of the rectangle?

_____

Name _____

Problem Solving • Area of Rectangles

Essential Question How can you use the strategy *find a pattern* to solve area problems?

Learning Objective You will use the strategy *find a pattern* to solve area problems by recording measurement data in a table and looking for a pattern of change in the relationships.

Unlock the Problem

Mr. Koi wants to build storage buildings, so he drew plans for the buildings. He wants to know how the areas of the buildings are related. How does the area change from the area of Building *A* to the area of Building *B*? How does the area change from the area of Building *C* to the area of Building *D*?

Use the graphic organizer to help you solve the problem.

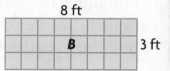

Read the Problem

What do I need to find?	**What information do I need to use?**	**How will I use the information?**
I need to find how the areas will change from *A* to *B* and from ____ to ____.	I need to use the _____ and _____ of each building to find its area.	I will record the areas in a table. Then I will look for a pattern to see how the _____ will change.

Solve the Problem

I will complete the table to find patterns to solve the problem.

	Length	Width	Area		Length	Width	Area
Building *A*	3 ft			Building *C*		4 ft	
Building *B*	3 ft			Building *D*		8 ft	

I see that the lengths will be the same and the widths will be doubled.

The areas will change from _____ to _____ and from _____ to _____.

So, when the lengths are the same and the widths are doubled,

the areas will be _____.

🔓 Try Another Problem

Mr. Koi is building more storage buildings. He wants to know how the areas of the buildings are related. How does the area change from the area of Building *E* to the area of Building *F*? How does the area change from the area of Building *G* to the area of Building *H*?

Use the graphic organizer to help you solve the problem.

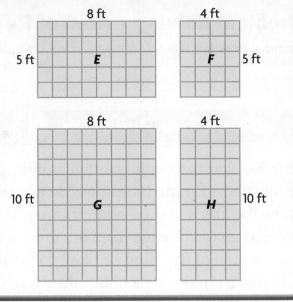

Read the Problem

What do I need to find?	What information do I need to use?	How will I use the information?

Solve the Problem

	Length	Width	Area		Length	Width	Area
Building *E*				Building *G*			
Building *F*				Building *H*			

- How did your table help you find a pattern?

_____

_____

_____

Math Processes and Practices ②

Reason Abstractly
What if the length of both sides is doubled? How would the areas change?

664

© Houghton Mifflin Harcourt Publishing Company

Name _____

Use the table for 1–2.

✓ **1.** Many pools come in rectangular shapes. How do the areas of the swimming pools change when the widths change?

First, complete the table by finding the area of each pool.

Think: I can find the area by multiplying the length and the width.

Swimming Pool Sizes			
Pool	Length (in feet)	Width (in feet)	Area (in square feet)
A	8	20	
B	8	30	
C	8	40	
D	8	50	

Then, find a pattern of how the lengths change and how the widths change.

The _____ stays the same. The widths

_____.

Last, describe a pattern of how the area changes.

The areas _____ by ____ square feet.

✓ **2.** What if the length of each pool was 16 feet? Explain how the areas would change.

_____

_____

3. (Math Processes and Practices 7) **Look for a Pattern** If the length of each pool in the table is 20 feet, and the widths change from 5, to 6, to 7, and to 8 feet, describe the pattern of the areas.

_____

_____

4. **Math Processes and Practices ①** **Analyze Relationships** Jacob has a rectangular garden with an area of 56 square feet. The length of the garden is 8 feet. What is the width of the garden?

_____

5. **GO DEEPER** A diagram of Paula's bedroom is at the right. Her bedroom is in the shape of a rectangle. Write the measurements for the other sides. What is the perimeter of the room? (Hint: The two pairs of opposite sides are equal lengths.)

_____

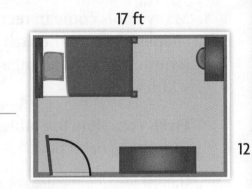

17 ft

12

6. **THINK SMARTER** Elizabeth built a sandbox that is 4 feet long and 4 feet wide. She also built a flower garden that is 4 feet long and 6 feet wide and a vegetable garden that is 4 feet long and 8 feet wide. How do the areas change?

_____

_____

_____

7. **THINK SMARTER** Find the pattern and complete the chart.

Total Area (in square feet)	50	60	70	80	
Length (in feet)	10	10		10	
Width (in feet)	5	6	7		

How can you use the chart to find the length and width of a figure with an area of 100 square feet?

_____

_____

Problem Solving • Area of Rectangles

Learning Objective You will use the strategy *find a pattern* to solve area problems by recording measurement data in a table and looking for a pattern of change in the relationships.

Use the information for 1–3.

An artist makes rectangular murals in different sizes. Below are the available sizes. Each unit square is 1 square meter.

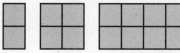

A   B   C   D

1. Complete the table to find the area of each mural.

Mural	Length (in meters)	Width (in meters)	Area (in square meters)
A	2	1	2
B	2	2	4
C	2		
D	2		

2. Find and describe a pattern of how the length changes and how the width changes for murals A through D.

_____

_____

3. How do the areas of the murals change when the width changes?

_____

4. **WRITE** ▸*Math* Write and solve an area problem that illustrates the use of the *find a pattern* strategy.

_____

_____

Lesson Check

1. Lauren drew the designs below. Each unit square is 1 square centimeter. If the pattern continues, what will be the area of the fourth figure?

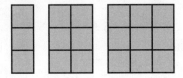

_____

_____

2. Henry built one garden that is 3 feet wide and 3 feet long. He also built a garden that is 3 feet wide and 6 feet long, and a garden that is 3 feet wide and 9 feet long. How do the areas change?

_____

_____

Spiral Review

3. Joe, Jim, and Jack share 27 football cards equally. How many cards does each boy get?

_____

4. Nita uses $\frac{1}{3}$ of a carton of 12 eggs. How many eggs does she use?

_____

5. Brenda made 8 necklaces. Each necklace has 10 large beads. How many large beads did Brenda use to make the necklaces?

_____

6. Neal is tiling his kitchen floor. Each square tile is 1 square foot. Neal uses 6 rows of tiles with 9 tiles in each row. What is the area of the floor?

_____

FOR MORE PRACTICE GO TO THE
Personal Math Trainer

Name _____

Area of Combined Rectangles

Essential Question How can you break apart a figure to find the area?

Learning Objective You will use the Distributive Property or a break apart strategy to find the areas of combined rectangles by adding the area of smaller rectangles to find the total area.

🔑 Unlock the Problem

Anna's rug has side lengths of 4 feet and 9 feet. What is the area of Anna's rug?

🔒 Activity Materials ■ square tiles

STEP 1 Use square tiles to model 4 × 9.

STEP 2 Draw a rectangle on the grid paper to show your model.

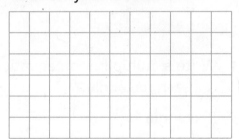

STEP 3 Draw a vertical line to break apart the model to make two smaller rectangles.

The side length 9 is broken into _____ plus _____.

STEP 4 Find the area of each of the two smaller rectangles.

Rectangle 1: _____ × _____ = _____

Rectangle 2: _____ × _____ = _____

STEP 5 Add the products to find the total area.

_____ + _____ = _____ square feet

STEP 6 Check your answer by counting the number of square feet.

_____ square feet

So, the area of Anna's rug is _____ square feet.

Remember

You can use the Distributive Property to break apart an array.

3 × 3 = 3 × (2 + 1)

Math Talk

Math Processes and Practices ⑥

Compare Did you draw a line in the same place as your classmates? Explain why you found the same total area.

CONNECT Using the Distributive Property, you found that you could break apart a rectangle into smaller rectangles, and add the area of each smaller rectangle to find the total area.

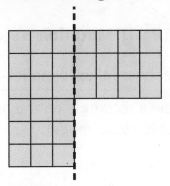

How can you break apart this figure into rectangles to find its area?

🔓 One Way Use a horizontal line.

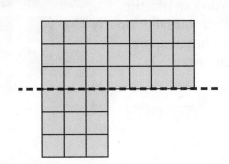

STEP 1 Write a multiplication equation for each rectangle.

Rectangle 1: ___ × ___ = ___

Rectangle 2: ___ × ___ = ___

_____

STEP 2 Add the products to find the total area.

___ + ___ = ___ square units

So, the area is _____ square units.

🔓 Another Way Use a vertical line.

STEP 1 Write a multiplication equation for each rectangle.

Rectangle 1: ___ × ___ = ___

Rectangle 2: ___ × ___ = ___

_____

STEP 2 Add the products to find the total area.

___ + ___ = ___ square units

Math Talk

Math Processes and Practices ①

Evaluate How can you check your answer?

Share and Show

1. Draw a line to break apart the figure into rectangles. Find the total area of the figure.

Think: I can draw vertical or horizontal lines to break apart the figure to make rectangles.

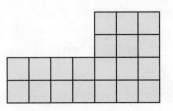

Rectangle 1: ___ × ___ = ___

Rectangle 2: ___ × ___ = ___

___ + ___ = ___ square units

Name _____

Use the Distributive Property to find the area. Show your multiplication and addition equations.

2.
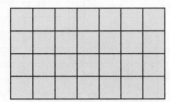

_____

_____ square units

3.
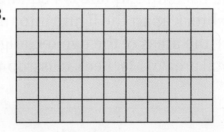

_____

_____ square units

On Your Own

Use the Distributive Property to find the area. Show your multiplication and addition equations.

4.

_____

_____ square units

5.
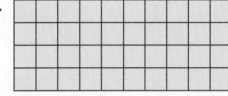

_____

_____ square units

Draw a line to break apart the figure into rectangles. Find the area of the figure.

6.
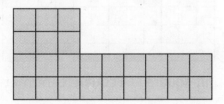

Rectangle 1: ___ × ___ = ___

Rectangle 2: ___ × ___ = ___

___ + ___ = ___ square units

7.
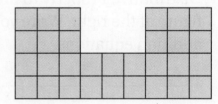

Rectangle 1: ___ × ___ = ___

Rectangle 2: ___ × ___ = ___

Rectangle 3: ___ × ___ = ___

___ + ___ + ___ = ___ square units

Problem Solving • Applications

8. **GO DEEPER**   A model of Ms. Lee's classroom is at the right. Each unit square is 1 square foot. Draw a line to break apart the figure into rectangles. What are the areas of the two rectangles? What is the total area of Ms. Lee's classroom?

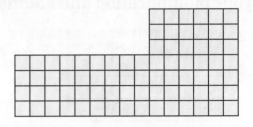

_____

9. David has a rectangular bedroom with a rectangular closet. Each unit square is 1 square foot. Draw a line to break apart the figure into rectangles. What is the total area of David's bedroom?

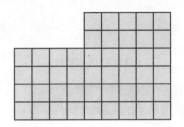

_____

10. **THINK SMARTER**   **Explain** how to break apart the figure to find its area.

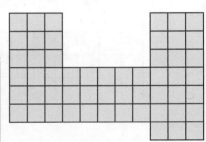

_____

_____

_____

1 unit square = 1 square meter

_____

11. **Math Processes and Practices ④**   **Interpret a Result**   Use the Distributive Property to find the area of the figure at the right. Write your multiplication and addition equations.

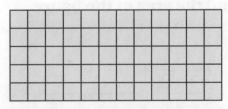

_____

1 unit square = 1 square centimeter

_____

Personal Math Trainer

12. **THINK SMARTER +**   Pete drew a diagram of his backyard on grid paper. Each unit square is 1 square meter. The area surrounding the patio is grass.

How much more of the backyard is grass than patio? Show your work.

_____ more square meters

Name _____

Area of Combined Rectangles

Learning Objective You will use the Distributive Property or a break apart strategy to find the areas of combined rectangles by adding the area of smaller rectangles to find the total area.

Use the Distributive Property to find the area. Show your multiplication and addition equations.

1.

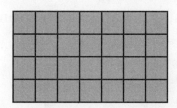

$4 \times 2 = 8; 4 \times 5 = 20$
_____

$8 + 20 = 28$
_____

____28____ square units

2.

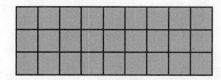

_____

_____

_____ square units

Draw a line to break apart the shape into rectangles. Find the area of the shape.

3.

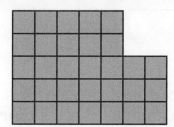

Rectangle 1: _____ $\times$ _____ = _____

Rectangle 2: _____ $\times$ _____ = _____

_____ + _____ = _____ square units

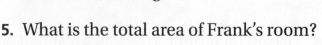
Problem Solving · Real World

A diagram of Frank's room is at right. Each unit square is 1 square foot.

4. Draw a line to divide the shape of Frank's room into rectangles.

5. What is the total area of Frank's room?

_____ square feet

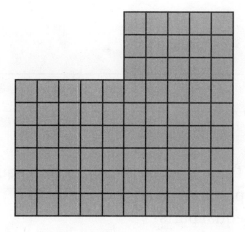

6. 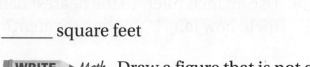 **WRITE** ▸ *Math* Draw a figure that is not a rectangle and find its area. Use grid paper and show each step.

_____

_____

Lesson Check

1. The diagram shows Ben's backyard. Each unit square is 1 square yard. What is the area of Ben's backyard?

    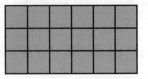

    _____

2. The diagram shows a room in an art gallery. Each unit square is 1 square meter. What is the area of the room?

    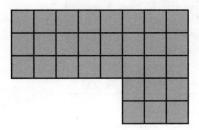

    _____

Spiral Review

3. Naomi needs to solve $28 \div 7 = \blacksquare$. What related multiplication fact can she use to find the unknown number?

    _____

    _____

4. Karen drew a triangle with side lengths 3 centimeters, 4 centimeters, and 5 centimeters. What is the perimeter of the triangle?

    _____

    _____

5. The rectangle is divided into equal parts. What is the name of the equal parts?

    _____

6. Use an inch ruler. To the nearest half inch, how long is this line segment?

    |———————————————|

    _____

Name _____

Same Perimeter, Different Areas

Essential Question How can you use area to compare rectangles with the same perimeter?

Learning Objective You will use square tiles and grid paper to identify and draw rectangles with the same perimeter and tell which rectangle has a greater area.

Unlock the Problem Real World

Toby has 12 feet of boards to put around a rectangular sandbox. How long should he make each side so that the area of the sandbox is as large as possible?

- What is the greatest perimeter Toby can make for his sandbox?

_____

Activity

Materials ■ square tiles

Use square tiles to make all the rectangles you can that have a perimeter of 12 units. Draw and label the sandboxes. Then find the area of each.

Sandbox 1

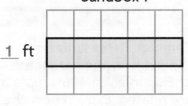

_1_ ft

_5_ ft

Sandbox 2

__ ft

__ ft

Sandbox 3

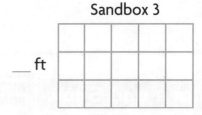

__ ft

__ ft

Find the perimeter and area of each rectangle.

	Perimeter	Area
Sandbox 1	_5_ + _1_ + _5_ + _1_ = _12_ feet	_1_ × _5_ = ___ square feet
Sandbox 2	__ + __ + __ + __ = ___ feet	__ × __ = ___ square feet
Sandbox 3	__ + __ + __ + __ = ___ feet	__ × __ = ___ square feet

The area of Sandbox ____ is the greatest.

So, Toby should build a sandbox that is

____ feet wide and ____ feet long.

 Math Talk

Math Processes and Practices 6

Compare How are the sandboxes alike? How are the sandboxes different?

❶ Examples Draw rectangles with the same perimeter and different areas.

Ⓐ Draw a rectangle that has a perimeter of 20 units and an area of 24 square units.

The sides of the rectangle measure

____ units and ____ units.

Ⓑ Draw a rectangle that has a perimeter of 20 units and an area of 25 square units.

The sides of the rectangle measure

____ units and ____ units.

Math Talk   Math Processes and Practices ❸

Compare Representations Explain how the perimeters of Example *A* and Example *B* are related. Explain how the areas are related.

Share and Show MATH BOARD

1. The perimeter of the rectangle at the right is

   ____ units. The area is ____ square units.

2. Draw a rectangle that has the same perimeter as the rectangle in Exercise 1 but with a different area.

3. The area of the rectangle in Exercise 2 is

   ____ square units.

✅ 4. Which rectangle has the greater area?

   _____

5. If you were given a rectangle with a certain perimeter, how would you draw it so that it has the greatest area?

   _____

Math Talk   Math Processes and Practices ❻

Explain how you knew what the rectangle for Exercise 5 would look like.

Name _____

**Find the perimeter and the area. Tell which
rectangle has a greater area.**

 6.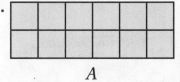

                    A: Perimeter = _____ ; Area = _____

                    B: Perimeter = _____ ; Area = _____

                    Rectangle _____ has a greater area.

**Find the perimeter and the area. Tell which
rectangle has a greater area.**

7. 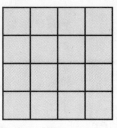   8.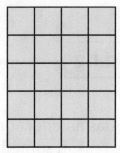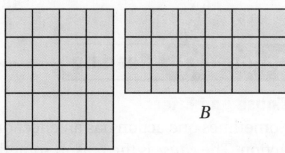

A: Perimeter = _____ ;   A: Perimeter = _____ ;

    Area = _____   Area = _____

B: Perimeter = _____ ;   B: Perimeter = _____ ;

    Area = _____   Area = _____

Rectangle ___ has a greater area.   Rectangle ___ has a greater area.

9. **Math Processes and Practices 6** **Use Math Vocabulary** Todd's flower garden
is 4 feet wide and 8 feet long. If the answer is 32 square
feet, what is the question?

_____

Problem Solving • Applications

10. THINK SMARTER Draw a rectangle with the same perimeter as Rectangle *C*, but with a smaller area. What is the area?

Area = _____

C

11. THINK SMARTER Which figure has a perimeter of 20 units and an area of 16 square units?

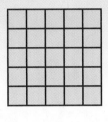

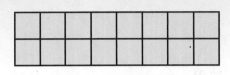

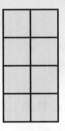

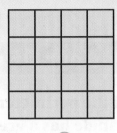

Ⓐ   Ⓑ   Ⓒ   Ⓓ

Connect to Reading

Cause and Effect

Sometimes one action has an effect on another action. The *cause* is the reason something happens. The *effect* is the result.

12. GO DEEPER Sam wanted to print a digital photo that is 3 inches wide and 5 inches long. What if Sam accidentally printed a photo that is 4 inches wide and 6 inches long?

Sam can make a table to understand cause and effect.

Cause	Effect
The wrong size photo was printed.	Each side of the photo is a greater length.

Use the information and the strategy to solve the problems.

a. What effect did the mistake have on the perimeter of the photo?

_____

b. What effect did the mistake have on the area of the photo?

_____

Name _____

Same Perimeter, Different Areas

Learning Objective You will use square tiles and grid paper to identify and draw rectangles with the same perimeter and tell which rectangle has a greater area.

Find the perimeter and the area.
Tell which rectangle has a greater area.

1.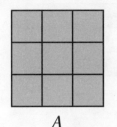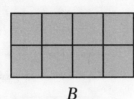

_A_

_B_

2.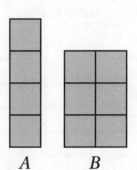

_A_ _B_

_A_: Perimeter = **12 units** ;

Area = **9 square units**

_B_: Perimeter = _____ ;

Area = _____

Rectangle _____ has a greater area.

_A_: Perimeter = _____ ;

Area = _____

_B_: Perimeter = _____ ;

Area = _____

Rectangle _____ has a greater area.

Problem Solving · Real World

3. Tara's and Jody's bedrooms are shaped like rectangles. Tara's bedroom is 9 feet long and 8 feet wide. Jody's bedroom is 7 feet long and 10 feet wide. Whose bedroom has the greater area? **Explain**.

_____

_____

4. **WRITE** ▸ _Math_ Draw three examples of rectangles that have the same perimeter, but different areas. Note which of the areas is greatest and which is the least.

_____

_____

Lesson Check

1. Draw a rectangle that has a perimeter of 12 units and an area of 8 square units.

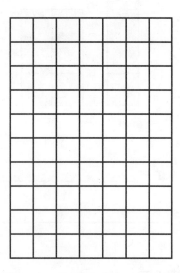

2. Find the perimeter and the area. Tell which rectangle has the greater area.

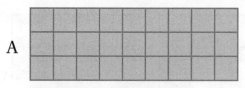

A

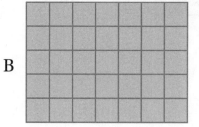

B

A: Perimeter = _____ units

Area = _____ square units

B: Perimeter = _____ units

Area = _____ square units

Rectangle _____ has a greater area.

Spiral Review

3. Kerrie covers a table with 8 rows of square tiles. There are 7 tiles in each row. What is the area that Kerrie covers in square units?

4. Von has a rectangular workroom with a perimeter of 26 feet. The length of the workroom is 6 feet. What is the width of Von's workroom?

FOR MORE PRACTICE
GO TO THE
Personal Math Trainer

Name _____

Same Area, Different Perimeters

Essential Question How can you use perimeter to compare rectangles with the same area?

Learning Objective You will use square tiles and grid paper to identify and draw rectangles with the same area and tell which rectangle has a greater perimeter.

Unlock the Problem Real World

Marcy is making a rectangular pen to hold her rabbits. The area of the pen should be 16 square meters with side lengths that are whole numbers. What is the least amount of fencing she needs?

• What does the least amount of fencing represent?

_____

Activity Materials ▪ square tiles

Use 16 square tiles to make rectangles. Make as many different rectangles as you can with 16 tiles. Record the rectangles on the grid, write the multiplication equation for the area shown by the rectangle, and find the perimeter of each rectangle.

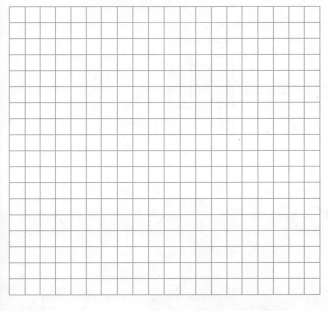

Math Talk Math Processes and Practices ④

Model Mathematics How did you determine what rectangles to draw?

Area: _____ × _____ = 16 square meters   Perimeter: _____ meters

Area: _____ × _____ = 16 square meters   Perimeter: _____ meters

Area: _____ × _____ = 16 square meters   Perimeter: _____ meters

To use the least amount of fencing, Marcy should make a rectangular

pen with side lengths of _____ meters and _____ meters.

So, _____ meters is the least amount of fencing Marcy needs.

Try This!

Draw three rectangles that have an area of 18 square units on the grid. Find the perimeter of each rectangle. Shade the rectangle that has the greatest perimeter.

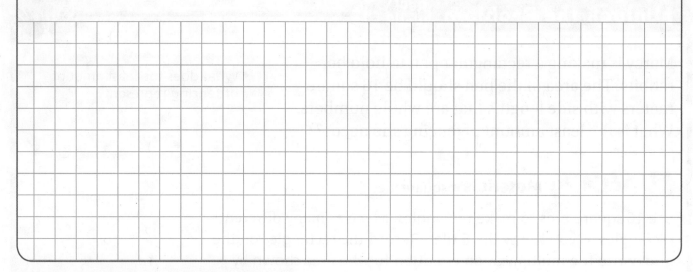

Share and Show

1. The area of the rectangle at the right is

   _____ square units. The perimeter is _____ units.

2. Draw a rectangle that has the same area as the rectangle in Exercise 1 but with a different perimeter.

3. The perimeter of the rectangle in Exercise 2 is

   _____ units.

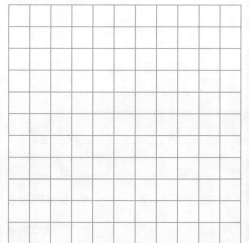

✓ 4. Which rectangle has the greater perimeter?

   _____

5. If you were given a rectangle with a certain area, how would you draw it so that it had the greatest perimeter?

   _____

Math Processes and Practices ③

Compare Representations
Did you and your classmate draw the same rectangle for Exercise 2?

Name _____

Find the perimeter and the area. Tell which rectangle has a greater perimeter.

6.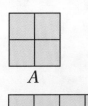

  A: Area = _____ ; Perimeter = _____

  B: Area = _____ ; Perimeter = _____

  Rectangle _____ has a greater perimeter.

On Your Own

Find the perimeter and the area. Tell which rectangle has a greater perimeter.

7.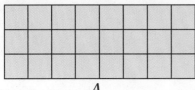

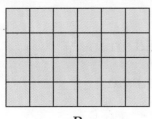

8.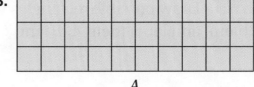

A: Area = _____ ;

  Perimeter = _____

B: Area = _____ ;

  Perimeter = _____

Rectangle _____ has a greater perimeter.

A: Area = _____ ;

  Perimeter = _____

B: Area = _____ ;

  Perimeter = _____

Rectangle _____ has a greater perimeter.

9. **THINK SMARTER** **Sense or Nonsense?** Dora says that of all the possible rectangles with the same area, the rectangle with the largest perimeter will have two side lengths that are 1 unit. Does her statement make sense? Explain.

Unlock the Problem

10. Roberto has 12 tiles. Each tile is 1 square inch. He will arrange them into a rectangle and glue 1-inch stones around the edge. How can Roberto arrange the tiles so that he uses the least number of stones?

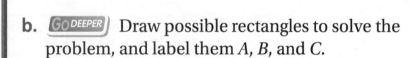

a. **Math Processes and Practices 6** **Explain a Method** How will you use what you know about area and perimeter to help you solve

the problem? _____

_____

_____

b. **GO DEEPER** Draw possible rectangles to solve the problem, and label them *A*, *B*, and *C*.

_____

_____

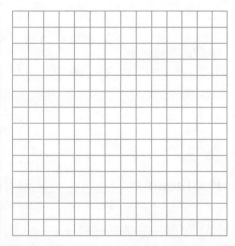

c. So, Roberto should arrange

the tiles like Rectangle _____ .

11. **THINK SMARTER** Draw 2 different rectangles with an area of 20 square units. What is the perimeter of each rectangle you drew?

Area = 20 square units

Perimeter = _____ units

Perimeter = _____ units

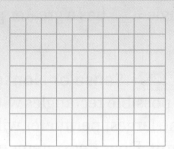

Name _____

Same Area, Different Perimeters

Learning Objective You will use square tiles and grid paper to identify and draw rectangles with the same area and tell which rectangle has a greater perimeter.

Find the perimeter and the area. Tell which rectangle has a greater perimeter.

1.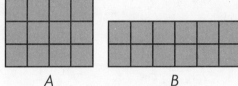

A

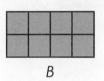

B

A: Area = __8 square units__ ;

Perimeter = __18 units__

B: Area = _____ ;

Perimeter = _____

Rectangle _____ has a greater perimeter.

2.

A   *B*

A: Area = _____ ;

Perimeter = _____

B: Area = _____ ;

Perimeter = _____

Rectangle _____ has a greater perimeter.

Problem Solving · Real World

Use the tile designs for 3–4.

3. Compare the areas of Design A and Design B.

_____

_____

4. Compare the perimeters. Which design has the greater perimeter?

_____

5. **WRITE** ▸ *Math* Draw two rectangles with different perimeters but the same area.

_____

_____

Beth's Tile Designs

A

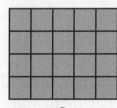

B

Lesson Check

1. Jake drew two rectangles. Which rectangle has the greater perimeter?

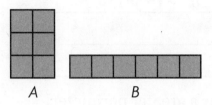

2. Alyssa drew two rectangles. Which rectangle has the greater perimeter?

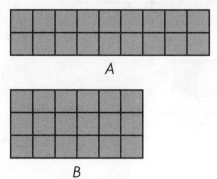

_____

_____

Spiral Review

3. Marsha was asked to find the value of $8 - 3 \times 2$. She wrote a wrong answer. What is the correct answer?

4. What fraction names the point on the number line?

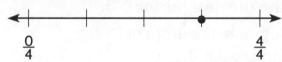

_____

_____

5. Kyle drew three line segments with these lengths: $\frac{2}{4}$ inch, $\frac{2}{3}$ inch, and $\frac{2}{6}$ inch. List the fractions in order from least to greatest.

6. On Monday, $\frac{3}{8}$ inch of snow fell. On Tuesday, $\frac{5}{8}$ inch of snow fell. Write a statement that correctly compares the snow amounts.

_____

_____

Name _____

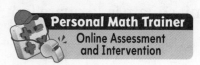
1. Find the perimeter of each figure on the grid. Identify the figures that have a perimeter of 14 units. Mark all that apply.

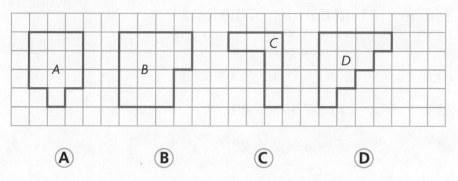

Ⓐ   Ⓑ   Ⓒ   Ⓓ

2. Kim wants to put trim around a picture she drew. How many centimeters of trim does Kim need for the perimeter of the picture?

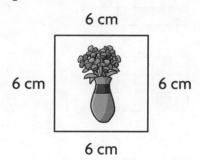

6 cm

6 cm   6 cm

6 cm

_____ centimeters

3. Sophia drew this rectangle on dot paper. What is the area of the rectangle?

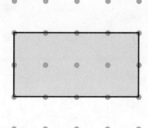

_____ square units

GO DIGITAL **Assessment Options**
Chapter Test

4. The drawing shows Seth's plan for a fort in his backyard. Each unit square is 1 square foot.

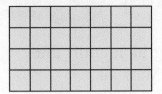

Which equations can Seth use to find the area of the fort? Mark all that apply.

Ⓐ $4 + 4 + 4 + 4 = 16$

Ⓓ $4 \times 4 = 16$

Ⓑ $7 + 4 + 7 + 4 = 22$

Ⓔ $7 \times 7 = 49$

Ⓒ $7 + 7 + 7 + 7 = 28$

Ⓕ $4 \times 7 = 28$

5. Which rectangle has a number of square units for its area equal to the number of units of its perimeter?

Ⓐ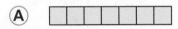

Ⓒ

Ⓑ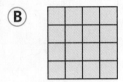

Ⓓ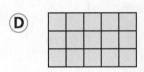

6. Vanessa uses a ruler to draw a square. The perimeter of the square is 12 centimeters. Select a number to complete the sentence.

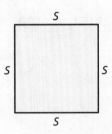

The square has a side length of
| 3 |
| 4 |
| 5 |
| 6 |
centimeters.

Name _____

7. Tomas drew two rectangles on grid paper.

Circle the words that make the sentence true.

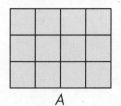
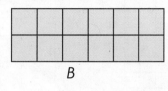

A   B

Rectangle *A* has an area that is

| less than |
| the same as |
| greater than |

the area of Rectangle *B*, and a perimeter that is

| less than |
| the same as |
| greater than |

the perimeter of Rectangle *B*.

8. Yuji drew this figure on grid paper. What is the perimeter of the figure?

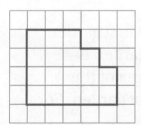

_____ units

9. What is the area of the figure shown? Each unit square is 1 square meter.

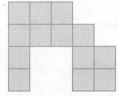

_____ square meters

10. Shawn drew a rectangle that was 2 units wide and 6 units long. Draw a different rectangle that has the same perimeter but a different area.

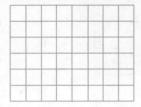

11. Mrs. Rios put a wallpaper border around the room shown below. She used 72 feet of wallpaper border.

What is the unknown side length? Show your work.

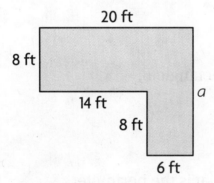

_____ feet

12. Elizabeth has two gardens in her yard. The first garden is 6 feet long and 4 feet wide. The second garden is double the width of the first garden. The area of the second garden is double the area of the first garden. For numbers 12a–12d, select True or False.

12a.	The area of the first garden is 24 square feet.	○ True	○ False
12b.	The area of the second garden is 48 square feet.	○ True	○ False
12c.	The length of the second garden is 12 feet.	○ True	○ False
12d.	The length of the second garden is 6 feet.	○ True	○ False

Name _____

13. Marcus bought some postcards. Each postcard had a perimeter of 16 inches. Which could be one of the postcards Marcus bought? Mark all that apply.

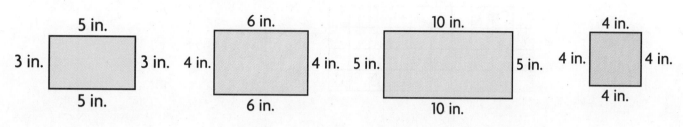

- (A)
- (B)
- (C)
- (D)

14. **THINK SMARTER +** Anthony wants to make two different rectangular flowerbeds, each with an area of 24 square feet. He will build a wooden frame around each flowerbed. The flowerbeds will have side lengths that are whole numbers.

Part A

Each unit square on the grid below is 1 square foot. Draw two possible flowerbeds. Label each with a letter.

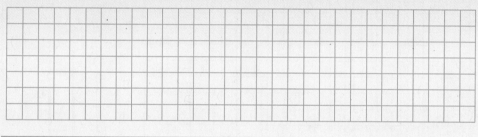

Part B

Which of the flowerbeds will take more wood to frame? Explain how you know.

_____

_____

_____

15. Keisha draws a sketch of her living room on grid paper. Each unit square is 1 square meter. Write and solve a multiplication equation that can be used to find the area of the living room in square meters.

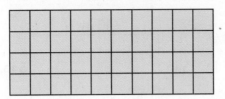

_____

_____ square meters

16. GO DEEPER Mr. Wicks designs houses. He uses grid paper to plan a new house design. The kitchen will have an area between 70 square feet and 85 square feet. The pantry will have an area between 4 square feet and 15 square feet. Draw and label a diagram to show what Mr. Wicks could design. Explain how to find the total area.

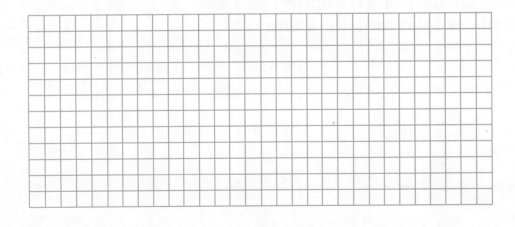

_____

_____

Geometry

BIG IDEA Describe, analyze, and compare two-dimensional shapes. Develop a conceptual understanding of dividing shapes into equal areas and writing the area as a fraction.

Students at Dommerich Elementary helped design and construct a mosaic to show parts of their community and local plants and animals.

Make a Mosaic

Have you ever worked to put puzzle pieces together to make a picture or design? Pieces of paper can be put together to make a colorful work of art called a mosaic.

Get Started

WRITE ▸ Math

Materials ■ construction paper ■ glue ■ ruler ■ scissors

Work with a partner to make a paper mosaic. Use the Important Facts to help you.

- Draw a simple pattern on a piece of paper.

- Cut out shapes, such as rectangles, squares, and triangles of the colors you need from construction paper. The shapes should be about 1 inch on each side.

- Glue the shapes into the pattern. Leave a little space between each shape to make the mosaic effect.

Describe and compare the shapes you used to make your mosaic.

Important Facts

- Mosaics is the art of using small pieces of materials, such as tiles or glass, to make a colorful picture or design.
- Mosaic pieces can be small plane shapes, such as rectangles, squares, and triangles.
- Mosaic designs and patterns can be anything from simple flower shapes to common objects found in your home or patterns in nature.

_____

_____

_____

_____

Completed by _____

Chapter 12
Two-Dimensional Shapes

 Show What You Know

Personal Math Trainer
Online Assessment and Intervention

Check your understanding of important skills.

Name _____

▶ **Plane Shapes**

1. Color the triangles blue.

2. Color the rectangles red.

▶ **Number of Sides** Write the number of sides.

3. ____ sides

4. ____ sides

5. Circle the shapes that have 4 or more sides.

 **Math in the Real World**

Whitney found this drawing that shows 9 small squares. Find larger squares in the drawing. How many squares are there in all? Explain.

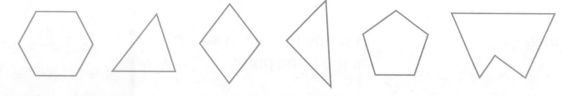

© Houghton Mifflin Harcourt Publishing Company

Vocabulary Builder

▶ **Visualize It** ••

Complete the tree map by using the words with a ✓.

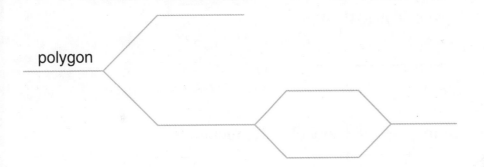

polygon

▶ **Understand Vocabulary** ••••••••••••••••••••••••••••

Draw a line to match the word with its definition.

1. closed shape •

2. line segment •

3. right angle •

4. hexagon •

5. angle •

6. polygon •

• A part of a line that includes two endpoints and all the points between them

• A shape formed by two rays that share an endpoint

• A shape that starts and ends at the same point

• An angle that forms a square corner

• A closed plane shape made up of line segments

• A polygon with 6 sides and 6 angles

Preview Words

angle

closed shape

hexagon

intersecting lines

line

line segment

open shape

parallel lines

perpendicular lines

point

polygon

✓ quadrilateral

ray

✓ rectangle

✓ rhombus

right angle

✓ square

trapezoid

✓ triangle

Venn diagram

vertex

• Interactive Student Edition
• Multimedia eGlossary

Chapter 12 Vocabulary

angle

ángulo

2

endpoint

extremo

19

intersecting lines

líneas secantes

36

line

línea

42

line segment

segmento

44

octagon

octágono

54

parallel lines

líneas paralelas

56

pentagon

pentágono

58

The point at either end of a line segment

endpoints

A shape formed by two rays that share an endpoint

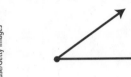

A straight path extending in both directions with no endpoints

Lines that meet or cross

A polygon with eight sides and eight angles

A part of a line that includes two points, called endpoints, and all of the points between them

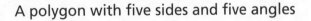

A polygon with five sides and five angles

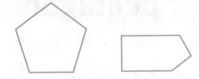

Lines in the same plane that never cross and are always the same distance apart

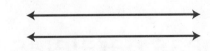

perpendicular lines

líneas perpendiculares

60

polygon

polígono

64

quadrilateral

cuadrilátero

66

ray

semirrecta

68

rhombus

rombo

71

trapezoid

trapecio

78

Venn diagram

diagrama de Venn

81

vertex

vértice

82

A closed plane shape with straight sides that are line segments

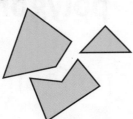

Lines that intersect to form right angles

A part of a line, with one endpoint, that is straight and continues in one direction

A polygon with four sides and four angles

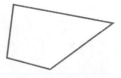

A quadrilateral with at least one pair of parallel sides

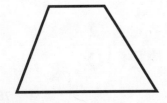

A quadrilateral with two pairs of parallel sides and four sides of equal length

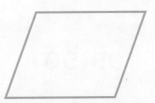

The point at which two rays of an angle or two (or more) line segments meet in a plane shape or where three or more edges meet in a solid shape

Examples:

vertex

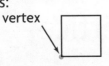

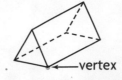

vertex

A diagram that shows relationships among sets of things

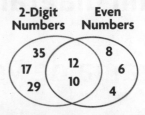

Going to an Art Museum

For 2 players

Materials

- 1 red playing piece
- 1 blue playing piece
- 1 number cube
- Clue Cards

How to Play

1. Choose a playing piece and put it on START.
2. Toss the number cube to take a turn. Move your playing piece that many spaces.
3. If you land on one of these spaces, follow the instructions.

   Blue Space Follow the directions printed in the space.

   Red Space Take a Clue Card from the pile. If you answer the question correctly, keep the Clue Card. If you do not, return the Clue Card to the bottom of the pile.
4. Collect at least 5 Clue Cards. Move around the track as many times as necessary.
5. Only when you have 5 Clue Cards, follow the closest center path to reach FINISH.
6. The first player to reach FINISH wins.

Word Box
angle
endpoints
intersecting lines
line
line segment
octagon
parallel lines
pentagon
perpendicular lines
polygon
quadrilateral
ray
rhombus
trapezoid
Venn diagram
vertex

TAKE A
CLUE CARD

Your favorite
artist's work is
on display.
Move ahead 1.

FINISH

TAKE A
CLUE CARD

You stand too close
to a painting and
set off the alarms.
Go back 1.

The museum is closed today. Go back 1.

TAKE A CLUE CARD

Free tours today! Move ahead 1.

FINISH

TAKE A CLUE CARD

START ▶

The Write Way

Reflect

Choose one idea. Write about it.

- In two minutes, draw and label as many examples of polygons that you can. Use a separate piece of paper for your drawing.
- Work with a partner to explain and illustrate parallel, intersecting, and perpendicular lines. Use a separate piece of paper for your drawing.
- A reader of your math advice column writes, "I confuse rhombuses, squares, rectangles, and trapezoids. How can I tell the difference between these quadrilaterals?" Write a letter to your reader offering step-by-step advice.

Describe Plane Shapes

Essential Question What are some ways to describe two-dimensional shapes?

Learning Objective You will describe the attributes of two-dimensional shapes and write whether a shape is open or closed.

 Unlock the Problem Real World

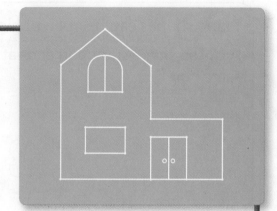

An architect draws plans for houses, stores, offices, and other buildings. Look at the shapes in the drawing at the right.

A **plane shape** is a shape on a flat surface. It is formed by points that make curved paths, line segments, or both.

point		**line**	
• is an exact position or location	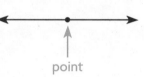	• is a straight path • continues in both directions • does not end	
endpoints		**line segment**	
• points that are used to show segments of lines		• is straight • is part of a line • has 2 endpoints	• •

ray •———————►

• is straight • is part of a line • has 1 endpoint • continues in one direction

Some plane shapes are made by connecting line segments at their endpoints. One example is a square. Describe a square using math words.

Think: How many line segments and endpoints does a square have?

A square has ____ line segments. The line

segments meet only at their _____.

Math Talk

Math Processes and Practices ❸

Apply Why can you not measure the length of a line?

Chapter 12   697

Plane shapes have length and width but no thickness, so they are also called **two-dimensional shapes**.

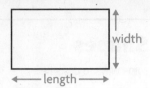

width

← length →

Try This! Draw plane shapes.

Plane shapes can be open or closed.

A **closed shape** starts and ends at the same point.

In the space below, draw more examples of closed shapes.

An **open shape** does not start and end at the same point.

In the space below, draw more examples of open shapes.

Math Talk

Math Processes and Practices ⑥

Explain whether a shape with a curved path must be a closed shape, an open shape, or can be either.

- Is the plane shape at the right a closed shape or an open shape? Explain how you know.

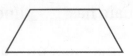

_____

_____

Name _____

1. Write how many line segments

   the shape has. _____

Circle all the words that describe the shape.

2.	3.	✓4.	5. 
ray	open shape	open shape	line
point	closed shape	closed shape	line segment

Write whether the shape is *open* or *closed*.

6.	7.	✓8.	9.
_____	_____	_____	_____

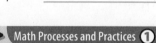

Math Talk — Math Processes and Practices ①

Describe How do you know whether a shape is open or closed?

On Your Own

Write how many line segments the shape has.

10.	11.	12.	13.
_____ line segments	_____ line segments	_____ line segments	_____ line segments

Write whether the shape is *open* or *closed*.

14.	15.	16.	17. 
_____	_____	_____	_____

Problem Solving • Applications

18. What's the Error? Brittany says there are two endpoints in the shape shown at the right. Is she correct? Explain.

_____

_____

19. (Math Processes and Practices 6) **Explain** how you can make the shape at the right a closed shape. Change the shape so it is a closed shape.

_____

_____

20. GO DEEPER Look at Carly's drawing at the right. What did she draw? How is it like a line? How is it different? Change the drawing so that it is a line.

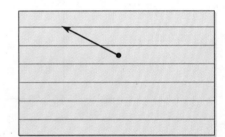

_____

_____

21. THINK SMARTER Draw a closed shape in the workspace by connecting 5 line segments at their endpoints.

22. THINK SMARTER Draw each shape where it belongs in the table.

Closed Shape	Open Shape

Name _____

Describe Plane Shapes

Learning Objective You will describe the attributes of two-dimensional shapes and write whether a shape is open or closed.

Write how many line segments the shape has.

1.

___4___ line segments

2.

_____ line segments

Write whether the shape is *open* or *closed*.

3.

_____

4.

_____

Problem Solving · Real World

5. Carl wants to show a closed shape in his drawing. Show and explain how to make the drawing a closed shape.

_____

_____

6. The shape of a fish pond at a park is shown below. Is the shape open or closed?

_____

7. **WRITE** ▸Math Draw an open shape and a closed shape. Label your shapes.

_____

_____

Lesson Check

1. How many line segments does this shape have?

_____

2. What is part of a line, has one endpoint, and continues in one direction?

_____

Spiral Review

3. What multiplication sentence does the array show?

▢▢▢▢▢▢▢
▢▢▢▢▢▢▢
▢▢▢▢▢▢▢
▢▢▢▢▢▢▢

_____

_____

4. What is the unknown factor and quotient?

$9 \times \boxed{} = 27$

$27 \div 9 = \boxed{}$

_____

_____

5. What fraction is equivalent to $\frac{4}{8}$?

_____

6. Mr. MacTavish has 30 students from his class going on a field trip to the zoo. He puts 6 students in each group. How many groups of students will he make?

_____

FOR MORE PRACTICE
GO TO THE
Personal Math Trainer

Name _____

Describe Angles in Plane Shapes

Essential Question How can you describe angles in plane shapes?

Learning Objective You will describe angles by telling how many of each type of angle a shape has and by measuring to compare an angle measure with the measure of a right angle.

🔑 Unlock the Problem

An **angle** is formed by two rays that share an endpoint. Plane shapes have angles formed by two line segments that share an endpoint. The shared endpoint is called a **vertex**. The plural of *vertex* is *vertices*.

vertex ⟶

Jason drew this shape on dot paper.

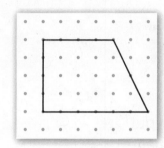

• How many angles are in Jason's shape?

_____

Look at the angles in the shape that Jason drew.

How can you describe the angles?

🔓 **Describe angles.**

This mark means *right angle*.

A **right angle** is an angle that forms a square corner.

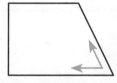

Some angles are less than a right angle.

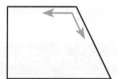

Some angles are greater than a right angle.

Look at Jason's shape.

Two angles are _____ angles, _____ angle

is _____ a right angle, and _____ angle

is _____ a right angle.

Math Talk Math Processes and Practices ❶

Analyze What are some examples of these types of angles that you see in everyday life? Describe where you see them and what types of angles you see.

Activity Model angles.

Materials ■ bendable straws ■ scissors ■ paper ■ pencil

- Cut a small slit in the shorter section of a bendable straw. Cut off the shorter section of a second straw and the bendable part. Insert the slit end of the first straw into the second straw.

cut slit   cut off   insert

straw 1   straw 2   straw 1   straw 2

- Make an angle with the straws you put together. Compare the angle you made to a corner of the sheet of paper.

- Open and close the straws to make other types of angles.

In the space below, trace the angles you made with the straws. Label each *right angle*, *less than a right angle*, or *greater than a right angle*.

Share and Show

1. How many angles are in the triangle at the right?

   _____

Math Talk Math Processes and Practices ②

Use Reasoning How do you know an angle is greater than or less than a right angle?

Use the corner of a sheet of paper to tell whether the angle is a *right angle, less than a right angle,* or *greater than a right angle.*

2.

_____

3.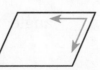

_____

✓4.

_____

Name _____

Write how many of each type of angle the shape has.

5.

_____ right

_____ less than a right

_____ greater than a right

6.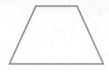

_____ right

_____ less than a right

_____ greater than a right

☑**7.**

_____ right

_____ less than a right

_____ greater than a right

On Your Own

Use the corner of a sheet of paper to tell whether the angle is a _right angle_, _less than a right angle_, or _greater than a right angle_.

8.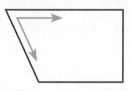

_____

9.

_____

10.

_____

Math Processes and Practices ① Analyze Relationships **Write how many of each type of angle the shape has.**

11.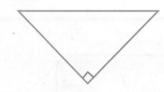

_____ right

_____ less than a right

_____ greater than a right

12.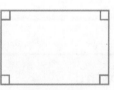

_____ right

_____ less than a right

_____ greater than a right

13.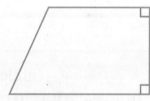

_____ right

_____ less than a right

_____ greater than a right

14. THINK SMARTER Describe the types of angles formed when you divide a circle into 4 equal parts.

_____

Unlock the Problem

15. Holly drew the four shapes below.
Which shape does NOT have a right angle?

Q   R   S   T

a. What do you need to know? _____

b. Tell how you might use a sheet of paper to solve the problem.

_____

_____

c. Shape *Q* has _____ right angle(s), _____ angle(s) greater than
a right angle, and _____ angle(s) less than a right angle.

Shape *R* has _____ right angle(s), _____ angle(s) greater than
a right angle, and _____ angle(s) less than a right angle.

Shape *S* has _____ right angle(s), _____ angle(s) greater than
a right angle, and _____ angle(s) less than a right angle.

Shape *T* has _____ right angle(s), _____ angle(s) greater than
a right angle, and _____ angle(s) less than a right angle.

So, shape _____ does not have a right angle.

16. **THINK SMARTER** Circle a number or word
from each box to complete the sentence
to describe all of the angles in this shape.

There are
| 2 |
| 3 |
| 4 |
right angles and
| 2 |
| 3 |
| 4 |
angles
| less |
| greater |

than a right angle.

Name _____

Describe Angles in Plane Shapes

Learning Objective You will describe angles by telling how many of each type of angle a shape has and by measuring to compare an angle measure with the measure of a right angle.

Use the corner of a sheet of paper to tell whether the angle is a _right angle, less than a right angle,_ or _greater than a right angle._

1.

   <u>less than a right angle</u>

2.

   _____

3.

   _____

Write how many of each type of angle the shape has.

4.

   _____ right

   _____ less than a right

   _____ greater than a right

5.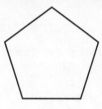

   _____ right

   _____ less than a right

   _____ greater than a right

6.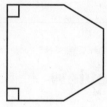

   _____ right

   _____ less than a right

   _____ greater than a right

 Problem Solving Real World

7. Jeff has a square piece of art paper. He cuts across it from one corner to the opposite corner to make two pieces. What is the total number of sides and angles in both of the new shapes?

8. **WRITE** ✏️ *Math* Draw an example of a shape that has at least one right angle, one angle less than a right angle, and one angle greater than a right angle. Label the angles.

_____

_____

_____

_____

Lesson Check

1. What describes this angle?
Write *right angle, less than a right angle,* or *greater than a right angle.*

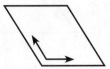

_____

_____

2. How many right angles does this shape have?

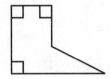

_____

_____

Spiral Review

3. What fraction of the group is shaded?

_____

4. Compare.

$\frac{4}{8} \bigcirc \frac{3}{8}$

5. What is straight, continues in both directions, and does not end?

6. How many line segments does this shape have?

_____

_____

708

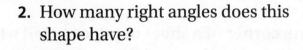

FOR MORE PRACTICE
GO TO THE
Personal Math Trainer

Name _____

Identify Polygons

Essential Question How can you use line segments and angles to make polygons?

Learning Objective You will use line segments and angles to name and describe polygons by telling the number of sides and the number of angles a shape has.

CONNECT In earlier lessons, you learned about line segments and angles. In this lesson, you will see how line segments and angles make polygons.

A **polygon** is a closed plane shape that is made up of line segments that meet only at their endpoints. Each line segment in a polygon is a **side**.

> ### Math Idea
> All polygons are closed shapes. Not all closed shapes are polygons.

🔑 Unlock the Problem

Circle all the words that describe the shape.

A	B	C	D

plane shape	plane shape	plane shape	plane shape
open shape	open shape	open shape	open shape
closed shape	closed shape	closed shape	closed shape
curved paths	curved paths	curved paths	curved paths
line segments	line segments	line segments	line segments
polygon	polygon	polygon	polygon

Try This!

Fill in the blanks with *sometimes*, *always*, or *never*.

Polygons are _____ plane shapes.

Polygons are _____ closed shapes.

Polygons are _____ open shapes.

Plane shapes are _____ polygons.

> **Math Talk**
>
> Math Processes and Practices ②
>
> **Reason Abstractly**
> Why are not all closed shapes polygons?

Name Polygons Polygons are named by the
number of sides and angles they have.

Some traffic signs are in the shape of
polygons. A stop sign is in the shape of
which polygon?

angle

side →

🔑 **Count the number of sides and angles.**

triangle	quadrilateral	pentagon
3 sides	4 sides	_____ sides
3 angles	_____ angles	5 angles
		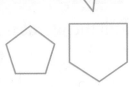

hexagon	octagon	decagon
_____ sides	8 sides	_____ sides
6 angles	_____ angles	10 angles

How many sides does the stop sign have? _____

How many angles? _____

So, a stop sign is in the shape of an _____.

Math Talk

Math Processes and Practices ⑧

Generalize Compare
the number of sides
and angles. What is a
true statement about
all polygons?

Share and Show 🖊 MATH BOARD

1. The shape at the right is a polygon. Circle all the words
that describe the shape.

   plane shape   open shape   closed shape   pentagon

   curved paths   line segments   hexagon   quadrilateral

710

Name _____

Is the shape a polygon? Write *yes* or *no*.

2.

_____

3.

_____

☑4.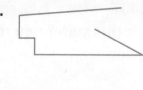

_____

Write the number of sides and the number of angles. Then name the polygon.

Math Talk

Math Processes and Practices ③

Apply How can you change the shape in Exercise 4 to make it a polygon?

5.

_____ sides

_____ angles

_____

6.

_____ sides

_____ angles

_____

☑7.

_____ sides

_____ angles

_____

On Your Own

Is the shape a polygon? Write *yes* or *no*.

8.

_____

9.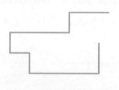

_____

10.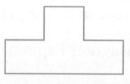

_____

Write the number of sides and the number of angles. Then name the polygon.

11.

_____ sides

_____ angles

_____

12.

_____ sides

_____ angles

_____

13.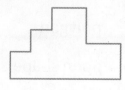

_____ sides

_____ angles

_____

Problem Solving · Applications

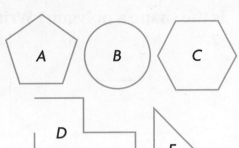

14. **WRITE** ›Math Jake said Shapes A—E are all polygons. Does this statement make sense? Explain your answer.

_____

_____

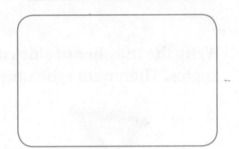

15. **GO DEEPER** I am a closed shape made of 6 line segments. I have 2 angles less than a right angle and no right angles. What shape am I? Draw an example in the workspace.

_____

16. **THINK SMARTER** Is every closed shape a polygon? Use a drawing to help explain your answer.

_____

_____

_____

17. **Math Processes and Practices 3 Make Arguments** Ivan says that the shape at the right is an octagon. Do you agree or disagree? Explain. _____

_____

18. **THINK SMARTER** For numbers 18a–18d, select True or False for each description of this shape.

18a. polygon   ○ True   ○ False

18b. open shape ○ True   ○ False

18c. hexagon   ○ True   ○ False

18d. pentagon   ○ True   ○ False

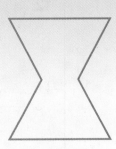

Identify Polygons

Learning Objective You will use line segments and angles to name and describe polygons by telling the number of sides and the number of angles a shape has.

Is the shape a polygon? Write *yes* or *no*.

1.

   ___no___

2.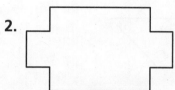

   _____

Write the number of sides and the number of angles. Then name the polygon.

3.

   _____ sides

   _____ angles

   _____

4.

   _____ sides

   _____ angles

   _____

Problem Solving Real World

5. Mr. Murphy has an old coin that has ten sides. If its shape is a polygon, how many angles does the old coin have?

   _____

6. Lin says that an octagon has six sides. Chris says that it has eight sides. Whose statement is correct?

   _____

7. **WRITE** *Math* Draw a pentagon. Explain how you knew the number of sides and angles to draw.

   _____

   _____

Lesson Check

1. What is a name for this polygon?

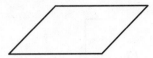

_____

2. How many sides does this polygon have?

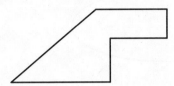

_____

Spiral Review

3. How many right angles does this shape have?

_____

4. Erica has 8 necklaces. One fourth of the necklaces are blue. How many necklaces are blue?

_____

5. What is straight, is part of a line, and has 2 endpoints?

_____

6. What describes this angle? Write *right angle, less than a right angle,* or *greater than a right angle.*

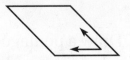

_____

714

FOR MORE PRACTICE
GO TO THE
Personal Math Trainer

Name _____

Describe Sides of Polygons

Essential Question How can you describe line segments that are sides of polygons?

Learning Objective You will describe line segments that are sides of polygons and determine whether they appear to be intersecting, perpendicular, or parallel.

⚿ Unlock the Problem (Real World)

Look at the polygon. How many pairs of sides are parallel?

- How do you know the shape is a polygon?

_____

_____

TYPES OF LINES	TYPES OF LINE SEGMENTS
Lines that cross or meet are **intersecting lines**. Intersecting lines form angles. 	The orange and blue line segments meet and form an angle. So, they are _____.
Intersecting lines that cross or meet to form right angles are **perpendicular lines**. 	The red and blue line segments meet to form a right angle. So, they are _____.
Lines that never cross or meet and are always the same distance apart are **parallel lines**. They do not form any angles. 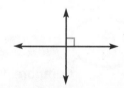	The green and blue line segments would never cross or meet. They are always the same distance apart. So, they appear to be _____.

So, the polygon above has _____ pair of parallel sides.

Math Talk

Math Processes and Practices ②

Use Reasoning Why can't parallel lines ever cross?

Try This! Draw a polygon with only 1 pair of parallel sides. Then draw a polygon with 2 pairs of parallel sides. Outline each pair of parallel sides with a different color.

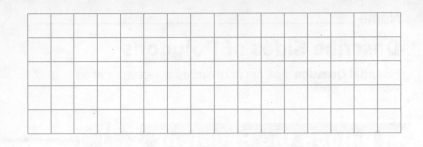

1. Which sides appear to be parallel?

_____

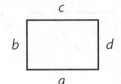

c

b   d

a

Think: Which pairs of sides appear to be the same distance apart?

Look at the green sides of the polygon. Tell if they appear to be *intersecting*, *perpendicular*, or *parallel*. Write all the words that describe the sides.

2.
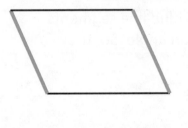

_____

_____

☑3.

_____

_____

☑4.
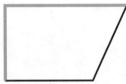

_____

_____

On Your Own

Look at the green sides of the polygon. Tell if they appear to be *intersecting*, *perpendicular*, or *parallel*. Write all the words that describe the sides.

Math Talk Math Processes and Practices ⑥

Compare How are intersecting and perpendicular lines alike and how are they different?

5.

_____

_____

6.

_____

_____

7.

_____

_____

716

Name _____

Use pattern blocks *A–E* for 8–11.

Chelsea wants to sort pattern blocks by the types of sides.

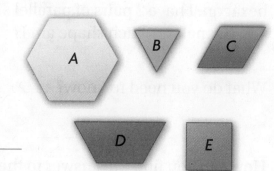

8. Which blocks have intersecting sides?

_____

9. Which blocks have parallel sides?

_____

10. Which blocks have perpendicular sides?

_____

11. Which blocks have neither parallel nor perpendicular sides?

_____

12. GO DEEPER   On the box at the right, how many pairs of edges are perpendicular line segments?

_____

▲ The red line segments show some pairs of perpendicular line segments.

13. THINK SMARTER   Can the same two lines be parallel, perpendicular, and intersecting? Explain your answer.

_____

_____

_____

🔑 Unlock the Problem

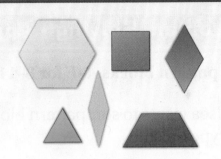

14. **Math Processes and Practices ③ Compare Representations** I am a pattern block that has 2 fewer sides than a hexagon. I have 2 pairs of parallel sides and 4 right angles. Which shape am I?

a. What do you need to know? _____

_____

b. How can you find the answer to the riddle? _____

_____

c. Write *yes* or *no* in the table to solve the riddle.

2 fewer sides than a hexagon					
exactly 2 pairs of parallel sides					
4 right angles					

So, the _____ is the shape.

15. **THINK SMARTER** Select the shapes that have at least one pair of parallel sides. Mark all that apply.

(A)

(C)

(B)

(D)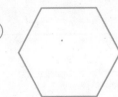

Describe Sides of Polygons

Learning Objective You will describe line segments that are sides of polygons and determine whether they appear to be intersecting, perpendicular, or parallel.

Look at the dashed sides of the polygon. Tell if they appear to be *intersecting*, *perpendicular*, or *parallel*. Write all the words that describe the sides.

1.

___parallel___

2.

_____

3.

_____

4.

_____

5.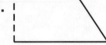

_____

6.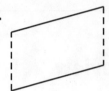

_____

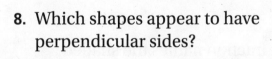

Use shapes *A–D* for 7–8.

7. Which shapes appear to have parallel sides?

_____

8. Which shapes appear to have perpendicular sides?

_____

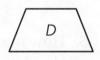

9. **WRITE** ▸*Math* Give some examples of perpendicular lines inside or outside your classroom.

_____

_____

Lesson Check

1. How many pairs of parallel sides does the quadrilateral appear to have?

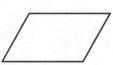

_____

2. Which sides appear to be parallel?

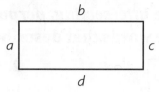

_____

Spiral Review

3. Mr. Lance designed a class banner shaped like the polygon shown. What is the name of the polygon?

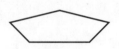

_____

4. How many angles greater than a right angle does this shape have?

_____

5. How many line segments does this shape have?

_____

6. What fraction names the shaded part?

_____

FOR MORE PRACTICE
GO TO THE
Personal Math Trainer

Name _____

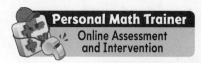

Vocabulary

Choose the best term from the box to complete the sentence.

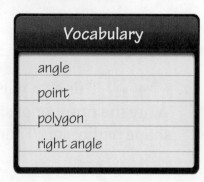

Vocabulary
angle
point
polygon
right angle

1. An _____ is formed by two rays that share an endpoint. (p. 703)

2. A _____ is a closed plane shape made up of line segments. (p. 709)

3. A _____ forms a square corner. (p. 703)

Concepts and Skills

Use the corner of a sheet of paper to tell whether the angle is a *right angle, less than a right angle,* or *greater than a right angle.*

4.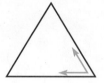

_____

5.

_____

6.

_____

Write the number of sides and the number of angles. Then name the polygon.

7.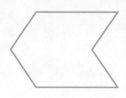

____ sides

____ angles

_____

8.

____ sides

____ angles

_____

9.

____ sides

____ angles

_____

10. Anne drew the shape at the right. Is her shape an open shape or a closed shape?

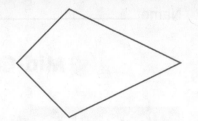

_____

11. GO DEEPER This sign tells drivers there is a steep hill ahead. Write the number of sides and the number of angles in the shape of the sign. Then name the shape.

_____

12. Why is this closed plane shape NOT a polygon?

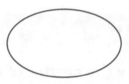

_____

_____

13. Sean drew a shape with 2 fewer sides than an octagon. Which shape did he draw?

_____

14. John drew a polygon with two line segments that meet to form a right angle. Circle the words that describe the line segments.

| intersecting |
| curved |
| parallel |
| perpendicular |

Classify Quadrilaterals

Essential Question How can you use sides and angles to help you describe quadrilaterals?

Learning Objective You will describe, classify, and compare quadrilaterals based on their attributes.

 Unlock the Problem

Quadrilaterals are named by their sides and their angles.

Describe quadrilaterals.

quadrilateral

_____ sides

_____ angles

 ! ERROR Alert

Some quadrilaterals cannot be classified as a trapezoid, rectangle, square, or rhombus.

trapezoid

at least _____ pair of opposite sides that are parallel
lengths of sides could be the same

rectangle

_____ pairs of opposite sides that are parallel

_____ pairs of sides that are of equal length

_____ right angles

square

_____ pairs of opposite sides that are parallel

_____ sides that are of equal length

_____ right angles

rhombus

_____ pairs of opposite sides that are parallel

_____ sides that are of equal length

 Math Talk

Math Processes and Practices 8

Generalize Why can a square also be named a rectangle or a rhombus?

Share and Show MATH BOARD

Look at the quadrilateral at the right.

1. Outline each pair of opposite sides that are parallel with a different color. How many pairs of opposite sides appear to be parallel? _____

2. Look at the parallel sides you colored.

   The sides in each pair are of _____ length.

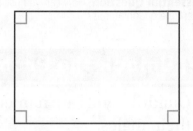

Think: All the angles are right angles.

✓ 3. Name the quadrilateral in as many ways as you can.

   _____

Circle all the words that describe the quadrilateral.

4.

rectangle

rhombus

square

trapezoid

5.

rhombus

quadrilateral

square

rectangle

✓ 6.

rectangle

rhombus

trapezoid

quadrilateral

On Your Own

Circle all the words that describe the quadrilateral.

7.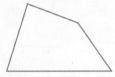

rectangle

trapezoid

quadrilateral

rhombus

8.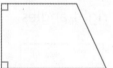

rectangle

rhombus

trapezoid

square

9.

quadrilateral

square

rectangle

rhombus

Math Talk

Math Processes and Practices ①

Analyze How can you have a rhombus that is not a square?

724

Name _____

Use the quadrilaterals at the right for 10–12.

10. Which quadrilaterals appear to have 4 right angles?

   _____

11. Which quadrilaterals appear to have 2 pairs of opposite sides that are parallel?

   _____

12. Which quadrilaterals appear to have no right angles?

   _____

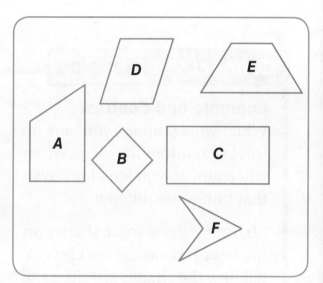

Write *all* or *some* to complete the sentence for 13–18.

13. The opposite sides of _____ rectangles are parallel.

14. _____ sides of a rhombus are the same length.

15. _____ squares are rectangles.

16. _____ rhombuses are squares.

17. _____ quadrilaterals are polygons.

18. _____ polygons are quadrilaterals.

19. **Math Processes and Practices ⑥** Circle the shape at the right that is not a quadrilateral. **Explain** your choice.

   _____

   _____

   _____

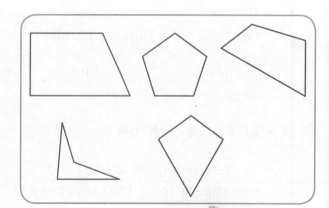

20. **THINK SMARTER** I am a polygon that has 4 sides and 4 angles. At least one of my angles is less than a right angle. Circle all the shapes that I could be.

   quadrilateral   rectangle   square   rhombus   trapezoid

21. *THINK SMARTER*   Identify the quadrilateral that can have two pairs of parallel sides and no right angles.

(A) rhombus   (B) square   (C) rectangle

Connect to Reading

Compare and Contrast

When you *compare*, you look for ways that things are alike. When you *contrast*, you look for ways that things are different.

Mr. Briggs drew some shapes on the board. He asked the class to tell how the shapes are alike and how they are different.

GO DEEPER   **Complete the sentences.**

- Shapes _____, _____, _____, _____, _____, _____, and _____ are polygons.

- Shapes _____, _____, and _____ are not polygons.

- Shapes _____, _____, _____, and _____ are quadrilaterals.

- Shapes _____, _____, and _____ appear to have only 1 pair of opposite sides that are parallel.

- Shapes _____, _____, and _____ appear to have 2 pairs of opposite sides that are parallel.

- All 4 sides of shapes _____ and _____ appear to be the same length.

- In these polygons, all sides do not appear to be the same length. _____

- These shapes can be called rhombuses. _____

- Shapes _____ and _____ are quadrilaterals but cannot be called rhombuses.

- Shape _____ is a rhombus and can be called a square.

Name _____

Classify Quadrilaterals

Learning Objective You will describe, classify, and compare quadrilaterals based on their attributes.

Circle all the words that describe the quadrilateral.

1.

   (square)

   (rectangle)

   (rhombus)

   (trapezoid)

2.

   square

   rectangle

   rhombus

   trapezoid

3.

   square

   rectangle

   rhombus

   trapezoid

Use the quadrilaterals below for 4–6.

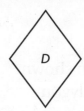

A   B   C   D   E

4. Which quadrilaterals appear to have no right angles?

   _____

5. Which quadrilaterals appear to have 4 right angles?

   _____

6. Which quadrilaterals appear to have 4 sides of equal length?

   _____

Problem Solving · Real World

7. A picture on the wall in Jeremy's classroom has 4 right angles, 4 sides of equal length, and 2 pairs of opposite sides that are parallel. What quadrilateral best describes the picture?

   _____

8. **WRITE** ▸ *Math* Explain how a trapezoid and a rectangle are different.

   _____

   _____

   _____

Lesson Check

1. What word describes the quadrilateral?

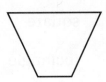

_____

2. Which quadrilaterals appear to have 2 pairs of opposite sides that are parallel?

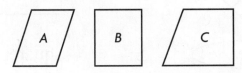

_____

Spiral Review

3. Aiden drew the the polygon shown. What is the name of the polygon he drew?

_____

4. How many pairs of parallel sides does this shape appear to have?

_____

5. What word describes the dashed sides of the shape shown? Write *intersecting, perpendicular,* or *parallel.*

_____

6. How many right angles does this shape have?

_____

FOR MORE PRACTICE GO TO THE Personal Math Trainer

Name _____

Draw Quadrilaterals

Essential Question How can you draw quadrilaterals?

Learning Objective You will use grid paper to draw and name quadrilaterals then draw polygons that do not belong in a set of quadrilaterals and explain why.

Unlock the Problem

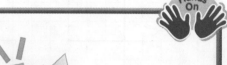

CONNECT You have learned to classify quadrilaterals by the number of pairs of opposite sides that are parallel, by the number of pairs of sides of equal length, and by the number of right angles.

How can you draw quadrilaterals?

Activity 1 Use grid paper to draw quadrilaterals.

Materials ▪ ruler

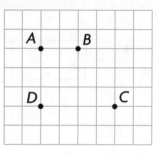

- Use a ruler to draw line segments from points *A* to *B*, from *B* to *C*, from *C* to *D*, and from *D* to *A*.

- Write the name of your quadrilateral.

_____

Activity 2 Draw a shape that does not belong.

Materials ▪ ruler

Ⓐ Here are three examples of a quadrilateral. Draw an example of a polygon that is not a quadrilateral.

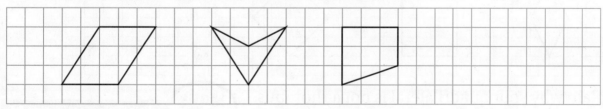

- Explain why your polygon is not a quadrilateral.

_____

_____

B Here are three examples of a square.
Draw a quadrilateral that is not a square.

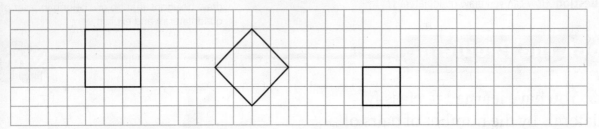

- Explain why your quadrilateral is not a square.

_____

_____

C Here are three examples of a rectangle.
Draw a quadrilateral that is not a rectangle.

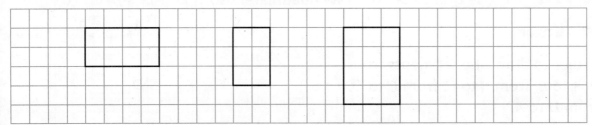

- Explain why your quadrilateral is not a rectangle.

_____

_____

D Here are three examples of a rhombus.
Draw a quadrilateral that is not a rhombus.

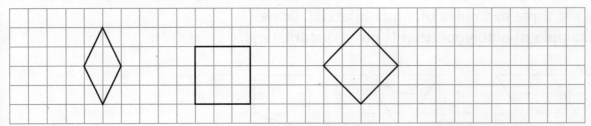

- Explain why your quadrilateral is not a rhombus.

Math Talk

Math Processes and Practices **3**

Compare Representations
Compare your drawings with your classmates. Explain how your drawings are alike and how they are different.

Name _____

1. Choose four endpoints, and connect them to make a rectangle.

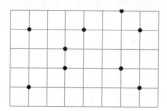

Think: A rectangle has 2 pairs of opposite sides that are parallel, 2 pairs of sides of equal length, and 4 right angles.

Draw a quadrilateral that is described.
Name the quadrilateral you drew.

☑ 2. 2 pairs of sides of equal length

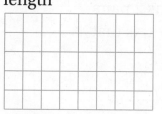

Name _____

☑ 3. 4 sides of equal length

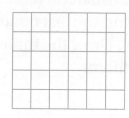

Name _____

Math Talk

Math Processes and Practices ⑥

Compare Explain one way the quadrilaterals you drew are alike and one way they are different.

On Your Own

Practice: Copy and Solve Use grid paper to draw a quadrilateral that is described. Name the quadrilateral you drew.

4. exactly 1 pair of opposite sides that are parallel

5. 4 right angles

6. 2 pairs of sides of equal length

Draw a quadrilateral that does not belong. Then explain why.

7.

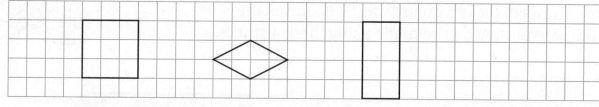

_____

8.

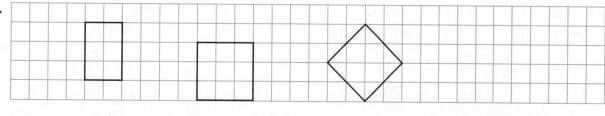

_____

© Houghton Mifflin Harcourt Publishing Company

Problem Solving • Applications

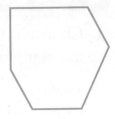

9. **Math Processes and Practices ❸** **Make Arguments** Jacki drew the shape at the right. She said it is a rectangle because it has 2 pairs of opposite sides that are parallel. Describe her error.

_____

_____

10. **GO DEEPER** Adam drew three quadrilaterals. One quadrilateral has no pairs of parallel sides, one quadrilateral has exactly 1 pair of opposite sides that are parallel, and the last quadrilateral has 2 pairs of opposite sides that are parallel. Draw the three quadrilaterals that Adam could have drawn. Name them.

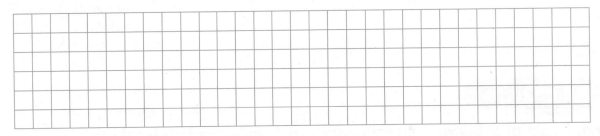

_____   _____   _____

11. **THINK SMARTER** Amy has 4 straws of equal length. Name all the quadrilaterals that can be made using these 4 straws.

_____ Amy cuts one of the straws in half. She uses the two halves and two of the other straws to make a quadrilateral. Name all the quadrilaterals that can be made using these 4 straws.

_____

12. **THINK SMARTER +** Jordan drew one side of a quadrilateral with 2 pairs of opposite sides that are parallel. Draw the other 3 sides to complete Jordan's quadrilateral.

Personal Math Trainer

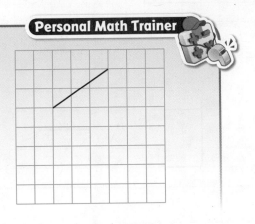

Draw Quadrilaterals

Learning Objective You will use grid paper to draw and name quadrilaterals then draw polygons that do not belong in a set of quadrilaterals and explain why.

**Draw a quadrilateral that is described.
Name the quadrilateral you drew.**

1. always has 4 sides of equal length

square or rhombus

2. only 1 pair of opposite sides that are parallel

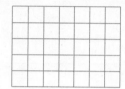

_____

**Draw a quadrilateral that does not belong.
Then explain why.**

3.

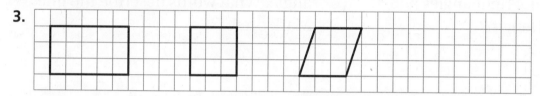

_____

_____

_____

Problem Solving Real World

4. Layla drew a quadrilateral with 4 right angles and 2 pairs of opposite sides that are parallel. What quadrilateral best describes her drawing?

_____

_____

5. **WRITE** ▸*Math* Draw a quadrilateral that is NOT a rectangle. Describe your shape, and explain why it is not a rectangle.

_____

_____

Lesson Check

1. Chloe drew a quadrilateral with 2 pairs of opposite sides that are parallel. Name all the shapes that could be Chloe's quadrilateral.

_____

_____

2. Mike drew a quadrilateral with four right angles. Name all the shapes he could have drawn.

_____

_____

Spiral Review

3. What is the name of the quadrilateral that always has 4 right angles and 4 sides of equal length?

_____

4. Mark drew two lines that form a right angle. What words describe the lines Mark drew?

_____

5. Dennis drew the rectangle on grid paper. What is the perimeter of the rectangle Dennis drew?

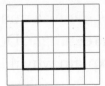

_____

6. Jill drew the rectangle on grid paper. What is the area of the rectangle Jill drew?

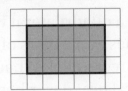

_____

FOR MORE PRACTICE
GO TO THE
Personal Math Trainer

Name _____

Describe Triangles

Essential Question How can you use sides and angles to help you describe triangles?

Learning Objective You will model, describe, and compare triangles based on the number of sides that have equal length and the types of angles they have.

🔑 Unlock the Problem

How can you use straws of different lengths to make triangles?

🔓 **Activity** **Materials** ■ straws ■ scissors ■ MathBoard

STEP 1 Cut straws into different lengths.

STEP 2 Find straw pieces that you can put together to make a triangle. Draw your triangle on the MathBoard.

STEP 3 Find straw pieces that you cannot put together to make a triangle.

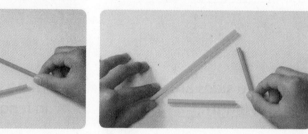

1. Compare the lengths of the sides. Describe when you can make a triangle.

_____

_____

Math Talk

Math Processes and Practices ②

Reason Abstractly What if you have three straws of equal length? Can you make a triangle?

2. **Math Processes and Practices ①** **Describe** when you cannot make a triangle.

_____

_____

_____

3. Explain how you can change the straw pieces in

Step 3 to make a triangle. _____

_____

Ways to Describe Triangles

What are two ways triangles can be described?

🔓 One Way

Triangles can be described by the number of sides that are of equal length.

Draw a line to match the description of the triangle(s).

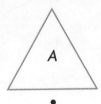 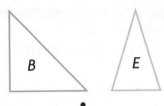 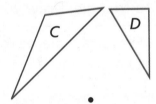

No sides are equal in length.

Two sides are equal in length.

Three sides are equal in length.

🔓 Another Way

Triangles can be described by the types of angles they have.

Draw a line to match the description of the triangle(s).

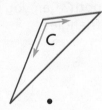  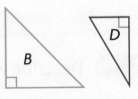

One angle is a right angle.

One angle is greater than a right angle.

Three angles are less than a right angle.

Math Talk

Math Processes and Practices ②

Use Reasoning Can a triangle have two right angles?

Name _____

1. Write the number of sides of equal length the triangle appears to have.

   _____

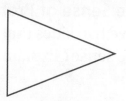

Use the triangles for 2–4. Write F, G, or H.

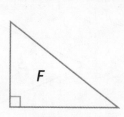  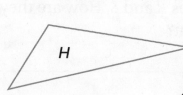

2. Triangle _____ has 1 right angle.

✓3. Triangle _____ has 1 angle greater than a right angle.

✓4. Triangle _____ has 3 angles less than a right angle.

Math Talk Math Processes and Practices ⑧

Generalize Explain the ways you can describe a triangle.

On Your Own

Use the triangles for 5–7. Write K, L, or M.
Then complete the sentences.

 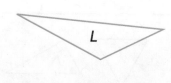 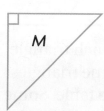

5. Triangle _____ has 1 right angle and appears to have

   _____ sides of equal length.

6. Triangle _____ has 3 angles less than a right angle and

   appears to have _____ sides of equal length.

7. Triangle _____ has 1 angle greater than a right angle and

   appears to have _____ sides of equal length.

Problem Solving • Applications

8. **Math Processes and Practices ①** **Make Sense of Problems** Martin said a triangle can have two sides that are parallel. Does his statement make sense? Explain.

_____

_____

9. **GO DEEPER** Compare Triangles R and S. How are they alike? How are they different?

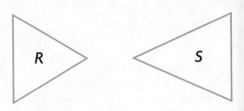

_____

_____

_____

10. **THINK SMARTER** Use a ruler to draw a straight line from one corner of this rectangle to the opposite corner. What shapes did you make? What do you notice about the shapes?

_____

_____

11. **THINK SMARTER** Write the name of each triangle where it belongs in the table. Some triangles might belong in both parts of the table. Some triangles might not belong in either part.

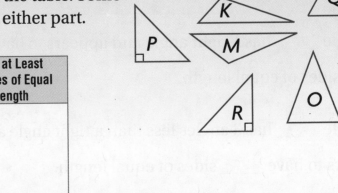

Has 1 Right Angle	Has at Least 2 Sides of Equal Length

Describe Triangles

> **Learning Objective** You will model, describe, and compare triangles based on the number of sides that have equal length and the types of angles they have.

Use the triangles for 1–3. Write *A*, *B*, or *C*.
Then complete the sentences.

  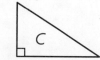

1. Triangle ___**B**___ has 3 angles less than a right angle and

   appears to have ___**3**___ sides of equal length.

2. Triangle _____ has 1 right angle and appears to have

   _____ sides of equal length.

3. Triangle _____ has 1 angle greater than a right angle

   and appears to have _____ sides of equal length.

Problem Solving · Real World

4. Matthew drew the back of his tent. How many sides appear to be of equal length?

5. Sierra made the triangular picture frame shown. How many angles are greater than a right angle?

_____

_____

6. **WRITE** ▸*Math* Draw a triangle that has two sides of equal length and one right angle.

_____

_____

Lesson Check

1. How many angles less than a right angle does this triangle have?

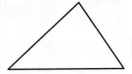

_____

2. How many sides of equal length does this triangle appear to have?

_____

Spiral Review

3. A quadrilateral has 4 right angles, 2 pairs of sides of equal length, and 2 pairs of opposite sides that are parallel. The pairs of opposite sides are not the same length. What quadrilateral could it be?

_____

_____

4. Mason drew a quadrilateral with only one pair of opposite sides that are parallel. What quadrilateral did Mason draw?

_____

_____

5. Draw a rectangle that has an area of 8 square units and a perimeter of 12 units. What are the side lengths of the rectangle?

_____

_____

6. What fraction of the square is shaded?

_____

_____

FOR MORE PRACTICE
GO TO THE
Personal Math Trainer

Name _____

Problem Solving • Classify Plane Shapes

Essential Question How can you use the strategy *draw a diagram* to classify plane shapes?

PROBLEM SOLVING
Lesson 12.8

Learning Objective You will use the strategy *draw a diagram* to classify plane shapes by using a Venn diagram to place shapes that share attributes in each category and determine which shapes fit in the section where the circles overlap.

🔑 🖐 Unlock the Problem · Real World

A **Venn diagram** shows how sets of things are related. In the Venn diagram at the right, one circle has shapes that are rectangles. Shapes that are rhombuses are in the other circle. The shapes in the section where the circles overlap are both rectangles and rhombuses.

What type of quadrilateral is in both circles?

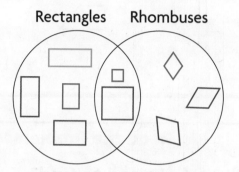

Rectangles   Rhombuses

Read the Problem	**Solve the Problem**
What do I need to find? _____ _____	What is true about all quadrilaterals? _____ Which quadrilaterals always have 2 pairs of opposite sides that are parallel? _____
What information do I need to use? the circles labeled _____ and _____	Which quadrilaterals always have 4 sides of equal length? _____ Which quadrilaterals always have 4 right angles? _____
How will I use the information? _____ _____ _____	The quadrilaterals in the section where the circles overlap always have _____ pairs of opposite sides that are parallel, _____ sides of equal length, and _____ right angles. So, _____ are in both circles.

Math Talk Math Processes and Practices ❶

Make Sense of Problems Does a ▱ fit in the Venn diagram? Explain.

Chapter 12 741

① Try Another Problem

The Venn diagram shows the shapes Andrea used to make a picture. Where would the shape shown below be placed in the Venn diagram?

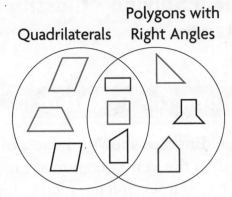

Read the Problem	Solve the Problem
What do I need to find?	**Record the steps you used to solve the problem.**
What information do I need to use?	
How will I use the information?	

1. How many shapes do not have right angles?

_____

2. How many red shapes have right angles but are not quadrilaterals? _____

3. Math Processes and Practices ② **Reason Abstractly** What is a different way to sort the shapes?

_____

_____

 Math Talk

Math Processes and Practices ①

Make Sense of Problems What name can be used to describe all the shapes in the Venn diagram? Explain how you know.

Name _____

Use the Venn diagram for 1–3.

✓ 1. Jordan is sorting the shapes at the right in a Venn diagram. Where does a ◇ go?

   First, look at the sides and angles of the polygons.

   Next, draw the polygons in the Venn diagram.

   The shape has _____ sides of equal length

   and _____ right angles.

   So, the shape goes in the

   _____ .

✓ 2. Where would you place a 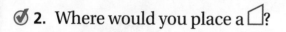?

   _____

3. What if Jordan sorted the shapes by Polygons with Right Angles and Polygons with Angles Less Than a Right Angle? Would the circles still overlap? Explain.

   _____

   _____

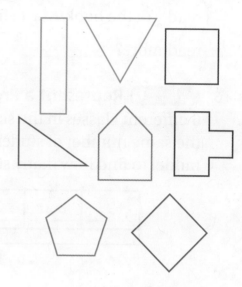

Polygons with Right Angles   Polygons with All Sides Equal in Length

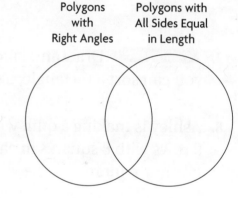

4. **GO DEEPER** Eva drew the Venn diagram below. Write labels she could have used for the diagram.

   _____   _____

   _____   _____

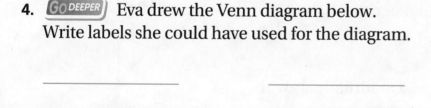

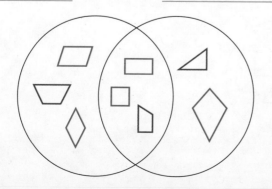

On Your Own

5. Ben and Marta are both reading the same book. Ben has read $\frac{1}{3}$ of the book. Marta has read $\frac{1}{4}$ of the book. Who has read more? _____

6. **Math Processes and Practices 2** **Represent a Problem** There are 42 students from 6 different classes in the school spelling bee. Each class has the same number of students in the spelling bee. Use the bar model to find how many students are from each class.

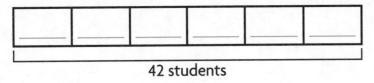

42 students

_____ ÷ _____ = _____

7. **THINK SMARTER** Draw and label a Venn diagram to show one way you can sort a rectangle, a square, a trapezoid, and a rhombus.

8. Ashley is making a quilt with squares of fabric. There are 9 rows with 8 squares in each row. How many squares of fabric are there?

_____

Personal Math Trainer

9. **THINK SMARTER +** Sketch where to place these shapes in the Venn diagram.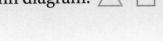

Polygons with All Sides of Equal Length   Quadrilaterals with Right Angles

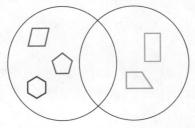

Problem Solving • Classify Plane Shapes

Learning Objective You will use the strategy *draw a diagram* to classify plane shapes by using a Venn diagram to place shapes that share attributes in each category and determine which shapes fit in the section where the circles overlap.

Solve each problem.

1. Steve drew the shapes below. Write the letter of each shape where it belongs in the Venn diagram.

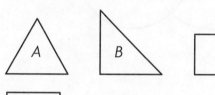

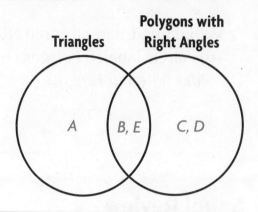

2. Janice drew the shapes below. Write the letter of each shape where it belongs in the Venn diagram.

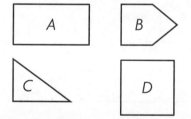

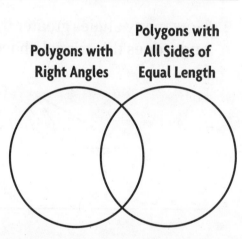

3. **WRITE** ▸*Math* Draw a Venn diagram with one circle labeled *Quadrilaterals* and the other circle labeled *Polygons with at Least 1 Right Angle*. Draw at least two shapes in each section of the diagram. Explain why you drew the shapes you chose in the overlapping section

Lesson Check

1. What shape could go in the section where the two circles overlap?

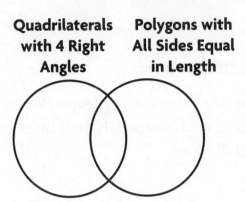

Quadrilaterals with 4 Right Angles   **Polygons with All Sides Equal in Length**

_____

2. What quadrilateral could NOT go in the circle labeled *Polygons with All Sides Equal in Length*?

_____

Spiral Review

3. How many angles greater than a right angle does this triangle have?

_____

4. How many sides of equal length does this triangle appear to have?

_____

5. Madison drew this shape. How many angles less than a right angle does it have?

_____

6. How many dots are in $\frac{1}{2}$ of this group?

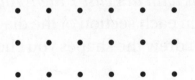

_____

FOR MORE PRACTICE
GO TO THE
Personal Math Trainer

Relate Shapes, Fractions, and Area

Essential Question How can you divide shapes into parts with equal areas and write the area as a unit fraction of the whole?

Learning Objective You will partition figures into parts with equal areas and express the area of each part as a unit fraction of the whole.

Investigate

Materials ▪ pattern blocks ▪ color pencils ▪ ruler

CONNECT You can use what you know about combining and separating plane shapes to explore the relationship between fractions and area.

A. Trace a hexagon pattern block.

B. Divide your hexagon into two parts with equal area.

C. Write the names of the new shapes. _____

D. Write the fraction that names each part of the whole you divided. _____
Each part is $\frac{1}{2}$ of the whole shape's area.

E. Write the fraction that names the whole area. _____

> **Math Idea**
> Equal parts of a whole have equal area.

Draw Conclusions

1. Explain how you know the two shapes have the same area.

   _____

   _____

2. Predict what would happen if you divide the hexagon into three shapes with equal area. What fraction names the area of each part of the divided hexagon? What fraction names the whole area?

   _____

3. *THINK SMARTER* Show how you can divide the hexagon into four shapes with equal area.

   Each part is _____ of the whole shape's area.

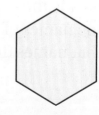

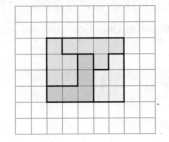

Make Connections

The rectangle at the right is divided into four parts with equal area.

- Write the unit fraction that names each part of the divided whole. _____

- What is the area of each part? _____

- How many $\frac{1}{4}$ parts does it take to make one whole? _____

- Is the shape of each of the $\frac{1}{4}$ parts the same? _____

- Is the area of each of the $\frac{1}{4}$ parts the same? Explain how you know.

_____

_____

Divide the shape into equal parts.

Draw lines to divide the rectangle below into six parts with equal area.

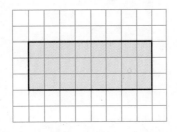

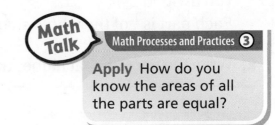

Math Talk

Math Processes and Practices ❸

Apply How do you know the areas of all the parts are equal?

- Write the fraction that names each part of the divided whole. _____

- Write the area of each part. _____

- Each part is _____ of the whole shape's area.

Share and Show

1. Divide the trapezoid into 3 parts with equal area. Write the names of the new shapes. Then write the fraction that names the area of each part of the whole.

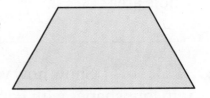

_____

748

Name _____

Draw lines to divide the shape into equal parts that show the fraction given.

2.
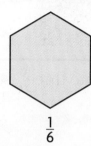
$\frac{1}{6}$

3.
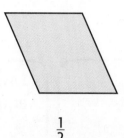
$\frac{1}{2}$

☑ 4.
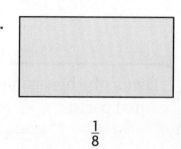
$\frac{1}{8}$

Draw lines to divide the shape into parts with equal area. Write the area of each part as a unit fraction.

5.
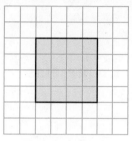
8 equal parts

☑ 6.
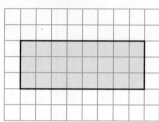
6 equal parts

7.
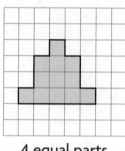
4 equal parts

Problem Solving • Applications (Real World)

8. **Math Processes and Practices ②** **Use Reasoning** If the area of three ◇ is equal to the area of one ⬡, the area of how many ◇ equals four ⬡? Explain your answer.

9. **THINK SMARTER** Divide each shape into the number of equal parts shown. Then write the fraction that describes each part of the whole.

2 equal parts
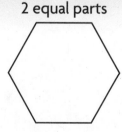

4 equal parts
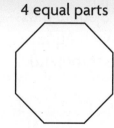

6 equal parts

10. **THINKSMARTER** **Sense or Nonsense?**

Divide the hexagon into six equal parts.

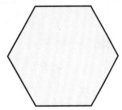

Which pattern block represents $\frac{1}{6}$ of the whole area?

_____

Divide the trapezoid into three equal parts.

Which pattern block represents $\frac{1}{3}$ of the whole area?

_____

Alexis said the area of $\frac{1}{3}$ of the trapezoid is greater than the area of $\frac{1}{6}$ of the hexagon because $\frac{1}{3} > \frac{1}{6}$. Does her statement make sense? Explain your answer.

_____

_____

_____

_____

- Write a statement that makes sense.

  _____

  _____

- **GO DEEPER** What if you divide the hexagon into 3 equal parts? Write a sentence that compares the area of each equal part of the hexagon to each equal part of the trapezoid.

  _____

  _____

Name _____

Relate Shapes, Fractions, and Area

Learning Objective You will partition figures into parts with equal areas and express the area of each part as a unit fraction of the whole.

Draw lines to divide the shape into equal parts that show the fraction given.

1.

$\frac{1}{3}$

2.

$\frac{1}{8}$

3.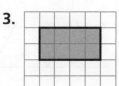

$\frac{1}{2}$

Draw lines to divide the shape into parts with equal area. Write the area of each part as a unit fraction.

4.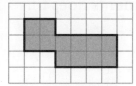

4 equal parts

_____

5.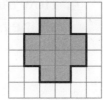

6 equal parts

_____

6.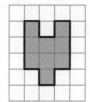

3 equal parts

_____

Problem Solving

7. Robert divided a hexagon into 3 equal parts. Show how he might have divided the hexagon. Write the fraction that names each part of the whole you divided.

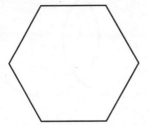

_____ _____

8. **WRITE** ▸ *Math* Trace a pattern block. Divide it into two equal parts, and write a unit fraction to describe the area of each part. Explain your work.

Lesson Check

1. What fraction names each part of the divided whole?

2. What fraction names the whole area that was divided?

_____

_____

Spiral Review

3. Lil drew the figure below. Is the shape open or closed?

4. How many line segments does this shape have?

_____

_____

Use the Venn diagram for 5–6.

5. Where would a square be placed in the Venn diagram?

_____

_____

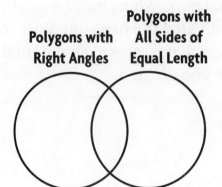

Polygons with Right Angles   Polygons with All Sides of Equal Length

6. Where would a rectangle be placed in the Venn diagram?

_____

_____

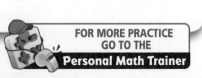

FOR MORE PRACTICE
GO TO THE
Personal Math Trainer

Name _____

✓ Chapter 12 Review/Test

1. Which words describe this shape? Mark all that apply.

   Ⓐ polygon

   Ⓑ open shape

   Ⓒ pentagon

   Ⓓ quadrilateral

2. Umberto drew one side of a quadrilateral with 4 equal sides and no right angles. Draw the other 3 sides to complete Umberto's shape.

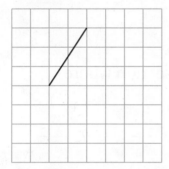

3. Mikael saw a painting that included this shape.

   For numbers 3a–3d, select True or False for each statement about the shape.

   3a. The shape has no right angles.   ○ True   ○ False

   3b. The shape has 2 angles greater than a right angle.   ○ True   ○ False

   3c. The shape has 2 right angles.   ○ True   ○ False

   3d. The shape has 1 angle greater than a right angle.   ○ True   ○ False

Assessment Options
Chapter Test

4. GO DEEPER   Fran used a Venn Diagram to sort shapes.

Part A

Draw another plane shape that belongs inside the left circle of the diagram but NOT in the section where the circles overlap.

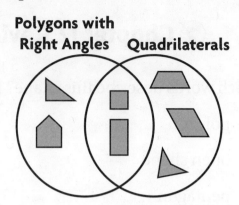

Polygons with Right Angles   Quadrilaterals

Part B

How can you describe the shapes in the section where the circles overlap?

_____

_____

5. Match each object in the left column with its name in the right column.

←——————————→ •   • point

•——————————• •   • line

•——————————→ •   • ray

•• •   • line segment

6. Describe the angles and sides of this triangle.

_____

7. Which words describe this shape. Mark all that apply.

rectangle   rhombus   quadrilateral   square

    Ⓐ   Ⓑ   Ⓒ   Ⓓ

8. Divide each shape into the number of equal parts shown. Then write the fraction that describes each part of the whole.

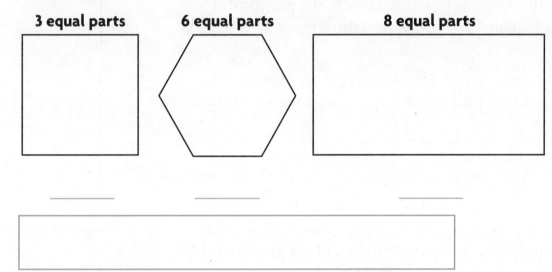

3 equal parts   **6 equal parts**   **8 equal parts**

9. Han drew a triangle with 1 angle greater than a right angle.

For numbers 9a–9d, choose Yes or No to tell whether the triangle could be the triangle Han drew.

9a.   ○ Yes   ○ No

9b. 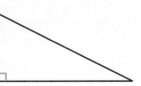   ○ Yes   ○ No

9c. 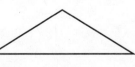   ○ Yes   ○ No

9d. 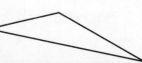   ○ Yes   ○ No

10. THINK SMARTER + Look at this group of pattern blocks.

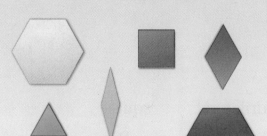

Part A

Sort the pattern blocks by sides. How many groups did you make? Explain how you sorted the shapes.

_____

_____

_____

Part B

Sort the pattern blocks by angles. How many groups did you make? Explain how you sorted the shapes.

_____

_____

_____

11. Teresa drew a quadrilateral that had 4 sides of equal length and no right angles. What quadrilateral did she draw?

_____

Name _____

12. Rhea used a Venn diagram to sort shapes. What label could she use for circle *A*?

Polygons with All
A   **Sides of Equal Length**

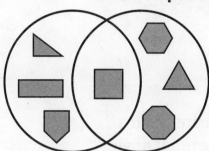

_____

13. Colette drew lines to divide a rectangle into equal parts that each represent $\frac{1}{6}$ of the whole area. Her first line is shown. Draw lines to complete Colette's model.

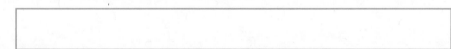

14. Brad drew a quadrilateral. Select the pairs of sides that appear to be parallel. Mark all that apply.

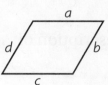

Ⓐ   *a* and *b*   Ⓒ   *c* and *a*

Ⓑ   *b* and *d*   Ⓓ   *d* and *c*

15. Give two reasons that this shape is **not** a polygon.

_____

16. The triangle at the right has one angle greater than a right angle. What statements describe the other angles? Mark all that apply.

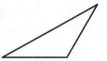

    Ⓐ   At least one is less than a right angle.

    Ⓑ   One is a right angle.

    Ⓒ   Both are less than a right angle.

    Ⓓ   One is greater than a right angle.

17. Ava drew a quadrilateral with 2 pairs of opposite sides that are parallel. The shape has at least 2 right angles. Draw a shape that Ava could have drawn.

18. For 18a–18d, select True or False for each description of a ray.

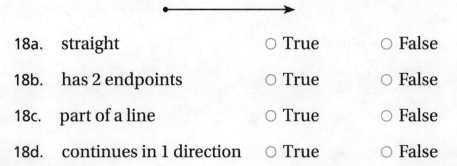

18a.	straight	○ True	○ False
18b.	has 2 endpoints	○ True	○ False
18c.	part of a line	○ True	○ False
18d.	continues in 1 direction	○ True	○ False

Name _____

In Our Corner of Space

Use with *ScienceFusion* pages 410–413.

Develop Vocabulary

1. Write the definition using your own words.

   solar system: _____

   _____

   _____

   planet: _____

   _____

   _____

Develop Concepts

2. Which characteristics do astronomers use to classify the different bodies found in the solar system?

   _____

   _____

   _____

3. Draw the sun and planets. Make sure that they are in their correct positions in relation to the sun.

Do the Math!

4. Look at the table below that tells each planet's distance from the sun, and use it to answer the questions.

Earth	150 million km	Mars	228 million km
Jupiter	778 million km	Mercury	58 million km

5. How much farther from the sun is Mars than Earth?

_____

_____

6. How much farther from the sun is Jupiter than Mercury?

_____

_____

7. List the planets in the table in order from the closest to the farthest from the sun. Which planet in the table is farthest from the sun?

_____

_____

8. Venus is 50 million km from Mercury. What is Venus's distance from the sun?

_____

_____

Summarize

9. Create a two-column chart and compare the different characteristics of inner and outer planets.

Inner Planets	Outer Planets

Name _____

Communities of Populations

Use with *ScienceFusion* pages 436–437.

Develop Vocabulary

1. Write the definition using your own words.

population: _____

_____

_____

community: _____

_____

_____

Develop Concepts

2. A park ranger says that there are about 150 grizzly bears in Yellowstone National Park. Is this a population or a community?

_____

_____

_____

3. When bison and wolves interact with each other in the same place, what do they make up?

_____

_____

_____

Do the Math!

4. Use the data in the table on the right to construct a bar graph.

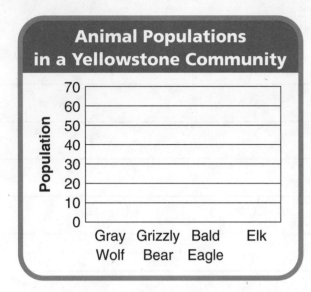

Animal	Population
Gray Wolf	35
Grizzly Bear	25
Bald Eagle	10
Elk	70

5. Which animal has the greatest population in the community? Which has the smallest?

_____

_____

_____

6. In the Yellowstone community, there are 45 Bull Snakes. How many more Bull Snakes than Gray Wolves are there?

_____

_____

_____

Summarize

7. What are some ways that animals and plants interact in a community?

_____

_____

_____

Name _____

Reflection and Refraction

Use with *ScienceFusion* pages 184–185.

Develop Vocabulary

1. Write the definition using your own words.

reflection: _____

_____

_____

refraction: _____

_____

_____

Develop Concepts

2. Give an example of an object that refracts light. How does it do this?

_____

_____

_____

3. Do binoculars reflect or refract light? What is the result of this reflection or refraction?

_____

_____

_____

Do the Math!

4. The table below lists how tall each of the objects appeared to be when Tom viewed them with and without binoculars. Complete the table by calculating the magnification of each item.

Object	Height without binoculars	Height with binoculars	Magnification
Robin	3 inches	9 inches	
American flag	5 inches	25 inches	
Cat	2 inches	6 inches	

5. Which object appeared to be the largest?

_____

_____

_____

6. Susie appeared to be 6 inches tall when Tom saw her without binoculars, but 18 inches tall with binoculars. How many times as tall as Susie looks without binoculars does she look with binoculars?

_____

_____

_____

Summarize

7. Name 4 different devices that depend on refracting lenses to work.

_____

_____

_____

Name _____

Big Changes: Fire, Water, Mud

Use with *ScienceFusion*
pages 288-289.

Develop Vocabulary

1. Write the definition using your own words. Write the first definition as a noun and the second as a verb.

flood (n): _____

_____

_____

flood (v): _____

_____

_____

Develop Concepts

2. What is a small change in water going to cause? What about a big change in water?

_____

_____

_____

3. When can fire cause a small change? When can fire cause a big change?

_____

_____

_____

Do the Math!

4. Skip count by fives to find the time it would take for a river to overflow if rain fell at 5 centimeters per hour and the river needed 55 centimeters of water to overflow.

_____

_____

_____

5. Write an equation for the problem above.

_____

_____

_____

6. Rain is falling at 5 centimeters each hour. Write an equation for each body of water given the rainfall needed for the water to overflow. Use this equation to determine the time until the water overflows.

	Rainfall needed to overflow	Equation	Time (in hours) until the water overflows
River	30 centimeters		
Stream	25 centimeters		
Lake	40 centimeters		

Summarize

7. Describe some conditions that can lead to flooding and mudslides.

_____

_____

_____

Name _____

Stargazing

Use with *ScienceFusion*
pages 404–405.

Develop Vocabulary

1. Write the definition using your own words.

telescope: _____

_____

_____

Develop Concepts

2. How do you think telescopes help scientists study space?

_____

_____

_____

3. What does *tele-* in *telescope* mean in Greek? What are some other words that use that word part *tele-* in them?

_____

_____

_____

4. How are a hand lens and a telescope alike? How are they different?

_____

_____

_____

Do the Math!

5. Max sees 8 stars each time he looks into the night sky behind his house. When he uses his telescope, he sees 7 times as many stars. Write an equation for how many stars Max sees through the telescope.

_____

_____

6. How many stars would Max see if he saw only 4 times as many stars?

_____

_____

_____

7. Which part of the sentence in problem 5 tells you which operation to use?

_____

_____

_____

8. Max's friend sees 6 stars without the telescope and 5 times as many stars with the telescope. How many stars does he see when he looks through the telescope?

_____

_____

_____

Summarize

9. Compare how stars look with your eyes and through a telescope.

_____

_____

_____

Name _____

Cool! It's Freezing!

Use with *ScienceFusion* pages 118–119.

Develop Vocabulary

1. Write the definition using your own words.

freezing: _____

_____

_____

change of state: _____

_____

_____

Develop Concepts

2. How can water in the liquid state change to water in the solid state?

_____

_____

_____

3. At what temperature does water change from liquid to solid?

_____

_____

_____

Do the Math!

4. The temperature of a puddle of water is 20°C. Draw a thermometer below and shade up to 20°C.

5. The temperature of the water in the puddle cools by 2 degrees every hour. At what temperature does water start to freeze?

_____

6. Predict how long it will take for the water in the puddle to start to freeze. Use division to help you find the answer.

_____

7. Predict how cooling will change the state of the water if the puddle doesn't reach 0°C.

_____

_____

8. How long will it take for the water in the puddle to start to freeze if the temperature is 10°C.

_____

Summarize

9. Refer back to the pictures on the last page of this activity. Identify the causes and effects in each picture.

_____

_____

Name _____

Chemical Changes

Use with *ScienceFusion* pages 134–137

Develop Vocabulary

1. Write the definition using your own words.

physical change: _____
_____
_____

chemical change: _____
_____
_____

Develop Concepts

2. What type of change is folding paper? Explain why.

_____
_____
_____

3. Name a physical and a chemical change that can occur when you eat an apple.

_____
_____
_____

4. In the activity, look at the picture of the rusted mailbox. How do you know that rusting is a chemical change?

_____
_____
_____

Do the Math!

5. Max placed three types of food on a plate and recorded how much mold he saw on each after 3 days. Complete the bar graph below by labeling the title and each axis.

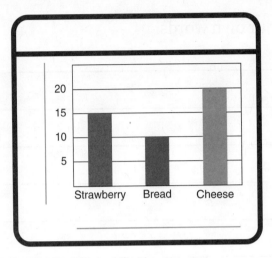

6. Which type of food had the most mold on it after 3 days? Is this a physical or a chemical change?

_____

_____

7. For a campfire, scouts want to burn 20 pieces of wood. If 1 match can light 4 pieces of wood on fire, how many pieces of wood can the scouts burn if they have only 5 matches? Do they need more matches?

_____

_____

8. Is burning wood an example of a physical or a chemical change?

_____

_____

Summarize

9. Compare a physical and a chemical change.

_____

_____

© Houghton Mifflin Harcourt Publishing Company

Name _____

Water Moves All Around

Use with *ScienceFusion* pages 344–345.

Develop Vocabulary

1. Write the definition using your own words.

salt water: _____

_____

_____

_____

fresh water: _____

_____

_____

_____

Develop Concepts

2. Is fresh water a natural resource? What do people use fresh water for?

_____

_____

_____

3. What are some places on Earth that contain fresh water?

_____

_____

_____

Do the Math!

4. Complete the table below. Write the fraction in the right-hand column.

Only 3 out of every 100 liters of water on Earth is fresh water. What fraction of Earth's water is fresh water?	
If Earth is divided into 10 equal parts, 7 of those would be covered by water. What fraction of Earth's surface is land?	

5. Draw a circle. Divide the circle into 10 equal parts. Color blue the number of parts of the circle that is equal to the number of parts of Earth covered by water. Color green the number of parts that are land.

6. If Earth's surface is $\frac{3}{10}$ land, what does this fraction help us understand?

_____

_____

_____

Summarize

7. Is Earth's surface mostly land or mostly water? Is most of Earth's water fresh water or salt water?

_____

_____

_____

Name _____

Using a Wheel-and-Axle

Use with *ScienceFusion* pages 214–215.

Develop Vocabulary

1. Write the definition using your own words.

   wheel-and-axle: _____

   _____

   _____

   _____

   fulcrum: _____

   _____

   _____

   _____

Develop Concepts

2. What part of the wheel-and-axle is like the fulcrum of the lever?

   _____

   _____

   _____

3. What is a real-world example of an object that uses a wheel-and-axle?

   _____

   _____

   _____

Do the Math!

4. A wheel turns on an axle. The arrow of each circle shows the direction in which the wheel turns. The shaded part shows how far the wheel turns. Write a fraction below each circle to indicate how far the wheel turned.

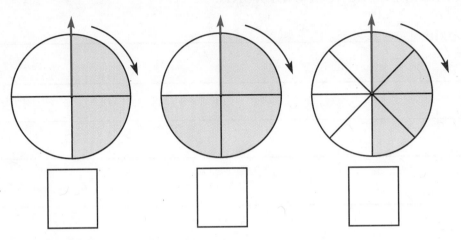

5. Compare the fractions you found for the circle on the left to the fraction you found for the circle on the right.

_____

_____

_____

6. Does the middle circle show the same whole as the last circle? Why?

_____

_____

_____

Summarize

7. How does a wheel-and-axle do work? Provide an example.

_____

_____

_____

Measure It!

Use with *ScienceFusion*
pages 20–21.

Develop Vocabulary

1. Write the definition using your own words.

gram: _____

_____

_____

_____

graduated cylinder: _____

_____

_____

_____

Develop Concepts

2. When you look at a recipe, how do you know how much of each ingredient to add?

_____

_____

_____

3. What is a good tool to use if you want to measure the length of your desk at school? What are some units of measurement that this tool uses?

_____

_____

_____

Do the Math!

4. Complete the table by thinking about what you are measuring on the left column and filling in what would be a good tool used to measure it and a possible unit of measurement you could use.

Measure	Tool used to measure it	Unit of measurement
Time		
Length		
Liquid		
Weight		

5. How many millimeters are in one centimeter? How many centimeters are in one meter?

_____

_____

_____

6. What are some uses of a graduated cylinder?

_____

_____

_____

Summarize

7. Name a tool to measure each of the following: length, liquid volume, mass.

_____

_____

_____

What's the Volume?

Use with *ScienceFusion* pages 98–99.

Develop Vocabulary

1. Define the following terms in your own words.

volume: _____

_____

_____

_____

cubic centimeter: _____

_____

_____

_____

Develop Concepts

2. How would you find the volume of a book?

_____

_____

_____

3. A book has a length of 13 cm, a width of 12 cm, and a height of 16 cm. What is the volume of the book?

_____

_____

_____

Do the Math!

4. A shell is added to a graduated cylinder with a specific volume of water. Complete the table by finding the volume of the shell.

	Volume of water	Volume of water + shell	Volume of the shell
Shell A	53 milliliters	64 milliliters	
Shell B	32 milliliters	35 milliliters	
Shell C	45 milliliters	70 milliliters	

5. What is the process called when a solid object is added to a liquid and the volume of the liquid is increased?

_____

_____

_____

6. A box is 4 cm long, 5 cm wide, and 8 cm high. What is the volume of that box?

_____

_____

_____

Summarize

7. What are some ways in which volume is measured?

_____

_____

_____

Planning and Building

Develop Vocabulary

1. Write the definition using your own words.

   prototype: _____

   _____

   _____

   _____

Develop Concepts

2. If a team of engineers is planning on building a new bridge, what will help them know what kind of bridge to build?

   _____

   _____

   _____

3. What are some objects around your house that might use a prototype when they are being designed and created?

   _____

   _____

   _____

4. Read the process for designing a bridge. What is the last step in the design process? What is the purpose of this step?

   _____

   _____

   _____

Do the Math!

5. Look at the bridge in the picture. What geometric shapes do you see?

_____

_____

_____

6. Are the angles at the top of the bridge greater than or less than a right angle? Are there any right angles on the bridge?

_____

_____

_____

7. In the space below, use geometric shapes such as triangles and rectangles to draw a bridge. Label the shapes and angles in your design.

Summarize

8. What is the main idea of the S.T.E.M. activity on pages 60 – 61?

_____

_____

_____

© Houghton Mifflin Harcourt Publishing Company

Glossary

Pronunciation Key

a	add, map	f	fit, half	n	nice, tin	p	pit, stop	û(r)	burn, term
ā	ace, rate	g	go, log	ng	ring, song	r	run, poor	yōō	fuse, few
â(r)	care, air	h	hope, hate	o	odd, hot	s	see, pass	v	vain, eve
ä	palm, father	i	it, give	ō	open, so	sh	sure, rush	w	win, away
b	bat, rub	ī	ice, write	ô	order, jaw	t	talk, sit	y	yet, yearn
ch	check, catch	j	joy, ledge	oi	oil, boy	th	thin, both	z	zest, muse
d	dog, rod	k	cool, take	ou	pout, now	<u>th</u>	this, bathe	zh	vision, pleasure
e	end, pet	l	look, rule	ōō	took, full	u	up, done		
ē	equal, tree	m	move, seem	ōō	pool, food	ù	pull, book		

ə   the schwa, an unstressed vowel representing the sound spelled *a* in *above*, *e* in *sicken*, *i* in *possible*, *o* in *melon*, *u* in *circus*

Other symbols:
- • separates words into syllables
- ' indicates stress on a syllable

A

addend [a′dend] **sumando** Any of the numbers that are added in addition
Examples: 2 + 3 = 5
                    ↑   ↑
                addend   addend

addition [ə•dish′ən] **suma** The process of finding the total number of items when two or more groups of items are joined; the opposite operation of subtraction

A.M. [ā•em] **a.m.** The time after midnight and before noon

analog clock [an′ə•log kläk] **reloj analógico** A tool for measuring time, in which hands move around a circle to show hours and minutes
Example:

angle [ang′gəl] **ángulo** A shape formed by two rays that share an endpoint
Example:

Word History

When the letter *g* is replaced with the letter *k* in the word **angle**, the word becomes *ankle*. Both words come from the same Latin root, *angulus*, which means "a sharp bend."

area [âr′ē•ə] **área** The measure of the number of unit squares needed to cover a surface
Example:

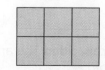

Area = 6 square units

Glossary   H1

array [ə•rā′] **matriz** A set of objects arranged in rows and columns
Example:

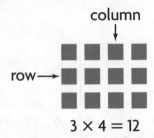

column

row →

$3 \times 4 = 12$

Associative Property of Addition [ə•sō′shē•āt•iv prāp′ər•tē əv ə•dish′ən] **propiedad asociativa de la suma** The property that states that you can group addends in different ways and still get the same sum
Example:
$4 + (2 + 5) = 11$
$(4 + 2) + 5 = 11$

Associative Property of Multiplication [ə•sō′shē•āt•iv prāp′ər•tē əv mul•tə•pli•kā′shən] **propiedad asociativa de la multiplicación** The property that states that when the grouping of factors is changed, the product remains the same
Example:
$(3 \times 2) \times 4 = 24$
$3 \times (2 \times 4) = 24$

bar graph [bär graf] **gráfica de barras** A graph that uses bars to show data
Example:

Favorite Food

Number of Votes

Tacos Pizza Chili Pasta
Food

capacity [kə•pas′i•tē] **capacidad** The amount a container can hold
Example:
1 liter = 1,000 milliliters

cent sign (¢) [sent sīn] **símbolo de centavo** A symbol that stands for *cent* or *cents*
Example: 53¢

centimeter (cm) [sen′tə•mēt•ər] **centímetro (cm)** A metric unit that is used to measure length or distance
Example:

1 cm

circle [sûr′kəl] **círculo** A round closed plane shape
Example:

closed shape [klōzd shāp] **figura cerrada** A shape that begins and ends at the same point
Examples:

Commutative Property of Addition [kə•myoot′ə•tiv prāp′ər•tē əv ə•dish′ən] **propiedad conmutativa de la suma** The property that states that you can add two or more numbers in any order and get the same sum
Example: $6 + 7 = 13$
$7 + 6 = 13$

Commutative Property of Multiplication [kə•myoot′ə•tiv prāp′ər•tē əv mul•tə•pli•kā′shən] **propiedad conmutativa de la multiplicación** The property that states that you can multiply two factors in any order and get the same product
Example: $2 \times 4 = 8$
$4 \times 2 = 8$

compare [kəm•pâr′] **comparar** To describe whether numbers are equal to, less than, or greater than each other

compatible numbers [kəm•pat′ə•bəl num′bərz] **números compatibles** Numbers that are easy to compute with mentally

cone [kōn] **cono** A three-dimensional, pointed shape that has a flat, round base
Example:

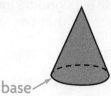

base

counting number [kount′ing num′bər] **número natural** A whole number that can be used to count a set of objects (1, 2, 3, 4 . . .)

cube [kyо̄о̄b] **cubo** A three-dimensional shape with six square faces of the same size
Example:

cylinder [sil′ən•dər] **cilindro** A three-dimensional object that is shaped like a can
Example:

data [dāt′ə] **datos** Information collected about people or things

decagon [dek′ə•gän] **decágono** A polygon with ten sides and ten angles
Example:

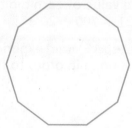

decimal point [des′ə•məl point] **punto decimal** A symbol used to separate dollars from cents in money
Example: $4.52

⎿ decimal point

denominator [dē•näm′ə•nāt•ər] **denominador** The part of a fraction below the line, which tells how many equal parts there are in the whole or in the group
Example: $\frac{3}{4}$ ← denominator

difference [dif′ər•əns] **diferencia** The answer to a subtraction problem
Example: $6 - 4 = 2$

⎿ difference

digital clock [dij′i•təl kläk] **reloj digital** A clock that shows time to the minute, using digits
Example:

digits [dij′its] **dígitos** The symbols 0, 1, 2, 3, 4, 5, 6, 7, 8, and 9

dime [dīm] **moneda de 10¢** A coin worth 10 cents and with a value equal to that of 10 pennies; 10¢
Example:

Distributive Property [di•strib′yо̄о̄•tiv präp′ər•tē] **propiedad distributiva** The property that states that multiplying a sum by a number is the same as multiplying each addend by the number and then adding the products
Example:
$5 \times 8 = 5 \times (4 + 4)$
$5 \times 8 = (5 \times 4) + (5 \times 4)$
$5 \times 8 = 20 + 20$
$5 \times 8 = 40$

divide [də•vīd′] **dividir** To separate into equal groups; the opposite operation of multiplication

dividend [div′ə•dend] **dividendo** The number that is to be divided in a division problem
Example: $35 \div 5 = 7$

⎿ dividend

division [də•vizh'ən] **división** The process of sharing a number of items to find how many groups can be made or how many items will be in a group; the opposite operation of multiplication

divisor [de•vī'zər] **divisor** The number that divides the dividend
Example: 35 ÷ 5 = 7
$$\underset{\text{divisor}}{\uparrow}$$

dollar [däl'ər] **dólar** Paper money worth 100 cents and equal to 100 pennies; $1.00
Example:

edge [ej] **arista** A line segment formed where two faces meet

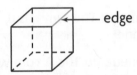
edge

eighths [ātths] **octavos**

These are eighths

elapsed time [ē•lapst' tīm] **tiempo transcurrido** The time that passes from the start of an activity to the end of that activity

endpoint [end'point] **extremo** The point at either end of a line segment

equal groups [ē'kwəl grо̄оpz] **grupos iguales** Groups that have the same number of objects

equal parts [ē'kwəl pärts] **partes iguales** Parts that are exactly the same size

equal sign (=) [ē'kwəl sīn] **signo de igualdad** A symbol used to show that two numbers have the same value
Example: 384 = 384

equal to (=) [ē'kwəl tо̄о] **igual a** Having the same value
Example: 4 + 4 is equal to 3 + 5.

equation [ē•kwā'zhən] **ecuación** A number sentence that uses the equal sign to show that two amounts are equal
Examples:
3 + 7 = 10
4 − 1 = 3
6 × 7 = 42
8 ÷ 2 = 4

equivalent [ē•kwiv'ə•lənt] **equivalente** Two or more sets that name the same amount

equivalent fractions [ē•kwiv'ə•lənt frak'shənz] **fracciones equivalentes** Two or more fractions that name the same amount
Example:

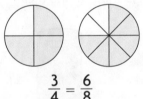

$$\frac{3}{4} = \frac{6}{8}$$

estimate [es'tə•māt] *verb* **estimar** To find about how many or how much

estimate [es'tə•mit] *noun* **estimación** A number close to an exact amount

even [ē'vən] **par** A whole number that has a 0, 2, 4, 6, or 8 in the ones place

expanded form [ek•span'did fôrm] **forma desarrollada** A way to write numbers by showing the value of each digit
Example: 721 = 700 + 20 + 1

experiment [ek•sper'ə•mənt] **experimento** A test that is done in order to find out something

F

face [fās] **cara** A polygon that is a flat surface of a solid shape

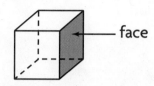

factor [fak′tər] **factor** A number that is multiplied by another number to find a product
Examples: $3 \times 8 = 24$

↑   ↑

factor   factor

foot (ft) [fŏŏt] **pie** A customary unit used to measure length or distance;
1 foot = 12 inches

fourths [fôrths] **cuartos**

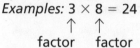

These are fourths

fraction [frak′shən] **fracción** A number that names part of a whole or part of a group
Examples:

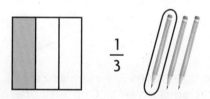

$\frac{1}{3}$

Word History

Often, a *fraction* is a part of a whole that is broken into pieces. *Fraction* comes from the Latin word *frangere*, which means "to break."

fraction greater than 1 [frak′shən grāt′ər <u>than</u> wun]
fracción mayor que 1 A number which has a numerator that is greater than its denominator
Examples:

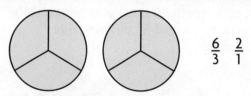

$\frac{6}{3}$ $\frac{2}{1}$

frequency table [frē′kwən·sē tā′bəl] **tabla de frecuencia** A table that uses numbers to record data
Example:

Favorite Color	
Color	**Number**
Blue	10
Green	8
Red	7
Yellow	4

G

gram (g) [gram] **gramo (g)** A metric unit that is used to measure mass;
1 kilogram = 1,000 grams

greater than (>) [grāt′ər <u>than</u>] **mayor que** A symbol used to compare two numbers when the greater number is given first
Example:
Read 6 > 4 as "six is greater than four."

Grouping Property of Addition [grōōp′ing präp′ər·tē əv ə·dish′ən] **propiedad de agrupación de la suma** *See* Associative Property of Addition.

Grouping Property of Multiplication [grōōp′ing präp′ər·tē əv mul·tə·pli·kā′shən] **propiedad de agrupación de la multiplicación** *See* Associative Property of Multiplication.

H

half dollar [haf dol'ər] **moneda de 50¢**
A coin worth 50 cents and with a value
equal to that of 50 pennies; 50¢
Example:

half hour [haf our] **media hora** 30 minutes
Example: Between 4:00 and 4:30 is one
half hour.

halves [havz] **mitades**

These are halves

hexagon [hek'sə•gän] **hexágono** A polygon
with six sides and six angles
Examples:

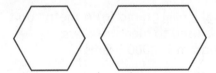

horizontal bar graph [hôr•i•zänt'l bär graf]
gráfica de barras horizontales A bar graph
in which the bars go from left to right
Examples:

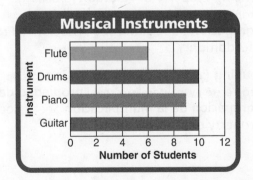

hour (hr) [our] **hora (h)** A unit used to measure
time; in one hour, the hour hand on an analog
clock moves from one number to the next;
1 hour = 60 minutes

hour hand [our hand] **horario** The short hand on
an analog clock

I

Identity Property of Addition [ī•den'tə•tē
präp'ər•tē əv ə•dish'ən] **propiedad de
identidad de la suma** The property that
states that when you add zero to a number,
the result is that number
Example: 24 + 0 = 24

Identity Property of Multiplication [ī•den'tə•tē
präp'ər•tē əv mul•tə•pli•kā'shən] **propiedad de
identidad de la multiplicación** The property
that states that the product of any number
and 1 is that number
Examples: 5 × 1 = 5
            1 × 8 = 8

inch (in.) [inch] **pulgada (pulg.)** A customary
unit used to measure length or distance
Example:

intersecting lines [in•tər•sekt'ing līnz] **líneas
secantes** Lines that meet or cross
Example:

inverse operations [in'vûrs äp•ə•rā'shənz]
operaciones inversas Opposite operations,
or operations that undo one another, such
as addition and subtraction or multiplication
and division

K

key [kē] **clave** The part of a map or graph
that explains the symbols

kilogram (kg) [kil'ō•gram] **kilogramo (kg)**
A metric unit used to measure mass;
1 kilogram = 1,000 grams

H6   Glossary

L

length [lengkth] **longitud** The measurement of the distance between two points

less than (<) [les <u>than</u>] **menor que** A symbol used to compare two numbers when the lesser number is given first
Example:
Read 3 < 7 as "three is less than seven."

line [līn] **línea** A straight path extending in both directions with no endpoints
Example:

←————————→

Word History

The word *line* comes from *linen*, a thread spun from the fibers of the flax plant. In early times, thread was held tight to mark a straight line between two points.

line plot [līn plät] **diagrama de puntos** A graph that records each piece of data on a number line
Example:

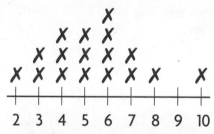

**Height of Bean Seedlings
to the Nearest Centimeter**

line segment [līn seg'mənt] **segmento** A part of a line that includes two points, called endpoints, and all of the points between them
Example:

●————————●

liquid volume [lik'wid väl'yoŏm] **volumen de un líquido** The amount of liquid in a container

liter (L) [lēt'ər] **litro (L)** A metric unit used to measure capacity and liquid volume;
1 liter = 1,000 milliliters

M

mass [mas] **masa** The amount of matter in an object

meter (m) [mēt'ər] **metro (m)** A metric unit used to measure length or distance;
1 meter = 100 centimeters

midnight [mid'nīt] **medianoche** 12:00 at night

milliliter (mL) [mil'i•lēt•ər] **mililitro (mL)** A metric unit used to measure capacity and liquid volume

minute (min) [min'it] **minuto (min)** A unit used to measure short amounts of time; in one minute, the minute hand on an analog clock moves from one mark to the next

minute hand [min'it hand] **minutero** The long hand on an analog clock

multiple [mul'tə•pəl] **múltiplo** A number that is the product of two counting numbers
Examples:

$$
\begin{array}{cccc}
6 & 6 & 6 & 6 \quad \text{counting} \\
\times\,1 & \times\,2 & \times\,3 & \times\,4 \leftarrow \text{numbers} \\
\hline
6 & 12 & 18 & 24 \leftarrow \text{multiples of 6}
\end{array}
$$

multiplication [mul•tə•pli•kā'shən] **multiplicación** The process of finding the total number of items in two or more equal groups; the opposite operation of division

multiply [mul'tə•plī] **multiplicar** To combine equal groups to find how many in all; the opposite operation of division

N

nickel [nik'əl] **moneda de 5¢** A coin worth 5 cents and with a value equal to that of 5 pennies; 5¢
Example:

noon [noŏn] **mediodía** 12:00 in the day

number line [num′bər līn] **recta numérica**
A line on which numbers can be located
Example:

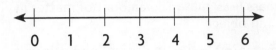

number sentence [num′bər sent′ns] **enunciado numérico** A sentence that includes numbers, operation symbols, and a greater than symbol, a less than symbol, or an equal sign
Example: $5 + 3 = 8$

numerator [noo′mər•āt•ər] **numerador** The part of a fraction above the line, which tells how many parts are being counted
Example: $\frac{3}{4}$ ← numerator

octagon [äk′tə•gän] **octágono** A polygon with eight sides and eight angles
Examples:

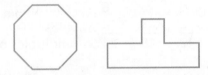

odd [od] **impar** A whole number that has a 1, 3, 5, 7, or 9 in the ones place

open shape [ō′pən shāp] **figura abierta** A shape that does not begin and end at the same point
Examples:

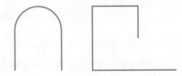

order [ôr′dər] **orden** A particular arrangement or placement of numbers or things, one after another

order of operations [ôr′dər əv äp•ə•rā′shənz] **orden de las operaciones** A special set of rules that gives the order in which calculations are done

Order Property of Addition [ôr′dər präp′ər•tē əv ə•dish′ən] **propiedad de orden de la suma** *See* Commutative Property of Addition.

Order Property of Multiplication [ôr′dər präp′ər•tē əv mul•tə•pli•kā′shən] **propiedad de orden de la multiplicación** *See* Commutative Property of Multiplication.

parallel lines [pâr′ə•lel līnz] **líneas paralelas** Lines in the same plane that never cross and are always the same distance apart
Example:

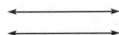

pattern [pat′ərn] **patrón** An ordered set of numbers or objects in which the order helps you predict what will come next
Examples:
2, 4, 6, 8, 10

pentagon [pen′tə•gän] **pentágono** A polygon with five sides and five angles
Examples:

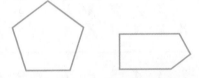

perimeter [pə•rim′ə•tər] **perímetro** The distance around a figure
Example:

perpendicular lines [pər•pən•dik′yoo•lər līnz] **líneas perpendiculares** Lines that intersect to form right angles
Example:

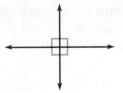

H8 Glossary

© Houghton Mifflin Harcourt Publishing Company

picture graph [pik'chər graf] **gráfica con dibujos** A graph that uses pictures to show and compare information
Example:

How We Get to School	
Walk	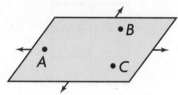
Ride a Bike	
Ride a Bus	
Ride in a Car	

Key: Each ⊛ = 10 students.

place value [plās val'yoo] **valor posicional** The value of each digit in a number, based on the location of the digit

plane [plān] **plano** A flat surface that extends without end in all directions
Example:

plane shape [plān shāp] **figura plana** A shape in a plane that is formed by curves, line segments, or both
Example:

P.M. [pē•em] **p.m.** The time after noon and before midnight

point [point] **punto** An exact position or location

polygon [päl'i•gän] **polígono** A closed plane shape with straight sides that are line segments
Examples:

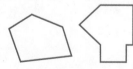

polygons

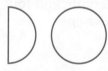

not polygons

Word History

Did you ever think that a *polygon* looks like a bunch of knees that are bent? This is how the term got its name. *Poly-* is from the Greek word *polys*, which means "many." The ending *-gon* is from the Greek word *gony*, which means "knee."

product [präd'əkt] **producto** The answer in a multiplication problem
Example: $3 \times 8 = 24$
product

quadrilateral [kwäd•ri•lat'ər•əl] **cuadrilátero** A polygon with four sides and four angles
Example:

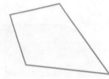

quarter [kwôrt'ər] **moneda de 25¢** A coin worth 25 cents and with a value equal to that of 25 pennies; 25¢
Example:

quarter hour [kwôrt'ər our] **cuarto de hora** 15 minutes
Example: Between 4:00 and 4:15 is one quarter hour.

quotient [kwō'shənt] **cociente** The number, not including the remainder, that results from division
Example: $8 \div 4 = 2$
quotient

R

ray [rā] **semirrecta** A part of a line, with one endpoint, that is straight and continues in one direction
Example:

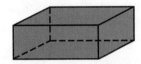

rectangle [rek'tang•gəl] **rectángulo** A quadrilateral with two pairs of parallel sides, two pairs of sides of equal length, and four right angles
Example:

rectangular prism [rek•tang'gyə•lər priz'əm] **prisma rectangular** A three-dimensional shape with six faces that are all rectangles
Example:

regroup [rē•grōōp'] **reagrupar** To exchange amounts of equal value to rename a number
Example: 5 + 8 = 13 ones or 1 ten 3 ones

related facts [ri•lāt'id fakts] **operaciones relacionadas** A set of related addition and subtraction, or multiplication and division, number sentences
Examples: 4 × 7 = 28   28 ÷ 4 = 7
                7 × 4 = 28   28 ÷ 7 = 4

remainder [ri•mān'dər] **residuo** The amount left over when a number cannot be divided evenly

results [ri•zults'] **resultados** The answers from a survey

rhombus [räm'bəs] **rombo** A quadrilateral with two pairs of parallel sides and four sides of equal length
Example:

right angle [rīt ang'gəl] **ángulo recto** An angle that forms a square corner
Example:

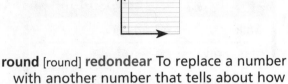

round [round] **redondear** To replace a number with another number that tells about how many or how much

S

scale [skāl] **escala** The numbers placed at fixed distances on a graph to help label the graph

side [sīd] **lado** A straight line segment in a polygon

sixths [siksths] **sextos**

These are sixths

skip count [skip kount] **contar salteado** A pattern of counting forward or backward
Example: 5, 10, 15, 20, 25, 30, . . .

solid shape [sä'lid shāp] **cuerpo geométrico** *See* three-dimensional shape.

sphere [sfir] **esfera** A three-dimensional shape that has the shape of a round ball
Example:

square [skwâr] **cuadrado** A quadrilateral with two pairs of parallel sides, four sides of equal length, and four right angles
Example:

square unit [skwâr yōo′nit] **unidad cuadrada**
A unit used to measure area such as square
foot, square meter, and so on

standard form [stan′dərd fôrm] **forma normal**
A way to write numbers by using the digits
0–9, with each digit having a place value
Example: 345 ← standard form

subtraction [səb•trak′shən] **resta** The process of
finding how many are left when a number of
items are taken away from a group of items;
the process of finding the difference when two
groups are compared; the opposite operation
of addition

sum [sum] **suma o total** The answer to an
addition problem
Example: 6 + 4 = 10

↑—sum

survey [sûr′vā] **encuesta** A method of gathering
information

tally table [tal′ē tā′bəl] **tabla de conteo** A table
that uses tally marks to record data
Example:

Favorite Sport	
Sport	**Tally**
Soccer	IIII III
Baseball	III
Football	IIII
Basketball	IIII I

thirds [thûrdz] **tercios**

These are thirds

three-dimensional shape [thrē də•men′shə•nəl shāp]
figura tridimensional A shape that has length,
width, and height
Example:

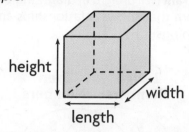

time line [tīm līn] **línea cronológica**
A drawing that shows when and in what
order events took place

trapezoid [trap′i•zoid] **trapecio**
A quadrilateral with at least one pair of
parallel sides
Example:

triangle [trī′ang•gəl] **triángulo** A polygon with
three sides and three angles
Examples:

two-dimensional shape [tōo də•men′shə•nəl shāp]
figura bidimensional A shape that has only
length and width
Example:

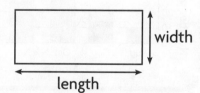

unit fraction [yōo′nit frak′shən] **fracción
unitaria** A fraction that has 1 as its top
number, or numerator
Examples: $\frac{1}{2}$ $\frac{1}{3}$ $\frac{1}{4}$

unit square [yōo′nit skwâr] **cuadrado de una unidad**
A square with a side length of 1 unit, used to
measure area

Venn diagram [ven dī′ə•gram] **diagrama de Venn**
A diagram that shows relationships among
sets of things
Example:

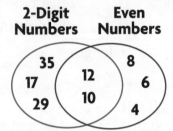

2-Digit Numbers   Even Numbers

35 17 29 | 12 10 | 8 6 4

vertex [vûr′teks] **vértice** The point at which
two rays of an angle or two (or more) line
segments meet in a plane shape or where
three or more edges meet in a solid shape
Examples:

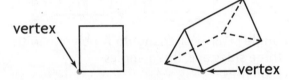

vertex   vertex

vertical bar graph [vûr′ti•kəl bär graf] **gráfica
de barras verticales** A bar graph in which the
bars go up from bottom to top

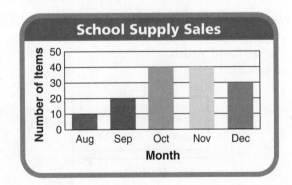

School Supply Sales

whole [hōl] **entero** All of the parts of a shape
or group
Example:

$\frac{2}{2} = 1$

This is one whole.

whole number [hōl num′bər] **número entero**
One of the numbers 0, 1, 2, 3, 4, . . .
The set of whole numbers goes on
without end

word form [wûrd fôrm] **en palabras** A way
to write numbers by using words
Example: The word form of 212 is
two hundred twelve.

Zero Property of Multiplication [zē′rō
präp′ər•tē əv mul•tə•pli•kā′shən] **propiedad
del cero de la multiplicación** The property
that states that the product of zero and
any number is zero
Example: $0 \times 6 = 0$

Index

Division

act it out, 301–304, 421–424

with arrays, 333–336, 340–341, 345–348,
389–391, 403–406

bar models, 319–322, 339–342

count back on number line, 326–328, 371,
377, 384

dividend, 320

dividing by

eight, 409–412

five, 377–380

four, 389–392

nine, 415–418

one, 351–354

seven, 403–406

six, 395–398

ten, 371–374

three, 383–386

two, 365–368

dividing with zero, 351–354

divisors, 320, 410

doubles, 378

equal groups, 301–304, 307–310,
313–316, 319–322, 333–336,
365–368, 383–386, 389, 395–398,
403–406, 415–418

equations, 320–322, 325–328,
334–335, 339–342, 345–348,
351–354, 365–368, 391

as inverse operation, 339–342

of liquid volume, 611–614

of mass, 611–614

with measurement quantities, 316, 410,
611–614

modeling, 301–304, 319–322

number lines, 326–328, 371, 384

quotients, 320

related facts, 345–348

related to multiplication, 339–342,
345–348, 372–374, 384–386, 390–392,
396–398, 404–406, 409–412, 416–418

repeated (successive) subtraction as,
325–328, 371–374, 409–412

rules for one and zero, 351–354

unknown factor problem, 372–374, 384,
390, 396, 404, 409, 416

using factors, 410

using related multiplication fact,
345–348, 372–378, 384, 390, 396, 404,
409, 416

Divisors, 320, 410

Doubles, 191–194, 204, 235

Draw a bar graph, 113–116

Draw a Diagram, 73–76, 159–162, 275–278,
493–496, 585–588, 741–744

Draw a picture graph, 99–102

Drawing

bar models, 73–75, 198–200, 319–322,
611–614

draw a bar graph, 113–116

draw a diagram, 73–76, 159–162,
275–278, 493–496, 741–744

draw a picture graph, 99–102

number lines, 23–26, 55–58, 147, 281–284

quadrilaterals, 697–700, 729–732

quick pictures, 147, 171–174, 177–180,
287–288, 309, 314, 351–354, 367, 445,
449, 452

shapes, 203, 698, 712, 716, 729–732,
747–750

solving problems, 73–76, 159–162, 475,
493–496

E

Eighths, 443

Elapsed time, 573–576, 579–582, 585–588

on clocks, 573–576, 579–582

defined, 573

find end time, 579–582, 585–588

find start time (begin), 579–582, 585–588

on number lines, 573–576, 579–582,
585–587

using subtraction, 574

Endpoints, defined 697

Equal groups

counting, 139–142, 145–148, 191–194,
301–304, 307–310, 313–316, 319–322,
333–336, 365–368, 383–386, 389–392,
395–398, 403–406, 415–418

defined, 139

division and, 301–304, 307–310, 313–316,
319–322, 333–336, 365–368, 383–386,
389–392, 395–398, 403–406, 415–418

multiplication and, 139–142, 145–148,
151–154, 339–342

number of, 313–316

size of, 307–310

skip counting, 139–142, 151–154

Equal parts, 443–446, 747–750

Equal parts of a whole, 443–446

problem solving, 73–74, 87–88, 159–160,
247–248, 275–276, 301–302, 421–424,
493–494, 507–508, 585–586, 663–664,
741–742
Tree Map, 138, 190, 260, 696
Venn diagram, 4, 364, 624

Graphs

bar graphs
analyzing and constructing, 107–110,
113–116
defined, 107
horizontal bar graphs, 107–108,
110–113, 116–121
scale, 107–110, 113–116
vertical bar graphs, 108–109, 114–115,
120–121, 122
key, 93–96, 99–102, 114, 162, 374
line plots
analyzing and constructing, 125–128
defined, 125
generating measurement data, 126,
593–596
picture graphs
analyzing and constructing, 93–96,
99–102, 113–116
defined, 93
key, 93
solving problems, 119–122

Greater than (>)

angles and, 703–706
fractions and, 507–510, 513–516,
519–522, 525–528

Grouping Property of Multiplication, 223–226

Groups

equal groups. *See* Equal groups
fractions of, 481–484, 487–490, 493–496

Half hours, 579, 585

Half symbol, 94

Halves, 443–446
measure to the nearest half inch, 593–596

Hexagons
angles of, 710–712
sides of, 710–712

Horizontal bar graphs, 107–108, 110–113,
116–121

Hour hand, 561–564

Hours

half, 559, 567–570, 579, 585
minutes after hour, 562
minutes before hour, 562

Hundreds

place value, 11–14, 18–20, 41–44, 50–52,
61–64, 67–70, 282–284, 288
round to nearest, 11–14

Identity Property

Addition, 5, 29–32
Multiplication, 177–180

Inches

as customary unit, 593–596
generating data in, 126, 593–596
measure to nearest fourth inch, 593–596
measure to nearest half inch, 593–596
measure to nearest inch, 126

Intersecting lines, 715–718

Inverse operations, 61, 339

Investigate, 333–336, 427–430, 539–542,
625–628, 747–750

Keys, 93–96, 99–102, 114, 162, 374

Kilograms

defined, 605
as metric unit, 605–608
solving problems in, 605–608, 611–614

Length

customary units for
feet, 151, 633, 637–640
inches, 593–596, 633
measure in centimeters, 631–634
measure to nearest fourth inch, 593–596
measure to nearest half inch, 593–596
measure to nearest inch, 126
metric units for
centimeters, 89, 631–634

Less than (<)
    angles and, 703–706
    comparing with greater than and equal to, 243, 507
    fractions and, 507–510, 513–516, 519–522, 525–528

Line plots
    defined, 125
    generating measurement data for, 126, 593–596
    making, 125–128
    read and interpret data in, 125–128

Lines
    defined, 697
    intersecting, 715–718
    parallel, 715–718
    perpendicular, 715–718

Line segments, 697
    describing, 699, 715–718

Liquid volume. *See also* Measurement; Units
    defined, 599
    estimating and measuring, 599–602
    liters, 599–602
    metric units for, 599–602
    solving problems, 599–602, 611–614

Liters
    defined, 599
    estimating and measuring, 599–602
    as metric unit, 599–602
    solving problems in, 599–602, 611–614

Make a table, 247–250
Make Connections, 334, 428, 540, 626, 748
Manipulatives and materials
    addition tables, 5, 6
    base-ten blocks, 281, 287
    beakers, 599, 600
    clock faces, 561–562, 567–570
    containers, 599, 600
    counters, 139, 307, 319, 365, 487
    crayons, 5–6, 230, 539, 594
    dot paper, 625
    fraction strips, 467, 489, 507
    geoboards, 625, 643
    glue stick, 613
    gram masses, 605, 606, 612
    1inch grid paper, 649

kilogram masses, 605, 606
    MathBoard. *See* MathBoard
    measuring tape, 126
    multiplication table, 229
    number lines, 11–14, 25, 55, 281–283, 467–470, 475–478, 514–515, 540–541, 546, 573–576
    pan balance, 605, 606, 612
    pattern blocks, 747
    pitchers. *See* Beakers
    rubber bands, 625, 643
    rulers, 126, 594, 631, 729, 747
        centimeter, 631–634
        inch, 593–596, 631–634
    square tiles, 165, 166, 171, 173, 209, 333, 345, 669, 675, 681
    straws, 704, 735
    two-color counters, 487

Mass. *See also* Measurement; Units
    defined, 605
    estimating and measuring, 605–608
    metric units for, 605–608
    solving problems, 605–608, 611–614

MathBoard, In every lesson. Some examples are: 43, 378, 410, 731, 748

Math Idea, 23, 29, 61, 94, 172, 223, 287, 334, 366, 461, 467, 475, 513, 540, 593, 637, 643, 709, 747

Math Processes and Practices
    1. Problem Solving. In many lessons. Some examples are: 11, 24, 90, 160, 173, 216, 230, 631, 724
    2. Abstract and Quantitative Reasoning. In many lessons. Some examples are: 7, 29, 87, 100, 209, 226, 651, 704, 735
    3. Use and Evaluate Logical Reasoning. In many lessons. Some examples are: 8, 50, 57, 114, 151, 198, 626, 699, 718
    4. Mathematical Modeling. In many lessons. Some examples are: 23, 94, 116, 145, 152, 168, 633, 652, 681
    5. Use Mathematical Tools. In many lessons. Some examples are: 38, 64, 127, 168, 242, 535, 596, 646, 710
    6. Use Precise Mathematical Language. In many lessons. Some examples are: 6, 25, 51, 113, 179, 237, 656, 716, 725
    7. See Structure. In many lessons. Some examples are: 5, 154, 171, 199, 217, 326, 428, 650, 655
    8. Generalize. In many lessons. Some examples are: 25, 95, 125, 215, 427, 599, 644, 710, 737

counting back on, 55, 326–328, 371–374, 377–380, 384

counting up on, 55, 378–379

dividing with, 325–328, 371, 377–380, 384

elapsed time. *See* Time

fractions greater than 1, 495–501

fractions on, 467–470

multiplying with, 151–154, 197–200, 235, 281–284

number line for hours in a day, 567

round numbers and, 11–14

skip counting, 151–154
    by eights, 235
    by fives, 197–198
    by sixes, 151
    by tens, 197–198
    time intervals. *See* Time
    by twos, 192

subtracting with, 55–58

take away tens and ones, 55–58

use to represent
    distances, 467–470
    elapsed time, 573–575, 579–582, 585–588

whole numbers on, 467–470, 475–478

Number patterns, 5–8, 229–232, 242, 261–264

Numbers

compatible, 17–20, 24–25, 49–52

counting, 281, 562, 438, 625

even, 5–8, 229–232, 235–236

expanded form of, 24, 35–38, 42, 56

fractions, 443–446, 449–452, 437–440, 455–458, 467–470, 475–478, 481–484, 487–490, 493–496, 507–510, 513–516, 519–522, 525–528, 533–536, 539–542, 545–548

hundreds, 11–14, 18–20, 35–38, 41–44, 50–52, 56–57, 61–64, 67–70, 281–284, 287–290

odd, 5–8, 229–232, 235–238

ones, 23–26, 29–32, 35–38, 41–44, 50–52, 55–58, 61–64, 67–70, 177–180, 351–354

ordering, 533–536

rounding, 11–14, 17–20

standard form of, 36

tens, 11–14, 23–26, 29–32, 35–38, 41–44, 55–58, 61–64, 67–70, 197–200, 287–290

unknown, 63, 193, 199, 225, 267–270, 367, 390–391, 396–397, 404–405, 410–411, 417, 429

zero, 177–180, 351–354

Numerators, 461

comparing fractions with same, 519–522, 525–528

defined, 461

fractions greater than 1, 476–478

ordering fractions with same, 533–536

O

Octagons

angles of, 709–712

sides of, 709–712

Odd numbers, 5–8, 229–232, 235–236

Ones, 12–14, 23–26, 29–32, 35–38, 41–44, 50–52, 55–58, 61–64, 67–70, 177–180, 287–290

On Your Own, In most lessons. Some examples are: 7, 43, 379, 411, 731, 744

Open shapes, 698–700

Ordering

fractions, 533–536

fraction strips, 533–536

liquid volume, 600

mass, 606

Order of operations, 427–430

Organize data, 87–90

P

Parallel lines, 715–718

Partitioning

fractions, 443–446, 449–452

shapes, 747–750

Patterns

addition, 5–8, 261–264

on the addition table, 5–8

arithmetic, 5–8, 229–232, 261–264

defined, 5

describing, 261–264

explaining using properties, 5–8, 229–232, 236

finding, 663–666

multiplication, 229–232, 242, 261–264

on the multiplication table, 229–232

with nine, 241–244

number, 5–8, 229–232

in a table, 261–264

© Houghton Mifflin Harcourt Publishing Company

© Houghton Mifflin Harcourt Publishing Company

Subtraction
> as inverse operations, 61
> bar models, 73–75
> break apart strategy, 56–57
> combining place values strategy, 67–70
> draw a diagram, 73–76
> elapsed time, 574
> equations, 423, 613, 640
> estimate differences, 49–52
> of liquid volume, 611–614
> of mass, 611–614
> of time intervals, 573–576, 579–582, 585–588
> mental math strategies, 55–58
> modeling, 55–58, 73–76
> place value strategy, 49–52, 55–58, 61–64
> regrouping, 61–64, 67–70
> related to division, 325–328
> repeated subtraction and division, 325–328, 371–374, 409–412
> rounding and, 49–52
> three-digit numbers, 49–52, 55–58, 61–64, 67–70, 73–76
> two-digit numbers, 49–52, 55–58
> using number lines, 55–58
> with compatible numbers, 49–52
> with friendly numbers, 55–58

Surveys, 93, 95, 100, 105, 108, 113, 125, 162

Table of Measures, H31

Tables and charts. *See also* Graphic
> Organizers
> addition tables, 5–6
> completing tables, 87–89, 247–250, 663–666
> frequency tables, 87–90
> input/output tables, 261–264
> make a table, 247–250
> making, 247–250
> multiplication tables, 204, 229–232
> for multiplying, 247–250
> patterns in, 5–8, 261–264, 663–666
> place-value charts, 49–52, 55–58, 61–64, 287–290
> show data in, 99–101, 113–116
> Table of Measures, H39
> tally tables, 87–90, 101

Tally tables, 87–90, 101

Technology and digital resources
> Go Digital, *In most lessons. Some examples are*: 5, 87, 191, 443, 561, 697. *See also* Chapter Review/Test; Show What You Know; Vocabulary Builder
> Math on the Spot Videos, In every Student Edition lesson. Some examples are: 26, 102, 200, 263, 380, 470, 542, 666, 712
> Multimedia eGlossary, *access through the Go Math! Interactive,* 4, 86, 136, 190, 260, 300, 364, 442, 506, 560, 624, 696

Tens
> round to nearest, 11–14, 50

Test and Review. *See* Review and test

Think Smarter, In every Student Edition lesson. Some examples are: 14, 101, 161, 231, 270, 310, 392, 464, 540, 581, 646, 705

Think Smarter +, In all Student Edition chapters. Some examples are: 52, 96, 137, 231, 290, 398, 602, 672

Thirds, 443–446

Three-digit numbers
> addition, 17–20, 23–26, 35–38, 41–44
> combining place values strategy, 67–70
> subtraction, 49–52, 55–58, 61–64, 67–70, 73–76

Time
> adding and subtracting, 573–576, 579–582, 585–588
> after midnight, 567
> after noon, 568
> A.M., 567–570
> clocks
>> analog, 561–564, 567–569, 574–575, 579–581
>> digital, 563, 568–569
>> telling time, 561–564, 567–570
> elapsed, 573–576, 579–582, 585–588
>> on clocks, 573–576, 579–582
>> defined, 573
>> find end time, 579–582, 585–588
>> find start time (begin), 579–582, 585–588
>> on number lines, 573–576, 579–582
>> using subtraction, 574
> intervals
>> adding, 573–576, 579–582, 585–588
>> measure in minutes, 573–576, 579–582, 585–588

Table of Measures

METRIC	CUSTOMARY

Length

1 centimeter (cm) = 10 millimeters (mm)

1 decimeter (dm) = 10 centimeters (cm)   1 foot (ft) = 12 inches (in.)

1 meter (m) = 100 centimeters   1 yard (yd) = 3 feet, or 36 inches

1 meter (m) = 10 decimeters   1 mile (mi) = 1,760 yards, or 5,280 feet

1 kilometer (km) = 1,000 meters

Capacity and Liquid Volume

1 liter (L) = 1,000 milliliters (mL)   1 pint (pt) = 2 cups (c)

1 quart (qt) = 2 pints

1 gallon (gal) = 4 quarts

Mass/Weight

1 kilogram (kg) = 1,000 grams (g)   1 pound (lb) = 16 ounces (oz)

TIME

1 minute (min) = 60 seconds (sec)   1 year (yr) = 12 months (mo), or about 52 weeks

1 hour (hr) = 60 minutes   1 year = 365 days

1 day = 24 hours   1 leap year = 366 days

1 week (wk) = 7 days   1 decade = 10 years

1 century = 100 years

MONEY

1 penny = 1 cent (¢)

1 nickel = 5 cents

1 dime = 10 cents

1 quarter = 25 cents

1 half dollar = 50 cents

1 dollar ($) = 100 cents

SYMBOLS

< is less than

> is greater than

= is equal to